MW01202203

This is a great book about MDM and its impact on our businesses, governments, and in many ways most of our lives. Written in a simple and effective style, it tells the story of how Master Data Management works, what it does, and why we should care very much how it is governed. If you have any interest in MDM, data or information governance, read this book.

—Steven B. Adler, CIPP
IBM Information Governance Solutions

In this book, Alex Berson and Larry Dubov convey the many facets of the value of adopting Master Data Management techniques while ably articulating an implementation roadmap. By maintaining the need to incorporate business process modeling, master data modeling, master metadata management, and data governance, the authors properly frame the necessary ideas for organizational preparation while still providing deep technical detail about both architecture and algorithms. This book is a definite addition to the MDM body of knowledge.

—David Loshin
President, Knowledge Integrity Incorporated

Alex and Larry have done it again: published a very comprehensive, highly applicable book on MDM and data governance that achieves an excellent balance between thought-provoking academic treatment of some very technical subjects, and highly relevant, usable advice on how to achieve success in implementing a successful MDM and data governance program. This is a must-read for any program sponsor, CIO, CTO, enterprise architect, information architect, data steward, program manager, or practitioner of MDM and data governance. This is not a read-and-forget book, but a great reference manual.

—Martin Moseley
Chief Architect, CTO, Information Agenda Tiger Team
IBM Software Group

This work is one of the most comprehensive, clear, well-researched, and insightful guidebooks on Master Data Management and data governance. Larry and Alex did an exceptional job covering these complex topics from many viewpoints, including technical, business, architectural, security, industry, social, international, product, and regulatory perspectives. I was so impressed at the level of detail and how much is in this book. The book covers critical principles, concepts, emerging trends, and misconceptions, based upon the authors' extensive experience and research, and clarifies keys in creating successful MDM and data governance programs.

—Len Silverston
Best-selling author of *The Data Model Resource Book*, Volumes 1, 2, and 3

Clearly, Alex Berson and Larry Dubov were hard at work tackling the tough topic of "master data governance" before the software vendor community had yet found religion (as the market now has "active," "passive," and my favorite "passive-aggressive" data governance flavors among the many marketing variations).

—Aaron Zornes
Chief Research Officer
The MDM Institute, San Francisco

About the Authors

Alex Berson is an internationally recognized expert, thought leader, author, and advisor in various areas of information technologies. Throughout his professional career, Alex held leadership technology and management positions in companies such as BearingPoint, Entrust, Merrill Lynch, enCommerce, Dun & Bradstreet, PricewaterhouseCoopers, Solomon Smith Barney, and others. He's currently a chief technology architect for a major global financial services institution.

Alex holds graduate and postgraduate degrees in Applied Math and Computer Sciences and has an extensive scientific background in applied research with specific concentration on advanced areas of algorithmic computations, linear programing, computer simulations, and computing architectures. He taught undergraduate and graduate classes and lectured on these topics throughout his career.

Alex combines his extensive scientific background and practical industry experience by focusing his professional activities on advanced multi-disciplined areas of information technology such as Identity Management and Information Security; Master Data Management (MDM) and Customer Data Integration (CDI); CRM and Business Intelligence; Database technologies, including Column-store and very large databases (VLDB); data warehousing and data mining; service-oriented architecture (SOA); mobile computing; enterprise application integration (EAI), messaging, and middleware. Throughout his career, Alex has continued to successfully apply his knowledge, experience, and vision to creating complex ground-breaking solutions for financial services, manufacturing, pharmaceutical and technology industries.

Alex is a member of the Board of Directors of the Wall Street Technology Association (WSTA) and is a member of Standard & Poor's Vista Research Society of Industrial Leaders (SIL). He actively participates in professional associations such as IEEE Computer Society, ACM, and Aberdeen Group's Technology Forecasting Consortium; standards organizations including OMG, OASIS, Open Group; various industry consortia such as the Data Warehousing Institute (TDWI), and technical advisory boards of several technology companies.

Alex has published numerous direction-setting technical articles in trade magazines and online publications, and is the author and coauthor of a number of best-selling professional books, including *Master Data Management and Data Governance; Master Data Management and Customer Data Integration for a Global Enterprise; Building Data Mining Applications for CRM; Data Warehousing, Data Mining and OLAP; Client/Server Architecture; SYBASE and Client/ Server Computing;* and *APPC: Introduction to LU6.2.*

Dr. Lawrence Dubov (Larry) is a recognized scientist, expert and thought leader in the implementation of complex business-driven technology solutions for financial services, banking, telecommunications, and pharmaceutical verticals, with the primary focus on Master Data Management (MDM), Customer Relationship Management (CRM), data warehousing, operational data stores, and service-oriented architecture. He has gained both depth and breadth of technical knowledge in multiple areas of Master Data Management, including data and solution architecture, matching technologies, customer-centric data transformations, data stewardship, and applications of information theory and advanced statistical methods to information quality. He has developed a strong holistic vision of the MDM problem domain and Master Data Governance implementation methodology based on practical experience gained through successful project implementations. He is an internationally recognized speaker and writer on the topics of Master Data Management and information management, quality, and governance. Larry has authored over 110 publications, with a recent focus on advanced mathematical methods in data governance, master data modeling, MDM roadmap development, business case definition, and accelerators for high complexity MDM programs and projects. In 2007 he coauthored a definitive book on MDM, *Master Data Management and Customer Data Integration for a Global Enterprise.*

Larry has held senior technology and management positions with IBM, Initiate Systems, Inc., and consulting companies, including BearingPoint and FutureNext ZYGA. Larry formerly worked as an independent consultant for a number of companies across various industry verticals. The list of Larry's clients includes but is not limited to Fortune 1000 companies and established mid-size organizations, such as Merrill Lynch, Bessemer Trust, Washington Mutual, Cenlar Bank, Merck, Johnson & Johnson, Hoffmann La Roche, Aventis, Estée Lauder, AT&T, Daimler-Benz.

Larry spent two years at Princeton University as a visiting research scientist working on mathematical models for optimal control of molecular processes. Earlier, during his career in Russia, he gained a strong scientific background with Ph.D. and Dr.Sci. degrees in Mathematical Physics.

A combination of multiple backgrounds—science (physics, chemistry, and advanced math), a deep knowledge of information technology, and an understanding of business processes—helps Larry see unique approaches to complex business problems and offer their solutions.

About the Technical Editors

Bernard K. Plagman is cofounder and chairman of TechPar Group (TPG), a technology advisory services company that consults on all facets of the information technology (IT) industry. TPG has delivered strategic and tactical advisory services to over 160 clients in eight years, serving technology investors, vendors, and enterprise users.

Paul Raskas has 30+ years of Fortune 500 consulting experience, working as a senior consultant at IBM and as an independent consultant. His work addresses application and data solutions in financial services, pharmaceutical, telecom, utilities, and transportation industries. He combines industry domain knowledge and cross-industry strategies, focusing on data architecture, data integration, data quality, Master Data Management, data governance, and Business Intelligence solutions.

Master Data Management and Data Governance
Second Edition

Alex Berson
Larry Dubov

New York   Chicago   San Francisco
Lisbon   London   Madrid   Mexico City
Milan   New Delhi   San Juan
Seoul   Singapore   Sydney   Toronto

The McGraw·Hill Companies

Library of Congress Cataloging-in-Publication Data

Berson, Alex.
  Master data management and data governance/Alex Berson, Larry Dubov.—
2nd ed.
           p.   cm.
  Rev. ed. of: Master data management and customer data integration for
a global enterprise/Alex Berson, Lawrence Dubov. 2007.
     Includes bibliographical references and index.
     ISBN 978-0-07-174458-4 (alk. paper)
     1. Customer relations—Data processing.   2. Data warehousing.   3. Data integration
(Computer science)   I. Dubov, Lawrence.   II. Berson, Alex.
Master data management and customer data integration for a global
enterprise.   III. Title.
     HF5415.5.B4835   2011
     658.8′120285574—dc22   2010049323

McGraw-Hill books are available at special quantity discounts to use as premiums and sales promotions, or for use in corporate training programs. To contact a representative, please e-mail us at bulksales@mcgraw-hill.com.

Master Data Management and Data Governance, Second Edition

4567890   DOC DOC   1543

ISBN   978-0-07-174458-4
MHID   0-07-174458-4

Associate Acquisitions Editor
  Meghan Riley

Editorial Supervisor
  Patty Mon

Project Manager
  Vasundhara Sawhney,
  Glyph International

Acquisitions Coordinator
  Stephanie Evans

Technical Editors
  Bernard Plagman
  Paul Raskas

Copy Editor
  Bart Reed

Proofreader
  Elise Oranges

Indexer
  Jack Lewis

Production Supervisor
  Jean Bodeaux

Composition
  Glyph International

Illustration
  Glyph International

Art Director, Cover
  Jeff Weeks

Contents at a Glance

Contents

Forewords

Finally we have the sequel! One that is from seasoned practitioners who have presciently zeroed in on the co-dependence of Master Data Management (MDM) and data governance.

Both Master Data Management and data governance programs are breaking new ground when it comes to complexity and business value justification for large-scale integration projects. Although established in the Global 5000–size financial service enterprises to some degree, Master Data Governance solutions are still an emerging area for both the vendor community and IT professionals. Moreover, there is a tremendous lack of published research on the convergence.

As chief research officer of The MDM Institute, I have been fortunate to work side by side with many of the same large enterprises that Alex and Larry have worked for and with in their MDM efforts. Early on, we commiserated about the lack of systemic rigor in providing the active data governance our clients were telling us they greatly needed. Clearly, our pioneering MDM ancestors were telling us to "go early, go governance" as we mutually came to the same determinations that:

- MDM and data governance are two vital IT initiatives that are both co-dependent and synergistic.

- Successful MDM requires a significant up-front data governance investment.

- Data governance as a discrete IT discipline benefits tremendously from the application of MDM.

At this point, potential readers should not need any more encouragement to read this book by two of the most experienced practitioners I know of. Clearly, Alex Berson and Larry Dubov were hard at work tackling the tough topic of "Master Data Governance" before the software vendor community had yet found religion (as the market now has "active," "passive," and my favorite "passive-aggressive" data governance flavors among the many marketing variations).

My team of research analysts and our Global 5000 IT clients greatly value the knowledge and skills that experienced pioneers such as Alex and Larry bring to our collective MDM consciousness. Now sit back and absorb… the industry's biggest and best download on the convergence of MDM and data governance.

Aaron Zornes

Aaron Zornes
Chief Research Officer, The MDM Institute, San Francisco,
and Conference Chairman, MDM & Data Governance Summit
(London, Madrid, New York, San Francisco, Singapore, Sydney, Tokyo)

T he single version of truth. The golden record. The 360-degree view. These buzzwords capture the nirvana state that data management professionals have strived to deliver to their business stakeholders for decades. Years of multimillion-dollar investments in large enterprise data warehousing, business intelligence, ERP, and CRM deployments and consolidations have only fanned the flames of discontent around data quality, data consistency, and ultimately, data trustworthiness. This was the environment that nurtured the birth and growth of the Master Data Management (MDM) market—including technology solutions such as Customer Data Integration (CDI) and Product Information Management (PIM), as well as consulting practices at management consultancies, systems integrators, and software vendors' professional services organizations.

These MDM technologies and best practices have matured significantly over the past decade, but the ability for data evangelists to secure executive sponsorship and funding for these investments—while also ensuring active collaboration and participation in the MDM initiative from their business partners—has been an ongoing challenge. Many organizations boast customer and/or product masters in production today, but while some are delivering needed business value, others unfortunately struggle with adoption, business justification, and a demonstrable return on an often large investment.

But from an MDM adoption standpoint, something good came out of the global economic downturn of the late 2000s. CEOs, CFOs, and CIOs, all in desperate need of any fine-tuning levers they could find to control their shrinking margins, reduce increasingly complex compliance and regulatory risk, and identify ways to differentiate their organizations from competition, increasingly embraced MDM. For years, these senior executives told their employees and shareholders that data is the organization's most critical asset, but finally they were providing resources to match the rhetoric. But having executive support is only step one. Knowing how to scope, plan, architect, implement, and administer an MDM capability remains a significant challenge. And MDM cannot deliver value and be effectively maintained without the implementation of a formal data governance program with active participation from both business and IT stakeholders—not an easy task in many corporate cultures with minimal business ownership and accountability for data quality.

To bridge this business/IT chasm, a key epiphany that all MDM evangelists must experience is the recognition that MDM and data governance initiatives should not be, and never should have been, about the data. Having a single trusted view of master data in some operational hub or analytical repository will never in fact directly deliver any of the strategic business drivers just listed. Trusted master data is only an enabler, and the goal of MDM and data governance must be to leverage trusted master data to improve the mission-critical business processes and decisions that actually run your business. So the key to MDM is something we at Forrester Research call "Process Data Management," which is the goal of aligning your MDM vision with the business processes and decisions that are inseparable from master data. Your MDM and data governance efforts must not only be aligned, but must be an embedded part of your organization's business process management and optimization strategies to ensure that trusted master data will in fact deliver the business value—and ultimately that prized single version of the truth we've been targeting for decades.

To help you on this journey through MDM's next stage of maturity, Alex Berson and Larry Dubov deliver this guide that can be leveraged by the MDM evangelist, architect, practitioner, and data governance program driver alike. Use this book as a resource to help you through each critical phase of your MDM initiative—from scoping and business case development, through architecture, implementation, and governance—and most importantly, as a tool to educate and recruit the business process professionals within your organization who need trusted master data to end the vicious cycle of process data management failure they have been experiencing for years.

Rob Karel,
Principal Analyst
Forrester Research, Inc.

Acknowledgments

First, I want to thank my friend and coauthor Larry Dubov for his knowledge, persistence, and dedication, without which this book would not have happened. Both Larry and I have formal scientific, academic background in mathematics, physics and computer science, and for this edition we unanimously decided to leverage this combined body of knowledge and introduce several concepts that are based on sound scientific principles such as the concept of information entropy for measuring information quality. We had a lot of fun writing these chapters and hope that this rewarding teamwork experience will drive our exploration of MDM and Master Data Governance into new depths in the near future.

I want to thank Aaron Zornes, founder and Chief Research Officer of The MDM Institute, for his kind words of encouragement, great quotes, support and help, and Rob Karol of Forrster Research for his insightful comments and advice. Both Aaron and Rob were kind enough to review the entire manuscript in detail and write the book's two Forewords, and I'm very grateful to have received their endorsements.

Very special thanks to my many friends and colleagues who I've worked with over the years, and who keep defining new challenges in and the vision of information management technology and, in particular, Master Data Management and Master data Governance. In particular, I want to express my gratitude to Gene Fernandez, my friend and colleague for many years, for his vision, energy, and continuous support. I also have to offer special thanks to Guy Chiarello, Adrian Kunzle, Mike Urciuoli, Craig Goulding, Ian Miller, Sachin Sangtani, Joe Rabbia, John Tabback, Steve Tsao, Mark Gaylord, David Laurance, Kevin Tyson, Dan Zinkin, Paul Yaron, Vince Feingold, Spencer Fine, Mark Appel, Buzz Moschetti, Peter Cherasia, Rich Burger, and many others for their continuous support and for giving me an opportunity to learn and work in a very stimulating and challenging environment on the leading edge of information technology.

I truly appreciate the opportunity to work with my friends Bernard Plagman and Charles Popper at TechPar Group, and to learn from their wisdom and lifelong experiences.

I also would like to express gratitude and appreciation to my numerous friends and colleagues at IBM, Merrill Lynch, Entrust, CitiGroup, The MDM Institute, Vertica, PriceWaterhouseCoopers, Trident Capital, and many other organizations that inspired me to write this book and helped with their knowledge, vision, optimism, perseverance, and invaluable insights. I want to specifically thank Michael Stonebraker, Peter Meekin, Alberto Yepez, David Ketsdever, Kris Bryant, Shanker Ramamurthy, Joe Hollander, Larry Caminiti, and my life-long friends Yakov and Lilia Tsalalikhin.

I would like to thank all those who have helped with clarifications, criticism, and valuable information during the writing of this book, and were patient enough to read the entire manuscript and make many useful suggestions. Special thanks and gratitude go to Bernard Plagman, Paul Raskas, and Jonathan Harris for their insightful edits. And I truly appreciate the reviews, valuable insights, advice, and quotes kindly provided by Steve Adler, Malcolm Chisholm, David Loshin, Marty Moseley, Len Silverston, and Robert Hillard

And, of course, we would have never finished this book without the invaluable assistance and thoroughness of McGraw-Hill's Lisa McClain, Meghan Riley, Patty Mon, and Bart Reed, and the great team from Glyph International led by Vasundhara Sawhney.

Finally, the key reason for writing this book is my family. My very special thanks to my wife Irina, my son Vlad and his wife Tara, my daughter Michelle, my grandchildren Colin Alexander, and Anna Valentina, who became an added inspiration for writing this book, my mother, and my mother- and father-in-law, who recently passed away and will always be loved and remembered. Thank you all for giving me time to complete the book and never-ending optimism, support, and love, and for understanding the book's importance.

—*Alex Berson*

I am grateful to my coauthor Alex Berson for the idea of writing this book and his enthusiasm that we could pull this book off despite the workloads we both have on our day jobs. It was a great pleasure working with Alex on summarizing our experiences, formulating the ideas, and reconciling our views. The views, sometimes different on the surface, were usually very similar when discussions were taken to the right depth. My work and discussions with Alex helped me a lot in deepening, summarizing, and systematizing my views on Master Data Management and Data Governance, their trends, and some key financial industry aspects around integration and synergies between MDM, data governance, and data warehousing.

Special thanks to Aaron Zornes, Chief Research Officer at The MDM Institute for his book review, the foreword and favorable quotes that reflect Aaron's enthusiasm and great insights into MDM and data governance.

I am thankful to Rob Karel, Senior Analyst at Forrester Research, for his support, book review, and discussions. I highly appreciate the book reviews, valuable insights, suggestions, and quotes provided by Steve Adler, Malcolm Chisholm, David Loshin, Marty Moseley, Len Silverston, and Robert Hillard. Special thanks to Marty—I have learned a lot partnering with him at Initiate Business Management Consulting.

I highly appreciate the work done by the technical editors of this book, Paul Raskas, Bernard Plagman, and Jonathan Harris, for their great comments and suggestions, which helped us improve the readability and overall quality of this book.

I would like to express my special gratitude to my friend and colleague Paul Raskas for helpful discussions on MDM-related topics and for partnership on a number of projects. Discussions with Paul, especially on the topics of Master Data Modeling and Data Governance were very fruitful.

I am thankful to Initiate Executive Management, Bill Conroy, Jeff Galowich, Jim Cushman, and Gina Sandon for their support of the idea of this book.

Special thanks to Dr. Scott Schumacher for fruitful discussions on the applications of Information Theory to data quality and some illustrative materials used in the book.

My knowledge of the Master Data Management and data governance comes mainly from practical project implementations, and everyday work with my clients and colleagues.

Therefore, many people who worked with me on MDM including implementation, sales, marketing, and product development contributed indirectly to this book. Many of my colleagues at Initiate contributed to the content of this book indirectly through numerous discussions of practical MDM and data governance problems, solution options and approaches. Special thanks to Jim Cushman, Jon Case, Alex Eastman, Upwan Chachra, and Bill Dorner.

Articulating MDM and Data Governance values and problem domains to different audiences is very challenging. We often face this type of challenges in sales cycles. I learned a lot from my MDM sales colleagues at Initiate and IBM. Among them Greg Shaw, Angela Losacco, Irene Nathan, Paul Schmerold, Neil Day, Linda Crump, Louis Hausle, Michael Fasciano, and Odilio Abreu. I am thankful to Crysta Anderson for her great work in assisting me with a number of blogs covering a few book topics.

I highly appreciate the work performed by the teams McGraw-Hill that helped us with the publishing lifecycle, which includes a broad range of activities from support for the book proposal to editing, art design, marketing, and other critical activities required to bring this book to the market. Among these individuals my special thanks to Lisa McClain, Meghan Riley, Vasundhara Sawhney, Bart Reed, Patty Mon, Bettina Faltermeier, and Karen Schopp.

I am very thankful to my wife Irene, as she inspired me to write this book, my son Anthony, and my daughter Anastasia for their encouragement and patience since this book took a lot of my time from the family. Indeed the book was written over the weekends and on vacation. I am also grateful to my mother and mother-in-law, and my sister Julia and her family for their encouragement and interest in this book.

—Larry Dubov

Introduction

About This Book

This book is about one of the top technology trends in the area of information management. This trend, known as Master Data Management, and its sister discipline—Master Data Governance—has evolved and become more pronounced over the last two to three years, and is considered by many analysts to be a high-impact, high-complexity, and broad-applicability technology that is focused on new ways of structuring, choosing, understanding, integrating, and disseminating information that is needed to run a business, service customers, and comply with numerous regulatory requirements.

To paraphrase Claude Shannon (the "father" of information theory and the concepts of information entropy), information is that which resolves uncertainty. Our entire existence is a process of gathering, analyzing, understanding, and acting on information. Progressive resolution of uncertainty is the key to the way we make business and personal decisions. The need to sustain new regulatory pressures and achieve competitive advantages by managing customer- or product-level profitability and risk-adjusted return on investment drives profound changes in the way business and government organizations operate. Traditional account-centric and application-specific silos of business processes restrict organizations' ability to meet the aforementioned challenge. Therefore, in order to succeed in today's highly competitive global and dynamic markets, businesses are making serious investments in the new business-entity-centric processes and technical capabilities. These new capabilities should allow organizations to effectively focus on selecting, acquiring, understanding, and managing accurate and relevant information about their primary business targets—customers, products, partners, patients, inventories, prices, services, and other areas of business concerns.

In doing so, enterprises are collecting and processing ever-increasing volumes of information, especially as business conditions change, markets shrink or expand, companies grow organically or by acquisitions, and customer retention and products' timely market introduction and competitiveness become some of the key business metrics.

As we entered the digital age, this accumulation of data has been accelerating. Now we have access to the ocean of information that was created by or stored in computer systems and networks over the last several years. This information now includes not just traditional structured data, but also semi-structured (that is, images, graphics, full-motion video, sounds) and unstructured data. Indeed, we brought with us data that previously existed only in nondigital form, such as books and paper documents. We have learned to digitize that data quickly and efficiently and thus created even more computer files and databases, all the time hoping that all this "stuff" will be managed transparently and effectively by our reliable, trusted computer systems and applications. The reasons for engaging in this data collection are obvious: We live in the age of digital information, where the Internet and the World Wide Web have made enterprise boundaries porous or fuzzy in order to attract a large number of customers and to enhance their experience. In this new digital age, an agile enterprise can become competitive only when it has access to more relevant, accurate, timely, and complete data about business conditions and performance metrics, enterprise customers, prospects and partners, products and markets, and a myriad of other things. Having the right data at the right time is even more imperative if you consider the challenges and the revolutionary nature of transforming a traditional account-centric business into a customer- or product-centric, global, agile, and intelligent enterprise.

Given the ever-growing amount of data that is collected and managed by the business units of global enterprises today, we are facing the difficult challenge of creating, finding, selecting, and managing data that is complete, accurate, relevant, and secure, and that is uniformly available to all enterprises and users who need this data to run their business. This challenge of creating and managing a new authoritative system of record is the focus of Master Data Management (MDM) and its closely related management discipline—Data Governance. The issues, approaches, concerns, drivers, benefits, architecture, applications, and trends of Master Data Management and Data Governance are the subject of this book.

About the Second Edition

The first edition of the popular book titled *Master Data Management and Customer Data Integration for the Global Enterprise,* by Alex Berson and Larry Dubov (McGraw-Hill, 2007), proved to be a timely, useful, and influential work that was widely accepted as the authoritative text on the subject of Master Data Management.

Since the first edition was published, Master Data Management has matured and advanced significantly. In fact, analysts, practitioners, and industry observers agree that Master Data Management is one of the fastest growing and dynamic areas of information technology. The advancements in Master Data Management include the approaches to building multidomain MDM systems, advancements in master data modeling, maturity of the approaches used to define the business case for MDM, recognition of the value and the importance of the relationships between MDM and its "sibling" Data Governance, and evolving architectural patterns in MDM.

These advancements and changes in MDM are quite profound, and have given rise to a whole new family of applications and solutions in the MDM space. In particular, MDM has evolved from its mostly individual-based Customer Data Integration to a truly Master Data Management solution for a broad variety of business domains, including individuals and institutions, complex accounts, products, financial instruments, and many others. In addition, MDM has been moving toward business-process-driven specialization, specifically toward operational and analytical MDM. As the result of these changes, the MDM practitioners and business stakeholders are looking for deep, proven thought leadership that can help them on their journey to implement MDM solutions.

Thus, the need for a major revision of the book in the form of a second edition that addresses all new developments in the MDM space has become a clear necessity.

This second edition is a significant revision and expansion of the first edition of the book: It adds several new chapters and covers a number of new or updated topics, including an introduction to MDM classification dimensions, discussions on Reference Master Data Management, hierarchy management, master data modeling, entity resolution for various domains, quantitative approaches to a justifiable business case, a discussion on the need for and composition of the MDM roadmap, use of information theory to measure and manage the quality of master data, an extensive discussion on the definition, approaches, and processes of Master Data Governance, and newly formulated MDM guiding principles. These new topics are explicitly mentioned in the table of contents for easy reference.

Who Should Read This Book

The topics of Master Data Management and Data Governance have very broad applicability across all industries. Indeed, the notion of transforming businesses from account-centric to customer- or product-centric enterprises applies equally well to any industry segment that deals with customers, products, and services, including financial services, healthcare, pharmaceutical, telecommunications, retail, and so on. MDM is beneficial and often necessary for any organization or industry that needs an authoritative source of customer, prospect, partner, patient, employee, information, product information, pricing and market, or reference data in general. The same argument applies to government entities that need to have a complete and accurate view of individuals for a variety of legitimate purposes, not the least of which are law enforcement and national security.

To discuss major issues related to Master Data Management and Data Governance, this book covers a broad set of topics, including the areas of business case definition, business transformations, data management, information security, regulatory compliance, Data Governance and data quality, and business process redesign. Therefore, this book is a must-read for a variety of business and technology professionals across all industry segments and the public sector. The audience for this book includes business unit managers; business process analysts and designers; technology project managers; infrastructure and operations staff; data analysts, data stewards, data quality managers, and database administrators; application developers; corporate strategists; information security specialists; corporate risk and regulatory compliance officers; and members of the offices of the CFO, CSO, CRO, and CIO.

Due to the complexity of the MDM problem space, many Master Data Management initiatives happen to be multiyear, multimillion-dollar projects that involve large teams of employees, external consultants, system integrators, and vendor-supplied professional services organizations. All these professionals will benefit from reading this book.

Finally, the topics of MDM and Data Governance are getting "hot" and attracting significant attention from the general and specialized industry analysts. All major industry research and analyst organizations, including Gartner Group and Forrester Research, have initiated appropriate coverage or created research services focusing on Master Data Management and Data Governance. Many vendors that have or plan to have MDM solutions in their portfolios are organizing user groups and vendor-sponsored conferences. Dedicated organizations such as The MDM Institute have leaped into existence and are aggressively organizing industry-wide forums and conferences. Technical and business professionals who plan to attend these types of conferences would find this book very useful.

The Style of This Book

This book is different from research and analysts' reports on the subject of MDM and Data Governance, in that it does not base its discussions strictly on industry-wide surveys and published statistics. Rather, the book is based on our actual professional experience, and we continue to be involved in some of the more advanced and large-scale implementations of MDM in the commercial sector, especially in financial services and pharmaceuticals. The book has been structured as a self-teaching guide that includes an introduction to the business problem domain related to MDM and Data Governance, and a discussion on the core architecture principles and concerns that should be interesting to those readers looking to learn not just the "how" but also the "why" of the MDM and Data Governance approaches. We have included a significant number of references to the key printed and online materials on Master Data Management and Data Governance. This will help the reader who wants to use this book as a single point of entry into the fields of MDM and Data Governance.

The book includes a rather detailed discussion of the issues related to information security and data protection in MDM environments. We feel very strongly that MDM designers and implementers should address these topics at the inception of every MDM initiative, regardless of whether a chosen vendor solution provides these capabilities directly or indirectly.

In addition to being an architectural primer for MDM, this book is also a practical implementation guide that can help MDM practitioners to avoid costly technical, business process, and organizational mistakes. To that end, the book includes several chapters that provide a step-by-step discussion of the practical issues and concerns relating to the defining the MDM business case and the MDM roadmap, implementation approaches of MDM projects, and an in-depth discussion on the key issues and concerns of Data Governance. And for those readers who are looking to select a vendor solution, the book offers a brief overview of the state of the art in the vendor solution marketplace for MDM.

The book concludes with a few thoughts about the trends and directions in the area of Master Data Management.

This book includes a fair amount of diagrams, figures, formulas, examples, and illustrations in an attempt to present a lot of rather complicated material in as simple a form as possible. Due to the relatively high degree of complexity of MDM and certain aspects of Data Governance, such as data quality measurements and metrics, wherever possible, the book combines theoretical and architectural discussion of a specific subject with some practical examples of how these issues could be addressed in real-life implementations.

The book is about a "hot" and very dynamic subject. All material included in the book was current at the time the book was written. We realize that as Master Data Management and Data Governance continue to evolve, and as the MDM vendor market matures, changes to the material covered in the book will be necessary. We intend to revise the book if and when significant developments in the areas of Master Data Management and Data Governance warrant changes.

What This Book Includes

The book contains five parts and two appendixes. Each chapter of the book contains a list of references specific to the content of the chapter.

Part I of the book defines the business imperative, drivers, and benefits of Master Data Management as well as the need for and role of Data Governance. It also discusses the challenges and risks associated with enterprise business model transformation inspired and enabled by MDM.

Part II of the book continues the MDM discussion by taking a closer look at the architecture and design concerns of MDM solutions, with a strong emphasis on the design issues of MDM Data Hub platforms and master data modeling. Part II offers an architecture background that introduces readers to several key concepts, including the enterprise architecture framework and service-oriented architecture.

Part III deals with major regulations, compliance requirements, and risks associated with implementing MDM solutions. This part offers a detailed discussion on general information security goals, techniques, and approaches. It concentrates on several important themes, including general data protection, intellectual property, and content protection using Enterprise Rights Management. This part of the book also provides an in-depth look at authentication, authorization, access control, policies, entitlements, and data visibility issues that have to be addressed in practically every MDM implementation.

Part IV of the book discusses a broad set of issues, concerns, and practical approaches to implement an MDM solution. It begins with the techniques and methods of defining an MDM business case and the roadmap, and specifically talks about how to start a successful MDM project. Part IV also provides an in-depth discussion on the implementation aspects of master entity resolution and processes designed to discover and leverage the totality of entity relationships with other entities and the enterprise. This part of the book also discusses Data Governance, with the primary focus on Master Data Governance processes and metrics, and introduces the reader to the advanced approaches to data quality metrics based on key concepts of the Information Theory. Part IV includes topics on the MDM implementation concerns related to data synchronization, data quality, and data management standards.

Part V concludes the book with a brief discussion of the market landscape and an overview of the relevant vendor solutions available on the market at the time of this writing. It also provides a brief discussion on future trends and directions for Master Data Management.

The appendixes include a list of common abbreviations and a glossary of key terms.

Introduction to Master Data Management

O ur civilization has evolved into a modern society by continuously acquiring and developing new knowledge and creating innovative ways to improve personal and business conditions. This evolution in large part is based on our ability and ever-growing need to collect and understand information in order to run businesses; predict the weather; analyze market performance; manage personal finances; define medical diagnoses in order to prescribe proper medication, and, in general, to do both mundane and new, exciting things.

Over the course of history, we have collected a huge amount of data; learned how to interpret it and transform it into useful, meaningful information; and even created a number of extremely sophisticated information theories and branches of information science. One interesting observation about the way we collect and use data is our reluctance to discard data that is either old or no longer relevant. For example, you may have a collection of old professional books, and most of them have some value. You have to decide which books are redundant and need to be discarded and which books should still be retained because some chapters or sections are still valuable. You might also be thinking that it is a good idea to create a catalog of books with pointers to their locations. Otherwise, you will not be able to find the book you want promptly when you need it.

Other examples of data that we tend to collect and keep include items of family history and sentimental value, such as photographs, letters from parents and grandparents, and certificates of awards we received in school—things we want to keep for a variety of reasons, all of which make the data more valuable as time goes on. Of course, there are other types of information we may have to keep in order to comply with the law (such as income tax returns) or for personal protection (paid promissory notes or signed legal papers). Finally, some of us like to keep documents that are no longer valid and are replaced by newer, more accurate versions—for example, old resumes or outdated wills. Keeping this old "stuff" eventually becomes a storage problem, and this is when people move the boxes with old documents into their attics and basements. As the amount of data stored this way grows, the task of finding the right document stored somewhere in the attic becomes a challenge. This can become more than just an inconvenience: Storing outdated or inaccurate documents may have some interesting and even unpleasant consequences. For example, if there are two significantly different versions of a Last Will and Testament document, using the wrong version during the settlement may have drastically different consequences from those intended by the owner of the will. And, of course, data is different from other "stuff"—you cannot have a garage sale to get rid of data you no longer need!

The business world has certainly experienced this dramatic data-growth phenomenon as well. And this trend has become even more pronounced as we have entered the digital age and now have access not only to the ocean of data naturally created by or stored in the computer systems but also to data that previously existed only in a paper form but has been digitized to be managed by computer systems and applications. This data proliferation in the business world has not been driven only by traditional organizational structures and processes where various application areas and lines of business created and managed their own versions or views of the data; other business and technical factors contributed to this phenomenon as well:

- The Internet and the World Wide Web have made enterprise boundaries "porous" or "fuzzy" in order to attract large numbers of customers and to enhance the customers' experience.

- The cost of disk storage dropped significantly in the 1990s. This prompted enterprises to collect increasingly vast amounts of data and develop complex data models with hundreds and thousands of entities at multiple levels of aggregation. Enterprises started storing ancillary data, providing much more context about the transaction or event.

- The number of entities and attributes managed by enterprises increased significantly. Enterprise architecture and data governance lagged behind and were poorly prepared for the tremendous increases in the volumes and complexity of the data. This has resulted in a significant accumulation of data issues over the decades.

In this new digital age, an agile enterprise can become competitive only when it has access to relevant, accurate, and complete information about business conditions and performance metrics, enterprise customers, prospects and partners, products and markets, and a myriad of other things. Given the ever-growing amount of data that is collected and managed by the business units of global enterprises today, we can draw an analogy similar to searching for old files in attics and basements. Enterprises have a hard time creating, finding, and managing data that is complete, accurate, relevant, and uniformly available to all businesses and users that need this data to run their businesses. In addition to the technical challenges of creating such a master data facility, there are several organizational and political obstacles to cleaning and rationalizing existing data stores. A common example would be the individual business unit's desire to hold on to its version of data because it is deemed unique to the business unit's goals, or because it helps eliminate dependencies of data management across business units. Some of these reasons are perfectly valid, but they do not eliminate the need to have an enterprise-wide, accurate, and complete view of the key entities and relationships of critical enterprise data.

Master Data Management

The need to clean up the "old stuff" and create an accurate, timely, and complete set of key business-critical data entities and relationships needed to manage and grow the business is the focus of Master Data Management (MDM).

The issues, approaches, concerns, and applications of Master Data Management and its strategic "sibling," data governance, are the subject of this book.

Overview of Master Data Management

I t is often said that Master Data Management enables an enterprise to create and use a "single version of the truth." As such, Master Data Management applies to almost all industries and covers a broad category of corporate data. Banks, insurance companies and brokerage houses, service companies, hospitality companies, airlines, car manufacturers, publishing houses, healthcare providers, telecommunication companies, retail businesses, high-technology organizations, manufacturing, energy providers, and law firms have at least one common need—the need to have access to complete, accurate, timely, and secure information about their respective businesses' financial and market performance, partners, customers, prospects, products, patients, providers, competitors, and other important business entities. Similarly, this need to create and use accurate and complete information about individuals and organizational entities applies equally well to the public sector. Governments at different levels across the globe need to know their citizens, patients, and persons of interest (POI) from multiple perspectives. They also need to understand what services are provided to which individuals and locations, where people and organizations reside, and so on.

Master Data Management (MDM)

As stated previously, the quest for a single version of the truth is not an industry or geography or data-domain specific. Therefore, the scope of Master Data Management is very broad and may cover customer data, product data, supplier data, employee data, reference data, and other key types of data that should be used to consistently manage the entire enterprise in an integrated fashion. And the primary vehicle by which Master Data Management enables this consistent and integrated management of the business is the ability to create and maintain an accurate and timely authoritative "system of record" for a given subject domain. In the case of customer data, for example, Master Data Management can support various aspects of customer, partner, and prospect information, including customers (both individuals and business entities), customer profiles, accounts, buying preferences, behavioral characteristics, service requests and complaints, contact information, and other important attributes.

Defining Master Data

The creation of a single version of truth and managing the quality of its data is a problem for almost every enterprise. The sheer number and variety of data quality issues and cross-system inconsistencies accumulated over long periods of time make it difficult even to list and prioritize the issues across the enterprise. This makes it practically impossible to focus on the data quality overall and concentrate on a single version of truth for every piece of information within one application or data domain. Who wants to boil the ocean? This rhetorical question reveals a great enterprise challenge: What categories of data should be a priority for the enterprise projects around the single version of truth and data quality?

Master Data Management resolves this uncertainty in priorities by clearly stating MDM focus.[1] MDM claims that some entities (master entities) are more important than others because they are widely distributed across the enterprise as well as reside and are maintained in multiple systems and application silos.

Master entities are critical for multiple business and operational processes. Although these entities and associated data domains may comprise only a small percent of an enterprise data model, their significance from the data-quality perspective is disproportionally high.

This point is particularly important when we consider the role of MDM in managing reference data. Reference data includes entities with fewer record counts than in traditional MDM entities. Reference data deals with identifiers, categories, types, classifications, and other "pick lists" defined by the business and/or data governance policies.

Bringing "order" to master data often solves 60–80 percent of the most critical and difficult-to-fix data quality problems. Thus, sound enterprise practices in management and governance of master data directly contribute to the success of the organization. Mismanagement of these practices and lack of master data governance pose the highest risk.

> **Master Data**
> *Master data* are those entities, relationships, and attributes that are critical for an enterprise and foundational to key business processes and application systems.

MDM and the "Single Version of Truth"

In a number of cases, "single version" has been interpreted literally and simplistically as a version having only one physical record representing a customer, product, location, and so on, that is equally useful, available, and accessible to all functional groups across the enterprise. In reality, enterprises typically require a holistic panoramic view of master entities that includes multiple (sometimes 10–15) definitions and functional views approved by data owners and maintained according to established data governance policies. These views can have different sets of attributes, different tolerances to false positives or false negatives, different latency requirements, and so on. For instance, the marketing department may have requirements different from those of customer service and different from compliance. A definition of a customer can vary significantly between shipments and billing. "Individual," "household," and "institution" can represent a customer in different contexts and scenarios. Similarly, the notion of a product or service can vary broadly based on the context of discussion within an enterprise. The notion of a holistic and panoramic master entity view represents real-life MDM requirements much better.

In essence, MDM is a great way to prioritize data quality and information development problems and focus resources properly to maximize the return on a data quality effort. Expressed differently, MDM is an efficient approach to fixing enterprise data quality problems (cherry picking in the area of data quality and data management, with master data being the cherry in a huge data quality garden).

In the early stages of MDM, two separate domain-specific streams had emerged: CDI (Customer Data Integration) and PIM (Product Information Management). Different software vendors focused on different data domains, and single-domain implementations were predominant. As MDM was maturing and evolving, the value of the multidomain MDM has become increasingly clear. For instance, it is much easier to build and maintain cross-domain relationships when MDM is implemented on a single multidomain MDM platform.

Party, customer, product, account, organization, and location top the list of choices of what most companies recognize as their master data. The terms "party" and "product" have a variety of industry-specific variants. These entity types are not just widely distributed across application silos but are also represented by high volumes of records, which creates additional challenges.

In the case of customer data, for example, Master Data Management can support various aspects of customer, partner, and prospect information, including customer profiles, accounts, buying preferences, service requests and complaints, contact information, and other important attributes.

MDM, Customer Centricity, and Data Quality

MDM strategy, architecture, and enabling technologies dealing with various aspects of customer data constitute the largest segment of the current Master Data Management market. One direct benefit of MDM is its ability to enable customer centricity and reach the often-elusive goal of creating and effectively using a "single and holistic version of the truth about customers." This single version of the truth is one of the requirements to support the fundamental transformation of an enterprise from an account-centric business to a new, effective, and agile customer-centric business—a transformation that has a profound impact on the way companies conduct business and interact with their customers.

Why Master Data Management Now?

Master Data Management emerged as an area of enterprise data management over the last decade, and now has become a broadly recognized and fast-growing discipline.

Although the aspirations of MDM are not new, the interest in developing MDM solutions has grown significantly. We can now see MDM-related initiatives being implemented across the wide spectrum of industries. This timing is not accidental, and is among several key reasons why implementing Master Data Management has become such a universal requirement for almost any business and industry. Some of these reasons are driven by recently adapted and emerging regulations.

Regulatory Compliance

A number of well-publicized corporate scandals and class-action shareholder lawsuits gave rise to new pieces of legislation and regulations, such as the Sarbanes-Oxley Act, the Basel II Capital Accord, and numerous Securities and Exchange Commission (SEC) rulings, all of which were focused on companies' need and requirement to provide, use, and report accurate, verifiable, and relevant data about their financial performance and significant material events that could impact company valuations and shareholder value. A few examples illustrate this point:

- On February 17, 2009, U.S. President Barack Obama signed the American Recovery and Reinvestment Act (ARRA) into law. ARRA funds ($789 billion) are targeted toward rebuilding infrastructure and positioning the country to grow the next-generation economy. The healthcare part of the bill includes health information technology ($19 billion) to stimulate early adopters of Electronic Health Record (EHR) standards and technologies.

- Interoperable Health Infrastructure—a ten-year plan to build a national electronic health infrastructure in the U.S. The idea is that with interoperable electronic health records, always-current medical information could be available wherever and whenever the patient and attending healthcare professional need it across the healthcare ecosystem. The plan improves efficiency and lowers costs in the healthcare system through the adoption of state-of-the-art health information systems and significantly improved data management with the primary focus on patient and provider data.

Privacy and Data Protection

In addition to overarching reporting regulations such as the Sarbanes-Oxley Act, companies have to comply with a multitude of local, state, federal, and international regulations focused on the following:

- Various aspects related to protecting enterprise data from unauthorized access, use, and compromise

- Capturing and enforcing customer privacy preferences

- Protecting customer data from malicious use and identity theft, the fastest-growing white-collar crime

Regulations such as the Gramm-Leach-Bliley Act, the Health Insurance Portability and Accountability Act (HIPAA), and state regulations such as California's SB 1386 require that companies implement effective and verifiable security controls designed to protect data, ensure data integrity, and provide appropriate notifications in case of a security breach resulting in data privacy and integrity compromise.

Safety and Security

The increased volume and global reach of money-laundering activities, the events of September 11, 2001, and growing appreciation of terroristic threats gave rise to regulations such as the USA Patriot Act with its Anti-Money Laundering (AML) and Know Your Customer (KYC) provisions. These regulations not only require an enterprise to maintain accurate and timely data on its customers and their financial transactions, but also to manage this data in such a way that it can be analyzed to detect and prevent money-laundering or other fraudulent activities before these transactions can take place. An attempt to blow up Northwest Airlines Flight 253 on Christmas day of 2009 and the widely publicized failure of the U.S. government agencies to provide timely actions to ensure safety and security of the flight indicate that significant and complex problems in these areas persist.

These regulations require that an organization maintain integrity, security, accuracy, timeliness, and proper controls over the content and usage of corporate operational and customer data—in effect, this is the requirement to implement Master Data Management for any data subject area that needs to be in compliance with key oversight tenets of Sarbanes-Oxley, Basel II, Gramm-Leach-Bliley, ARRA, and others.

Growing Complexity and Increased Velocity of Business and Government Activities

In addition to the nondiscretionary requirements of regulatory compliance, the need for Master Data Management can be easily traced to the more traditional goal of improving customer service and customer experience management. Having an accurate "single version of the truth" allows an organization to understand the factors and trends that may affect the business. Here are some particulars:

- Having an authoritative master data set allows an organization to reduce costs by sunsetting and discontinuing old application systems that create and use various "local" versions of the data.

- Having accurate and complete data about customers and their interactions with the enterprise allows an organization to gain better insight into the customers' goals, demands, abilities, and their propensity to request additional products and services, thus increasing the cross-sell and up-sell revenue opportunities.

- Having a complete picture of the customer allows an enterprise to offer a rich set of personalized services and appropriate treatments—the factors leading to improved customer experience and reduced customer attrition.

These goals and benefits, in turn, are driven by a number of factors related to the growing complexity and increased velocity of business and government activities, as discussed next:

- Business and government structures are evolving over time, and both the size and complexity of the organizations continue to grow to reflect the global, dynamic, and interconnected nature of the business and regulatory environments. In the case of business, we see increasing need to understand key business facts in a consistent, holistic way that integrates both cross-LOB (line of business) and cross-channel views. For example, a diversified global financial institution may create and maintain views of their customers that are specific to a particular line of business such as retail bank, investment bank, credit card division, and risk management division.

- Creating a panoramic, holistic view of the customer is a real business imperative that can significantly improve customer service, allow for better analysis of customer needs and credit risk exposure, and would allow the organization to better understand the totality of the relationships it has or may have with the customer.

- A similar situation arises when an organization creates a specific customer view based on the channel it uses to interface with the customer (bank branch, online channel, broker-driven interactions, and so on). In this case, MDM can become an enabler of cross-channel integration.

- The need for an integrated, accurate, and consistent view of the customers, products, locations, vendors, and suppliers is further exacerbated in cases of industry consolidations via mergers and acquisitions (M&A), an activity that is affecting many industry segments and equally impacting small, medium, and very large enterprises.

These points apply not just to customers but to patients and service providers in the healthcare industry, travelers in the travel and leisure industry, citizens and persons of interest in government and law enforcement areas, and many other data domains, thus covering all the major types of Master Data Management.

Challenges of Creating and Managing Master Data

Understanding the reasons for embarking on a Master Data Management initiative does not make it easier to accomplish the goals of MDM. Some significant challenges have to be overcome in order to make Master Data Management a reality. As the term "Master Data Management" implies, one of these challenges is centered on how to make data under management a "golden," authoritative version known as the "master."

For example, in the case of building Customer Relationship Management (CRM)[2] solutions across sales, marketing, and customer service channels, master data may consist of customer personal information (for example, name, address, and tax identification number), their assets and account numbers, service/warranty records, and history of service or product complaints. In the healthcare industry, consider Enterprise Master Patient Index (EMPI), the healthcare-specific variant of MDM for patient data widely used in hospitals, medical centers, and Integrated Delivery Networks (IDNs). There, master data may include not only patient personal information but also some diagnostic and prescription data, data on healthcare providers (such as doctors and hospitals), health insurance information, and similar data points. In the consumer retail business, master data may include information on products, product codes, suppliers, contracts, stores, sales, inventory levels, current and planned sales promotions, and so on. Even within the organization, master data varies from one business unit to another. For example, the scope of the master data subset for the accounting department within a retail enterprise may include information on budgets, cost centers, department codes, company hierarchies, invoices, accounts payable, and accounts receivables. Of course, in this case, the goal of Master Data Management would be to eventually integrate various subsets of department-level master data into an enterprise-wide master data superset.

Whether it is about customers, products, partners, or invoices, having relevant information in the form of master data allows businesses to capture key performance indicators, analyze all business transactions, and measure results to increase business effectiveness and competitiveness.

MDM and Business Processes

In order to create domain-specific, complete, accurate, and integrated master data, an organization needs to develop and institutionalize processes that help to discover and resolve inconsistencies, incompleteness, and other data quality issues caused in significant part by the way the established enterprises collect, store, and process data. Typically, the data that should be used to build the enterprise master is collected, stored, and processed by different business units, departments, and subsidiaries using different application systems; different definitions for the same data attributes; and different technologies, processes, formats, and transformation rules. The result is disjoined islands of data that manifest data quality issues in a number of ways, including the following:

- Semantic inconsistencies at the data attribute level include the following symptoms:
  - Different business units often use the same data attributes to describe different entities. For example, a customer identifier for CRM master data may point to a social security number but could be a Dun & Bradstreet DUNS number for a supply-chain business area.
  - Data attributes that describe business entities (product names, total revenue, and so on) often contain different values for the same attributes across different applications and lines of business. For example, a product name in one application may mean a product type in the other, and a product code in a third application.
  - Business entities may be identified differently across the enterprise because different applications systems may use different reference data sources.

- Inconsistencies in attribute-level data often go hand in hand with the inconsistencies across data-related business rules that define the way the data has to be formatted, translated, and used; these rules often vary from one business unit and application system to another.

- Data relationship inconsistencies impact the ability to identify explicit and/or inferred relationships between business entities (for example, accounts and payments, customers and households, and products and suppliers). These relationships are often defined differently in different applications and across lines of business. This is not a pure technology issue, although it is not unusual to find an organization that over time created various data stores designed strictly to support the business requirements of an individual business unit. This "stovepipe" design approach often results in situations that naturally create inconsistencies in data definitions, content, and structures, such as expressions of how various entities are related to one another.

- Business entities such as products, partners, and suppliers are sometimes inherently organized into hierarchies. For example, the corporate structure of a large supplier may contain a parent company and several levels of subsidiaries. Traversing these hierarchies is one of the requirements for applications that, for example, need to understand and manage intercompany relationships and to measure the total value of the transactions conducted with all business entities of a given corporate structure. Depending on the scope and design of an individual application, these hierarchies may be represented differently across system domains.

And the list can go on and on …

This discussion of data quality may appear to be of a more traditional nature and only slightly related to the goals of Master Data Management. In fact, the issues of data quality raised here are the primary factors in making the MDM goal of data integration across the enterprise much harder.[3]

To put it another way, MDM is much more than traditional data quality initiatives: Whereas most of the data quality initiatives are concerned with improving data quality within the scope of a particular application area or at a level of the specific line of business, MDM is focused on solving data-quality concerns in an integrated fashion across the entire enterprise.

Moreover, MDM is intrinsically linked with enterprise business processes and Business Process Management (BPM) technologies. Indeed, many business processes are designed assuming that accurate, complete data that can be trusted to execute business transactions and make key business decision is available as and when needed, preferably in the form of a trusted authoritative "system of record" (SOR). As defined in the previous sections, this system of record is created by an MDM solution. Conversely, the business process owners need to realize that, more often than not, the business processes have to be designed and aware of not only having access to the master data from the MDM system, but also that data created by these business processes can be of very questionable quality as it gets consumed by an MDM system. In short, MDM and BPM together have a profound impact on each other as well as on the overall data quality and the resulting effectiveness and behavior of the business.

This enterprise-wide impact of MDM on data quality of established and newly enabled business processes is a direct consequence of the MDM goal of achieving a "single (holistic) version of the truth." The way Master Data Management approaches this goal of delivering an integrated data view is by matching key data attributes across different application systems, lines of business, and enterprise entities in order to identify and link similar data records into uniquely identified groups of records, sometimes called "affinity clusters." For example, a customer-focused MDM solution for a financial institution would attempt to find all records about an individual customer from all available data sources that come from various lines of business, such as banking, credit cards, insurance, and others, and link them into a group of all individuals who comprise that customer's household. Fundamentally, this matching and linking activity is infeasible or at least unreliable if the data that is being matched displays the properties of inconsistency, inaccuracy, incompleteness, and other data quality issues discussed earlier in this section.

To sum up, one of the goals and challenges of Master Data Management is to allow organizations to create, manage, and deliver a master data platform that can demonstrate acceptable and measurable levels of data quality and that enables the consistent and effective integration of various data entities into cohesive and complete data views.

Defining Master Data Management

We have now reached the point where we can formally define Master Data Management. Although a number of MDM definitions are available, we need to define MDM in a way that is agnostic of the particular data subject area and provides a sufficiently complete description representing both the business and technology views.

> **Defining MDM**
> *Master Data Management (MDM)* is the framework of processes and technologies aimed at creating and maintaining an authoritative, reliable, sustainable, accurate, and secure data environment that represents a "single and holistic version of the truth" for master data and its relationships, as well as an accepted benchmark used within an enterprise as well as across enterprises and spanning a diverse set of application systems, lines of business, channels, and user communities.

Alternative Definition

For the purpose of completeness, we also include the following definitions of master data and Master Data Management by the Gartner Group [4]:

- "Master data is the official, consistent set of identifiers, extended attributes and hierarchies of the enterprise."
- "MDM is the workflow process in which business and IT work together to ensure the uniformity, accuracy, stewardship and accountability of the enterprise's official, shared information assets."

Slightly alternate definitions are given in well-known books.[5-7]

This need to achieve a "single version of the truth" is not a particular property of one industry. In the next chapter we will show that MDM has extremely broad applicability not only across industries but also across various types of organizations, including private and public companies as well as government organizations.

In achieving this ambitious goal of creating a "single holistic version of the truth," Master Data Management helps any organization that has disparate data sources and data stores, various applications, and multiple lines of business. In doing so, MDM can be viewed as an evolutionary, next-generation data management and data quality discipline, and we'll show some components of that evolution in the example of Master Data Management for Customer Domain (also known as Customer Data Integration or CDI) later in this chapter. At the same time, given the breadth, depth, and profound consequences of implementing Master Data Management, we can see it as a revolutionary, disruptive approach to data management, and we'll show later in the book that the impact of MDM is reaching deep into the core of many established business processes. These revolutionary properties of MDM require significant financial, time, and organizational commitment across the entire enterprise, including participation from both the business and technology sides of the company. Indeed, Master Data Management is an enterprise-wide data- and system-integration activity that requires a multidisciplinary, extremely well-planned and executed program that involves business process analysis; data analysis and mapping; data cleaning, enrichment, and rationalization; data matching, linking, and integration; data synchronization and reconciliation; data security; and data delivery.

In addition, we'll show in Part II of the book that an enterprise-class MDM solution should be implemented as an instance of a service-oriented architecture (SOA), and thus the program would include the design, development, testing, and deployment of both business and technical services that enable an MDM platform to function and continuously manage the new "system of records." Although this is far from a complete list of activities required to implement an MDM solution, many of these activities have to be planned, managed, and executed in a holistic fashion, whether an MDM initiative is focused on a small or large organization as well as whether its focus is on customer data, product reference data, or other data domains. Moreover, MDM provides significant value not only within an enterprise but also across enterprises when new efficiencies, standards, or regulations demand that two or more companies need to share data across enterprise boundaries—for example, when various government agencies need to share data about potential threats to national security, or when financial services companies need to support global industry initiatives such as Straight Through Processing (STP). On the one hand, when we look at the wide-open field of MDM opportunities, it is hard to imagine any enterprise, large or small, that has only a single source of data that it uses to manage the business. However, when we talk about initiatives of the scale and impact of MDM, size does matter, and many small to midsize companies have to limit the scope and investment of their MDM initiatives to avoid the challenges of justifying a significant level of commitment and investment.

In general, cleaning, standardizing, rationalizing, matching, linking, and managing records and their relationships are some of the key challenges and key differentiations of Master Data Management solutions.

Master Data Management for Customer Domain: Customer Data Integration (CDI)

As previously mentioned, situations where Master Data Management is focused on creating and managing an authoritative system of records about customers is the subject of the MDM variant known as Customer Data Integration (CDI). This term, however, may be misleading in that it may create an impression that CDI only deals with customer information, where customers are individuals who have predefined, known, and usually account-based relationships with the enterprise.

In fact, even though CDI stands for Customer Data Integration, the word "Customer" is used as a generic term that can be replaced by industry or LOB-specific terms, such as Client, Contact, Party, Counterparty, Patient, Subscriber, Supplier, Prospect, Service Provider, Citizen, Guest, Legal Entity, Trust, or Business Entity. We will use terms such as "customer" and "party" as primary descriptors of the customer master entities interchangeably throughout the book.

In addition to the broad scope of the term "customer," the CDI architecture and terminology have been evolving to reflect rich MDM capabilities that extend beyond data integration. As a result, the customer-focused MDM solutions known as CDI are sometimes called "Customer MDM" or "Customer Master."

Once we clearly define the data domain as the one dealing with the generic term "customer," we can provide a working definition of Customer Data Integration. As follows from the previous discussion, this definition builds on the definition of MDM presented in the preceding section.

> **Defining CDI**
> *Customer Data Integration (CDI)* is a Master Data Management framework focused on the customer data domain. It is a comprehensive set of technology components, services, and business processes that create, maintain, and make available an accurate, timely, integrated, and complete view of a customer across lines of business, channels, and business partners.

To state it slightly differently, a customer-focused MDM (CDI) solution takes customer data from a variety of data sources, discards redundant data, cleanses the data, and then rationalizes and aggregates it together. We can graphically depict such an MDM system as a hub-and-spokes environment. The spokes are information sources that are connected to the central hub as a new "home" for the accurate, aggregated, and timely data that, in the case of CDI, represents customer data (see Figure 1-1). Clearly, this hub-and-spoke topology is generally applicable to all MDM data domains; thus we often use the term "Data Hub" when discussing MDM solution space.

As stated earlier, CDI is a special, customer-data-focused type of Master Data Management, with the same goals, objectives, and benefits. Because this type of MDM deals with customer information that it collects, cleanses, rationalizes, and aggregates into a holistic customer view, a comprehensive CDI initiative can have a profound impact on the way any enterprise conducts its business and interacts with its customers.

Specifically, a customer-focused MDM solution can allow the enterprise to discover various relationships that the customers may have with one another, relationships that can allow the enterprise to understand and take advantage of potential opportunities offered by customer groups that define households, communities of interest, and professional affiliations. For example, a CDI solution implemented by a financial services firm can indicate that a group of its customers have created a private investment club, and that club could present a very attractive opportunity for the new services and product offerings.

The benefits of discovering and understanding relationships among individuals apply not just to commercial businesses. Understanding the relationships between individuals has direct and profound implications on various government activities, including law enforcement, risk management for global financial transactions, and national security. Indeed, if the full spectrum of MDM capabilities for recognition, identification, and relationships discovery of

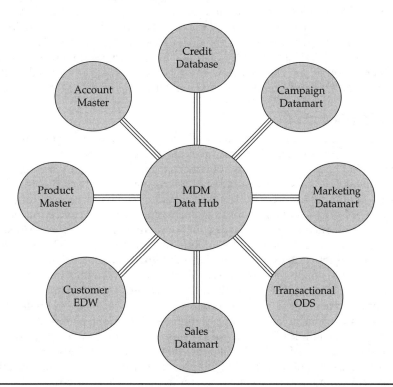

FIGURE 1-1   MDM customer data hub

individuals and their activities had been available globally, the tragic events of September 11, 2001, might not have happened because we now know that there was a sufficient amount of information available about the hijackers and their relationships. Unfortunately, this information was collected and analyzed by different government services but never integrated and delivered to the right people at the right time.

Although discovering and managing the relationships is a very useful capability, CDI benefits don't stop there. A CDI solution (often referred to as a Customer Data Hub, or CDH) can allow an enterprise to drastically change its business model from a traditional, account-centric approach to a new, more effective, and rewarding customer-centric model that can significantly improve the customer experience, reduce customer attrition, strengthen customer relationships with the enterprise, and even increase the customer's share of the wallet for the enterprise.

> **CDI and Customer-Centric Enterprise Transformation**
> CDI-enabled transformation from the account-centric to the customer-centric model is revolutionary, and it can drastically impact the established business processes and change the way the enterprise treats its customers, competes in the market, and grows its core customer-driven revenue.

We'll discuss account-centric-to-customer-centric transformations in more detail in Chapter 2.

Given that MDM enables a near-real-time, accurate, and complete "single holistic version of the truth," its customer-focused variant—CDI—enables a single version of the truth about the customer. The properties and benefits of having the accurate and complete view of the customer make it abundantly clear that CDI solutions are much more than simply another customer database or a new enterprise CRM platform, even though we can find the genesis of MDM and CDI in these and similar customer management technologies.

Evolution of MDM and CDI

Business and government entities have historically striven to create and maintain authoritative and timely information sources. This natural enterprise requirement has been further emphasized by a number of regulatory requirements that include the Sarbanes-Oxley Act and the Basel II Capital Accord (see discussion on these regulations in Part III of the book).

In the case of moving toward a holistic and accurate "system of record" for customer information organizations had been working on creating customer-centric business models and applications and enabling infrastructure for a long time. However, as the business complexity, number of customers, number of lines of business, and number of sales and service channels continued to grow, and because this growth often proceeded in a tactical, nonintegrated fashion, many organizations evolved into a state with a wide variety of customer information stores and applications that manage customer data.

The customer data in those "legacy" environments was often incomplete and inconsistent across various data stores, applications, and lines of business. Although in many cases individual applications and lines of business (LOB) were reasonably satisfied with the quality and scope of customer data that they managed, the lack of completeness, accuracy, and consistency of data across LOB prevented organizations from creating a complete, accurate, and up-to-date view of customers and their relationships.

Recognizing this customer data challenge and the resulting inability to transform the business from an account-centric to a customer-centric business model, organizations embarked on developing a variety of strategies and solutions designed to achieve this transformation. They offered new customer insights, new ways to improve customer service, and increased cross-selling and up-selling. Yet they were limited to being deployed within the boundaries of the existing organizational units and lines of business and were not positioned to become true enterprise-wide, cross-LOB global solutions.

The continuous discovery of cross-industry opportunities that could leverage customer centricity have helped define Master Data Management in general and its customer-focused CDI strategies and architecture in particular. We can see today that MDM has emerged to become not just a vehicle for creating the authoritative system of key business information, but, in the case of customer data, it became an enabler of achieving customer centricity.

Let's briefly look at what has been done and what elements, if any, can be and should be leveraged in implementing a CDI solution. The most notable CDI predecessors include Customer Information File (CIF); Extract, Transform, and Load (ETL) technologies; Enterprise Data Warehouse (EDW); Operational Data Store (ODS); data quality (DQ) technologies; Enterprise Information Integration (EII); and Customer Relationship Management (CRM) systems. Many of these CDI predecessors have been described in numerous books[8] and publications [9]:

- **Customer Information File (CIF)** is typically a legacy environment that represents some basic, static information about the customers. CIF systems have a number of constraints, including limited flexibility and extensibility; they are not well suited to capturing and maintaining real-time customer data, customer privacy preferences, customer behavior traits, and customer relationships. CIF systems are often used to feed the company's Customer Relationship Management systems.

- **Extract, Transform, and Load (ETL) tools** are designed to extract data from multiple data sources, perform complex transformations from source formats to the target formats, and efficiently load the transformed and formatted data into a target database such as an MDM Data Hub. Contemporary ETL tools include components that perform data consistency and data quality analysis as well as providing the ability to generate and use metadata definitions for data elements and entities.[10] Although not pure MDM solutions, ETL tools have been a part of the typical MDM framework and represent an important functionality required to build an MDM Data Hub platform, including Customer Data Integration systems.

- **Enterprise data warehouse (EDW)**[11,12] is an information system that provides its users with current and historical decision support information that is hard to access or present in traditional operational data stores. An enterprise-wide data warehouse of customer information was considered to be an integration point where most of the customer data can be stored for the purpose of supporting Business Intelligence applications and Customer Relationship Management systems. Classical data warehouses provide historical data views and do not support operational applications that need to access real-time transactional data associated with a given customer and therefore are falling short of delivering on the MDM promise of an accurate and timely system of record for key business data domains, including customer information.

- **Operational data store (ODS)**[13] is a data technology that allows transaction-level detail data records to be stored in a nonsummarized form suitable for analysis and reporting. Typical ODS does not maintain summarized data, nor does it manage historical information. Similar to the EDW, an ODS of customer data can and should be considered a valuable source of information for building an MDM Customer Data Hub.

- **Data quality (DQ) technologies,**[14,15] strictly speaking, are not customer data platforms, but they play an important role in making these platforms useful and useable, whether they are built as data warehouses, operational data stores, or customer information files. Given the importance of data quality as one of the key requirements to match and link customer data as well as to build an authoritative source of accurate, consistent, and complete customer information, data quality technologies are often considered not just as predecessors but as key MDM and CDI enablers.

- **Enterprise Information Integration (EII)**[16,17] tools are designed to create a virtually federated view of distributed data stores and provide access to that data as if it was coming from a single system. EII tools can isolate applications from the concerns related to the distributed and heterogeneous nature of source data stores and allow users to aggregate distributed data in memory or nonpersistent storage, thus potentially delivering a "just-in-time" customer data view. Depending on the data sources, data quality, and data availability, these EII solutions could be used as components of a full-function MDM Customer Data Hub.

- **Customer Relationship Management (CRM)** is a set of technologies and business processes designed to understand customers, improve customer experience, and optimize customer-facing business processes across marketing, sales, and servicing channels. As such, CRM solutions are probably the closest to what an MDM Customer Data Hub can offer to its consumers. CRM has been adopted by many enterprises as a strategy to integrate information across various customer data stores and to deliver appropriate analytics and improve customer interactions with the enterprise across all major channels. Unfortunately, experience shows that CRM systems positioned for enterprise-wide deployment could not scale well as an integrated system of complete and timely customer information.

Each of these predecessor technologies has its particular advantages and shortcomings. A detailed discussion of these technologies is beyond the scope of this book, but we offer some additional considerations regarding these technologies in Chapter 4.

Other MDM Variants: Products, Organizations, Hierarchies

In addition to MDM Customer, recent years have seen the emergence of several other MDM variants and specialized solutions. Most prominent among them is Master Data Management solution for Product Information. This variant is sometimes referred to as Product Information Master, or PIM, and it addresses a number of issues that by the very nature of the product data domain tend to have an enterprise-wide scope. PIM solutions support business processes that deal with the definition, creation, introduction, marketing, sales, servicing, supply-chain management, spend and inventory management, and product catalog management of product data. Often, the MDM Product Master has to deal with managing product definitional or reference data across multiple lines of business, where each LOB may have a unique terminology and structure of things that an organization may call "products," but reconciling and integrating data about these products is not a trivial task. For example, a retail bank may have a product called Money Market Mutual Fund that it sells to its retail customers. The fund may consist of several components (subfunds or securities), some of which are defined and managed by the investment bank that uses different names and product hierarchies/structures for these underlying security products. When the organization has to review and report on the revenue and expenses associated with each product by category, the reconciliation of the different product views across lines of business is the goal of the MDM PIM solution.

Challenges of MDM Implementation for Product Domain

The challenges of product information mastering are significant and often require approaches and capabilities that exceed those available for mastering customer information. Indeed, one of the key MDM capabilities is the ability to match and link data records in order to find and integrate similar records. The natural question of what is similar is the subject of extensive research, and its answer in large part depends on the domain of data that is being matched. For example, matching records about individuals is a relatively well-known problem, and a large number of matching techniques and solutions use a variety of attributes of the individual (for example, name, address, date of birth, social security number, work affiliation, and even physical attributes, if they are known) to deliver a high-confidence matching result. We discuss matching and linking in more detail in Parts II and IV of this book.

The situation changes when we move to other domains, such as product reference data and hierarchies of entities within various domains. Current published research shows that product matching, for example, can be much more complex than name and/or address matching. This complexity is driven by the fact that, although product attributes may represent a standard set for each product category (for example, consider a TV set as a product whose features and technical characteristics are well known), different manufacturers or suppliers may use different expressions, abbreviations, and attribute values to describe the same feature. Likewise, in the example of the financial products, different lines of business define and manage different aspects of a product, and often organize the products in hierarchies based on established business processes and practices (the structure of a sales team, geopolitical constraints, and so on). From a consumer perspective, if you try to review a detailed description of a product, you may end up with an incomplete or one-sided definition of the product (for example, an LCD HDTV set may have a feature described one way in a manufacturer's catalog but described differently or simply omitted in a store catalog). Similarly, in financial services, a product called a "High-Yield Bond" may be described differently or called something different, depending on the level of detail available from a given bank or broker.

This product reference incompatibility is magnified at the business level when you have to deal with a variety of suppliers or business partners. That is why a number of industry initiatives are underway to develop a library of common standards that describe entities for business-to-business (B2B) commerce in general (for example, global supplier networks such as 1SYNC, ebXML, radio-frequency identification [RFID]) or for a given domain (for example, RosettaNet for various vertical industries such as electronic components, manufacturing, and supply-chain automation; HL7 for the pharmaceutical industry; ACORD for the insurance industry; FpML, XBRL, and FixML for the financial services industry; and so on).

Another challenge that an MDM solution should be able to handle is the ability of an MDM Data Hub to define, recognize, and reconcile hierarchical structures of a given entity domain. For example, the process of aggregating and reconciling product expenses and revenue across a large, globally distributed organization is complicated because individual product information coming from a single LOB and/or from a given geographical region may describe the product (for example, Personal Loan) that is not only called something different but is at a different level than a conceptually similar product offered by another LOB of the bank (for example, Credit Management Basket, which may have a component that corresponds to the Personal Loan). Likewise, a large organization may consist of numerous legal entities/subsidiaries, each of which reports its own profit and loss statements to the corporate headquarters for the annual reports. A straightforward aggregation may produce erroneous results because some of the legal entities are subsidiaries of others, thus resulting in an over-counting of the numbers. Cases such as these illustrate that full-function MDM solutions not only have to create and manage master data for a given domain, but also enable understanding and management of master data hierarchies and reconciliation of hierarchy-level–defined data.

Customer Masters, Product Information Masters, Hierarchy Masters and associated Hierarchy Management , as well as other MDM variants have emerged to deal with these complex issues, sometimes involving the management and integration of not just structured, reference data but also unstructured data such as documents describing investment instruments, features and functions of new or existing products, and the management and navigation of complex entity groupings that may or may not be hierarchical in nature. We'll discuss many of these issues in Part IV of the book.

Introduction to MDM Classification Dimensions

The previous sections illustrated the complex, broad, and multifaceted nature of MDM. As defined previously, MDM is a framework that addresses complex business and technical problems, and as such it is a complex, multifaceted subject that can be described and viewed from various angles. The amount of information about MDM is quite large, and in order to make sense of the various and sometimes contradictory assertions about MDM, we need to apply one of the principles of organizing and managing information—classification or categorization. This allows us to organize available information and discuss various aspects of MDM according to a well-defined structure. Thus, in this section, we introduce several commonly accepted MDM classification schemes or dimensions. These classification dimensions include the Design and Deployment dimension, the Use Pattern dimension, and the Information Scope or Data Domain dimension. We see these dimensions as persistent characteristics of any MDM solution, regardless of the industry or master data domain. Clearly, there are other approaches to classifying such a complex subject, but we feel that these three dimensions cover most of the major differences between various MDM variants:

- **Design and Deployment**   This classification describes MDM architecture styles that support a full spectrum of MDM implementation—from a thin MDM reference-only layer to a full master data store that can support all business processes, including online transaction processing. These styles—Registry, Coexistence, Full Transaction Hub—are discussed in greater detail in Part II of the book.

- **Use Pattern**   This classification differentiates MDM solutions based on how the master data is used. We see three primary use patterns for MDM data usage:
  - **Analytical MDM**   This use pattern supports business processes and applications that use master data primarily to analyze business performance and provide appropriate reporting and insight into the data itself, perhaps directly interfacing with Business Intelligence suites. Analytical MDM tends to be read mostly, in that it does not change/correct source data in the operational systems but does cleanse and enrich data in the MDM store; from the data warehousing perspective, Analytical MDM builds complex data warehousing dimensions.
  - **Operational MDM**   This use pattern allows master data to be collected, changed, and used to process business transactions. Operational MDM is designed to maintain the semantic consistency of master data affected by the transactional activity. Operational MDM provides a mechanism to improve the quality of data in the operational systems, where the data is usually created.
  - **Collaborative MDM**   This use pattern allows its users to author master data objects and collaborate in the process of creation and maintenance of master data and associated metadata.
- **Information Scope or Data Domain**   This dimension describes the primary data domain managed by the MDM solution. In the case of customer MDM, the resulting solution is often called Customer Data Integration, or CDI; in the case of product MDM, the solution is known as Product Information Management, or PIM; other data domains may not have formal names yet, but they could have an impact on how the MDM solution is designed and deployed.

These MDM classification dimensions help us to better understand the relevance and importance of various factors affecting the product selection, architecture, design and deployment choices, impact on the existing and new business processes, and overall MDM strategy and readiness for the enterprise. The latter is based on the MDM Capability Maturity Model (MDM CMM), discussed in Part IV of the book.

Key Benefits of Master Data Management

An introduction to Master Data Management cannot be complete unless we look at the benefits these types of solutions bring to the enterprise. Companies embark on major MDM initiatives because of their natural need to establish a single, authoritative, accurate, timely, and secured master data system. In turn, they can create more accurate and timely key performance metrics, measure and manage risks, and develop competitive winning strategies. Furthermore, MDM allows enterprises to be compliant with appropriate regulatory requirements, including those defined by the Gramm-Leach-Bliley Act, the Sarbanes-Oxley Act, the Basel II Capital Accord, and many others (a discussion of these regulations can be found in Part III of the book). This compliance allows organizations to avoid costly penalties and bad publicity.

From a financial point of view, having a single authoritative system of record positions the enterprise to gradually sunset a number of legacy systems and applications and thus realize significant cost savings.

In addition to potential cost savings and gaining compliance, Master Data Management offers a number of critical capabilities to enterprises and government agencies alike, including the ability to detect and prevent illegal money-laundering activities and other fraudulent financial transactions in accordance with regulations such as AML and the KYC provisions of the USA Patriot Act. Moreover, the ability of customer-focused MDM (CDI) to discover and expose previously unknown relationships between individuals can be extremely useful in the global fight against terrorist organizations.

Likewise, creating and managing an authoritative system of record for product information and the ability to create and manage complex hierarchies of master data has a profoundly positive effect on all aspects of the enterprise business—from conceptualizing and introducing new, more effective, and highly competitive products to improving supply-chain metrics and efficient, just-in-time product delivery processes that save costs and improve customer satisfaction levels, to reconciling organizational and structural differences between various definitions of products, customers, organizational entities, and the like.

As a vehicle for discovering and addressing data quality issues, MDM is impacted by and has a direct impact on established business processes and can improve their effectiveness, efficiencies, timeliness, and reduce complexity, all of which can have a profound positive impact on the enterprise agility, cost structure, and competitiveness.

Master Data Management is not just about data accuracy and compliance. MDM helps to create new opportunities and ways to drastically improve customer experience and increase top-line revenue. Indeed, many new and established enterprises are looking to differentiate themselves from the competition by significantly increasing customer satisfaction and improving customer experience. Having an accurate and complete system of record for customer information and for products and services that can be offered and personalized for various customer groups allows enterprises to gain new and more actionable intelligence into the customer's buying behavior and thus allows companies to create and offer better and more accurate personalized products and services. Master Data Management solutions allow enterprises to capture and enforce the customer's privacy preferences and ensure the protection of the customer's confidential data—actions that result in the enterprise's ability to establish and strengthen trusted relationships with their customers, thus creating an additional competitive advantage.

In any customer-facing business, MDM not only helps to retain profitable customers but also addresses the challenge of any enterprise to grow its customer base. This customer base growth opportunity comes from several different directions:

- Accurate and complete customer data allows the enterprise to better leverage various cross-sell and up-sell opportunities.

- Master data that contains information about prospects allows enterprises to increase their prospect-to-customer conversion ratio, thus increasing the customer base.

- MDM's ability to discover and understand the complete picture of current and potential customer relationships allows an enterprise to create a targeted set of marketing campaigns and product and service offers that may prove to be more cost effective and demonstrate higher lift than traditional mass marketing.

Finally, any discussion about the benefits of Master Data Management would not be complete without mentioning the disruptive, transformational nature of its CDI variant for customer-facing business, which allows an enterprise to change its core business model and customer-facing products and services by transforming itself from an account-centric to a customer-centric enterprise. This new, transformed enterprise no longer views, recognizes, and services customers by account number.

The old account-centric model does not enable an enterprise to easily and reliably identify individuals who are associated with the account. Moreover, the old model does not enable an enterprise to discover associations and relationships between individuals owning the accounts and other individuals and businesses that own other accounts. For example, an individual may have several accounts with a bank, and some of these accounts may have designated an individual in the role of beneficiary or with power of attorney who may own another set of accounts, some of which may be managed by another business unit. Ideally, the enterprise would gain a significant competitive advantage if these intra- and inter-LOB relationships were discovered and leveraged, to increase the customer base and corresponding share of the customer wallet.

Discovering these relationships may have an extremely high impact on the way the enterprise should treat the individual. Indeed, recognizing the total lifetime value of the customer would allow the enterprise to provide an appropriate set of products, services, and special treatments that are commeasurable with the total value of the relationships that the customer may have with the enterprise. For example, an individual who opens a low-value savings account may be treated differently by the bank if it is known that this individual is also a high-net-worth customer of the bank's wealth management business, or if the customer is also a president of a medium-size company, or if the customer's spouse has a separate high-value account, or if this customer's child, who does not yet have an account with the bank, has inherited a multimillion-dollar trust fund.

In short, MDM-enabled transformation from the account-centric to the customer-centric model is revolutionary, and it can drastically impact established business processes and change the way the enterprise treats its customers, competes in the market, and grows its core customer-driven revenue.

References

1. Dubov, Lawrence. "MDM as a Technique to Prioritize Data Quality Problems." http://blog.initiate.com/index.php/2009/12/08/mdm-as-a-technique-to-prioritize-data-quality-problems/.

2. Berson, Alex, Stephen Smith, and Kurt Thearling. *Building Data Mining Applications for CRM*. McGraw-Hill (December 1999).

3. Dubov, Lawrence. "MDM Data Quality Processes." http://blog.initiate.com/index.php/2009/12/15/mdm-data-quality-processes/.

4. White, Andrew and John Radcliffe. "Mastering Master Data Management." Gartner Research (May 2008).

5. Dyche, Jill, Evan Levy, Don Peppers, and Martha Rogers. *Customer Data Integration: Reaching a Single Version of the Truth* (SAS Institute, Inc.) Wiley (August 2006).

6. Loshin, David. *Master Data Management*. The MK/OMG Press (September 2008).

7. Berson, Alex and Larry Dubov. *Master Data Management and Customer Data Integration for a Global Enterprise.* McGraw-Hill (May 2007).

8. Berson, Alex, Stephen Smith, and Kurt Thearling. *Building Data Mining Applications for CRM.* McGraw-Hill (December 1999).

9. Berson, Alex and Stephen J. Smith. *Data Warehousing, Data Mining, and OLAP.* McGraw-Hill (November 1997).

10. Kimball, Ralph and Joe Caserta. *The Data Warehouse ETL Toolkit: Practical Techniques for Extracting, Cleaning, Conforming, and Delivering Data.* Wiley (September 2004).

11. Kimball, Ralph, Margy Ross, Bob Becker, and Joy Mundy. *Kimball's Data Warehouse Toolkit Classics: The Data Warehouse Toolkit, 2nd Edition; The Data Warehouse Lifecycle, 2nd Edition; The Data Warehouse ETL Toolkit.* Wiley (April 2009).

12. Inmon, William H. *Building the Data Warehouse.* Wiley (Oct 2005).

13. Inmon, William H. *Building the Operational Data Store, 2nd Edition.* Wiley (May 1999).

14. English, Larry P. *Improving Data Warehouse and Business Information Quality: Methods for Reducing Costs and Increasing Profits.* Wiley (March 1999).

15. McGilvray, Danette. *Executing Data Quality Projects: Ten Steps to Quality Data and Trusted Information.* Morgan Kaufmann (July 2008).

16. Morgenthal, JP. *Enterprise Information Integration: A Pragmatic Approach.* Lulu.com (May 2005).

17. Morgenthal, JP. *Enterprise Information Integration: A Pragmatic Approach.* Lulu.com (January 2009).

MDM: Overview of Market Drivers and Key Challenges

I n the first chapter of this book, we discussed the reasons for and the evolution of Master
Data Management and Customer Data Integration. We also offered a working definition
of MDM. Specifically, we defined Master Data Management as the framework of
processes and technologies aimed at creating and maintaining an authoritative, reliable,
sustainable, accurate, and secure data environment that represents a holistic version of the truth
for master data. Master data are those entities, relationships, and attributes that are critical
for an enterprise and foundational to key business processes and application systems across
multiple lines of business.

We stated that MDM in general and its variants such as the customer-centric version
known as Customer Data Integration and the product-centric version often referred to as
Product Information Master are especially effective in modernizing a global enterprise, and
that the need for an authoritative, accurate, timely, and secure "holistic version of the truth"
is pervasive and is not particular to a specific industry, country, or geography.

We also mentioned that Master Data Management, although evolutionary from the pure
technological point of view, is revolutionary in its potential business impact and represents
a particularly interesting opportunity to any business-to-consumer (B2C), government-to-
consumer/citizen (G2C), and even business-to-business (B2B) entity.

Using all these factors as background, we are now ready to focus on a business view of
MDM and discuss the reasons for its rapid proliferation, the challenges that its adopters
have to overcome in order to succeed in implementing MDM initiatives, and the way the
market has been growing and reacting to the demands and opportunities of MDM.

Specifically, this chapter will concentrate on the following subjects:

- Market growth and adoption of MDM
- Business and operational drivers of MDM
- Challenges of MDM

We will also focus on the ability of MDM solutions to help transform an enterprise from
an account-centric to a customer-centric, agile business model.

Market Growth and Adoption of MDM

MDM is rapidly maturing and its adoption is growing strong. In the first edition of this book, published in 2007, we referenced a survey conducted by The MDM Institute (www .tcdii.com). The survey found that 68 percent of Fortune 2000 companies were actively evaluating or building MDM solutions. The adoption of MDM was much lower outside of these 2,000 large companies. At that time the survey focus was on both business and technical aspects of MDM. The survey tried to weigh the potential benefits of implementing an MDM platform against the cost, implementation, and operational risks of new technologies; the potential shortage of qualified resources; and the impact on established business processes. Many organizations that subscribe to the "buy before build" principle were also evaluating MDM vendors and system integrators as potential technology partners. The survey also found that many MDM initiatives that may have started as small pilots and were developed in-house were rapidly growing in size and visibility and have been repositioned to use best-in-class commercially available solutions.

Three years later, at the beginning of 2010, when this second edition of the book was written, according to the new MDM Institute report,[1] by 2012, 80 percent of Fortune 5000 companies will have committed to MDM as a core business strategy and have implemented at least one master entity solution (typically, a party or a product). From the comparison of the surveys performed in 2007 and 2010, it is fairly clear that MDM's adoption increased significantly over these years. The MDM that first started within Fortune 2000 has moved downstream to include "smaller" large companies outside Fortune 2000 and has begun penetration into the mid-market. Many companies are looking to move from a single-domain MDM to a more comprehensive multi-domain MDM, to leverage an MDM solution to resolve and manage relationships and hierarchies, and to integrate MDM with unstructured information.

And this MDM growth trend is not just about moving from a single-domain MDM to a multi domain MDM. In this chapter, we'll show that the most common drivers and challenges of MDM apply across many industry verticals and public sectors. In other words, we can see clearly now that MDM is indeed a horizontal discipline.

MDM Is a Horizontal Discipline
Master Data Management is horizontal in nature and applies equally well to any commercial market segment as well as to the public sector.

In the MDM space, the "buy before build" principle has evolved even more to a clear dominance of the "buy" over the "build." MDM products have been quickly maturing and currently provide numerous advanced capabilities "out of the box." These capabilities cannot typically be easily matched by homegrown solutions.

Although this "buy over build" trend is encouraging and points to an MDM market expansion, we need to recognize that embarking on an MDM journey is not a small or easy task. From a business perspective, building or buying an MDM solution is a significant undertaking that has to be supported by a comprehensive and compelling business case. Indeed, considering the high degree of technical and business risk, the significant software licenses and implementation costs, the (typically) long multiphase duration, and the high level of visibility and organizational commitment required to implement a full-fledged Master Data Management initiative, an MDM project should be considered if it can provide an enterprise with a well-defined and measurable set of benefits and a positive return on investment (ROI) in a reasonable amount of time. In short, a completed and deployed MDM solution should provide the enterprise with a tangible competitive advantage. Chapter 12 in Part IV of this book discusses the business case, the MDM roadmap, and its challenges in more detail. You can find more information using the references given at the end of this chapter.[2,3,4,5]

Every major IT industry analysis organization indicated that market demand for MDM remains healthy even during the economy downturn of 2009. As per Gartner Research,[6,7] demand for MDM technology remains strong, with 93 percent of businesses sustaining or increasing MDM spending. MDM business case, vision, strategy, processes, governance, and technology remain the focus of the MDM community worldwide.

MDM Growth and Customer Centricity

One way for customer-facing enterprises to achieve a competitive advantage is to know their best and largest customers, and be able to organize them into groups based on explicit or implied relationships, including corporate and household hierarchies. Knowing customers and their relationships allows an enterprise to assess and manage customer lifetime value, increase effectiveness of marketing campaigns, improve customer service, and thus reduce attrition rates. It is also important to recognize "bad" customers, including relationships involved in fraudulent activities (or "spinners"). This term applies to former customers dropped due to a history of delinquencies and unpaid debts. Spinners attempt to open new accounts under another name or use other tricks to conceal their true identity. A customer, individual, or a company that receives a significant credit for an enterprise's products or services by means of opening multiple accounts under different identities creates a significant credit risk for the enterprise, thus jeopardizing its financial stability.

In the account-centric world, depicted on the left side of Figure 2-1, there is no systemic way to determine whether the Joe who holds an employment insurance account (Account 123) is the same Joe that signed the student loan (Account 456). Similarly, does the record for the Mary from the employment insurance account represent the same Mary who owns the pension plan account (Account 789)? In the traditional account-centric scenario, the government agency cannot see the total of benefits that a citizen and his household receive from the government. Using the government agency as an example, in the future world, presented on the right side of Figure 2-1, a new entity "Citizen" is resolved and maintained, which makes the agency "customer centric" (more accurately, "citizen centric" in this example). In the future state, the organization that implements MDM is enabled to support a holistic, panoramic view of a customer or a party, including relationships between people, relationships between people and accounts, and the roles citizens play on the accounts. We see similar needs in customer-centricity patterns across multiple industries: financial services, telecommunications, insurance, hospitality, and so on. This transformation, revolutionary from the business perspective, represents the Holy Grail of MDM for many organizations and promises significant competitive advantages.

Although it may appear that the same can be accomplished using a more traditional CRM system, a full-function customer-centric MDM solution can extend the scope of already familiar CRM sales-services-marketing channels by integrating additional information sources that may contain customer-related data, including back-office systems, finance and accounting departments, product master references, and supply-chain applications. This broad and far-reaching scope of MDM data coverage provides a number of opportunities for an MDM-empowered enterprise to achieve a sustainable competitive advantage. Let's look at some prominent components of this competitive advantage.

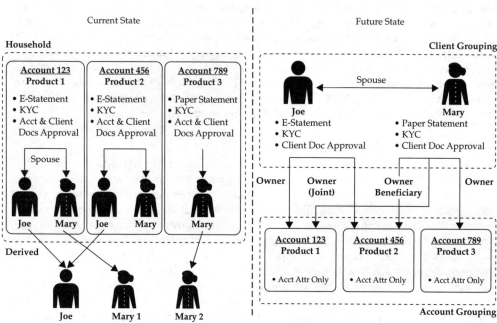

FIGURE 2-1   Transformation from account-centric to customer-centric enterprise

Even though Figure 2-1 depicts a customer-centric transition for citizens or retail customers, organizations serving commercial or institutional customers can equally benefit from MDM and obtain considerable competitive advantage by enabling the organizations to address the following questions and problems:

- **Value of a customer and product**   Does your organization measure the value of a client and product correctly by including all the subsidiaries, divisions, sites, brands, and so on? Do you classify/categorize your customers correctly and provide a value-based level of service?

- **Marketing**   Are there up-selling or cross-selling opportunities that your organization is missing? If your organization has relationships with Company A and some of its subsidiaries, but is not aware of the existence of some other subsidiaries in the complex hierarchical structure of Company A, marketing opportunities may have been missed.

- **Credit risk**   Does your organization correctly evaluate relationship risks? The knowledge that a midsize company is a subsidiary of a larger corporation is critical in evaluating the risk associated with the given relationship.

- **Pricing and fees**   Do your commercial customers receive the right pricing and fees? Lack of understanding of B2B hierarchies can cause errors in pricing and fees, impact customer satisfaction, and result in considerable overhead.

- **Data-cleansing efforts**   Does your organization spend money on data-cleansing efforts aimed at fixing your client and product hierarchy data? This problem can be permanently resolved by MDM

In Parts II and IV of this book, we will discuss specifics of an MDM architecture, its components, and the MDM roadmap as it applies to organizations serving individual customers and commercial enterprises.

Business and Operational Drivers of MDM

In order to define the value proposition and end-state vision, we have to clearly understand both business and operational drivers. Table 2-1 lists typical business drivers grouped by high-level categories such as Business Development, Sales and Marketing; Cost Reduction; Customer Service; and Compliance and Control. Organizations can use this list as a starting point to prioritize and quantify the importance of the business drivers as they apply to the company.

For more information, see "The Business Case for Master Data Management,"[8] as well as "Creating a Business Case for Master Data Management."[9]

Driver Categories	Drivers
Business Development, Sales and Marketing	Screening new prospects Cross-sell/up-sell to existing customers Effectiveness of marketing campaigns Recurring revenue from existing customers Retention of "good" customers Recognition of "bad" customers
Customer Service	Account setup time Customer service time Customer intelligence and level of service Consolidated statements Sales territory alignment Pricing and fees
Risk, Privacy, Compliance and Control	Risk management Accurate books and records Compliance with AML, KYC, ARRA, and so on Compliance with corporate standards and policies Regulatory fines and penalties
Operational Efficiency	Account setup costs Customer acquisition costs Administrative overhead of redundant and inconsistent data entry Operational costs (duplication, redundancies, transaction errors, data-processing errors, and exceptions) Agility to implement other projects Reduced likelihood of failed tactical initiatives Reduced costs of planned initiatives due to MDM M&A efficiency and enablement

TABLE 2-1   Common MDM Drivers

Once the drivers and the areas of impact are understood and documented, the project team in conjunction with the business stakeholders should perform an in-depth applications and business process analysis that answers the following questions:

- What business requirements drive the need to have access to better quality and more accurate and complete master data while still relying on existing processes and applications?

- What business activities would gain significant benefits from changing not just applications but also key business processes that deal with customer interactions and customer services at every touch point and across front- and back-office operations?

To illustrate these points, consider a retail bank that decides to develop an MDM platform to achieve several business goals, including better customer experience, better compliance posture, and reduced maintenance costs for the IT infrastructure. The bank may deploy an MDM Data Hub solution that enables the aggregation and integration of customer, product, and location data across various channels, application systems, and lines of business. As a result, existing and new applications may have access to a new customer master that should contain more accurate and complete customer information. The bank's Customer Relationship Management (CRM) and various Business Intelligence (BI) systems may have to be modified to leverage this new data. Improved insights into complete customer profile and past behavior as well as better anticipation of the customer's needs for products and services translate into better customer service and higher customer satisfaction. These are all valid and valuable benefits that allow the bank to quantify and measure a tangible return on investment. However, the core banking business still revolves around the notion of customer accounts, and the bank will continue to service its customers on the basis of their account type and status.

Moving to a customer-centric business model would allow the bank to understand and manage not just customer accounts but the totality of all current and potential customer relationships with the bank, to drastically improve the effectiveness and efficiency of customer interactions with the bank, and even to improve the productivity of the bank's service personnel. To achieve these goals, the bank would have to not only create a new customer master, but also redesign and deploy new, more effective and efficient business processes. For example, in the past the bank may have had an account-opening application that was used to open new customer accounts and modify existing ones. In the new customer-centric world, the bank may have to change its business processes and operational workflows in order to "create a customer" and modify his or her profile, assets, or relationships (accounts). These new processes will be operating in the context of the integrated holistic customer view. The efficiencies may come from the fact that if the bank deals with the existing customer, it can effectively leverage information already collected about that customer. The bank can leverage this information to shorten the time required to perform the transaction, and to offer better, more personalized, and more compelling products and/or services that are configured and priced based on the total view of the customer. Clearly, these new processes are beneficial to the customer and the bank, but they may represent a significant change in the behavior of the bank's application systems and customer service personnel. This is where the customer-centric impact analysis should indicate not only what processes and applications need to change, but what would be the financial impact of the change, and what would be the expected cost-benefit ratio if these changes are implemented as part of the MDM initiative.

Improving Customer Experience

Customer experience has emerged as a clear competitive differentiator. In the Internet-enabled e-business world, customer experience is viewed as one of the key factors that can strengthen or destroy trusted relationships that a customer may have with the enterprise. Customer experience includes a variety of tangible and intangible factors that collectively can make a customer a willing and eager participant or a dissatisfied party looking to take his or her business to a competitor as soon as possible. And in the era of e-banking, e-sales, and other Internet-enabled businesses, customers can terminate their relationship with the enterprise literally at a click of a button.

As a master customer data facility that manages all available information about the customer, MDM enables an enterprise to recognize a customer at any "point of entry" into the enterprise and to provide an appropriate level of customer service and personalized treatment—some of the factors improving customer experience and increasing enterprise's brand "stickiness." Let's illustrate this point with an example of a financial services company.

This company has created a wealth management business unit that deals with affluent customers, each of whom gets services from a dedicated personal financial advisor (PFA). When such an affluent customer calls his or her financial advisor, it is extremely important for the advisor to be able to access all the required information promptly, should it be information about a new product or service, a question about investment options, or a concern about tax consequences of a particular transaction. Unfortunately, in many cases, lack of customer data integration does not allow companies to provide an adequate level of service.

For example, it is customary in wealth management to have a variable-fee structure, with the amount of service fees inversely proportional to the amount of money under management (in other words, it is not unusual to waive fees for a customer who has total balances across all accounts that exceed a certain company-defined threshold). Of course, such a service would work much more effectively if the enterprise can readily and accurately recognize a customer not as an individual account holder but as an entity that owns all her or his accounts. What if a high-net-worth client calls because his fees were calculated incorrectly? The advisor could not obtain the necessary information during the call, and thus would not be able to provide an explanation to the customer and would ask for extra time and possibly an additional phone call to discuss the results of the investigation. This is likely to upset the customer who, as an affluent individual, has become used to quick and effective service. This situation can deteriorate rapidly if, for example, the investigation shows that the fee system interpreted the customer's accounts as belonging to multiple individuals. The corrective action may take some time, several transactions, and, in extreme cases, a number of management approvals, all of which can extend the time required to fix the problem, and thus make the customer even more unhappy.

This is a typical symptom indicating that a sound customer-centric MDM solution is required. If the situation is not resolved and occurs frequently, this may weaken the customer's relationship with the organization and eventually cause increased attrition rates.

Improving Customer Retention and Reducing Attrition Rates

To achieve sustainable growth, a company needs to focus on the customer segments with the highest growth potential in the area in which the company specializes—and build high loyalty by helping customers to realize their expectations from products and services offered by the company. Conceptually, these segments can be classified as follows:

- New, high-revenue-potential customers
- Existing customers whose total revenue potential has not yet been realized

In the case of new customer segments, every customer-facing enterprise has to solve the challenge of finding and acquiring new customers at the lowest possible acquisition cost. However, whether it is a new or an existing customer, enterprises have to find ways to improve customer retention rates at even lower costs. This last point is very important: Experience and market studies show that the cost of new customer acquisition could be many times the cost of retaining the existing customer, so the enterprise needs to understand the reasons that cause an existing customer to leave and go to a competitor. As mentioned in the preceding section, among the reasons for attrition are cumbersome or inconvenient ways of doing business (for example, an inefficient or aesthetically unappealing web portal, few retail bank branches, inconvenient locations or working hours, and a large number of high or "unfair" fees), poor customer service, lack of personalized or specific product and services offerings, lack of trust caused by violation of the customer's privacy and confidentiality, overly aggressive sales and marketing, and other factors that individually or collectively comprise the customer experience.

The cause of many of these factors is the lack of accurate business intelligence about the customer. Business intelligence has always been a valuable competitive differentiator, and best-in-class BI solutions such as customer analytics and customer data mining are critical to achieve a competitive advantage. The accuracy of business intelligence, in turn, depends on the availability, quality, and completeness of customer information. The value of accurate business intelligence became even more important as the result of the global financial crisis of 2008–2009, where the number of retail and commercial customers defaulting on their financial obligations (loans, mortgages, and so on) increased dramatically, and directly impacted the bottom line of any business that had an exposure to this risk. Thus, the role of an MDM solution designed to acquire and deliver complete, timely, and accurate customer information to appropriate users and BI applications has become ever more important.

Growing Revenue by Leveraging Customer Relationships

Enterprises have come to realize that customer loyalty is eroding, and with shortening product life cycles, most markets are facing intense competition and commoditization. In addition, and especially in financial services, the institutions have made a significant effort to acquire what is known as the "most profitable customers." However, because the total population of "best customers" is finite (that is, there are only so many customers that are worth doing business with), the businesses have realized that the new sources of revenue may come not from new customers but from the ability to understand and leverage the totality of the relationships a given customer may have with the enterprise. Therefore, the companies have to manage the life cycle of their customers beyond the acquisition. To state it differently, the strategy involves the notion of acquiring, understanding, and servicing the customer *in the context* of his or her relationships with the enterprise. This is different from the commonly used segmentation approach of CRM systems, which is based primarily on the history of customer transactions.

Understanding and leveraging relationships is one of the ways MDM can help to grow the business through increasing the "share of the wallet," by extending additional services to the existing customers individually and as part of various customer groups. This goal can be accomplished if the enterprise has developed and maintains accurate, complete, and actionable customer intelligence—a set of analytical insights and predictive traits indicating the best customers and the types of services and products that need to be offered to them in order to gain an increased share of the wallet. This customer intelligence is especially effective if it is gathered in the context of customer relationships with the enterprise and other customers. Examples of a relationship include a household, family, business partners, or any other group of customers that can be viewed as a single group from the service perspective. This relationship-based intelligence allows the enterprise to interact with customers based not only on their requirements and propensity to buy products and services, but also on the added opportunity of leveraging customer relationships for increased revenue as a percent of the entire relationship group's share of the wallet. The importance of understanding the relationships applies equally well to the corporate customers and partners that the company works with in the normal course of business. In the case of corporate customers, the relationships tend to be bi-directional (that is, the company offers products and services to a customer and buys that customer's products and services for its own use), thus creating an important management metric often called "balance of trade."

In addition to the increased "share of the wallet" and better value of the "balance of trade," an MDM solution can help to grow the customer base by identifying opportunities for acquiring new customers through actionable referrals. These MDM-enabled revenue growth opportunities drive market demand for MDM data integration products and services.

Improving Customer Service Time: Just-in-Time Information Availability

As mentioned in Chapter 1, one of the drivers behind Master Data Management is the need to make accurate data available to the users and applications more quickly. In many cases, the latency of information has a significant negative impact on various business processes, service quality and delivery, and customer experience. Indeed, imagine a customer contacting a service center with a question or complaint only to hear that the customer service representative cannot get to the right information because "our system is slow" or "this information is in our marketing systems and we don't have access to it." Likewise, a trading partner may contact the company's representative complaining about an unauthorized or invalid transaction, without getting a timely and satisfactory answer to the query. These situations do not improve the customer's or partner's confidence in the way the enterprise manages its business.

Timely availability of accurate data is clearly a requirement for any enterprise, especially customer-facing businesses that support a variety of online channels. This data availability and timeliness has two key components:

- Physical, near-real-time access to data is a function of operating systems, applications, and databases. Practically every organization has deployed these systems and the underlying technical infrastructures to enable the near-real-time execution of online transactions.

- Accurate and timely data content is created by aggregating and integrating relevant information from a variety of data sources, and this integration is the job for an MDM solution.

The latter point is one of the reasons enterprises seriously consider significant investment into MDM initiatives. Having just-in-time, accurate, and complete master data can not only improve customer service, but can also enable the enterprise to create near-real-time cross-sell and up-sell opportunities across various online channels. Successful cross-sell and up-sell activities have a significant positive impact on cost of sales and result in increased sales revenue. Likewise, just-in-time, accurate, and complete information about transactions, products, accounts, and customers is key to fraud detection, risk management, compliance requirements for unauthorized access, customer onboarding, and a host of other key business activities.

The typical overnight batch-cycle data latency provided by traditional data warehouses is no longer sufficient to support some business demands. Enterprises are looking for ways to cross-sell or up-sell immediately when a customer is still in the store or shopping online on the company's website. Today, sophisticated customer analytics and fraud detection systems can recognize a fraudulent transaction as it occurs. MDM-enabled data integration allows an enterprise to build sophisticated behavior models that provide real-time recommendations or interactive scripts that a salesperson could use to entice the customer to buy additional products or services.

For instance, suppose you have just relocated and purchased a new home. You need to buy a number of goods. The store should be able to recognize you as a new customer in the area and impress you with a prompt offering of the right products that fit your family's needs. In order to do this efficiently, an MDM system would find and integrate your customer profile, household information, and buying patterns into one holistic customer view.

Using this integrated data approach, an advanced sales management system would be able to recognize an individual as a high-potential-value customer regardless of the channel the customer is using at any given time.

Improving Marketing Effectiveness

Marketing organizations develop MDM solutions to improve the effectiveness of their marketing campaigns and enable up-sell and cross-sell activities across the lines of business. It is not unusual for an MDM solution to increase the effectiveness of marketing campaigns by an order of magnitude. According to Michael Lowenstein,[10] the Royal Bank of Scotland reduced the number of marketing mailings from 300,000 to 20,000 by making marketing campaigns more intelligent, targeted, and event driven.

At a high level, marketing campaigns are similar across industries. There are some industry-specific marketing areas, though (for example, Communities of Practice). This marketing solution is well known in the pharmaceutical industry. The Communities of Practice solution is based on a methodology aimed at identifying medical professionals considered to be "thought leaders" by their professional communities within a given geography and specialization area (specific infectious diseases, certain inflammatory diseases, areas of oncology, and so on). As soon as the thought leaders are identified, the pharmaceutical company can launch a highly selective marketing campaign targeting the thought leaders who are expected to influence their colleagues on the merits of the drug or product. One of the key challenges in implementing the Communities of Practice approach is to recognize medical professionals and maintain the required profile information and information about their professional relationships and organizations. For more information, refer the article by to Etienne Wenger, et al.[11]

Reducing Administrative Process Costs and Inefficiencies

A significant MDM driver is its ability to help reduce the administrative time spent on account administration, maintenance, and processing. It is not unusual that every time a new account for an existing customer needs to be opened, the customer profile information is entered redundantly again and again. Many current processes do not support the reuse of the data that has already been entered into the account profile opened at a different time or by a different line of business. One of the reasons for not reusing the data is the complexity associated with finding a customer's other account or profile data across various application silos.

An MDM solution capable of maintaining the client profile and relationships information centrally can significantly reduce the overhead of account opening and maintenance.

In addition, a comprehensive MDM solution can help to improve data quality and reduce the probability of errors in books and records of the firm. This improved accuracy not only helps maintain a high level of customer satisfaction but also enables an enterprise to be in a better position to comply with the requirements of government and industry regulations, such as the Sarbanes-Oxley Act for the verifiable accuracy and integrity of financial reporting. Some financial service organizations invest in MDM with the goal of reducing the administration time spent by the sales force by 50 percent.

Reducing Information Technology Maintenance Costs

In addition to the business drivers described in the preceding section, enterprise-wide MDM initiatives focused on the creation of a new, authoritative, complete, and accurate source of master data records are often driven by the objective to reduce the cost of ongoing maintenance of the IT infrastructure, applications, and operations. Lack of common system architecture, lack of systemic controls, and data inconsistencies cause data-processing errors and increase the cost of IT maintenance and operations. In addition, from the information technology perspective, the absence of a holistic authoritative system of record results in the limited ability of the enterprise to adapt to the ever-changing business requirements and processes, such as those driven by new and emerging regulatory and compliance demands. The need for system and application agility to support business and regulatory demands is a powerful MDM driver. Properly implemented MDM solutions enable more agile application development and reduce system implementation costs and risks. Many enterprise-wide initiatives, such as CRM and Enterprise Data Warehouse, often fail because in the pre-MDM days the issues of data accuracy, timeliness, and completeness had not been resolved proactively or, in some cases, successfully.

MDM Challenges

This section offers a high-level view of the challenges and risks that a company faces on its way toward mature Master Data Management and customer centricity. Parts II, III, and IV of this book will deal with these issues in more depth.

We start by offering two perspectives that organizations should acknowledge and address in adopting and executing a successful MDM strategy:

- The first perspective addresses business issues, such as defining a compelling value proposition that encompasses a cross-functional perspective championed by data governance and sound data policies, project drivers, the new end-state business vision, the project organization, competing stakeholder interests, and overcoming socialization obstacles.

- The second perspective addresses technical issues such as architecture, data profiling and quality, data synchronization, visibility, and security. In addition, it examines regulatory and compliance project drivers.

One of the general observations we can make by analyzing how MDM solutions are implemented across various industries is the strong desire on the part of the enterprise to embark on an MDM initiative in a way that properly addresses MDM challenges, manages and mitigates implementation risk, while at the same time realizing tangible business benefits. In practical terms, it often means that MDM initiatives start small and focus on a single high-priority objective such as improving data quality or creating a unified customer profile or product hierarchies based on available data. Often, these initial MDM implementations are done using in-house development rather than a vendor MDM tool, and they try to leverage existing legacy systems to the extent possible. For example, many organizations try to reuse existing business intelligence, reporting, and profile management applications while providing them with better, more accurate, and more complete data.

Many MDM implementations start with the primary focus of enabling data warehousing by building the content of data warehousing dimensions, oftentimes referred to as "analytical MDM." Indeed, for complex data warehousing dimensions such as Customer, Product, Service, Provider, and Location, traditional ETL technologies may not be able to create and maintain high-quality dimensions. As a result of this problem, the main data warehousing promise of enabling an enterprise with "slice and dice" reporting and analytics capabilities to calculate the total value of a relationships, and other customer- and product-centric metrics, remains unrealized. The paradigm of "slice and dice" heavily relies on the perfection of multidimensional data structures containing all possible levels of measures. These structures are often referred to as "multidimensional cubes" or simply "cubes." In reality, the cubes may be far from perfection, as illustrated on the right side of Figure 2-2.

In the case of Customer dimensions, for example, required "slice and dice" capabilities can provide correct results only if all expected customers and nodes of the corporate hierarchy are accounted for and no double-counting is performed.

FIGURE 2-2
"Slice and dice" capabilities depend on the quality of complex dimensions.

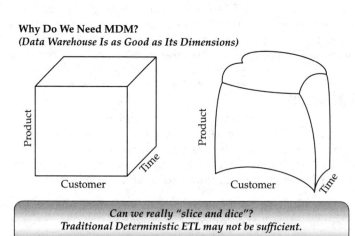

Why Do We Need MDM?
(Data Warehouse Is as Good as Its Dimensions)

Can we really "slice and dice"?
Traditional Deterministic ETL may not be sufficient.
This is where Probabilistic MDM enabled by Data Hubs comes in.

As the initial pilots begin to prove their usefulness to the business community, we see a common trend of expanding the scope of the project by including additional data sources and new consuming applications. This may include functionality that can leverage new customer identity information and create new service improvement and revenue opportunities driven by more complete knowledge of the customers and their relationships. Ultimately, MDM initiatives mature enough to have a profound impact on the business model of the enterprise by enabling enterprise transformation from account-centric to customer-centric processes.

From the technology point of view, we see that after projects that were initially developed in-house succeed in implementing an MDM proof of concept, enterprises start evaluating and implementing best-in-class vendor solutions. Many enterprises ensure that this transition is relatively smooth by adapting a service-oriented architecture (SOA) approach and proven MDM architecture patterns, even to the in-house MDM pilot implementations. In fact, we see that those enterprises that follow the SOA approach can relatively easily grow their MDM framework by replacing MDM components that were developed in-house with longer-term SOA-based MDM vendor products combined with the enterprise-wide SOA infrastructures, common messaging frameworks, common process management, and even common enterprise-wide information security.

To summarize, some common high-level MDM approaches include implementation strategies aimed at reducing project and investment risk, and a broad adoption of the service-oriented architecture to build, integrate, and deploy an MDM Data Hub as a component of the overall enterprise architecture.

On the business side, enterprises are beginning to see significant benefits that MDM solutions offer, including growth of revenue and up-sell and cross-sell opportunities, improved customer service, consistent cross-channel customer experience, increased customer-retention rates, better visibility into key performance indicators for business relationship and partner management, and a better regulatory and compliance posture for the enterprise. At the same time, enterprises quickly realize the complexity and multidisciplinary nature of an MDM initiative and therefore often treat an MDM program as a multiphase corporate initiative that requires large cross-functional teams, multiple work streams, robust and active project management, and a clearly defined set of strategic measurable goals.

The following list presents some of the key technical challenges facing every organization that plans to implement MDM:

- Technical aspects of data governance and the ability to measure and resolve data quality issues.

- The need to create and maintain enterprise-wide semantically consistent data definitions.

- The need to create and maintain an active and accurate metadata repository that contains all relevant information about data semantics, location, and lineage.

- Support and management of distributed and/or federated master data, especially as it requires business rules–driven synchronization and reconciliation of data changes across various data stores and applications.

- Uniformed architecture approach of integrating, federating, and distributing master data, especially reference data, in a way that does not proliferate methods and techniques that result in creating redundant data.

- The complexity of the processes required to orchestrate composite business transactions that span systems and applications, not only within the enterprise but also across the system domains of its business partners.

- Scalability challenges that require an MDM solution to scale with data volumes, especially as new entity-identification tokens such as radio frequency identification (RFID) solutions for products, universal identification cards for citizens, and GPS coordinates for locations become available.

- Scalability of data types. The need to rationalize and integrate both structured and unstructured content is rapidly becoming a key business requirement, not only in the areas of product, trading, and reference data, but even when dealing with customer information, some of which can be found in unstructured files such as documents and images, as in a photo gallery.

- The need to implement process controls to support audit and compliance reporting.

- The challenges of leveraging an existing enterprise security framework to protect the new MDM platform and to enable function-level and data-level access control to master data that is based on authenticated credentials and policy-driven entitlements.

Senior Management Commitment and Value Proposition

Enterprise-scale MDM implementations tend to be lengthy, expensive, complex, and laden with risks. A typical MDM initiative takes at least a year to deliver, and the initiative's cost can easily reach several million U.S. dollars. Senior management's real commitment in terms of strategy, governance, and resources is essential for the success of the initiative. Only a compelling value proposition with clearly defined challenges and risks can secure their commitment.

On the surface, defining and socializing a compelling value proposition appears to be a straightforward task. In practice, however, given the diversity of project stakeholders and new concepts that an MDM project often brings to the table, this step will likely take time and energy and may require multiple iterations. Projects may have to overcome a few false starts until finally the organization gains the critical mass of knowledge about what needs to be achieved in all key domains. Only then can the project team obtain and confirm required levels of executive sponsorship, management commitment, and ownership.

Customer Centricity and a 360-Degree View of a Customer

The stakeholders often use popular terms such as "360-degree view of a customer," "single version of the truth," "golden customer record," and so on. We used this terminology in Chapter 1 as well. It takes time for the organization to understand what these frequently used terms mean for the company and its business. For one thing, these terms by themselves do not necessarily imply customer centricity. Indeed, many CRM systems had a holistic customer view as one of their design and implementation goals, but achieving this 360-degree customer view without changing fundamental business processes did not transform an organization into a customer-centric enterprise, and the traditional account-centric approach continued to be the predominant business model. One way to embark on the road to becoming a customer-centric enterprise is to clearly articulate the reasons for the transformation. To accomplish that goal, the project's stakeholders should answer a number of questions:

- What business processes currently suffer from a lack of customer centricity?
- Do different lines of business or business functions, such as compliance, marketing, and statement processing, have identical definitions of a customer, including cases that deal with an institutional customer?
- Can the company share customer information globally and still comply with appropriate global and local regulatory requirements?
- What are the benefits of the new customer-centric business processes and how can the company quantify these benefits in terms of ROI?

Answering these questions may not be as simple as it sometimes appears, and often represents a challenge for an organization embarking on an MDM project. Indeed, many of these questions, if answered correctly, imply a significant financial, resource, and time commitment, so they should not be taken lightly. On the other hand, not answering these questions early in the project life cycle may result in a significant risk to the project when the stakeholders begin to review the project status, goals, budget, and milestones.

Justifying Customer Centricity
Customer-centric impact analysis is one of the key vehicles that should be used to understand and justify the time, resource, and budgetary requirements of the transformational change toward customer centricity.

Challenges of Selling MDM Inside the Enterprise

By their very nature, MDM projects enable profound and far-reaching changes in the way business processes are defined and implemented. At the same time, experience shows that enterprise-scale MDM initiatives tend to take a long time and significant expenditure to implement. These factors make the challenges of socializing the need and benefits of MDM ever more difficult.

Because MDM initiatives are often considered to be infrastructure projects, the articulation of business benefits and compelling value proposition represents an interesting management challenge that requires considerable salesmanship abilities and a clear and concise business case. Without any application that can rapidly take advantage of a new MDM environment, and without clearly articulated, provable, and tangible ROI, it could be difficult to sell the concept of the MDM (and justify the funding request) to your senior management and business partners. In fact, selling the idea of a new application that can quickly take advantage of the MDM solution could prove to be the most effective way to define a compelling value proposition. This consumption-based approach often becomes a preferred vehicle for getting the buy-in from the internal stakeholders, especially if the new application delivers certain mandated, regulatory functionality.

In some cases, MDM initiatives start as IT process improvement/new system platform projects (moving from a mainframe to an open-system platform, moving from one database management system to another, and so on). In these situations, the projects may not have a clearly articulated set of business requirements, and the primary justification is based on the enterprise technology strategy direction, cost avoidance, partner integration requirements, or the objectives of improving the internal infrastructure, rationalizing the application portfolio, improving data quality, and increasing processing capacity and throughput. If these drivers are sufficiently important to the enterprise, the organization responsible for the delivery of the new capabilities becomes a vocal and powerful champion, and the MDM project can start without too much resistance.

Whether there are clear and compelling business requirements, or the MDM tasks and deliverables are defined within a more traditional technology-driven project, one thing is clear: Large, complex, and costly initiatives such as MDM projects typically fail without comprehensive buy-in from senior management and other stakeholders. We will discuss this in more detail in Chapter 12.

It is important to point out that the answers to the questions for the stakeholders that are listed in the previous section are expected to be multifaceted and would depend on the context and the stakeholder role. Indeed, initiatives and projects of MDM caliber involve multiple stakeholder groups (see Figure 2-3 for a graphical representation of the stakeholder groups).

This stakeholder landscape includes executive management and sponsors; line-of-business leaders; front, middle, and back office; corporate and LOB data governance professionals; technology managers, architects, and engineers; finance; regulatory compliance; legal department; information security; technical infrastructure; external technology partners; and possibly other participants. Given their diversity and differences in priorities and goals, these stakeholders will most likely have different opinions and will thus provide different answers to the questions listed earlier. It is crucial to the success of the project that even though the views are different, they must represent different sides of

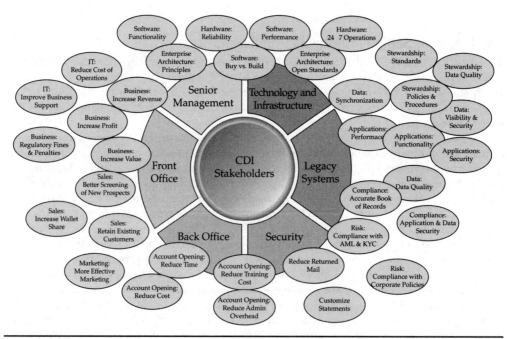

FIGURE 2-3   Variety of stakeholders and functional areas of MDM

a single consistent "story" about the project's goals, objectives, strategy, priorities, and the end-state vision. It is the ultimate challenge of the project's executive sponsors and project management team to establish, formulate, and disseminate project messages consistently to the appropriate team members, stakeholders, and project sponsors.

From the risk management perspective, human factors outweigh technical factors. For example, the IT organization might decide to implement the MDM project without obtaining an organizational buy-in. Even if the resulting solution is technically sound and perfectly implemented, the efforts would be viewed as a failure if the project is not socialized properly within the organization. Only about 20 percent of all MDM failures are caused by poor technology or architecture decisions. An estimated 80 percent have a root cause in political, management, user acceptance, and other human and cultural issues. In order to mitigate this risk, the initiative should be aligned with business objectives. In this case, project sponsors can "sell" the effort as a major improvement in business processes, customer experience, customer intelligence, business development, marketing, compliance, and so on.

Socializing MDM as a Multidimensional Challenge

The socialization challenge of a large-scale initiative like MDM is a multidimensional problem (see Figure 2-4).

We see the socialization problem as having at least three dimensions. The first dimension illustrates a variety of stakeholder groups.

The phases of the project life cycle are shown as the second dimension. The role of each group evolves over time as the initiative progresses through the life-cycle phases. For example, business analysts who represent various business units and define business requirements at the beginning of the initiative may later participate in business acceptance testing. The challenges

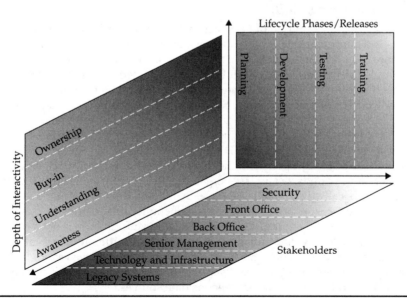

FIGURE 2-4   The three-dimensional socialization problem

continue in the roadmap development and architecture phase when the solution is defined and the road to the end state is determined. The challenges vary as the project evolves, but they continue to be present throughout the project life cycle. To ensure the success of the MDM initiative, the project team has to make sure to obtain and regularly renew the organizational commitment from multiple stakeholder groups throughout all phases of development, implementation, deployment, and training.

> **Need for Organizational Buy-In**
> Even technically successful MDM projects can be perceived as failures if the project team fails to socialize project goals and benefits as well as properly organize and orchestrate training for the end-user community.

The third dimension represents the depth of interactivity or the level of user buy-in and involvement. The user involvement begins with awareness. At this level, a stakeholder group becomes aware of the upcoming change but may have a limited high-level understanding of the initiative. The next level includes understanding the magnitude and complexity of the effort and its primary implications. Finally, the key stakeholders should participate in the initiative at the ownership level. These stakeholders actively participate in the effort and are responsible for assigned deliverables. On some projects the level of interaction between stakeholders is insufficient, and oftentimes stakeholders are taken by unpleasant surprise when they eventually learn about some decisions made without their involvement. On the other hand, having numerous standing meetings attended by 50–70 people, due to an attempt to engage all parties in MDM project discussions, is counterproductive. Proper understanding of the depth of interactivity helps in building and maintaining a balanced project communications plan.

Technical Challenges of MDM

MDM projects represent a myriad of technical challenges and risks to IT managers, systems, applications and data architects, security officers, data governance officers, data stewards, and operations. This section focuses on high-level implementation challenges and risks.

For example, customer-centricity solutions are trivialized by suggesting that the problem can be solved by placing all customer data in a single repository. This approach has been known not to work in all cases. Similarly, the best way to build a product master may not lie in making a central product database for all product information as a single data repository. In reality, this approach is limited and may be appropriate for small department-level projects. However, MDM projects become much more complex and difficult as the size of the company and the diversity of customer, product, service, and location data grows. In midsize and large organizations, it is not unusual to find that master data is physically distributed and logically federated across multiple application systems that provide existing and new business functions and support various lines of business. Rationalizing, federating, and aggregating this information is not a trivial task, and dealing with the legacy data and applications brings additional complications into the mix. This is especially true if you consider that in many cases legacy systems lack complete and accurate process documentation and stable data definitions—the principal obstacles to seamless semantic integration of heterogeneous data sources.

Of course, an enterprise may adopt a strategy of decommissioning some legacy systems to help deal with this challenge, and can put together an end-state vision for the MDM project that allows for some of these legacy application systems to be phased out over time. However, this strategy can be successful *only* if the candidate legacy systems are carefully analyzed for the potential impact on remaining upstream and downstream application systems. In addition to the impact of decommissioning, a careful analysis needs to take place to see the impact of introducing an MDM platform into the existing application environment, even if decommissioning is not going to take place. The project team should develop an integrated project plan that contains multiple parallel work streams, clearly defined dependencies, and carefully allocated resources. The plan should help to direct the implementation of an MDM platform in a way that supports coexistence between the old (legacy) and the new (MDM) environments, until such time as the organization can decommission the legacy applications without invalidating business processes. We discuss these and other implementation challenges in Part IV of the book.

Most of the technical MDM challenges to achieving consistent master data quality deal with the following:

- Implementation costs and time-to-market
- Data governance
- Data quality, synchronization, integration, and federation
- Data visibility, security, and regulatory compliance

The sections below provide additional details on some of these challenges. We'll discuss the challenges of data governance in more detail in Chapter 17.

Implementation Costs and Time-to-Market Concerns

As we have already stated, large-scale MDM projects are risky. The risk is even higher because these projects are supposed to result in significant changes in business processes and impact structural, architectural, and operational models. Achieving all stated objectives of an MDM project may take several iterations that can span years. Therefore, it is not realistic to assume that the project team can deliver a comprehensive end-to-end solution in a single release. Such an unreasonable expectation would represent a significant implementation risk.

The project team can mitigate this risk by devising a sound release strategy. The strategy should include the end-state vision and an implementation plan that defines a stepwise approach in which each step or phase should deliver clear tactical benefits. These benefits should be tangible, measurable, and aligned with the strategic roadmap and business demands. Project plans should ensure that each release provides a measurable incremental business value on a regular, frequent basis, preferably every six to nine months. When multiple lines of business are involved in the MDM initiative, the first production release should be defined as a trade-off between the business priority of a given line of business and implementation feasibility that minimizes the delivery risk of the first release. We can extend this model by devising a strategy that maintains a trade-off between the business value of the release and the release manageability, risk, and complexity, as illustrated in Figure 2-5.

Another implementation risk of an MDM project is caused by a project plan or approach that does not take into account the issues related to existing legacy data stores and applications. For example, consider an MDM project with the goal of delivering a brand-new Data Hub.

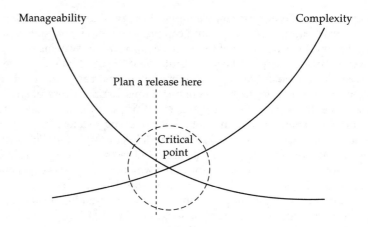

Figure 2-5
Trade-off between
release complexity
and manageability

If the project plan does not account for the need to either integrate with or phase out the existing application legacy systems, the resulting MDM Data Hub environment may have questionable value because it will be difficult to synchronize it with various legacy systems and use it as an accurate authoritative master. In the case of MDM for Customer Domain, the challenge of concurrently supporting the new customer-centric universe and the old account-centric "legacy world" may be unavoidable. Both universes must coexist and cooperate in delivering business value, but the risks associated with this approach have to be understood and mitigated through careful planning. For instance, the coexistence and cooperation approach may require significant integration and synchronization efforts, may complicate application and data maintenance, and thus may increase operational risk. Not planning for these efforts may result in a highly visible project failure and could negatively affect the enterprise's ability to transform itself into a new customer-centric business model and develop a sound MDM solution.

Another concern related to the drive toward customer centricity is its potential organizational impact due to the implementation of new system platforms and new business processes. As we show in Part IV of this book, major MDM implementations lead to significant changes in the business processes that can greatly impact stakeholders' responsibilities and required skills. Some jobs can be significantly redefined. For example, a legacy mainframe application that was the system of record for customer information may lose its significance or may even be decommissioned when the MDM Data Hub becomes available as the new system of record for master data.

Partnerships with Vendors

Given the complexity of many MDM projects, it is reasonable to assume that no single vendor can provide an all-in-one, out-of-the-box comprehensive MDM solution that fits the business and technical requirements of every enterprise. This should not be looked upon as a limitation of continuously evolving vendor products but rather as another call for the acceptance of a service-oriented architecture philosophy. Conceptually speaking, each vendor provides a service or a combination of services used by an enterprise within its service-oriented infrastructure. This approach is aligned with a vision of an agile enterprise architecture optimized for an evolutionary change. As we know, reliance on a single product that fits all demands or a vendor that serves all enterprise needs leads to monolithic inflexible solutions that cannot evolve to support the changing business needs and open-architecture standards.

This puts MDM implementers in a position where they have to look for a combination of vendor products and home-grown solutions in order to meet the business demands of the enterprise. Involving multiple vendors is not unusual for any major MDM implementation. This approach requires that the organization implement a formal process of product evaluation and selection to determine which best-in-class products can make a short list of potentially acceptable solutions. Typically, once the short list is finalized, the organization may start a proof-of-concept activity where one or more vendors would implement working prototypes that demonstrate both functional and nonfunctional capabilities. Although this approach can protect the enterprise from blindly choosing a product based solely on the vendor's claims, it does create significant management overhead due to running one or more proof-of-concept projects, managing additional resources, dealing with the shortage of skilled resources, and balancing conflicting priorities. Strong architectural and data governance oversight for the activities that include multiple vendors and implementation partners is a must, and the lack of such oversight represents a very common and significant implementation risk.

Data Quality, Data Synchronization, and Integration Challenges

Generally speaking, data has a tendency to "decay" and become stale with time as changes in business and technology occur on a regular or sporadic basis (products change names, financial systems change accounting rules, and so on). This is especially true for customer data. Indeed, a 2003 study completed by The Data Warehousing Institute titled "Data Quality and the Bottom Line" stated the following: "The problem with data is that its quality quickly degenerates over time. Experts say 2 percent of records in a customer file become obsolete in one month because customers die, divorce, marry, and move."

To put this statistic into perspective, assume that a company has 500,000 customers and prospects. If 2 percent of these records become obsolete in one month, that would be 10,000 records per month, or 120,000 records every year. So, in two years, about half of all records are obsolete if left unchecked.

Master Data Management solutions can create and maintain consistent, accurate, and complete customer views, product hierarchies, reference records, and locations. Critical business decisions such as promotions, price changes and discounts, marketing campaigns, credit decisions, and daily operations revolve around key market, customer, and product data. Without an accurate and complete view of the master entities, efforts to provide targeted, personalized, and compelling products and services may prove to be ineffective.

In no small measure, a company's success or failure is based on the quality of its master data. The challenge of MDM is to be able to quickly and accurately capture, standardize, and consolidate the immense amount of data that comes from a variety of channels, touch points, and application systems.

Many organizations have separate sales, operations, support, and marketing groups. If these groups have different databases of master data—and different methods for recording and archiving this information—it is extremely difficult for the enterprise to rationalize and understand all of the key business processes and data infrastructure issues simultaneously.

The crux of the problem most companies face is the inability to compile complete master entity views when most of the systems are isolated from each other in their stovepipes and operate independently. By definition, an MDM system effectively bridges the gap between various master data views by rationalizing, integrating, and aggregating master data collected from disparate data sources and applications in order to provide a single, properly resolved, accurate, consolidated view of the master data.

MDM solutions benefit the enterprise by pulling critical master information from existing internal and external data sources and validating that the data is correct and meets the business needs and data-quality standards of the enterprise. Over time, MDM solutions can further enrich master data with additional internal and external information, as well as store, manage, and maintain the master data as a benchmark for enterprise use.

One approach for maintaining data quality and integrity would be to tackle the problem at the operating system level. This seems to be a practical approach. After all, operating systems support applications that manage and execute transactions and maintain transactional properties of atomicity, consistency, isolation, and durability (ACID). To sustain these properties, operational, transactional applications tend to be isolated from nonoperational applications such as data warehousing and business intelligence systems. This "isolation" helps discover and resolve data-integrity issues one system at a time.

Correcting data quality in each of the operational systems is only part of the problem that does not address the MDM cross-system issues holistically. Once the data in a single system has been corrected, the data changes have to be synchronized and integrated with various data sources. Moreover, various data records about the same individual or product need to be aggregated into a single master database, often logically, creating a federated data store. Although data-integration challenges are not new and are not unique to the MDM space, Master Data Management emphasizes their criticality. The challenges of data integration include the following:

- **Lack of standardization of customer or company names and addresses**   If this information isn't standardized, it is difficult to resolve customer lifetime value, because customers may have different representations within the various application databases.

- **No common identifier or linking of customers across systems**   For example, an individual customer record may be stored in several operational systems, and thus the customer can be represented differently in every system, even using different names and aliases. This representation mismatch may prevent an MDM solution from recognizing the same individual across various applications and data stores.

- **Anonymous data**   Master data solutions often use special codes to signify anonymous or default data. For example, a phone number of "999-999-9999" or a birth date of "01/01/01" may represent common shortcuts for unspecified or missing data. These special codes may have to be treated in a way that escalates data content questions to the appropriate data steward.

- **Stale, outdated data**   As we stated earlier, data has a tendency to change over time. Left unchecked and unmanaged, these changes do not get reflected in the master database, thus significantly reducing the value of data.

One of the stated goals and key requirements of any MDM solution is to create and maintain the best possible information about the master data regardless of the number and type of source data systems. To achieve this goal, Master Data Management should support an effective data-acquisition process (discussed in more detail in Chapter 5). The MDM process requires different steps and rules for different data sources. However, the basic process is consistent and at a minimum should answer the following questions:

- What points of data collection might have master data?
- What systems are impacted by master data and what master data is used by each of the affected systems?
- How does each data source store, validate, and audit master data?
- What sources contain the best master data for a given domain, entity, and possibly attribute?
- How can data be integrated across various data sources?
- What master data entities and attributes are required for current and future business processes?

Of course, there are many questions surrounding data quality concerns. Answering these questions can help an MDM solution to determine what business and integration rules are required to bring the best data from the various sources together. This best-available master data is integrated under the MDM umbrella and should be entity-resolved, cleansed, rationalized, integrated, and then synchronized with the operational data systems.

Data Visibility, Security, and Regulatory Compliance

Solving challenges of data quality and data integration allows MDM solutions to enable entity-centric business process transformation. In the case of MDM for Customer Domain and as part of this transformation, the MDM platform creates a fully integrated view of the customers and their relationships with the enterprise, information that most likely has to be protected according to a multitude of various government and industry regulations. Or, stating it slightly differently, integrating customer information in an MDM Data Hub supports enterprise-wide customer-centric transformations that in turn create significant competitive advantages for the enterprise. At the same time, however, precisely because an MDM system integrates master data, including customer data, in one place called a "Data Hub," these implementations face significant security and compliance risks.

The majority of the relevant regulations discussed here focus on the financial services segment and deal with the need to protect customer data from corruption as well as compromised, unauthorized access and use. In addition, a number of government and industry regulations require an enterprise to capture and enforce customer privacy preferences. Parts III and IV of this book provide a detailed look into the requirements for data protection and their impact on the technology of MDM solutions.

We offer a brief overview of the data protection and privacy regulations in this section for the purposes of completeness and ease of reference.

Basel II and FFIEC

Basel II defines operational risk to include the risk of compromise and fraud. Therefore, when the Federal Financial Institutions Examination Council (FFIEC) stipulated its latest guidance, it immediately affected the scope of Basel II's operational risk in these specific ways:

- In order to combat fraud, on October 12, 2005, the FFIEC issued new guidance on customer authentication for online banking services. The guidance stated that U.S. banks would be expected to comply with the rules by the end of 2006.
- These new regulations guided banks to apply two major methods:
  - **Risk assessment**   Banks must assess the risk of the various activities taking place on their Internet banking sites.
  - **Risk-based authentication**   Banks must apply stronger authentication for high-risk transactions.
- Specific guidelines required banks to implement the following:
  - Layered security
  - Monitoring and reporting
  - Configurable authentication, where its strength depends on degree of risk
  - Customer awareness and reverse authentication
  - Single-factor and multifactor authentication
  - Mutual authentication

The USA Patriot Act's KYC Provision

MDM data-protection concerns are driven by regulations such as the USA Patriot Act and the Basel Committee's "Customer Due Diligence for Banks," issued in October 2001. The USA Patriot Act specifies requirements to comply with Know Your Customer (KYC) provisions. Banks with inadequate KYC policies are exposed to significant legal and reputation risks. Sound KYC policies and procedures protect the integrity of the bank and serve as remedies against money laundering, terrorist financing, and other unlawful activities. KYC is an important part of the risk-management practices of any bank, financial services institution, or insurance company. KYC requires a customer acceptance policy (opt-in/opt-out), customer identification, ongoing monitoring of high-risk accounts, and risk management. MDM-enabled customer identification is one of the key drivers for the enterprises to implement systems known as the Customer Identity Hub platform.

Customer Fraud Protection

One of the tenets of customer fraud protection is based on sound customer identification and recognition capabilities offered by MDM. According to IdentityGuard.com,[12] over 28 million Americans have had their identity stolen in the past three years. According to the California research firm Javelin Strategy & Research, in 2005 there were 8.9 million identity theft victims in the U.S. alone, costing $56.6 billion! Fraud protection measures resulted only in some marginal improvements in recent years. According to the Privacy Rights Clearinghouse,[13] the total one-year fraud amount decreased to $55.7 billion in 2006 and then to $49.3 billion in 2007.

The Sarbanes-Oxley Act

The Sarbanes-Oxley Act of 2002 requires public companies to implement internal controls over financial reporting, operations, and assets. The Securities and Exchange Commission (SEC) requires that companies make regular disclosures about the strengths, weaknesses, and overall status of these controls. The implementation of these controls is heavily dependent on information technology. Sarbanes-Oxley's demands for operational transparency, reporting, and controls fuel the needs for MDM implementations.

OFAC

The Office of Foreign Asset Control (OFAC) of the U.S. Department of the Treasury administers and enforces economic and trade sanctions against target countries, terrorists, international narcotic trafficking, and those entities engaged in activities related to the proliferation of weapons of mass destruction. Executive Order 13224 requires the OFAC to make available to customer-facing institutions a list of "blocked individuals" known as Specially Designated Nationals (SDNs). The executive order requires institutions to verify the identity of their customers against the "blocked list." Clearly, an MDM solution is a valuable platform that can help to achieve OFAC compliance.

Gramm-Leach-Bliley Act (GLBA)

The Financial Modernization Act of 1999, also known as the Gramm-Leach-Bliley Act, includes provisions to protect consumers' personal financial information held by financial institutions. There are three parts to the privacy requirements: the Financial Privacy Rule, the Safeguard Rule, and Pretexting provisions. The Financial Privacy Rule regulates the collection and disclosure of customer information. The Safeguards Rule requires enterprises to design, implement, and maintain safeguards to protect customer information. The Pretexting provisions of the GLBA protect consumers from individuals and companies that obtain the consumers' personal information under false pretenses.

GLBA requires disclosure on what information a company can collect, the usage of the collected information, what information can or cannot be disclosed, and the customer-specific opt-in/opt-out options. The Safeguard Rule includes a disclosure of the procedures used to protect customer information from unauthorized access or loss. For Internet users, the company must disclose the information collected when the user accesses the company's website.

Given the potential scope and information value of data stored in MDM Data Hubs, it is easy to see why MDM implementations should consider GLBA compliance as one of the key risk-mitigation strategies.

The UK Financial Services Act

The UK Financial Services Act (1986) requires companies to match customer records against lists of banned individuals (terrorists, money launderers, and others) more rapidly and accurately. An MDM Data Hub is an effective data enabler to conduct these matches.

DNC Compliance

As part of their privacy protection campaign, the United States and later Canada accepted Do Not Call (DNC) legislation. In order to avoid penalties, telemarketers must comply with this regulation, which may also require some level of customer recognition and identification.

The legislation requires the companies to maintain their customers' opt-in/opt-out options. Customer-centric MDM implementations allow the enterprise to capture and enforce DNC preferences at the customer level as well as at the account level. Chapter 7 illustrates this concept by discussing a high-level MDM data model.

CPNI Compliance

The Consumer Proprietary Network Information (CPNI) regulation prohibits telephone companies from using information identifying whom customers call, when they call, and the kinds of phone services they purchased for marketing purposes without customer consent. This creates the need for the opt-in/opt-out support and offers a platform to drive CPNI compliance.

HIPAA

The Health Insurance Portability and Accountability Act (HIPAA) of 1996 (45 CFR Parts 160 and 164) requires the federal government to protect the privacy of personal health information by issuing national standards. An MDM Data Hub for a healthcare provider or a pharmaceutical company may contain comprehensive and complete personal health information at the customer/patient levels. Thus, HIPAA directly affects the design and implementation of MDM solutions that deal with customer health information.

ARRA

The American Recovery and Reinvestment Act (ARRA) is an economic stimulus package signed by President Barack H. Obama into law in February of 2009. One of the five stated intents of the ARRA is to provide investments needed to increase economic efficiency by spurring technological advances in science and health. The $19 billion allocated to Health Information Technology are expected to accelerate the adoption of MDM and other technologies.

Internationalization of Data Protection

Many countries have been developing their own data-protection regulations. There is a clear need for internationalization of these regulations. In its absence, all nations experience additional costs associated with a variety of information-sharing laws. The 31st International Data Protection Commissioners Conference,[14] hosted by the Spanish Data Protection Agency (AEPD) in Madrid, Spain, in 2009, discussed movement toward an international regulation on privacy.[15] These types of international regulations can have a significant impact on many areas of global information management, including MDM.

In conclusion, these sections demonstrate that although MDM solutions can offer significant benefits to an enterprise, these solutions are not easy to develop and deploy. Furthermore, an organization has to address many challenges when it embarks on an MDM initiative, including significant benefits; competitive advantages; and major additional technical, organizational, and business challenges related to an MDM-enabled transformation toward entity centricity and, in particular, customer centricity. We discuss many of these challenges, issues, and approaches in more details in Parts II, III, and IV of this book.

Challenges of Global MDM Implementations

The discussion about MDM challenges would not be complete without looking at the global MDM implementations. The complexities of global MDM deployment exist at multiple levels and are caused by the following:

- Country-specific regulations can restrict information sharing outside the country.

- Cultural differences, if they exist between different corporate sites across the globe, result in more diverse MDM needs that may require significant reconciliation efforts.

- Multilingual MDM issues can create additional complexities for record matching and entity resolution, reconciliation of reference codes and metadata, use of different character sets, support for multilingual user interfaces, and so on.

- Even though many MDM implementations are mission critical and require 24×7 operations, global implementation requirements contribute to the availability and peak performance needs.

To date, the number of implemented MDM solutions and the level of MDM maturity in North America, the UK, and the English-speaking world overall is much higher than that in the countries where English is not the predominant language. The number of MDM implementations in French language–dominated geographies has been gradually growing over the last few years.

We will be covering the complexities of global MDM throughout the book, focusing on specific issues and how they can be resolved. In this chapter we will limit our discussion to a few examples that illustrate the cultural differences in how individual names vary by the individual's ethnic background and country. These differences can have considerable MDM implications.

Russia, Ukraine, and Eastern Europe

In Russia, the Ukraine, and some Eastern European countries, the second name points to the individual's father's first name. Typically the wife takes her husband's last name, but her last name will have an additional gender-specific suffix—for example, Ivanov (husband) and Ivanova (wife).

Clearly these rules differ from those typically used domestically in the U.S. and inherited from the European English-, Dutch-, German- and French-speaking countries, where people often have two or more given names. When the wife takes her husband's name, their last names are exactly identical without any additional suffixes.

Spain and Italy

In Spain and Spanish-speaking countries, people have one or more given names and two family names—one from the father and one from the mother.

In Italy, people may have one or more given names, no middle name, and a family name.

Thailand

According to WindowOnTheWorldInc.com,[16] last names have been used in Thailand for only the past 50 years and are difficult even for the Thai people to pronounce. Two people with the same last name are almost certainly related. As per APMForum.com,[17] when immigrants from other countries apply for a Thai last name, they have to obey the following procedure that regulates registrations of the new Thai last names:

- The applicants submit five alternatives to the government officer. Each one has a maximum of ten Thai characters.
- The officer will search in the database for identical last names. The law requires the uniqueness of the last name.
- About one month later, the applicant will check with the officer. If there is no duplication, the applicant can use the new last name. If there is any duplication, the applicant needs to resubmit the application with a new set of proposed surnames. Because Thailand has many immigrants, particularly from China, subsequent applicants have to create new unique last names. This explains why the Thai people have long surnames—and they are getting longer.

There are significant consequences of these rules from an MDM project perspective. Indeed, it is much easier to resolve customer identification issues with the rules just described.

Korea

According to GamingGeeks.org,[18] until the eighteenth century, only about half the population of Korea had surnames. There are only about 300 or 400 family names used in Korea, of which Lee, Kim, and Park/Pak are particularly common, accounting for almost half the population. People with the same surname are divided into branches often identified by a place name (about 280 in the Kim family and around 5 in most others), and members of these branches could not intermarry until recently, when the Korean Supreme Court made a ruling that people from the same clan could marry outside Korea. Women do not take their husband's surname. In addition, Korean names are formed differently than Western names, with the family name first, followed by the two-part given name. The first of the two given names is shared by everyone of the same generation in the family, and the second is the individual's given name.

As you can see from these examples (which just scratch the surface of international, multilingual, and multicharacter set of MDM attributes), global MDM initiatives have to deal with a wide variety of challenging and fascinating rules, some of which we will discuss in more detail in Part IV. Differences in standards, languages, privacy, compliance, and security regulations, as well as cultural differences drive the complexity of international and global MDM solutions to new heights. In order to be successful in implementing global MDM solutions, enterprises and MDM vendors have to gain a deep understanding of country-specific and cultural rules and regulations. Clearly, global MDM products and solution approaches are still maturing, and a lot of work lies ahead. It is certainly a significant area of growth for Master Data Management. Emerging global MDM solutions may have to leverage the trends in developing and deploying global identifiers for individuals as well as advances in authentication technologies that rely on truly global identification attributes that transcend geography and language differences. Examples of these global identification attributes and their usage include multifactor authentication using biometrics such as fingerprints, iris scans, and retina scans. Practical use of many of these technologies is still in its infancy. Multifactor authentication is discussed in more detail in Part III.

References

1. "Enterprise Master Data Management: Market Review and Forecast for 2008–2012."

2. Rob Karel. "The ROI for Master Data Management." Forrester Research, Inc., October 29, 2008.

3. Dubov, Lawrence. "Estimating the Benefits for MDM." Mastering Data Management, February 23, 2010. http://blog.initiate.com/index.php/2010/02/23/estimating-the-benefits-of-mdm/.

4. Nitin Joshi. "Quantifying Business Value in Master Data Management." 9/3/2009 http://www.information-management.com/infodirect/2009_137/master_data_management-10016016-1.html.

5. Henrik Liliendahl Sorensen. "55 Reasons to Improve Data Quality." 11/22/2009 http://liliendahl.wordpress.com/2009/11/22/55-reasons-to-improve-data-quality/.

6. Andrew White. "MDM Spend Remains Healthy, Despite Economic Slow Down." September 22, 2009. http://blogs.gartner.com/andrew_white/2009/09/22/mdm-spend-remains-healthy-despite-economic-slow-down/.

7. White, Andrew, et al. "Key Themes and Hot Topics from Gartner Master Data Management Summit." November 23, 2009.

8. Mark Smith, "The Business Case for Master Data Management." April 2007, Ventana Research. http://www.ventanaresearch.com/uploadedFiles/The%20Business%20Case%20for%20Master%20Data%20Management.pdf.

9. John Radcliffe and Michael Smith. "Creating a Business Case for Master Data Management," 2008, Gartner Research.

10. Lowenstein, Michael. "CDI: The CRM Dance Every Marketer Must Learn" *CRM News*, February 2, 2002. http://searchcrm.techtarget.com/originalContent/0,289142,sid11_gci799952,00.html.

11. Etienne Wenger, et al. *"Cultivating Communities of Practice."* Harvard Business Press (2002).

12. www.identityguard.com.

13. http://www.privacyrights.org/ar/idtheftsurveys.htm.

14. http://www.privacyconference2009.org/home/index-iden-idweb.html.

15. http://www.priv.gc.ca/resource/int/conf_09_e.cfm.

16. http://www.windowontheworldinc.com/countryprofile/ thailand.html.

17. http://www.apmforum.com/ columns/thai4.htm.

18. http://www.gaminggeeks.org/Resources/KateMonk/Orient/Korea/Surnames.htm.

3

CHAPTER

MDM Applications by Industry

I n Chapter 1, we defined master data as the data represented by the key enterprise data
entities, attributes, and relationships. We defined Master Data Management (MDM) as
a discipline that resolves master data to maintain the golden record—a holistic and
panoramic view of master entities and relationships, the benchmark for master data that
can be used across the enterprise, and sometimes between enterprises, to facilitate data
exchanges. Master Data Management applies equally well to any commercial market
segment, such as financial services, the healthcare industry, telecommunications, consumer
retail, and many others. Moreover, MDM can be beneficial to any public sector business,
including government agencies that deal with citizens, employees, tourists, immigration,
law enforcement, and others. In other words, using the definitions of master data and
MDM as a guide, we showed that Master Data Management is a horizontal discipline and
technology that applies to all industries and markets and is global in nature.

In Chapter 2, we discussed the key drivers and challenges that are also mostly horizontal
in nature and apply to all industries that face challenges of improving customer service;
improving management of their products, servicers, and assets; enhancing the accuracy of
reporting and analytics; reducing customer churn and attrition; increasing efficiency of
operations; reducing risks; strengthening compliance; and so on. We showed that increasing
sales productivity and revenue, improving customer satisfaction, and reducing IT
infrastructure costs represent intrinsic MDM properties and thus can be found in MDM
implementations for practically every market segment. We also discussed key business,
organizational, and technical challenges at a high level.

Although the scope of Master Data Management is extremely broad and includes
customers, products, hierarchies, reference data, and other data types and domains, we put a
significant focus of the discussions in Part I on the party domain. A focus on the party domain
does not make the scope of the discussion smaller. Indeed, customer master (or, more
generally, party master) is a requirement for any business-to-consumer (B2C) or government-
to-citizen (G2C) organization, which of course is a very broad field. Based on market size, the
customer domain is the largest MDM market domain and, hence, deserves the highest level
of attention. Many considerations applied to the customer domain are equally applicable to
other domains. We are discussing several other non-customer-domain-specific considerations
in the context of industry-specific needs.

Industry Views of MDM

When dealing with such a large area of MDM coverage, it is important to recognize both the similarities and differences, not only in business and data semantics, but also in the way MDM is viewed and implemented across various industries and government sectors. Therefore, we will look at the MDM requirements, approaches, and challenges that different industries and organizations have to deal with in order to achieve the stated MDM goal of creating an authoritative, accurate, timely, and comprehensive master data resource. Clearly, each industry brings its own set of requirements and challenges that are specific to the industry.

As individuals, we deal with MDM problems in everyday life:

- When we interact with our phone, TV services, or the Internet provider
- When we call a bank or interact with a financial advisor
- When we call a credit card company as a credit card holder to resolve an issue or to apply for a card
- When we call a mortgage servicer or are looking to apply for a mortgage or loan
- When we buy medicine, contact a healthcare provider, are treated in a hospital, or get reimbursed by a health insurance company
- When we shop in a retail store or a supermarket
- When we travel by air, train, or bus
- When we call an insurance company for quotes or a claim
- When we make a hotel reservation or buy a vacation package
- When we send a FedEx or UPS package
- When we interact with social security services, law enforcement, public education, and other government agencies

And this list can grow easily with other examples.

With a lot of commonality across a variety of industry verticals that can benefit from MDM, our MDM overview in Part I of the book would not be complete without a discussion of specific vertical MDM variants and applications. Every company embarking on an MDM project or program is looking to understand what MDM can do specifically for their industry, the adoption of MDM in their industry area of interest, how MDM has been leveraged by their industry competitors, and what MDM would mean for their enterprise business processes, systems, applications, capabilities, competitiveness, and the bottom line. Even though it is practically impossible to provide a comprehensive list of usage scenarios by industry, there is a need to articulate the predominant case studies and scenarios. In order to address this need, in this chapter we focus on several industry verticals to discuss specific case studies as they apply to multiple commercial enterprises and the public sector.

In the sections that follow, we limit the discussion to the following categories and examples of industry sectors and subsectors:

- **Services**   Financial services, telecommunications companies, healthcare, hospitality and the gaming industry
- **Products**   Manufacturing, software publishing, and pharmaceutical companies

- **Transportation**   Airlines, shipping and logistics companies
- **Retail sales**
- **Public sector**

Commercial Sector

Let's start this discussion with a review of the MDM suitability and usage in various industries of the commercial sector. In this discussion, we focus on the information management needs of a given industry rather than on the interactions/delivery channels and marketing viewpoints, such as those typically found in B2B and B2C models. Although B2B and B2C differ from each other in several ways—including longer sales cycles and more structured, often bi-directional relationships for B2B, and the relatively more dynamic, almost "social" nature of B2C interactions—the similarities between B2B and B2C are meaningful enough to benefit from an MDM solution that creates, maintains, and makes available an accurate, timely, and secure authoritative source of information about customers, service providers, suppliers, products, and other relevant domains.

Financial Services, Banking, and Insurance

For the purpose of our discussion, financial services include banks, brokerages, wealth management organizations, credit card companies, mortgage companies, and insurance firms. The financial services industry has been one of the early adopters of MDM concepts and technologies, including MDM Data Hubs. The industry has significant interests in both individual (retail) customers and institutional or commercial organizations. In the previous chapters, we discussed financial services institutions as good illustrative examples of how a customer-facing enterprise can benefit from implementing an MDM solution. Here, we take a more detailed view of the needs of the financial services industry.

Retail financial services institutions (FSIs) such as consumer banks, life insurance companies, and retail brokerage houses have always faced the challenge of dealing with thousands and even millions of their customers and prospects in a highly competitive marketplace. In that respect, these types of FSIs are similar to consumer retail businesses such as Walmart and Sears, and they have been at the forefront of creating and using the concept of a single-customer view. This need to have an accurate and complete customer view is not new—as stated in Chapter 1, MDM precursors designed to create a single-customer view included Customer Information Files (CIF), Enterprise Data Warehouses (EDW), and Operational Data Stores (ODS). Financial services organizations were some of the first companies to pioneer and effectively use customer analytics, data mining, and multichannel CRM systems to better understand customer behavior and the factors enforcing customers' brand loyalty, propensity to buy, and reasons for customer attrition. Today, financial services institutions embark on MDM initiatives to overcome the inefficiencies and limitations of CIF and other MDM precursors and to collect, manage, and analyze hundreds of financial metrics that heavily rely on the accuracy, consistency, and timeliness of corporate reference data and various views of corporate hierarchies. In addition to managing financial metrics, modern MDM initiatives enable the delivery of accurate, cross-channel-integrated, and current customer information to the point of sales, service, or online channel in a timely fashion to have an impact on the outcome of a customer transaction.

Financial services organizations servicing retail customers do not limit the scope of the solution on individual customers and prospects. The party model for financial services organizations is typically complex and comprehensive in order to address the enterprise's needs for customer relationships and customer and account groupings. Consequently, in addition to individual customers, the party model oftentimes includes formal and informal organizational entities such as mutual funds, informal investment groups or clubs, associations, trusts, estates, tax groups, and other entities representing more than one customer. Wealth management and financial advisory organizations often operate as multiple financial advisory teams serving their customers under the umbrella of a large financial services corporation. The financial advisors may not even be the company's employees; they may operate as a collection of small virtual companies (teams) under the umbrella of another established financial institution. For large wealth management and financial services organizations, where the number of financial advisors can be measured in the thousands, MDM has significant data security, visibility, and eligibility requirements that we will concentrate on in Parts II and III of this book.

MDM enables customer on-boarding as well as global account opening and management processes. These processes and the supporting user interfaces include the ability to look up the reference data in the Data Hub before a new customer or prospect record is created. The process helps to prevent the creation of multiple records that refer to one customer, even if the records have different information. This improvement at the point of entry introduces efficiencies downstream. We will discuss this approach to Data Hub Design and Use Pattern in more detail when we discuss MDM architecture styles in Parts II and IV of this book.

The same approach applies to insurance firms for a policy issuance process and some other industries, such as mutual funds. For insurance, this method (look up before create) is used when MDM is integrated with claim-processing applications and other key insurance operational systems in all areas of insurance—Property and Casualty (P&C), Life, and Auto. Many established insurance companies operate globally and provide a variety of insurance products. In doing so, insurance companies need the ability to associate new customer applications with already existing accounts and manage a variety of corporate hierarchies (legal, sales, marketing, risk, and so on) with arbitrary hierarchy levels. By design, MDM is a major enabler of these capabilities for insurance firms.

As do most banks, credit, loan, and mortgage companies leverage MDM to match applicant records against the Office of Foreign Assets Control (OFAC) list,[1] Specially Designated Nationals (SDN) lists,[2] and other watch lists to get a holistic view of a customer and make substantiated application decisions.

Banks often embark on MDM projects because MDM is looked upon as an important and foundational capability when a bank intends to re-platform from legacy system environments to a new, more efficient, cost-effective, or more functionally rich environment—for example, a move to a new core banking system[3] or trust accounting system. These systems are typically the key operational systems that own the most important and complex business rules and transactions managed by the organization. Similarly, claim-processing systems[4,5] represent the engine of operational processing in insurance companies. A successful completion of a re-platforming project or migration from an obsolete legacy system to a new claim-processing or core banking system can utilize the MDM Data Hub to ensure continued operations and improve the agility of the enterprise architecture to support quickly evolving business needs.

Until recently, the single-customer view was the predominant driver of data integration initiatives throughout financial services institutions. However, ever since financial services organizations became subject to numerous regulations such as the Gramm-Leach-Bliley Act, the Sarbanes-Oxley Act, the Basel II Capital Accord, the USA Patriot Act's AML and KYC provisions, and many others, a new and compelling reason to implement MDM has emerged. Indeed, because these and other regulations deal with accuracy of financial information, protection of customer data, and the need to capture and enforce customer privacy preferences, the need to have accurate, complete, secure, and available master data about customers, their portfolios, transactions, sales, and service records became a mandatory requirement. Financial services organizations that develop their MDM solutions to comply with the regulations and laws find the justification for building an MDM system to be relatively straightforward.

Large financial services institutions have grown through several mergers and acquisitions (M&A) and as such have consolidated multiple lines of businesses within their organizations. For example, the companies that started as purely insurance businesses focused on some specific line of business (Life, P&C, or Auto) started offering lending and wealth management and advisory services. Similarly, many banks broadened their offerings to include life insurance and other services traditionally provided by insurance. Although M&A is not an exclusive business strategy reserved for financial services organizations, the business strategy of many financial services institutions considers M&A as an effective growth vehicle and a competitive differentiator. Obviously, one of the challenges of the merged organization is the integration of its customer bases and harmonization of financial instruments and associated procedures. This is where MDM capabilities become highly beneficial; in fact, an MDM solution can quickly become a system of record for the new, merged enterprise or can be used to arbitrate entity resolution when data entry is done through the legacy operational systems of each firm. In Part IV we will discuss what MDM can do for M&A in more detail.

MDM and Securities Master

Financial services institutions manage complex products known as financial instruments. Financial instruments continuously grow in their complexity and variety (currently about 8.4 million). These products include securities, bonds, stocks, deposits, loans, options, futures, derivatives, swaps, collars, and so on. Derivatives are complex products that derive their value from the underlying assets; new derivatives are created frequently by financial services firms, whenever the firm sees an opportunity to offer a new product with attractive characteristics that can help the firm to differentiate itself from the competition and to establish or strengthen customer relationships in the process.

But the issue with derivatives is only one concern. Generally speaking, accurate, timely, and reliable information about the financial instruments is a core reference source for practically all financial services companies, and it should be treated as a special domain of the Master Data Management environment. There are several reasons for this treatment, including a wide variety of identifiers that require rationalization and may be difficult to reconcile. For example, when we look at the most popular identifiers of securities, we can easily see how numerous and diverse these identifiers are.

The Committee on Uniform Security Identification Procedures (CUSIP)[6] manages CUSIP as a unique nine-character (alphanumeric) security identifier used for all North American securities and their issuers for the purpose of the clearing and settlement of trades. The CUSIP system is owned by the American Bankers Association. In addition to CUSIP, financial services companies sometimes use CUSIP's international equivalent, CINS,[7] the International Securities Identification Numbering (ISIN) system,[8] and other standard and sometimes internal, organization-specific identifiers for financial instruments.

NOTE *The International Securities Identification Numbering (ISIN) system is an international standard set up by the International Organization for Standardization (ISO) and used for numbering specific securities, such as stock, bonds, options, and futures. ISIN numbers are administered by a National Numbering Agency (NNA) in each country, and they work just like serial numbers for those securities.*

In addition to the identifier problem for existing securities, information on new securities and updates on existing securities is often unavailable in a timely fashion, and it's not unusual that the information about the securities is incomplete or inaccurate. In the absence of a systematic MDM solution, inconsistencies in securities description and indicative information can be reconciled only through manual processes. As a result, many trading activities can be negatively impacted by the lack of accurate and timely securities reference data. This poor data quality and unavailability delays trades clearing and settlement, and in general can prevent real-time trade matching, Straight-Through Processing, and next day settlement (T+1) activities.

This discussion, although focused on the financial instruments and securities, clearly illustrates that with the variety and complexity of financial instruments, product-centric variants of MDM are growing in importance. In combination with the need to manage positions, issuers, and other entities associated with product-centric MDM, its data models can be fairly complex.

Telecommunications Industry

The telecommunications sector includes companies that provide voice, data, and video communications services. These services can be delivered via wired, wireless, cable, or satellite communications.

Telecommunications companies deal with customers that include individuals as well as business entities. From the individual customer-support point of view, telecommunications companies face mostly the same issues as retail financial services, and having a single-customer view is considered a primary driver to improve customer service and create up-sell and cross-sell opportunities. Telecommunication companies are experiencing significant market transformation where the competition for communications products and services has intensified drastically over the last several years, and today their customers are able to choose and switch to a different service provider with relative ease.

In the days of telecommunication monopoly, customer attrition was not even a possibility, but today telecommunication companies are looking into MDM solutions to get a better understanding of customer retention drivers, and to deliver personalized, specially configured and priced service packages that would help increase the customer retention rates.

Other drivers for MDM in telecommunications include support for customer self-service, detection of fraudulent transactions, and communication and integration of customer accounts and customer billing for those customers who chose to purchase multiple services from the same provider, but who did that not as a package but rather as individual transactions (it is not unusual today for a customer to receive numerous separate invoices for various telecommunications services from the same provider). Moreover, the telecommunications industry has been going through significant changes driven not just by deregulation and the introduction of new communication technologies, but also by significant mergers and acquisition activities. These drivers have naturally resulted in the need to integrate and rationalize both product and service offerings as well as customer bases.

Looking at the product domain in particular, we can see that many telecommunications companies developed two major groups of products and lines of business supporting them: wire-line (TV cable, phone landline service, and so on) and wireless (mobile, satellite service, and so on). Historically these services grew independently, with the traditional wire-line service having been in existence for decades while the wireless services have been quickly growing in the last 15–20 years. Wire-line and wireless services may be managed by different departments or divisions that used to be different independent companies in the past and then merged as a result of an M&A transaction. As is not unusual in any M&A situation, these divisions are likely to have different operational models and organizational cultures. They use different systems to manage accounts and customers. Clearly, an MDM challenge is to provide a holistic, panoramic view of products and services offerings as well customers across the divisions and lines of business. This is something that traditionally was addressed by different MDM projects and different MDM technology solutions.

However, as the MDM technologies and approaches mature, we have started to see that MDM initiatives in the telecommunication sector usually include several MDM domains, such as Customer and Services/Products, in order to deliver a master environment that can support an integrated authoritative source of customer references in conjunction with critical product and service bundles.

Leading telecommunications companies engage in multidomain, multiphase programs addressing one or two master data domains in each phase. Frequently, these MDM programs begin with the customer domain (consumer and commercial) and then deal with products, locations, services, assets, and suppliers in the consequent phases.

To sum up, MDM enables a holistic view of the telecommunication company's products, assets, and locations. As new, advanced telecommunications products pour into the market, the complexity of resources and assets required to support these products grows, too. The companies need to understand which of their individual and corporate customers at given sites and locations can benefit from the new advanced products, services, and upgrades. The offers should be extended only to the customer groups and locations that meet asset and resource qualifications criteria (for example, network requirements). Furthermore, the telecommunication industry is often said to be "process driven," including robust and well-defined service provisioning, order processing, and billing. Thus, many MDM projects require tight integration with established process flows and business rule engines to support these complex business processes.

Healthcare Services Ecosystem

In the U.S., the healthcare ecosystem includes hospitals, medical centers, medical offices and providers, Integrated Delivery Networks (IDNs), Regional Healthcare Information Organizations, medical insurance companies (payers), medical labs, pharmacies (this is where healthcare overlaps with the pharmaceutical industry), and other segments.

Over 17% of the U.S. Gross Domestic Product (GDP) falls under the healthcare ecosystem,[9] and this number keeps growing. Similar estimates apply to most other developed countries and economic zones.

The term "interoperable health" was introduced by Tommy Thompson, head of Health and Human Services in the George W. Bush administration (2004), in a ten-year plan to build a national electronic health infrastructure in the U.S. The idea is that with interoperable electronic health records, always-current medical information could be available wherever and whenever the patient and attending health professional needed it across the healthcare ecosystem. As per the Obama-Biden plan,[10] health insurance premiums have doubled in the past eight years, rising 3.7 times faster than wages. Over half of all personal bankruptcies are caused by medical bills, and about 100,000 Americans die from medical errors every year.

The notion of interoperable health is closely related to the terms Electronic Medical Record (EMR), Electronic Health Record (EHR), and Electronic Personal Health Record (ePHR). The National Alliance for Health Information Technology (NAHIT) established definitions for these terms.[11] The term EMR refers to the electronic record of health-related information on an individual that is created, gathered, managed, and consulted by licensed clinicians and staff from a single organization that is involved in the individual's health and care. An EMR can be limited to a single system or an office.

An Electronic Health Record (EHR) is defined as the aggregate electronic record of health-related information on an individual that is created and gathered cumulatively across more than one healthcare organization and is managed and consulted by licensed clinicians and staff involved in the individual's health and care. By these definitions, an EHR includes an interoperability of EMR records across multiple organizations and systems. Sometimes the term EHR is used in the U.S. nationwide context as an electronic record for a patient available nationally.

The term Electronic Personal Health Record (ePHR) refers to an electronic, cumulative record of health-related information about an individual, drawn from multiple sources, which is created, gathered, and managed by the individual. The integrity of the data in the ePHR and control of access to that data is the responsibility of the individual and can be used for patient electronic portals. An ePHR should include cumulative health information ranging from past and current illnesses, demographics, allergies, prescriptions, and more. The patient makes a decision on what information is stored and who has access to it. Microsoft's HealthVault[12] and Google Health[13] are two prominent examples of ePHRs.

On December 30, 2009, the Office of the National Coordinator for Health Information Technology (ONC) and the Centers for Medicare & Medicaid Services (CMS) released documents that outline what physicians and hospitals must do to qualify for EHR incentive payments under the information technology section of ARRA.[14] To qualify for incentives, physicians and hospitals must be using EHR technologies in a "meaningful manner."[15] The providers who adopt EHRs earlier may be eligible to receive greater incentive payments over time, while late adopters will be penalized beginning in 2015. For providers that implement EHRs and demonstrate meaningful use,[16] the highest incentive payments will be available from 2011 through 2013. Additional, but reduced incentive payments will be available in 2014 and 2015, and penalties will begin in 2015.

MDM, and more specifically its patient-centric variant, Enterprise Master Patient Index (EMPI), along with other interoperability certification standards (CCHIT, HL7, Information Healthcare Exchanges [IHE] profiles)[17] are at the very heart of what is required to enable a holistic, panoramic view of patient information and accomplish the EMR, EHR, and ePHR goals.

According to FactCheck.org, President Obama cited a RAND study[18] stating that if most hospitals and doctor offices adopted electronic health records, up to $77 billion of savings would be realized each year through improvements such as reduced hospital stays, avoidance of duplicative and unnecessary testing, more appropriate drug utilization, and other efficiencies.

In the U.S., 785 million health care tests are conducted each year.[19] The lack of interoperable systems to effectively communicate the results among the various providers who need to review them is consuming 1 billion hours of administrative processing time just to get the data in the right place, according to one estimate.

Unstructured Master Data in the Healthcare Ecosystem

Integration of patient registration[20] and clinical[21] and medical claim–processing systems[22] with MDM, EMPI, document management systems, imaging systems, and other unstructured information are the key steps in the move to interoperability and EHR.

Hospitals and medical centers are on the forefront of MDM integration with unstructured information. This type of integration is much less adopted by other industries—for example, financial services, pharmaceutical companies, manufacturing, telecommunications—even though there exists a demand to integrate MDM with document management systems, contract management systems, image repositories, and so on.

The primary focus on a single entity (patient) in hospitals and medical centers is evolving to include other master entities, such as provider, medical office, and other critical healthcare entities.

Additional classes of healthcare data are expected to come into the scope of MDM in healthcare, including medical procedures, diagnoses, treatments, and medication. MDM needs in healthcare are likely to grow beyond clinical departments and include marketing, supply and inventory management, biosurveillance, and other areas important for the operations of hospitals and medical centers.

Pharmacy health information exchanges enable physicians and pharmacists to electronically exchange prescription information, match physician requests for patient medication history, deliver patient formulary and eligibility across multiple systems, and make information available at the point of care in real time. MDM improves pharmacy operations due to a reduction of follow-up calls from pharmacists and Pharmacy Benefits Management (PBM). MDM solutions with their holistic panoramic view of patients and providers enable the Drug Enforcement Administration (DEA) to screen medicine seekers, fill prescriptions in all stores using a single MDM Data Hub, and improve patient safety by identifying potentially harmful prescription interactions across stores.

MDM needs of pharmacy chains are somewhat similar to the needs of retail stores, which will be covered in later sections. In fact, the largest retail stores run pharmacies as part of their operations.

Hospitality and Gaming Industry

The hospitality and gaming industry includes hotels and gambling establishments. It is clear that having an accurate and complete guest master that delivers a timely single-customer view is as beneficial to hotel chain management as it is to a retail bank. At a minimum, a single-customer view can help hotel management to provide better customer service, enable bigger cross-sell and up-sell opportunities, increase marketing campaign effectiveness, and enable better management of hotel inventory. However, this segment (and its gaming component in particular) brings an additional MDM requirement—to provide a complete guest view, together with all his or her relationships, and integrate this information with prior history of gambling activities linked with this guest in order to detect fraudulent gamblers and potential collusion between casino employees and players, employees and vendors, employees who are players, and so on. In this case, an MDM system would source information from a variety of applications, build and maintain the resolved entity, and make a new guest master available for advanced analytics.

Established casino firms are geographically diverse with scores of locations worldwide. A single company's operations may include casino hotels, dockside and riverboat casinos, and other establishments. A significant part of the revenue often comes from casino gambling. This revenue stream heavily relies on the quality of the company's loyalty programs. Recognizing and understanding the customer in the gaming and hospitality industry is critical. Therefore, MDM drives loyalty, revenue, and profitability. Improvement of guest data quality is a significant challenge in the hospitality industry due to the data volumes, sparseness, and inaccuracy of the data.

International hospitality organizations have developed complex operating models aimed at driving demand to their subsidiaries and brands. This includes advertising and marketing campaigns, call centers, websites that support multiple languages, large sales force organizations, and advanced hotel loyalty programs that count millions of members. Strategic information and re-platforming initiatives often begin with the consolidation of customer information.

MDM Data Hubs leverage sophisticated probabilistic capabilities to match disparate guest records despite misspellings, transpositions, dropped or extra characters in customer names and addresses, nicknames, and other inconsistencies. This enables the hospitality industry enterprises to effectively and accurately match guest records, resolve customer relationships in real time, and prevent duplicate guest entries.

Many established hotel chains are still lacking real-time guest-recognition capabilities. They lack an ability to track guests and assemble a holistic view for the guests that do not have the top parent loyalty program identifier, even if the guests have long-term loyalty relationships with one or several company brands. This is due to the fact that many large hospitality companies have grown through multiple acquisitions of smaller hotels, casinos, and so on. As a result, the hospitality industry faces a challenge due to the extremely high number of systems and brands that are to be integrated into the scope of MDM. Whereas for most other industries the integration of 20–40 operational systems under the MDM Data Hub umbrella may be a meaningful enterprise scope, the hospitality industry companies may require an MDM integration of thousands of systems across multiple brands.

Manufacturing and Software

This sector includes the companies that produce a wide variety of products, such as chemicals, hardware, devices, parts, cars, planes, cosmetics, software, home products, electronics, food, and furniture.

Manufacturing companies implement MDM solutions that often begin with the product domain to support their complex supply-chain requirements. Specifics depend on what the company produces. For instance, cosmetics and chemical manufacturing companies develop their products in highly collaborative environments required to maintain the continuity of supply-chain processes. These processes may include chemical synthesis, chemical analysis, technical operations, supplier management, quality assurance, labeling, packaging, marketing, billing, shipments, and so on. The Bill of Materials (BOM) is the single most import element of master data for many manufacturing organizations. Bill of Materials management can be especially challenging for global companies with multiple geographic sites and locations that manage the BOM with different granularity, systems, standards, and languages. Even the governance around BOM is a complex issue that requires a balanced approach, combining a centralized management of some generic aspects of the BOM with other more specific aspects that should be managed in a federated fashion and controlled by divisions, brands, and sites. Once the key challenges of the product domain are addressed, manufacturing companies can concentrate on the customer domain.

Manufacturing companies strive to create additional distribution channels for their products and services. Traditionally, many manufacturers distribute their products through distribution centers, department stores, and other channels. Until recently, the manufacturing companies did not maintain direct relationships with the consumers, delegating this role to department stores and other distribution channels. In order to enable additional channels, manufacturing companies build customer portals. These portals, depending on the nature of the manufacturing products, can service individual consumers or businesses. Naturally, customer portals use an e-mail address as an important account identifier. This e-mail identifier is well maintained, along with the credit card or bank account information used for billing, while other pieces of information about the account holder can be populated very sparsely and inaccurately. Consequently, manufacturing companies are lacking complete, accurate, and holistic information about their customers, which impacts the efficiency of marketing, risk management, and ultimately the profitability.

More recently, many manufacturers are selling directly to their customers using the Internet portal. Therefore, the challenge to maintain a single-customer view, whether the customer bought from a store or the portal, is even more challenging. An MDM approach that combines the use of data gathered from the Internet about customer behavior, along with using data collected from traditional channels, can be used to address this challenge. Car manufacturers deal with the challenges that arise from the fact that car dealerships are typically independent companies that guard their customer data. Still, these dealerships can benefit from marketing campaigns developed by the car manufacturer centrally. MDM helps preserve the balance between the dealerships' demands to protect the access to their customer data in dealership-specific systems and a holistic customer view required by the manufacturing company to perform marketing campaigns. MDM resolves highly fragmented customer data and enriches it to enable cross-sell and up-sell opportunities during servicing; it improves campaign management processes while maintaining security of customer data in the local dealerships' systems.

Software Publishing

Software mega-vendors operate somewhat similarly to large manufacturing companies. Software giants have developed hundreds of products, and they license these products globally to millions of customers, including individual consumers and commercial organizations. MDM for corporate hierarchies allows software companies to understand what products their business customers decided to license and what discounts their customers are eligible for. MDM helps with reliable pricing, credit risk estimates, and marketing aspects for subsidiaries and divisions of large corporations. Many software companies serve customers around the globe, which makes their customer base multilingual and results in very high volumes of customer data. One of the important specifics of software companies is that their products can be downloaded over the Internet. Consequently, many customers who place their orders online do not have to provide accurate postal address information for delivery purposes, which creates additional challenges for customer matches across systems and accounts and ultimately makes it extremely challenging to build a single-customer view. The MDM market in the software vertical until recently has been limited mostly by very large software companies. Today, MDM adoption is moving downstream toward smaller-size companies.

Pharmaceutical Industry

The pharmaceutical industry deals with research, development, production, and the sale of various products for approved medical use. Typically, pharmaceutical companies do not deal directly with consumers but rather with physicians and service providers, who in turn prescribe and deliver the company's products to their customers (patients). To a certain degree the pharmaceutical industry can be considered under the umbrella of manufacturing. From the pharmaceutical manufacturing perspective this would be a fare categorization. Because the pharmaceutical products (drugs and vaccines) require a very specialized, highly regulated, lengthy, and costly research and development process, this industry deserves a separate discussion, which is why we have placed the pharmaceutical industry in a separate section. Furthermore, the unique three-cornered process of manufacturer, customer (provider and physician), and consumer (patient) presents special MDM opportunities.

Pharmaceutical companies are challenged by the task of rationalizing and integrating physician/customer information from multiple systems and business units in order to deliver a comprehensive view of their consumers' network and better insight into the competitive landscape.

In this industry segment, where the customers (physicians) also act as participants in the supply chain, MDM is viewed as an enabler of increased efficiency and effectiveness of supply-chain operations. Pharmaceutical companies see MDM as an enabler to reconcile various industry-standard identifiers, thus creating an integrated view of the customer (that is, physician, healthcare provider organization, medical group).

Having an accurate healthcare provider (physician, medical office, hospital, and so on) master data set that contains all relevant information in one place allows a pharmaceutical company to increase the effectiveness of the company's sales representatives; to increase the acquisition, retention, and profitability rates of its customers (physicians and physician groups); and to enable better regulatory and compliance controls. For example, pharmaceutical companies need to adhere to strict regulations that require them to monitor and limit the total amount of various forms of compensation to their customers (that is, a physician may attend a conference sponsored by the company, give a for-pay lecture discussing the latest company product, and so on). And these activities can be performed using different names, including a medical group of which this physician is a member. Traditionally, these activities were recorded in different, disconnected systems, and this is where an MDM solution would enable information integration across these disparate systems into a single view in order to assess the total compensation.

Pharmaceutical and large biotechnology companies have to deal with the complexities of their product pipelines that begin with drug target identification, identification and screening of active substances, and screening of drug candidates for drug development.

This complex process often takes over ten years before the company can bring a drug or vaccine to the market. Each of the functional areas across the drug discovery and development process uses its dedicated Laboratory Information Management Systems (LIMS) and other applications. These functions include, but are not limited to, lead generation, active compound screening and drug development, candidate selection, pharmaco-kinetics, toxicology, teratology, drug metabolism, drug formulation, pathology, stability studies, chemical analysis, and so on. During this process, multiple entities come into play: drug, indication, route of administration, and so on. Although some of these entities may change rather frequently, the need for an accurate, consistently available authoritative source of these entities nevertheless makes these entities good candidates for master data in drug discovery, development, clinical research, and manufacturing.

In clinical research and pharmaco-vigilance, patient-centric MDM is also important. Disparate LIMS systems limit the holistic view of the product (drug or vaccine candidate) across the variety of pharmaceutical enterprise functions. As a drug candidate moves along the pipeline, the R&D process becomes increasingly regulated, subjected to the practices required for Investigational New Drug (IND) applications and New Drug Applications (NDAs). Complex submission processes regulated by the FDA CFR part 11 in the U.S. domestically and other country-specific regulations internationally exacerbate the complexity of the process. Ultimately, pharmaceutical companies not only need to integrate all structured data about a drug candidate, drug, vaccine candidate, or vaccine, but also provide a panoramic view of unstructured data associated with the product. This unstructured content is not limited to formal submission documentation residing typically in document management systems, but also includes informal memos, e-mails, images of chemical structures, graphs, intermediate test results, and so on.

Pharmaceutical companies oftentimes outsource certain types of studies and tests to contract research organizations (CROs). Master Data Management can help to manage the contracts and other vendor and supplier information if integration with unstructured information is in the scope of MDM.

Shipping and Logistics

Shipping companies need to understand not only customers' special pricing eligibility at present but also the eligibility status at a point in time in the past (support for temporal hierarchies), which makes MDM even more challenging. Location is a critical entity for shipping companies. Advances in GPS technologies have created additional opportunities when a location is identified by both postal address and GPS coordinates.

Understanding corporate hierarchies in conjunction with very high volumes of data and global, multilingual implementations is also a challenge for leading shipping companies. From the business perspective, these shipping companies embark on MDM implementations to better understand customer eligibility for special rates and discounted pricing for postal packages. This intelligence results in increased revenue and loyalty through price optimization and effective differentiation of services and products between the B2B and B2C models.

Airlines

Airlines are under tremendous pressure to reduce their operational costs while retaining their best, most profitable customers. For the U.S. domestic airline companies, it is critical to survive during a long-term recession (2008–2010) and in the face of intense competition domestically and internationally with the largest European airlines. To accomplish this objective, the airlines offer loyalty programs to their customers that include a number of benefits, such as upgrades from Economy to Business or First Class. Frequent-flier miles can be used for free-of-charge plane tickets. In addition to mergers and acquisitions (for example, the recent merger of Delta Air Lines and Northwest Airlines), airlines develop alliances (Star Alliance, Skyteam, and so on). All airline consolidation and partnership scenarios drive the demand to merge loyalty programs and better recognition of a customer across merged companies and across the companies in the alliance. The airlines establish partnerships with hospitality companies, credit card firms, rental companies, and so on. These partnerships also contribute to the need of a panoramic view of a customer and household.

Airline security is an additional driver for a holistic passenger view. El Al is the recognized gold standard in this area. All airlines could benefit from better and timely intelligence about their passengers. In the U.S., the burden of passenger security lies mostly on the government and specifically on the Transportation Security Administration (TSA). We will continue our discussion of airline security in the section that focuses on MDM in the public sector.

In earlier days, airline ticket reservation systems were managed exclusively by the airlines. The Computer Reservation Systems (CRS) used to store, retrieve, and process air travel information were extended for use by travel agencies. The need to book and sell tickets for multi-airline trips drove the demand for Global Distribution Systems (GDS). GDS companies make their systems accessible to consumers over the Internet. Modern GDSs enable users to book not just plane tickets but also hotel rooms and rental cars. There is a significant potential in the integration of these global systems with MDM Data Hubs to improve airline security and other applications.

Retail Sales

Retail stores often tackle multiple domains—customer, location, product, and supplier—in the scope of their MDM solutions. The primary goal in the customer domain is to resolve (match, link, and merge) scores of millions or even hundreds of millions of customer records across systems and store locations. The complexity of the high volumes is often exacerbated by high transactional volumes that can reach and even exceed a million transactions per day with peak rates nearing 1,000 transactions per second. Retail stores use MDM as the enterprise source of panoramic information about their customers to make better and faster credit decisions based on a holistic view of a customer. The view takes into account the house-holding and relationships aspects of the customer's profile. MDM helps to enhance customer experience, minimize fraud, and gather business intelligence about the customer's spending patterns.

Although data warehouses have had a long history in retail chain operations, real-time capabilities provided by MDM are relatively new and on the rise. Despite the fact that these real-time capabilities have a short history, they have already proven themselves to be a powerful enabler. These capabilities help sales organizations to provide timely customer intelligence in order to make immediate offerings to a customer based on the purchasing patterns at the point and time of sales. When a customer buys or even expresses an interest in a certain product in one department of the store, other departments receive this information in real time, which positions the sales representatives to promptly offer relevant additional products to the customer.

The relationships between correlated products that are often purchased together can also be maintained by MDM and is referred to as Market Basket Analytics. As an illustrative example, similar capabilities are employed on Amazon.com when the website offers books and other products that are often purchased with the product the customer search was originally focused on.

Customer data, along with locations, product hierarchies, and supplier data are fed to operational systems. This way, MDM maintains the content of the most complex data warehousing dimensions. From the business perspective, MDM improves risk management, customer intelligence, and marketing.

It is not feasible, or even practical, to try to cover all commercial verticals and industry segments that can benefit from MDM. Having said that, we believe that the industry segments described thus far represent the most significant areas of MDM adoption. Industry segments such as energy, gas, and utilities companies, even though they have not been covered, have similar MDM requirements as telecommunications companies when they support similar customer groups or bases. Other industry segments that have not been covered in this section may have some specific characteristics, but, generally speaking, have similar MDM requirements, drivers, and challenges.

Public Sector

When we discuss MDM implementation in the public sector, we include not only the departments and agencies of various national governments, but also businesses run by governments (various utilities, research establishments, transportation companies, and so on). Similar to the commercial sector, government organizations dealing with businesses and individuals (G2B and G2C) are also looking to improve efficiencies, reduce expenses, and improve levels of customer service. Government-sponsored businesses and various agencies are concerned that poor service levels may lead to a public outcry that can impact the policies, rules, regulations, staffing levels, and even the management teams running these organizations. Therefore, government organizations are looking to implement MDM solutions that deliver a single-customer view (or, as the case may be, a single-citizen view) in order to better understand the needs and behavior traits of their constituencies.

In essence, many of the commercial industry verticals described earlier in this chapter can be presented in the public sector. For instance, some healthcare organizations can be in the private or public sector. In most of the European countries, Canada, and Australia, the role of the public sector in healthcare and other verticals is much higher than that in the U.S. For example, many telecommunications, utilities, and energy companies in Canada are Crown corporations. Crown corporations are state-owned companies. This ownership can reside at the federal, provincial, or territorial level.[23] And for most of the industries, the need for MDM remains mostly the same, regardless of whether an enterprise belongs to the private sector or is a government-owned organization.

Among the great variety of functions and areas where different levels of government are involved include social services, law enforcement, border protection, and intelligence agencies. All of these are the primary consumers of MDM.

We will focus on MDM applications in social services first and then continue with MDM in law enforcement, border protection, and intelligence agencies.

Social Services

Social Services departments, Human Services departments, and their country-specific equivalents represent an inherent government function typically responsible for a wide range of services to diverse groups of citizens and residents across the country, state, or province. The primary function of the department may involve the delivery of a range of health services, including primary health, mental health, alcohol and drugs, retirement/ aged care, disability services, children/youth care, family services, and housing for homeless. The purpose of these departments is to provide for the most needy groups of the population by helping them with certain basic needs: healthcare, food, shelter, special education for disabled children, and so on.

Social Services departments provide multiple variations of services. Eligibility to receive certain services by individuals and households is governed by complex rules defined in government regulations and guidance documents. Social Services agencies need to create a holistic view of a citizen who is in fact a client of the social service, understand what social services are already provided to the individual and the household or were provided in the past, and what agency or organization provides or provided each service. Therefore, from the MDM perspective, three complex entities dominate social services: Client, Service, and Agency or Organization.

This holistic, panoramic view of a client (individual and the household) and the services he or she receives are critical for services coordination to prevent delays in providing timely vital services. This is also important for timely recognition of individuals who receive services they are not eligible for and have possibly obtained due to incorrect or even fraudulent information provided when applying for the service. Understanding the relationships is important for Departments of Social Services so that these departments can get a holistic view of the providers in the context of the services they deliver. Relationships between a provider and a client are important for understanding who provides the services for each client.

Typically, multiple client databases and systems are used by Departments of Social Services. Each of the systems serves a single function in the department. The systems are generally not integrated due to privacy concerns or a lack of a holistic strategy. An increasing complexity in client data and regulatory rules and requirements often leads to a client accessing several different services delivered by both the department directly and by a service provider indirectly. For example, a mental health patient occupying a public housing unit may face eviction due to behavioral problems. Because this information may reside in different service-specific systems, the department is not aware of a pending problem that can cause new hardships to the Social Services client.

In another scenario, a patient may receive some equipment in a hospital after an injury for short-term disability needs. The client may be unaware what needs to be done to secure this equipment for longer term disability services. Lack of systems integration makes it very difficult to generate automatic alerts in these scenarios. This lack of integration and coordination can leave a disabled person without a required piece of equipment. There exist multiple scenarios that require alerts and coordination between the systems and functions of Departments of Social Services or Human Services in government organizations at different levels worldwide.

Overall, Departments of Social Services leverage MDM capabilities to improve service levels and client intelligence, move from product-/account-/policy-centric processes to party-/client-centric operations, support fast-evolving risk and compliance needs, reduce operational costs, reduce errors by enabling cross-functional alerts, and improve the outcomes of services and the client/citizen experience overall.

A widely known MDM program implemented in the UK nationally is ContactPoint.[24] ContactPoint is a key element of the Every Child Matters initiative in the UK, transforming child services through prevention and early intervention. The MDM Data Hub holds information about all children under the age of 18 in England. The system was created under the Children Act 2004. The history of this program began in 2000. Victoria Climbié, an 8-year-old girl, was abused and murdered by her guardians in London. Separate agencies, including the police, many local social services, the NHS, and local churches all had contact with her and noted signs of abuse. All failed to properly investigate the abuse, and little action was taken.

A government study recommended that the government investigate the feasibility of a database covering all children, providing basic identifying details and contact details for practitioners and services involved with the child. ContactPoint has been developed as a quick way for a practitioner to find out who else is working with the same child, making it easier to deliver more coordinated support and enabling more effective prevention and early intervention. Contributing systems include schools, doctors, social services, benefits, and official records.

Despite children privacy concerns and multiple regulations restricting information sharing between providers, the solution design has found a balance between children privacy needs and the required level of information sharing, which ultimately resulted in a successful program implementation.

Law Enforcement, Border Protection, and Intelligence Agencies

Law enforcement organizations, border protection, intelligence and national security agencies, homeland security, antiterrorist organizations, and some other agencies can leverage MDM capabilities to provide a comprehensive view of a person of interest (POI). Law enforcement and intelligence agencies are established consumers of MDM. Person of Interest is a fast-growing MDM domain in law enforcement and intelligence agencies.

In the U.S., the Law Enforcement National Data Exchange (N-DEx)[25] is based on MDM Data Hub technologies that link and bring together data from law enforcement agencies throughout the U.S. As per the referenced N-DEx website, this includes "incident and case reports, booking and incarceration data, and parole/probation information. N-DEx detects relationships between people, vehicle/property, location, and/or crime characteristics. It 'connects the dots' between data that is not seemingly related. And it supports multi-jurisdictional task forces—enhancing national information sharing, links between regional and state systems, and virtual regional information sharing."

The needs of intelligence agencies go far beyond POI, weapons, and vehicles. MDM, in conjunction with advanced entity-resolution technologies, can resolve complex composite entities such as an incident report, a collection of containers on a ship, and even a terrorist network.[26–30] Extremely high volumes of data and the complexity of entities and relationships are some of the characteristics and challenges of MDM applications for global law enforcement and intelligence agencies.

In addition to improved service levels and operations, MDM in the government sector holds tremendous promise for providing necessary just-in-time insight into individual behavior, transactions, relationships, and linkages with various terrorist groups and their supporters.

A properly designed MDM solution can help to identify and track individuals both inside the country and across the globe. Despite the absence of a national identifier in the U.S., an MDM solution used by a public sector entity (Person of Interest) can be integrated with technologies that implement strong biometrics-based authentication and identification of individuals at points of entry into the country. These capabilities of an MDM solution are very attractive to international, federal, and local law enforcement as well as to various intelligence agencies, and hopefully could be used in the future to prevent acts of terrorism and other harmful activities.

Given the highly confidential nature of some of the information handled by most of the government agencies, it is not surprising that data security, privacy, confidentiality, and integrity concerns are some of the top priorities for implementing MDM solutions in the public sector.

From the entity-resolution and matching perspective, MDM probabilistic algorithms are more tuned to minimize false negative matches, whereas in most other industry-specific MDM applications the primary concern is not to allow false positive matches. Indeed, for example, in financial services a false match on customer records can cause a check, statement, or other sensitive material to be sent to the wrong person. In healthcare, even worse, a false positive match can cause life-threatening scenarios when a person receives the wrong medication, gets a blood transfusion with an incompatible blood type, and so on. Conversely, for law enforcement, counterterrorism organizations, and intelligence agencies, false negative scenarios are very important to avoid. They result in failures to recognize a Person of Interest.

Due to their sensitive nature, successful MDM applications for the POI and the corresponding case studies are not readily available in public domains. Having said that, when the capabilities that are supposed to be enabled by MDM fail to prevent terrorism, the importance of MDM for the POI gets crystal clear. A misspelled name caused a false negative match, which in turn caused a failure that resulted in the issuance of a U.S. entry visa to Umar Farouk Abdulmutallab, known as the "underwear bomber," a 23-year-old Nigerian man accused of trying to blow up Northwest Airlines Flight 253 from Amsterdam to Detroit on Christmas Day, 2009. This story was widely discussed on all world news channels and analyzed in the mass media.

Various articles discuss the event from the MDM perspective.[31-35] Politics aside, a few considerations important from the MDM perspective should be mentioned:

- Abdulmutallab was not on the No-fly List or the Selectee List. He was only on the Terrorist Identities Datamart Environment (TIDE) list as a Person of Interest with possible terrorist ties. As a result, the answer to the yes/no question of whether Abdulmutallab should be allowed to fly was "yes."

- A probabilistic MDM approach in combination with entity resolution should replace the notion of a static "watch list." Scoring entity-resolution algorithms should be able to bring together multiple indications about the terrorist despite this information being scattered around multiple databases. Using all the relevant information about Abdulmutallab and applying the concept of probability to the question of whether he should have been granted the entry visa and allowed on the plane leads to much better decision making. However, it requires that all the relevant information be shared and available to the algorithm that should be able to alert the decision maker.

- In the case of Abdulmutallab, the systems should have been able to take into account the following circumstances by scoring them from the terrorist threat perspective:
  - The person was barred from entering a foreign country because he was on that country's (the UK) "watch lists."
  - The passenger was reportedly associated with a radical terrorist group. His father told U.S. authorities he believed Abdulmutallab was being radicalized in Yemen.
  - The person paid cash for the plane ticket. Not many people do that. A cash payment for a fairly expensive flight may indicate an intent to conceal one's identity.
  - The passenger boarded the transatlantic flight without any baggage, which is another indication.
- In order to bring together all these data points, the disparate indicative pieces of information should have been matched and assembled to connect the dots. A high terrorist threat probability score was supposed to raise the alert, prompting the denial of the entry visa in the U.S. or triggering an extra screening for the individual. This could have led to his detention in case a bomb or any other suspicious explosive device or hazardous material was found.

Timely access and dynamic assembly of *all* the available information like what was known about Abdulmutallab is a daunting information technology task. But from the technology perspective, this task can be resolved by modern MDM Data Hub systems.

There is another aspect that should be taken into account. Commentators have recently been calling vociferously for better information sharing. Information sharing is clearly a necessary part of the solution to prevent another terrorist attack, but it is not as easy as it sounds. Information sharing can be potentially damaging and involves risks. Let's assume, as some people propose, that the government starts sharing all its lists across multiple agencies and branches of government. We can't envision all the complications but it is fairly clear that some "list sharing" can result in serious adverse consequences. As information sharing is spread among many individuals and agencies, the chances of information leaks grow. A simplistic uncontrolled "list sharing" can help terrorists to understand what names are on the "lists" and what names are not. This may shed some light for them on how this information got collected and the methods used by agencies to gather the information. This can unintentionally aid terrorist operations, and possibly reveal the techniques and individuals responsible for making the terrorist names available to the intelligence agencies. Politics aside, it is fairly clear that "list sharing" across agencies is a complex master data governance problem applied to multiple "lists" (or, in more "physical" terms, "multiple MDM Data Hubs"). Obsolete, outdated thinking in terms of static "watch lists" is one of the barriers that governance agencies must overcome to correctly approach the problem.

Master data governance is a control discipline with the primary focus on cross-functional master data quality, consistency, and sharing of master data. This includes technologies, processes, and control options that enable master data sharing while balancing the risks of information sharing with the risks of *not* sharing. This is an opportunity to use entity resolution in conjunction with advanced master data governance to connect the dots across intelligence and law enforcement data sources while minimizing the risks of information sharing.

Following the attempt to bring down the airliner, President Obama directed Assistant to the President for Homeland Security and Counterterrorism John Brennan to conduct a review of the circumstances leading to the airline security failure.[36] Here's what it found:

- The report found that significant progress had been made since 9/11/2001. The report states the data integration and information sharing had been significantly improved. Information Technology within the U.S. counterterrorism community "did not sufficiently enable the correlation of data," which is a clear indication that more complex problems around MDM as well as entity and relationships resolution remain unsolved by the counterterrorism community.

- The summary report also suggests that the current process involves many manual procedures performed by "watch listing personnel" who use deterministic rules to define "minimum derogatory standards," as opposed to quantitative matching thresholds to place the person of interest on the No-Fly List.

- Finally, the fact that the U.S. entry visa was given to Abdulmutallab was a typical MDM matching problem from the MDM perspective. His name was misspelled, and the technologies that were used for screening failed to detect the similarity between the name on the visa application and the name on one of the "watch lists."

MDM and Public Sector

MDM-enabled solutions around master entities such as Citizen or Client, Social Service, and Agency can be used by the government to significantly improve the usability and accuracy of the client's self-service channels, thus reducing government costs of service.

An MDM-enabled Person of Interest master can be used to increase the effectiveness of law enforcement, intelligence, and counterterrorism operations.

References

1. http://www.ustreas.gov/offices/enforcement/ofac/.

2. http://www.ustreas.gov/offices/enforcement/ofac/sdn/.

3. http://www.inntron.co.th/corebank.html.

4. http://www.fineos.com/solutions/claims.htm?gclid=COjhjcf_sZ8CFQYeDQodenXy1g.

5. http://mvsc.com/contact.cfm?gclid=CLabxJ-Asp8CFQMNDQoduH_Rzw.

6. https://www.cusip.com/static/html/webpage/welcome.html.

7. https://www.cusip.com/static/html/webpage/cusip_based_iden.html#002.

8. http://www.investopedia.com/terms/i/isin.asp.

9. http://politifi.com/news/Healthcare-spending-17-percent-of-economy-171793.html.

10. http://www.barackobama.com/pdf/issues/HealthCareFullPlan.pdf.

11. http://www.softwareadvice.com/articles/medical/ehr-vs-emr-whats-the-difference/.

12. http://www.healthvault.com/personal/index.html?WT.mc_id=M10011214&WT
    .ad=text::HealthVault::GoogSrch::HvPHp::Goo&WT.srch=1&WT.seg_1=healthvault.

13. https://www.google.com/accounts/ServiceLogin?service=health&nui=1&continue=
    https%3A%2F%2Fhealth.google.com%2Fhealth%2Fp%2F&followup=https%3A%2F
    %2Fhealth.google.com%2Fhealth%2Fp%2F&rm=hide.

14. http://hitechanswers.net/about.

15. http://www.softwareadvice.com/articles/medical/the-stimulus-bill-and-meaningful-
    use-of-qualified-emrs-1031209/.

16. Fernandes, Lorrain. "Discover Meaningful Use." http://www.healthcareitnews.com/
    news/discover-meaningful-use.

17. http://ihewiki.wustl.edu/wiki/index.php/Connectathon_Testing_PIX_PDQ_XDS.

18. http://www.factcheck.org/elections-2008/obamas_inflated_health_savings.html.

19. http://www.comport.com/healthcare_provider.html.

20. http://www.jazdhealthcare.com/healthtech/leaf/Hospital-Management/
    Patient-Registration-Systems.htm.

21. http://www.epic.com/.

22. http://verticals.botw.org/Software/Insurance/Claims-Processing/.

23. http://en.wikipedia.org/wiki/Crown_corporations_of_Canada.

24. http://en.wikipedia.org/wiki/ContactPoint.

25. http://www.fbi.gov/hq/cjisd/ndex/ndex_home.htm.

26. Schumacher, Scott. "Complex Entities: Tracking a Vehicle Across State Lines."
    http://blog.initiate.com/index.php/2009/12/16/complex-entities-tracking-a-
    vehicle-across-state-lines/.

27. Talburt, John. "Entity-Based Integration Model." http://identityresolutiondaily.com/
    684/entity-resolution-integration-model/.

28. "Identity Resolution Daily Links 2010-01-11." http://identityresolutiondaily.com/
    683/identity-resolution-daily-links-2010-01-11/.

29. Calvert, Brian. "Actionable Identity Intelligence from Identity Resolution Identity
    Resolution Daily Links 2010-01-11."

30. Schumacher, Scott. "Agencies Sharing Information with Entity Resolution."
    http://blog.initiate.com/index.php/2009/12/02/agencies-sharing-information-
    with-entity-resolution/.

31. Dubov, Lawrence, Alex Eastman, and Jeffrey Huth. "Connecting the Dots Before
    Boarding." http://blog.initiate.com/index.php/2010/01/05/connecting-the-dots-
    before-boarding/.

32. Loshin, David. "President Obama: Problems Connecting the Dots? How About a
    Master Terrorist Management System?" http://www.b-eye-network.com/blogs/
    loshin/archives/2010/01/president_obama.php.

33. Eastman, Alex. "A Reference Architecture for Connecting the Dots." http://blog.initiate
.com/index.php/2010/01/25/a-reference-architecture-for-connecting-the-dots/.

34. Dubov, Lawrence, Alex Eastman, and Jeffrey Hugh. "Entity Resolution to
Build a Better 'Watch List.'" http://blog.initiate.com/index.php/2010/01/06/
entity-resolution-to-build-a-better-watch-list/.

35. Chen, Ramon. Systemic Failure—Will the Government Put in a Decent MDM
System Already!" http://www.ramonchen.com/?p=1968.

36. "Summary of the Whitehouse Review of the December 25, 2009 Attempted Terrorist
Attack." http://msnbcmedia.msn.com/i/MSNBC/Sections/NEWS/summary_of_
wh_review_12-25-09.pdf.

Architectural Considerations

I n the introductory part of this book, we offered a broad-brush description of the
purpose, drivers, and key benefits of Master Data Management and used some specific
examples of its customer-focused variant, Customer Data Integration. This part of the
book discusses the issues of MDM architecture as a key logical step to building enterprise-
wide solutions.

An architecture discussion is important for several reasons:

- A comprehensive end-to-end MDM solution is much more than just a database of
  customer or product information organized by some kind of a unique key. Some
  MDM capabilities and components are "traditional" and are a part of a common
  best-practice design for integrated data solutions, whereas other, new features came
  to light primarily in the context of MDM problem domains. An architectural vision
  can help organize the "old" and the "new" features into an integrated, scalable, and
  manageable solution.

- MDM is not just a technology problem—a comprehensive MDM solution consists
  of technology components and services as well as new business processes and even
  organizational structures and dynamics. There are many architecture viewpoints,
  significant complexity, and a large number of interdependencies to warrant a
  framework-based approach to the architecture. This multifaceted, multidimensional
  architecture framework looks at the overall problem domain from different but
  complementary angles.

- Any solution intended to create an authoritative, accurate, and timely system of
  record that should eventually replace existing legacy sources of the information
  must be integrated with the overall enterprise architecture and infrastructure. Given
  the heterogeneity and the "age" of legacy systems, this requirement is often difficult
  to satisfy without a comprehensive architecture blueprint.

Thus, we organized this part of the book in the following fashion: First, we discuss the
architectural genesis of MDM. Then, we take a closer look at the enterprise architecture
framework and explain how this framework helps us to see different aspects of the solution
as interconnected and interdependent views. This discussion is followed by an overview of
traditional data management and emerging concerns of MDM architecture, MDM data
modeling, data management architecture, and the newer concept of MDM services.

4

CHAPTER

MDM Architecture Classifications, Concepts, Principles, and Components

I n order to understand "how" to build a comprehensive Master Data Management solution, we need to define the "what" of Master Data Management.

We have already offered high-level definitions of MDM and its customer-focused variant, CDI, in Part I of this book. We also stated that CDI and other MDM variants share many architecture principles and approaches; therefore, in this part of the book we concentrate on common architecture aspects of Master Data Management. Where appropriate, we'll mention specific architecture features of key MDM variants—in particular, Customer Data Integration and Product Information Master.

Architectural Definition of Master Data Management

As shown in previous chapters, the scope of Master Data Management by its very nature is extremely broad and applies equally well to customer-centric, product-centric, and reference data–centric business problems, to name just a few. A common thread among the solutions to these problems is the ability to create and maintain an accurate, timely, and authoritative "system of record" for a given subject domain. Clearly, such a definition can be refined further for each situation and problem domain addressed by Master Data Management.

Let's start with a fresh look at the definitions of master data and Master Data Management offered in Chapter 1:

- *Master data* is composed of those entities, relationships, and attributes that are critical for an enterprise and foundational to key business processes and application systems.

- *Master Data Management (MDM)* is the framework of processes and technologies aimed at creating and maintaining an authoritative, reliable, sustainable, accurate, and secure data environment that represents a "single and holistic version of the truth," for master data and its relationships, as well as an accepted benchmark used within an enterprise as well as across enterprises and spanning a diverse set of application systems, lines of business, channels, and user communities. To state it slightly differently, an MDM solution takes the master data of a given domain from a variety of data sources' discards redundant data; and then cleanses, rationalizes, enriches, and aggregates it to the extent possible. We can illustrate such an MDM environment as a "hub and spokes," where the spokes are information sources connected to the central hub as a new "home" for the accurate, aggregated, and timely master data (see Figure 4-1). This description helps explain why we often use the term "Data Hub" when discussing an MDM solution space.

Interestingly, using this definition of "what" MDM is does not make our goal of creating architecture much easier to achieve. Indeed, this definition points to the fact that, for example, a CDI solution is much more than just a database of customer information, a solution known by many as a Customer Information File (CIF), a data warehouse of customer information, or an operational data store (ODS). In fact, this definition describes an enterprise-scale system that consists of software components, services, processes, data models and data stores, metadata repositories, applications, networks, and other infrastructure components.

Thus, in order to develop a clear understanding of the "how" of the MDM solution, we will review the historical roots of Master Data Management and its evolution from early attempts to deliver on the MDM promise to what it has become today.

FIGURE 4-1
MDM Customer/
Product Data Hub

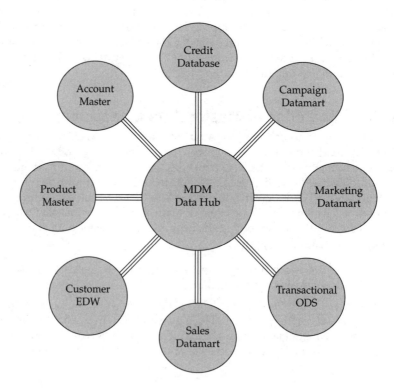

Evolution of Master Data Management Architecture

As we discussed in Chapter 1, the need to create and maintain an accurate and timely "information system of record" is not new, and it applies equally well to businesses and government entities. Lately, a number of regulatory requirements, including the Sarbanes-Oxley Act, the Basel II Capital Accord, and the emerging Basel III Accord (see the discussion on these regulations in Part III of the book), have emphasized this need even further.

In the case of Customer Data Integration, organizations have been engaged in creating customer-centric business models and applications and enabling infrastructure for a long time. However, as the business complexity, number and type of customers (retail customers, individuals, institutional customers, and so on), number of lines of business, and number of sales and service channels continued to grow, this growth often proceeded in a tactical, nonintegrated fashion. As result, many organizations ended up with a wide variety of customer information stores and applications that manage customer data. As an example, one medium-sized service/distribution company maintained no less than eight customer databases that had to be rationalized and cleansed in order to achieve targeted goals for efficiency and quality of the customer service.

The customer data in that "legacy" environment was often incomplete and inconsistent across various data stores, applications, and lines of business. In many other cases, individual applications and lines of business were reasonably satisfied with the quality and scope of customer data they managed. However, the lack of completeness and accuracy and the lack of consistency across lines of business continued to prevent organizations from creating a complete and accurate view of customers and their relationships with the servicing organization and its partners.

Similarly, product information is often scattered across multiple systems. Products and services are modeled in product design and analysis systems where product functionality, bills of materials, packaging, pricing, and other characteristics are developed. Once the product modeling is complete, product information along with product-specific characteristics are released for cross-functional enterprise use.

NOTE *In the scope of MDM for customer domain, we often discuss business transformation to achieve customer centricity as a major goal and benefit of MDM. However, given the domain-agnostic nature of MDM, it is more accurate to talk about transforming the enterprise from an account-centric to an entity-centric model, and, where possible, we'll be using the term "entity centricity" when discussing this transformational feature of MDM.*

Recognizing the entity-centricity (e.g., customer, product) challenge and the resulting inability to transform the business from an account-centric to an entity-centric model, organizations first developed a variety of solutions that attempted to help move the organizations into the new entity-centric world. Although in general these solutions added some incremental value, many of them were deployed in the constraints of the existing lines of business, and very few were built with a true enterprise-wide focus in mind. Nevertheless, these solutions and attempts to achieve entity centricity have helped define MDM in general and CDI and PIM in particular to become a real enabler of such business model transformations. Therefore, we need to understand what has been done prior to the emergence of MDM, and what, if any, portions of the existing solutions can and should be leveraged in implementing MDM. The good news is that many of these solutions are not data-domain specific and can be viewed as foundational technologies for MDM in general.

These solutions include but are not limited to Customer Information File (CIF); Extract, Transform, and Load technologies (ETL); Enterprise Data Warehouse (EDW); an operational data store (ODS); data quality (DQ) technologies; Enterprise Information Integration (EII); Customer Relationship Management (CRM) systems; and Product Master environments, to name just a few. Although some of these solutions and technologies were discussed briefly in Chapter 1, we want to offer a slightly deeper and more architecture-focused review of them, with a view toward their suitability to act as components of a Master Data Management platform.

- **Customer Information File (CIF)**   Many companies have established LOB-specific or company-wide customer information file environments. Historically, CIF solutions used older file management or database management systems (DBMS) technology and represented some very basic point-in-time (static) information about the customers. In other words, CIFs offer limited flexibility and extensibility and are not well suited to capturing and maintaining real-time customer data, customer privacy preferences, customer behavior traits, and customer relationships. Moreover, traditional CIF does not support new complex business processes, event management, and data element–level security constraints known as "data visibility" (see Part III for a detailed discussion on this topic). Shortcomings like these prevent traditional CIF environments from becoming a cross-LOB integration vehicle of customer data.

  Although CIF systems do not deliver a "single version of the truth" about the customer, in most cases existing CIF systems are used to feed the company's Customer Relationship Management systems. Moving forward, a CIF can and should be treated as a key source data file that feeds a new Master Data Management Customer Data Hub system.

- **Extract, Transform, and Load (ETL)**   These tools are typically classified as data-integration tools and are used to extract data from multiple data sources, transform the data to a required target structure, and load the data into the target data store. A key functionality required from the ETL tool is its ability to perform complex transformations from source formats to the target; these transformations may include Boolean expressions, calculations, substitutions, reference table lookup, support for business rules for aggregation and consolidation, and many other features. Contemporary ETL tools include components that perform data consistency and data quality analysis as well as the ability to generate and use metadata definitions for data attributes and entities. Many tools can create output data in XML format according to the predefined schema. Finally, the enterprise-class ETL tools are designed for high scalability and performance and can parallelize most of their operations to achieve acceptable throughput and processing times when dealing with very large data sets or complex transformations.

  Although many ETL processes run in batch mode, best-in-class ETL tools can support near-real-time transformations and load functionality. Given that description, it is quite clear that an ETL component can and should be used to transform and load data into an MDM platform—Data Hub—both for the initial load and possibly for the incremental data updates that keep the Data Hub in sync with existing sources. We discuss MDM data synchronization approaches using ETL in Chapter 16 of the book.

- **Enterprise Data Warehouse (EDW)** Strictly speaking, a data warehouse is an information system that provides its users with current and historical decision-support information that is hard to access or present using traditional operational data stores. An enterprise-wide data warehouse of customer information can become an integration vehicle where most of the customer data can be stored. Likewise, an enterprise data warehouse of product information can act as an integration point for many product-related transactions. Typically, EDW solutions support business intelligence (BI) applications and, in the case of customer domain, Customer Relationship Management (CRM) systems. EDW's design, technology platform, and data schema are optimized to support the efficient storage of large amounts of data and the processing of complex queries against a large number of interconnected data tables that include current and historical information. Traditionally, companies use EDW systems as informational environments rather than operational systems that process real-time, transactional data.

  Because EDW cleanses and rationalizes the data it manages in order to satisfy the needs of the consuming BI and CRM systems, an EDW becomes a good platform from which data should be loaded into the Data Hub.

- **Operational data store (ODS)** This technology allows transaction-level detail data records to be stored in a nonsummarized, query accessible, and long-lasting form. An ODS supports transaction-level analysis and other applications that deal with the low level of details. An ODS differs from a data warehouse in that it does not maintain summarized data, nor does it manage historical information. An ODS allows users to aggregate transaction-level data into higher-level attributes but does not support a drill-down into the underlying detail records. An ODS is frequently used in conjunction with the Enterprise Data Warehouse to provide the company with both historical and transactional real-time data.

  Similar to the EDW, an ODS that contains customer or product data can and should be considered a valuable source of information for constructing an MDM solution.

- **Data quality (DQ) technologies** From the point of view of a business value proposition, the focus of data quality technologies and tools is to help all applications to produce meaningful and reliable results. These tools are especially important for delivering accurate business intelligence and decision support as well as improving customer retention, sales and customer service, customer experience, risk management, compliance, and fraud detection. Companies use data quality technologies to profile data, to report anomalies, and to standardize and "fix" data in order to correct data inconsistencies and known data quality issues, such as missing or invalid data.

  Although data quality tools are especially effective when dealing with the name and address attributes of customer data records, they are also very useful for managing data quality in other data domains. Thus, data quality tools and technologies are key components of most Master Data Management solutions.

- **Enterprise Information Integration (EII)** Enterprise Information Integration tools are frequently used to aggregate subsets of distributed data in memory or nonpersistent storage, usually in real time. Companies use EII solutions to perform search queries across distributed databases and aggregate the results of the queries at the application or presentation layer. Contrast that with the data-integration solutions that aggregate and persist the information at the back end (that is, in a data warehouse or an MDM Data Hub). An EII engine queries a distributed database environment and delivers a virtualized aggregated data view that appears as if it came from a single source. EII engines are also used often in a service-oriented architecture (SOA) implementation as the data access and abstraction components (we discuss SOA later in this chapter).

  Some MDM implementations use EII technologies to provide users with a virtualized total view of a master data without creating a persistent physical image of the aggregation, thus providing additional data model flexibility for the target Data Hub.

- **Customer Relationship Management (CRM)** Customer Relationship Management uses a set of technologies and business processes designed to help the company understand the customer, improve customer experience, and optimize customer-facing business processes across marketing, sales, and servicing channels. From the architecture perspective, CRM systems often act as consumers of customer data and are some of the primary beneficiaries of the MDM Data Hubs.

- **Product Master** Manufacturing companies manage a variety of complex products and product hierarchies. Complex products consist of multiple parts, and those parts contain lower-level components, materials, or parts. This hierarchy represents what is often called a "Bill of Materials" (BOM). BOM management software helps centralize and control complex BOM processes, reduce error rates, and improve control over operational processes and costs.

  An MDM system that is integrated with BOM management software can significantly enhance an integrated multidomain view of the master data. For example, a product characterized by BOM components can be integrated with suppliers' component data.

MDM Architectural Philosophy and Key Architecture Principles

MDM has evolved from and is a direct beneficiary of the variety of solutions and approaches described in the previous section. In this context, MDM enables an evolutionary approach to constructing a comprehensive architectural vision that allows us to define many different viewpoints, each of which represents a particular architecture type.

Moreover, we can create an MDM architecture view that addresses a variety of architectural and management concerns. Specifically, we can develop an architectural view that defines components responsible for the following functional capabilities:

- Creation and management of the core data stores
- Management of processes that implement data governance and data quality
- Metadata management

- Extraction, transformation, and loading of data from sources to target
- Backup and recovery
- Customer analytics
- Security and visibility
- Synchronization and persistence of data changes
- Transaction management
- Entity matching and generation of unique identifiers
- Resolution of entities and relationships

The complexity of the MDM architecture and the multitude of architectural components represent an interesting problem that is often difficult to solve: how to address such a wide variety of architectural and design concerns in a holistic, integrated fashion. One approach to solving this type of challenge is to use the classical notion of a top-down, abstracted representation of the MDM functionality as a stack of interdependent architecture layers, where a given layer of functionality uses services provided by the layers below and in turn provides services to the layers above.

Defining Service-Oriented Architecture

Service-oriented architecture (SOA) is the architecture in which software components can be exposed as loosely-coupled, fine-grained, or coarse-grained reusable services that can be integrated with each other and invoked by different applications for different purposes through a variety of platform-independent service interfaces available via standard network protocols.

We can further enhance the notion of the layered architecture by expressing the functional capabilities of each of the architecture layers in the stack as a set of abstracted services, with a degree of abstraction that varies from high (at the upper layers of the stack) to low (for the bottom layers of the stack). The notion of abstracted services is very powerful and provides architects, designers, and implementers with a number of tangible benefits. We discuss these benefits and the principles of service-oriented architecture (SOA) later in this chapter.

Applying the notion of service-level abstraction to the MDM architecture, we now define its key architecture principles as follows:

- An effective MDM solution should be architected as a metadata-driven SOA platform that provides and consumes services that allow the enterprise to resolve master entities and relationships and move from traditional account-centric legacy systems to a new entity-centric model rapidly and incrementally.
- We can define several key tenets of the information management aspects of the MDM architecture that have a profound impact on the design, implementation, and use of the MDM platform:
  - Decouple information from applications and processes to enable its treatment as a strategic asset.
  - Support the notion that the information content (master data) shall be captured once and validated at the source to the extent permissible by the context.

- Support propagation and synchronization of changes made by MDM system to key master attributes so the changes are available to the consuming downstream systems.

- Enable measurement, assessment, and management of data quality in accordance with information quality standards established by the organization and articulated as part of business needs and data governance.

- Ensure data security, integrity, and appropriate enterprise access.

- Support the retention of data at the appropriate level of granularity.

- Provide an effective vehicle for standardizing content and formats of sources, definitions, structures, and usage patterns.

- Enable consistent, metadata-driven definitions for all data under management.

- Preserve data ownership and support well-defined data governance rules and policies administered and enforced by an enterprise data governance group.

Although the notion of supporting these key information management tenets and using service-level abstraction is fundamental and even necessary in architecting enterprise-scale MDM solutions, it is not totally sufficient. Other aspects of the MDM architecture are better described using alternative architecture representations, or architecture viewpoints, that differ in the content, context, and levels of abstraction. In order to formalize the process of defining and using various architecture viewpoints, we need to introduce the notion of a multidimensional enterprise architecture framework. Readers already familiar with the principles and concepts of the architecture framework can skip the following section.

Enterprise Architecture Framework: A Brief Introduction

As stated earlier in this chapter, the complex multifaceted nature of an MDM solution cannot be described using a single architecture view, but instead requires a number of architectural perspectives organized in a multidimensional architecture framework. Let's illustrate this framework notion using an analogy of building a new community within existing city boundaries. In this case, the city planners and the architects need to create a scaled-down model of the new area, including buildings, streets, parks, and so on. Once this level of architecture is completed and approved, the building architects would start developing building blueprints. Similarly, the road engineers would start designing the streets and intersections. Utilities engineers would start planning for underground cabling, water, and sewerage. City planners would start estimating the number and types of schools and other public facilities required to support the new community. And this list goes on.

Clearly, before the work can get started, the city planners will have to create a number of architecture views, all of which are connected together to enable a cohesive and complete picture of *what, when, where,* and *how* the individual parts of the new city area will be built.

To state it differently, any complex system can be viewed from multiple angles, each of which can be represented by a different architecture perspective. To organize these various architecture perspectives into a holistic and connected picture, we will use the enterprise architecture framework first pioneered by John Zachman. This framework helps architects, designers, and engineers to develop a complex solution in a connected, cohesive, and comprehensive fashion.

Zachman's principal insight is the way to solve the complexity of the enterprise architecture by decomposing the problem into two main dimensions, each of which consists of multiple subcategories. The first dimension defines the various levels of abstraction that represent business scope, conceptual level (business model), logical level (system model), and physical level (technology model). The second dimension consists of key decision-driving questions—what, how, where, who, when, and why. In the context of the enterprise architecture, these questions are considered at the different levels of the first dimension as follows:

- "What" answers the question about what data flows throughout the enterprise.
- "How" describes the functions and business processes performed by the different parts of the enterprise.
- "Where" defines the network that provides interprocess and intercomponent connectivity and information delivery.
- "Who" defines the people and organizational structures affected by the target architecture.
- "Why" represents business drivers for this architecture-based initiative.
- "When" defines the timing constraints and processing requirements.

Each question of the second dimension at every level of the first dimension represents a particular architecture viewpoint—for example, a logical data model view or a physical network architecture view. All these 30 viewpoints are organized together in the framework to comprise a complete enterprise architecture. Figure 4-2 shows a graphical representation of Zachman's framework.

The representation in Figure 4-2 is based on the work published by Zachman's Institute for Framework Advancement (ZIFA).[1]

The value of such an architecture framework is its ability to act as a guide for organizing various design concerns into a set of separate but connected models. The framework benefits become apparent as the complexity and the heterogeneity of the system that is being designed increase. In the case of Master Data Management, this framework approach helps address the complexity of the individual functions and components; the integration of the new MDM environment with the legacy systems; and the need to implement an effective, efficient, secure, and manageable solution in a stepwise, controlled fashion.

Architecture Patterns

The other approach to solving complex system design and architecture challenges is the notion of architecture and design patterns. A pattern is a proven, successful, and reusable approach to solving a well-defined problem. Here are some specifics:

- A pattern is an approach to the solution that has been implemented successfully a number of times in the real world to solve a specific problem space.
- Typically, patterns are observed and documented in the course of successful real-life implementations.

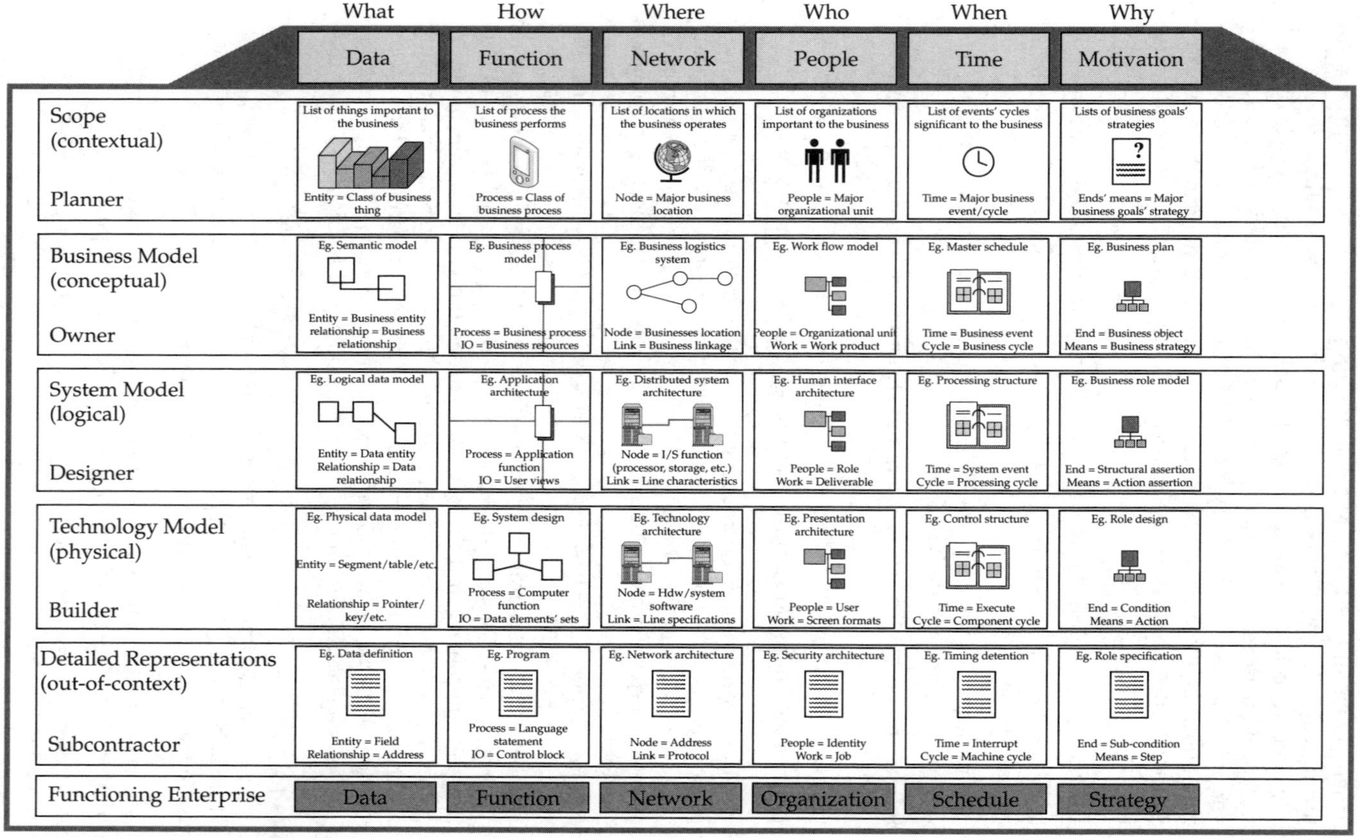

	What — Data	How — Function	Where — Network	Who — People	When — Time	Why — Motivation
Scope (contextual) / Planner	List of things important to the business. Entity = Class of business thing	List of process the business performs. Process = Class of business process	List of locations in which the business operates. Node = Major business location	List of organizations important to the business. People = Major organizational unit	List of events' cycles significant to the business. Time = Major business event/cycle	Lists of business goals' strategies. Ends' means = Major business goals' strategy
Business Model (conceptual) / Owner	Eg. Semantic model. Entity = Business entity relationship = Business relationship	Eg. Business process model. Process = Business process, IO = Business resources	Eg. Business logistics system. Node = Businesses location, Link = Business linkage	Eg. Work flow model. People = Organizational unit, Work = Work product	Eg. Master schedule. Time = Business event, Cycle = Business cycle	Eg. Business plan. End = Business object, Means = Business strategy
System Model (logical) / Designer	Eg. Logical data model. Entity = Data entity, Relationship = Data relationship	Eg. Application architecture. Process = Application function, IO = User views	Eg. Distributed system architecture. Node = I/S function (processor, storage, etc.) Link = Line characteristics	Eg. Human interface architecture. People = Role, Work = Deliverable	Eg. Processing structure. Time = System event, Cycle = Processing cycle	Eg. Business role model. End = Structural assertion, Means = Action assertion
Technology Model (physical) / Builder	Eg. Physical data model. Entity = Segment/table/etc. Relationship = Pointer/key/etc.	Eg. System design. Process = Computer function, IO = Data elements/ sets	Eg. Technology architecture. Node = Hdw/system software, Link = Line specifications	Eg. Presentation architecture. People = User, Work = Screen formats	Eg. Control structure. Time = Execute, Cycle = Component cycle	Eg. Role design. End = Condition, Means = Action
Detailed Representations (out-of-context) / Subcontractor	Eg. Data definition. Entity = Field, Relationship = Address	Eg. Program. Process = Language statement, IO = Control block	Eg. Network architecture. Node = Address, Link = Protocol	Eg. Security architecture. People = Identity, Work = Job	Eg. Timing detention. Time = Interrupt, Cycle = Machine cycle	Eg. Role specification. End = Sub-condition, Means = Step
Functioning Enterprise	Data	Function	Network	Organization	Schedule	Strategy

Figure 4-2 Zachman's enterprise architecture framework

- Patterns don't solve every single aspect of every problem, and typically are focused on core, main aspects of the problem (following the law of the "trivial many and the critical few," better known as Pareto's Law, or the 80-20 Rule).[2]

- When defined correctly, patterns are easy to apply to service-oriented architectures because they leverage object-oriented design principles, especially the notion of inheritance, by often inheriting components (objects) from already defined patterns.

When we discuss architecture patterns, their primary benefit is in helping architects of complex systems such as MDM to identify various design options and understanding which options are most appropriate for a given problem domain. More often than not, individual patterns have to be combined with other patterns to define a solution to a particular business problem.

Patterns are different from architecture viewpoints. They tend to solve a well-defined, discrete problem space by providing proven, reusable choices. Architecture viewpoints, on the other hand, offer an opportunity to the architects and designers to view the problem from different angles to understand the interrelationships among the components, services, and other system objects and to formulate an approach to solve problems when the directional decisions have been made. In other words, a typical architecture viewpoint represents an aspect of the problem space that needs to be broken into a set of patterns that can be implemented with high confidence.

In MDM space, we use both architecture viewpoints and patterns, although patterns, by representing a more constraint problem domain, tend to provide a lower level of technical design.[3]

MDM Architecture Viewpoints

Because of its broad coverage of the business-to-technology dimensions, an architecture framework can help organize and promote different points of view for an enterprise. Different groups within the organization may express these points of view based on their organizational affiliation, skill sets, and even the political landscape of the workplace. Because a full-function MDM solution tends to be truly an enterprise-scale initiative that spans organizational and lines-of-business boundaries, one benefit of using the framework approach is to help gain organizational buy-in and support for expensive and lengthy MDM projects.

Of course, we do not want to create an impression that any MDM solution has to be architected using Zachman's framework. In fact, very few enterprise-wide initiatives use this framework in its entirety with all its 30 viewpoints. Many architecture-savvy organizations use a subset of the complete enterprise architecture framework or different architecture viewpoints. The goal of the preceding discussion was simply to illustrate the principles and benefits of the enterprise architecture framework and patterns approach as a way to solve the design and implementation challenges of any large and complex software system.

We would like to use the principles of the architecture framework to define the most relevant architecture viewpoints for a successful design and implementation of an MDM solution, with a specific emphasis on the MDM Data Hub implementations. In this context, we will focus the framework viewpoints discussion on the conceptual and logical levels of the architecture, and shall consider the following set of architecture viewpoints:

- Architecture viewpoints for various classification dimensions, in particular the consumption and reconciliation dimension and the use pattern dimension
- Conceptual architecture
- High-level reference architecture
- Services architecture
- Data architecture

From the framework perspective, we recognize many different but equally important architecture viewpoints. However, because describing a complete framework set is beyond the scope of this book, we'll focus the follow-on discussion in this chapter on three viewpoints: the services view, architecture views of MDM classification dimensions (we introduced this topic in Chapter 1), and the reference architecture view. We discuss additional architecture details and specific data architecture views in Chapters 5, 6, and 7, whereas data security and visibility architecture views are discussed in Chapter 11.

Services Architecture View

A services architecture viewpoint is probably one of the most relevant to the architecture discussion of the MDM system. Indeed, we have stated repeatedly that an MDM system should be an instance of the service-oriented architecture (SOA). Using this viewpoint has an additional benefit in that it helps us illustrate how we can extend the very approach of the enterprise architecture framework to describe complex systems such as MDM systems. Indeed, even though Zachman's framework does not explicitly show a services architecture viewpoint, we will define such a viewpoint for a Data Hub system and show how this viewpoint can be mapped to Zachman's framework.

Introduction to Service-Oriented Architecture

We define *service-oriented architecture (SOA)* as an architecture in which software components can be exposed as loosely-coupled, coarse-grained, reusable services that can be integrated with each other and invoked by different applications for different purposes through a variety of platform-independent service interfaces available via standard network protocols.

This is a practical definition but not the only valid definition of SOA. There are a number of alternative definitions of SOA,[4] and it's beyond the scope of this book to described them all or offer arguments about the merits of individual definitions. Therefore, we should consider a standard bearer in the SOA space. The World Wide Web Consortium (W3C) has developed a comprehensive definition of the service-oriented architecture in its February 2004 Working Group publication.

> ### W3C Definition of Service-Oriented Architecture
> A service-oriented architecture (SOA)[5] is a form of distributed systems architecture that is typically characterized by the following properties:
>
> - **Logical view**   The service is an abstracted, logical view of actual programs, databases, business processes, and so on, defined in terms of *what* it does, typically carrying out a business-level operation.
>
> - **Message orientation**   The service is formally defined in terms of the messages exchanged between provider agents and requester agents, and not the properties of the agents themselves.
>
> - **Description orientation**   A service is described by machine-processable metadata.
>
> - **Granularity**   Services tend to use a small number of operations with relatively large and complex messages.
>
> - **Network orientation**   Services tend to be oriented toward use over a network, although this is not an absolute requirement.
>
> - **Platform-neutral**   Messages are sent in a platform-neutral, standardized format delivered through the interfaces.

Similar to the architecture framework discussion, we can define SOA in a way that recognizes multiple views of service orientation and clearly relies on the messaging paradigm implemented over a network. Moreover, because services are composed from service components, and can be organized to work together to perform a given task, we need to introduce two additional concepts: service orchestration and service choreography. These concepts are key for the notion of service management. There are numerous, often conflicting definitions of these terms. We offer here one definition set as a reference. Readers interested in this subject can review other definitions available on the Web.[6]

> ### SOA and Service Management: Orchestration and Choreography
> *Orchestration* refers to the automated execution of a workflow. An orchestrated workflow is typically exposed as a set of services that can be invoked through an API. It does not describe a coordinated set of interactions between two or more parties.
> *Choreography* refers to a description of coordinated interactions between two or more parties.

The definition of SOA and its key concepts help define a services view of the MDM system in a way that makes it clear which services, functions, and components need to be considered and included for a full-function MDM SOA implementation. We discuss this point in more detail later in this chapter.

In addition to the regular SOA viewpoint, we can also show that the service-oriented architecture can be mapped to the viewpoints of an enterprise architecture framework. Specifically, consider that SOA is not a specific technology or product. Rather, it can be described as a design philosophy for the application architecture portion of the framework. If we use the SOA definition to represent information technology assets as services, then SOA can be mapped to the framework at the Logical level within the Function domain.

We can logically extend this approach to show that the set of functional services represents business processes, and because SOA is based on the network-aware messaging paradigm, the notion of the service orientation can be realized in several architecture framework viewpoints that connect process models and network-based messaging.

We offer these considerations simply to demonstrate that the framework approach and service-oriented architecture are closely connected and continuously evolving concepts that together can be used to help describe and plan the design and implementation of complex systems such as Master Data Management.

SOA Benefits

Additional insights into the SOA include the following key principal benefits:

- SOA offers access mechanisms to the application logic as a service to users and other applications where
  - Service interfaces are independent of user interfaces.
  - Services are business-process-oriented.
  - Business-level services are coarse-grained and can be easily mapped to business functions.
  - Coarse-grained services can be combined or assembled from lower-level, fine-grained service primitives at run time.
  - Services are published in a standard fashion for discovery and execution.
  - Services can be used and reused by existing applications and systems.
- SOA permits the construction of scalable applications over the network.
- SOA supports asynchronous communications.
- SOA supports application-level conversations as well as process and state management.

SOA can significantly simplify and accelerate the development of new applications by invoking a variety of published services and organizing or orchestrating them to achieve the desired business functionality. Because SOA allows business-level services to be assembled at run time, developers do not have to design all possible variations of services in advance. This reduces the development time and helps minimize the number of errors in the application code.

One of the benefits of SOA is its ability to leverage the power and flexibility of Web Services across the enterprise by building loosely-coupled, standards-based applications that produce and consume services.

Introduction to Web Services

Web Services is another important concept that enables a shift in distributed computing toward loosely-coupled, standards-based, service-oriented architectures that help achieve better cross-business integration, improved efficiency, and closer customer relationships.

The short definition of *Web Services* offered here states that Web Services are *encapsulated, loosely-coupled, contracted* software objects that are published and consumed using standard interfaces and protocols.

The true power of Web Services lies in three related concepts that describe how Web Services change the fundamental nature of distributed computing:

- Web Services offer a standard way of supporting both synchronous and asynchronous messages—a capability essential to perform *long-running* B2B transactions.

- Web Services are loosely coupled, enabling a *reduction in the integration costs* as well as facilitating a *federation of systems.*

- Web Services support *coarse granularity* of the application programming interfaces (APIs). A coarse-grained interface rolls up the functions of many different API calls into a small number of business-oriented messages—a key to *business process management and automation.*

A good discussion on Web Services, SOA, and Web Services Architecture (WSA) can be found in the W3C Architecture documents.[7] For simplicity, we'll define Web Services as encapsulated, loosely-coupled, contracted software objects that are published and consumed using standard interfaces and protocols.

> **Web Services**
> *Web Services* are encapsulated, loosely-coupled, contracted software objects that are published and consumed using standard interfaces and protocols.

A high-level view of a service-oriented architecture is shown in Figure 4-3.

Another, more structured view of the service-oriented reference architecture has been developed by a standards organization called the Organization for the Advancement of

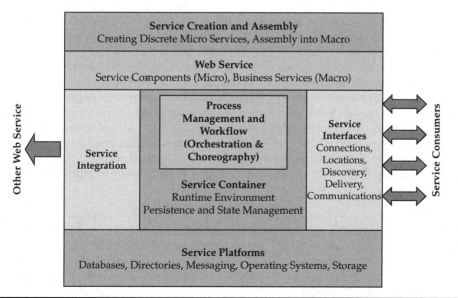

FIGURE 4-3   Service-oriented architecture

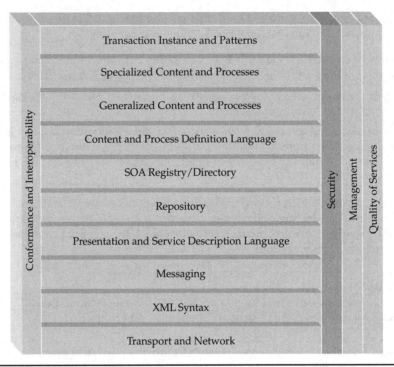

FIGURE 4-4 OASIS service-oriented reference architecture

Structured Information Standards (OASIS).[8] One of the OASIS SOA reference architecture views is depicted in Figure 4-4.

SOA and Web Services are rapidly evolving from intra-enterprise usage to inter-enterprise communities of interest to general-purpose business-to-business environments, thus enabling significant reductions in the cost of integration among established business partners. SOA and Web Services have changed the way companies do business. For example, business transactions that use Web Services can offer new per-use or subscription-based revenue opportunities by exposing value-added services via public, Internet-accessible directories.

Combined with the benefits of the entity-centric transformations offered by the MDM Data Hub solutions, Web Services and SOA are powerful tools that can have a direct and positive impact on the design, implementation, and benefits of new entity-centric business strategies.

MDM and SOA MDM is a direct beneficiary and at the same time an enabler of the service-oriented approach and Web Services. Indeed, MDM's complexity and variability of features and options all benefit from the ability to "assemble" or compose an MDM system from a pallet of available services by leveraging service reusability, service granularity, and loose coupling. SOA and Web Services by their very nature promote standards compliance as well as service provisioning and monitoring.

Moreover, SOA requires and enables service identification and categorization—features that represent a natural affinity to the capabilities of the MDM platform. Services categorization by itself is a valuable concept, because it helps define and understand service taxonomy, which in turn can guide architects and designers to the most effective placement and composition of services and their interdependencies. We show how these capabilities can be mapped onto the MDM system's services view later in this chapter.

In other words, there are significant synergies between MDM and SOA. At a high level, these synergies can be summarized as follows:

- SOA defines a fabric that helps deliver operational and analytical master data from the MDM system to all business application systems and users.
- MDM is a core engine of SOA master data services (MDS) and uses SOA components and principles to make master data available to it's applications and users via services.

CAUTION *These synergies between MDM and SOA are not automatic. It is important to understand that SOA programs aimed at Master Data Management sometimes fail because the enterprise group responsible for the services framework does not align the SOA strategy, framework, and components with the enterprise data strategy and specifically the MDM strategy. MDM, with its cross-functional context, is a perfect area of application for SOA. When an SOA does not support MDM data services, the value of the SOA, even if it is implemented well from the technology perspective, is marginal.*

Applying SOA principles to MDM solutions, we can construct a high-level service-oriented view of the MDM Data Hub (see Figure 4-5). Here, the Data Hub acts as a services platform that supports two major groups of services: internal, infrastructure-type services that maintain Data Hub data integrity and enable necessary functionality; and external, published services. The latter category of services maps well to the business functions that can leverage the MDM Data Hub. These services are often considered business services, and the Data Hub exposes these external business services for consumption by the users and applications.

As we stated in the section on defining MDM architectural philosophy, we can organize all the services into a layered framework, with the services consumers on the top requesting and using the coarse-grained business services on the second layer. These published, business-level services invoke appropriate internal, fine-grained services in the layer(s) below. In this context, Data Hub internal services enable data access and maintain data integrity, consistency, security, and availability. The internal services interact with the Data Hub as a data service provider, and potentially with other data stores for the purpose of data acquisition, synchronization, and delivery.

The services invoke executable components and implement methods that perform requested actions. Following the principles of the service-oriented architecture and Web Services, the lower-level Data Hub services can be combined to form more coarse-grained, composite, business-level services that execute business transactions. In general, the service-oriented nature of the Data Hub platform would allow this service assembly to take place at run time. In this case, a Data Hub would help establish an appropriate execution environment, including the support for transactional semantics, orchestration/choreography, composition

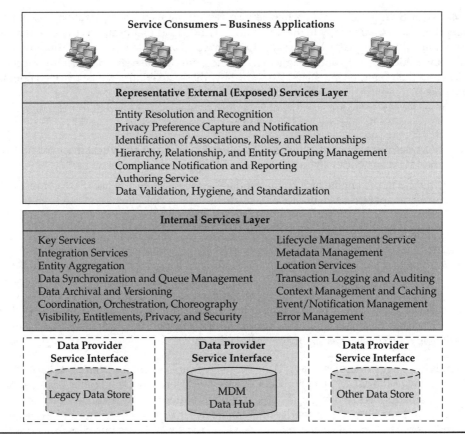

Figure 4-5   MDM Data Hub as a service platform

and remediation of failed actions, and security services. A full-function MDM Data Hub system would deliver these features through a dedicated set of internal services and functional components.

An important benefit of the SOA approach is that it allows for significant flexibility in the way the MDM services are selected and delivered, and the SOA approach does not require or imply that all services have be a part of a single product. In fact, SOA allows MDM designers to select best-in-class solutions for the services. For example, an organization may select an MDM vendor product implemented as a service platform but may decide to use an entity-matching engine and data integration services from another vendor based on features, price points, existing inventory, familiarity with the product, and a host of other reasons.

Although many MDM vendor products support service-oriented functionality, support for the scalability, flexibility, and granularity of the business services varies significantly from product to product.

We discuss additional details of the Data Hub as an instance of a service-oriented architecture in Chapter 6. We describe the Data Hub components view in the context of the reference architecture later in this chapter.

MDM and SOA Misconceptions   One of the key differences between modern services-oriented MDM solutions and their ODS predecessors is that an MDM Data Hub is much more a service platform than just a data repository. The term "MDM Data Hub" is often inaccurately used to mean the same thing as the more traditional operational data stores of the 1980s and 1990s.[9] Misusing the term adversely affects understanding of the modern design options of Enterprise Data Management (EDM) and MDM solutions that are enabled by MDM Data Hub systems.

There are some key characteristics and features of Data Hubs that often are underestimated or misunderstood by enterprise architects and systems integrators. Here are two of the most common misconceptions:

- **Misconception 1: An MDM Data Hub is just another data repository or a database used for storage of cleansed data content, often used to build data warehousing dimensions.**

  Indeed, data must be cleansed and standardized before it is loaded into the Data Hub. For many professionals brought up on the concepts of operational data stores, data warehouses, and ETL (Extract, Transform, and Load), this is an undisputable truth. But it's not the only concern of Data Hub data content. Modern MDM architectures support a much more active approach to data than just the storage of a golden record. The Data Hub makes the best decisions on entity and relationship resolution by arbitrating the content of data created or modified in the source systems. Expressed differently, a Data Hub operates as a master data service responsible for the creation and maintenance of master entities and relationships.

  The concept of a Data Hub as the enterprise master data service (MDS) applies the power of advanced algorithms and human input to resolve entities and relationships in real time. In addition, data governance policies and data stewardship rules and procedures define and mandate the behavior of the master data service, including the release of reference codes and code translation semantics for enterprise use.

  The services nature of the MDM Data Hub provides an ideal way for managing data within an SOA environment. Using a hub-and-spoke model, the MDS serves as the integration method to communicate between all systems that produce or consume master data. The MDS is the hub, and all systems communicate directly with it using SOA principles.

  Participating systems are operating in a loosely-coupled, federated fashion and are "autonomous" in SOA parlance, meaning that they can stay independent of one another and do not have to know the details of how other systems manage master data. This allows disparate system-specific schemas and internal business rules to be hidden, which greatly reduces tight coupling and the overall brittleness of the MDM ecosystem. It also helps to reduce the overall workload that participating systems must bear to manage master data.

- **Misconception 2: The system of record must be persisted in the MDM Data Hub.**

  The notion of a Data Hub as a data repository erroneously presumes that the single version of the truth, the golden record, must be persisted in the Data Hub. The notion of the MDM Data Hub as a service platform does not make this presumption. Indeed, as soon as the master data service can deliver master data to the enterprise, the Data Hub may persist the golden record or assemble it dynamically instead.

One of the arguments for persistently stored master data in the Data Hub is that performance for master data retrieval will suffer if the record is assembled dynamically on request. The reality is that the existing Data Hub solutions have demonstrated that dynamic master data content can be assembled with practically no performance impact if the master data model is properly implemented.

One of the advantages of dynamically assembled records is that the Data Hub can maintain multiple views of the master data aligned with line-of-business and functional requirements, data visibility requirements, tolerance to false positives and negatives, and latency requirements. Mature enterprises increasingly require multiple views for the golden record, and the dynamic record assembly works better to support this need.

Conversely, we can offer a strong argument in favor of a persistently stored master data records. This argument is driven by the need to support the history and auditability of the master data life cycle. There are at least two major usage patterns for the history of master data:

- The first pattern is driven by audit requirements. The enterprise needs to be able to understand the origin, the time, and possibly the reason for a change. These audit and compliance requirements have to be supported by the Data Hub at the attribute level. MDM solutions that maintain the golden record can dynamically address this need by supporting the history of changes in the source system's record content.

- The second usage pattern for history support results from the need to support database queries on data referring to a certain point in time or certain time range— for example, what was the inventory on a certain date, or sales over the second quarter? A classic example of this type of history support is the implementation and management of slowly changing dimensions in data warehousing. In order to support this usage pattern, the golden version of the master record must be persisted. It is just a question of location. Many enterprises decide this question in favor of data warehousing dimensions while avoiding the persistently stored golden record in the Data Hub.

In short, modern MDM Data Hub systems function as active components of service-oriented architecture by providing master data services, rather than being passive repositories of cleansed data. This consideration should help the enterprise architects and systems integrators build sound Master Data Management solutions. An additional discussion about these differences can be found in Chapter 6.

Architecture Viewpoints of Various MDM Classification Dimensions

As we defined in Chapter 1, MDM addresses complex business and technical problems and, as such, is a complex, multifaceted framework that can be described and viewed from various angles. The amount of information about MDM goals, benefits, design viewpoints, and challenges is quite large, and in order to make sense of various, sometimes contradictory assertions about MDM, we introduced several MDM classification dimensions that allow us to organize available information, and we discussed various aspects of MDM according to a well-defined structure. In this section, we consider the architectural implications of various classification dimensions introduced in Chapter 1, as follows:

- The Design and Deployment dimension (consumption and reconciliation architecture viewpoint)
- The Use Pattern dimension
- The Information Scope or Data Domain dimension

MDM practitioners and industry analysts see these dimensions as persistent characteristics of any MDM solution, regardless of the industry or master data domain.

MDM Design and Deployment Dimension

The Design and Deployment viewpoint addresses MDM consumption and reconciliation architecture concerns, and the resulting MDM architecture styles. Armed with the architecture framework approach, we can recognize that these "styles" represent architecture viewpoints that determine the way the MDM system is intended to be used and be kept reliably in sync with its data providers (data sources) and data consumers. These viewpoints represent an intersection of the functional and data dimensions of the enterprise architecture framework at the logical, conceptual, and contextual levels. The resulting design constructs are a direct consequence of the different breadth and depth of the MDM data model coverage. We will discuss master data modeling in more detail in Chapter 7.

The architecture styles vary in the context of other dimensions of the enterprise architecture framework, including the organizational need and readiness to create and fully deploy a new system of records about customer data. And, of course, these architecture styles manifest themselves in different service-oriented architecture viewpoints.

Let's briefly describe the four predominant MDM architecture styles in the context of master data scope management, consumption, and reconciliation services. These styles have been introduced by several prominent industry analysts, including the Gartner Group.[10] We discuss the implementation concerns of these architecture styles later, in Part IV of the book.

MDM Architecture Styles

The MDM architecture, design, and deployment styles include the following:

- External reference
- Registry
- Reconciliation engine
- Transaction hub

The underlying principle behind these styles is the fact that an MDM Data Hub data model may contain *all* data attributes about the data domain it manages, or just *some* attributes, while other attributes remain in their original data stores. It is logical to assume that the Data Hub can be the "master" of those master entities whose data attributes it manages or just arbitrates the entities and attributes across operational systems where the master data is created and maintained. This assumption is one of the drivers defining the MDM architecture styles. Let's look at this issue in detail.

External Reference Style   In this case, an MDM Data Hub is a reference database pointing to all source data stores but does not usually contain actual data for a given domain—for example, customer data for a customer domain, product for product domain, and so on:

- This is the most extreme case, where a Data Hub contains only a reference to the source or system of record data that continues to reside in the legacy data stores. In this case, the Data Hub acts as a special "directory" and points to the master data that continues to be created and updated by the existing legacy applications. This design option, known as the "External Reference Data Hub," is the least complex of the Data Hub styles.

- One of the main architecture concerns of this style is the ability of the MDM Data Hub to maintain accurate, timely, and valid references to the master data at all times, which may require design focus on a reliable, just-in-time interconnection between source systems and the Data Hub, perhaps by using an enterprise-class messaging mechanism.

- A significant limitation of this architectural style is that the Data Hub does not hold any attributes, even those needed for matching and entity resolution. The Data Hub service responsible for matching has to access matching attributes across multiple systems in a federated fashion.

Even though this design is theoretically possible and a few attempts have been made to implement it, federated matching has been proven ineffective and most MDM Data Hub vendors discontinued its support.

Registry Style   This style of the MDM Data Hub architecture represents a Registry of unique master entity identifiers (created using identity attributes). It maintains only the identifying attributes. These attributes are used by an entity resolution service to identify which master entity records should be linked because they represent the same entity (i.e., customer, product, location, and so on). The Data Hub matches and links the records that share the same identity. The Data Hub creates and maintains links with data sources that were used to obtain the identity attributes. The MDM Data Hub exposes a service that returns a fully assembled holistic entity view to the consuming application either as retrieval or an assembly operation (for example, a customer, at run time). Using MDM for customer domain as an example, a Registry-style Data Hub should support the following features:

- Maintain some, at least matching customer profile attributes that it uses to generate a unique customer identifier. Such attributes may include customer name, address, date of birth, and externally assigned identifiers (social security number, an employer identification number, a business reference number such as a DUNS number, and so on).

- Automatically generate and maintain links with all upstream systems that maintain data about the customers. Consuming applications query the Registry for a given customer or a set of customers, and the Registry would use its customer identification number and legacy pointers or links and record merge rules to allow the application to retrieve and construct a view of the customer from the underlying data.

- Act as the "master" of the unique identifiers, and support arbitration of data conflicts by determining which attribute values in the source systems are better than others by applying attribute survivorship rules across multiple systems.

A limitation of this MDM architecture style is that it relies on the data available in the operational systems to assemble the best possible view of data. The Data Hub is not used for data entry and does not own the master data, but rather arbitrates the values that should be available in the operational source systems to be displayed by the Data Hub. If the data is not available in the source systems, the Registry-style Data Hub cannot create the right attribute values by itself. The records and correct attribute values have to be created and maintained in one of the feeding operational systems. Then the Data Hub will process the changes originated in the source system in real time and display an improved view of the benchmark record.

Reconciliation Engine This MDM architecture style is a system of record for some entity attributes; it provides active synchronization between itself and the legacy systems.

- In this case, the Data Hub is the master for those data attributes that it actively maintains by supporting authoring of master data content. The Reconciliation Engine Data Hub style relies on the upstream source systems to maintain other data attributes. One implication of this approach is the fact that *some* applications that handle source or master data may have to be changed or redesigned based on the business processes, application interfaces, and the data they use. The same is true for the corresponding business processes. The other implication is that the Data Hub has to maintain, create, and change those data attributes for which it is the master. The Data Hub has to propagate changes for these attributes to the systems that use these attributes. The result is a data environment that continuously synchronizes the data content among its participants to avoid data inconsistencies.

- A shortcoming is that the complexity of synchronization increases as some of the data attributes maintained in the Data Hub are derived from the data attributes maintained in other systems. For example, a typical Reconciliation Engine–style Data Hub for customer domain has to create and maintain unique customer identifications as well as references to the legacy systems and data stores where the customer data is sourced from or continues to reside.

This architecture style is more sophisticated than the Registry-style Data Hub, and in many situations is a viable evolutionary step toward the full Transaction Hub.

Transaction Hub This is the most sophisticated option, in which the Data Hub becomes the primary source of and the system of record for the entire master data domain, including appropriate reference pointers:

- This is the case where the Data Hub maintains practically *all* data attributes about the entity. For a given entity domain, such as a customer domain (individuals or businesses), the Data Hub becomes a "master" of the master entity information, and as such should be the source of all changes to any attribute about the master entity. In this case, the Data Hub has to be engineered as a complete transactional environment that maintains its data integrity and is the sole source of changes that it propagates to all downstream systems that use the customer data.

- The Transactional Hub has some profound implications for the overall environment, the existing applications, and business processes already in place. For example, an existing account maintenance application may have to undergo modifications to update the Data Hub instead of an existing legacy system, and appropriate synchronization mechanisms have to be in place to propagate and apply the changes from the Data

Hub to some or all downstream systems. Moreover, most of the previously deployed transactions that change entity information should be redesigned to work directly with the Data Hub, which may also change existing business processes, workflows, and user navigation. This is the most complex case, which is known as a Full Transaction Hub.

- Practically speaking, the intrusiveness of the Transaction Hub style makes it a viable choice mostly in two scenarios:
  - When dealing with a new enterprise that does not have a massive legacy infrastructure maintaining the master entity the Data Hub is supposed to resolve.
  - When the current processes and applications already manage the master entity as a Transaction-style Data Hub. In this scenario, the new Data Hub is built to replace the existing master entity management system with a new system (for example, a customer-centric solution). For instance, it can be the case where the enterprise has already been using a home-grown Transaction-style MDM Data Hub and is looking to replace it with a more advanced vendor solution.

With the exception of the first, the External Reference style, these architecture and design styles have one thing in common—they define, create, and manage a centralized platform where master data is integrated either virtually (Registry) or physically (Reconciliation Engine and Transaction Hub) to create a reliable and sustainable system of record for master data.

MDM and Use Pattern Dimension

The Use Pattern classification dimension differentiates MDM architectures based on how the master data is used. We see three primary use patterns for MDM data usage: Analytical MDM, Operational MDM, and Collaborative MDM.

- *Analytical MDM* supports business processes and applications that use master data primarily to analyze business performance and provide appropriate reporting and analytical capabilities, often by directly interfacing with business intelligence (BI) tools and packages. Analytical MDM tends to be read-mostly, it usually does not change or create source data in the operational systems, but it does cleanse and enrich data in the MDM Data Hub. From the overall system architecture view, Analytical MDM can be architected as a feed into the data warehouse and can create or enrich an accurate, integrated view of the master data inside the data warehouse. BI tools are typically deployed to access this cleansed, enriched, and integrated data for reporting, perform deep analytics, and provide drill-through capabilities for the required level of detail.

- *Operational MDM* allows master data to be collected, changed, and used to process business transactions; Operational MDM is designed to maintain the semantic consistency of the master data affected by the transactional activity. Operational MDM provides a mechanism to improve the quality of the data in the operational systems, where the data is usually created. By design, Operational MDM systems ensure that the accurate, single version of the truth is maintained in the MDM Data Hub and propagated to the core systems used by existing and new processes and applications.

- *Collaborative MDM* allows its users to author master data objects and collaborate in the process of creation and maintenance of master data and its associated metadata.

These Use Pattern–based architecture viewpoints have common concerns and often use common or similar technologies, especially the components of technology related to data extraction, transformation, and load, as well as data quality.

At the same time, we can clearly see how the architectural implications of these three Use Pattern dimensions impact the way the MDM Hub has to handle data synchronization concerns, implement cross-application interoperability, deliver data changes to upstream and/or downstream systems, detect and improve data quality issues, and enable and support data governance processes.

Data Domain Dimension

The Information Scope or Data Domain dimension describes the primary data domain managed by the MDM solution. In the case of MDM for the customer data domain, the resulting solution is often called Customer Data Integration, or CDI. In the case of MDM for product data domain, the solution is known as Product Information Management, or PIM. Other data domains may not have formal acronym definitions yet, but could have an impact on how the MDM solution is designed and deployed. Primary architectural implications related to implementing customer, product, or other domains include:

- Design for entity resolution and identification. Techniques for these data domains can vary drastically based on the requirements for semantic consistency, speed, accuracy, and confidence.

- Ability to acquire and manage sources of external entity references, such as authoritative sources of individual names and addresses, business names, as well as identifiers and industry classifications (for example, D&B DUNS numbers).

- Information security and privacy concerns that apply differently to different data domains based on a particular risk profile of a given data domain within the context of business requirements as well as those governed by a variety of rules, policies, and governmental regulations.

Reference Data and Hierarchy Management

When we discuss the architectural implications of an MDM solution in the context of the data it manages, we need to recognize that the data scope alone does not address all variations of what data needs to be managed in what way. For example, most MDM implementations deal with creating a master environment of *reference* data, such as product reference, account reference, customer reference, and so on. However, it is not unusual for an organization to try to build an authoritative master data environment that supports enterprise-wide business attributes, such as customer revenues, expenses, risk exposure, and so on. Technically speaking, this is not traditional reference data, and the MDM Data Hub architecture should provide for features, functions, and services that can calculate, maintain, and ensure the quality of these key business metrics. Clearly, this adds an additional layer of complexity to an already complex system. This is where proven architecture patterns for creating such metrics can be inherited from existing business systems and "adopted" into the MDM Data Hub.

MDM and Hierarchy Management   Many business problems addressed by the MDM architecture include the management of data domain hierarchies. It is a common situation when an organization manages multiple views of the business based on a specific business focus, such as marketing view of customers, financial views of a global organization, various views of products, and so on. In these cases, we see an organizational hierarchy that consists of a parent (for example, legal entity) and multiple dependents (for example, accounts or other legal entities). Similarly, businesses tend to structure their sales organizations based on either products or geographies or cost centers. The challenge here is that these hierarchies are not static over time, and can and do change with business restructuring, mergers and acquisitions, new product introductions, and other events. Several formal definitions of hierarchies are available, but the following working definition of hierarchies is most relevant to general data management, and Master Data Management in particular.

In the context of MDM, we define a *hierarchy* as an arrangement of entities (parties, accounts, products, cost centers, and so on) where entities are viewed in relationship to each other as "parents," "children," or "siblings/peers" of other entities, thus forming a conceptual tree structure where all leaf nodes in the hierarchy tree can be rolled into a single "root."

Further, the entities of a given domain can often support several hierarchical arrangements based on a particular classification schema (legal entity level, geography/location, role/rank, scope of authority, and so on). A direct consequence of this fact is that changes in a classification schema or the introduction of another schema will result in the creation of a different hierarchy, sometimes referred to as an alternate hierarchy.

In order to create and maintain an authoritative, verifiable system of record, an MDM system has to be able to recognize and manage hierarchies based on the classification schemas; to compare, match, and link master entities that may exist at different levels of hierarchy; to manage the creation, maintenance, and versioning of different alternative hierarchies; and to provide relevant and timely changes in the hierarchies of reference data to the MDM users and consuming applications.

MDM Hierarchy Management and Data Warehousing   The discussion on hierarchy management of reference data offered in the preceding section is particularly relevant to the relationship between MDM and data warehousing. Let's compare the principles of hierarchical structures with the concepts of facts and dimensions in the data warehousing discipline.[11] Indeed, the notion of a hierarchy applies directly to the dimensions in a data warehouse's data model, frequently referred to as a dimensional data model in the form of a "star" or "snowflake" schema, with the fact entities organized in a set of central tables that are "surrounded" by dimension tables, where the dimensional data contains attributes used as keys that point to the facts in the Fact Table.[12] For example, a customer data warehouse may contain information about customer account values (facts) and dimensions such as customer identifiers, customer locations, and time. As the dimensional attributes change, the facts may change or new facts may get created. And in cases where dimensional values change infrequently, the data warehousing discipline recognizes the concept of Slow Change Dimensions, or SCD, the constructs that allow a data warehouse to maintain the historical view of the values of the facts (sometimes referred to as "time travel").

> **Hierarchies and Data Dimensions**
> In the context of denormalized dimensional data models such as the star or snowflake schemas widely used in data warehousing, *hierarchies* are arrangements of records in the data model's dimensions.

Data warehousing is a complex and mature technical discipline, and a detailed discussion of this topic is beyond the scope of this book. However, we briefly discuss the relationship between MDM hierarchy management and data warehousing concepts for the following reasons:

- As stated in preceding chapters, data warehousing is one of the predecessor technologies to MDM.

- In many instances, an MDM system is implemented "upstream" from data warehouses and data marts that are used to collect and aggregate master data and to provide reporting, analytical, and business intelligence capabilities to support an organization's business and financial management needs.

Therefore, it is important to understand what MDM architecture features are required to support a large multidimensional data warehouse as a downstream system. Architecturally, these features are organized into a collection of hierarchy management services, and these services are used to maintain the integrity and accuracy of various hierarchies; to work in conjunction with entity resolution services to properly recognize, match, link, and aggregate entities in accordance with their hierarchical relationships; and to enable the efficient delivery of hierarchy changes to appropriate downstream consuming applications. Hierarchy management services and their uses are discussed in more detail in Chapters 5 and 6.

NOTE *The classification domains introduced in this chapter have clear implications on MDM architecture. Specifically, although MDM architecture styles defined by these various viewpoints are different, they have many things in common. In reality, it is not unusual to find an MDM implementation that exhibits properties of one or more architecture styles at the same time—for example, acting as a Registry for some master data domain while being a coexistence-style MDM Data Hub for others. Likewise, aside from some very specific capabilities and implementation patterns, the architecture of an MDM Data Hub for a customer domain is significantly similar to that of the product domain, and so on. The latter is one of the enablers of evolving MDM from a single-domain master data management solution to a multidomain Data Hub operating on the same technology platform.*

The relevance of this note is in that it points to the significant flexibility and versatility of the MDM architecture. It also confirms our previous discussion on the value of the architecture frameworks and architecture viewpoints that provide different insights into the same large and complex system.

Reference Architecture Viewpoint

In the previous sections we looked at the key components and architecture viewpoints of the MDM architecture, and showed its complexity and the variety of approaches you could take to select, build, and implement an MDM solution.

However, this discussion would not be complete if we didn't consider another key architectural artifact—a reference architecture viewpoint. Reference architecture is one of the best-known complexity-reducing architecture viewpoints. Let's informally define reference architecture as follows:

> *Reference architecture* is a high-level abstraction of a technical solution to a particular problem domain; it is a set of interlinked components, services, processes, and interfaces organized into functional layers, where each layer provides services to the layers above and consumes services from the layers below. As such, reference architecture does not define specific technologies or implementation details.

The key value proposition of reference architecture is in its ability to help architects and designers to define the functionality and placement of all architecture components in the context of the overall system and problem domain. In other words, reference architecture provides a blueprint and helps create a set of patterns for designing specific solution/system

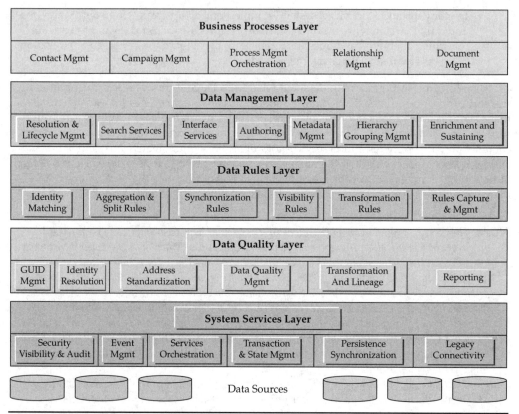

Figure 4-6   MDM reference architecture

components and their interactions. That is why a reference architecture viewpoint is such a powerful tool for designing systems of MDM-level complexity and interdependencies.

Using this definition of the reference architecture, we can define an MDM reference architecture viewpoint as an industry- and data domain–agnostic architectural multilayered abstraction that consists of services, components, processes, and interfaces (see Figure 4-6).

As an instance of an SOA, this MDM reference architecture contains a significant number of key service components. Some of these services are discussed in further detail in Chapters 5 and 6 of the book, but we offer a brief list of higher-level service layers in this section for the purpose of completeness.

- The Data Management layer includes:
  - Interface services, which expose a published and consistent entry point to request MDM services.
  - Entity resolution and lifecycle management services, which enable entity recognition by resolving various levels of identities, and manage life stages of master data by supporting business interactions including traditional Create, Read, Update and Delete (CRUD) activities.
  - Search services, for easy access to the information managed by the MDM Data Hub.

- Authoring services, which allow MDM users to create (author), manage, customize/change, and approve definitions of master data (metadata), including hierarchies and entity groups. In addition, Authoring services enable users to manage (CRUD) specific instances of master data.

- The metadata management service, which provides support for data management aspects of metadata creation, manipulation, and maintenance. The metadata management service supports a metadata repository and relies on and supports internal Data Hub services such as attribute and record locator services and even key generation services.

- Hierarchy, relationships, and groupings management services, which deliver functions designed to manage master data hierarchies, groupings, and relationships. These can process requests from the authoring services.

- Enrichment and sustaining services, which are focused on acquiring and maintaining the correct content of master data, controlled by external data references and user-driven adjustments.

- The Data Rules layer includes key services that are driven by business-defined rules for entity resolution, aggregation, synchronization, visibility and privacy, and transformation.

- The Data Quality layer includes services that are designed to validate and enforce data quality rules, resolve entity identification and hierarchical attributes, and perform data standardization, reconciliation, and lineage. These services also generate and manage global unique identifiers as well as provide data quality profiling and reporting.

- The System Services layer includes a broad category of base services such as security, data visibility, event management (these are designed to react to predefined events detected within the master data by triggering appropriate actions), service management (orchestration, choreography), transaction and state management, system synchronization, and intersystem connectivity/data integration services, including Enterprise Information Integration services for federated data access (discussed in more detail in Chapters 5 and 6).

Despite this long list of services defined in the MDM reference architecture viewpoint, at a high level this reference architecture appears to be deceptively simple. However, a closer look will reveal that most of the components and services of the architecture have to be present in order to accomplish the goal of creating an MDM system. Moreover, many of these components are complex objects that, in turn, contain many lower-level components and services. We will offer a more detailed discussion of some of the components in the subsequent chapters of the book. To set the stage for the detailed discussion, we will organize the components, services, and layers of this high-level conceptual reference architecture into two major groups: traditional architecture concerns of information management and new, advanced concerns driven by the goals of Master Data Management.

The traditional architecture concerns focus on the area of data and data management. These concerns include data architecture and data modeling; data extractions, transformation, and loading; metadata repository and metadata management; database management system performance and scalability; transaction management; backup and recovery; and others (see Figure 4-7).

Advanced MDM-specific concerns include areas such as identity recognition, matching and generation of global unique entity identifiers, persistence of entity identification,

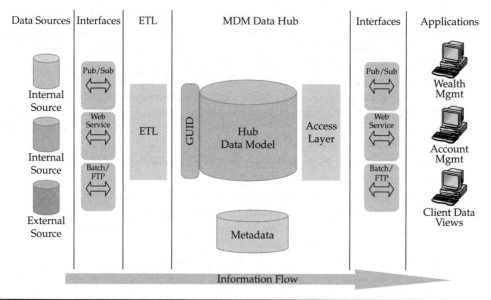

FIGURE 4-7   Traditional data-centric view of MDM architecture.

rules-based and data content–based synchronization to/from legacy, reconciliation and arbitration of data changes, data security and data visibility, service implementation and management integration with legacy environments, and many others (see Figure 4-8).

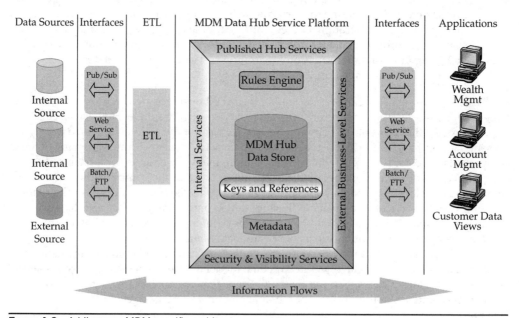

FIGURE 4-8   Adding new MDM-specific architecture concerns

We discuss these traditional and advanced concerns of the MDM architecture in more detail in the remaining chapters of this part of the book and also in Part III. The material in these chapters offers additional insights and architecture viewpoints that should help MDM managers, designers, and implementers to achieve measurable results using a structured and disciplined architecture approach.

References

1. Zachman Enterprise Architecture Framework, Zachman's Institute for Framework Advancement (ZIFA).

2. http://homepage.newschool.edu/het//profiles/pareto.htm.

3. Dreibelbis, Allen, Ivan Milman, Paul van Run, Eberhard Hechler, Martin Oberhofer, and Dan Wolfson. *Enterprise Master Data Management: An SOA Approach to Managing Core Information.* IBM Press (2008).

4. "IBM SOA Foundation, An Architectural Introduction and Overview," 2005. http://www.ibm.com/developerworks/webservices/library/ws-soa-whitepaper/.

5. http://www.w3.org/TR/ws-arch/.

6. http://www.infoq.com/news/2008/09/Orchestration.

7. http://www.w3.org/TR/ws-arch/.

8. http://docs.oasis-open.org/soa-rm/v1.0/soa-rm.pdf.

9. Dubov, Larry, "Guest View: Old Thinking Does a Disservice to New Data Hubs," *SD Times*, October 15, 2009. http://www.sdtimes.com/GUEST_VIEW_OLD_THINKING_DOES_A_DISSERVICE_TO_NEW_DATA_HUBS/By_LARRY_DUBOV/About_DATABASES/33828.

10. www.gartner.com.

11. Berson, Alex, and Stephen J. Smith. *Data Warehousing, Data Mining, & OLAP.* McGraw-Hill (1997).

12. Kimball, Ralph, Margy Ross, Bob Becker, and Joy Mundy. *Kimball's Data Warehouse Toolkit Classics: The Data Warehouse Toolkit, 2nd Edition; The Data Warehouse Lifecycle, 2nd Edition; The Data Warehouse ETL Toolkit.* Wiley (2009).

Data Management Concerns of MDM Architecture: Entities, Hierarchies, and Metadata

T he preceding chapters discussed the enterprise architecture framework as the vehicle that helps resolve a multitude of complex and challenging issues facing MDM designers and implementers. As we focused on the complexity of the MDM architecture, we showed how to apply the enterprise architecture framework to the service-oriented view of the MDM platform, often called an MDM Data Hub. And we also discussed a set of services that any Data Hub platform should provide and/or support in order to deliver key data integration properties of matching, linking detail-level records, and entity and relationship resolution—services that enable the creation and management of a complete view of the products, organizational entities, accounts, customers, parties, and associations and relationships among master entities.

We also started a discussion of the services required to ensure the integrity of the data inside the Data Hub as well as the services designed to enable the synchronization and reconciliation of data changes between the Data Hub and the surrounding systems, applications, and data stores. The synchronization and reconciliation services are especially important because the value of the MDM solution becomes fully recognized only when the master data can be accessed by or delivered to the business consumers, and the delivery mechanisms have to be designed to streamline and improve enterprise-wide business processes using master data.

We discuss master data modeling in Chapter 7. There we explain what data models are to be maintained to support the whole spectrum of MDM requirements, including requirements for the master data models, their key characteristics, and design styles.

We have now reached the point where the discussion of the Data Hub architecture cannot continue without considering the issues and challenges of integrating a Data Hub platform into the overall enterprise information environment. To accomplish this integration, we need to analyze the Data Hub architecture components and services that support cross-system and cross-domain information management requirements. These requirements include challenges of the enterprise data strategy, data governance, data quality, a broad suite of data management technologies, and the organizational roles and responsibilities that enable the effective integration and interoperability between the Data Hub, its data sources, and its consumers (users and applications).

NOTE *As we continue to discuss key issues and concerns of the MDM architecture, services, and components, we focus on the logical and conceptual architecture points of view, and thus we express the functional requirements of MDM services and components in architecture terms. These component and service requirements should not be interpreted literally as the prescription for a specific technical implementation. Some of the concrete implementation approaches—design and product selection guidelines that are based on the currently available industry best practices and state of the art in the MDM product marketplace—are provided in Part IV of this book.*

Data Strategy

This chapter deals primarily with issues related to data management, data delivery, and data integration between a Data Hub system, its sources, and its consumers. In order to discuss the architecture concerns of data management, we need to expand the context of the enterprise architecture framework and its data management dimensions by introducing key concerns and requirements of the enterprise data strategy. Although these concerns include data technology and architecture components, the key insights of the enterprise data strategy are contained in its holistic and multidimensional approach to the issues and concerns related to enterprise-class information management. Those readers already familiar with the concepts of data strategy, data governance, and data stewardship can easily skip this section and proceed directly to the section titled "Managing Data in the Data Hub."

The multifaceted nature of the enterprise data strategy includes a number of interrelated disciplines such as data governance, data quality, data modeling, data management, data delivery, data synchronization and integrity, data security and privacy, data availability, and many others. Clearly, any comprehensive discussion of the enterprise data strategy that covers these disciplines is well beyond the scope of this book. However, in order to define and explain MDM Data Hub requirements to support enterprise-level integration with existing and new applications and systems, at a minimum we need to introduce several key concepts behind data governance, data quality, and data stewardship. Understanding these concepts helps explain the functional requirements of those Data Hub services and components that are designed to find the "right" data in the "right" data store, to measure and improve data quality, and to enable business rules–driven data synchronization between the Data Hub and other systems. We address the concerns of data security and privacy in Part III of this book and additional implementation concerns in Part IV.

Guiding Principles of Information Architecture

Let's start the discussion on data management concerns of MDM with a brief look at the definition and guiding principles of the information architecture.

The Gartner Group defines *enterprise information architecture* as that part of the enterprise architecture process that describes—through a set of requirements, principles, and models—the current state, future state, and guidance necessary to flexibly share and exchange information assets to achieve effective enterprise change.[1]

To paraphrase this, we can define enterprise information architecture (EIA) as the blueprint describing an approach to the creation, management, delivery, and analysis of semantically consistent information structures across existing data sources to find meaningful relations and enable opportunities for effectively exchanging, sharing, and leveraging information.

Using this definition as the guide, we're now in a position to put forward key principles of enterprise information architecture. These principles are based on the analysis of best practices in enterprise information management, and we offer them here as an example and a recommendation only, with the understanding that there are numerous alternate sets of EIA principles. That said, we believe that principles like these are necessary for the enterprise to excel at leveraging data for the benefit of all of its stakeholders by providing better service and better financial returns.

The last point is a general statement about the value of EIA principles. However, because this discussion is offered in the context of Master Data Management, wherever possible, we have tried to be specific and concentrate on Master Data Management as one of the core components of the enterprise information architecture.

- **Principle #1** Information architecture shall be driven by clearly articulated and properly documented business processes.

- **Principle #2** No matter what application is used to create a piece of master data content, this content must be validated against the existing master data.

- **Principle #3** Any data modifications/corrections to master data can be made only according to the rules and policies established by the business, including the rules of resolving data change conflicts; these changes will be made available to all downstream systems based on agreed upon SLAs.

- **Principle #4** Every data item shall have an identified business owner, a custodian (steward), and a single authoritative source that is used by all enterprise stakeholders. We are not making any assumptions about how many systems will be used to capture and update the master data operationally. The authoritative source should obtain all updates in real time and make policy-based decisions about acceptance or rejection of the change for the purpose of enterprise use.

- **Principle #5** The quality of data shall be measured in accordance with information quality standards established by the organization.

- **Principle #6** Information architecture shall ensure data security, integrity, and appropriate access controls.

- **Principle #7** Information architecture shall support the appropriate retention of data at the appropriate level of granularity.

- **Principle #8** Sources, definitions, structures, and usage of shared and common information shall be standardized.

- **Principle #9** Information architecture shall support the definition, assignment, persistence, and synchronization of unique identifiers for all business objects supported and used by the enterprise.

- **Principle #10** Information architecture shall support flexible, accurate, and timely data integration, and promote the creation and maintenance of Master Data Management environments as authoritative systems of record ("single version of the truth").

- **Principle #11**   Information architecture shall provide for consistent, metadata-driven definitions for all data under management.

- **Principle #12**   Information management will include and be based on well-defined data governance rules and policies administered and enforced by appropriately structured and empowered groups, including an Enterprise Data Governance group.

As you can see, these principles of information architecture are prescriptive and help articulate the role of Master Data Management in the overall enterprise information architecture context.

Data Governance

As we discuss Master Data Management, the notion of governance becomes one of the key concepts of effective, proactive, and predictable information management. In general, nontechnical terms, we can define governance as the set of processes and activities that manifest themselves in decisions that define expectations, grant power, or verify performance. In Chapter 17 we focus on data governance in more detail and focus on advanced concepts important for MDM specifically.

In the domain of Information Technology, we can find various branches of governance, including application governance, network governance, and information or data governance. The latter is an important discipline that has profound implications on the way MDM technology is selected, used, and creates value for the enterprise.

Using the general definition of governance shown in the preceding paragraph, we can offer the following working definition of data governance (sometimes called "information governance").

> **Data Governance**
> *Data governance* is a process and quality control discipline focused on managing the quality, consistency, usability, security, and availability of information. This process is complex, multifaceted, and closely linked to the notions of data ownership and stewardship, data quality management, metadata management, and the definition of effective organizational structures to support data governance efficiently and in an agile fashion.

Clearly, according to this definition, data governance becomes a critical component of any MDM initiative. Data governance helps organizations in making decisions about how to manage data, realize value from it, minimize cost and complexity, manage risk, and ensure compliance with ever-growing legal, regulatory, and other requirements. Governance allows organizations not only to create rules about information use, but also to apply effective processes and controls to make sure that the rules are being followed, and to deal with noncompliance and other issues. Data governance is at the forefront of many Information Technology initiatives and activities. The Data Governance Institute is one of the independent organizations that define the principles, standards, and frameworks of data governance.[2]

An integrated MDM data architecture emphasizes the need for and importance of data governance, especially if you consider that even successful MDM initiatives have to deal with a typical enterprise information landscape that contains not only the Data Hub but also many applications and databases that more often than not were developed independently, in a typical stovepipe fashion, and the information they use is often inconsistent, incomplete, and of different quality.

Data governance strategy helps deliver appropriate data to properly authorized users where and when they need it. Moreover, data governance and its data quality component are responsible for creating data quality standards, data quality metrics, and data quality measurement processes that together help deliver acceptable quality data to the consumers—applications and end users.

Data quality improvement and assurance are no longer optional activities. For example, the 2002 Sarbanes-Oxley Act requires, among other things, that a business entity should be able to attest to the quality and accuracy of the data contained in its financial statements. Obviously, the classical "garbage in, garbage out" truism is still alive, and no organization can report high-quality financial data if the source data used to produce the financial numbers is of poor quality. To achieve compliance and to successfully implement an enterprise data governance and data quality strategy, the strategy itself should be treated as a value-added business proposition and sold to the organization's stakeholders to obtain a management buy-in and commitment like any other business case. The value of improved data quality is almost self-evident and includes factors such as the enterprise's ability to make better and more accurate decisions, to collect and analyze competitive trends, to formulate a better and more effective marketing strategy, to define a more attractive and compelling product, to gain deeper insights into the customer's behavior, to understand the customer's propensity to buy products and services, the probability of the customer's engaging in high-risk transactions, the probability of attrition, and so on. The data governance strategy is not limited to data quality and data management standards and policies. It includes critically important concerns of defining organizational structures and job roles responsible for monitoring and enforcing compliance with these policies and standards throughout the organization.

Committing an organization to implement a robust data governance strategy requires an implementation plan that follows a well-defined and proven methodology. Several effective data governance methodologies are available, and we will discuss some of them in Chapter 17. No matter what data governance methodology is used, we can stipulate that a high-level data governance strategy should be aligned with and based on the key principles of the enterprise information architecture, discussed in the previous section. For the sake of completeness, this section reviews the key steps of a generic data governance strategy program as it may apply to the MDM Data Hub:

- *Define a data governance process.* This is the key in enabling monitoring and reconciliation of data between the Data Hub and its sources and consumers. The data governance process should cover not only the initial data load but also data refinement, standardization, and aggregation activities along the path of the end-to-end information flow. The data governance process includes such data management and data quality concerns as the elimination of duplicate entries and the creation of linking and matching keys. We will show in Chapter 6 that these unique identifiers help aggregate or merge individual records into groups or clusters based on certain criteria (for example, a household affiliation or a business entity). As the Data Hub is integrated into the overall enterprise data management environment, the data governance process should define the mechanisms that create and maintain valid cross-reference information using approaches such as Record Locator metadata that enables linkages between the Data Hub and other systems. In addition, a data governance process should contain steps that support manual corrections of false positive and negative matches as well as the exception processing of errors that cannot be handled automatically.

- *Design, select, and implement a data management and data delivery technology suite.* In the case of an MDM Data Hub, both data management and data distribution/delivery technologies play a key role in enabling a fully integrated MDM solution regardless of the MDM Use Pattern (Analytical or Operational MDM) and the architecture style of the Data Hub, be it a Registry, a Reconciliation Engine, or a Transaction Hub. Later in this chapter we use the principles and capabilities of service-oriented architecture (SOA) to discuss the data management and data delivery aspects of the Data Hub architecture and the related data governance strategy.

- *Enable auditability and accountability for all data under management that is in scope for data governance strategy.* Auditability is extremely important because it not only provides verifiable records of the data access activities but also serves as an invaluable tool to help achieve compliance with the current and emerging regulations, including the Gramm-Leach-Bliley Act and its data protection clause, the Sarbanes-Oxley Act, and the Basel II and III Capital Accords. Auditability works hand in hand with accountability of data management and data delivery actions. Accountability requires the creation and empowerment of several data governance roles within the organization, including data owners and data stewards. These roles should be created at appropriate levels of the organization and assigned to the dedicated organizational units or individuals.

Let's briefly look at the concept of data stewards and their role in assessing, improving, and managing data quality. We will focus on these topics again in Part IV to discuss them in more detail.

Data Stewardship and Ownership

One of the key principles of the enterprise information architecture (Principle #4) states that every data item shall have an identified business owner and a custodian (steward).

As the name implies, data owners are those individuals or groups within the organization that are in the position to obtain, create, and have significant control over the content (and sometimes, access to and the distribution of) the data. Data owners often belong to a business rather than a technology organization. For example, an insurance agent may be the owner of the list of contacts of his or her clients and prospects.

The concept of data stewardship is different from data ownership. Data stewards do not own the data and do not have complete control over its use. Their role is to ensure that adequate, agreed-upon quality metrics are maintained on a continuous basis. In order to be effective, data stewards should work with data architects, database administrators, ETL (Extract, Transform, Load) designers, business intelligence and reporting application architects, and business data owners to define and apply appropriate data usage policies and data quality metrics. These cross-functional teams are responsible for identifying deficiencies in systems, applications, data stores, and processes that create and change data and thus may introduce or create data quality problems. One consequence of having a robust data stewardship program is its ability to help the members of the IT organization to enhance appropriate architecture components to improve data quality, availability, and integrity.

Data stewards must help create and actively participate in processes that would allow the establishment of business context–defined, measurable data quality goals. Only after an organization has defined and agreed with the data quality goals can the data stewards devise appropriate data quality improvement programs.

These data quality goals and improvement programs should be driven primarily by business units, so it stands to reason that in order to gain full knowledge of the data quality issues, their roots, and the business impact of these issues, a data steward should be a member of a business team. Regardless of whether a data steward works for a business team or acts as a "virtual" member of the team, the data steward has to be very closely aligned with the Information Technology group in order to discover and mitigate the risks introduced by inadequate data quality.

Extending this logic even further, we can say that a data steward would be most effective if he or she can operate as close to the point of data acquisition as technically possible. For example, a steward for customer contact and service complaint data that is created in a company's service center may be most effective when operating inside that service center.

Finally, and in accordance with information architecture and data governance principles, data stewards have to be accountable for improving the data quality of the information domain they oversee. This means not only appropriate levels of empowerment but also the organization's willingness and commitment to make the data steward's data quality responsibility his or her primary job function, so that data quality improvement is recognized as an important business function that treats data as a valuable corporate asset.

Data Quality

Whether an enterprise is deploying an MDM solution or is using more traditional data management approaches (data warehouses, operational data stores, and so on), one undisputable fact about the value and use of data remains—any business process that is based on the assumption of having access to trustworthy, accurate, and timely data will produce invalid, unexpected, and meaningless results if this assumption is false and the processes that capture and manage the input data don't recognize data quality shortcomings and don't have mechanisms or steps in place to ensure the required data quality levels.

MDM Data Hub is a powerful concept with a rich set of value-added capabilities. But even the most sophisticated MDM solution can deliver a single view of master data only if it can trust the source data and the processes and systems that deliver that data into the Data Hub. In Part IV, we get into more implementation details on the topic of relationships between MDM and data quality and discuss master data quality processes and metrics.

In other words, we cannot discuss Master Data Management without paying serious attention to the issues of data quality, and recognizing that data quality for Master Data Management can be affected by two related factors—data quality of the input data collected from a variety of internal and external sources, and the impact on data quality that results from the shortcomings of the upstream business processes that handle input data before it is entered into the Data Hub. The notion that MDM data quality is linked to the efficiency and effectiveness of the upstream business processes is a profound concern that has become a topic of extensive discussions in the business and technology community that deal with not just data management but also with Business Process Management (BPM).

In this chapter, however, we concentrate on the data side of the data quality issues, because BPM is a large and complex topic in its own right and is outside the scope of this book.

> ### Data Quality
> *Data quality* is one of the key components of any successful data strategy and data governance initiative, and is one of the core enabling requirements for Master Data Management. Conversely, MDM is a powerful technique that helps enterprises improve the quality of master data.

Creating a new authoritative source from information of low quality is almost an impossible task. Similarly, when data quality is poor, matching and linking records for potential aggregation will most likely result in low match accuracy and produce an unacceptable number of false negative and false positive outcomes.

Valuable lessons about the importance of data quality are abundant, and data quality concerns confronted data architects, application designers, and business users even before the problem started to manifest itself in such early data integration programs as Customer Information Files (CIF), early implementations of data warehouses, Customer Relationship Management (CRM), and Business Intelligence (BI) solutions. Indeed, if you look at a data integration solution such as a data warehouse, published statistics show that as high as 75 percent of the data warehouse development effort is allocated to data preparation, validation, extraction, transformation, and loading (e.g., by using ETL tools). Over 50 percent of these activities are spent on cleansing and standardizing the data.

Although there is a wide variety of ETL and data-cleansing tools that address some of the data quality problems, data quality continues to be a complex, enterprise-wide challenge. Part of the complexity that needs to be addressed is driven by the ever-increasing performance requirements. A data-cleansing tool that would take more than 24 hours to cleanse a customer file is a poor choice for a real-time or a Web-based customer service application. As the performance and throughput requirements continue to increase, the functional and technical capabilities of the data quality tools sometimes struggle to keep up with the demand.

But performance is not the primary issue. A key challenge of data quality is an incomplete or unclear set of semantic definitions of what the data is supposed to represent, in what form, with what kind of timeliness requirements, and so on. These definitions are ideally stored in a *metadata repository*. However, our experience shows that even when an enterprise adapts a metadata strategy and implements a metadata repository, it often contains incomplete or erroneous (poor quality) definitions. We discuss metadata issues in more detail later in this chapter.

The quality of metadata may be low, not because organizations or data stewards do not work hard on defining it, but primarily because there are many data quality dimensions and contexts, each of which may require a different approach to the measurement and improvement of the data quality. For example, if we want to measure and improve address information about customers, there are numerous techniques and reference data sources that can provide an accurate view of a potentially misspelled or incomplete address. Similarly, if we need to validate a social security number or a driver license number, we can use a variety of authoritative sources of this information to validate and correct the data. The problem becomes much harder when we have to deal with names or similar attributes for which there is no predefined domain or a business rule. For example, "Alec" may be a valid name or a misspelled version of "Alex." If evaluated independently, and not in the context of, say, postal information about a name and the address, this problem often requires human intervention to resolve the uncertainty.

Finally, as the sophistication of the data quality improvement process grows, so do its cost and processing requirements. It is not unusual to hear that an organization would be reluctant to implement an expensive data quality improvement system because, according to them, "So far the business and our customers have not complained, so the data quality issue must not be as bad as you describe." This is not an invalid argument, although it may be somewhat shortsighted from the strategic point of view, especially because many aspects of data quality fall under government- and industry-regulated requirements.

Data Quality Tools and Technologies

Many tools automate portions of the tasks associated with cleansing, extracting, loading, and auditing data from existing data stores into a new target environment—be it a data warehouse or an MDM Data Hub. Most of these tools fall into one of several major categories:

- **Profiling tools** They tools enhance the accuracy and correctness of the data at the source. These tools generally compare the data in the source database to a set of business rules that are either explicitly defined or automatically inferred from a scan operation of the data file or a database catalog.

  Profiling tools can determine the cardinality of certain data attributes, value ranges of the attributes in the data set, and the missing and incomplete data values, among other things. These tools would produce various data quality reports and can use their output to automate certain data-cleansing and data correction operations.

- **Data-cleansing tools** These tools employ various deterministic, probabilistic, or machine learning techniques to correct the data problems discovered by the profiling tools. These tools generally compare the data in the data source to a set of business rules and domain constraints stored in the metadata repository or in an external rules repository. Traditionally, these tools were designed to access external reference data such as a valid name and address file from an external "trusted" data provider (for example, Acxiom or Dun & Bradstreet) or an authoritative postal information file (for example, a National Change of Address [NCOA] file) or to use a service that validates social security numbers. The data-cleansing process improves the quality of the data and potentially adds new, accurate content. Therefore, this process is sometimes referred to as "data enrichment."

- **Data-parsing and standardization tools** The parsers break a record into atomic units that can be used in subsequent steps. For example, such a tool would parse one contiguous address record into separate street, city, state, and ZIP code fields. Data standardization tools convert the data attributes to what is often called a canonical format or a canonical data model—a standard format used by all components of the data acquisition process and the target Data Hub.

Canonical Data Format

Canonical data format is a format that is independent of any specific application. It provides a level of abstraction from applications' native data formats by supporting a common format that can either be used by all applications or may require transformation adapters that convert data between the canonical and native formats. Adding a new application or a new data source may only require a new adapter or modifying an old one, thus drastically reducing the impact on applications. A canonical data format is often encoded in XML.

- **Data Extract, Transform, and Load (ETL) tools** These are not data quality tools in the pure sense of the term. ETL tools are primarily designed to extract data from known structures of the source systems based on prepared and validated source data mapping, transforming input formats of the extracted files into a predefined target data store format (for example, a Data Hub), and loading the transformed data into a target data environment (for example, the Data Hub). Because ETL tools are aware of the target schema, they can prepare and load the data in a way that preserves various integrity constraints, including referential integrity and the domain integrity constraints. ETL tools can filter out records that fail a data validity check and usually produce exception reports used by data stewards to address data quality issues discovered at the load stage. This functionality helps ensure data quality and the integrity of the target data store, which is the reason we mentioned ETL tools in this section.

- **Hybrid packages**   These packages may contain a complete set of ETL components enriched by a data parser and a standardization engine, the data profiling components, and the data-cleansing components. These extract, parse, standardize, cleanse, transform, and load processes are executed by a hybrid packaged software in sequence and load consistently formatted and cleansed data into the Data Hub.

Managing Data in the Data Hub

Armed with the knowledge of the role of the enterprise data strategy, we can discuss MDM Data Hub concerns that have to deal with acquiring, rationalizing, cleansing, transforming, and loading data into the Data Hub as well as the concerns of delivering the right data to the right consumer at the right time over the right channel. In this chapter, we also discuss interesting challenges and approaches of distributing and synchronizing data in the Data Hub with applications and systems used to source the data in the first place.

Let's start with the already familiar Data Hub conceptual architecture that we first introduced in Chapter 4. This architecture shows the Data Hub data store and supporting services in the larger context of the data management architecture (see Figure 5-1). From the data strategy point of view, this architecture view depicts data sources that feed the loading process, the data access and data delivery interfaces, the ETL service layer, the Data Hub platform, and some generic consuming applications.

However, to better position our discussion of the data-related concerns, let's transform our Data Hub conceptual architecture into a view that is specifically designed to emphasize data flows and operations related to managing data in and around the Data Hub.

Data Zone Architecture Approach

To address data management concerns of the Data Hub environment, we introduce the concept of the data zones and the supporting architectural components and services. The Data Zone architecture, illustrated in Figure 5-2, employs sound architecture principles of the separation of concerns and loose coupling.

Separation of Concerns

In software design, the principle of *separation of concerns* is linked to specialization and cooperation: When one is designing a complex system, the familiar trade-off is between a few generic modules that can perform various functions versus many specialized modules designed to work together in a cooperative fashion. In complex systems, specialization of components helps address the required functionality in a focused fashion, organizing groups of concerns into separate, designated, and specifically designed components.

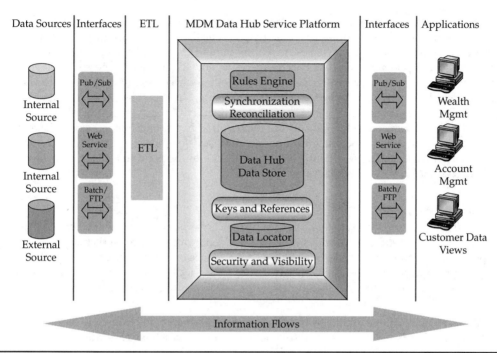

Figure 5-1   Conceptual Data Hub components and services architecture view

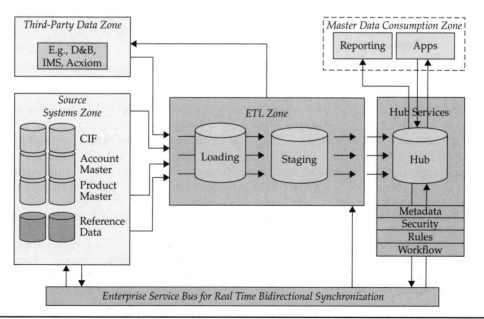

Figure 5-2   Data Hub architecture—Data Zone view

Turning to nature, consider the differences between simple and complex organisms. Whereas simple organisms contain several generic cells that perform all life-sustaining functions, a complex organism (for example, an animal) is "built" from a number of specialized "components" such as heart, lungs, eyes, and so on. Each of these components performs its functions in a cooperative fashion, together with other components of the body. In other words, when the complexity is low to moderate, having a few generic components simplifies the overall design. However, as the complexity of the system grows, the specialization of components helps address the required functionality in a focused fashion, by organizing groups of concerns into separate, designed-for-purpose components.

We briefly discussed the principle of loose coupling in the previous chapter when we looked at service-oriented architectures.

Loose Coupling
In software design, *loose coupling* refers to the design approach that avoids rigid, tightly coupled structures where changes to one component force some related changes to propagate throughout the systems, and where a failure or the poor performance of one component may bring the entire system down. Often, loosely coupled components or services can be exposed to the enterprise for reuse in multiple systems.

When we apply these architecture principles to the data architecture view of the Data Hub, we can clearly delineate several functional domains, which we call "zones." The data zones shown in Figure 5-2 include the following:

- Source Systems zone
- Third-Party Data Provider zone
- ETL/Acquisition zone
- Hub Services zone
- Master Data Consumption zone
- Enterprise Service Bus zone

To make it very clear, this zone structure is a logical design construct that should be used as a guide to help solve the complexity of data management issues. The Zone Architecture approach allows architects to consider complex data management issues in the context of the overall enterprise data architecture, but address them within the context of a relevant zone. As a design guide, it does not mean that a Data Hub implementation has to include every zone and every component. A specific MDM implementation may include a small subset of the data zones and their respective processes and components.

Let's review the key concerns addressed by the data zones shown in Figure 5-2.

- *The Source Systems zone* is the province of existing data sources, and the concerns of managing these sources include good procedural understanding of data structures; content; timeliness; update periodicity; and such operational concerns as platform support, data availability, data access interfaces, access methods to the data sources, batch window processing requirements, and so on. In addition to the source data, this zone contains enterprise reference data, such as code tables used by an organization to provide product name–to–product code mapping, state code tables, branch numbers, account type reference tables, and so on. This zone contains "raw material" that is loaded into the Data Hub and uses information stored in the metadata repository to determine data attributes, formats, source system names, and location pointers.

- *The Third-Party Data Provider zone* deals with external data providers and their information. An organization often purchases this information to cleanse and enrich input data prior to loading it into a target environment such as a Data Hub. For example, if the Data Hub is designed to handle customer information, the quality of the customer data loaded into the Data Hub would have a profound impact on the linking and matching processes as well as on the Data Hub's ability to deliver an accurate and complete view of a customer. Errors, the use of aliases, and a lack of standards in customer name and address fields are most common and are the main causes of poor customer data quality. To rectify this problem an organization may decide to use a third-party data provider that specializes in maintaining an accurate customer name and address database (Acxiom, D&B, and so on). The third-party data provider usually receives a list of records from an organization, matches them against the provider's database of verified and maintained records, and sends updated records back to the organization for processing. Thus, the third-party zone supporting this processing is concerned with the following processes:

  - Creating a file extract of entity records to be sent to the provider
  - Ensuring that the extracted records are protected and that only absolutely minimal necessary information is sent to the provider in order to protect confidential data
  - Receiving an updated file of cleansed records enriched with accurate and perhaps additional information
  - Making the updated file available for ETL processing
  - Making appropriate changes to the content of the metadata repository for use by other data zones

  Alternatively, an enterprise may look for third-party data to verify and enrich a set of financial instruments—for example, getting market or pricing information from authoritative sources of such data, including feeds from stock exchanges. In this case, the processes implemented inside the third-party zone may include the generation of service requests to receive necessary data from the external provider based on a previously established contract. Such requests may be executed as request-response messages using standard protocols, as real-time streaming data feeds, or as Web Services calls.

- *The ETL/Acquisition zone* is the province of ETL tools and their corresponding processes. These tools are designed to extract data from known structures of the source systems based on prepared and validated source-to-target data mapping; transforming input formats of the extracted files into a predefined target data store format (for example, a Data Hub); and loading the transformed data into the Data Hub using either a standard technique or a proprietary one. The transformations may be quite complex and can perform substitutions, aggregations, and logical and mathematical operations on data attribute values. ETL tools may access an internal or external metadata repository to obtain the information about the transformation rules, integrity constraints, and target Data Hub schema, and therefore can prepare and load the

PART II

data while preserving various integrity constraints. Many proven, mature solutions can perform ETL operations in an extremely efficient, scalable fashion.

Modern ETL tools can parallelize all operations to achieve very high performance and throughput on very large data sets. These solutions can be integrated with an enterprise metadata repository and a BI tool repository.

- An effective design approach to the Acquisition/ETL data zone is to use a multistage data acquisition environment. To illustrate this point, we consider a familiar analogy of a loading dock for a "brick-and-mortar" warehouse facility. Figure 5-2 shows a two-stage conceptual Acquisition/ETL data zone, where the first stage, called the *Loading zone,* is acting as a recipient of the data extraction activities. Depending on the complexity and interdependencies involved in data cleansing, enrichment, and transformation, a Loading zone may serve as a facility where all input data streams are normalized and consolidated into a common, canonical format. The third-party data provider usually receives an appropriate set of data in such a canonical format. The Loading zone is a convenient place where the initial audit and profiling of input records can take place.

- *The Staging zone,* on the other hand, is a holding area for the already cleansed, enriched, and transformed data received from the Loading zone as well as the data processed by and received from a third-party data provider. The Staging zone data structure could be similar to that of the Data Hub. The benefits of having a Staging zone include efficiency in loading data into the Data Hub (often using a database-specific utility function, because the transformations are already completed). The Staging zone offers access to a convenient area to perform a record-level audit before completing the load operation. Finally, a Staging zone provides for an easy-to-use, efficient, and convenient Data Hub reload/recovery point that does not depend on the availability of the source systems.

- *The Hub Services zone* deals with the data management services that create and maintain the structures and the information content inside the Data Hub. We described the SOA reference architecture and several of these services in Chapter 4. In this chapter, we discuss Data Hub services that support data synchronization, data distribution, reconciliation of conflicting data changes, system and information integration, and metadata services that use a metadata repository to enforce semantic consistency of the information. Other MDM services (including Linking, Matching, Record Locator, and Attribute Locator services) are discussed in Chapter 6, and more implementation details of these services are provided in Part IV.

- *The Master Data Consumption zone* is concerned with data delivery–related issues such as formats, messages, protocols, interfaces, and services that enable effective and easy-to-use access to the required information, whether it resides in the Data Hub or in the surrounding systems. The Master Data Consumption zone is designed to provide data to support business applications including Business Intelligence applications, CRM, and functional applications such as account opening and maintenance, aggregated risk assessment, and others. The Master Data Consumption zone enables delivery and distribution of master data, especially reference data, to the requesting applications based on predefined and agreed-upon protocols. This distribution is governed by the service-level agreements (or Web Service contracts) between a Data Hub as a service provider and various service consumers. The Master Data Consumption zone supports persistent data delivery and virtual, just-in-time data integration technologies, including Enterprise Information Integration (EII) solutions. Like other zones, the Master Data Consumption zone takes advantage of the metadata repository to determine data definitions, data formats, and data location pointers.

- *The Enterprise Service Bus (ESB) zone* deals with technologies, protocols, message formats, interfaces, and services that support a message-based communication fabric between all components and services of the MDM data architecture. The goal of the ESB is to support the loosely coupled nature of the Data Hub service-oriented architecture (SOA) by providing a message-based integration mechanism that ensures guaranteed, once-and-only-once, sequence-preserving message delivery that can support transactional semantics if and when appropriate.

Now that we have reviewed the contents and purposes of the architecture zones, we can expand these concepts by including several high-level services that are available to various data architecture components, including the Data Hub. Many of these services are shown in the MDM Reference Architecture diagram (see Figure 5-3). Most of these services are a part of the Data Management Layer of the reference architecture, while some are located in the lower layers of the architecture.

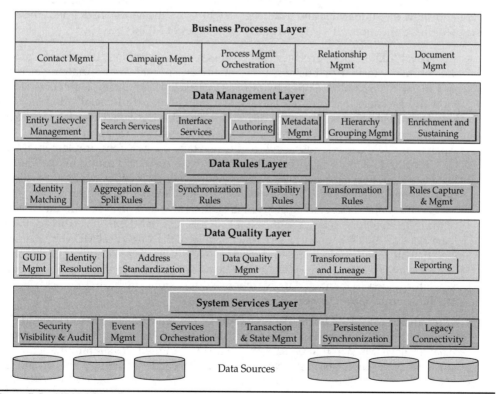

FIGURE 5-3 MDM SOA reference architecture

The list of MDM Data Hub service groups dealing with data management include:

- Integration services and Legacy Connectivity services
- Data Normalization and Enrichment services
- Data Hub Lifecycle Management services
- Data Synchronization and Reconciliation services
- Data Location and Delivery services

Many of these services are briefly described in Chapter 4. We discuss additional details of some of these services in the following sections as we continue the Data Zone architecture discussion.

Operational and Analytical MDM and Data Zones

As we described in Chapter 4, MDM is a complex set of technologies and design patterns. We described an approach to analyze MDM complexity that is based on various MDM classification dimensions. One of the dimensions that is particularly relevant to the discussion of information architecture and data management is the Use Pattern dimension, which differentiates MDM architectures based on how the master data is used—specifically, as an Analytical, Operational, or Collaborative MDM. In this section, we will map the two primary types of MDMs—Analytical and Operational—to the Data Zone architecture concept and show the similarities and differences in the ways the zones are defined. To set the stage for this discussion, let's briefly review these types of MDMs:

- **Analytical MDM** Supports business processes and applications that use master data primarily to analyze business performance and provide appropriate reporting and analytical capabilities, often by directly interfacing with Business Intelligence tools and packages. Analytical MDM tends to be read-mostly. It usually does not change or create source data in the operational systems but does cleanse and enrich data in the MDM Data Hub. From the Data Zone architecture point of view, Analytical MDM can be architected to fully leverage the ETL zone, implement Data Cleansing and Lifecycle services in the Hub Services zone, and configure the Master Data Consumption zone and Data Delivery/Distribution services to act as a feeder into the enterprise data warehouse and domain-specific data marts. Clearly, Data Synchronization services aimed at keeping upstream systems in sync with the content of the Data Hub don't play a significant role in this type of MDM. Nevertheless, the Data Zone architecture enables core functionality of the Analytical MDM by making sure that all zones' components and services work in concert to create or enrich an accurate, integrated view of the master data inside the data warehouse, and provide key information to manage data warehouse dimensions, including necessary attributes to support slow-changing dimensions.

- **Operational MDM** Allows master data to be collected, changed, and used to process business transactions. The principal difference between Operational and Analytical MDMs is in that Operational MDM is designed to maintain the semantic consistency of the master data throughout the transactional activity and provides a mechanism to correct data quality issues by communicating necessary changes to the operational systems, where the data is usually created. By design, Operational MDM systems uses the full power of all data zones and leverage their services and functions to ensure that the accurate, single version of the truth is maintained in the MDM Data Hub and propagated to the core systems. Data Integration, Legacy Connectivity, Synchronization, Delivery and Distribution, Data Cleansing, Enrichment, and Lifecycle services all work in concert to support this MDM architecture.

In summary, although both Analytical and Operational MDM architecture styles map equally well onto the concept of the Data Zone architecture, their similarities and differences are clearly underlined and brought into focus by the way the data zones should be configured and integrated into the overall enterprise information architecture.

Loading Data into the Data Hub

The data architecture concerns discussed in the beginning of this section have a profound impact on the overall Data Hub architecture and, in particular, its data management and data delivery aspects. The Data Zone architecture view shown in Figure 5-2 can help define new, effective design patterns; additional services and components that would support any generic data integration platform; and, in particular, a Data Hub system for Master Data Management.

The level of abstraction of the Data Zone architecture is sufficiently high to be applicable equally well not only to the major types of MDMs—that is, Analytical and Operational MDMs—but also to all major styles of the Data Hub design, including Registry style, Reconciliation Hub style, and, ultimately, full Transaction Hub style. However, as we take a closer look at these design styles, we discover that the way the data is loaded and synchronized varies significantly from one style to another (see Chapter 4 for more details on these MDM architecture styles). Indeed, consider the key difference between these styles—the scope of data for which the Data Hub is the master. Here are some specifics:

- The *Registry style* of the MDM Data Hub architecture represents a Registry of unique master entity identifiers (created using identity attributes). It maintains only the identifying attributes. These attributes are used by an entity resolution service to identify which master entity records should be linked because they represent the same customer, product, location, and so on. The Data Hub matches and links the records that share the same identity. The Data Hub creates and maintains links with data sources that were used to obtain the identity attributes. The MDM Data Hub exposes a set of services that return a fully assembled holistic entity view to the consuming application to either retrieve or assemble a holistic entity view (for example, a customer, at run time). In the case of MDM for customer domain, the Registry-style Data Hub maintains some at least matching customer profile attributes that the Hub uses to generate a unique customer identifier; it can automatically generate and maintain links with all upstream systems that maintain data about the customers, and acts as the arbiter that determines which attribute values in the source systems are better than others by applying attribute survivorship rules across multiple systems.

- The *Reconciliation Engine style* (sometimes also called the Coexistence Hub) supports an evolutionary stage of the Data Hub that enables coexistence between the old and new masters, and by extension provides for a federated data ownership model that helps address both inter- and intra-organizational challenges of who controls which data. The Data Hub of this style is a system of record for *some* but not all data attributes. It provides active synchronization between itself and the systems that were used to create the Hub data content or still maintain some of the Hub data attributes inside their data stores. By definition of the "master," the data attributes for which the Data Hub is the master need to be maintained, created, and changed in the Data Hub. These changes have to be propagated to the upstream and downstream systems that use these data attributes. The goal is to enable synchronization of the data content between the Data Hub and other systems on a continuous basis. The complexity of this scenario increases dramatically as some of the data attributes maintained in the Data Hub are not simply copied but rather *derived* using business-defined transformations on the attributes maintained in other systems.

- The *Transaction Hub* represents a design style where the Hub maintains *all* data attributes about the target subject area. In the case of a MDM Data Hub for customer domain, the subject area is the customer (individuals or businesses). In this case, the Data Hub becomes a "master" of customer information, and as such should be the source of all changes that affect any data attribute about the customer. This design approach demands that the Data Hub is engineered as a complete transactional environment that maintains its data integrity and is the sole source of changes that it propagates to all systems. This design also dictates that the systems integrated with the MDM Data Hub disable their data entry and maintenance interfaces as they relate to the given master data domain.

The conceptual Data Hub architecture shown in Figure 5-1 and its Data Zone viewpoint shown in Figure 5-2 should address the following *common* data architecture concerns:

- **Batch and real-time input data processing**   Some or all data content in the Data Hub is acquired from existing internal and external data sources. The data acquisition process affects the Source System zone, the Third-Party Data Provider zone, and the Acquisition/ETL data zone. It uses several relevant services, including Data Integration services, Data Normalization and Enrichment services, Lifecycle Management services, Entity Resolution services (including Linking, Matching, and Key Generation services), and Metadata Management services that use Record Locator and Attribute Locator services. Moreover, the data-acquisition process can support two different modes—initial data load and delta processing of incremental changes. The former implies a full refresh of the Data Hub data content, and it is usually designed as a batch process. The data-processing mode may support either batch or real-time processing. In the case of batch design, the data processing, at least for the newly inserted records, can leverage the same technology components and services used for the initial data load. The technology suite that enables the initial load and batch data processing has to support high-performance, scalable ETL functionality that architecturally "resides" in the Acquisition/ETL data zone and usually represents a part of the enterprise data strategy and architecture framework. Real-time data processing, on the other hand, should take full advantage of service-oriented architecture, including the Enterprise Service Bus zone, and in many cases is implemented as a set of transactional services that include Data Hub Lifecycle Management services, Transaction and State Management services, and Synchronization services.

- **Data quality processes**   To improve the accuracy of the matching and linking process, many Data Hub environments implement data cleansing, standardization, and enrichment preprocessing in the Third-Party Data Provider and Acquisition/ETL zones before the data is loaded into the Data Hub. These processes use Integration services and Data Normalization and Enrichment services, and frequently leverage external, industry-accepted reference data sources such as Dun & Bradstreet for business information or Acxiom for personal information. It should be noted that some Data Hub vendor solutions are very effective in record matching and linking without prior standardization. Any standardization process has a risk of loosing valuable information, which can adversely impact the quality of match if advanced matching algorithms are used. Still, standardization is often required for reasons other than record matching and linking.

NOTE   *Mapping Data Hub service to the data zones by using a service-oriented architecture approach allows Data Hub designers to abstract and isolate services from the actual location of the methods and functions that execute them regardless of which architecture zone these methods reside in.*

Data Synchronization

As data content changes, a sophisticated and efficient synchronization activity between the "master" and the "slaves" has to take place on a periodic or an ongoing basis depending on the business requirements. Where the Data Hub is the master of some or all attributes of the entities in question, the synchronization flows have to originate from the Hub toward other systems. Complexity grows if existing business processes treat some applications and/or data stores as a master for certain attributes that are also stored in the Data Hub. In this case, every time one of these data attributes changes in the existing system, this change has to be delivered to the Data Hub for synchronization. One good synchronization design principle is to implement one or many unidirectional synchronization flows, as opposed to a more complex bidirectional synchronization. In either approach, the synchronization process may require transactional conflict-resolution mechanisms, compensating transaction designs, and other synchronization and reconciliation functionality, and often causes a revision or change to the existing business processes that rely on the availability of the golden record of master data.

A variety of reasons drive the complexity of data synchronization across multiple distributed systems. In the context of an MDM Data Hub, synchronization becomes difficult to manage when the entire data environment that includes the Data Hub and the legacy systems is in a peer-to-peer relationship. This is not an MDM-specific issue; however, if it exists, it may defeat the entire purpose and benefits of building an MDM platform. In this case, there is no clear master role assigned to a Data Hub or other systems for some or all data attributes, and thus changes to some "shared" data attributes may occur simultaneously but on different systems and applications. Synchronizing these changes may involve complex business rules–driven reconciliation logic. For example, consider a typical non-key attribute such as telephone number. Let's assume that this attribute resides in the legacy Customer Information File (CIF), a customer service center (CRM) system, and also in the Data Hub, where it is used for the matching and linking of records. An example of a difficult scenario would be as follows:

- A customer changes his or her phone number and makes a record of this change via an online self-service channel that updates the CIF. At the same time, the customer contacts a service center and tells a customer service representative (CSR) about the change. The CSR uses a CRM application to make the change in the customer profile and contact records but mistypes the number. As the result, the CIF and the CRM systems now contain different information, and both systems are sending their changes to each other and to the Data Hub for the required record update.

- If the Data Hub receives two changes simultaneously, it will have to decide which information is correct or should take precedence before the changes are applied to the Hub record.

- If the changes arrive one after another over some time interval, the Data Hub needs to decide if the first change should override the second, or vice versa. This is not a simple "first-in first-serve" system because the changes can arrive into the Data Hub after the internal CIF and CRM processing is completed, and their timing does not have to coincide with the time when the change transaction was originally applied.

- Of course, you can extend this scenario by imagining a new application that accesses the Data Hub and can make changes directly to it. Then all systems participating in this change transaction are facing the challenge of receiving two change records and deciding which one to apply, if any.

This situation is not just possible but also quite probable, especially when you consider that the Data Hub has to be integrated into an existing enterprise data and application environment. Of course, should the organization implement a comprehensive data governance strategy and agree to recognize and respect data owners and data stewards, it will be in a position to decide on a single ownership for each data attribute under management. Unfortunately, not every organization is successful in implementing these data management principles. Therefore, we should consider defining conceptual Data Hub components that can perform data synchronization and reconciliation actions in accordance with a set of business rules enforced by a business rules engine (BRE).

Overview of Business Rules Engines

There are many definitions of *business rules engine*. The simplest one says that a business rules engine is a software system that executes one or more business rules in a runtime production environment.[3] If we want to be more specific about business rules engines in the context of MDM Data Hub architecture, we can offer the following definition.

Business Rules Engine

A *business rules engine (BRE)* is a software application or a system that is designed to manage and enforce business rules based on a specified stimulus (for example, an event of attribute value changes). Business rules engines are usually architected as software components that separate the business rules from the application code. This separation helps reduce the time, effort, and costs of application maintenance by allowing the business users to modify the rules as necessary without the need for application changes.

In general, a BRE supports functionality that helps register, classify, and manage the business rules it is designed to enforce. In addition, a BRE can provide functionality that detects inconsistencies within individual business rules (for example, a rule that violates business logic) as well as rule sets.

Rule Set

A *rule set* is a collection of rules that apply to a particular event and must be evaluated together.

In the context of the MDM Data Hub Synchronization services, BRE software manages the rules that define how to reconcile the conflicts of bi-directional synchronization (clearly, a BRE software can be used to support other MDM capabilities, such as linking and matching, attribute survivorship, and so on). For example, if a date-of-birth attribute is changed in the CRM system supporting the service center and in the self-service Web channel, an organization may define a business rule that requires the changes to this attribute that came from the self-service channel to take precedence over any other changes. A more complex rule may dictate to accept changes to the date of birth only if the resulting age of the customer does not exceed the value of 65. There may be another business rule that would require a management approval in the case where the age value is greater than 65. The BRE would evaluate and enforce all rules that apply to a particular event. BRE technologies can also be used to define the workflows around data issues resolution, data stewardship, and in some applications typically powered by MDM (for example, customer on-boarding, account opening and management, and product modeling).

At a minimum, a full-function BRE will include the following components:

- **Business rules repository**   A database that stores the business rules defined by the business users

- **Business rules designer/editor**   An intuitive, easy-to-use, front-end application and user interface that allows users to define, design, document, and edit business rules

- **A query and reporting component**   Allows users and rules administrators to query and report on existing rules

- **Rules engine execution core**   The actual code that enforces the rules

Several types of business rules engines are available today that differ by at least the following two dimensions: by the way they enforce the rules and by the types of rules they support. The first dimension differentiates the engines that *interpret* business rules in a way similar to a script execution from the engines that "compile" business rules into an internal executable form to drastically increase the performance of the engine. The second dimension is driven by the types of rules—that is, inference rules and reaction rules. Here are some specifics:

- *Inference engines* support complex rules that require an answer to be inferred based on conditions and parameters. For example, an Inference BRE would answer a question such as, "Should this customer be offered an increased credit line?"

- *Reaction rules engines* evaluate reaction rules automatically based on the context of the event. The engine would provide an automatic reaction in the form of a real-time message, directive, feedback, or alert to a designated user. For example, if the customer age in the Data Hub was changed to qualify for mandatory retirement account distribution, the Reaction BRE would initiate the process of the retirement plan distribution by contacting an appropriate plan administrator.

Advanced BRE solutions support both types of business rules in either translator/ interpreter or compilation mode. In addition, these engines support rules conflict detection and resolution, simulation of business rules execution for "what-if" scenarios, and policy-driven access controls and rule content security. Clearly, such an advanced BRE would be useful in supporting the complex data synchronization and conflict reconciliation requirements of the MDM Data Hub. Architecturally, however, a BRE may be implemented as a component of a Data Hub or as a general business rules engine that serves multiple lines of business and many applications. The former approach leads to a specialized BRE that is fine-tuned to effectively process reconciliation rules of a given style and context of the Data Hub. The latter is a general-purpose shared facility that may support a variety of business rules and applications, an approach that may require the BRE to support more complex rules-definition language syntax and grammar, and higher scalability and interoperability with the business applications. To isolate Data Hub design decisions from the specifics of the BRE implementation, we strongly recommend that companies take full advantage of the service-oriented approach to building a Data Hub environment and to encapsulating the BRE and its rules repository as a set of well-defined services that can be consumed by the Data Hub on an as-needed basis.

Data Delivery and Metadata Concerns

The complexities and issues of loading data into the Data Hub give rise to a different set of concerns. These concerns have to be solved in order to enable data consumers (systems, applications, and users) to find and use the right data and attest to its quality and accuracy. The Master Data Consumption zone addresses these concerns by providing a set of services that help find the right data, package it into the right format, and make available the required information to the authorized consumers. Although many of these concerns are typical for any data management and data delivery environment, it is important to discuss these concerns in the context of the MDM Data Hub and its Data Location service.

Data Zone Architecture and Distribution of Reference Data

One concern of master data distribution is centered on the distribution of a particular domain of master data—reference data. Although this concern applies to all types of master data, the reference data issues clearly underline the problem, primarily because practically every organization has a reference data system even if the MDM Data Hub is not yet implemented or even planned. We will discuss a number of implementation and governance issues that are specific to reference data as a subset of master data in Part IV.

A Reference MDM Data Hub, by definition, maintains a golden, accurate, and timely reference data record of ensured, measured data quality. This reference data needs to be delivered to consumers not only when it changes (as in data synchronization MDM processing) but also on demand. One approach that some organizations use to distribute reference data is to implement a data replication mechanism that allows each consuming application to acquire a "local" copy of the data and use it to support business processes. However, it is easy to see the problems with this approach:

- Using standard data replication techniques may create significant data redundancies, which result in extra storage, processing, and integration costs.

- Applications that acquired a "local" copy of the reference data may find it convenient to repurpose some of reference data attributes for a particular business process, thus potentially violating the data quality of the reference data because the Data Hub is not a part of this process.

- Changes to "local" copies of reference data don't always get communicated back to the reference master, thus creating serious and often difficult-to-reconcile data quality and consistency issues.

Ignoring these issues and relying on an MDM engine to continue to maintain the required data quality of reference data is a short-sighted approach to reference data distribution. Indeed, MDM has capabilities to ensure the appropriate data quality, and its Master Data Consumption zone can implement various effective mechanisms to deliver the data to consumers automatically or on demand (either as a request or as a business event–driven action), but it cannot do it alone. The organization needs to recognize the problem and institute a set of policies and controls that address this reference data distribution issue at its core. For example, when an organization decides to implement a reference master data environment, it may stipulate the following:

- All reference data changes are versioned, and version references are available to all consumers.

- If the reference data is changed in the Reference Data Hub, its distribution should be implemented as an event-driven process, thus enabling the accurate view of reference data and the context of the change in business terms.

- Mass replication of reference data to all consumers without considering the semantics of the event that cause the distribution action and without implementing proper data quality controls should be avoided wherever possible.

- Data governance principles for reference data should clearly define the responsibilities and accountability of reference data owners, stewards, publishers, and consumers.

Data Zone Architecture and Hierarchy Management

As we discussed in Chapter 4, one important aspect of reference data is the hierarchical structure of many reference data domains. A hierarchy is defined according to some classification scheme, and changes to the scheme or the introduction of a new scheme results in creation of a new hierarchy. It is not unusual for an enterprise to organize its key reference data in different hierarchies according to the business requirements of a particular line of business. For example, consider a classical case of a customer reference master, where the customer entities represent institutional customers. In this case, a sales organization may use a customer hierarchy that reflects the legal entity structure of a parent company and its subsidiaries. At the same time, a marketing organization may use a location-based hierarchy that helps the marketing organization to refine its messages and campaigns according to the specific geographic and political concerns of a customer entity that operates in various regions of the global marketplace. Thus, we just defined two different hierarchies for the same domain. As business requirements change, and sales and marketing territories get realigned because of potential reorganization or a merge activity, these two hierarchies will have to change to reflect the changes in business conditions. In addition, a sales organization may decide to change the legal entity–based hierarchy to a version that is also based on the products that customers are using. It is easy to see that in the normal course of business activities, an enterprise can create several alternate hierarchies and continue to change them on a frequent basis.

Clearly, an MDM system will have to support these changes and maintain an appropriate degree of reference data integrity, versioning, and traceability, which is the province of the MDM Hierarchy Management services. Equally as important, however, an MDM system, and in particular its Master Data Consumption zone, has to implement a set of reference data delivery services that would provide a change impact analysis and deliver these hierarchy changes to downstream business systems that use the reference data to provide the enterprise with vitally important management and analytical data.

These requirements become particularly important in the case where the downstream system that consumes master data is an enterprise data warehouse and a set of dependent data marts that enable reporting, business intelligence, and other key business management functionality. As we showed in Chapter 4, the notion of hierarchy applies directly to the dimensions in a data warehouse data dimensional model, frequently referred to as a "star schema" or a "snowflake schema," with the fact entities organized in a central table(s) and "surrounded" by dimensions that provide keys that point to each fact in the Fact Tables.[4] A typical data warehouse design includes a robust dimensional data model and a set of services that support the acquisition, maintenance, relationships, and integrity of the fact data and dimensional data.

In some cases, these services and data models need to be rather complex to support complex business process that cause changes in the underlying dimensions and, therefore, in the values of the facts (for example, in cases where dimensional values change infrequently, the data warehousing system should define and maintain Slow Change Dimensions, or SCDs, which are the modeling constructs that enable a data warehouse to maintain the historical view of the values of the facts and allow the users to see the data as of a specific date, an activity referred to as "time travel").

One benefit of MDM Hierarchy Management in conjunction with the Reference Data Delivery services deployed in the Master Data Consumption zone is that this architecture supports a system design option that allows the MDM system to maintain the data warehousing dimensions, including the management of their hierarchies in the MDM Data Hub instead of the data warehouse. As long as the Hierarchy Management service maintains the timely, accurate, and auditable view of hierarchy changes in a given dimension and supports the automatic synchronization of these changes across all related dimensions, the Master Data Consumption zone can implement a Data Delivery model that does the following:

- Propagate these reference data changes to the data stores that maintain the facts.
- Distribute the latest set of reference data directly to data marts that are used for management reporting and analytics.

Clearly, replacing data warehouse dimensions with the MDM Data Hub is just one design option, and not a mandatory configuration. However, because the Data Zone approach allows an MDM system to implement a loosely coupled connection between

Hierarchy Management services in the Hub Services zone and Data Delivery services in the Master Data Consumption zone, it may be beneficial in some cases to allow for on-demand delivery of the accurate reference data rather than develop hierarchy management features inside the data warehousing environment.

Metadata and Attribute Location Services

As we look at the overall enterprise data landscape, we can see the majority of data values spread across the Data Hub and many heterogeneous source systems. Each of these systems may act as a master of some data attributes, and in extreme cases it is even possible that some data attributes have many masters. Every time a consumer requests a particular data record or a specific data attribute value, this request can be fulfilled correctly only when the requesting application "knows" what system it should access to get the requested data. This knowledge of the master relationship for each data attribute, as well as the knowledge of the name and location of the appropriate masters, is the responsibility of the *Attribute Location service*. Architecturally, it is an internal MDM Data Hub data service that is used by several higher-order services, including the Metadata Management service. Conceptually, the Attribute Location service acts as a directory for all data attributes under management, and this directory is active; that is, the directory is continuously updated as data attributes migrate or get promoted from old masters to the Data Hub—a natural evolution of an MDM environment from a Registry style to the Transaction Hub. Logically, however, this service is a subset of a larger service group called Metadata Management Services that supports and relies on an enterprise-wide *metadata repository*—a key component of any enterprise-wide data strategy and data architecture. The Metadata Repository role is much broader than just providing support for the Attribute Locator service, and also includes such internal Data Hub services as Record Locator and even Key Generation services.

Although a detailed discussion of metadata is beyond the scope of this book, we briefly discuss the basic premises behind metadata and the metadata repository in the section that follows. This section describes how a metadata repository helps enable just-in-time data delivery capabilities of some Data Hub implementations as well as some end-user applications such as real-time or operational Business Intelligence applications.

Metadata Basics

The most common definition of metadata is "data about data." However, we can refine this definition to include more details. For example, we can define metadata as information about data's structure (syntax) and meaning (semantics). Structural definitions describe the structure of the data objects and how the data is used, and include such familiar constructs as system catalogs for relational database management systems and XML schemas.

Semantic metadata provides a means to understand the meaning of data. For example, semantic metadata includes an explanation or description of the data entity in a data dictionary, commentary and annotations in documents, the content of the thesauri, and advanced information management concepts such as taxonomies of information patterns and ontologies.[5]

The power of metadata concepts includes metadata's ability to be applied to itself by defining the structure and semantics of the metadata. In other words, if metadata is data about data, meta-metadata (also known as "meta-model") is metadata about metadata—that is, it defines the structure and semantics of metadata. Examples of standardized meta-models include Unified Modeling Language (UML),[6] Common Warehouse Meta-model (CWM),[7] and Meta Object Facility, or MOF[8] (a standard for meta-meta-models).

In principle, metadata is generated whenever data is created, acquired, added to, deleted from, or updated in any data store and data system in scope of the enterprise data architecture. Metadata provides a number of very important benefits to the enterprise, including the following:

- **Consistency of definitions**   Metadata contains information about data that helps reconcile the differences in terminology such as "clients" and "customers," "revenue" and "sales," and so on.

- **Clarity of relationships**   Metadata helps resolve ambiguity and inconsistencies when determining the associations between entities stored throughout the data environment. For example, if a customer declares a "beneficiary" in one application, and this beneficiary is called a "participant" in another application, metadata definitions would help clarify the situation.

- **Clarity of data lineage**   Data lineage is one of the key capabilities of metadata management and provides the functionality to determine where data comes from, how it is transformed, and where it is going. Data lineage metadata maintains the trace of information as it traverses various systems. Specifically, the data lineage aspect of metadata maintains information about the origins of a particular data set and can be granular enough to define information at the attribute level; metadata may maintain allowed values for a data attribute as well as its proper format, location, owner, and steward. Operationally, metadata may maintain auditable information about users, applications, and processes that create, delete, or change data, the exact timestamp of the change, and the authorization that was used to perform these actions.

In addition to the structural and semantic classifications of metadata, we also recognize three broad categories of metadata:

- **Business metadata**   This includes definitions of data files and attributes in business terms. It may also contain definitions of business rules that apply to these attributes, data owners and stewards, data quality metrics, and similar information that helps business users to navigate the "information ocean." Some reporting and business intelligence tools provide and maintain an internal repository of business-level metadata definitions used by these tools.

- **Technical metadata**   This is the most common type of metadata. Technical metadata is created and used by the tools and applications that create, manage, and use data. For example, some best-in-class ETL tools maintain internal metadata definitions used to create ETL directives, mappings, or scripts. Technical metadata is a key metadata type used to build and maintain the enterprise data environment. Technical metadata typically includes database system names, table and column names and sizes, data types and allowed values, and structural information such as primary and foreign key attributes and indices. In the case of MDM architecture, technical metadata will contain subject areas defining attribute and record location reference information.

- **Operational metadata**   This type of metadata contains information that is available in operational systems and runtime environments. It may contain data file size, date and time of last load, updates, and backups, as well as the names of the operational procedures and scripts that have to be used to create, update, restore, or otherwise access data.

All these types of metadata have to be persistent and available in order to provide necessary and timely information to manage often heterogeneous and complex data environments such as those represented by various Data Hub architecture styles. A metadata management facility that enables the collection, storage, maintenance, and dissemination of metadata information is called a "metadata repository."

Topologically, metadata repository architecture defines one of the following three styles:

- Centralized metadata repository
- Distributed metadata repository
- Federated or hybrid metadata repository

The centralized architecture is the traditional approach to building a metadata repository. It offers efficient access to information, adaptability to additional data stores, scalability to capture additional metadata, and high performance. However, like any other centralized architecture, a centralized metadata repository is a single point of failure. It requires continuous synchronization with the participants of the data environment, it may become a performance bottleneck, and it may negatively affect the quality of the metadata. Indeed, the need to copy information from various applications and data stores into the central repository may compromise data quality if the proper data validation procedures are not a part of the data acquisition process.

A distributed architecture avoids the concerns and potential errors of maintaining copies of the source metadata by accessing up-to-date metadata from all systems' metadata repositories in real time. Distributed metadata repositories offer superior metadata quality because the users see the most current information about the data. However, because a distributed architecture requires real-time availability of all participating systems, a single system failure may potentially bring the metadata repository down. Also, as source systems' configurations change, or as new systems become available, a distributed architecture needs to adapt rapidly to the new environment, and this degree of flexibility may require a temporary shutdown of the repository.

A federated or a hybrid approach leverages the strengths and mitigates the weaknesses of both distributed and centralized architectures. Like a distributed architecture, the federated approach can support real-time access to metadata from source systems. It can also centrally and reliably maintain metadata definitions or at least references to the proper locations of the accurate definitions in order to improve performance and availability.

Regardless of the architecture style of the metadata repository, any implementation should recognize and address the challenge of semantic integration. This is a well-known problem in metadata management that manifests itself in the system's inability to integrate information properly because some data attributes may have similar definitions but have completely different meanings. The reverse is also true. A trivial example is the task of constructing an integrated view of the office staff hierarchy for a company that was formed because of a merge of two entities. If you use job titles as a normalization factor, a "vice president" in one company may be equal to a "partner" in another. Not having these details explained clearly in the context becomes a difficult problem to solve systematically. The degree of difficulty grows with the diversity of the context. Among the many approaches to solving this challenge is an effective application of information semantics concepts such as ontologies. From the metadata repository point of view, the repository design has to be "ontology aware" and provide the capability to link the context to the information itself and the rules by which this context should be interpreted.

Enterprise Information Integration and Integrated Data Views

Enterprise Information Integration (EII) is a set of technologies that leverage information collected and stored in the enterprise metadata repository to deliver accurate, complete, and correct data to all authorized consumers of such information without the need to create or use persistent data storage facilities.

The fundamental premise of EII is to enable authorized users with just-in-time and transparent access to all the information they are entitled to. Part III of this book discusses the concepts of the "authorized user" and "entitlements."

This capability of delivering transparent access to information that is distributed across several, possibly heterogeneous data stores is what makes EII technology a viable and attractive data access component of the service-oriented architecture (SOA) that supports these types of distributed data environments (for example, an enterprise MDM system). We can further state that, conceptually, EII technologies complement other solutions found in the Master Data Consumption zone by defining and delivering virtualized views of integrated data that can be distributed across several data stores, including an MDM Data Hub.

EII data views are based on the data requests and metadata definitions of the data under management. These views are independent from the technologies of the physical data stores used to construct these views.

Moreover, advanced EII solutions can support information delivery across a variety of channels, including the ability to render the result set on any computing platform, including various mobile devices. Looking at the MDM Reference Architecture (refer to Figure 5-2), we can see that EII components that deliver requested data views to the consumers (users or applications) should be designed, implemented, and supported in conjunctions with the Data Location and Data Delivery services discussed in the previous sections of this chapter.

Although, strictly speaking, EII is not a mandatory part of the MDM Data Hub architecture, it is easy to see that using EII services allows a Data Hub to deliver the value of an integrated information view to the consuming applications and users more quickly, at a lesser cost, and in a more flexible and dynamic fashion.

In other words, a key part of any MDM Data Hub design is the capability of delivering data to consuming applications periodically and on demand in agreed-upon formats. However, being able to deliver data from the Data Hub is not the only requirement for the Master Data Consumption zone. Many organizations are embarking on the evolutionary road to a Data Hub design and implementation that supports both the Analytical and Operational styles of MDM. In this scenario, the Data Hub becomes a source of analytical and operational data for the Business Intelligence suites (Analytical MDM) and Servicing CRM (Operational MDM). This approach expands the role of the Data Hub from the data integration target to the master data source that feeds value-added business applications. This expanded role of the Data Hub and the increased information value of data managed by the Data Hub require an organizational recognition of the importance of an enterprise data strategy; broad data governance; clear and actionable data quality metrics, especially appointed data stewards that represent business units; and the existence and continuous support of an enterprise metadata repository.

The technical, business, and organizational concerns of data strategy, data governance, data management, and data delivery that were discussed in this chapter are some of the key factors necessary to make any MDM initiative a useful, business value–enhancing proposition.

References

1. Newman, David, Nicholas Gall, and Anne Lapkin. "Gartner Defines Enterprise Information Architecture." February 2008. http://www.gartner.com/DisplayDocument?doc_cd=154071.

2. http://www.datagovernance.com/fw_the_DGI_data_governance_framework.html.

3. http://en.wikipedia.org/wiki/Business_rules_engine.

4. Kimball, Ralph, Margy Ross, Bob Becker, and Joy Mundy. *Kimball's Data Warehouse Toolkit Classics: The Data Warehouse Toolkit, 2nd Edition; The Data Warehouse Lifecycle, 2nd Edition; The Data Warehouse ETL Toolkit.* Wiley (April 2009).

5. http://www.merriam-webster.com/dictionary/ontology.

6. http://www.uml.org/.

7. http://www.omg.org/technology/documents/modeling_spec_catalog.htm.

8. http://www.omg.org/mof/.

PART II

MDM Services for Entity and Relationships Resolution and Hierarchy Management

I n the previous chapters, we discussed several general topics related to Master Data Management architecture.

We organized these discussions in the context of the enterprise architecture framework and its various viewpoints, which we used to help address the complexity and the interconnected nature of components of the MDM solutions. Using the principles and goals of the architecture framework, we demonstrated several key requirements and features of the MDM architecture. We also showed key differences and common features between two classes of data management solutions: Master Data Management on the one hand, and the technologies from which MDM has evolved, including Customer Information File, data warehousing, operational data stores, and Customer Relationship Management, on the other hand.

The features and functions that have evolved into contemporary MDM solutions from their various predecessor technologies are driving our approach to leverage already-familiar data architecture and data management concepts and components. These concepts and components include, among other things, scalable and manageable database technology; metadata management; Extract, Transform, and Load (ETL) technologies; and data quality measurement and improvement technologies. We discuss the architecture viewpoints and design constructs dealing with these technologies in Chapters 4 and 5 and master data modeling constructs in Chapter 7.

Architecting an MDM System for Entity Resolution

We're now ready to discuss those aspects of the MDM architecture that enable MDM-specific functionality. Using the MDM definition offered in Chapter 4, we can assert that Master Data Management architecture cannot be complete without considering components, functions, and services that enable the transformation of record-level detail data into a cleansed, rationalized, aggregated, sustainable, and leverageable system of record.

Defining MDM

Master Data Management (MDM) is the framework of processes and technologies aimed at creating and maintaining an authoritative, reliable, sustainable, accurate, and secure data environment that represents a "single and holistic version of truth" for master data and its relationships, as well as an accepted benchmark used within an enterprise as well as across enterprises and spanning a diverse set of application systems, lines of business, channels, and user communities.

The architecture constructs discussed in previous chapters are primarily relevant to Master Data Management and may not apply to predecessor technologies such as CIF, EDW, and others. In order to discuss these MDM-specific architecture concerns, we will use the already-familiar approach of analyzing and defining MDM features, functions, components, and architecture viewpoints in the context of the enterprise architecture framework. Furthermore, we will look at how enterprise architecture framework concepts apply to the specific, well-defined variants of Master Data Management, including MDM for Customer Domain (sometimes referred to as Customer Data Integration, or CDI) and MDM for Product Domain (sometimes referred to as Product Information Management, or PIM), and concentrate our discussions on the design and requirements for the service components of MDM Data Hubs.

Recognizing Individuals, Groups, and Relationships

Although the scope of Master Data Management is extremely broad and includes parties and customers, products, hierarchies, reference data, and other data types and domains, we dedicate a significant effort to the discussion of the Customer or Party domain, where the Party is a type of entity that represents individuals, families/households, groups, and corporate or institutional customers.

NOTE *For convenience and in order to avoid confusion of multiple terms, we'll refer to MDM for Customer domain when we discuss both Customer and Party entities.*

One of the reasons for this focus on the Party is due to the fact that Party or Customer master is a requirement for any business-to-consumer (B2C), government-to-citizen (G2C), or business-to-business (B2B) organization. Secondarily, the market size of the MDM for Customer Domain represents the largest MDM market share and thus deserves the highest level of attention. Many considerations relevant to MDM's ability to recognize and manage entities in the Customer domain apply equally well to other domains. The specific concerns relevant to MDM Data Hub for Customer domain include capabilities that allow an organization to uniquely identify, recognize, and possibly aggregate (or enable aggregation of) individual records about the customers into groups or clusters of records, all of which describe a particular aspect of the entity that represents a given party.

> ### Recognizing Individuals, Groups, and Relationships
> One of the key design goals of the MDM solution for the Customer domain is the ability to identify and recognize not just individual customers but all of their existing and potential relationships with the organization.
>
> Equally important, an MDM system for the Customer domain has to be able to recognize when two or more detail-level records belong to the same Party (individual or an organization).

For example, let's consider a hypothetical family—the Johnson family. We will start with Mike Johnson, who has just become a customer of the neighborhood bank by opening a savings account with a minimum deposit. Such an action is considered trivial by the bank, and Mike is categorized by the bank's CRM platform as a low-priority customer. However, the situation would change drastically if the bank knew that Mike Johnson is a member of a very affluent family and has relationships with other, already established customers of the bank's Wealth Management and Private Banking business units. The immediate implication of this situation is that Mike Johnson and his extended household represent high-net-worth customers that may already provide or in the future will provide significant revenue to the bank.

Let's further assume that Mike Johnson's network of relationships includes family relationships, business relationships, and investment/trust relationships, as follows:

- Mike Johnson's extended family consists of six individuals:
  - Dan (Daniel) Johnson and Kathy Johnson (parents)
  - Mike Johnson and his wife Susan
  - Mack Johnson (Mike and Susan's son)
  - George Patterson (Susan's brother)
  - Ann Patterson (George's wife)
- Mike Johnson's family owns two businesses:
  - Advanced Computer Graphics Inc.
  - Leading Edge Marketing, LLP
- Mike Johnson's family established and owns three trusts:
  - Dan and Kathy Johnson Trust
  - Mack Johnson Trust
  - Patterson Trust Company
- Mike Johnson is a chief designer in the Advanced Computer Graphics company, where his father is the CEO. He is also a board member of the Patterson Trust Company and is a senior technical advisor for Leading Edge Marketing.
- Dan and Kathy Johnson have several accounts with the bank, and Dan often uses his nickname (Rusty). The bank classifies Dan and Kathy as high-net-worth, high-priority customers.
- George Patterson has established a business account with the bank and is considering opening a joint Wealth Management account with his wife.

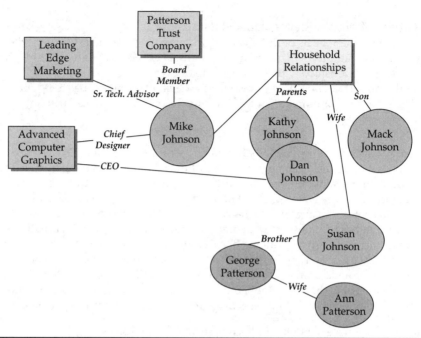

Figure 6-1 Johnson-Patterson family

A simplified graphical representation of the Johnson-Patterson family is shown in Figure 6-1.

An effective MDM solution would deliver an integration platform for customer data that contains a complete, integrated view not only of each individual in the Johnson household but also of the entire extended Johnson family. In order to accomplish this goal, the MDM platform has to support data models and functional capabilities that, for example, can recognize all relationships that Dan Johnson has with the bank as belonging to the same individual, even though Dan used an alias when he opened his private banking account. In the context of the Party data model, an account is a typical type of relationship that a party may have with the organization. Of course, there exist other relationship types, such as legal entities (see Chapter 7 for additional details on the MDM data model and the relationships it supports).

Even more importantly, the bank should recognize any member of the extended Johnson family as belonging to this extended family, and should be able to obtain a data view that shows the totality of the relationships the Johnson family and its members have already established and may establish with the bank in the future. Family relationships with businesses and organizations are key to understanding and leveraging the actual and potential relationships between a customer and the organization.

From the business model point of view, these capabilities in fact mean that an MDM system that manages not just individual customers but also all of their current and potential relationships would enable a transformation of an account-centric view of the Johnson household to an entity-centric (in this case, customer-centric) view that facilitates the new, better, and more rewarding customer experience that the bank can provide to both the Johnson and Patterson households and their business associations (see Figure 6-2).

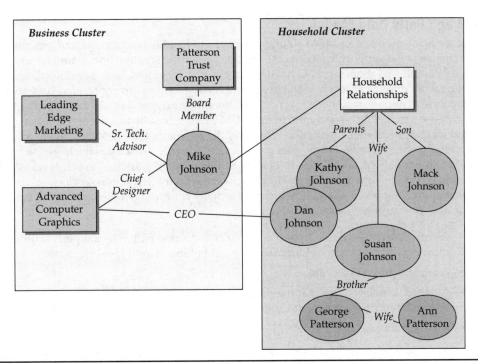

FIGURE 6-2   Customer relationship clustering

The ability to recognize and maintain these relationships is one of the key properties of the MDM Data Hub solutions no matter what architecture style is used (Registry, Reconciliation Engine/Hybrid, or full Transaction Data Hub). The process of creating the relationship links, which collects or groups individual records into higher-level clusters, starts with the very granular, low-level entity data (that is, accounts) and can extend its scope to include higher levels of abstractions, such as households, business associations, and other customer groups. This process requires that an MDM system implements a comprehensive data model and provides a set of functional services designed to support entity recognition, matching, and linking (these activities are collectively called "entity resolution" and are enabled by the corresponding Entity Resolution service of the MDM system). We discuss MDM data modeling concerns in Chapter 7, and entity recognition capabilities in more detail later in this chapter and in Chapters 14 and 15.

Entity Groupings

The ability to recognize individual entities as members of arbitrary complex groups (for example, households and extended families for individuals, holding companies, and other organizational hierarchies for business entities) is one of the key properties of Master Data Management. This feature applies equally well to MDM for Customer domain, Reference Data Masters, Product Master Hubs, and so on, with the complexity of the associations and groupings depending in large part on the completeness and accuracy of the data, the richness of the semantics of the data domain, and the business rules driving the resolution of conflicting or undetermined links.

MDM and Party Data Model

One of the key features of an MDM solution designed to handle the matching and grouping requirements is the support for a data model that allows the creation and maintenance of arbitrary complex relationships. Such a data model may be reused from previous data modeling work done as part of a data management activity. Alternatively, an enterprise may develop an appropriate data model from scratch internally, acquire a model from an external source, or use a model that is included in the MDM product bundle that the enterprise has selected for the project implementation. Whatever the approach, the MDM data model should address the specific business needs of an organization. Chapter 7 discusses the key aspects of data modeling for MDM, and Chapters 14 and 15 offer additional discussion points on MDM data models and the impact of data model design on the Entity Resolution services.

To support complex functional requirements, many conceptual MDM data models contain at least the following major subject areas:

- A party/customer profile subject area that is populated with relevant party attributes, some of which are required for matching and linking of individual records

- A relationships subject area

- A metadata subject area that maintains record-level and attribute-level location information, attribute formats, domain constraints, and other relevant information

- An audit subject area

The first two subject areas are often industry specific and may be customized to support a particular line of business. For example, several industry-proven data models support property and casualty insurance or a retail banking business. These data models maintain customer/party profiles and relationships in the context of the industries they support. We briefly illustrate the key components of the conceptual domain-specific subject area in this chapter and offer more implementation-level concerns in Part IV of the book.

The remaining subject areas are created to support the Data Hub's ability to become a reliable, accurate, and timely system of record. Some of these subject areas are created as part of the Data Hub data model, whereas others are created as separate data domains. For example, the metadata subject area is often implemented not as a part of the Data Hub data model but rather as a logical component of the metadata repository (metadata and other supporting subject areas of the Data Hub are discussed in more detail in Chapter 5).

A conceptual MDM data model that can support an entity-centric business such as retail banking, institutional banking, personal insurance, or commercial insurance is known as a "party-centric" model, and it may consist of a number of entities and attributes, including party/customer, party profile, account, party group, location, demographics, relationships, channels, products, events, and privacy preferences. Some of the key attributes of this model include identity attributes used to uniquely identify the party as a collection or cluster of individual detail-level records. Such a party-centric data model supports multiple party types, including organizations, customers, prospects, and so on. Figure 6-3 illustrates a highly simplified version of this conceptual model that is aligned with the insurance domain. Fundamental entities in this conceptual party model include the following:

- The Party entity, which represents a person or an organization, and can support an existing customer or a prospect. In our relationship example (see previous section in this chapter), a party could represent a member of the Johnson family.

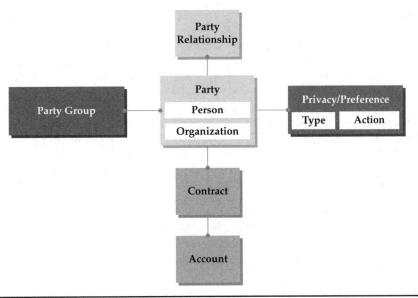

FIGURE 6-3   Simplified generic MDM party data model

- The Party group, which is an entity that represents a collection of individual parties affiliated with each other based on specific, well-defined criteria (for example, a household).
- Relationship-enabling entities, which support party-to-party relationships.
- Party-level privacy preferences, which can differ from one contract or account to another.
- The Party entity may have one or more contracts, each of which may have one or more accounts.

In practice, MDM implementations have to support party models that are much more extensive and complex.[1,2]

Entity Groupings and Hierarchies

One consequence of identifying, matching, and linking entities based on a predefined set of attributes is the ability to create entity groups. As mentioned, in the case of the individual customer/party domain, entities that represent individuals can be naturally grouped into clusters of households or families. Likewise, in the case of an institutional customer, some entities that represent various divisions of the same company can be grouped together to reflect a legal structure of the company. To illustrate this point, consider a large global organization that has multiple subsidiaries, some separated by the business focus (for example, a global diversified financial services firm may have an insurance subsidiary, a wealth management subsidiary, and so on) and by geography/location (for example, a U.S. bank, a Latin American broker-dealer, an Australian credit bureau, and so on). This situation is not an exclusive province of financial institutions; we see the same phenomenon in manufacturing, pharmaceutical, auto, advanced technologies, and other areas. For example, Ford Motor Company is a parent of a number of smaller manufacturers of Ford and other brands, such as Jaguar in United Kingdom (recently sold by Ford to Tata). All these legal entities can be grouped together to represent one common, global parent company, and MDM technology provides such identification, matching, and grouping capabilities to various domain types.

An important consideration for this "natural" grouping is related to the fact that these domain entities are related to one another in a hierarchical fashion. We discussed hierarchies and MDM hierarchy management in Chapters 5, and in this chapter, and the relevant implication on the MDM data model in Chapter 7. Just to recap, in many cases a given data domain has at least one "official" hierarchy based on a specific, business-defined classification schema, sometimes supporting alternative views of the entities for different business purposes. For example, businesses tend to structure their sales organizations based on either products or geographies or cost centers. Modern MDM solutions are designed to not only support primary and alternative hierarchies; they can automatically create and manage entity groups based on the hierarchies to which these entities belong.

This entity grouping topic becomes more complicated if you consider the need to organize entities into groups that do not follow the "natural" affinity (for example, members of the household) or are not aligned with standard (for a given domain and business) hierarchies. Consider an example where an aircraft manufacturer decides to set up a group of some of its suppliers and partners in order to develop a new product as a virtual team. In this case, members of the groups can engage in research and development activities and start acquiring supplies and hiring personnel using a credit facility. In this case, an MDM system should recognize individual expense or revenue transactions performed against one of the group members as belonging to a larger virtual entity for the purpose of aggregating this data into a combined balance sheet.

Moreover, this group may enter into an agreement where the share of the revenue or the expenses is not split evenly among the members, so a straightforward aggregation may be inappropriate.

One approach to support these arbitrary complex entity groups is to create *custom hierarchies* (these may not be hierarchies in the pure sense of the term but rather define the rules of linking and aggregating for the group at large and each individual member) and then leverage the MDM system to manage the resulting balance sheets, combined risk exposures, and other business metrics.

Such entity groups can be defined both in the individual and institutional customer domains. For example, an investment club may invite members that are not related in any obvious way, but have to be treated as a group for the purpose of negotiating better brokerage commissions or a larger credit line with more advantageous terms.

Clearly, the challenge of managing entity groups is often related to the challenge of managing hierarchies. This challenge is exacerbated by the fact that hierarchies are not static, and can and do change with business restructuring, mergers and acquisitions, new product introductions, and other events. As we stated in Chapter 4, hierarchies are key aspects of creating and managing master data entities and entity groups, and a typical MDM system implements a certain level of hierarchy management, including entity-level matching, aggregation, and hierarchy realignment, by providing a rich set of services and management capabilities that can create and manage multiple hierarchies, including alternative hierarchies and custom, user-defined structures that can in turn support various types of entity groups.

We discuss hierarchies and entity groups in this chapter because their existence makes the challenge of entity resolution much harder. Indeed, the problem of entity resolution is multidimensional, where the matching process has to be designed to support both simple, same-grain-of-detail comparison of entities (such as two customer records) and the much more complex task of discovering whether two entities are related according to some hierarchical arrangement or because they belong to an implicit or explicit entity group.

Challenge of Product Identification, Recognition, and Linking

When we discuss the need to recognize, match, and link entities from the customer domain, the existing MDM solutions have been shown to do a reasonably good job. The primary enablers of entity resolution in MDM for customer domain include advancements in data quality technologies as well as the maturity of the techniques and algorithms focused on solving name- and address-matching problems. The majority of these techniques are syntax and/or pattern based, and are very successful in detecting and correcting typical data entry errors; in recognizing misspellings caused by phonetic interpretations of a given word; and in the handling of professional terminology, abbreviations (for example, St. and Street), synonyms, nicknames and alternative representations (for example, Mike and Michael), invalid postal codes, and other name and address issues.

Likewise, the challenge of matching entities in the customer domain that are organized into different hierarchies is addressed by many MDM products, and relies to a large extent on the patterns and explicit rules.

When we deal with the product domain, the challenge of matching and linking entities is much harder, and not just for managing hierarchies of product entities, but also in the fundamental activities of matching product entities that appear to be at the same levels of grainularity (hierarchy).

The root of the problem lies in the wide variety, intrinsic complexity, and limited standardization of product data. Because product data is not just domain specific but often source data specific (that is, often the same product is defined and described differently by the product manufacturer, developer, or provider), the typical syntax-based analysis and matching techniques prove to be ineffective. Indeed, product data, by its very nature, contains rich semantics that are based on the product purpose, the materials and components used for its development, the processes and instructions defining the product's use, and a host of other factors. Moreover, the product definition standards are often limited to a given product type, and even then are often incomplete or not being followed. Examples abound: Consider computer products and accessories, clothing and shoes, furniture, and so on. Each of these product groups is described by its own set of attributes, and the value of these attributes is often driven by marketing considerations, and therefore tends to be different even in the same group. The result is the realization that there is almost no single and accurate way to describe products and thus leverage common product definition syntax to perform identification and matching.

For example, let's look at a class of computer electronics products—specifically, laptop computers and accessories. In this case, "extended port replicator," "quick connect docking station," and "USB port extender" may be equally accurate descriptions and perfectly understandable to an educated buyer, but not very useful to a classical MDM system that requires syntax-based, structured information that is organized as a set of well-defined attributes, such as "class = Computer Accessory, item = Port Replicator, type = USB attached," and so on, unless equivalent terms are explicitly defined for the matching software.

Moreover, some of these attributes only apply to specific product models/versions (in our example, not all port replicators can work with all laptop brands and models). This further complicates the product-matching problem because a successful matching technique should recognize, maintain, and use links between the related products (in our example, a complete list of laptop computers and the supported docking stations).

The conclusion is straightforward: In order for an MDM system to support entity resolution for a product domain, it should use a semantically driven approach to product recognition, matching, and linking that would reliably and effectively extract not just the product data attributes but would also extract and rationalize the "meaning" of these attributes in a way that eliminates ambiguity and provides consistency of definitions.

Semantics-based solutions for processing such complex data domains as product data have emerged from the area of academic research into the mainstream, and are now used in various areas of information technology, including Semantic Web, Artificial Intelligence, and many others. The key concept of semantics-based processing—ontology—is defined as a formal representation of a set of concepts within a given domain and the relationships between those concepts that can be used to make assertions about the properties of that domain.[3] Modern MDM solutions can take advantage of the tools that are based on processing information ontologies to derive and operate on the semantic content as effectively as traditional tools operate on syntax-based constructs. Moreover, the realization of the need for semantics-based processing has a profound effect on the entity resolution design of MDM systems for the product domain, and also provides a new way to address data quality by measuring and managing the quality of data in the context of its meaning.

MDM Architecture for Entity Resolution

In the preceding chapter we showed that in order to create and maintain an authoritative, accurate, timely, and secure system of record, an MDM solution must support a number of capabilities that are designed not only to maintain the content, scope, and integrity of the core data model but also to enable the MDM Data Hub to be integrated and interoperate with established business processes, systems, and applications.

Figure 6-4 illustrates these service-based capabilities in the form of functional components at a conceptual level. Here, we show that the core MDM data store is surrounded by additional functional components that work in concert to enable the desired MDM functionality.

However, this picture represents only high-level conceptual component architecture. It does not show a view in which MDM functionality is available as a set of services that are published and consumed by the Data Hub in accordance with the service-oriented architecture (SOA) paradigm. In Chapter 4, we discussed the rationale and the benefits of the service-oriented architecture approach to designing complex integration-enabled software systems. Master Data Management solutions, by their very nature, belong to the category of complex integration-enabled systems. Therefore, applying SOA principles and concepts to the architecture of the MDM system is not only an appropriate but also an effective approach. The next section describes a high-level view of the MDM services aimed at solving identification, matching, linking, and grouping of master entities.

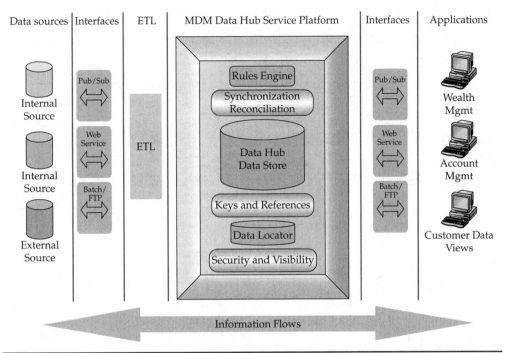

FIGURE 6-4   The conceptual architecture view addresses MDM-specific problem domains.

Key Services and Capabilities for Entity Resolution

Let's start the discussion of the functional aspects of the MDM platform in the context of the MDM Data Hub reference architecture viewpoint described in Chapter 4. The MDM Reference Architecture viewpoint shown in Figure 6-5 is focused on key services that enable MDM entity management–related functionality. As a reminder, we offer an abbreviated definition of services-oriented architecture.

> **SOA**
> *Service-oriented architecture (SOA)* is the architecture in which software components can be exposed as loosely-coupled, fine-grained, or coarse-grained reusable services that can be integrated with each other and invoked by different applications for different purposes through a variety of platform-independent service interfaces available via standard network protocols.

As shown in Figure 6-5, the MDM Reference Architecture includes a number of components and services designed to enable enterprise-scale MDM solutions. We arrange these components and services into functional architecture layers that emphasize the MDM services taxonomy. From a business point of view, the MDM Data Hub publishes and consumes coarse-grained functional business services that usually correspond to business functional requirements. Additionally, at the top layer of the architecture stack, the MDM

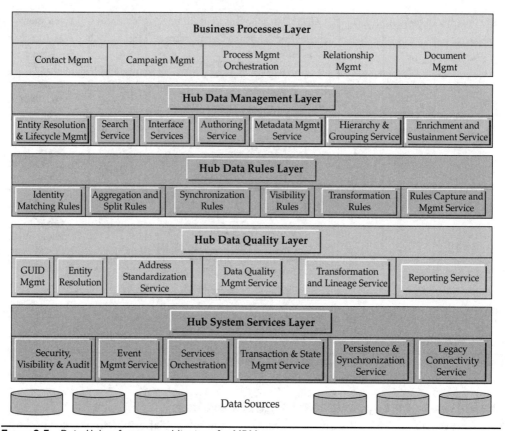

FIGURE 6-5   Data Hub reference architecture for MDM

services platform supports coarse-grained technical services. However, under the covers, the MDM platform supports fine-grained, lower-level services, some of which represent primitive, atomic services used to compose higher-level business services (we discuss this important point in Chapter 4). Some of the services provided by the MDM platform include internal, system-level, and infrastructure-level services that make the entire environment operational and manageable by the enterprise in a production environment. These supporting, infrastructure-level services include service coordination and orchestration, legacy integration service, systems instrumentation and management, error processing, and many others.

Entity Resolution and MDM Reference Architecture

Let's review these layers of services as they're defined in the MDM Reference Architecture.

- The Data Management layer includes the following services:
  - Interface services, which expose a published and consistent entry point to request MDM services.

- Entity Resolution and Life-Cycle Management services, which enable entity recognition by processing various levels of identities, and manage life stages of master data by supporting business interactions including traditional Create, Read, Update, and Delete (CRUD) activities.

- Search services, for easy access to the information managed by the MDM Data Hub.

- Authoring services, which allow MDM users to create (author), manage, customize/change, and approve definitions of master data (metadata), including hierarchies and entity groups. In addition, Authoring services enable users to manage (CRUD) specific instances of master data.

- Metadata Management service, which provides support for data management aspects of metadata creation, manipulation, and maintenance. The Metadata Management service supports a metadata repository and relies on and supports internal Data Hub services such as Attribute and Record Locator services and even Key Generation services.

- Hierarchy, Relationships, and Groupings Management services, which deliver functions designed to manage master data hierarchies, groupings, and relationships. These services can process requests from the Authoring services.

- Enrichment and sustaining services, which are focused on acquiring and maintaining the correct content of master data, controlled by external data references as user-driven adjustments.

- The Data Rules layer includes key services that are driven by business-defined rules for entity resolution, aggregation, synchronization, visibility and privacy, and transformation.

- The Data Quality layer includes services that are designed to validate and enforce data quality rules; resolve entity identification and hierarchical attributes; perform data standardization, reconciliation, and lineage; generate and manage global unique identifiers; and provide data quality profiling and reporting.

- The System Services layer includes a broad category of base services such as security, data visibility, event management (these are designed to react to predefined events detected within the master data and to trigger appropriate actions); service orchestration; transaction and state management; system synchronization; and intersystem connectivity/data integration services, including Enterprise Information Integration services for federated data access.

In preceding chapters, we have shown that the richness of this SOA-based MDM architecture allows an MDM Data Hub to create and maintain an authoritative system of master entities for one or more domains. In this chapter, however, we will focus our discussion on those MDM capabilities that are data-domain independent and are relevant to MDM Data Hub systems that integrate and manage customer data, organization data, reference data, and product data alike.

Key MDM Capabilities

Several key MDM capabilities have to be supported by all major Data Hub Architecture styles from registry to Transaction Hub. These capabilities are data domain independent and are relevant to Data Hub systems that integrate and manage customer data, organization data, reference data, and product data alike. In the context of Master Data Management for Customer Domain, these capabilities include (but are not limited to) the following:

- Entity resolution, which includes identity recognition as well as matching and generation of global unique customer identifiers
- Persistence and maintenance of the entity identifiers and other information for which the Data Hub is the master
- Rules-based and data content–based synchronization to/from legacy systems
- Reconciliation and arbitration of data changes
- Attribute location service
- Data security and visibility

Let's illustrate these key MDM capabilities and services by offering an alternative view of SOA-based MDM Data Hub Reference Architecture. This view is a high-level conceptual framework that attempts to group all MDM services into external and internal sets of services (see Figure 6-6). We will use this high-level view to discuss several additional considerations on how the MDM services framework enables both business functionality and enterprise-level integration between an MDM Data Hub and other systems and applications.

Specifically, in addition to the published business services, we can differentiate between two major groups of interoperable internal services. The first group includes atomic functional services such as Create, Read, Update, and Delete (CRUD). These atomic services are a part of the MDM Life-Cycle Management service but also can be combined to assemble higher-level, coarse-grained composite business services that execute business transactions (for example, a coarse-grained business service such as Search would provide "Find a Customer by Name" functionality, and the Authoring service would allow users to "Create Customer Profile"). This abstraction is very powerful; it enables the reuse of services and components and easy, almost declarative-style integration.

The second group is a set of technical management and operational services that hide the technical complexity of the design from the application and business service developers. The services in this group include support for transactional semantics, coordination, compensation, orchestration, synchronization, recovery, error management, auditing, and so on. Although these services abstract application developers from the underlying technical complexity, they interoperate with both atomic and business services in order to manage and execute business transactions against an MDM Data Hub.

Following the same approach defined in Chapter 4, we can illustrate the service-oriented nature of an MDM Data Hub by "wrapping" the core Data Hub platform in the layers of internal and external services. We have shown a high-level graphical representation of this

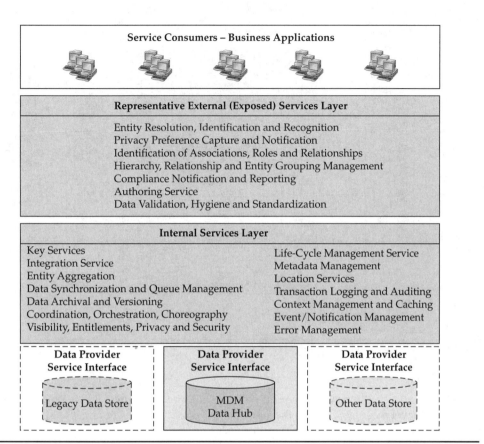

Service Consumers – Business Applications

Representative External (Exposed) Services Layer

Entity Resolution, Identification and Recognition
Privacy Preference Capture and Notification
Identification of Associations, Roles and Relationships
Hierarchy, Relationship and Entity Grouping Management
Compliance Notification and Reporting
Authoring Service
Data Validation, Hygiene and Standardization

Internal Services Layer

Key Services
Integration Service
Entity Aggregation
Data Synchronization and Queue Management
Data Archival and Versioning
Coordination, Orchestration, Choreography
Visibility, Entitlements, Privacy and Security

Life-Cycle Management Service
Metadata Management
Location Services
Transaction Logging and Auditing
Context Management and Caching
Event/Notification Management
Error Management

Data Provider
Service Interface

Legacy Data Store

Data Provider
Service Interface

MDM
Data Hub

Data Provider
Service Interface

Other Data Store

Figure 6-6   Data Hub as a service platform

SOA wrapping in Chapter 4 (refer to Figure 4-8). Figure 6-7 builds on the view shown in Figure 4-8 and provides additional service details.

Entity Recognition, Matching, and Generation of Unique Identifiers

The preceding sections of this chapter talked about the challenges and goals of identifying, matching, and linking master data entities, and set the stage to move from the general discussion about delivering key MDM capabilities for entity management to the point where we can focus our attention on the specific capabilities and services for entity resolution.

As before, we'll use Customer domain as a background on which we explain key MDM services for entity resolution. As we stated earlier, one of the primary goals of an MDM solution for the Customer domain is to enable business transformation from an account-centric to a customer-centric enterprise by creating an authoritative system of record that provides an accurate and complete view of the customers, their groups, their relationships, and the way they may be organized into hierarchies.

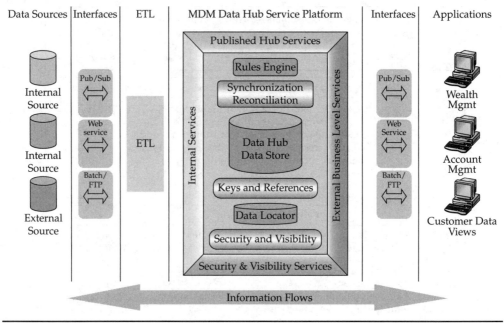

FIGURE 6-7 Services and MDM platform

When we deal with the Customer domain, the ability to recognize the fact that two or more detail-level records belong to the same party (individuals or organizations) is a paramount requirement for any MDM solution.

MDM technologies and services that enable this type of recognition are collectively known as entity resolution services and include the matching and linking of detail records and the creation and maintenance of unique identifiers as primary links to indicate the affinity of detail records to the same party.

Matching and Linking Services and Techniques

In the context of MDM for Customer domain, matching and linking is a highly specialized set of technologies that allows the user to identify party entities with a high degree of confidence.

The operation resulting in party identification allows a user of the MDM platform to construct a total view of a party from the detail-level records. Matching and linking technologies are very sophisticated, and many commercial products that offer these capabilities try to differentiate their matching and linking engines by using three value dimensions: *accuracy* of the match, *speed* of the match, and processing *scalability*. These characteristics are the result of the techniques and implementation approaches of the matching algorithms. It is not surprising, therefore, that many vendors keep their matching algorithms and techniques a closely guarded secret! We will discuss specific implementation concerns of the matching and linking services in Part IV.

NOTE *As we discussed in previous sections, the matching and linking of product records is conceptually similar to the process of matching party records, but the techniques used for the product domain tend to be semantics based, rather than syntax, rule, and pattern based, which are predominant techniques for party matching.*

The variety of matching and linking techniques for the Customer domain is rather large, and it would be beyond the scope of this book to cover them all. Therefore, in this chapter, we take a closer look at some of the best-known techniques used to achieve a high degree of accuracy in matching individual records. The algorithms we discuss in this section are proven to be very effective for entity resolution in the Customer domain; they are highly regarded within the area of the academic research and are effectively used in various technology solutions related to data quality.

At a high level, we can classify all algorithmic approaches to record matching into the following groups:

- **Deterministic algorithms**   These algorithms offer predictable behavior of the comparison and matching process that is based on the data itself. In a deterministic algorithm, each attribute is compared against the same attribute in another record, which results in either a match or a no-match. For example, the deterministic algorithm would compare a social security number in one record with the social security number in another—an operation that would find a match if these two values are equal. Because of this relative simplicity, a deterministic algorithm can deliver very high performance and throughput. Deterministic algorithms often require cleansing of the input data and format standardization in order to perform the match. Traditionally, deterministic algorithms had limited capability to handle such common data anomalies as blank fields, transposition of characters, common misspellings of known names and addresses, and abbreviations. Today, however, advanced deterministic algorithms can overcome this limitation by employing various fuzzy logic techniques and using phonetic functions and lists of equivalencies.

- **Probabilistic algorithms**   These matching algorithms are based on various statistical probability theories; for example, see Scott Schumacher's article.[4] The advantage of the probabilistic algorithm is that it can learn to match records that initially had to be resolved by a direct user intervention. The matching process of a probabilistic algorithm consists of several steps:

  - An analysis of the input data to determine precise frequencies for weighting and matching individual data elements

  - A determination of the outcome of matching between records using derived statistical distribution of value frequencies

  - An assignment of the weight values for match attributes and a predefined match threshold

  - A refinement of the match values through the user-guided value assignment process for those cases where the match confidence level is below the threshold

- **Machine learning algorithms** These sophisticated techniques are based on advanced research and development in the area of machine learning and artificial intelligence. These techniques allow the system not only to detect similarities between two entities based on a number of factors and rules, but also to learn to refine the matching process automatically over time. Many machine learning approaches are somewhat similar to fuzzy logic techniques, typically include probabilistic techniques, and allow the matching engine to learn how to match records based on calculated proximity values. These algorithms can discover and measure similarities between attributes and entire record values in a way similar to how a human brain may recognize two objects as being similar.

NOTE *Machine learning and artificial intelligence algorithms that can process information ontologies could also support entity matching in the product domain.*

- **Hybrid algorithms** As the name implies, these algorithms may use multistep processes that combine deterministic, probabilistic, and machine learning techniques that can also be enhanced by applying more advanced techniques, including phonetic conversion and matching. Hybrid algorithms may use formal matching rules in a deterministic fashion. Alternatively, they can enhance the probabilistic relevance of the variables (attributes) and weights to achieve higher matching rates. Many advanced algorithms may use heuristics (algorithmic techniques that use the observed and understood experience of searching for matches within a given domain), pattern-based matching techniques, and a number of other techniques. Of course, as new techniques become available, their implementations could be either a hybrid or a "pure" deterministic or probabilistic matching engine.

Regardless of how sophisticated and innovative the matching algorithms are, in practice no single technique or single algorithm can satisfy all the diverse matching requirements of the enterprise, especially if the enterprise already developed and successfully used empirical, proven, business area–specific matching rules that may contain a large number of exceptions. This is especially true when dealing with a multidomain MDM that includes complex matching challenges of product information.

In general, however, when deciding on which linking and matching technique is best suited for any given environment, the MDM designers and match solution architects should consider the following factors:

- **Match accuracy** This requirement is self-explanatory. Higher accuracy allows the enterprise to construct a more complete integrated view of the entity such as a customer—be it an individual or an organization—and to reduce the errors associated with assigning false positives (for example, incorrectly recognizing an individual as a member of a wrong household) or false negatives (for example, missing a key member of the household).

- **Linking and matching speed** This requirement is especially important in the case of online applications designed to recognize an entity (for example, an individual) in real time—for instance, a patient who is being admitted to the hospital and requires an emergency blood transfusion, or an airport security control point that has to recognize an individual as a potential threat before airplane boarding starts.

- **Uniqueness and persistence of the link keys**   The linking and matching process can be very fast and accurate, but if the results of the match cannot be stored reliably in the Data Hub or another facility for follow-on processing, then the value of the matching becomes questionable. Therefore, a matching engine needs to be able to generate a unique identifier that the Data Hub would persist in its data store as a unique key. These key values must be unique in the name space of all possible Data Hub entity keys. In other words, if we're dealing with an MDM Data Hub for a global retail enterprise that serves 100 million customers, each of which has one or more detail records (for example, account-level records), the link key should have a sufficient range of values to support the cardinality of all Hub customer entities (in our example, 100 million) rather than all detail-level records.

- **Deterministic outcome**   The key generation service must be deterministic in the sense that if the underlying data did not change, then the key value for the same cluster of records should not change either.

- **Scalability of the solution**   This is a classical system requirement. In the case of the linking and matching engine, it has to address numerous scalability concerns. These include the number of records to be matched, the number of various data sources, the number of user-defined matching rules, and the number of concurrent users that may request the matching operation either to recognize individuals or to generate unique identification keys. The latter requirement should address the concurrency and throughput concerns of the Data Hub environment where the matching engine has to support a prerequisite number of concurrent users, each of which is able to perform a required number of tasks in a unit of time— for example, a predefined number of transactions per second (TPS).

- **Ease of use**   The algorithm and the engine that implements it should provide an easy-to-use, intuitive way for the users to define or customize matching criteria, to understand the reasons for the matching outcome, and to resolve potential uncertainties. The engine should not require the user to be an expert in mathematics or computer science. The intuitive way users can employ the tool may make all the difference between user acceptance and rejection.

Ease of Implementation and Administration

If the matching engine is external to the MDM platform (that is, not built in as a component of the MDM application or an MDM vendor product), the engine should not require a highly specialized computing platform such as a supercomputer, FPGA-based appliance (FPGA stands for Field Programmable Gate Array—a special purpose, high-performance computing device), and so on. The engine should comply with the enterprise infrastructure standards and should be easily integrated into the enterprise system architecture and infrastructure environments. And, finally, an external matching engine should interoperate with the MDM platform of choice (server hardware, software, and the DBMS).

Flexibility

The matching engine should be flexible to conform to ever-changing business requirements. For example, if the organization decides not to use certain data elements in order to protect customer privacy and confidentiality and to comply with applicable privacy regulations (for example, not to use social security numbers or unlisted telephone numbers), the MDM administrator should be able to easily configure the matching engine to implement these changes.

Ability to Adapt to the Business Requirements and to Implement Proven Existing Matching Rules

Many matching algorithms are very sophisticated and are finely tuned to achieve high matching accuracy. The engines that implement these algorithms are designed to preserve the integrity (and, in many cases, significant intellectual property) of these algorithmic techniques. This approach works for many organizations that would like to rely on the matching engine rather than on home-grown matching rules. However, there are organizations and/or business situations where custom-defined matching rules and manual processes must be followed to achieve the desired business outcome. In these cases, the matching engine should be able to use user-defined custom rules in conjunction with the internal algorithms in such a way that the custom rules could override the internal processing or, at a minimum, defer the match decision to a user-driven manual process of asserting the matching result.

Ability to Support Linking and Matching as a Service

This is a technical requirement of the service-oriented architecture (SOA) that helps implement and manage the linking and matching engine as a part of the enterprise architecture. If the engine makes its capabilities available as services, then the consumer (a user or an application) is isolated from the intricacies and complexities of the underlying algorithms and is only concerned with the consumption of the service and the interpretation of the results.

To summarize, the most effective matching engine will utilize a combination of deterministic, probabilistic, and machine learning algorithms to achieve the highest accuracy in the shortest time. And at the end of the day, the flexibility of the matching engine to support the business rules of the enterprise creates a winning combination of sophisticated technology and intuitive behavior that enables the best linking and matching process for the enterprise.

Matching and Linking Service

The outcome of the matching and linking process is the identification of groups or clusters of records associated with each other based on some criteria. An effect of this process on the MDM data content is the ability of the Matching and Linking service to generate, insert, and persist for each record a unique identifier that can be used to organize individual records into clusters of affinity known as "match groups." The Matching and Linking service applies the notion of uniqueness to the match groups rather than to the individual detail records themselves.

Aggregating Entity Information

Using the Matching and Linking service described in the preceding section, the Data Hub will recognize similar records and assign unique link keys to all records in such a way that all records with a given link key value can be grouped together or aggregated into a single entity. In the case of the MDM Party model shown in Figure 6-3, this entity is the Party, and the link key becomes the Party's unique identifier and its primary key.

In principle, this process can be iterative, and it can match and link Party entities using some business-defined criteria. Therefore, a Matching and Linking service can use various business rules to generate different identifiers used to aggregate individual Party objects into even higher-level entities. Examples of these higher-level entities are households, business associations, and other types of customer groups. Depending on the desired depth of aggregation, the Matching and Linking service can generate a number of keys or identifiers that are unique in the corresponding name space of entities for which the matching operation is performed.

Once the identifiers are generated, the MDM Data Hub can use its internal Entity Aggregation service to merge appropriate records into the next-level entity. This merge operation can be automatic or user guided. For example, the Entity Aggregation Service component of the MDM Data Hub may use the unique identifiers to automatically "merge" account-level records into clusters representing individuals, and use next-level identifiers to merge individual-level records into uniquely identified groups such as households (see Figure 6-8). We discuss the merge process in more detail in Chapter 15.

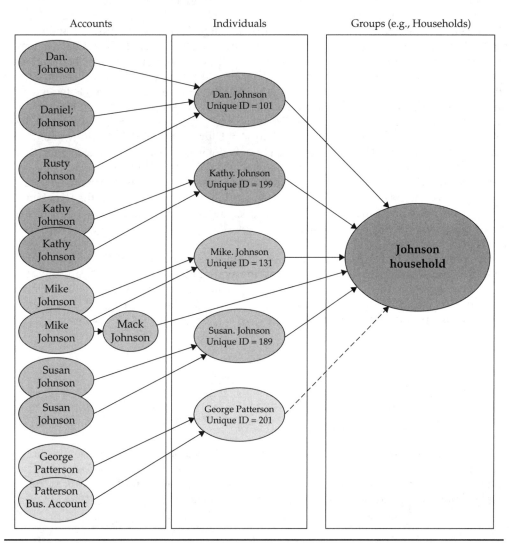

FIGURE 6-8   Mapping accounts to individuals and group

In practice, however, an automatic merge may be undesirable. This is because the matching algorithm may create false positive and false negative outcomes. Another consideration for not using an automatic merge is that, in some cases, the matching business rules are so complex and the number of exceptions is so great that the users would prefer that the system suggest a potential merge suspect while leaving the final decision to the user. Thus, the Entity Aggregation Service of the MDM Data Hub should be able to support both modes of operation: automatic and user-guided (or supervised) aggregation.

Data Hub Keys and Life-Cycle Management Services

The previous sections discussed the MDM Data Hub services designed to match and link individual records by generating persistent unique identifiers. These identifiers, while critically important, are not sufficient to synchronize and maintain the content of the Data Hub in relationship to the upstream and downstream data stores and applications. Indeed, the MDM Data Hub is not an isolated and disconnected environment. It should be a system of record for some information such as customer profile, organizational profile, organizational hierarchies, product reference, and other data domains. Depending on the MDM architecture style, the Data Hub may be just a Registry of the identification information, or a federated data environment that allows the Data Hub to "peacefully" coexist with other systems by maintaining some information inside the Data Hub and some pointers to data in external data stores, data for which the Data Hub is *not* the master. Ultimately, an MDM platform could be the full Transaction Data Hub and a completely self-contained master of the information that it manages. Regardless of the architecture style, an MDM Data Hub has to support a comprehensive data model and a number of specialized services designed to maintain data integrity inside the Data Hub. These specialized services also have to support the Data Hub's ability to keep its content in sync with the providers and consumers of the master data that is stored in the Hub (the data management aspects of MDM data synchronization are discussed in Chapter 5).

Keeping a Data Hub in sync with its sources and consuming applications is not a trivial task. It requires a comprehensive design and the availability of a number of carefully orchestrated services and well-defined processes. To illustrate this point, let's define several *interdependent cooperative* service classes designed to work in concert to support Data Hub synchronization consistency and data integrity:

- Key Generation service
- Record Locator service
- Synchronization service
- Reconciliation service
- Attribute Location service

We briefly discuss the Key Generation and Record Locator services in the next sections. The other services and additional architecture considerations of the MDM Data Hub solution are discussed in Chapter 5. Part IV of this book offers an in-depth look at the implementation aspects of these and other MDM services.

Key Management and Key Generation Service

First, let's review some basic concepts related to the creation and management of Data Hub keys. As we stated in the beginning of this chapter, the MDM Data Hub data model contains a number of data entities and the relationships between the entities. The general principles of the enterprise data architecture and the relational data model dictate that every entity has at least one unique key, and depending on how the model is defined, one of these unique keys is known as the "primary key." A *data modeler* defines the interrelationships between entities through the assignment and maintenance of the primary and foreign keys. These keys enable a key data model constraint of *referential integrity*, where a primary key of one entity (for example, a customer table) should exist in a related table as a foreign key.[5] For example, a Party Profile table may have a unique Profile key. This table may be related to the Account table, which in turn contains unique Account keys. Further, each Profile may have one or more accounts. To link these two tables, Profile keys are inserted into the Account table as foreign keys for easy reference in such a way that for each Profile key in the Account table, there is a record in the Party Profile table with this key value.

Referential integrity is one of the principal features of the majority of Relational Database Management Systems (RDBMS) that support the MDM system. Many MDM solutions are deployed on standards-based commercial RDBMS platforms. However, because a typical MDM solution uses a number of other keys, many MDM engines offer additional key management services designed to maintain the integrity and consistency of the MDM Data Hub.

As shown in Chapter 7, at design time, a Data Hub data modeler constructs the logical and physical data models that include primary and foreign keys. However, having a key placeholder is not enough—the values of these keys need to be available for any operation where data in the Data Hub is added, changed, or deleted. Moreover, the values of these keys need to be created and placed in appropriate records in such a way that they do not violate referential integrity and other constraints. These key values need to be available prior to loading data into the Data Hub so that the load operation can create a well-formed Data Hub data store. Likewise, any action that results in the addition of a data record (for example, a new account) has to be carefully designed to make sure that the appropriate values for the primary and foreign keys are available and that the resulting operation does not violate the referential integrity of the Data Hub.

The generation and maintenance of all keys required for the operation and the sustainability of the MDM Data Hub is the responsibility of the Key Generation service. This service has to be flexible, adaptable, and scalable, and should support any number of keys defined in the MDM Data Hub data model. For example, the Key Generation Service should efficiently generate primary keys for every record stored in the Data Hub and insert foreign keys for all related entities inside the Data Hub data model. This service also needs to capture and maintain "natural" keys that get loaded into the Data Hub from all data sources. The Key Generation service needs to interface with the Matching and Linking service (discussed in previous sections) in order to store and manage various unique identifiers created by the Matching and Linking process.

As the Data Hub matures and begins to support additional data attributes and entities, the Key Generation service would need to rapidly and easily adapt to new requirements and generate new sets of keys as required by the service consumers, which include data load processes as well as business applications that can add, change, and delete records.

Record Locator Services

An MDM Data Hub is an information integration platform that, by definition, integrates information collected from various data sources. A Data Hub data model is designed to easily aggregate individual records that came into the Data Hub from a variety of sources into linked groups. The resulting logical and physical data structures inside the Data Hub are different from the data stores used to load the Data Hub. In other words, in the majority of all MDM implementation cases, there is no simple one-to-one mapping between the records in the Data Hub and its sources. And this is the reason why an MDM Data Hub needs to support a service capability that enables such mapping.

This mapping becomes necessary as soon as the Data Hub is loaded with data and correctly seeded with entity keys. At that point, the Data Hub can act as the authoritative reference of the information for which it is the master. However, as the consuming applications begin to use Data Hub information, a number of use cases need to be considered to maintain the integrity and accuracy of the data (many of these cases are discussed in Chapter 5):

- Consuming applications may request information that is only partially stored in the Data Hub, with the remainder still residing in the source system from which the Data Hub was initially loaded—a typical scenario for the Registry and Coexistence Hub architecture styles.

- As data in the Data Hub gets updated by users and application, the Data Hub would have to propagate the changes to the systems that were used to load the Data Hub in the first place (Hub-to-Source synchronization).

- The data for which the Data Hub is not the master resides in the old legacy systems of record. If this data is also loaded into the Data Hub, it has to be updated in step with the updates to the original source system (Source-to-Hub synchronization).

The challenge of these use cases is to find appropriate records in the source systems based on the records stored in the Data Hub, and vice versa. This is the responsibility of another important Data Hub service—the Record Locator service.

The Record Locator service is a metadata-based service that creates and maintains a persistent transactional subject area inside a metadata repository store. The Record Locator service leverages a metadata repository and maps Data Hub keys and keys used by other systems as they participate in the loading and updating of data inside the Data Hub. This mapping represents a special type of metadata that may be implemented as a subject area in the Data Hub metadata repository (metadata is briefly discussed Chapters 4 and 5).

Conceptually, this metadata area is a directory that can be represented as a table that contains a row for each Data Hub record. Each row contains a primary key of the Data Hub detail record, and as many columns as there are external record keys. Again, this is certainly only a conceptual view. Logical and physical models would require normalization. The key values are loaded into this table during operations that create records in the Data Hub. The primary key can be obtained from the Linking and Matching service or, if desired, from the Key Generation service, as long as that key value exists in the Data Hub record.

In our Source-to-Hub use case, the Record Locator service would identify the impacted records in the Data Hub caused by the changes received by one or more source systems.

In the Hub-to-Source scenario, the Record Locator service would perform a reverse operation and would identify external (to the Hub) systems and individual records impacted by changes applied to the Data Hub.

The Key Generation service and Record Locator service are necessary functional components of any MDM solution, whether developed in-house or implemented as an MDM vendor product. The architecture requirements for these services include service-oriented implementation, scalability, reliability, flexibility, and support for transactional semantics. The latter means that when, for example, a Data Hub creates, updates, or deletes a data record, this operation will succeed only if the update operations for Key Generation and Record Locator services also complete successfully. In this case, the Data Hub will commit all the changes to the Data Hub data store and to the metadata repository. If any of the component transactions (Hub data operation, Key Generation, or CRUD operations on Record Locator metadata) fail, then the entire transaction should fail, and the Data Hub has to roll the partial changes back to their pre-transaction state.

The foregoing discussion of Data Hub services would not be complete if we did not mention other MDM functions and services such as Transaction Coordination, Synchronization and Reconciliation service, Rules Management service, Metadata-driven Attribute Location service, Change Management service, Hub Data Load service, Security and Visibility service, and many others. We discuss some of these services in the Chapters 4 and 5, and their implementation aspects are covered in Part IV of the book.

References

1. Silverston, Len. *The Data Model Resource Book*, Revised Edition, *Vol. 1: A Library of Universal Data Models For All Enterprises*. Wiley Computer Publishing (March 2001).

2. Silverston, Len and Agnew, Paul. *The Data Model Resource Book, Vol. 3: Universal Patterns for Data Modeling*. Wiley Computer Publishing (January 2009).

3. http://en.wikipedia.org/wiki/Ontology_(information_science).

4. Schumacher, Scott. "Probabilistic Versus Deterministic Data Matching: Making an Accurate Decision." Information Management Special Reports, January 2007. http://www.information-management.com/specialreports/20070118/1071712-1.html.

5. Berson, Alex and Smith, Stephen. *Data Warehousing, Data Mining, and OLAP*. McGraw-Hill (November 1997).

Master Data Modeling

At this point in our MDM architecture discussion, we are ready to take a closer look at a particularly important and foundational concern of any data management framework—the discipline of data modeling and specific issues related to data modeling in MDM environments.

Importance of Data Modeling

In the corporate world, enterprise data resides mostly in relational databases. Similarly to the cities, towns, villages, housing developments, and individual buildings that require architects to create the structures and then control structural changes, the organization of data requires sound architectural standards and principles. Data modeling is the key part of data architecture that defines the structures in which the enterprise data resides and evolves. Enterprise data modeling is considered a powerful technique to define, create, and maintain data structures and enable data integrity; gather business requirements; and communicate and socialize the scope of enterprise data; its organization, levels of aggregation, and constraints.

Furthermore, a robust and scalable data architecture enables meaningful and timely change. Historically, every era has witnessed an accelerated rate of change and scope from many perspectives such as business, technology, regulatory, social, and political. To flourish or even simply survive in this environment requires real business agility to respond to market threats and opportunities as well as regulatory challenges. Strategic and tactical business strategies, business operations, and supporting technologies must all be malleable and aligned.

Over the past four decades, since Edgar F. Codd introduced the notion of a relational database and its normalization principles,[1-3] data modeling has evolved into a discipline that defines a common data modeling "language" widely accepted by various enterprise users: data modelers, business analysts, database administrators, application and database developers, data governors, and data stewards. Data modeling is used in a variety of contexts and scenarios, ranging from conceptual and canonical models that determine the entities and relationships in a system-agnostic way, to logical and physical data models that represent specific systems and applications.

For a data modeler, a data model provides valuable business and architectural insight into the scope of the enterprise data, data integrity rules, information on how the data modeling universe will be able to support business processes and determine what data can be retrieved, and the paths to join pieces of information to bring them together. For business and systems analysts, a data model can play an important role in gathering and documenting business requirements.

Data modeling tools supporting modern physical data models allow database administrators and database developers to model and maintain a variety of objects (tables, indexes, attributes of various data types, views, triggers, stored procedures, functions, constraints, and other more complex objects) for an assortment of database vendors and products.

In order to support a variety of needs and views at different levels of abstraction and granularity, the data modeling discipline introduced a number of modeling styles that differ by the goal for which each of the styles is optimized. In this chapter we briefly discuss the styles that dominate the current data modeling market. We concentrate on the strengths of these data modeling styles and some of their weaknesses, especially as these weaknesses apply to Master Data Management, which is the focus of this book.

We analyze master data modeling–specific needs to understand which data modeling methodologies, techniques, and patterns developed over the decades are best fit to model the master data, and how. Then, based on this analysis, we focus on the modeling styles in the context of their relevance and optimization for master data. This will help us arrive at conclusions as to what data modeling styles can be used for different master data solution scenarios. We discuss a number of practical and important master data aspects around the dependencies between MDM data modeling styles and the goals they have to support, including such important considerations as change control issues, data model readability, required history support, and support for entity resolution and relationship resolution, and contrast this with the needs of applications that consume MDM services, on-going support for master data model synchronization, and so on.

Predominant Data Modeling Styles

The third normal form (3NF) modeling introduced by Edgar F. Codd has been the most widely adopted standard for several decades. The 3NF normalized models are optimized to ensure minimal data redundancy. For instance, if a doctor's office or hospital captures and re-enters the patient's name, address, date of birth, and other static or infrequently changing pieces of information for every patient visit, along with visit-specific information, the patients' data will be redundant. Not only will such redundancy require extra data storage; what is more important, data redundancy may cause data inconsistencies and complicate data maintenance. Indeed, if a data element value is incorrect, in order to fix the issue the data must be corrected in multiple places where the data element is stored. Similarly, if a company's order processing system requires or allows the information about its frequent customers to be re-entered every time a customer places an order or opens a new account, this situation will lead to data redundancy.

The burden and subsequent costs to an organization are often significant. Change is stifled. Redundancy masks the fundamental problem of accessing an entire data domain in terms of its original purpose and also utilizing it for new business purposes.

Data normalization techniques and 3NF normalization techniques, specifically, tackle the problem by breaking large data into relatively small normalized tables where the data attributes depend on the primary key and only the primary key. For example, an Order table that contains both customer- and order-level data in its denormalized form may be split into two tables as a result of normalization. These are the Customer table and the Order table, with the customer-specific attributes residing in the Customer table while the order-specific attributes remain in the Order table. The Order table would have a reference key (foreign key) that points to a uniquely identified customer in the customer table.

Because 3NF modeling minimizes or eliminates data redundancy, the 3NF modeling style is considered a good choice for transactional systems, where the primary goal is to input and update the data in the database and maintain the data consistency. When the data is stored without redundancy, data consistency issues are addressed naturally. Expressed differently, 3NF is the preferred and predominant modeling style for On-Line Transaction Processing (OLTP).

If the goal of data modeling is to optimize the data model for reporting and analytics, a normalized model may not be the best choice. With the data modeled in the 3NF format, bringing data from different tables together for a report may require many tables to be queried in a joint fashion (in RDBMS, this operation is called a "join," and it can be a very expensive operation in terms of computing resources and the performance impact). In addition to the potential performance problems, joins represent challenges for the database developer responsible for making the tables to join with each other correctly and efficiently, using the least amount of resources and creating a minimal an amount of intermediate, temporary tables as possible.

As the cost of storage dropped significantly over the last several decades, enterprises started gathering increasingly more information about their businesses, customers, products, and other data domains, both broader in scope and deeper in the detail levels of granularity. This has resulted in the material increase in the number of data records, elements, and attributes that need to be stored and processed. From the data modeling perspective, this trend that started in 1990s led to a tremendous increase in the complexity of enterprise data models, often having to manage thousands of entities and relationships in a single model.

In an extreme case, one simple report metric, such as total sales, can span numerous tables from multiple internal and external sources in multiple geographic and functional domains. Moreover, each of these data sources can have different technical architectures and different business definitions.

Figure 7-1 illustrates a typical representation of a 3NF data model with the number of entities around 50.

Even with 50 entities, it is not easy to navigate through such a model and correctly join the tables to retrieve the results of a complex reporting query. When the number of tables grows to reach hundreds and even thousands of tables or entities, the complexity of the model defeats the purpose of the data model stated at the beginning of this chapter as a common "language" that can be used by many data modeling stakeholders across the enterprise.

Robert Hillard[4] proposed measuring the complexity of the data model by looking at it as a graph within the Small World theory. The Small World theory had been earlier applied to networking in biology, sociology, telephony, and other types of networks. The theory evaluates the complexity of the network in terms of the number of steps required to assemble information distributed across the network. The Small World approach uses the graph theory terms *vertex* (node) and *edge* (connection between nodes). These two terms can be easily interpreted in terms of the more traditional data modeling concepts of *entity* and *relationship*, respectively. This approach introduces the following terms:

- Vertex (node) = entity
- Edge (connection between nodes] = relationship
- Order = number of entities/vertices

Enterprise data modeling is considered a powerful technique to define, create, and maintain data structures and data integrity, and communicate and socialize the scope of the enterprise da its organization, and its levels of aggregation and constraints.

- Enterprise data models, when 3NF normalized, include many hundreds and oftentimes thousands of entities connected in many different ways.
- Simple business questions become very difficult with the 3NF enterprise model.
- There are no clearly defined processes and procedures for how the data model is going to be used and maintained.
- Expensive industry data models oftentimes end up unused.

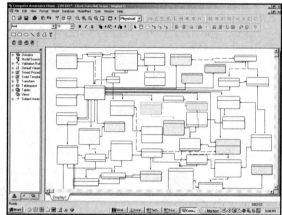

FIGURE 7-1   An illustrative example of a normalized data model

- Size = number of relationships/edges
- Geodesic distance = minimum number of relationships/edges to be traversed
- Average degree = average number of edges (connections) per node
- Average distance = averaging the geodesic distance of all entity pairs
- Maximum distance = maximum number of edges/relationships needed to traverse between the two most remote entities in the model

Figure 7-2 illustrates the concept of the Small World theory and its metrics.

▶ Data model complexity measurement according to Mike2.0:
   http://mike2.openmethodology.org/index.php/Small_Worlds_Data_
   Transformation_Measure

   • Data model as a graph where each table is a node/vertex and relationships
     are looked upon as connections or edges

   • Order = 5
   • Size = 4
   • Average Degree = (1+2+3+1)/5=1.4
   • Average Distance
     (1+2+3+3+1+2+2+1+1+2)/10=1.8
   • Maximum Distance = 3

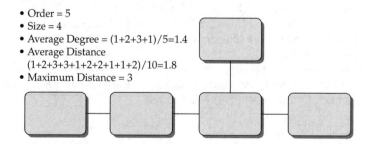

FIGURE 7-2   The Small World theory metrics

From more traditional data modeling and database development perspectives, these measures evaluate a potential complexity of the joins that may be required to bring the data together and to read the model intelligently. The theory suggests that if the average geodesic distance is less than 4, the graph (in this case, the data model) is relatively easy to read and navigate. A graph with an average distance approaching 10 makes it extremely challenging to navigate the model, even for individuals who do it on a daily basis as a full-time job. Hence, in order for multiple stakeholder groups to use the data model as a common language, the average geodesic distance should not exceed 4. The data model with an average geodesic distance between 4 and 10 can be used only by trained and tenured database developers and administrators. As the average geodesic distance approaches 10 and exceeds it, the data model as a readable network environment becomes inefficient.

Strengths and Weaknesses of 3NF Data Modeling

3NF is a powerful data modeling technique that accomplishes the following:

- Minimizes data redundancy within the model.
- Simplifies maintenance when data records are updated or deleted. This makes the 3NF modeling design optimized for applications that concentrate on data entry and record-at-a-time processing, which is typical of On-Line Transaction Processing (OLTP).

This modeling technique has its limitations:

- 3NF models are not optimized for data retrieval, reporting, and analytics. Consequently, simple business questions may become difficult to answer, even if the data is available in the database.
- The model is not optimized to support a historical view of the data. The traditional normalization methodology models the current state data. Requirements to support historical views are typically addressed separately and later.
- The traditional 3NF normalization methodology does not focus on the data volumes that are expected for each database table. The methodology suggests that denormalization should be applied later, when the 3NF model is complete and database queries are optimized and possibly denormalized for performance.

NOTE *3NF is not the only normalization modeling schema, just the most popular. Other, next-level normalization forms exist, with 4NF addressing normalization that considers multivalued dependencies[5] and 5NF designed to reduce redundancy related to multivalued facts.[6] These are very advanced normalization topics. They are beyond the scope of this book and have somewhat limited practical significance.*

The aforementioned difficulties with the 3NF data modeling design drove the need to develop alternative data modeling techniques optimized for data retrieval, reporting, and decision making. The star schema modeling approach was championed by Ralph Kimball in his first data warehousing book[7] and the books and numerous articles that followed.

Figure 7-3
Illustration of the
star schema
design

An Illustrative Star Schema Design

Star Schema with N dimensions:

- Order = N+1
- Size = N
- Average Degree = (N*1+1*N)/(N+1)=2*N/(N+1) → 2 when N → ∞
- Average Distance [1*N +2*N*(N–1)/2]/[(N+1)*N/2]=2*N/(N+1) → 2 when N → ∞
- Maximum Distance = 2

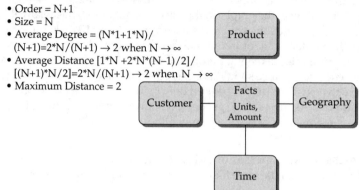

The star schema modeling is optimized for data retrieval and therefore is much better suited to support business intelligence, analytics, data warehousing, and ultimately decision making. Consequently, the star schema modeling design is often considered as an integral part of On-Line Analytical Processing (OLAP). We have briefly mentioned the concept of a star schema data model as it relates to data warehousing in Chapters 4 and 5. Figure 7-3 illustrates the typical star schema design.

This modeling design makes it much easier to read and retrieve data. The central table (fact table) usually holds numeric metrics—for example, sales revenue, sold units count, number of shipments, and so on. The tables around the center of the star are known as dimensional tables or dimensions (often representing reference data). The simple illustrative star schema in Figure 7-3 depicts Customer, Product, Geography, and Time dimensions. We will assume that the Time dimension is built with a granularity of calendar date, as is often done in data warehousing. Let's assume that there are two metrics (facts) in the fact table. The first metric represents the number of units sold, and the second metric represents the amount spent by a customer on a specific product on a given date. This model is easy to read and is often interpreted using the "slice and dice" metaphor. It is intuitively clear that the structure is designed for reporting on unit counts and dollar amount spent by a given customer on a given product at a given geography or location on a given date. Note that even with millions of records in the data store, the star schema design can enable a sub-second execution time for the query:

```
select UnitCount from Facts, Customer, Product, Geography, Time,
where
CustomerID = 'Given CustomerID',
ProductID = 'Given ProductID',
Geography = 'Given GeographyID',
TimeID = 'GivenDateID'
```

Although this query joins five tables, as long as each join predicate can be evaluated using simple equality operator (=), the type of join where a large table in the middle of the star (fact table) is joined with its immediate neighbors (dimensions) turns out to be very efficient from the performance, readability, and ease-of-use perspectives. Consequently, all major database vendors have developed proprietary star-join query optimization techniques.

> **Star Schema Definition**
> *Star schema* is a data modeling design that places a table with facts (typically numeric measures) in the middle of the star (fact table), while placing reference tables (dimensions) providing business contexts of the facts in the vertices of the star. Each dimension can be denormalized and presented by a single physical table, which maximizes the performance of the star-join.

We can interpret readability and the ease of use of the star schema model in terms of the Small World theory.

> **Star Schema Readability in Terms of the Small World Theory**
> For a star schema with N dimensions:
>
> ```
> Order = N+1 (N dimensional tables plus the fact table),
> Size = N (the number of relationships),
> Average Distance = (1*N + 2*N*(N-1)/2)/[(N+1)*N/2] → 2
> ```
>
> When the number of dimensions is high (N → ∞):
>
> ```
> Maximum Distance = 2 (between any two dimensions)
> ```

In the preceding formulas, (1*N) stands for N distances equal to 1 between each of the N dimensions and the fact table. 2*N*(N–1)/2 comes from the contribution of N*(N–1)/2 distances between the dimensions, with each distance being equal to 2. (N+1)*N/2 is the total number of distances between N+1 nodes (one fact table and N dimensions).

A star schema design assumes that the fact table is much larger by data volume (and certainly by the number of records) than the dimensional tables. This drives the recommendation to keep the dimensions denormalized since data redundancy in dimensions does not significantly impact the overall database size because the volume of the fact table mainly determines the total volume of the database. Still, data modelers sometimes denormalize dimensions and connect them with related fact tables, which results in a design known as a "snowflake" schema.

Star and snowflake schemas are built on a common design principle: separation of facts and references about the facts into two connected types of structures—fact and dimension tables. To avoid confusion, we will refer to both of these model types using a common name: the *dimensional* model.

NOTE *The assumption that the fact table is much larger in volume than dimensional tables doesn't always hold true (for example, consider a customer reference data dimension that may contain millions of records and can grow significantly if there is a requirement for historical reference data). The trend has been to persist history, thus significantly increasing business value, but at the cost of increased complexity and performance burden.*

Strengths and Weaknesses of Dimensional Modeling

The modeling techniques supporting star and snowflake schemas (typically referred to as "dimensional" schema) have evolved as a powerful alternative to the 3NF data modeling standard by offering several key benefits:

- They optimize the model for reporting on business metrics.
- They make the model easier to read and understand even if the model contains many dimensions.
- They support history (iterative views of reference data). They allow for and support dimensions that are relatively static, and make it easier to track these changes over time (slowly changing dimensions, or SCD).

Still, dimensional models such as the star schema are not perfect and have certain limitations:

- When the size of the dimensions is significant and close to the size of the fact tables, a typical data warehousing system design may have to be enhanced to address the difficulties associated with the growing dimensional cardinality and complexity.
- When the dimensions change frequently, the concept of slowly changing dimensions is no longer valid, and the resulting dynamic nature of the analytical data environment creates additional challenges and complications.
- Overall, data warehousing approaches have challenges in terms of the means for creating and maintaining high data volumes and the complexity in the content and structure of data warehousing dimensions, including the dimensions (Customer, Product, Location, and so on) that are the areas of focus of Master Data Management.

It should be noted that the 3NF structures and the dimensional model structures are so different that it is not a recommended practice to gradually move your model between these two formats. Many modelers have tried it without success. Data modelers often maintain both model formats (that is, star schema and 3NF) to make sure that their transactional needs and reporting needs are adequately supported.

As we can see, data modeling design requirements depend upon the data model purpose. In addition to the widely known 3NF and dimensional model designs (that is, the star and snowflake schemas), some alternative data modeling techniques have been developed. For instance, data vault modeling for enterprise data warehousing has been gaining popularity over the last decade.[8] It's a hybrid approach that utilizes the concepts of 3NF and star/ snowflake schema.

NOTE *A number of data modeling design styles and levels of abstraction must be maintained by data modelers and architects to support a variety of data modeling purposes, roles, and stakeholder groups.*

MDM Data Modeling Requirements

In the previous section we discussed the predominant data modeling patterns and reviewed the criteria of what scenarios these patterns are optimized for. Now we are in a position to focus on the key MDM data modeling requirements. These requirements will lead us to the master data modeling patterns and an understanding of what they can leverage from the normalization techniques, dimensional schema design, and other architecture patterns.

In the discussion that follows, we will assume that a master data model meets the following requirements:

- It must be optimized for entity resolution, relationship resolution, and fast searches of master entity records.

- It must be flexible to support multiple data domains with a variety of master entities and relationships.

- It should be able to support consuming applications such as data warehouses, data marts, operational data stores, and so on.

Let's analyze these three requirements and use them as a guide to understand master data modeling principles and patterns.

One of the primary tenets of the previous chapters has been the idea of entity resolution and relationship resolution. In order to efficiently support entity resolution and relationship resolution, a master data model must be optimized to expose and manage master data entities, their keys and identifiers, and the dynamic relationships between the entities. As we already know, these entities include Party, Product, Location, Instrument, Organization, and other entities, where the record count is expected to be at least in the thousands and can climb to many millions and even billions. For some applications (such as Person of Interest in law enforcement, counterterrorism, and intelligence gathering), these entities can be more complex than the "classical" entity types listed above, as we discussed in Chapter 3.

It is important to understand that when we discuss MDM from the entity resolution perspective, the notion of an "MDM entity" is different from the notion of an "entity" in the 3NF world. In the 3NF world, it is assumed that there is a way to define a record uniquely and the modeler is not responsible for figuring out how this is going to be done. The 3NF model asserts the existence of the primary key for each entity while not specifying how this primary key is created or inferred. A traditional 3NF modeling process does not divide the attributes into those that will be used for matching, entity resolution, and relationship resolution and those that will not be used for these purposes. Technically speaking, two or more records can have totally identical nonkey attributes. This is perfectly "legal" from the 3NF perspective to have all identical non-key attributes while two or more records have different primary keys.

This is quite different in dimensional modeling. Ralph Kimball's definitive book on the subject[7] defines the key steps of how a star schema model is developed. The process begins with the identification of business flows that drive the selection of the facts and their granularity. Then the data modeler defines the dimensions, levels of aggregation, and so on.

Let's follow this pattern by defining and discussing in detail the steps that need to be followed to develop the model optimized for entity resolution and relationship resolution:

1. *Define entity domains.* High-level definitions of these domains and the domain implementation sequence are typically aligned with and driven by business strategies. Party, Product, Location, Supplier, and Account are the most frequent candidates in the list of MDM data domains.

2. *For each master data domain, define the entities that need to be resolved algorithmically due to their complexity.* Let's take a look at the entities and attributes of a Party model and discuss the differences in how these constructs are presented in the 3NF model and in the master data model optimized for entity resolution and relationship resolution. For example, for the Party domain we need to define what entities we will need to resolve algorithmically due to their volume and complexity and what entities we will extensively search on in MDM-enabled applications across the enterprise.

   Unlike 3NF modeling, where all entities are equal and volume agnostic, master data modeling optimized for entity resolution concentrates on the entities that have high volumes of data and require advanced algorithms. We touched on these algorithm categories in Chapter 6 (probabilistic, machine learning, and so on). For instance, from the 3NF perspective, the entities Customer, Country, and Gender would normally be represented as three entities depicted as "boxes" in an Entity Relationship Diagram (ERD) with the primary keys CustomerID, CountryID, and GenderID. Unlike that, from the entity resolution perspective, the entity Customer (with thousands and oftentimes millions of records) is typically the "first-class citizen" that requires an entity resolution algorithm, whereas entities such as Country and Gender do not qualify for this "first-class citizen" entity category.

   Many enterprises serve both individual and commercial or institutional customers. This makes "Individual" and "Organization" the most likely candidates for the "first-class citizen" entities in the Party domain. An identification of the "first-class citizen" entities must take into account business definitions of the terms "Customer," "Product," and so on. An enterprise division or line of business that services retail customers (individuals), in addition to having individual customers in the MDM Data Hub, may also want to see "Household" as a separate entity to support marketing needs. For many organizations and business functions, the notion of a Household is a preferred definition of a Customer. The division that serves commercial customers may have multiple definitions of the entities comprising the Party domain, too. For instance, a billing department may consider the parent company that is responsible for bill processing a Customer whereas the shipment department may have a more granular definition of a Customer based on the site or location.

3. *For each "first-class citizen" entity, define identity attributes.* The identity attributes are the attributes that will be used to match and discriminate records, and to separate entity types and record types. Expressed differently, these are all the attributes that can help resolve master entities and assign a unique identifier to each set of records that represent the same object (customer, product, and so on). For instance, Name and Address are typical matching attributes. The attribute Gender is not good for record matching on its own but can help discriminate two records from matching when husband and wife or different gender siblings or twins live at the same address.

This is especially important if only the initials are available for their first names. Entity type or record type attributes are important to separate records that may look similar but represent different entity subtypes that should never be matched—for example, John Smith (a person) to John Smith, Foundation.

4. *Define attribute history needs and versioning requirements.* Record history is critical for entity resolution and relationship resolution. Indeed, if Mary Smith changed her last name three years ago and her new name is Mary Johns, from the entity resolution perspective it is important to know that she was Mary Smith in the past. Some systems may recognize Mary by her new last name whereas some other systems may still hold the old last name (Smith) that Mary had three years ago. Address history is even more important. Statistically, in the U.S. an individual changes primary residence once every five years.

Importance of History for Entity Resolution

From the entity resolution perspective, the past attribute values are almost equally as important as the present values. This should be taken into account by the master data modeler.

An exception to this rule is when an attribute value was entered by mistake.

When modeling for history support with a focus on entity resolution, the modeler has to decide what groups of fields constitute an attribute from the versioning perspective. For instance, the attributes Address and Location would typically consist of a set of fields. This set may include street, city, state/province, ZIP or regional code, and GPS coordinates. The modeler should define the set of address fields as a single attribute of a complex data type. When an address changes, a new version of the composite address attribute will be created. Even if a customer has moved to another apartment and all address fields other than "Apartment" remain unchanged, a new version of the entire address still will be created by the system.

Figure 7-4 illustrates how address records are versioned. There are many attributes that should be versioned like complex data types, including addresses, names, pieces of identification, credit card information, and so on.

Address

IndividualID	Version	Street	City	State	ZIPCode	Status	Create Date	Update Date
100	1	2012 Main St	Hightstown	NJ	08520	Inactive	1/19/2007	2/22/2010
100	2	1015 Mercer St	Hightstown	NJ	08520	Active	2/22/2010	01/01/9999

Address is an example of an attribute of a complex type. Even though only the street address changed, a new version of the address attribute is created.

FIGURE 7-4 Versioning of complex data attributes (address as an illustrative example)

5. *Add non-identity attributes.* These are the attributes required for reasons other than entity resolution and relationship resolution. Payload attributes are one of the categories of non-identity attributes. Payload attributes are those that need to be in the model due to the way the enterprise intends to use the MDM Data Hub to support portals and other applications that operate on the MDM Data Hub directly or require the payload data in the data feeds from the MDM Data Hub. For instance, payload data may include the customer's investment goals for a wealth management company, product description and pricing, and so on. Another group of non-identity attributes includes the attributes that are maintained in the MDM Data Hub to support the needs of data governance dashboard and data quality.

   It should be noted that when an MDM Data Hub is already in production, it is much easier to add or drop a non-identity attribute than an identity attribute. Indeed, the addition or removal of an identity attribute can change the primary identifiers linking the source system records. This change can be fairly intrusive, especially if changes in the enterprise identifiers are accepted and processed in MDM consuming applications. From this perspective, the addition of payload attributes is much less intrusive. Therefore, a modeler should do his or her best to make sure that all of the identity attributes are included in the model to support the entity resolution algorithm. Payload attributes can be easily added later.

6. *Create an MDM-Star schema.* In the MDM world, an *MDM-Star* schema is a natural representation of the concept of a master entity. Figure 7-5 represents an MDM-Star with an entity Customer that can have multiple names, multiple addresses, and multiple pieces of identification. Relatively few attributes have a one-to-one relationship to the center of the star Customer (examples include Date of Birth and Gender).

   In the previous paragraph we introduced a new term: "MDM-Star." Indeed, instead of being presented as a single entity box in a typical relational model, the model in Figure 7-5 represents a master entity, Customer, as an MDM-Star with the customer identifier in the center of the star and the attributes hanging around the center with one-to-many relationships between the CustomerID and each of the attributes. The direction of one-to-many relationships from the center of the star to the attributes makes the MDM-Star look different from a data warehousing star schema structure, where one-to-many relationships are directed from the dimensions to the center of the star (fact table). Despite that, the MDM-Star possesses the same benefits as the traditional data warehousing star schema design. The MDM-Star schema design is optimized for entity resolution and relationship resolution, and supports very high performance for search, matching, and linking for millions and even billions of records. Figure 7-5 depicts only one star representing one entity: Customer. Similarly, an MDM-Star should be created for each MDM entity that requires algorithmic entity resolution or relationship resolution.

   Identification in Figure 7-5 represents pieces of identification such as Social Security Number, Driver's License, Passport, and so on.

   The MDM-Star design is not optimized for complex cross–MDM-Star analytical queries. Applications modeled with the MDM-Star modeling style provide cross-entity navigation functionality through relationships, which typically meets the operational needs of MDM Data Hub users.

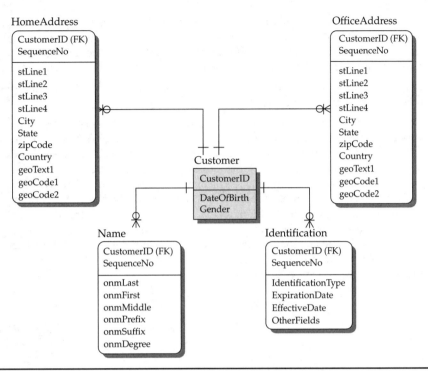

FIGURE 7-5 An MDM-Star for a single entity (Customer)

It is appropriate to mention that the Small World theory can be applied to the MDM-Star model to evaluate its readability the way we did earlier in this chapter for the data warehouse star schema design. For an MDM-Star schema with N attributes, we can define the following:

- Order = N+1 (N attributes plus the center of the star table).
- Size = N (the number of connections between the center of the star and the attributes).
- Average Distance → 2 when the number of attributes is high (N → ∞).
- Maximum Distance = 2 (between any two attributes).

MDM-Star Schema Readability in Terms of the Small World Theory

Order = N+1 (N attributes plus the center of the star table).

Size = N (the number of connections between the center of the star and the attributes).

Average Distance = $(1*N + 2*N*(N–1)/2)/[(N+1)*N/2]$ → 2 when the number of attributes is high (N → ∞).

Maximum Distance = 2 (between any two attributes).

7. *Model relationships.* The MDM-Star design enables the modeler to create relationships. Relationships in the MDM-Star design are allowed only between the centers of the stars. Figure 7-6 represents four entities (Individual, Account, Household, and Organization) with a few relationships supported as relationship tables.

Potentially some other relationships can be defined in Figure 7-6 (for example, a relationship between an Individual and Household).

The notion of a relationship in the entity resolution and relationship resolution world is richer than that in the traditional relational world (3NF or data warehouse star schema). In the relationship resolution process, it is important to know how a relationship is created and maintained. In the traditional logical data modeling, the modeler defines a relationship by its cardinality and ordinality (in this context, *ordinality* refers to the order of records or some of its attributes). In the physical data model, this translates into the foreign key and primary key constraints. For example, if two entities—Brand and Product—are related by a one-to-many relationship, the physical model tells us that the foreign key (BrandID) defines a relationship between Brand and Product. The model does not tell us how this foreign key, and therefore the relationship, is created and maintained.

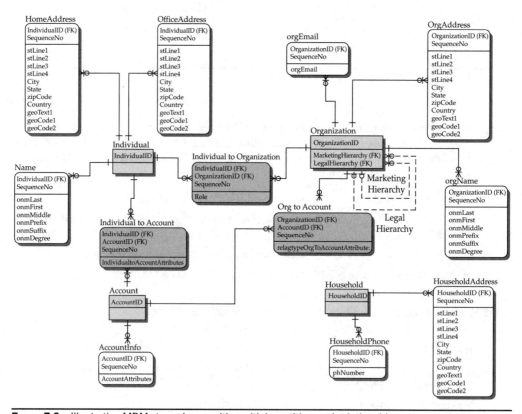

FIGURE 7-6 Illustrative MDM-star schema with multiple entities and relationships

In contrast to that, the MDM Data Hub software can algorithmically resolve relationships by applying deterministic, probabilistic, or fuzzy logic to a set of attributes responsible for a relationship; for example, the attribute "Employer" in the entity "Individual" can trigger a resolution of a relationship between the "Individual" and the "Organization."

As we can see, this consideration is similar to what we discussed earlier in this chapter for the notion of entity resolution and how the primary keys are defined or inferred.

At a high level there exist three methods for relationship resolution, and ideally an MDM-Star model should support some or all of them even though at present traditional data modeling tools do not support such functionality:

- **A relationship resolved as an exact match**   A foreign key constraint is an example of this relationship. The relationships in this category are resolved based on the rule that an attribute value or a key value in one entity is exactly equal to an attribute value or a key value in another entity. The value can be represented by a complex data type and composite key.

- **A relationship resolved by an advanced algorithm**   When we discussed entity resolution, we touched upon advanced algorithms (fuzzy, probabilistic, learning algorithms). A similar approach can be applied to relationship resolution.

   These algorithms resolve relationships by linking entities. The goal of the algorithm in this scenario is not to determine that two or more records represent the same entity, but rather to determine or infer relationships.

   For instance, a relationship between a customer and an organization or between a customer and a household can be inferred. A Person of Interest can be related algorithmically to a terrorist network, and so on.

- **A relationship defined by a human**   Even though advanced entity and relationship resolution algorithms can demonstrate quasi-human intelligence, it is a common requirement that an end user can override an algorithmically derived or inferred relationship. This includes the ability to create a new relationship that has not been established algorithmically or to unlink two entities that the algorithm linked to create a relationship. For example, a human resource manager can define a relationship between several employees based on a set of common interests (for example, a running club).

Oftentimes, all three methods are used in combination to accomplish the best results.

8. *Model hierarchies.* A hierarchy is a special case of relationships. We started discussing hierarchies in Chapters 5 and 6, and provide additional considerations of hierarchies in the context of master data modeling in this section. To recap, in the context of MDM we can define a *hierarchy* as an arrangement of entities (parties, accounts, products, cost centers, and so on) where entities are viewed in relationship to each other as "parents," "children," or "siblings/peers" of other entities according to a certain classification schema, thus forming a conceptual tree structure where all leaf nodes in the hierarchy tree can be rolled into a single "root." Further, each hierarchy has one and only one root node. Each hierarchy node can have zero, one, or many children nodes. Each node other than the root node has one and only one parent. A hierarchy can have an unlimited number of layers.

In the MDM world, corporate hierarchies are especially important. Risk management organizations and marketing departments need to understand the corporate hierarchies of their prospects and clients to manage relationship risks and credit risks as well as to improve the intelligence of marketing and marketing outcomes. A number of vendors offer corporate hierarchy data (Dun & Bradstreet, Equifax, and so on). These hierarchies are used to resolve hierarchical relationships. This resolution follows the three methods outlined earlier where we discussed relationships. It is particularly important in Master Data Management to be able to support multiple hierarchies required by different functions in the enterprise (sales hierarchy, legal hierarchy, marketing hierarchy, and so on). Two hierarchies are shown in Figure 7-6 as illustrative examples (legal and marketing). The need for hierarchies is not limited to organizational hierarchies. For instance, employees of a company are organized in hierarchies that show reporting relationships. Product hierarchy representation is a convenient way to see a breakdown structure of complex products or bills of materials. Geographies can also be organized in hierarchies for sales territory management.

9. *Define and model reference data.* This step concentrates on the modeling of reference data. Reference data processes include the following:

- A definition of reference data entities (for example, Account Type, Brand, Gender, Country, and Territory).

- A definition of the lists of allowed or accepted values recognized by the enterprise across multiple functions for the reference data entities selected in the first bullet. These are typically the entities with lower record counts, ranging from very few allowed values (for example, Gender) to a few hundred records (such as Territory codes). At the same time, it is not unusual to find reference data files that are much larger; for example, a financial services securities master can contain thousands of records. And, of course, a customer or account reference file can have millions of records, where the records contain externally or internally established identifiers such as customer ID, account numbers, and so on. Regardless of the size of the reference data, managing these entities is based on the idea that only certain distinct values are allowed from the business process and data governance perspectives. The business and data governance organization working together define the distinct values that should be allowed for the reference data.

- A definition of standards and formats that the attributes and list values must comply with. Definitions of standards can apply to short lists of allowed values and the entities with very high distinct value counts, such as social security number, phone number, and e-mail address. Account numbers and credit card numbers also follow specific formats that must be validated. This type of validation is one of the data governance functions.

The model presented in Figure 7-6 is easily readable. Given that a mature enterprise may have hundreds of reference data entities and rules, their inclusion in the diagram in Figure 7-6 would hamper the model readability. This issue can be addressed by using multiple views of the MDM canonical (systems- and applications-agnostic) data model. Different views should be able to turn on or off the display of the reference data. The existing data modeling tools do not adequately support this type of data modeling need.

10. *Map the model to source systems and define the source systems' entities and attributes that will be stored in the MDM Data Hub.* So far, we have been focusing our data modeling steps on the development of master data structures for the canonical master data model, which is independent of operational source systems. Typically an MDM Data Hub redundantly stores the source system data used in the process of matching, linking, and entity/relationship resolution to infer master entity records and relationships. Early versions of MDM Data Hub products made some attempts not to store the source system records in the MDM Data Hub redundantly, but rather access the source system records directly in the source systems. This type of federated architecture has not been adopted in the field due to performance problems. Therefore, the modeler should be able to model a representation of data where the model explicitly shows which systems, tables, and attributes contribute to the attributes in the canonical MDM-Star model depicted in Figure 7-6.

Figure 7-7 provides the source system–specific view of the MDM-star schema presented in Figure 7-6.

Let's analyze the differences between the canonical (system-agnostic) representation in Figure 7-6 and the system-specific model representation in Figure 7-7:

• Figure 7-7 shows that the centers of the stars for the source-specific models have additional identifiers: the identifier that shows which system each record is originated from (SystemID) and the system-specific identifiers for the record

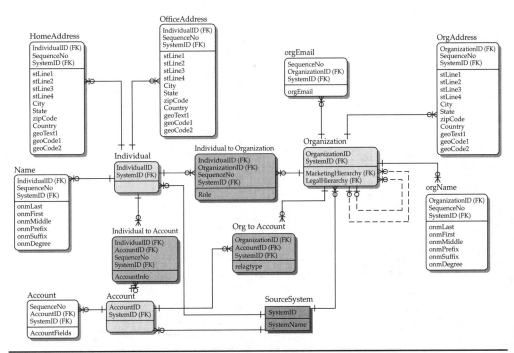

FIGURE 7-7   An illustrative MDM-Star schema (source-specific representation)

(SystemCustomerID, SystemAccoutID, SystemOrganizationID, and SystemProductID). This model is more granular than the one in Figure 7-6 and allows more than one source system record to contribute to the canonical master entity representation (system-agnostic) depicted in Figure 7-6.

Another significant difference between Figures 7-6 and 7-7 is that Figure 7-6 contains four MDM-Stars, whereas Figure 7-7 displays only three MDM-Stars. Figure 7-8 explains the reason for this. The Individual MDM-Star in the source-specific model yields two entities: Individual and Household. The entity Customer in Figure 7-6 is obtained by entity resolution that takes into account all of a person's identity attributes, and the entity Household is obtained from Household identity attributes. The Household identity attributes do not include attributes such as First Name, Social Security Number, and any other attributes of an individual Customer.

The way the source system attributes can contribute to the values of the canonical entity attributes is by following the attribute survivorship rules that we will discuss in more detail in Part IV. Ideally, it would be great to keep these attribute survivorship rules in a data modeling tool. Unfortunately, many existing data modeling tools do not present a convenient way of doing this.

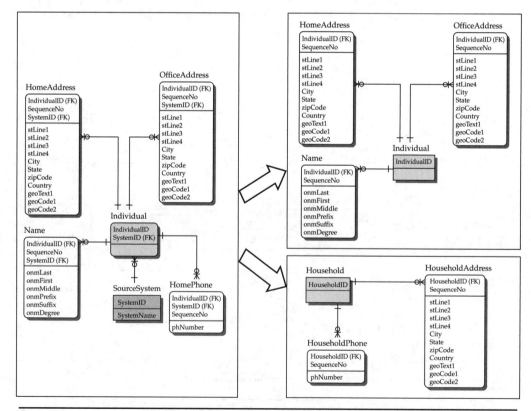

FIGURE 7-8   Mapping between the canonical model and a source-specific model

It should be noted that the MDM-Star system-specific structures in Figure 7-7 are so efficient from the entity resolution and relationship resolution perspectives that the canonical model in Figure 7-6 (system agnostic) may not even be persisted but rather created dynamically. This design is proven to support use cases with many millions of records. In Part IV, we will discuss the pros and cons of having the canonical-level record persisted in the MDM Data Hub versus the solution where the canonical-level record is retrieved dynamically.

Reference code reconciliation is an important part of reference data mapping. The reference codes, allowed values, and standards defined in the reference data section must be mapped to the values and codes used in the source systems. It is an architectural decision which component is responsible for reference code reconciliation semantics. This can be done inside the Data Hub or by an external component.

To a significant extent the data governance organization decides which reference codes, values, and standards have enterprise significance and which enumerations, codes, and standards should be managed in specific functional areas. We will discuss the issues of data governance in more detail in Part IV.

From the Master Data Management perspective, third-party data sources that help resolve entities and relationships and enrich data should also be considered as data sources and their attributes modeled in the source-specific schema. Third-party data sources are typically considered trusted master data sources. This means that the third-party records cannot be linked by a single enterprise identifier, unlike the internal enterprise records residing in operational systems.

11. *Model landing and staging areas.* Landing and staging area data models are often used to load the data into the Data Hub (refer to the Data Zone architecture discussion in Chapter 5 for additional details on these areas). There is a trend to make these areas less significant, especially when real-time integration between the source systems and the MDM Data Hub is required. The source system record is sent to the MDM Data Hub through an Enterprise Service Bus (ESB). Modern MDM Data Hub products support a set of services to transform the data and present the canonical data correctly and dynamically (Figure 7-6), even if the records are not perfectly cleansed in the system-specific layer (Figure 7-7).

12. *Model for master data consumption, including data warehousing dimensions.* The MDM-Star model optimized for entity resolution, relationship resolution, and entity-specific searches, with the need to find a particular customer, product, location, and so on, is not optimized for other types of queries. For instance, queries that require joins of multiple MDM-Star entities are not efficient. The relationships between the centers of the MDM-Stars are typically used to navigate between the MDM-Stars rather than for the queries that execute multientity MDM-star joins.

Consequently, there is a need for a model or models optimized for multientity joins. This can include operational data stores and data warehouses. A variety of industry-specific model libraries exist that can be leveraged as a starting point for developing operational data stores and data warehouses. Some examples of these libraries include:

- IBM Insurance Information Warehouse[9]
- Libraries of industry models developed by Len Silverston[10,11,12]
- Insurance models developed by Prima Solutions[13]
- Oracle industry data models[14]
- ESRI data models[15]

At the time of this writing, many MDM Data Hub products offer limited support for integration with industry-standard models. This fact is also an opportunity for MDM vendors to enhance their MDM Data Hub products to support industry-standard data models in future releases.

To further illustrate MDM data modeling requirements let's focus on the needs of the analytical MDM. We can view the analytical MDM as a separate class of consuming applications that implement some standard architectural patterns. One highly important pattern of the analytical MDM is the ability of the MDM Data Hub to create and maintain the content of data warehousing dimensions. An important question comes up as to what extent MDM should be responsible for the creation and maintenance of master data in the traditional data warehousing formats required for dimensional modeling and support for slowly changing dimensions. Figures 7-9 depicts a scenario where source systems feed a data warehouse.

The data warehouse is used to consolidate, standardize, and conform dimensional information as well as to bring the dimensional data into the required data warehousing formats used to support slowly changing dimension and other data warehousing requirements. The data warehouse is also responsible for storing and managing the fact data.

FIGURE 7-9
Data warehousing
data flow in the
absence of MDM

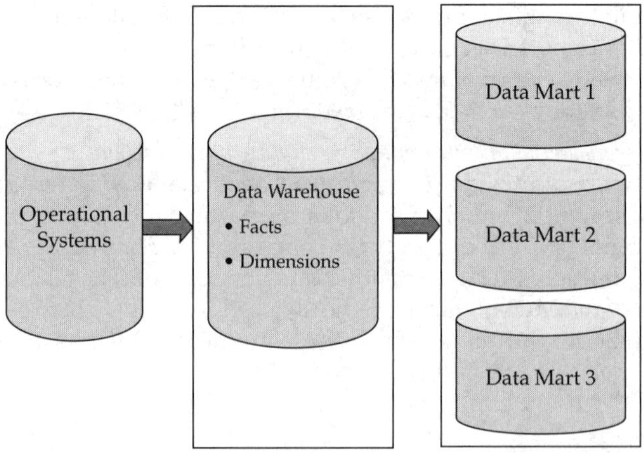

In a typical data warehouse–data mart scenario, subsets of facts and dimensions are fed into data marts that are used for reporting and analytics. It is important to understand that as a common best practice, the data warehouse is not used for reporting and analytics directly.

An MDM Data Hub can be used to manage data warehousing dimensions, as shown in Figure 7-10.

The architectural change that resulted from the introduction of an MDM Data Hub is illustrated by a comparison of Figures 7-9 and 7-10. Figure 7-10 shows that the data warehouse is no longer managing dimensional data but rather only the fact data and dimensional keys. The ownership of dimension management, including key functionality of dimensional hierarchy management, has moved to the Data Hub.

Let's discuss the nature of the changes required to translate the MDM-Star structures into a data warehousing format supporting slowly changing dimensions.

As we discussed earlier in this chapter, every change in the MDM-Star applied at the source system level is translated into the canonical-level structure. From the dimensional modeling perspective, it is important to capture dimensional snapshots within certain time intervals (for example, daily). If multiple changes occur during a day, intermediate daily changes are not captured in the dimensional world. The effective dates for the changes to take effect must be calculated for both versions of the record.

Specifically, prior to the change, only a one dimensional record exists: version 1. The record is *Active* before the change, and the start date shows the date when the record was originally created, whereas the end date (01/01/9999) signifies some unknown date in the future. After the change, version 1 of the record becomes *Inactive*, and the end date is set to the date when the change occurred (02/19/2010). The new record is created (version 2) and becomes *Active* with the new start date (02/20/2010) and the end date (01/01/9999). This type of transition requires a process that identifies the records changed over a predefined period (for example, a business day), deactivates the updated version, and creates the new active version as described in this paragraph.

FIGURE 7-10
Data warehousing
data flow after
an MDM
implementation

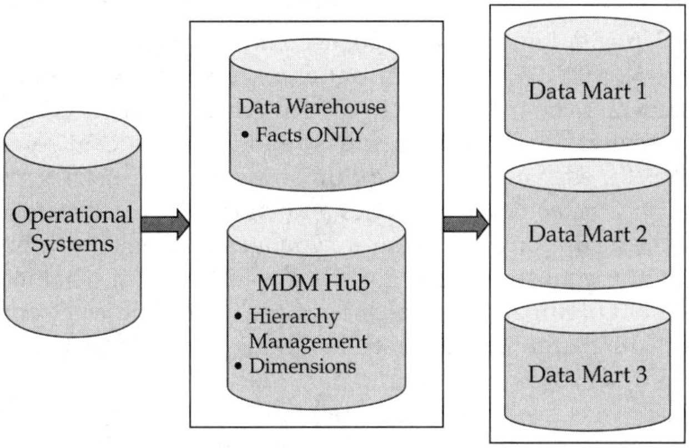

MDM-Star Model Optimized for Entity and Relationship Resolution

Master data modeling requires properly architected and managed data redundancy represented by a number of data models:

- Source system models. Typically, master data modeling efforts do not explicitly include source system modeling. The source systems exist prior to the commencement of the master data modeling effort along with their data models. Still, the master data modeler should have good level of understanding of the source data models.

- Landing and staging area models used by ETL processes. These models are normally developed by the data modeler as part of the MDM data modeling project.

- A canonical (source system–agnostic) MDM-Star model representing the authoritative source of resolved master entities and relationships. This is the most critical deliverable the data modeler should be responsible for.

- A source-specific version of the MDM-Star model representing the source system data stored in the MDM Data Hub.

- Optionally, master data models can include data formats optimized for the consuming system that require cross-entity queries. This may include the management of data warehousing dimensions in the MDM Data Hub. Most MDM implementations manage this data modeling area outside of the MDM Data Hub. There is a growing demand to improve support for consuming applications—for example, by managing data warehousing dimensions inside the MDM Data Hub in the scenarios that focus on analytical MDM.

Data Modeling Styles and Their Support for Multidomain MDM

Early MDM implementations primarily focused on a single MDM domain: most frequently Party or Product. As MDM adoption continues to grow across all industry segments, other domains have proven to be important: Location, Service, Asset, and so on. It is important to take into the account the fact that in addition to the significant commonalities of data modeling features for each of the named domains across industries, there are also some significant differences specific to industries and enterprises. For instance, the Party model for Person of Interest supporting law enforcement can differ significantly from the Party model required for a retail store. Both models may differ from what is required to support wealth management organization needs. Similarly, in the product domain, financial services products differ significantly from manufacturing products, which can translate into significant differences in the required data models. It should be noted that even if an MDM data model meets the original requirements at the MDM program initiation, the model may not be able to meet evolving MDM requirements. If an MDM initiative started with one or two domains originally defined by business requirements, other domains may become priorities of the future implementation phases. Generally speaking, this discussion focuses on the need for flexibility of the data model required to support multiple domains, functional areas, entities, attributes, relationships, and evolving business requirements.

This flexibility should be built into the model while at the same time retaining robustness, support for performance, and the maintainability of the MDM Data Hub.

Each of the data modeling styles can and should be implemented using the service-oriented architecture (SOA). The nature of the services and their granularity, to a significant extent, depend on the data modeling style.

Figure 7-11 depicts the primary MDM data modeling styles used by MDM vendors. Understanding these styles is important and may drive the selection of the MDM product and vendor.

These modeling styles differ by the degree of model abstraction and flexibility to support a variety of data modeling requirements.

- Approach 1: The "Right" Data Model
- Approach 2: Metadata Model
- Approach 3: Abstract MDM-Star Model

Approach 1: The "Right" Data Model

The first of the data modeling styles (on the left in Figure 7-11) approaches the data model with a specific data domain or domains in mind. For example, if the model concentrates on the Party domain, the model would typically include database objects (tables) such as Party, Customer, or Contact with the corresponding primary key (PartyID, CustomerID, or ContactID). Such a model is not intended to support the product domain. Many business domain–specific products were originally focused on a single domain. If a customer has acquired an MDM Data Hub product supporting only the Party domain, the need for the Product, Location, or Asset domain would drive the need for another MDM product. There are a number of disadvantages in having multiple products supporting different MDM data domains including costs, the needs to deal with potentially overlapping data modeling areas and functions offered by different MDM products, and the resulting needs to extend governance and integration efforts. To address these shortcomings, domain model–specific MDM products have evolved by supporting and integrating additional data domain areas (for example, adding and integrating the product domain to the party data model). The data

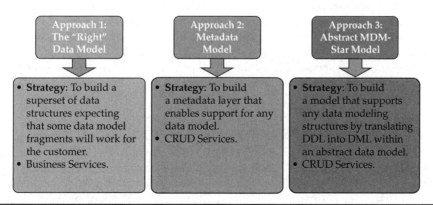

Figure 7-11   Master data modeling styles

domain model integration is a key because, oftentimes, data domain–specific products grew not organically but through the acquisitions of the MDM Data Hub products supporting different data domains.

Data Domain–Specific MDM Models and Products

MDM products with data domain–specific models face difficulties with data model flexibility and cross-domain integration because it is practically impossible to pre-build a data model supporting a variety of MDM needs for multiple industries, domains, and enterprises.

Business domain–specific models typically lead to business domain–specific services (data services and more complex composite business services).

Approach 2: Metadata Model

The second MDM data modeling style (in the middle in Figure 7-11) does not persist any data structures (tables) "out of the box." Data tables are defined in a metadata layer for each MDM project as needed. The flexibility of such metadata-driven MDM products allows the MDM modelers and architects to build multidomain MDM products and apply on-going changes to the composite data model. Clearly, this approach requires complex metadata management because the physical data model may not comply with the MDM-Star modeling rules. Consequently, the metadata should be able to map attributes from multiple tables that comprise a logical MDM entity. The complexity of this design may make it difficult to resolve errors in the metadata, which affects the ease of maintenance of the product. The overall performance of the product designed this way may suffer from the need to perform multiple table joins even within a single data domain or entity. This performance problem grows with the number of data domain records and can cause significant difficulties if entity resolution for millions of records is required.

Metadata-Only MDM Products

Metadata-only MDM products demonstrate the highest flexibility to support practically any data modeling business domain and structure required for an MDM implementation. There exists an inherent complexity of the metadata that can cause some maintainability and performance problems for complex models with high volumes of master data.

These products are often built to support multiple domains. Therefore, key services are defined at the atomic Create, Read, Update, Delete (CRUD) level for both fine-grain and coarse-grain data services. Typically, this type of product does not support complex business services "out of the box."

Approach 3: Abstract MDM-Star Model

The third data modeling style is an abstracted MDM-Star model. This data modeling style converts the typical SQL Data Definition Language (DDL) constructs such as entity names and primary key definitions into the constructs of the SQL Data Manipulation Language (DML). For instance, all entity names (Product, Customer, Broker, Service, Asset, Account, and so on) are stored as rows in a dedicated database table. The primary keys (ProductID, CustomerID, BrokerID, ServiceID, AccountID, and so on) are stored in a separate table, too. The association between the entity name and the primary key is resolved by storing the entity identifier on the record. Such a record, for the canonical-level model, may include the primary key and the key identifying the entity the primary key belongs to. The source-specific level of the model, in addition, holds the system identifier. This master data modeling style is optimized for entity and relationship resolution and can be used for an unlimited number of data domains and entities within the MDM-Star modeling style.

Because physical table names and attribute names are abstracted, the data model would not display the names like Product, Customer, and so on, which complicates the readability of the model. Business analysts would have to deal with the business services or data services layer to understand the model and its scope from the data domain perspective. As an alternative, MDM-Star abstracted models require additional components known as "bridges."[16] Such a bridge enables the product to integrate with many data modeling and database designer tools and display the abstracted model as a traditional Entity Relational Diagram (ERD).

Abstracted MDM-Star Model Products

The Abstracted MDM-star model provides flexibility to support any data domains and entities within the MDM-Star schema paradigm, which makes this data model design efficient for entity resolution and relationship resolution. This data modeling style represents some challenges in reading the data model and its interpretation from the business perspective.

The products supporting this modeling style are often built for multiple domains. Data services are defined at the fine-grain and coarse-grain levels. Typically, out of the box the list of services does not include composite business services.

We started this chapter with an overview of the predominant data modeling patterns. We used these patterns to describe a variety of MDM needs and translate these needs into a number of data modeling structures and components that must be maintained with properly architected redundancy. Our goal was to make it clear why a widely accepted data modeling practice to limit data modeling effort by a 3NF canonical model is not sufficient to address the complexity of Master Data Modeling needs. As data warehousing modeling techniques evolved in the 1990s and continued to evolve in the last decade, we can see the beginning of a similar data modeling trend for master data modeling in recent years, and we see that master data modeling is growing as a separate specialized data modeling discipline. This fact is often underestimated by the data modelers assigned to MDM initiatives.

We have discussed and defined the process of master data modeling and explained each of the data modeling steps along with why these steps are required and what makes them and master data modeling in general different from OLAP and OLTP. We have concluded with a discussion of three primary approaches used by the MDM Data Hub product vendors, and offered a comparison of these data modeling design approaches by highlighting their strengths, weaknesses, and areas of focus. As we could see, different MDM vendors concentrate on different types of data models and data modeling abstraction layers.

The data modeling "philosophy" with which an MDM Data Hub is built drives significant differences in the structure, the level of granularity of services, and the functionality and performance offered by the MDM Data Hub products.

References

1. Codd, E.F. (June 1970). "A Relational Model of Data for Large Shared Data Banks." *Communications of the ACM* **13** (6): 377–387.

2. Codd, E.F. "Further Normalization of the Data Base Relational Model." (Presented at Courant Computer Science Symposia Series 6, "Data Base Systems," New York City, May 24–25, 1971.) IBM Research Report RJ909 (August 31, 1971). Republished in *Data Base Systems: Courant Computer Science Symposia Series 6* (Randall J. Rustin, Editor). Prentice-Hall (1972).

3. Codd, E.F. "Recent Investigations into Relational Data Base Systems." IBM Research Report RJ1385 (April 23, 1974). Republished in *Proc. 1974 Congress* (Stockholm, Sweden, 1974). North-Holland (1974).

4. Hillard, Robert. "Small Worlds." http://mike2.openmethodology.org/index.php/Small_Worlds_Data_Transformation_Measure.

5. Fagin, Ronald. "Multivalued Dependencies and a New Normal Form for Relational Databases." *ACM Transactions on Database Systems* **2** (1): 267. September 1977. http://www.almaden.ibm.com/cs/people/fagin/tods77.pdf.

6. Kent, William. "A Simple Guide to Five Normal Forms in Relational Database Theory," *Communications of the ACM, (1983)* **26**: 120–125.

7. Kimball, Ralph. *The Data Warehouse Toolkit: Practical Techniques for Building Dimensional Data Warehouses.* Wiley (1996). 162.

8. Linstedt, Dan E. "Data Vault Series 1—Data Vault Overview." July 1, 2002. http://www.tdan.com/view-articles/5054/.

9. http://www-01.ibm.com/software/data/industry-models/insurance-data/.

10. Silverston, Len. *The Data Model Resource Book*, Revised Edition, *Vol. 1: A Library of Universal Data Models For All Enterprises.* Wiley Computer Publishing (March 2001).

11. Silverston, Len. *The Data Model Resource Book*, Revised Edition, *Vol. 2: A Library of Universal Data Models For Specific Industries.* Wiley Computer Publishing (March 2001).

12. Silverston, Len and Angew, Paul. *The Data Model Resource Book, Vol. 3: Universal Patterns for Data Modeling.* Wiley Computer Publishing (January 2009).

13. http://www.prima-solutions.com/frontOffice/produits/primaIBCS.jsp?gclid=CObu3e7ug6ACFVl35QodXlsYvQ.

14. http://blogs.oracle.com/datawarehousing/2009/04/oracle_releases_industry_data.html.

15. http://support.esri.com/index.cfm?fa=downloads.datamodels.gateway.

16. http://www.metaintegration.net/Products/MIMB/OMGXMI.html.

Data Security, Privacy, and Regulatory Compliance

PART
III

A s we stated in the beginning of the book, one of the major goals of Master Data
       Management strategy is the creation of an authoritative, cleansed, and integrated
       system of record for a specific business domain such as customers, products,
partners, and so on. Collecting and integrating such information in one place creates an
extremely useful, valuable, and highly leverageable information management opportunity.
At the same time, it makes these integrated data platforms attractive targets for unauthorized
access and subject to various types of information security risks, including risks of
noncompliance with numerous government and industry regulations and laws.

This heightened risk exposure has become a key concern of information security officers
and regulatory compliance groups and therefore has to be well understood in order to create
business-driven, value-added MDM solutions that don't put the enterprise in jeopardy. This
part of the book, therefore, will review various aspects of information security risks and the
key regulatory compliance requirements driving the issues of security and privacy to the
forefront of MDM implementations, with an emphasis on Master Data Management for
Customer Domain solutions such as MDM Data Hubs that integrate and need to protect
confidential data and personally identifiable information (PII) about customers, prospects,
business partners, service providers, and other parties. In addition, this part discusses
approaches and strategies for managing and mitigating information security risks. This
discussion includes information technology architecture and infrastructure implications of
developing and deploying secure and integrated MDM solutions. The discussion of these
topics is organized in the following fashion: Chapter 8 discusses regulatory requirements for
security, privacy, and confidentiality of information. Chapter 9 provides an introduction to
information security and identity management technologies, Chapter 10 talks about
information content protection, and Chapter 11 concludes with a discussion of data security
and visibility concerns and implications for the MDM architecture and design.

CHAPTER 8

Overview of Risk Management for Master Data

In business, we recognize and are concerned about various types of risks, including financial, legal, operational, transactional, reputational, and many others. While these types of risks don't represent formal risk taxonomy, it is easy to see that they all have some elements in common and are closely related. Unfortunately, more often than not various risk types are treated differently by different organizations within the enterprise, often without proper coordination between the organizations and without the ability to effectively recognize and aggregate the risks to understand the root causes and thus the most effective approaches to mitigate the risks.

This chapter offers a high-level overview of various types of risk, risk management strategies, and the implications of the major risk types for Master Data Management across various data domains. It is not intended to provide readers with a complete set of definitions, processes, and concerns of the integrated risk management and regulatory impact analysis. Rather, the goal of this chapter is to help information technology teams and MDM designers to be aware of the concerns and high-level requirements of the integrated risk management. This awareness should help MDM practitioners to better understand the impact of integrated risk management on the architecture, design, and implementation of Master Data Management solutions.

Risk Taxonomy

The interconnected nature of various risk types became highly visible with the emergence of a broad set of government regulations and standards that focus on increased information security threats related to criminal and terrorist activities that can result in unintended and unauthorized information exposure and security compromise. The types of risks companies are facing include:

- **Transaction risk** Sometimes also referred to as operational risk, transaction risk is the primary risk associated with business processing. Transaction risk may arise from fraud, error, or the inability to deliver products or services, maintain a competitive position, or manage information. It exists in each process involved in the delivery of products or services. Transaction risk includes not only production operations and transaction processing, but also areas such as customer service, systems development and support, internal control processes, and capacity planning. Transaction risk may affect other risk types such as credit, interest rate, compliance, liquidity, price, strategic, and reputational risks.

- **Reputational risk**   Errors, delays, omissions, and information security breaches that become public knowledge or directly affect customers can significantly impact the reputation of the business. For example, a failure to maintain adequate business resumption plans and facilities for key processes may impair the ability of the business to provide critical services to its customers.

- **Strategic risk**   Inaccurate or incomplete information can cause the management of an organization to make poor strategic decisions. We will focus on this type of risk in Part IV when discussing data quality and the methods to improve it.

- **Compliance (legal) risk**   Inaccurate or untimely data related to consumer compliance disclosures or unauthorized disclosure of confidential, material non-public information (MNPI) about the business transaction or personally identifiable customer information could expose an organization to significant financial penalties and even costly litigation. Failure to track regulatory changes and provide timely accurate reporting could increase compliance risk for any organization that acquires, manages, and uses customer data.

NOTE *There are other ways to represent various types of risks. We will discuss a different representation of the risk taxonomy later in this chapter, when we review how the emerging regulatory and compliance requirements are driving risk management approaches.*

To address these various risks, companies have to develop and maintain a holistic risk management program that coordinates various risk management activities for a common goal of protecting the company and its assets.

Defining Risk and Risk Management

In general, we can define *risk* as the probability that a threat agent will be able to exploit a defined vulnerability that would adversely impact the business.

Risk management is defined as policies, procedures, and practices involved in identification, analysis, assessment, control, avoidance, minimization, or elimination of unacceptable risks.[1]

Using these definitions, an organization can calculate the risk if it understands the possibility that a vulnerability will exist, the probability that a threat agent will exploit it, and the resulting cost to the company. In practical terms, the first two components of this equation can be analyzed and understood with a certain degree of accuracy. The cost component, on the other hand, is not always easy to figure out since it depends on many factors, including business environments, markets, competitive positioning of the company, and so on. Clearly, not having a cost component makes the calculation of the risk management ROI a challenging proposition.

For example, in the case of the risk of a computer virus attack, one option to calculate the cost could be based on how many computers have to be protected using appropriate antivirus software—the total cost will include the costs of software licenses, antivirus software administration, configuration and distribution/deployment, and software patch management. The other option could be to calculate the cost based on the assumption that infected computer systems prevent the company from serving their customers for an extended period of time, let's say one business day. In that case, the cost could be significantly larger than the one assumed in the first option.

Furthermore, consider the risk of a computer system theft or a data compromise. The resulting potential exposure and loss of customer data may have significant cost implications, and the cost to the company could vary drastically from a reasonable system recovery expense to the hard-to-calculate cost of potentially irreparable damage to the company's reputation. Combining this cost with the cost of a highly probable case of litigation against the company, this risk can result in loss of potential and unrealized customer revenue, loss of market share and, in the extreme case, even liquidation of the business.

Risk Analysis

Risk analysis brings together all the elements of risk management (identification, analysis, and control) and is critical to an organization for developing an effective risk management strategy. There are two types of risk analysis: qualitative and quantitative. *Qualitative risk analysis* is scenario driven and does not attempt to assign values to components. *Quantitative risk analysis* attempts to assign an objective numeric value (cost) to components (assets and threats.)

While quantitative risk analysis could be quite an involved process, in principle it uses the following variables to calculate the risk exposure:[2]

- **SLE** is the single loss expectancy (expressed as the monetary value of the loss).
- **ARO** is the annualized rate of occurrence.
- **ALE** is the annualized loss expectancy.

Using these variables we can define the following expression for risk calculations:

ALE = SLE × ARO

The implication of the definitions shown above is clear: To manage the risks properly, the company must understand all of its vulnerabilities and match them to specific threats. This can be accomplished by employing any formal risk management methodology and a formal risk management process that at a minimum includes the following four steps:

1. Identify the assets and their relative value.
2. Define specific threats and the frequency and impact that would result from each occurrence.
3. Calculate annualized loss expectancy (ALE).
4. Prioritize risk reduction measures and select appropriate safeguards.

This high-level process allows an organization to be in a position to define a risk management strategy that includes options to either find a way to avoid the risk, accept the risk, transfer the risk (for example, by purchasing the insurance), or mitigate the risk by identifying and applying the necessary actions (known as "countermeasures").

While a comprehensive discussion of risk management and various types of risks is well beyond the scope of this book, understanding and managing information security risks by defining appropriate countermeasures is key to designing and deploying Master Data Management solutions, especially MDM Data Hub solutions that deal with customer information. Therefore, we will discuss the notion of customer-level risks, the causes of information security risks, regulatory and compliance drivers that elevate the concerns of the information security risks to the highest levels of the organization, and the principles used to develop information risk management strategies.

Regulatory Compliance Landscape

Businesses in general, and financial services firms in particular, are beginning to recognize and adopt the concept of Integrated Risk Management (IRM) as a means to manage the complex process of identifying, assessing, measuring, monitoring, and mitigating the full range of risks they face. One of the drivers for IRM is the expansion of the traditional risk management scope to include the notion of "customer risk" for individual and institutional customers alike—a notion that, in addition to the already-familiar personal credit risk and probability of default, now includes the risks of fraudulent and terrorism-related behavior, the risk of exposing confidential personal and business-related information and violating customer privacy, as well as the risk of customer identity theft. Many of these customer-level risk concerns have become significantly more visible and important as organizations have started to integrate and aggregate all information about their customers using advanced MDM solutions.

The reason for this elevated level of concerns is straightforward: Customer privacy and protection of personally identifiable customer information, protection of material non-public information (MNPI), and concerns related to information confidentiality and integrity have become subject to new regulatory and compliance legislations and industry-wide rules. In many cases, compliance is mandatory, with well-publicized implementation deadlines. Depending on a particular regulation and legal interpretation, noncompliance may result in stiff penalties, expensive litigation, damaged reputation, and even an inability to conduct business in certain markets. To achieve timely compliance, to manage these and other types of risks in a cohesive, integrated fashion, companies around the world are adopting technology, data structures, analytical models, and processes that are focused on delivering effective, integrated, enterprise-wide risk management solutions. But the technology is just an enabler of IRM. IRM cannot be implemented without the direct participation of the business units. For example, the Office of the Comptroller of the Currency (OCC) is forcing financial organizations to place risk management directly at the business unit level. These IRM-related regulations are forcing companies to ensure that the business managers own and manage risk. This approach results in integrated risk management solutions that provide a single, cohesive picture of risk exposure across the entire organization.

Integrated Risk Management: Benefits and Challenges

An effective information risk management strategy provides improved accuracy for risk and compliance reporting, and can mitigate transaction risk by reducing operational failures. Some of the benefits of an integrated information risk management strategy are shown in the following list:

- The ability to provide accurate, verifiable, and consistent information to internal and external users and application systems.

- The ability to satisfy compliance requirements using clean, reliable, secure, and consistent data.

- The ability to mitigate transaction risk associated with the data issues. For example, in financial services, companies embarked on implementing IRM strategies are better positioned to avoid data-related issues that affect the successful implementation of Straight Through Processing and next-day settlement environments (STP and T+1).

- Flexibility in implementing and managing new organizational structures and the cross-organizational relationships that can be caused by the increase in the Merger and Acquisition (M&A) activities as well as in forming new partnerships.

- The ability to define, implement, and measure enterprise-wide data governance and quality strategy and metrics.

- The ability to avoid delays related to data issues when delivering new products and services to market.

Many organizations struggle when attempting to implement a comprehensive and effective information risk management strategy, often because they underestimate the complexity of the related business and technical challenges. Moreover, these risks and challenges have to be addressed in the context of delivering integrated master data solutions such as those enabled by MDM platforms. Some of these challenges include:

- Business Challenges

  - Some risk management and information strategy solutions may have a profound impact on the organization at large, and thus may require continuous executive-level sponsorship.

  - Data ownership and stewardship have organizational and political implications that need to be addressed prior to engaging in implementation of the information risk management strategy.

  - Determining real costs and calculating key business metrics such as Return on Investment (ROI), Return on Equity (ROE), and Total Cost of Ownership (TCO) is difficult; the calculations are often based on questionable assumptions and thus produce inaccurate results and create political and budgetary challenges.

  - New regulatory requirements introduce additional complexity into the process of defining and understanding intra- and inter-enterprise relationships; this is one of the areas where Master Data Management can help mitigate the complexity risks.

  - The product and vendor landscape is changing rapidly. Although technology solutions continue to mature, this causes additional uncertainty and increases the risk of not achieving successful, on-time, and on-budget project delivery.

- Global enterprises and international business units often face conflicting regulatory requirements, cross-border data transfer restrictions, and various local regulations pertaining to outsourcing and off-shoring data that include access, content masking, storage, and transfer components.

- Technical Challenges

    - Risk management solutions must be scalable, reliable, flexible, and manageable. This challenge is particularly important for financial services institutions with their need to support the enterprise-level high throughput required for the high-value global transactions that traverse front-office and back-office business systems (for example, globally distributed equities or currency trading desks).

    - Risk-related data already resides in a variety of internal repositories, including enterprise data warehouses and CRM data marts, but its quality and semantic consistency (different data models and metadata definitions) may be unsuitable for business transaction processing and regulatory reporting.

    - Similarly, risk-related data is acquired from a variety of internal and external data sources that often contain inconsistent or stale data.

    - Risk data models are complex and are subject to new regulations and frequently changing relationships between the organizations and its customers and partners.

    - Even business-unit–specific risks can have a cascading effect throughout the enterprise, and risk mitigation strategies and solutions should be able to adapt to rapidly changing areas of risk impact. Specifically, a business unit (BU) may be willing to accept a particular risk. However, a security compromise may impact the company brand name and reputation well beyond the scope of a particular channel or a business unit. For example, a major bank may have tens of business units. A security breach within a mortgage BU can affect retail sales, banking, wealth management, consumer lending, credit card services, auto finance, and many other units.

All these challenges have broad applicability to all enterprise-class data management issues, but they are particularly important to organizations that embark on implementing MDM solutions.

Regulatory Compliance Requirements and Their Impact on MDM IT Infrastructure

As we stated in previous sections, a number of new regulatory and compliance legislations have become the primary drivers for the emergence and adoption of the Integrated Risk Management concept. Generally speaking, access to and use of any information that is classified as restricted, confidential, or private needs to be regulated and controlled, and a number of broadly defined regulations address these controls. The situation becomes even more critical when we consider two industry segments that by definition have to deal with a customer's privacy and confidentiality concerns by protecting personally identifiable information (PII): financial services and healthcare. In this case, regulations that are focused on protecting customer financial and personally identifiable data, as well as the risks associated with its misuse, include but are not limited to the following:

- **The Sarbanes-Oxley Act of 2002 (SOX)** defines requirements for the integrity of the financial data and availability of appropriate security controls.

- **The USA Patriot Act** includes provisions for Anti-Money Laundering (AML) and Know Your Customer (KYC).

- **The Gramm-Leach-Bliley Act (GLBA)** mandates strong protection of personal financial information through its data protection provisions.

- **The Basel II and Basel III Capital Requirements** define various requirements for operational and credit risks.

- **FFIEC guidelines** require strong authentication to prevent fraud in banking transactions.

- **The Payment Card Industry (PCI) Standard** defines the requirement for protecting sensitive cardholder data inside payment networks.

- **California's SB1386** is a state regulation requiring public written disclosure in situations when a customer file has been compromised.

- **Do-Not-Call** and other opt-out preference requirements protect customers' privacy.

- **International Accounting Standards Reporting IAS2005** defines a single, high-quality international financial reporting framework.

- **The Health Insurance Portability and Accountability Act (HIPAA)** places liability on anyone who fails to properly protect patient health information including bills and health-related financial information.

- **New York Reg. 173** mandates the active encryption of sensitive financial information sent over the Internet.

- **Homeland Security Information Sharing Act (HSISA, H.R. 4598)** prohibits public disclosure of certain information.

- **The ISO 17799 Standard** defines an extensive approach to achieve information security including communications systems requirements for information handling and risk reduction.

- **The European Union Data Protection Directive** mandates the protection of personal data.

- **Japanese Protection for Personal Information Act.**

- **Federal Trade Commission, 16 CFR Part 314** defines standards for safeguarding customer information.

- **SEC Final Rule, Privacy of Consumer Financial Information (Regulation S-P)**, 17 CFR Part 248 RIN 3235-AH90.

- **OCC 2001-47** defines third-party data-sharing protection.

- **17 CFR Part 210** defines rules for records retention.

- **21 CFR Part 11** (SEC and FDA regulations) define rules, for electronic records and electronic signatures.

PART III

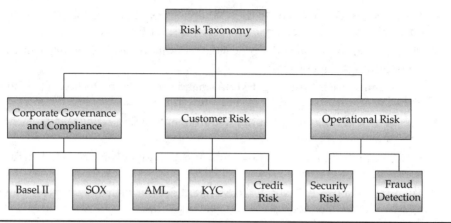

Figure 8-1   Risk taxonomy

- **NASD rules 2711 and 3010** define several supervisory rules, including the requirement that each member establish and maintain a system to supervise the activities of each registered representative and associated person.

This is far from a complete list, and it continues to grow and expand its coverage and impact on the way businesses must conduct themselves and protect their customers.

Many of these regulations are "connected" to each other by their risk concerns and the significant implications for the IT infrastructure and processes that are required to comply with the applicable laws. If we were to map the types of risks discussed in this chapter to the key regulations that are designed to protect the enterprise and its customers from them, we might end up with the mapping shown in Figure 8-1.

Using this risk taxonomy diagram as a guide, the following sections discuss some of the regulatory compliance requirements and their impact on the information management infrastructures.

The Sarbanes-Oxley Act

The Sarbanes-Oxley Act (SOX) addresses a set of business risk management concerns and contains a number of sections defining specific reporting and compliance requirements.[3] Some of the key requirements of the Act are defined in Sections 302, 404, 409, and 906, and they require that the company's CEO/CFO must prepare quarterly and annual certifications that attest that:

- The CEO/CFO has reviewed the report.
- The report does not contain any untrue or misleading statement of a material fact or omit to state a material fact.
- Financial statements and other financial information fairly present the financial condition.

- The CEO/CFO is responsible for establishing and maintaining disclosure controls and has performed an evaluation of such controls and procedures at the end of the period covered by the report.
- The report, discloses to the company's audit committee and external auditors:
  - Any significant deficiencies and material weaknesses in Internal Control over Financial Reporting (ICFR)
  - Any fraud that involves personnel that have a significant role in the company's ICFR

    SOX, requires each annual report to contain an "internal control report" that:
    - Defines management's responsibilities for establishing and maintaining ICFR
    - Specifies the framework used to evaluate ICFR
    - Contains management's assessment of ICFR as of the end of the company's fiscal year
    - States that the company's external auditor has issued an attestation report on management's assessment

  SOX also requires that:
- The company's external auditor reports on management's internal control assessment.
- Companies have to take certain actions in the event of changes in controls.

In addition, Section 409 specifies the real-time disclosure requirements that need to be implemented by every organization. This represents a challenge for those companies that have predominantly offline, batch business reporting processes.

The events requiring real-time disclosure include:

- Loss of major client (bundled service purchaser or significant component of product portfolio)
- Increased exposure to industries that are "in trouble" (significant portion of portfolio)
- Impact of external party changes (for example, regulators, auditors)
- Write-offs of a significant number of loans or portfolios
- Cost over-runs on IT or other major capital projects

These and similar material events will require reporting to interested parties within 48 hours of the event's occurrence. From a technical capabilities point of view, Section 409's real-time disclosure requires:

- Real-time analytics instead of or in addition to batch reporting
- The ability to report on a wide range of events within 48 hours
- Real-time notification and event-driven alerts
- Deep integration of information assets

Clearly, achieving SOX compliance, and especially compliance with Section 409 requirements, would be easier using an MDM solution to provide flexible and scalable near-real-time reporting capabilities.

Gramm-Leach-Bliley Act Data Protection Provisions

The Gramm-Leach-Bliley Financial Modernization Act was signed into law on November 11, 1999 as Public Law 106-102.[4] The GLBA contains a number of sections and provisions that specify various data protection requirements, including protection of nonpublic personal information, obligations with respect to disclosures of personal information, disclosure of institution's privacy policy, and a number of other related requirements.[5]

Of particular interest to the preceding discussion is GLBA Section 501, which is focused on establishing standards for protecting the security and confidentiality of financial institution customers' nonpublic personal information. Specifically, GLBA Section 501[6] defines the Data Protection Rule and subsequent safeguards that are designed to:

- Ensure the security and confidentiality of customer data
- Protect against any reasonably anticipated threats or hazards to the security or integrity of the data
- Protect against unauthorized access to or use of such data that would result in substantial harm or inconvenience to any customer

GLBA key privacy protection tenets are defined in the following paragraphs:

- **Paragraph A**   "Privacy obligation policy—It is the policy of the Congress that each financial institution has an affirmative and continuing obligation to respect the privacy of its customers and to protect the security and confidentiality of those customers' nonpublic personal information."
- **Paragraph B3**   "… to protect against unauthorized access to or use of such records or information which could result in substantial harm or inconvenience to any customer."

In the context of GLBA, the term "nonpublic personal information" (NPI) referenced in Paragraph A means personally identifiable information (PII) that is

- Provided by a customer to a financial institution,
- Derived from any transaction with the customer or any service performed for the customer, or
- Obtained by the financial institution via other means.

In January 2003, the Federal Financial Institutions Examination Council (FFIEC) issued new guidance that expanded GLBA. The new guidance requires financial institutions to protect *all* information assets, not just customer information. The FFIEC recommended a security process that the financial institutions have to put in place to stay compliant with the expanded requirements. This process includes the following components:

- Information security risk assessment including employee background checks
- Security strategy development including:
  - Response programs for unauthorized events
  - Protective measures against potential environmental hazards or technological failures

- Implementation of security controls (these controls and technologies enabling the controls are discussed in some detail in Chapters 9–11):
    - Access controls and restrictions to authenticate and permit access by authorized users only
    - Encryption of data-in-transit (on the network) and data-at-rest (on a storage device)
    - Change control procedures
- Security testing
- Continuous monitoring and updating of the security process, including monitoring systems and procedures for intrusion detection

GLBA makes an organization responsible for noncompliance even if the security breach and the resulting data privacy violation are caused by an outside vendor or service provider.

Specifically, according to GLBA, the organization must establish appropriate oversight programs of its vendor relationships, including:

- Assessment of outsourcing risks to determine which products and services are best outsourced and which should be handled in-house
- Creation and maintenance of an inventory list of each vendor relationship and its purpose
- Prioritization of the risk of each relationship consistent with the types of customer information the vendor can access
- Routine execution of proper due diligence of third-party vendors
- Execution of written contracts that outline duties, obligations, and responsibilities of all parties

A number of federal and state agencies are involved in enforcing GLBA, for example:

- Federal banking agencies (that is, Board of Governors of the Federal Reserve System, Comptroller of the Currency, FDIC, Office of Thrift Supervision, and others)
- National Credit Union Administration
- Secretary of the Treasury
- Securities and Exchange Commission
- Federal Trade Commission
- National Association of Insurance Commissioners

It is easy to see that the requirements imposed by the Sarbanes-Oxley and Gramm-Leach-Bliley acts have clear implications for the way organizations handle customer and financial data in general and, by extension, how the data is managed and protected in data integration platforms such as Master Data Management systems.

Other Regulatory/Compliance Requirements

Of course, in addition to SOX and GLBA, there are numerous other regulations that have similarly profound implications for the processes, technology, architecture, and infrastructure of the enterprise data strategy and particularly on the initiatives to develop MDM solutions. We'll discuss some of these regulations briefly in this section for the purpose of completeness.

OCC 2001-47

GLBA makes an organization responsible for noncompliance even if the breach in security and data privacy is caused by an outside vendor or service provider. Specifically, the Office of the Comptroller of the Currency (OCC) has defined the following far-reaching rules that affect any institution that plans to share sensitive data with an unaffiliated third party:

- A financial institution must take appropriate steps to protect information that it provides to a service provider, regardless of who the service provider is or how the service provider obtains access.

- The Office of the Comptroller of the Currency defines oversight and compliance requirements that require company management to:

  - Engage in a rigorous analytical process to identify, measure, monitor, and establish controls to manage the risks associated with third-party relationships.

  - Avoid excessive risk-taking that may threaten the safety and integrity of the company.

The OCC oversight includes a review of the company's information security and privacy protection programs regardless of whether the activity is conducted directly by the company or by a third party. OCC's primary supervisory concern in reviewing third-party relationships is whether the company is assuming more risk than it can identify, monitor, manage, and control.

USA Patriot Act: Anti–Money Laundering (AML) and Know Your Customer (KYC) Provisions

Money laundering has become a serious economic and political issue. Indeed, the International Monetary Fund has estimated that the global proceeds of money laundering could total between 2 and 5 percent of the world gross domestic product, which is equivalent to 1 to 3 trillion USD every year.

The USA Patriot Act is one of a number of legislations that deal with issues of money laundering. The long list of related legislations includes the 1970 Bank Secrecy Act (BSA), the 1986 Money Laundering Control Act, the 1988 Money Laundering Prosecution Improvement Act, and the 1990 Bank Fraud Prosecution and Taxpayer Recovery Act of 1990 (Crime Control Act), to name just a few.

The USA Patriot Act of 2001 is an abbreviation of the 2001 law with the full name "Uniting and Strengthening America by Providing Appropriate Tools to Restrict, Intercept and Obstruct Terrorism Act." It requires information sharing among the government and financial institutions, implementation of programs that are concerned with verification of customer identity, implementation of enhanced due-diligence programs; and implementation of anti–money laundering programs across the financial services industry.[7]

With the advent of the International Money Laundering Abatement and Anti-Terrorism Financing Act of 2001 (Title 3 of the USA Patriot Act), the U.S. Department of the Treasury has enacted far-reaching regulations aimed at detecting and deterring money-laundering activities and events. These regulations apply to all financial institutions, and have direct implications for all Master Data Management initiatives as activities that deal with the totality of customer financial and personal information.

The USA Patriot Act affects all financial institutions, including banks, broker-dealers, hedge funds, money service businesses, and wire transfers, by requiring them to demonstrate greater vigilance in detecting and preventing money-laundering activity. It defines implementation milestones that include mandatory suspicious activity reporting (SAR) and mandatory adoption of due-diligence procedures to comply with these regulations.

USA Patriot Act Technology Impact   Business process requirements of the USA Patriot Act include:

- Development of the AML policies and procedures.
- Designation of a compliance officer.
- Establishment of a training program.
- Establishment of a corporate testing/audit function.
- Business units that manage private banking accounts held by noncitizens must identify owners and sources of funds.
- For the correspondent accounts processing, implement restrictions that do not allow account establishment with foreign shell banks; implement strict and timely reporting procedures for all corresponding accounts with a foreign bank.
- Organizations must develop and use "reasonable procedures" to know their customer when opening and maintaining accounts.
- Financial institutions can share information on potential money-laundering activity with other institutions to facilitate government action; this cooperation will be immune from privacy and secrecy-based litigations.

The USA Patriot Act requires banks to check a terrorist list provided by the Financial Crimes Enforcement Network (FinCEN). Another list to be checked is provided by the Treasury's Office of Foreign Assets Control (OFAC). Additional information sources may become available as the system matures.

Key technical capabilities that support the USA Patriot Act requirements include:

- Workflow tools to facilitate efficient compliance procedures, including workflow processes to prioritize and route alerts to appropriate parties
- Analytical tools that support the ongoing detection of hidden relationships and transactions among high-risk entities, including the ability to detect patterns of activity to help identify entities utilizing the correspondent account (the customer's customer)
- Creation and maintenance of account profiles and techniques like scenario libraries to help track and understand client behavior throughout the life of the account
- Support of risk-based user segmentation and a full audit trail to provide context for outside investigations
- Policy-driven comprehensive monitoring and reporting to provide a global view and to promote effective and timely decision making

Many of the required capabilities can be enabled by effective leveraging the data collected and maintained by the existing CRM or new MDM systems. However, the USA Patriot Act and its "Know Your Customer" (KYC) directive require additional customer-focused information.

This requirement of knowing your customers and being able to analyze their behavior quickly and accurately is one of the benefits and a potential application of the MDM for Customer Domain.

Basel II Capital Accord Technical Requirements

In 1988, the Basel Committee on Banking Supervision introduced a capital measurement system, commonly referred to as the Basel Capital Accord. This system addressed the design and implementation of a credit risk measurement framework for a minimum capital requirement standard. This framework has been adopted by more than a hundred countries.

In June 1999, the Committee issued a proposal for a New Capital Adequacy Framework to replace the 1988 Accord. Known as "Basel II," this capital framework consists of three pillars[8]:

- **Pillar I**   Minimum capital requirements
- **Pillar II**   Supervisory review of an institution's internal assessment process and capital adequacy
- **Pillar III**   Effective use of disclosure to strengthen market discipline as a complement to supervisory efforts

One key departure from the 1988 Basel Accord is that banks are required to set aside capital for operational risk. The Basel Committee defines operational risk as "the risk of direct or indirect loss resulting from inadequate or failed internal processes."

The Basel II Accord seeks to align risk and capital more closely, which may result in an increase in capital requirements for banks with higher-risk portfolios.

To comply with Basel II requirements financial institutions have begun creating an *Operational Risk Framework and Management Structure.* A key part of this structure is a set of facilities that would track and securely store loss events in Loss Data Warehouses (includes Loss, Default, and Delinquency data) so that at least two years of historical data are available for processing. A Loss Data Warehouse (LDW) is a primary vehicle to provide an accurate, up-to-date analysis of capital adequacy requirements, and is also a source of disclosure reporting.

In the context of Master Data Management, an LDW should become an integrated platform of accurate, timely, and authoritative data that can be used for analysis and reporting.

NOTE *In December 2009, the Basel Committee on Banking Supervision published two consultative documents that have been widely considered as the foundation of a new "Basel III Accord" that is focused on the strengthening of the global banking system. At the time of this writing the work on defining specific Basel III requirements was ongoing.*

FFIEC Compliance and Authentication Requirements

On October 12, 2005, the Federal Financial Institutions Examination Council (FFIEC) issued new guidance on customer authentication for online banking services. According to the FFIEC guidance, the authentication techniques employed by the financial institution should be appropriate to the risks associated with those products and services used by the authenticated users. The new regulation guides banks to apply two major methods:

- **Risk assessment**   Banks must assess the risk of the various activities taking place on their Internet banking site.

- **Risk-based authentication**   Banks must apply stronger authentication for high-risk transactions.

Technical implications of the FFIEC regulations include:

- The ability to provide multifactor authentication for high-risk transactions
- Monitoring and reporting capabilities embedded into all operational systems
- Appropriate strength of authentication that is based on the degree of risk
- Customer awareness and ability to provide reverse authentication where customers are assured they communicate with the right institution and not a fraudulent site
- Implementation of layered security framework

Let's consider these requirements in the context of MDM. An MDM Data Hub solution designed and deployed by a financial institution will most likely represent the authoritative source of customer personal and financial data. Therefore, a Data Hub platform must be designed to support the adaptive authentication and information security framework required by the FFIEC regulations. Key details of this enterprise security framework are discussed in Chapter 11.

State Regulations: California's SB1386

In addition to U.S. federal regulations, individual states have adopted various legislations that deal with data privacy and confidentiality. Among these state-level legislations, California's Senate Bill 1386 (SB1386) was one of the first state laws on this topic, and we'll briefly describe it in this section to illustrate the interdependencies between state and federal legislations.

SB1386 was introduced in 2002,[9] and it requires that companies dealing with residents of the State of California disclose breaches of their computer systems, when such breaches are suspected of compromising certain confidential information of the California customers. The most unique feature of this law is that it allows for class-action lawsuits against companies in the event of noncompliance.

SB1386 and Sarbanes-Oxley Compliance   In the beginning of this chapter we stated that many of the regulations affecting the processes and methods of information management are interconnected. This section describes one such example of the connected nature of the regulations.

The Committee of Sponsoring Organizations of the Treadway Commission (COSO) has established a framework[10] against which a company's internal controls may be benchmarked for effectiveness and compliance with the Sarbanes-Oxley Act and other applicable laws. According to the COSO framework, the companies are required to identify and analyze risks, establish a plan to mitigate each risk, and have well-defined policies and procedures to ensure that management objectives are achieved and risk mitigation strategies are executed.

The implication of these requirements is that failure to deal with regulations such as California SB1386 effectively could be interpreted as the failure of a company's management in establishing and maintaining appropriate internal controls to deal with the risk of customer data compromise, thus violating the principal requirements of the Sarbanes-Oxley Act. Litigation and the resulting SB1386 judgments could potentially trigger Sarbanes-Oxley–related violations and its consequences.

Key Information Security Risks and Regulatory Concerns

The networked, interconnected, and global nature of today's business and technology ecosphere has created incredible opportunities for organizations to increase their customer bases and market share, create new effective partnerships, improve their effectiveness and agility, rapidly introduce new products and services, and in general successfully grow their businesses. Likewise, customers are able to take full advantage of the interconnected, Internet-based channels, products, and services to become willing participants in this networked economy. However, the convenience and availability of the network-based products and services come with new complications and risks, including viruses, worms, and hackers of all types. These risks are growing and multiplying and are impacting not just individual customers but also business and government organizations (for example, widely publicized denial-of-service attacks and other acts of cyber-terrorism). The reality is such that the number of types of risks is growing faster than what security technologies can build countermeasures for.

This is an ever-growing area of concern for all risk management and law enforcement professionals globally, and the analysis of all types of information security risks is clearly beyond the scope of a single book. However, one area of this risk is directly connected to the privacy and information protection discussion in the previous sections, and it represents the fastest-growing white-collar crime: identity theft.

Identity Theft

Numerous government and private sector reports from sources such as the Federal Trade Commission (FTC), the Federal Bureau of Investigation (FBI), and the Computer Security Institute (CSI) repeatedly indicate that identity theft is rapidly becoming one of the fastest-growing white-collar crimes on the Internet. According to the FBI, the number of Internet sites that spread various forms of "crimeware" designed to steal PC passwords reached an all-time high of 31,173 in December of 2008, an 827 percent increase from January of 2008.[11]

Even more disturbing, identity theft continues to be on the rise, and the size of the problem is becoming quite significant.

For example, according to the 2009 Gartner Report, about 7.5 percent of U.S. adults lost money to some sort of financial fraud in 2008, and data losses cost companies an average of $6.6 million per breach. The direct effect of the identify theft is that for the same time period, customer attrition across industry sectors due to a data breach almost doubled from the regular rate of 3.6 percent to 6.5 percent, and in the financial services sector in particular the turnover rate reached 5.5 percent.[12] And the Identity Theft Statistics website[13] offers the following disturbing facts:

- There were 10 million victims of identity theft in 2008 in the U.S. (Javelin Strategy and Research, 2009).

- One in every ten U.S. consumers has already been victimized by identity theft (Javelin Strategy and Research, 2009).

- Over a million households experienced fraud not related to credit cards (that is, their bank accounts or debit cards were compromised; U.S. Department of Justice, 2005).

- Those households with incomes higher than $70,000 were twice as likely to experience identity theft than those with salaries under $50,000 (U.S. Department of Justice, 2005).

- Seven percent of identity theft victims had their information stolen to commit medical identity theft.

There are two primary classes of economic crime related to identity theft:

- *Account takeover* occurs when a thief acquires a person's existing credit or bank account information and uses the existing account to purchase products and services. Victims usually learn of account takeover when they receive their monthly account statement.

- In true *identity theft*, a thief uses another person's SSN and other identifying information to fraudulently open new accounts and obtain financial gain. Victims may be unaware of the fraud for an extended period of time—which makes the situation that much worse.

In general, credit card fraud is the most common application of the account takeover style of identity theft, followed by phone or utility fraud, bank fraud, real estate rent fraud, and others.

Phishing and Pharming

Traditionally, the most common approach to stealing one's identity was to somehow get hold of the potential victim's personal information and confidential data such as passwords. In pre-Internet days thieves went after one's wallet or a purse. Then they increased the area of "coverage" by collecting and analyzing the content of the trash of the intended victims. With the advent of electronic commerce, the Internet and the Web, the thieves embarked on easy-to-implement phishing scams, in which a thief known as a "phisher" takes advantage of the fact that some users trust their online establishments such as banks and retail stores. The phisher creates compelling e-mail messages that lead unaware users to disclose their personal data. For example, a frequent phishing scam is to send an e-mail to a bank customer that may look like a totally legitimate request from the bank to verify the user's credentials (for example, user ID and password) or worse, to verify the individual's social security number. Phishers use frequent mass mailings in the hope that even a small percentage of respondents will financially justify the effort.

Useful information about phishing can be found on the Anti-Phishing Working Group (APWG) website.[14] The APWG is the global pan-industrial and law enforcement association focused on eliminating the fraud and identity theft that result from phishing, pharming, and e-mail spoofing of all types. APWG 2009 report shows that:

- The number of unique phishing websites detected in June 2009 rose to 49,084—the highest since April 2007's record of 55,643 and the second-highest recorded since APWG began reporting this measurement.

- The number of hijacked brands ascended to an all-time high of 310 in March 2009 and remained at an elevated level.

- The total number of infected computers rose more than 66 percent to 11,937,944—now more than 54 percent of the total sample of scanned computers.

Payment services became phishing's most targeted sector, displacing general financial services, and institutional customers still are a primary target of electronic criminals, with the majority of electronic record breaches linked to organized crime. A variant of phishing known as *spear-phishing* targets a phishing attack against a selected individual. The phishing text contains correct factual elements (personal identifiers) that correspond to the target/reader. Such targeted phishing messages are quite effective in convincing their intended victims of the presumed authenticity of the message.

Pharmers, on the other hand, try to increase the success ratio of stealing other people's identification information by redirecting as many users as possible from legitimate commercial websites to malicious sites. The users get redirected to the false websites without their knowledge or consent, and these pharming sites usually look exactly the same as the legitimate site. But when users log in to the sites they think are genuine by entering their login name and password, the information is captured by criminals.

Of course, there are many other types of scams that are designed to steal people's identities. These criminal actions have reached almost epidemic proportions and have become subject to numerous laws and government regulations. The variety of scams is so large that a number of advisory websites publish new scam warnings on a regular basis. Examples of these watchdog sites include www.LifeLock.com, the Identity Theft Resource Center (www.idtheftcenter.org), and Anti-Phishing Working Group (www.antiphishing.org).

MDM and Identity Theft

The key reason we're discussing identity theft in this chapter is the fact that, by design, Master Data Management solutions are some of the most attractive targets for identity thieves, including phishers and pharmers. To protect customers' identities from being stolen from an MDM system, these solutions have to be designed and deployed in such a way that access to and the content of the information these solutions manage are protected and that proper security controls are put in place as MDM Data Hubs are being deployed.

GLBA, FCRA, Privacy, and Opt-Out

Other relevant regulations include National Do Not Call lists and the ability of customers to declare their privacy preferences as well as to opt-out from sharing their personal information with other companies or nonaffiliated third parties. The ability to opt-out is a provision of legislations such as the Gramm-Leach-Bliley Financial Modernization Act (GLBA) and the Fair Credit Reporting Act (FCRA).

The term *opt-out* means that, *unless and until* the customers inform their financial institution that the customer does not want them to share or sell customer data to other companies, the company is free to do so. The implication of this law is that the initial burden of privacy protection is on the customer, not on the company.

Contrast this with a stronger version of expressing the same choices—*opt-in*. This option prohibits the sharing or sale of customer data *unless* the customer explicitly agreed to allow such actions.

In addition to the opt-out option, additional privacy protection regulations are enabled by the National Do Not Call (DNC) Registry. The National Do Not Call Registry (www.DoNotCall.org) is a government organization that maintains a protected registry of individual phone numbers that their owners have opted to make unavailable for most telemarketing activities.

Recognizing customer privacy preferences such as opt-ins, opt-outs, and DNC allows companies to enhance the customer's perception of being treated with respect and thus improves customers' experience and strengthens their relationships with the organization. The ability to capture and enforce customer privacy preferences including opt-in/out choices is one of the design requirements for data integration solutions in the form of customer information files, enterprise data warehouses, CRM systems, and MDM Data Hubs.

Key Technical Implications of Data Security and Privacy Regulations on MDM Architecture

As you can see from the foregoing discussion, regulations such as the Sarbanes-Oxley Act, the Gramm-Leach-Bliley Act, and many others, have profound implications for the technical architecture and infrastructure of any data management solution. Of course, Master Data Management is becoming a focal point where these implications are clearly visible and have a significant impact. If we focus on the issues related to the protection of and controlling access to the information managed by a Master Data Management solution, we can summarize the technical implications of key regulations into a concise set of requirements that should include the following:

- Support for a layered information security framework.
- Support for flexible multifactor authentication with the level of authentication strength aligned to the risk profile.
- Support for policy-based, roles-based, and entitlements-based authorization.
- The ability to protect data managed by an MDM platform whether data is in transit (on the network) or at rest (on a storage device or in memory).
- Support for data integrity and confidentiality.
- Business-driven data availability.
- The ability to aggregate personal profile and financial reporting data only to an authorized individual.
- Auditability of the transactions and all data access and manipulation activities.
- Support for intrusion detection, prevention, and monitoring systems.
- Support for an inventory list of each third-party vendor relationship and its purpose.
- Support for event and workflow management.
- Support for real-time analytics and reporting.
- The ability to recognize and categorize all data that needs to be protected, including customer records, financial data, product and business plans, and similar information that can impact the market position of the organization.
- Support for a structured process that can keep track of all input and output data to mitigate business risk associated with disclosing private, confidential information about the company and its customers. This includes not only the authoritative data source but also all copies of this data. Indeed, unlike other auditable assets, a copy of data has the same intrinsic value as the original. Therefore, the tracking process should include an active data repository that maintains a current, up-to-date inventory of all data under management that needs to be protected and accounted for.

To sum up, the regulatory landscape that defines the "rules of engagement" related to the protection of information assets and identities of customers and parties has some profound implications for any IT infrastructure. By their very nature, Master Data Management solutions are targets of the majority of the regulations mentioned in this chapter. Thus, an MDM solution that is designed to integrate private confidential or financial data has to be architected and implemented to achieve a verifiable compliance state that supports PII and MNPI requirements. The remaining chapters of this part of the book describe design approaches that mitigate various information security risks while addressing the multitude of regulatory and compliance requirements.

References

1. http://www.businessdictionary.com/definition/risk-management.html.

2. http://security.practitioner.com/introduction/infosec_5_3_7.htm.

3. http://www.sec.gov/about/laws/soa2002.pdf.

4. http://banking.senate.gov/conf/.

5. http://www.ftc.gov/privacy/glbact/glbsub1.htm.

6. http://www.fdic.gov/news/news/financial/2001/fil0168.html.

7. http://www.fdic.gov/regulations/examinations/bsa/bsa_3.html.

8. http://www.basel-ii-risk.com/Basel-II/Basel-Three-Pillars/index.htm.

9. http://info.sen.ca.gov/pub/01-02/bill/sen/sb_1351-1400/sb_1386_bill_20020926_chaptered.html.

10. http://www.coso.org/Publications/ERM/COSO_ERM_ExecutiveSummary.pdf.

11. Anti-Phishing Working Group, March 2009.

12. Gartner, Inc. February 2009, ID: 165825, "Data breach and financial crimes scare consumers away."

13. http://www.spendonlife.com/guide/identity-theft-statistics.

14. http://www.antiphishing.org/.

Introduction to Information Security and Identity Management

I n medieval times, commerce was conducted in city-states that were well protected by city walls, weapons, and an army of guards and soldiers. In modern times, as commerce rapidly moved to a global marketplace, the goal of keeping potential participants out was replaced by the desire to invite and keep potential customers in.

In today's business environment, we see a similar transformation—instead of keeping everything hidden behind proprietary, secure networks protected by firewalls, commerce is done on the public Internet, and every business plans to take advantage of the potentially huge population of prospective customers. Denying access to corporate information is no longer a viable option—inviting new customers and enticing them to do business is the new imperative.

Traditional and Emerging Concerns of Information Security

The new imperative of Internet-driven secure inclusion brings with it a new set of security challenges—challenges that are reinforced by numerous pieces of legislation that promote various forms of e-commerce and even e-government and require new approaches to security that can protect both the customer and corporate information assets. We discussed a number of these regulations in Chapter 8.

What Do We Need to Secure?

The Internet has become a de facto standard environment where corporations and individuals conduct business, "meet" people, perform financial transactions, and seek answers to questions about anything and everything. In fact, all users and all organizations that have some form of Internet access appear to be close (and equidistant) to each other.

The Internet has moved the boundaries of an enterprise so far away from the corporate data center that it created its own set of problems. Indeed, together with the enterprise boundaries, the traditional security mechanisms have also been moved outward, creating a new "playing field" for customers, partners, and unwanted intruders and hackers alike. As a result, enterprise security requirements have become much more complex.

One way to discuss these requirements is to look at what areas of the business environments need to be secured, and from what kind of danger. Figure 9-1 illustrates the areas of security concerns and corresponding security disciplines that are defined in the following section.

> **Layered Security Framework**
> Security domains can be organized into a layered framework that looks at security from "outside in": perimeter security, network security, platform (host) security, application security, data security, and user security.

The model of a layered security framework describes security "zones" that need to be protected regardless of whether the threat is originating from outside or from within the organization.

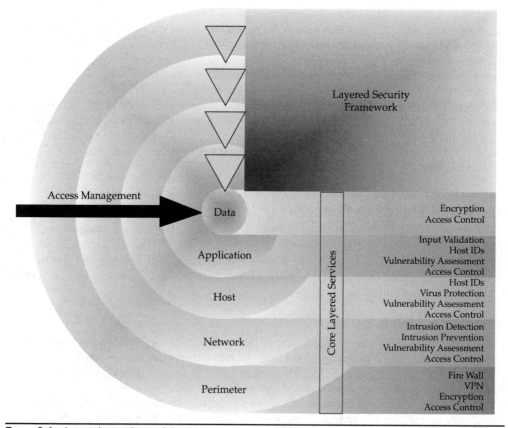

FIGURE 9-1   Layered security model

Technologies that enable the implementation of a layered security framework may offer overlapping functionality and can span several security domains. For example, the security disciplines of authentication, authorization, and administration (3A) play equally important roles in securing the network resources, the enterprise perimeter, the computing platform, and the applications, data, and users.

Perimeter Security

Perimeter security deals with the security threats that arrive at the enterprise boundary via a network. By definition, perimeter security has to handle user authentication, authorization, and access control to the resources that reside inside the perimeter. The primary technology employed to achieve perimeter security is known as *firewalls*.

A firewall is placed at the network node where a secure network (for example, an internal enterprise network) and an insecure network (for example, the Internet) meet each other. As a general rule, all network traffic, inbound and outbound, flows through the firewall, which screens all incoming traffic and blocks that which does not meet the restrictions of the organization's security policy.

In its most simple form, the role of the firewall is to restrict incoming traffic from the Internet into an organization's internal network according to certain parameters. Once a firewall is configured, it filters network traffic, examines packet headers, and determines which packets should be forwarded or allowed to enter and which should be rejected.

Network Security

Network security deals with authenticating network users, authorizing access to network resources, and protecting the information that flows over the network.

Network security involves authentication, authorization, and encryption and often uses technologies like Public Key Infrastructure (PKI) and Virtual Private Network (VPN). These technologies are frequently used together to achieve the desired degree of security protection. Indeed, no security tool, be it authentication, encryption, VPN, firewall, or antivirus software, should be used alone for network security protection. A combination of several products needs to be utilized to truly protect the enterprise's sensitive data and other information assets.

Network and Perimeter Security Concerns   A common approach to network security is to surround an enterprise network with a defensive perimeter that controls access to the network. However, once an intruder has passed through the perimeter defenses, he, she, or it may be unconstrained and may cause intentional or accidental damage. A perimeter defense is valuable as a *part* of an overall defense. However, it is ineffective if a hostile party gains access to a system inside the perimeter or compromises a single authorized user.

Besides a defensive perimeter approach, an alternative network security model is a model of mutual suspicion, where every system within a critical network regards every other system as a potential source of threat.

Platform (Host) Security

Platform or host security deals with security threats that affect the actual device and make it vulnerable to external or internal attacks. The platform security concerns include the already-familiar authentication, authorization, and access control disciplines, and the security of the operating system, file system, application server, and other computing platform resources that can be broken into, or taken over, by an intruder.

Platform security solutions include security measures that protect physical access to a given device. For example, platform security includes placing a server in a protected cage; using sophisticated authentication and authorization tokens that may include biometrics; using "traditional" physical guards to restrict access to the site to the authorized personnel only; developing and installing "hardened" versions of the operating system; and using secure application development frameworks like the Java Authentication and Authorization Service, or JAAS. (JAAS defines a pluggable, stacked authentication scheme. Different authentication schemes can be plugged in without having to modify or recompile existing applications.)

Application, Data, and User Security

Application, data, and user security concerns are at the heart of the overall security framework. Indeed, the main goal of any malicious intent is to get a hold of the protected resource and use it, whether it is information about a company's financial state or an individual's private activities, functionality of the electronic payment funds transfer, or, as the case may be, the identity of a person the intruder wants to impersonate for personal, political, or commercial gains.

The security disciplines involved in this are already familiar: the 3As (authentication, authorization, administration), encryption, digital signatures, confidentiality, data integrity, privacy, accountability, and virus protection.

End-to-End Security Framework

To sum up the discussions in the previous sections, when we talk about security, we may want to look at the entire security space from "outside in," using the diagram in Figure 9-1. An important point that needs to be emphasized here is that neither of the disciplines taken separately—network, perimeter, platform, application, data and user security—could offer a complete security assurance.

The events of recent history and the heightened awareness of the real dangers that can be exploited by various terrorist organizations and unscrupulous opportunists have taught us that in order to be and feel secure, we need to achieve "end-to-end security"—an environment that does not intentionally or by omission expose security holes and can provide the business benefits of security—privacy, confidentiality, integrity, and trust (see Figure 9-2).

Only a strong understanding of potential security vulnerabilities and an effective combination of various security technologies and disciplines can ensure that this goal can be achieved.

Traditional Security Requirements

Today's business environment has different security requirements than traditional "brick and mortar" commerce. Enterprise networks are no longer defined by the physical boundaries of a single company location but often encompass remote sites and include mobile and remote users all over the world. Also, organizations often use many contractors who are not employees and thus do not undergo employee-level screening and vetting, but may have similar or even greater access to enterprise systems and applications than many employees.

Traditional security requirements include:

- **Authentication**   The ability to verify that an individual or a party is who they claim they are; authentication is a verification component of the process known as identification.

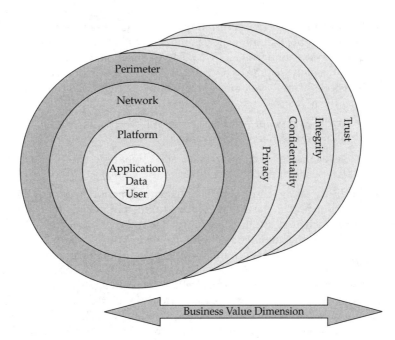

FIGURE 9-2
Security and
business value
dimensions

- **Authorization**   A business process of determining what data and computing resources the authenticated party is allowed to access; authorization processes and technologies enforce the permissions expressed in the user authorization schema known as *entitlements*. An authorization mechanism automatically enforces entitlements that are based on a security policy dealing with the use of the resource, and, in general, the policy could be roles-based, rules-based, or a combination of the two. Clearly, authorization is driven by and depends on reliable authentication (see the discussion on various authorization concerns later in this and the following chapters).

- **Confidentiality**   A business requirement that defines the rules and processes that can protect certain information from unauthorized use. A more formal definition of confidentiality has been offered by the International Organization for Standardization (ISO) in its ISO-17799 standard[1] as "ensuring that information is accessible only to those authorized to have access."

NOTE   *Confidentiality is necessary but not sufficient for maintaining the privacy of the personal information stored in the computing system. This is based on the definition of* privacy *as the proper handling and use of personal information (PI) throughout its life-cycle, consistent with the preferences of the individual and with data protection principles of accountability, collection limitations, disclosure, participation, relevance, security, use limitations, and verification.*

- **Integrity**   A business requirement that data in a file or a database, or a message traversing the network remain unchanged unless the change is properly authorized; data integrity means that any received data matches exactly what was sent; data integrity deals with the prevention of accidental or malicious changes to data.

- **Verification and Nonrepudiation**   This requirement deals with the business and legal concepts that allow a systematic verification of the fact that an action in question was undertaken by a party in question, and that the party in question cannot legally dispute or deny the fact of the action (*nonrepudiation*); this requirement is especially important today when many B2C and B2B transactions are conducted over the network.

  - Traditional paper-based forms are now available over the network and are allowed to be signed electronically.

  - Legislation such as eSign made such signatures acceptable in the court of law (see section on eSign law later in the chapter).

- **Auditing and Accountability**   The requirement that defines the process of data collection and analysis that allows administrators and other specially designated users, such as IT auditors, to verify that authentication and authorization rules are producing the intended results as defined in the company's business and security policies. Individual accountability for attempts to violate the intended policy depends on monitoring relevant security events, which should be stored securely and time-stamped using a *trusted time source* in a reliable log of events (also known as an audit trail or a chain of evidence archive); this audit log can be analyzed to detect attempted or successful security violations. The monitoring process can be implemented as a continuous automatic function, as a periodic check, or as an occasional verification that proper procedures are being followed. The audit trail may be used by security administrators, internal audit personnel, external auditors, government regulatory officials, and in legal proceedings.

- **Availability**   This requirement provides an assurance that a computer system and the information it manages are accessible by authorized users whenever needed.

- **Security management**   This requirement includes user administration and key management:

  - In the context of security management, user administration is often referred to as *user provisioning*. It is the process of defining, creating, maintaining, and deleting user authorizations, resources, and the authorized privilege relationships between users and resources. Administration translates business policy decisions into an internal format that can be used to enforce policy definitions at the point of entry, at a client device, in network devices such as routers, and on servers and hosts. Security administration is an ongoing effort because business organizations, application systems, and users are constantly changing.

  - Key management deals with a very complex process of establishing, generating, saving, recovering, and distributing private and public keys for security solutions based on PKI (see more on this topic later in the chapter).

These traditional security concerns apply to any software system or application that has to protect access to and use of information resources regardless of whether the system is Internet based, internal intranet based, or is a more traditional client-server design. However, as businesses and government organizations continue to expand their Internet channels, new security requirements have emerged that introduce additional complexity into an already complex set of security concerns.

Emerging Security Requirements

Let's briefly discuss several security concerns and requirements that have emerged in recent years. These requirements include identity management, user provisioning and access certification, intrusion detection and prevention, antivirus and antispyware capabilities, and concerns about privacy, confidentiality, and trust.

Identity Management

This security discipline is concerned with some key aspects of doing business on the Internet. These aspects include:

- The need to develop and use a common and persistent identity that can help avoid endless checkpoints that users need to go through as they conduct business on different websites
- The need to prevent the theft and unauthorized use of user identities

The first requirement is not just a user convenience—the lack of a common identity management results in multiple instances of the same user being known but being treated differently in different departments of the same organization. For example, a services company may have a Mike Johnson in its sales database, an M. W. Johnson in its services database, and Dr. Michael Johnson and family in its marketing database—clearly, this organization would have a difficult time reconciling this individual's sales and services activity, and may end up bombarding him and his household with marketing offers for the products he already has—the result is a negative customer experience and poor customer relationship!

The second requirement is also very important. As we stated in Chapter 8, identity theft continues to be on the rise, and the size of the problem is becoming quite significant. For example, according to the 2009 Gartner Report, about 7.5 percent of U.S. adults lost money to some sort of financial fraud in 2008, and data losses cost companies an average of $6.6 million per breach. The direct effect of the identify theft is that for the same time period, customer attrition across industry sectors due to a data breach almost doubled from the regular rate of 3.6 percent to 6.5 percent, and in the financial services sector in particular the turnover rate reached 5.5 percent.[2] This growth of identity theft incidents is estimated to continue at an alarmingly high rate, and many analysts agree that identity theft has become the fastest-growing white-collar crime in the U.S. and probably around the world.

Identity management is also a key requirement for the success of Web Services. For Web Services to become a predominant web-based e-business model, companies need to be assured that web-based applications have been developed with stringent security and authentication controls. Not having strong identity management solutions could prevent Web Services from evolving into mature web-based solutions.

Identity management consists of many components, services, and complex interrelated processes. In order to better visualize the complexity and multitude of identity management, we use a notion of the conceptual reference architecture. Such an identity management reference architecture is shown in Figure 9-3.

There are a number of standards-based and industry-driven initiatives that attempt to address various aspects of identity management, including such initiatives as Liberty Alliance and the recently announced Kantara Initiative[3]. However, the topic of identity, anonymity,

Federated Identity Layer		
Cross-enterprise Provisioning	Cross-enterprise Identity Mapping	Cross-enterprise Trust Models

Identity Provisioning and Life-Cycle Management Layer				
Provisioning	Customer Self Service	Policy Management	Credentials & Profile Management	Customer Preferences Management

Access Control and Management Layer				
Authentication	Access Control	Authorization	Entitlements	Monitoring
SSO	RBAC	Permissions	Roles & Rules Management	Auditing and Reporting

Identity and Security Infrastructure Layer			
Directory Services	Workflow Management	XML Web Services	Data Security PKI, Tokens
Network Security	Perimeter Security		Platform Security

System Directory Store	User Identity Store	Policy Store

FIGURE 9-3   Identity management reference architecture

and privacy involves the sociology of personal information and of information more generally. Therefore, identity management should by itself be considered as a cross-discipline, multifaceted area of knowledge and technology. The diagram in Figure 9-4 shows a typical architecture of identity management.

User Provisioning and Access Certification

This requirement has emerged to address identity life-cycle management and its user administration aspects that deal with the creation, maintenance, and termination of digital identities. User provisioning deals with automating the process of granting users access rights (entitlements) to computing and network resources. Therefore, it is also referred to as *entitlements provisioning*. By automating time-consuming and costly manual procedures, user provisioning can sharply reduce the costs of provisioning new employees, customers, partners, and suppliers with the necessary credentials, tools, and access privileges. Conversely, the process can also be used in reverse to deprovision ex-employees, customers, partners, suppliers, and expired accounts. User provisioning provides a greater degree of corporate efficiency and lowers administrative costs by facilitating account creation and tightly controlling access privileges, and enhances security by tracking, managing, and controlling access. It is also very important to note that by automating the processes of creating and removing user accounts and their entitlements, user provisioning and deprovisioning are

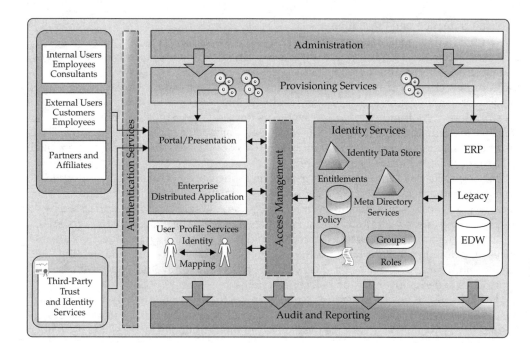

FIGURE 9-4   Identity management logical architecture

widely viewed as some of the key capabilities that are required to enable compliance with various regulations, including those defined in GLBA, SOX, and the USA Patriot Act's Know Your Customer (KYC).

Provisioning and deprovisioning users and assigning their access privileges in the form of entitlements represent only one side of the issue. On-boarding new users, modifying existing entitlements, and removing users and entitlements can become a very complex process, especially when the number of security rules, the number of users and their roles, and the number of protected resources grow with business maturity in a globally competitive marketplace. The new challenge of verifying the outcome of user provisioning gave rise to a companion discipline—*Access Certification*. This security discipline is often considered in conjunction with user provisioning and frequently implemented as a product bundle. Products and solutions implementing access certification support extensive capabilities for user role modeling, provide an accurate view of access privileges provisioned to the users, verify that these privileges are assigned according to the security policies of the enterprise, and detect conflicts in assigned privileges against the policies, as well as detect changes in user access that can result in an increase in risk profiles.

Access certification helps organizations to quickly determine who has access to what resource, why this access was granted, the impact of adding a new set of roles and entitlements to already established user groups, and in general helps manage identity governance and supports compliance reporting and access control implementation requirements of the enterprise.

Intrusion Detection and Prevention

This truly is a traditional requirement that has been revitalized in recent years due to increased incidents of break-ins and similar security violations, all due to the networked and interconnected nature of today's business. According to a 2009 survey conducted by the Computer Security Institute (CSI),[4] organizations detected large increases in incidences of password sniffing, financial fraud, and malware infection, and 33 percent of the surveyed organizations were fraudulently represented as the sender of a phishing message. These statistics are growing significantly year after year. Considering the typical enterprise's reluctance to admit to incidents or their inability to detect them, the true figures are likely to be higher than what has been reported.

Intrusion detection is the process of monitoring the events occurring in a computer system or network and analyzing them for signs of intrusion. Intrusion detection is a necessary business, technical, and even legal requirement that cannot be addressed by simply relying on firewalls and Virtual Private Networks. Indeed, as the attackers are getting smarter and their intrusion techniques and tools are getting more effective, reliable intrusion detection solutions have to offer a degree of sophistication and adaptability that requires unprecedented levels of industry collaboration and innovative "out-of-the-box" approaches to designing intrusion detection systems.

While intrusion detection systems were designed to detect unauthorized access or misuse of computing resources, the new breed of security systems, called *Intrusion Prevention Systems (IPS)* has emerged to change the focus from the detection of attack to the prevention of an attack before actual damage has occurred. Contemporary IPS solutions are designed to protect against such common threats as worms, viruses, and Trojan horses; installation and activation of back doors; modifications to system files; changes in user entitlements and privilege levels; buffer overflow attacks; various spyware applications; and many others.

Information and Software Integrity and Tamper-Resistance

Protection of software and data against illegitimate use and modifications is a pressing security issue for software developers, software publishers, and intellectual property distributors (for example, music, digital video, DVD) alike. Many existing software-based mechanisms are too weak (for example, having a single point of failure) or too expensive to apply (for example, heavy runtime performance penalty). Software tamper-resistance deals with a serious threat, where a malicious user obtains a copy of the software and modifies its protection mechanism so that the modified software can change its original behavior to satisfy the attacker's intent. For example, a program can be modified to create an unauthorized copy of the software that can be illegally distributed to the public, to a business competitor, to a criminal organization, etc.

Privacy, Confidentiality, and Trust

These requirements became critical as more organizations and users started to use the Internet for many aspects of business and personal life. We briefly described the confidentiality and privacy requirements in the preceding section. The issue of trust adds additional requirements of keeping confidential information confidential, respecting and maintaining user privacy according to his or her privacy preferences, and providing a systematic means of verifying that the privacy and confidentiality aspects of the trusted relationship are not violated. In general, different forms of trust exist to address different types of problems and mitigate risk in certain conditions. Various forms of trust have to be managed and reinforced differently based on the nature of the business and its corporate policies. When we look at the traditional network security solution, we can identify two principal forms of trust: direct trust and third-party trust.

- *Direct trust* refers to a situation in which two entities (for example, individual users) have established a trusted relationship in order to exchange information. When direct trust is applied to secure communications, it is the responsibility of each entity to ensure that they are comfortable with their level of personal trust in one another.

- *Third-party trust* refers to a situation in which two entities implicitly trust each other even though they have not previously established a personal relationship. In this situation, two entities implicitly trust each other because they each share a relationship with a common third party, and that third party vouches for the trustworthiness of the two entities in question. As an example, when classical security users named Alice and Bob want to exchange trustworthy credentials, they can use passports and/or driver licenses since they implicitly trust the government agencies that issued those credentials. Third-party trust is a fundamental requirement for any large-scale implementation of a network security solution based on public key cryptography since it's impractical and unrealistic to expect each user to have previously established relationships with all other users.

Trust and Business Semantics

The nature of trust in relationship to security varies based on the business processes that require different degrees and procedures to establish trust. A Russian proverb, adopted by former U.S. President Ronald Reagan, says, "Trust, but verify." This is especially true for the financial services industry, and more specifically, for securities trading. The notion of trust is paramount there and is the key to enable securities trading. However, the business trust in securities trading is different from the trust relationship between two individuals. Business trust implies the ability to rely on others to assume certain risks, the assurance that business commitments will be honored, and the certainty that there is an effective avenue of recourse. To establish and maintain these trusted relationships, a security system should support the notion that *acting as if* you don't trust the *counterparty* forces you to find ways to trust the *transaction*. This concept of trust drives new developments in security standards, systems, and solutions.

Overview of Security Technologies

This section provides a cursory overview of several major security technologies. This overview is by necessity brief—a complete and comprehensive discussion on this topic is well beyond the scope of this book.

Confidentiality and Integrity

Let's start the overview of security technologies with a high-level discussion of two key security requirements—information confidentiality and integrity—and the techniques that support these requirements.

Cryptography, Cryptology, and Cryptanalysis

Cryptography is the process of converting data into an unreadable form via an *encryption algorithm*. Cryptography enables information to be sent across communication networks that are assumed to be insecure, without losing confidentiality or the integrity of the information being sent. Cryptography also can be used for user authentication by enabling verification of the sender identity to the recipient.

Cryptanalysis is the study of mathematical techniques designed to defeat cryptographic algorithms. Collectively, a branch of science that deals with cryptography and cryptanalysis is called *cryptology*.

An encryption algorithm transforms plain text into a coded equivalent, known as the cipher text, for transmission or storage. The coded text is subsequently decoded (decrypted) at the receiving end and restored to plain text. The encryption algorithm uses a key, which typically is a large binary number. The length of the key depends on the encryption algorithm and is one of the factors that determines the strength of the encryption.

The data that needs to be protected is "locked" for sending by using the bits in the key to transform the data bits using some mathematical operation. At the receiving end, the same or a different but related key is used to unscramble the data, restoring it to its original binary form. The effort required to decode the unusable scrambled bits into meaningful data without knowledge of the key—known as "breaking" or "cracking" the encryption—typically is a function of the complexity of the algorithm and the length of the keys. In most effective encryption schemes, the longer the key, the harder it is to decode the encrypted message.

Two types of algorithms are in use today: shared key (also known as "secret key" or symmetric key) and public key (or asymmetric key).

Symmetric vs. Asymmetric Key Encryption

There are two principally different approaches to creating, applying, and managing the encryption keys: One is known as *symmetric cipher* (the encryption and decryption keys are identical, and all communicating parties have to know the key in order to communicate successfully and confidentially); the second one is an *asymmetric* cipher, and it is the foundation of the *Public Key Infrastructure (PKI)*.

The obvious problems with the symmetric cipher include:

- The key distribution problem
  - The need to exchange the secret key between all intended recipients of the sender
  - Communication difficulties between unknown parties (that is, the challenge is for the sender to distribute a secret key to a party unknown to the sender)
- The scalability issue; for example, in a group of 100 participants, a sender may have to maintain 99 secret keys

These problems of symmetric ciphers were addressed by the discovery made by Whitfield Diffie and Martin Hellman in the mid-1970s. Their work defined a process in which the encryption and decryption keys were mathematically related but sufficiently different that it would be possible to publish one key with very little probability that anyone would be able to derive the other. This notion of publishing one key in the related key pair to the public gave birth to the term Public Key Infrastructure (PKI). The core premise of PKI is based on the fact that while deriving the other key is possible, it is computationally and economically infeasible.

While symmetric encryption is using a shared secret key for both encryption and decryption, PKI cryptography is based on the use of public/private key pairs. A public key is typically distributed in the form of a certificate that may be available to all users wishing to encrypt information, to be viewed only by a designated recipient using his or her private key.

A *private key* is a distinct data structure that is always protected from unauthorized disclosure and is used by the owner of the private key to decrypt the information that was encrypted using the recipient's public key. The elegance of the PKI is in its mathematics, which allows the encryption key to be made public, but it still would be computationally infeasible to derive a private decryption key from the public key.

Allowing every party to publish its public key PKI solves the major key distribution and scalability problems of symmetric encryption that we mentioned earlier.

The mathematical principles, algorithms, and standards used to implement public key cryptography are relatively complex and their detailed description is well beyond the scope of this book. Moreover, creation and management of the public-private key pairs is a complex and elaborate set of processes that include key establishment, key life-cycle management, key recovery, key escrow, and many others. These and other details about various aspects of PKI are too complex and numerous to be discussed in this book. However, there are a number of mature PKI products on the market today, and in many cases the technology has been made sufficiently easy to use to become practically transparent to the user.

PKI, Nonrepudiation, and Digital Signatures

Digital signatures are one of the major value-added services of the Public Key Infrastructure. Digital signatures allow the recipient of a digitally signed electronic message to authenticate the sender and verify the integrity of the message. Most importantly, digital signatures are difficult to counterfeit and easy to verify, making them superior even to handwritten signatures.

Digital Signatures

A digital signature fundamentally relies on the concept of a key pair, where a private "signing" key is known only to the sender (Alice), so that when she signs some data, the data is uniquely and explicitly tied to her. Alice's public key is available to a broad audience of potential recipients, so that the signature can be verified and associated with the owner of the private key (Alice). Because of the nature of public key encryption algorithms, only the public key can decrypt a message encrypted with the corresponding private key. This process thus establishes that only the holder of the private key (Alice) could have created the digitally signed message.

Most analysts and legal scholars agree that digital signatures will become increasingly important in establishing the authenticity of the record for admissibility as evidence. The adoption of the Electronic Signatures in Global and National Commerce Act (eSign) legislation into law by the U.S. Congress is one confirmation of the importance of digital signatures. However, the status of explicit digital signature legislation varies from country to country. For example, the European Union has set different levels of legal recognition for different forms of electronic signatures that meet different legal and technology requirements, from limited acceptance to broad applicability.

Digital signatures received serious legal backing from organizations such as the American Bar Association (ABA), which states that to achieve the basic purpose of a signature, it must have the following attributes:

- **Signer authentication**   A signature should indicate who signed a document, message, or record, and should be difficult for another person to produce without authorization.

- **Document authentication**   A signature should identify what is signed, making it impracticable to falsify or alter either the signed matter or the signature without detection.

The ABA clarifies that these attributes are mandatory tools used to exclude impersonators and forgers and are essential ingredients of a "nonrepudiation service."

Nonrepudiation

Nonrepudiation is the term used for a service that assures, to the extent technically possible, that entities cannot deny the fact that a particular action has been taken by the entity in question. In the context of PKI, we can distinguish several types of nonrepudiation:

- *Nonrepudiation of origin*, in which a user cannot falsely deny having originated a message or a document

- *Nonrepudiation of receipt*, in which a user cannot falsely deny having received a message or a document

- Other forms of nonrepudiation, including nonrepudiation of *creation*, *delivery*, and *approval*

Network and Perimeter Security Technologies

This group of security technologies is relatively mature and widely deployed throughout corporate and public networks today.

Firewalls

Network firewalls enforce an enterprise's security policy by controlling the flow of traffic between two or more networks. A firewall system provides both a perimeter defense and a control point for monitoring access to and from specific networks. Firewalls often are placed between the corporate network and an external network such as the Internet or a partnering company's network. However, firewalls are also used to segment parts of corporate networks.

Firewalls can control access at the network level, the application level, or both. At the network level, a firewall can restrict packet flow based on such protocol attributes as the packet's source address, destination address, originating TCP/UDP port, destination port, and protocol type. At the application level, a firewall may base its control decisions on the details of the conversation (for example, rejecting all conversations that discuss a particular topic or use a restricted keyword) between the applications and other available information, such as previous connectivity and user identification.

Firewalls may be packaged as system software, hardware and software bundles, and, more recently, dedicated hardware appliances (embedded in routers, for example). Known as firewall "appliances," they are easy-to-configure integrated hardware and software packages that run on dedicated platforms. Firewalls can defend against a variety of attacks, including:

- Unauthorized access
- IP address "spoofing" (a technique where hackers disguise their traffic as coming from a trusted address to gain access to the protected network or resources)
- Session hijacking
- Spyware, viruses, and Trojans
- Malicious or rogue applets
- Traffic rerouting
- Denial of Service (DoS)

With the emergence of spyware and malware as some of the fastest-growing security threats, advanced firewalls and other perimeter defense solutions are extending their features to support the capability to recognize and eradicate spyware modules that reside on end-user computers and corporate servers.

Many popular firewalls include VPN technology, where a secure "tunnel" is created over the external network via an encrypted connection between the firewalls to access the internal, protected network transparently.

Virtual Private Networks

Virtual Private Network (VPN) solutions use encryption and authentication to provide confidentiality and data integrity for communications over open and/or public networks such as the Internet. In other words, VPN products establish an encrypted tunnel for users and devices to exchange information. This secure tunnel can only be as strong as the method used to identify the users or devices at each end of the communication, and the method used to protect data that is transmitted over the tunnel.

Typically, each VPN node uses a secret session key and an agreed-upon encryption algorithm to encode and decode data, exchanging session keys at the start of each connection using public key encryption. Both end points of a VPN link check data integrity, usually using a standards-compliant cryptographic algorithm (for example, SHA-1 or MD-5).

Secure HTTP Protocols/SSL/TLS/WTLS

These communication protocols address issues of secure communication between clients and the server on the wired (and in the case of WTLS, wireless) network. We discuss these protocols very briefly in this section for completeness.

Secure HyperText Transport Protocols   These protocols include popular HTTP Secure (HTTPS) and its less used alternative—Secure HTTP or S-HTTP. Both use, as their basis, the primary protocol used between web clients and servers—the HyperText Transport Protocol (HTTP). HTTP Secure, or HTTPS, is a combination of HTTP and SSL/TLS protocols (the latter is described in the next section). HTTPS provides encryption and secure identification of the server. It uses a dedicated port (i.e., Port 443) and therefore is often used to secure sensitive communications such as payment transactions, identity establishment and verification, and so on. Similarly to **HTTPS,** Secure HTTP (S-HTTP) extends the basic HTTP protocol to allow both client-to-server and server-to-client encryptions. Both protocols provide three basic security functions: digital signature, authentication, and encryption. Any message may use any combination of these (as well as no protection). These protocols provide multiple-key management mechanisms including password-style manually distributed shared secret keys, public key key exchange, and Kerberos ticket distribution. In particular, provisions have been made for prearranged symmetric session keys to send confidential messages to those who have no established public-private key pair.

Secure Sockets Layer (SSL)   SSL is the most widely used security technology on the web. SSL provides end-to-end security between browsers and servers, always authenticating servers and optionally authenticating clients. SSL is application-independent because it operates at the transport layer rather than at the application layer. It secures connections at the point where the application communicates with the IP protocol stack so it can encrypt, authenticate, and validate all protocols supported by SSL-enabled browsers, such as FTP, Telnet, e-mail, and so on. In providing communications channel security, SSL ensures that the channel is private and reliable and that encryption is used for all messages after a simple "handshake" is used to define a session-specific secret key.

Transport Layer Security Protocol (TLS)   The Internet Engineering Task Force renamed SSL as the Transport Layer Security protocol in 1999. TLS is based on SSL 3.0 and offers additional options for authentication such as enhanced certificate management, improved authentication, and new error-detection capabilities. Its three levels of server security include server verification via digital certificate, encrypted data transmission, and verification that the message content has not been altered.

Wireless Transport Layer Security   The Wireless Transport Layer Security (WTLS) protocol is the security layer of the Wireless Application Protocol (WAP). The WAP WTLS protocol was designed to provide privacy, data integrity, and authentication for wireless devices. Even though the WTLS protocol is closely modeled after the well-studied TLS protocol, there are a number of potential security problems in it, and it has been found to be vulnerable to several attacks, including a chosen plaintext data recovery attack, a datagram truncation attack, a message forgery attack, and a key-search shortcut for some exportable keys.

Security experts are continuously working on addressing these concerns, and new wireless security solutions are rapidly becoming available, not only to corporate local area networks, but to all wireless devices including personal computers, PDAs, and even mobile phones. Therefore, information stored in an MDM Data Hub can be accessed securely as long as the wireless access point or a router and the wireless users exercise appropriate precautions and employ wireless security protocols of enterprise-defined strengths. These protocols include Wireless Equivalent Privacy (WEP), Wi-Fi Protected Access (WPA), Extensible Authentication Protocol (EAP), and others.

Application, Data, and User Security
In this section, we'll discuss application, data, and user security technologies and their applicability to the business requirements of authentication, integrity, and confidentiality.

Introduction to Authentication Mechanisms

Authentication mechanisms include passwords and PINs, one-time passwords, digital certificates, security tokens, biometrics, Kerberos authentication, and RADIUS.

Passwords and PINs   Authentication most commonly relies on passwords or personal identification numbers (PINs). Passwords are typically used while logging into networks and systems. To ensure mutual authentication, passwords can be exchanged in both directions.

Challenge-Response Handshakes   These techniques offer stronger authentication than ordinary passwords. One side starts the exchange, and is presented with an unpredictable challenge value. Based on a secretly shared value, an appropriate response is then calculated and sent. This procedure defeats the unauthorized use of simple passwords.

One-Time Password   One-time passwords are designed to remove the security risks presented by traditional, static passwords and PINs. The same password is never reused, so intercepted passwords cannot be used for authentication. Implementations of this approach vary, often using time values to provide the basis on which the current password is based. For example, RSA Security's SecurID solution generates a key value that changes every 60 seconds and can be displayed on the RSA SecureID small hardware token or presented to the user on a screen of a device that runs a SecureID "soft token" application (this RSA application can be installed on a PDA or a smartphone device). This value, plus an optional PIN, is submitted to an authentication server, where it is compared to a value computed for that user's SecureID at that particular time. This form of authentication is sometimes referred to as "two-factor authentication."

Digital Certificates   Digital certificates work like their real-life counterparts that are issued by a trusted authority to contain and present the user's credentials (for example, passports and driver's licenses). Digital certificates contain encryption keys that can be used to authenticate digital signatures. Certificates are often based on PKI technology and mathematically bind a public encryption key to the identity (or other attribute) of a principal. The principal can be an individual, an application, or another entity such as a web server. A trusted certificate authority creates the certificate and vouches for its authenticity by signing it with the authority's own private key. There are several commercial certificate issuers, such as RSA Security (now a part of EMC^2) and VeriSign. An organization can issue certificates for its own applications by using an internally managed Certificate Authority. A certificate-issuing server can also be installed as a part of the Web Server suite (for example, IBM, Lotus, and Microsoft integrate a certificate server with their web server software). PKI security vendors such as VeriSign and RSA Security/EMC^2 offer a variety of mature certificate-enabled products for businesses.

Other authentication techniques include Kerberos and Remote Authentication Dial-In User Service (RADIUS) Authentication.

Multifactor Authentication Technologies

In principle, any authentication process deals with one or more questions that help define the user's identity. These questions include:

- Something you have (for example, a smart card or a hardware token)
- Something you know (for example, a password or a PIN)

- Something you are (for example, an intrinsic attribute of your body including fingerprint, iris scan, face geometry)
- Something you do (for example, typing characteristics, handwriting style)

The concept of multifactor authentication uses more than one of these options. Clearly, multifactor authentication systems are more difficult for the user to get used to. However, the security benefits of multifactor authentication are significant. Multifactor authentication can successfully withstand a number of impersonation attacks, and therefore can eventually overcome many perceived drawbacks of this technology.

Biometrics   The goal of biometric identification is to provide strong authentication and access control with a level of security surpassing password and token systems.[5] This goal is achievable because access is allowed only to the specific individual, rather than to anyone in possession of the access card.

Biometric techniques usually involve an automated process to verify the identity of an individual based on physical or behavioral characteristics. The first step in using biometrics is often called the *enrollment*. Predefined biometric templates, such as a voiceprint, fingerprint, and iris scan, are collected for each individual in the enrollment database. The template data then is used during a verification process for comparison with the characteristic of the person requesting access. Depending on the computer and network technologies used, verification can take only seconds. Biometric techniques fall into two categories: physiological and behavioral.

- **Physiological biometrics**   Face, eye, fingerprint, palmprint, hand geometry, and thermal images
- **Behavioral biometrics**   Voiceprints, handwritten signatures, and keystroke/ signature dynamics

Biometric measures are used most frequently to provide hard-to-compromise security against impersonation attacks, but they also are useful for avoiding the inconveniences of needing a token or of users forgetting their passwords.

When considering biometric techniques, care must be taken to avoid a high rate of false positives (erroneous acceptance of the otherwise compromised identity) and false negatives (erroneous rejections of the otherwise valid identity). For example, a fingerprint scan can produce a false negative because the individual's finger was dirty, covered with grease, etc. Among the biometric techniques available to date, the iris scan produces the highest degree of confidence[6] (indeed, an iris scan is unique for each eye for each individual for as long as the individual is alive; the number of all possible iris scan codes is in the order of 10^{72}—a very large number that exceeds the number of observable stars in the universe!).

Smart Cards

Smart cards represent another class of multifactor authentication solutions that offer a number of defenses against password-based vulnerabilities.

Smart cards—plastic cards about the same size as a credit card, but with an embedded computer chip—are increasingly used in a wide variety of applications, from merchant loyalty schemes to credit/debit cards, to student IDs, to GSM phones. According to several reports by the Gartner Group and other research organizations, smart cards are the highest-volume semiconductor-based product manufactured today, with GSM phones and financial-service applications leading this boom—the GSM subscriber information module (SIM) remains the single-largest smart card application.

Authentication, Personalization, and Privacy

Personalization has long been recognized as one of the key elements of an improved customer experience and enhanced customer relationships with the enterprise. However, organizations need to strike the right balance between the customers' desire for personalized services and the need for privacy protection. In other words, we can recognize the tension between *privacy*, with its intrinsic property of not disclosing personal information unless and to the extent absolutely necessary, and *personalization*, which requires access to personal information, transactional behavior, and even knowledge of the party-to-enterprise relationships. To put it slightly differently, enabling personalization requires a certain amount of privacy disclosure.

But personalization is not the only threat to privacy. We have stated repeatedly that effective, strong authentication is a prerequisite to protecting an individual's privacy. However, it can also threaten privacy since, depending on the situation, the risk profile of the users, and their transactions, the stronger the authentication, the more personal, sensitive, identifying information may be needed before access to an information resource or permission to execute a transaction can be granted. Solving these tensions is one of the drivers for an integrated MDM solution that can support the privacy preferences of the users as a part of the MDM data model and the extension of the data governance rules and policies.

Integrating Authentication and Authorization

While PKI addresses the issues of authentication, integrity, confidentiality, and nonrepudiation, we need to define an overarching conceptual framework that addresses a set of issues related to the authorization of users and applications to perform certain functions, to access protected resources, to create and enforce access control policies, and to "provision" users to automatically map appropriate policies, permissions, and entitlements at the time of their enrollment into a security domain.

As we mentioned earlier, a successful authorization relies on the ability to perform reliable authentication. In fact, these two disciplines should go hand in hand in order to create a robust and fully functional and auditable security framework. To help discuss these topics, let's take a brief look at access control mechanisms and Single Sign-On (SSO) technologies as a contemporary access control solution for the web and beyond.

Access control simplifies the task of maintaining the security of an enterprise network by cutting down on the number of paths and modes through which attackers might penetrate network defenses. A more detailed discussion on access control can be found in Chapter 11.

SSO Technologies

Single Sign-On (SSO) is a technology that enables users to access multiple computer systems or networks after logging in once with a single set of authentication credentials. This setup eliminates the situation where separate passwords and user IDs are required for each application. SSO offers three major advantages: user convenience, administrative convenience, and improved security. Indeed, having only one sign-on per user makes administration easier. It also eliminates the possibility that users will keep their many passwords in an easily accessible form (for example, paper) rather than try to remember them all, thereby compromising security. Finally, SSO enhances productivity by reducing the amount of time users spend gaining system access.

SSO is particularly valuable in computing environments where users access applications residing on multiple operating systems and middleware platforms and, correspondingly, where its implementation is most challenging.

One disadvantage of the SSO approach is that when it is compromised, it gives the perpetrator access to all resources the user can access via a single sign-on.

Federated SSO and SAML

Enabling effective and seamless access to computing environments where users access applications residing on multiple operating systems and middleware platforms is the challenge addressed by Federated SSO—a set of authentication technologies that support and manage identity federation by enabling the portability of identity information across otherwise autonomous security domains. Identity federation offers a number of business benefits to the organization, including a reduction in the administration costs of identity provisioning and management, increased security and improved user experience by reducing the number of identification and authentication actions (ideally to a single action), and improved privacy compliance by allowing the user to control or limit what information is shared.

From a technology point of view, identity federation and seamless cross-domain authentication (federated SSO) are enabled through the use of open industry standards such as the Security Assertion Markup Language (SAML).[7]

SAML is the standard for exchanging authentication and authorization data between security domains. SAML has been developed by the Organization for the Advancement of Structured Information Standards (OASIS) and is an XML-based protocol that uses security tokens containing assertions to pass authentication and authorization information about a principal (usually an end user) between an identity provider and a Web Service. There are essentially three fundamental components of the SAML specification:

- SAML assertions
- SAML protocol
- SAML bindings

The SAML specification includes an XML schema that defines SAML assertions and protocol messages. The specification also describes methods for binding these assertions to other existing protocols (HTTP, SOAP) in order to enable additional security functionality. A detailed discussion of SAML is beyond the scope of this book.

SAML is not the only standard addressing identity federation. There are a number of other standards and technologies, many of which are available as standalone products or as part of other environments. Most popular solutions include:

- **Windows CardSpace**[8]   A Windows application available in the latest versions of Microsoft Windows (starting with the Vista operating system). The Windows CardSpace application allows users to provide their digital identity to online services in a simple and secure way by creating a secure online virtual information card that is used to prove a user's identity and is difficult for the intruder to acquire or change.

- **OpenID**[9]   A lightweight identity system designed around the concept of Internet identifier (URI-based) identity. OpenID was initially designed to address a very simple use case—enabling blog commenting in a controlled manner to protect against blog abuse, spam, and invalid/misstated attribution. OpenID's primary benefits are the simplicity of its trust model and ease of integration.
- **ID-WSF (The Liberty Alliance's ID-Web Services Framework)**[10]   A platform for the discovery and invocation of identity services implemented as Web Services associated with a given identity. ID-WSF's security model is very flexible and supports use cases with distributed identity services.

Web Services Security Concerns

We discussed Web Services in Part II, when we looked at service-oriented architecture (SOA). While Web Services offer a number of truly significant benefits, they bring with them interesting and challenging security concerns that need to be addressed in order to design, develop, and deploy a security Web Services system.

Authentication

Since Web Services, like any other services and interfaces, should allow only authorized users to access service methods, authenticating those users is the first order of business. This is similar to the username and password authentication of users that ordinary websites may require. However, the main difference here is that in the context of Web Services, the users are other computers that want to use the Web Service.

Data Integrity and Confidentiality

If an organization decides to expose an internal application as a Web Service, it may have to also expose supporting data stores (databases, registries, directories). Clearly, special care is necessary to protect that data, either by encryption (which may come with a performance impact) or by guarding its accessibility.

Similarly, data may be in danger of interception as it is being processed. For example, as a Web Service method gets invoked on user request, the temporary data that the Web Service uses locally may be exposed to an attacker if unauthorized users gain access to the system.

Eavesdropping in a Web Services context implies acquiring the information that users get back from a Web Service. If the Web Services output can be intercepted on its way to the user, the attacker may be in a position to violate the confidentiality and integrity of this data. One preventive measure is to use data-in-transit encryption (for example, SSL) for returned information.

Attacks

In the Web Services model, special care needs to be taken with regard to input parameter validation. In a poorly designed service, an attacker can insert a set of invalid input parameters that can bring the service or a system down. One solution to this problem could be to use a standard object transport protocol such as Simple Object Transport Protocol (SOAP) to define an acceptable value for all input parameters in a Web Service.

Denial-of-service (DoS) attacks, especially the ones where an attacker can overload the service with requests, will prevent legitimate users from using the service and thus disrupt the business. Furthermore, a flood of requests on one component or service can propagate to other components, affecting them all in a cascading, "domino" effect. Since component A may receive requests from sources B and C, this means that an attack on B disrupts A, and may also affect users of C.

The loosely coupled nature of Web Services also leads to other security issues. The chain of components always has a component that is most vulnerable to attack (the weakest link). If attackers can compromise such a weak-link component, they can exploit this opportunity in a variety of ways:

- Intercept any data that flows to that particular component from either direction.

- Acquire sensitive, personal, or valuable information.

- Manipulate the streams of data in various ways, including data alteration, data redirection, and using "innocent" servers to mount denial-of-service attacks from the inside.

- Shut down the component, denying its functionality to the other components that depend upon it; this will effectively disrupt many users' activities from many different access points.

WS-Security Standard

As we discussed in the preceding section, the security of Web Services includes concern about authenticity, integrity, and confidentiality of messages, and understanding of and protection from various penetration and denial-of-service attacks. A dedicated OASIS standard—*WS-Security*—has been developed to provide options for Web Services protection through message integrity, message confidentiality, and single-message authentication. These mechanisms can be used to accommodate a wide variety of security models and encryption technologies.

WS-Security also provides a general-purpose mechanism for associating security tokens with messages. No specific type of security token is required by WS-Security. It is designed to be extensible (for example, to support multiple security token formats). For example, a user might provide proof of identity and proof of a particular business certification. Additional information about WS-Security can be found on the OASIS Web Services Security Technical Committee website.[11]

Putting It All Together

Given the multitude and complexity of security technologies and the size constraints of the book, we were able only to "scratch the surface" of security concerns. However, general security practices and common sense dictate that enterprises should develop a comprehensive end-to-end security framework and reference architecture in order to protect data, users, and application platforms to a degree that makes good business, economic, and even legal sense. The key concerns of information security that are driven by risk management imperatives as well as regulatory and compliance requirements can and should be addressed by carefully designing and implementing a holistic, integrated, and manageable information security architecture and infrastructure that are based on established and emerging standards as well as industry- and enterprise-specific policies. Experience shows that as long as you design your security solution holistically and do not concentrate only on one aspect of security, be it authentication, firewall, or encryption, the current state of the art in security technologies can enable you to create robust and secure Master Data Management solutions. This approach of the ground-up end-to-end security design helps protect the MDM system and the master data it manages, even though all modern MDM implementations are architected as SOA instances and thus the security concerns of Web Services are directly applicable to the design of an MDM Data Hub. From the architecture framework point of view, the layered security framework shown in Figure 9-1 should be considered as an integral part of the MDM solution; in fact, the security framework shows that the outer layers of security are "wrapped" around the data core that naturally represents a Data Hub.

The last two chapters in this part of the book focus on two key aspects of information security that are particularly important to Master Data Management solutions: protecting MDM information and functionality from a security breach and unintended, unauthorized access and use.

To that end, we'll show how to design an MDM solution to enable appropriate levels of information security and security-related compliance. We'll also show how to integrate MDM information management architecture, which was discussed in Part II of the book, with the security and compliance concerns discussed in this and the previous chapters.

References

1. http://www.iso.org/iso/catalogue_detail?csnumber=39612.

2. Gartner, Inc. "Data breach and financial crimes scare consumers away." (February 2009).

3. http://kantarainitiative.org/confluence/display/GI/Mission.

4. http://gocsi.com/survey.

5. http://ctl.ncsc.dni.us/biomet%20web/BMIndex.html.

6. http://ctl.ncsc.dni.us/biomet%20web/BMIris.html.

7. http://www.oasis-open.org/committees/tc_home.php?wg_abbrev=security.

8. http://www.microsoft.com/windows/products/winfamily/cardspace/default.mspx.

9. http://openid.net/get-an-openid/what-is-openid/.

10. http://www.projectliberty.org/specs/.

11. www.oasis-open.org/committees/wss/.

Protecting Content for Secure Master Data Management

The Internet has brought about an information and connectivity revolution where enterprises, governments, and individuals all act as participants in the global interconnected, networked information ecosphere. The information assets available in this networked ecosphere continue to grow and expand their scope. Moreover, as enterprises aggregate data into large data warehouses and MDM Data Hub systems that use networked storage devices, these information assets become increasingly more valuable and at the same time more accessible. This networked ecosphere and the information it contains have become an attractive target for identity thieves, information thieves, and other malicious attackers who have learned to take advantage of the ubiquitous nature of the Internet, and therefore have defined new challenges for the entire spectrum of data security.

Data Security Evolution

Even as security practitioners are working diligently to develop new security solutions, the hackers do not stay idle. They continue to develop new security compromise techniques and approaches. These approaches include not only phishing and pharming (we discussed these in the previous chapter). The hackers and information thieves keep on building and distributing new spyware and malware at an ever-increasing rate. As a result, the number, the variety, and the size of security breaches continue to grow with no signs of slowing down.

For example, consider a high-profile 2009 security breach at Princeton, NJ, payment processor Heartland Payment Systems. According to the company, which processes payments for more than 250,000 businesses, this incident may have compromised tens of millions of credit and debit card transactions. If accurate, such figures may make the Heartland incident one of the largest data breaches ever reported. And this incident is not unique. The 2009 *Washington Post* article "Payment Processor Breach May Be Largest Ever"[1] described the Heartland Payment System incident and offered a number of alarming facts:

- On December 23, 2008, RBS Worldpay, a subsidiary of Citizens Financial Group Inc., said a breach of its payment systems may have affected more than 1.5 million people.

- In March 2008, Hannaford Brothers Co. disclosed that a breach of its payment systems—also aided by malicious software—compromised at least 4.2 million credit and debit card accounts.

- In early 2007, TJX Companies Inc., the parent of retailers Marshalls and TJ Maxx, said a number of breaches over a three-year period exposed more than 45 million credit and debit card numbers.

- In 2005, a breach at payment card processor CardSystems Solutions jeopardized roughly 40 million credit and debit card accounts.

In 2009, the PGP Corporation and the Ponemon Institute published results of their annual *U.S. Cost of a Data Breach Study*.[2] According to the study, data breach incidents cost U.S. companies $202 per compromised customer record in 2008, compared to $197 in 2007. Overall, the cost per compromised record has grown by 40 percent since 2005, with an average total per-incident cost in 2008 of $6.65 million, compared to an average per-incident cost of $6.3 million in 2007. These numbers include explicit and implicit costs attributed to the following:

- Discovery of the breach
- Escalation procedures
- Notification of the potential victims
- Recovery from security incidents in the form of fraud write-offs, legal costs, investigation costs, audits, credit report monitoring, IT and operational costs, and other redress activities
- Impact of customer defections

The overall cost of a security breach would also include other implicit costs often characterized by lost opportunities, legal liabilities, and noncompliance with federal and state regulations. The result could be not just a significant loss of revenue but the potential termination of business as customers lose trust in the business's ability to protect personal and financial data and may decide to change their service providers, trading partners, and suppliers.

Incidents of data compromise are often classified as identity theft—the fastest-growing white-collar crime in the U.S. (we introduced identity theft in Chapter 8). The U.S. Federal Bureau of Investigation (FBI), the Computer Security Institute (CSI), and various identity theft watchdog organizations estimate that organized crime globally makes more money from identity theft than from selling illegal drugs.

What appears to be even more alarming is that the sources of these incidents and the security threats to organizations are no longer coming from outside the enterprise. Disgruntled or irresponsible employees and contractors can easily bypass traditional perimeter defenses and cause significant, long-lasting damage to organizations, their customers, and their reputation. According to published FBI reports, internal threats that originated inside the enterprise account for 50–80 percent of all security attacks.

Emerging Information Security Threats

The vast majority of information that is stored in digital form contains some confidential data—data that is the real target of a wide variety of security threats. We described some of these threats in previous chapters and the preceding section. In addition, the rapid growth of spyware and various forms of viruses has become one of the major threats to the security of the enterprise information.

> **Spyware**
> *Spyware* is malicious software that installs itself onto a user's computer and sends information from that computer to a third party without the user's permission or knowledge.

Some of the better-known types of spyware include:

- General compromise enablers such as
  - Botnet worms that can create a network of infected computers that can work in concert to perform any malicious activity, including but not limited to running Distributed Denial-of-Service (DDoS) attacks
  - Downloaders that are designed to install potentially malicious programs on computers without the user's knowledge or consent
- Identity grabbers that "complement" phishing and pharming activities by performing such actions as
  - Theft of user identification, passwords, and other sensitive or confidential personal information
  - Monitoring and capturing keystrokes that can enable a thief to steal user information such as passwords (this type of spyware is known as a "keylogger")
  - Hijacking a web browser in order to modify browser settings so that it can redirect the user to a pharming location or another bogus site
- Data theft enablers include:
  - **Banking Trojans**   Specialized software agents that monitor information entered into banking applications
  - **Backdoor Trojans**   A type of spyware that may allow hackers unrestricted remote access to a computer system when it is online

These and other types of spyware represent a real threat to enterprises and individual users alike. However, those spyware programs that are focused specifically on data compromise represent a serious challenge to the enterprise's ability to comply with data protection regulations (many of these regulations are mentioned in Chapter 8 and also listed in the next section). These regulations are designed to protect sensitive and confidential customer and business financial data, including the following data categories:

- Customer and patient data
- Financial transactions
- Finance and accounting data
- Human resource data

- Confidential company performance and planning data
- Military data
- Legal data
- Intellectual property including design and research data

Interestingly, these data categories represent primary areas of the activities surrounding Master Data Management initiatives. As we discussed in Part II of the book, MDM solutions are information integration platforms that create and manage authoritative, accurate, timely, and secure systems of record for their respective areas of focus (customer, product, and so on). The goal of these MDM Data Hub solutions is to collect, integrate, and manage confidential data from a wide variety of sources in order to create a new system of record for the enterprise. Obviously, enterprises implementing these MDM solutions need to protect information stored in Data Hub systems from the compromise of unauthorized access and use.

Moreover, this information may represent highly confidential intellectual property that requires additional considerations for protecting the use of the information content even after the data is legitimately delivered to an authorized user. The latter information protection concern is the province of a special category of information asset protection technology known as Digital Rights Management (DRM) or Enterprise Rights Management (ERM). We briefly discuss ERM later in this chapter. In general, however, the need to protect information assets is driven by a number of factors, including customer expectations, business demands, competitive pressures, industry regulations, business policies, and so on. Recent adoption of regulatory compliance requirements—some of which are general, while others are specific to a particular domain such as public sector, life sciences, and financial services—has further emphasized this need for data protection.

Regulatory Drivers for Data Protection

Concerns over confidential data in general and customer data privacy and data security in particular have resulted in a broad range of legislative and regulatory requirements for data security. Failure to comply with these rules can result in civil and criminal liability. We have discussed some of these regulations in previous chapters of this book, and they are listed here for ease of reference. Examples of regulatory requirements that directly or indirectly focus on information security include:

- **The Sarbanes-Oxley Act** requires that executives know who has access to what information, and that proper security controls are in place to ensure data confidentiality and integrity.
- **The Gramm-Leach-Bliley Act (GLBA)** dictates that organizations must preserve the security and confidentiality of nonpublic personal information including personal financial data.
- **The Health Information Portability and Accountability Act (HIPAA)** directs health care providers to preserve the confidentiality of individual medical records. To the extent that some of this data becomes visible to the benefits departments of any organization (for example, the Human Resources and Payroll departments), HIPAA may have broader applicability than just health care providers.

- **21 Code of Federal Regulations (CFR) Part 11** In the pharmaceutical industry, the Federal Drug Administration (FDA) has established guidelines for any individual or organization governed by the FDA that uses electronic recordkeeping and electronic signatures, including requirements for auditable procedures to ensure the integrity of that data.

- **The Children's On-Line Privacy Protection Act (COPPA)** establishes privacy protection guidelines for any organization holding information about children.

- **California Senate Bill 1386** requires that any organization that loses a California citizen's personal data must alert its California customers via "notification to major statewide media."

- **Nevada Law NRS 597.970** took effect October 1, 2008. It explicitly states that any business in the State of Nevada cannot transfer any personal information of a customer through an electronic transmission other than a facsimile to a person outside of the secure system of the business, unless the business uses encryption to ensure the security of electronic transmission.

- **Massachusetts Law 201 CMR 17.00**, scheduled to take effect in the first quarter of 2010, requires that any person or business dealing with the creation, access, delivery, and use of personal information about state residents has to implement a number of security protection measures, including user authentication protocols, secure access control measures, encryption on all wireless networks linked to personal information repositories, monitoring and encryption for all portable devices with personal information, and firewall protection for any database containing PII. The law further dictates that all system security software must be installed on all devices dealing with PII and be kept current; moreover, this law includes the requirement to implement and provide timely education and training of all persons affected by this law.

- **The European Data Protection Directive** establishes a set of rules that address the handling of *all* types of personal data. This directive requires organizations to ensure that

  - Personal data must be kept confidential.

  - Individuals should know in advance what information is collected about them, how it will be used and by whom, who has access/permissions to change that data, and how it will be stored.

Risks of Data Compromise

To summarize the concerns discussed in the preceding section, data security, privacy, integrity, and confidentiality are no longer optional requirements, and data compromises that violate these requirements can put an organization at significant risk. Some risk types associated with data security compromises include:

- **Reputation risk**   Risk to earnings or revenue arising from negative public opinion.

- **Compliance risk**   Companies are now subject to numerous federal regulations such as the Sarbanes-Oxley Act, the Basel II Accord, the USA Patriot Act, the Gramm-Leach-Bliley Act, as well as state and local regulations such as California's SB 1386, Nevada Law NRS 597.970, and Massachusetts Law 201 CMR 17.00, to name just a few.

- **Operational/transactional risk**   Risk of direct or indirect loss from inadequate or failed internal processes, people, and systems, or from external events, including fraud. Data compromised at the enterprise level can increase operational risk by potentially impacting the stability and availability of the key enterprise systems.

- **Third-party information sharing risk**   According to the letter and spirit of GLBA and the Office of the Comptroller of Currency (OCC) regulations such as OCC 2001-47, an organization is responsible for data privacy and confidentiality breaches even if these events happened at or were caused by an unaffiliated third-party data or service provider. This risk is particularly relevant as organizations move toward outsourcing and offshore implementation of many customer service and support tasks.

Managing these risks is a focus of data security and identity and access management or IAM (we introduced the concepts of IAM in Chapter 9). IAM and data security are complementary technology disciplines that offer a number of significant business benefits including organizational ability to

- Minimize fraud
- Meet compliance requirements of existing and emerging legislation
- Minimize legal exposure
- Improve competitive advantage
- Increase brand equity
- Enhance customer retention/loyalty

Technical Implications of Data Security Regulations

Although many of the data protection regulations do not cover all information, and rather concentrate only on business-confidential or personal information that could be used for identity theft or financial crime, the technical implications of these regulations are quite broad and impact many systems, applications, and data stores in a profound way. Obviously, MDM Data Hubs, as systems of authoritative information about various data domains, are at the center of these data protection concerns. Let's consider what processes and technical capabilities have to be put in place in order to comply with the data protection requirements:

- Implement a data inventory and classification program and store the information about data location and usage in a securely controlled data inventory system (this could be implemented and managed as a component of the MDM Data Hub).

- Review/audit, document, and create a secure repository of records related to third-party providers to make sure they are aware of the data protection regulations and are ready to comply with them, including support for data encryption and policy-driven auditable access controls.

- Install and configure a strong perimeter defense solution, including a firewall and intrusion protection or (better yet) intrusion detection system.

- Configure the use of encryption on all wireless networks, preferably implementing WPA2 or stronger protocols.

- Use SSL/TLS to encrypt all network traffic, especially when your network is connected to the external Internet.

- Encrypt any data-at-rest, including both internal storage systems and data that is stored on remote sites, especially sites managed by third-party providers. This includes both traditional remote storage facilities and the infrastructure-as-a-service (IaaS) facilities, such as cloud storage solutions.

- Encrypt all backup offline media, such as tapes.

- Install security software that would encrypt all laptop computers and mobile devices such as BlackBerry PDAs, because these devices often carry personal or confidential data and are subject to loss and theft.

- Implement data obfuscation/data masking procedures that would render confidential data useless when the data files are used for offsite or offshore development and testing.

Even a cursory review of these actions shows that implementing an authoritative system of record, such as the MDM Data Hub, that is designed from the ground up as a data protection compliant system is not a small undertaking. We discuss various aspects of data security in the remainder of this chapter and in Chapter 11.

Data Security Overview

The foregoing discussion shows that data protection is a key business requirement of any organization. However, solving the data protection problem is a massive and very complex undertaking that requires a holistic view of information security and, in particular, knowledge of identities that can either cause harm or become victims of these new types of crime. As stated earlier, the set of technologies and processes dealing with issues related to digital identities is known as identity and access management. Information security is an overarching concept that, in addition to identity and access management, includes multilayered defense-in-depth approaches of defending a system against any particular attack using several different but complementary methods, including authentication, authorization and access control, entitlements and provisioning, enterprise rights management, and various data encryption solutions. The defense-in-depth strategy was developed by the National Security Agency (NSA)[3] as a comprehensive approach to security using a variety of protection mechanisms, methods, and countermeasures.

This chapter deals with one particular aspect of identity management and information security—data security and protection.

> **Data Security**
> *Data security* refers to the protection of data from either accidental or unauthorized viewing, modification, destruction, duplication, or disclosure during input, processing, storage, transmission, or output operations.

The practice of safeguarding data is at the core of the Information Security discipline and is primarily concerned with the following factors (please see Chapter 9 for additional details on these factors):

- **Data privacy and confidentiality**   Information should be available only to those who rightfully have access to it.

- **Data integrity**   Information should be modified only by those who are authorized to do so via authorized actions.

- **Data availability**   Information should be accessible to those who need it, when they need it.

In the context of data security, the term "data" includes, but is not limited to, data in databases or files, transactional data, operational policies and procedures, system design, organization policies and procedures, system status, and personnel schedules.

Layered Security Framework

The protection of data can only be effective if considered as part of a comprehensive security strategy and end-to-end security framework. We started a general discussion of the layered security framework in Chapter 8. This chapter will take a closer look at this framework from the perspective of data protection. In the context of data protection, a layered security framework considers information as the core that needs to be protected from outside attackers and internal compromises caused by incompetence, lack of appropriate due diligence, or malicious intent.

The comprehensive end-to-end security framework defined in Chapter 8 offers a multilayered "defense-in-depth" approach that surrounds data and its users in several layers of security controls. This layered security framework consists of the following layers:

1. Perimeter
2. Network
3. Platform (host)
4. Application
5. Data
6. User

The diagram shown in Figure 10-1 depicts the security layers as well as the core security services for each layer.

We discussed specific security concerns for each layer of the framework in Chapters 8 and 9 of this book, and summarize these concerns in the following list for ease of reference:

- **Perimeter security** deals with security threats that arrive at the enterprise boundary via a network. Perimeter security has to support user authentication, authorization, and access control to the resources that reside inside the perimeter. The perimeter may consist of one or more firewalls protecting a network perimeter demilitarized zone (DMZ). The DMZ may contain web servers, e-mail gateways, network antivirus software, and Domain Name Servers (DNS) exposed to the Internet. It may also implement intrusion detection and intrusion prevention systems.

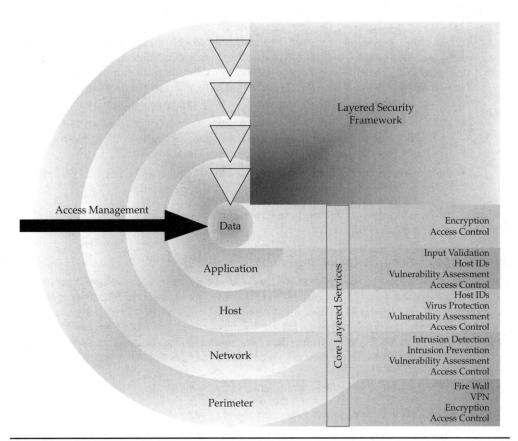

FIGURE 10-1   Layered security framework

- **Network security** deals with the authentication of the network user, authorizing access to the network resources, and protecting the information that flows over the network. Network security often uses technologies like transport layer security (SSL/TLS or IPSec), Public Key Infrastructure (PKI), and Virtual Private Network (VPN). It may also implement intrusion detection and intrusion prevention systems.

- **Platform/host security** deals with the security threats that affect the actual device and make it vulnerable to external or internal attacks. Platform security issues include authentication, authorization, and access control disciplines, and the security of the operating system, file system, application server, and other computing platform resources that can be broken into or taken over by a hostile agent.

- **Application security** deals with the need to protect not just access to the application execution environment but also access to the application code itself. Poorly protected applications can provide easy access to confidential data. Unprotected application code can be stolen or modified to create "back doors," to insert spyware, worms, and Trojans. Therefore, it is very important to define and enforce a comprehensive set of application security standards and controls.

- **Data security** addresses the means and methods to protect the *content* of transactional, historical, dynamic, and static data that organizations acquire, create, store, and manipulate in order to conduct business operations. This includes not only traditional data files and databases but also the software that may represent significant information assets. Generally speaking, content security for all data under management falls into two categories: data-in-transit and data-at-rest.

  - **Data-in-transit** is defined as any data moving between systems over network connections as well as data transferred between applications using file transfer mechanisms, messaging and queuing mechanisms, and/or ETL tools.

  - **Data-at-rest** is defined as data residing in locally attached or networked data stores as well as data in archives (for example, tape backup).

Data security concerns for each of these two major categories are described in more detail in the following section.

Data-in-Transit Security Considerations

The techniques and technologies of data-in-transit protection represent a mature area of data protection and are reasonably well understood. These technologies include transport layer security (SSL/TLS or IPSec) as well as secure tunneling using Virtual Private Networks (VPNs). In the case of proprietary network protocols (for example, IBM Systems Network Architecture APPC/LU6.2), encryption options are available in some implementations, and typically these protocols are implemented over nonpublic wide-area networks that offer a certain degree of security by design.

The main principles behind the techniques used for data-in-transit protection include:

- Authentication between the sender and the receiver
- Encryption of the message payload while it traverses the network fabric

The advantages of using these data-in-transit techniques include:

- Maturity of the technology solutions.
- Protection of data content while in transit.
- Predictable performance impact.
- Application transparency: As a rule, networked applications don't have to be changed to send messages/data over a secure network protocol.

One consideration concerning data-in-transit solutions includes the need for client-resident components. For example, in a web-based environment, SSL/TLS solutions rely on the Web browser's security features and usually do not require additional client-side software.

IPSec, on the other hand, requires client-side software installation. Since a typical legacy environment is not Web-based, IPSec may be the right choice for data-in-transit protection for legacy applications.

Another interesting approach to protecting data-in-transit deals with the message-level security that can be implemented on top of the transport layer protection. The message payload itself can be protected using a variety of techniques, for example, by using encryption for messages that are moving into and from message queuing systems. One approach to secure e-mail messaging is to use S/MIME (this feature is available in popular e-mail clients such as Microsoft Outlook and Outlook Express, and does not require additional software distribution).

A key consideration for data protection relates to the scope of protection. For example, some data-in-transit techniques protect data only between the client and the server (for example, between a Web browser and a Web server), thus leaving data in the open on the sending and receiving systems. An attacker can exploit these exposure points with relative ease. Therefore, security architects need to consider additional security measures that can complement "out-of-the-box" transport-level security to ensure a reasonable degree of data protection.

Security architects and system designers have to consider the following key requirements and considerations for data-in-transit protection:

- Minimize the number of encryption/decryption points to ensure a reasonable level of performance, throughput, and latency.

- Develop an integrated key management strategy across different network segments, especially if they use different encryption algorithms (for example, TLS and IPSec between Web-based networks and legacy systems).

To sum up, data-in-transit protection addresses some of the security concerns about data that is moving over networks. However, by itself, this protection is limited and does not address a number of the security concerns discussed earlier. For example, a network can be compromised, data payload can be intercepted (hijacked), data can be replayed or redirected to unintended destinations, and the network can become unavailable or can be used for denial-of-service or other types of attacks.

Therefore, relying on just data-in-transit protection is a necessary but not a sufficient approach to protecting data privacy, confidentiality, integrity, and availability.

Data-at-Rest Protection

Even if the network is secure, and appropriate access controls are in place, the sophistication of the attackers continues to outpace the defenders' ability to detect and prevent new types of attacks in a timely manner, which can put the entire enterprise at risk.

Therefore, the scope of data security includes an approach that aims to protect data if/ when all other security controls failed and the attacker got hold of data that is stored on a storage device. The goal of data-at-rest protection is to address this risk by making data unusable to unauthorized users even if such a user has managed to obtain proper network access credentials. Data-at-rest protection provides complementary protection capability that works equally well for defending the enterprise from both external and internal compromises. The latter point is very important since a significant number of all security breaches occur because of inappropriate, erroneous, or malicious actions on the parts of the employees.

In general, the technologies of data-at-rest security rely on authentication, access authorization and control, and payload encryption techniques. This section looks closely at the data-at-rest techniques that make the data unusable when the access controls and perimeter defenses are compromised. These techniques include:

- **Data masking** or **data obfuscation**   As mentioned in the previous section, data masking procedures transform some or all data attributes in a source file or a database into a form that would change confidential data content or render confidential data useless. Data masking is often used as a preferred method of delivering data to an off-site facility for application and system testing. Depending on the technique used for data masking, data masking operation can be irreversible and the masked data becomes unusable by the business applications, which limits data masking applicability as a data protection technique. Therefore, we focus on the two other data-at-rest protection techniques – compression and encryption.

- **Compression**   Data-loss-less protection schemes are often used to provide certain levels of protection while improving the operational throughput of data due to the reduced record/message length.

- **Encryption**   Data encryption schemes are commonly implemented at the data, application, and operating-system levels. Almost all schemes involve encryption/decryption keys that must be available to all parties accessing the data. When the data is at-rest on a storage device, we can apply these general techniques at the following levels of granularity:

  - **Field-level protection**   In this case, the protection mechanism would encrypt or scramble the data in place, thus protecting each sensitive field individually. The data type and the field length would not change. This technique would not require any addition of new fields to any files.

  - **File or database protection**   In this case, the protection mechanism would encrypt the entire file or database, without separating sensitive data from the total data content.

  - **Block-level protection** encrypts the entire device block.

In addition, as a general principle we should also consider physical security as an accepted means of protecting any facilities including data centers and data storage facilities (security gates, hard-to-compromise identification badges, background checks, security guards, and so on).

We need to consider these levels of data-at-rest protections in the context of the business and technical requirements that help determine technical and economical viability. The key requirements for software- and hardware-based data-at-rest security approaches include:

- **Data type support**   Support for any form of data-at-rest, including files, databases, messages, and so on.

- **Total application transparency**   If data is encrypted on a storage device, it has to be decrypted for every access to preserve and sustain application functionality; applications that use the protected data should not be aware of the cryptographic operations.

- **Preserved database functionality**   If attributes used for database access are encrypted (for example, primary and foreign keys, indexes, and search arguments), then the database may become unusable.

- **Encryption**   Use of strong encryption that is based on industry standards and proven encryption algorithms.
- **Key management**   This is a key requirement for any data-at-rest encryption to be viable; for example, key management needs to address the following:
  - Encryption/decryption keys have to be available to all applications producing and consuming protected data; this requirement presents a key distribution challenge.
  - Keys have to change regularly so that the data protection scheme does not become stale and thus become vulnerable to being broken by a brute force attack.
  - Keys have to be available for a long period of time so that the data can be recovered and used long after it was first encrypted (for example, recovery from archive storage).
- **Performance**   The encryption/decryption operations are very computing-cycles-intensive and can drastically impact the performance of the entire environment.
- **Manageability**   Support for operations and system/network management.
- **Scalability**   Data-at-rest security solutions should scale up functionally and technically to cover the current and future data landscapes.

Data-at-Rest Solution Selection Considerations

When choosing a data-at-rest solution, we have to map the requirements listed in the preceding section and the business needs of the organization to the solution's capabilities.

We should consider and assess these capabilities in line with the organization's risk management strategy. For example, we can start by analyzing whether the solution is configurable and customizable in order to protect the highest risk areas first. Once the most vulnerable areas are covered, we have to assess the scalability and flexibility of the solution to easily and quickly cover other areas of data protection concerns. Some of the considerations for choosing a solution may be as follows:

- In general, field-level encryption has the largest negative impact on performance and may affect application transparency.
- Newer operating systems offer file-level encryption (for example, Microsoft's Encrypted File System [EFS]).
- Some database management systems have built-in encryption capabilities.
- Some storage vendors offer proprietary encryption engines that operate on the storage device to perform encrypt/decrypt operations.
- Some specialized data-at-rest security vendors offer dedicated software and hardware appliances that operate on the entire storage subsystem.

While the last three options offer application transparency and deliver better performance than a field-level encryption, they are specific to the data formats and platforms supported. For example, database encryption will not support protection of non-database file structures. Similarly, EFS is not supported outside Microsoft operating environments. And built-in crypto-engines only work with the storage devices they are built for.

Specialized vendors of data-at-rest solutions differ in the choices of technologies, approaches, capabilities, performance, and supported platforms. Many support block-level encryption on the device. A large number of vendors offer hardware-based appliances that are installed on the I/O channel between the computer and the storage subsystem. These appliances deliver the best performance and the least performance penalty (some solutions claim to have under 1 percent performance penalty), total application transparency, manageability of the devices, scalability for the size of the protected data, and the number of consuming applications. Most of the current limitations of the appliance-based solutions revolve around the types of storage subsystems and the channel protocols used to exchange data between the CPU and the storage. For instance, almost all vendor solutions support Storage Area Network (SAN) and Network Attached Storage (NAS) architectures over Fibre Channel. Examples of the hardware-based data-at-rest security appliances include solutions from NetApp, SafeNet, and others.

Enterprise Rights Management

The collaborative nature of work in today's global enterprise results in the need for individual workers and organizations to engage in frequent interactions with their colleagues, partners, suppliers, government agencies, and other parties. These interactions often include the need to exchange information over the network in order to achieve common business goals.

The information exchanged between collaborating parties is often of a very sensitive nature, and enterprises have to protect it to satisfy regulatory requirements and the company's fiduciary obligations to its customers and other owners of this information.

In addition to the collaboration scenario, an organization that needs to distribute highly confidential data to its authorized customers has to be concerned about protecting this information is such a way that the information's access and use are aligned with the organization's business goals, customer legal rights, and service agreements (for example, a financial services company can distribute sensitive equity research reports to its top tier customers via a public network).

Three main concerns related to protecting data in the collaborative and information distribution environments have become painfully obvious. We already discussed two key concerns in this and the previous chapters:

- Access to any data that requires protection needs to be controlled, enforced, and audited based on the appropriate policies, user entitlements, and regulations.

- The information content needs to be protected from unauthorized use both while it traverses communication networks and while it "rests" on storage devices.

The third concern is a direct consequence of the proliferation of the digital content, a collaborative nature of the work, a sensitive content distribution business model, and the recognition of the intrinsic information value of data regardless of whether it is in the "original" form or in copies. To put it slightly differently, any copy of the data is as valuable as the "original" data itself.

Indeed, according to numerous studies, over 90 percent of all information created by corporations now exists in electronic form. Moreover, a significant portion of this information contains intellectual property that represents key market value for many business and individual content creators (such as authors, artist, researchers and analysts) alike. According to studies by companies such as PricewaterhouseCoopers, a significant component of the market value of a typical U.S. company resides in its intellectual property assets.

Thus, the third concern deals with the need to understand and protect the rights of access to and use of data content and to prevent potential IP leakage. Such concern becomes a reality when, for example, the data is initially acquired by an authorized user and then shared with a person who has no authority to use all or some of this data.

This concern often comes to light when a business defines a collaborative process that creates or uses protected intellectual property information. Such information may include research, discovery, or patent description; legal documents requiring protection; business transactions or business plans related to a proposed merger or acquisition; medical diagnosis and medical history of a patient being referred to another physician or a hospital; and many similar cases. In a collaborative situation, an authorized user can legitimately create and access this information, and then share it with a recipient outside the protected enterprise in order to perform a particular business task (for example, an external reviewer of the patent application). Clearly, sharing the protected information in this case creates opportunities for data leakage, misuse, and outright theft.

Likewise, a customer of a financial services organization may purchase a highly sensitive research report about a particular market situation; the customer may decide to make a copy of the report and to share it with some of the coworkers or friends, who in turn can share their copies with others. As a result, the information becomes widely distributed without proper controls, and the financial services company will be at risk of not being able to collect the revenue associated with the distribution of this report as well as the risk of uncontrolled distribution of sensitive information that can contain material non-public information.

For example, imagine that confidential information regarding a merger between two companies has been organized and stored as an Excel spreadsheet document. This document can be stored in a highly secured enterprise server that is protected by robust policy-based authentication and access control mechanisms. However, if this highly confidential document is accessed legitimately by a member of the M&A team and then given to an unauthorized third party either via e-mail, as a printed document, or as a copy on a removable storage device, the document no longer enjoys the protection it requires.

In other words, while secure data access can prevent unauthorized users from accessing confidential information, this may not stop the authorized user from copying the information and sharing it with others. And once that information moves outside the protection of the secured enterprise network, anyone can do with it what they will, and the owner's ability to control that information is lost. This last point has become a business driver for the intellectual property protection of digital content in the retail marketplace. A well-known example of the need for IP and copyright protection includes electronic distribution and sharing of music and/or books over the Internet.

The area of concern we've just described is the focus of technologies collectively known as Digital Rights Management (DRM). And as the interconnected and collaborative nature of today's networked business continues to embed itself tighter and tighter into the daily enterprise activities, DRM has often been referred to using a broader term, Enterprise Rights Management (ERM). Since the focus of this book is on enterprise solutions for Master Data Management, we will use the term ERM when discussing issues related to the protection of the digital content. To be specific, let's define ERM.

Enterprise Rights Management

Enterprise Rights Management (ERM) is a set of technologies designed to manage and enforce information access policies, protect intellectual property embedded in the electronic documents, and enforce usage rights of electronic documents. ERM provides protection persistence that enforces information access policies. ERM-enforced polices allow an organization to control access to information that needs to be secured for privacy, competitive, or compliance reasons. ERM's protection persistence should prevent users and administrators from disabling protection mechanisms.

In order to show specific functional components of ERM, we can restate the ERM definition as follows:

Enterprise Rights Management (ERM) is a set of technologies designed to

- Secure content using strong encryption.

- Enable protection persistence that prevents users and administrators from disabling the protection mechanisms.

- Provide security controls that automatically and assuredly monitor and audit all data access operations and events, including traditional Create, Read, Update, Delete (CRUD) operations as well as print, e-mail, copy/paste, file transfer, and screen capture.

- Minimize the impact of content protection on users and applications from both usability and performance points of view.

- Leverage existing enterprise authentication and authorization methods, including enterprise directory and provisioning systems to manage and control authorized users.

Master Data Management environments by their very nature require that the authoritative master data created and managed by MDM systems should be protected in a comprehensive and holistic way. This includes user authentication, authorization and access controls, data-in-transit and data-at-rest protections, and the post-retrieval protection of the secured content based on the concepts of ERM. To put it another way, secure Master Data Management should integrate several information security disciplines and technologies, including ERM.

It's important to note that similar to the requirements of data protection for data in-transit and at-rest (see previous sections), one of the key requirements in developing an ERM-capable MDM system system is the potential impact of ERM technologies and processes on user experience. Any system that creates drastically different or difficult-to-use methods to gain access to the content will make ERM adoption at best long and at worst impractical.

Combining these factors with the high visibility and strategic positioning of any Master Data Management initiative makes the transparency and the ease of use of the ERM solution some of the key success factors not only for selecting and deploying an ERM solution but for the entire MDM initiative.

ERM Processes and MDM Technical Requirements

Since an MDM solution may contain confidential or sensitive information assets, an MDM data integration platform such as a Data Hub for customer or product information would have to enable or implement some key ERM/DRM capabilities, including data model extensions, processes, and technologies.

Contemporary ERM systems can leverage basic ideas of symmetric and asymmetric encryption algorithms of the Public Key Infrastructure (PKI) technology and the rights management policy and the XML licensing standard known as XrML.

An ERM-enabled MDM system that uses XrML-expressed policies and rules should support at least two key processes: authoring and viewing.

An example of the authoring process that uses both symmetric and asymmetric key encryption would include the following steps:

- Create a publishing license that uses the XrML standard to define content entities and their rights.
- Encrypt the content, usually with a symmetric content key.
- Protect the content key by encrypting it with the public key of the ERM server.
- Digitally sign the publishing license and the encrypted content key.
- Attach the package that contains the signed publishing license to the content.

A corresponding viewing process will act in reverse and should include the following steps:

- Authenticate the user.
- Extract the content key and decrypt it using the user's private key.
- Create a use license specifying the rights outlined in the publishing license.
- Decrypt the content and apply the use license to it to comply with the publishing license restrictions.

These processes may appear complex. However, there are a number of ERM products on the market today that implement these types of processes and transparently enforce ERM rules. Examples of these DRM products include Microsoft's Rights Management System (RMS), Adobe Lifecycle Rights Management, IBM's Content Manager, and many others.

ERM Use Case Examples

Let's illustrate the way an ERM/DRM solution could be deployed in a Master Data Management Data Hub environment that is designed to store and manage confidential and sensitive data.

Ensuring Regulatory Compliance of Customer Information

Master Data Management solutions that collect and aggregate customer information in the data integration systems are known as MDM systems for Customer domain or Customer Data Integration (CDI) Data Hubs. As we stated in the previous chapters of this book, an MDM Data Hub for Customer domain is the integration point of *all* information about the customer. As such, the MDM Data Hub must enable the following functions:

- Protect customer information in the Data Hub from inappropriate or unauthorized access by internal and external users.

- In financial services in particular, a Data Hub must enforce strict visibility rules where a broker or an account manager must be able to access the information associated only with their customer and accounts, and prevent users from accessing information about other customers (we discuss visibility concerns and architecture approaches in greater detail in Chapter 11).

- Protect customer information from unintended use by those who have been authorized to access the information.

HIPAA Compliance and Protection of Personal Health Information

At a high level, the Health Insurance Portability and Accountability Act (HIPAA)'s Security and Privacy Rules define similar concerns. According to HIPAA regulations, health care organizations must, among other controls, implement the following:

- Establish policies, procedures, and technical measures that protect networks, computers, and other electronic devices.

- Protect the privacy of all individually identifiable health information that is stored and/or transmitted electronically.

- Restrict disclosures of protected health information (PHI) to the minimum needed for healthcare treatment and business operations.

- Establish new business agreements with business partners that would safeguard their use and disclosure of PHI.

- Assess and modify systems to ensure they provide adequate protection of patient data.

End users, healthcare providers, and organizations can easily violate these requirements if the appropriate controls are not put in place. Indeed, consider the following: A hospital's office manager may have a perfectly legitimate reason to access patient health, insurance, and financial information. A common business practice may be to capture the patient's profile, account, medical diagnosis, and treatment information into specially designed Microsoft Office documents or forms for planning, referral, or contact management purposes. However, since these documents can be printed or e-mailed, the very fact of their existence creates a new risk of exposure that can put the hospital at risk of noncompliance and privacy preference violations. These risks could easily translate into significant reputational damage to the hospital and potentially to the parent company managing a network of healthcare providers.

Other ERM Examples

Other examples of situations where ERM/DRM can play a significant role include Master Data Management implementations that support highly confidential information about impending mergers and acquisitions, equities research, scientific research, and patent processing and filing. In the government sector, ERM/DRM may protect information assets of military, law enforcement, and national security agencies as well as other government organizations. As you can see, the area of ERM applicability is very large, and as MDM solutions began to proliferate across various industries and areas of business focus, their respective implementations have to enable the protection of the information assets that these solutions are designed to aggregate and integrate.

To sum up, sophisticated information security and visibility architecture is a key component of any MDM implementation, especially those Data Hub systems that deal with personally identifiable or business-confidential information. Therefore, in addition to authentication, authorization, access control, and content protection, the security architecture for an MDM solution should consider and include an implementation of the ERM/DRM processes and technology as a part of the overall information security design.

Sound information-protection architecture should enforce policy-based and roles-based security to protect access to information from unauthorized users. Such architecture should enable an audit of data access actions and archiving of information for a legally required or enterprise-defined duration based on industry and government regulations. In addition, such comprehensive security architecture should employ an ERM/DRM solution to identify information objects such as documents and e-mail messages that contain regulated content (such as account numbers and social security numbers), apply appropriate protection techniques, and ensure that authorized users use confidential protected information in approved ways.

Let us conclude this discussion with the following observations:

- The need for information protection has become one of the key priorities of government agencies and commercial organizations—a priority that is driven and reinforced by regulatory and compliance pressures. However, while enforcing information protection is no longer an option for any commercial or government organization, there is no single "silver bullet" to accomplish this goal. Therefore, we strongly recommend using a layered "defense-in-depth" approach to protecting information assets.

- In the area of information protection, data-at-rest protection and ERM have emerged as hotly competitive areas of information security, areas that could easily become a competitive differentiator in situations when customers and organizations are looking for assurances that even if a security breach has occurred, the data acquired by such an action continues to be secure. This confidence in information security, confidentiality, and integrity reinforces the notion of trusted relationships between organizations and their customers.

References

1. http://voices.washingtonpost.com/securityfix/2009/01/payment_processor_breach_may_b.html.

2. http://www.pgp.com/insight/newsroom/press_releases/2008_annual_study_cost_of_data_breach.

3. http://www.nsa.gov/ia/_files/support/defenseindepth.pdf.

Enterprise Security and Data Visibility in Master Data Management Environments

A s we stated in previous chapters, a core component of any Master Data Management solution is its data integration platform, which is designed to provide a complete and accurate view of one or several data domains, including the customer, product, account, and so on. MDM solutions for Customer Domain (sometimes referred to as CDI) and MDM solutions for Product Domain are perfect examples of such platforms.

By design an MDM Data Hub contains a wealth of information about individuals, companies, or products, all in a convenient, integrated form, and thus represents an attractive target for various forms of information security attacks. Thus, as a repository maintaining an authoritative system of record for the enterprise, an MDM Data Hub would require extra levels of protection for the information it manages.

The preceding chapters discussed various concerns and approaches to the protection of the information content.

This chapter will focus on protecting and controlling access to the Data Hub and the information stored there.

Access Control Basics

In general, when we talk about controlling access to a resource, be it a computer, network device, a program, or an application, we intuitively accept that such a control should be based on the individual or group credentials and permissions that are defined according to the security policies.

As we showed in the previous chapters, the credentials that are acquired or assigned through the process called provisioning, and then are verified through the activities called *authentication*. We also discussed that authentication can be weak or strong, single factor or multifactor. Whatever the approach, the end result of the authentication action is twofold: the user is identified using supplied credentials such as user ID and password, hardware or a biometric token; and the user's identity is verified (authenticated) by comparing the supplied credentials with the ones stored in the authentication store such as an enterprise directory.

However, the authentication alone does not solve the access control portion of the security equation unless authenticated users are given total access to all resources in the system for which they are authenticated.

In practice, most users should have access to some but not all resources, and we need to find a way to limit access rights per user based on some form of authorization rule that is based on authenticated credentials and the security policy in force at the time of the access request. To state it differently, each authenticated user should be able to access only those resources that he or she is authorized to use. The authorization decision is based on who the user is and on the security policy that defines the access.

This decision-making process could be implemented and enforced easily if an enterprise has individual policies for each user. Clearly, this approach is not realistic since the number of authenticated users can easily reach thousands (that is, employees and contractors) or even millions in the case of customers of large enterprises or government agencies. Managing such a large number of policies is a labor-intensive and error-prone activity that can also create significant security vulnerabilities.

One way to "avoid" creating and managing this large policy set is to implement access control logic inside the applications. Many applications have traditionally been developed with these access control capabilities as a part of their application logic—an approach that historically has proved to be expensive, inflexible, and hard to maintain.

A better approach is to abstract the authorization functionality away from applications into a common set of authorization functions. This approach would deliver a much more flexible and scalable solution. There are design patterns that implement common authorization functionality while reducing the number of policies that need to be managed. The goal of these designs is to provide sufficient flexibility, scalability, and fine-level granularity for functions and data access. Naturally, these techniques and design options are the domain of the security discipline called authorization. And as we stated in previous chapters, authentication, authorization, access control, and related concerns including entitlements and provisioning are all components of the information security discipline known as *Identity and Access Management*, or *IAM*.

Groups and Roles

One of the main principles in reducing the required number of policies is to introduce the notion of user groups and roles, and to provide access decisions based on a user's membership in groups and/or assignment of one or more roles. Since the number of groups and roles is typically much smaller than the overall number of users, this approach can be quite effective. Groups can help reduce errors in permissions and opportunities for a user to have unnecessary and potentially dangerous access.

Group-Based Access Control

The basic principles of group-based access controls are as follows:

- A security administrator creates groups and roles with the various permissions.
- Then the administrator assigns users to one or more groups/roles.

- An individual's access permission set is the aggregate of all group/role permissions to which the person is assigned.
- Updating user access is as simple as adding/deleting the user to a group, or changing the permissions for a defined group/role.

Some of the group-based approaches for a common authorization facility are based on what is known as Access Control Lists (ACLs), where the typical ACL structure would maintain a name-value pair with the "name" being the user or a group identifier, and the "value" being the reference or an address of the resource this user or this group can access, and a set of actions the group is allowed to perform. For example, an ACL may contain a list of functional groups such as Managers, HR Administrators, and Database Administrators, and where each employee is assigned to one or more groups. Each of the groups will have one or more resources they are allowed to access, with the specific access authorization (Create, Read, Update, Delete, Execute [CRUDE]). Such ACL structures have been widely implemented in many production environments protected by legacy security systems including Resource Access Control Facility (RACF), ACF2, and Top Secret. Several popular operating systems such as UNIX and ACL-controlled Windows Registry also use Access Control List–based authorization schemas.

ACLs work well in situations with well-defined and stable (persistent) objects, such as the IBM DB2 subsystem or the Windows System Registry. In these cases, the ACL can be mapped to the object, and access decisions can be made based on group membership and the CRUDE contents of the ACL. However, ACLs have some well-documented shortcomings. Among them are the following items:

- The ACL model does not work well in situations where the authorization decisions are often based not only on the group membership but also on business logic. For example, an authorization may depend on the value of a particular attribute (for instance, outstanding payment amount), where if a value exceeds a predefined threshold it can trigger a workflow or an authorization action.

- A common administrative task of reviewing and analyzing access given to a particular user or group can become difficult and time-consuming as the number of objects/resources grows, since the ACL model will require reviewing every object to determine if the user has access to the object. Generally speaking, the administration of large ACL sets can become a management nightmare.

- ACLs do not scale well with an increase in the number of users/groups and resources. Similarly, ACLs do not scale well as the granularity of the user authorization requests grows from a coarse to a fine level. In other words, to take full advantage of the group metaphor, the administrator would create a small number of groups and assign all users to some or all of the groups. However, if the organization has a relatively large number of individuals that are organized in a number of small teams with a very specialized set of access permissions, the ACL administrator would have to define many additional groups, thus creating the same scalability and manageability issues stated in the preceding list. An example of the last point can be a brokerage house that defines groups of traders specialized in a particular financial instrument (for example, a specific front-loaded mutual fund). The business rules and policies would dictate that these traders can only access databases that contain information about this particular mutual fund. To support these policies, the ACL administrator may have to define a group for each of the specialized instruments.

Roles-Based Access Control (RBAC)

A more scalable and manageable approach to authorization is to use user roles as the basis for the authorization decisions. Roles tend to be defined and approved using a more rigorous and formalized process known as *roles engineering*, which can enable the enterprise to better align the roles with the security policies. The approach and technologies of providing access control based on user credentials and roles are known as Roles-Based Access Control (RBAC). Although some of the goals of Roles-Based Access Control can be accomplished via permission groups, we will focus on RBAC since it offers a framework to manage users' access to the information resources across an enterprise in a controlled, effective, and efficient manner. The goal of RBAC is to allow administrators to define access based on a user's job requirements or "role." In this model an administrator follows a two-step process:

1. Define a role in terms of the access privileges for users assigned to a given role.

2. Assign individuals to a role.

As the result, the administrator controls access permissions to the information assets at the role level. Permissions can be queried and changed at the role level without touching the objects that have to be protected. Once the security administrator establishes role permissions, changes to these permissions will be rare compared to changes in assigning users to the roles.

Clearly, for RBAC to be effective the roles of the users have to be clearly defined and their access permissions need to be closely aligned with the business rules and policies.

Roles-Engineering Approach

When we discuss user roles, we need to recognize the fact that similarly named roles may have different meanings depending on the context of how the roles and permissions are used. For example, we may be able to differentiate between roles in the context of the Organization, Segment, Team, and a Channel:

- The *Organization* role defines the primary relationship between the user and the organization. An example of the organization role could be an Employee, Customer, Partner, Contractor, and so on. Each user can only have one Organization role for a given set of credentials.

- The *Segment* role defines the user's assignment to a business domain or segment. For example, in financial services a segment could be defined by the total value of the customer's portfolio, such as high priority customers, active traders, and so on. Each of these segments can offer its members different types of products and services. Segment roles can be set either statically or dynamically, and each user may be assigned to multiple Segment roles.

- The *Team* role defines the user's assignment to a team, for example, a team of software developers working on a common project, or a team of analysts working on a particular M&A transaction. The Team role can be set either statically or dynamically. Each user may be assigned multiple Team roles.

- The *Channel* role defines user permissions specific to a channel (channel in this context means a specific platform, entry point, application, and so on). For example, a user may have a role of a plan administrator when having personal interactions with the sales personnel (for instance, a financial advisor). At the same time, in the self-service online banking channel the same user can be in the role of a credit card customer who can perform online transactions including funds transfers and payments. Each user may be assigned multiple Channel roles.

The role classification shown in the preceding list is only one example of how to view and define the roles. More formally, we need a rigorous roles-engineering process that would help define the roles of the users in the context of the applications and information assets they need to access.

There are a number of methodological approaches and references[1] on how to define roles and to engineer roles-based access controls. The details of these approaches are beyond the scope of this book. However, it would be helpful to further clarify these points by reviewing some key role-designing principles:

- The roles need to be defined in the context of the business and therefore should not be done by the IT organization alone.

- Like any other complex cross-functional activity, the roles-engineering process requires sound planning and time commitment from both business and IT organizations. Planning should start with a thorough understanding of security requirements, business goals, and all the components essential to the implementation of the RBAC.

- Some core roles-engineering components include:
  - Classes of users
  - Data sources
  - Applications
  - Roles
  - Business rules
  - Policies
  - Entitlements

The last three components are discussed in greater detail later in this chapter.

Sample Roles-Engineering Process Steps   The roles-engineering process consists of several separate steps necessary to build the access management policies. The following steps illustrate how the process can be defined:

- Analyze the set of applications that would require role-based access controls. This analysis should result in a clear inventory of application features and functions, each of which can be mapped to a specific permission set.

- Identify a target user base and its context dimensions (organizations, segment, team, and so on). Use a generally accepted enterprise-wide authoritative source of user credentials to perform this task, for example, a human resources database for employees.

- Create role definitions by associating target functional requirements with a target user base.

Once the role definitions are created, we recommend identifying and mapping business rules that should be used for user-role assignment. For example, a rule may state that a user is assigned the role of a teller if the HR-supplied credentials are verified and if the user operates from the authorized channel (for example, a branch). Another example can be a business rule that states that an employee does not get assigned a Segment role.

RBAC Shortcomings
While roles-based access control can be very effective in many situations and represents a good alternative to Access Control Lists, it does have a number of shortcomings. Some of these shortcomings are described in the following list:

- Roles-Based Access Control does not scale well as the granularity of protected resources grows. In other words, if you need to define access controls to sensitive data at the record or even attribute levels, you should define a set of roles that would map to each possible data record and/or attribute, thus resulting in a very large and difficult-to-manage set of roles.

- Roles can be difficult to define in an enterprise-wide uniform fashion, especially if the enterprise does not have a formal process that guides the creation and differentiation of roles. For example, an enterprise may define a role of an analyst in its marketing department and a similarly named role of the analyst for the IT department. However, these roles represent different capabilities, responsibilities, compensation, and so on.

- Roles alone do not easily support access constraints where different users with equal roles have access only to a portion of the same data object. This particular requirement is often called "data visibility" and is discussed in more detail later in this chapter.

Policies and Entitlements
The limitations of Roles-Based Access Control that we discussed in the preceding section make it difficult to implement many complex business-driven access patterns. These access patterns are particularly important when you consider all the potential uses of a Master Data Management environment. MDM designers should consider these use cases and usage patterns in conjunction with the need to protect information from unauthorized access. At the same time, MDM solutions should streamline, rationalize, and enable new, more effective and efficient business processes. For example, let's consider an MDM Data Hub implementation that is positioned to replace a number of legacy applications and systems that support customer management processes. In this case, in order to take full advantage of the MDM Data Hub as a system of record for the customer information, an enterprise should change several core processes (for example, the account-opening process). So, instead of accessing

legacy data stores and applications, a modified account-opening process should use the MDM Data Hub's data, services, and RBAC-style access controls as a centralized trusted facility. But in a typical enterprise deployment scenario, existing legacy applications contain embedded business-rules-driven access controls logic that may go beyond RBAC. Thus, the Data Hub cannot replace many legacy systems without analyzing and replicating the embedded functionality of the access control logic in the Data Hub first. This means that all access decisions against Data Hub need to be evaluated based on the user attributes, the content of the data to be accessed, and the business rules that take all these conditions into considerations before returning a decision.

Analysis of typical legacy applications shows that access permissions logic uses a combination of user roles and the business rules, where the business rules are aligned with or derived from the relevant security and business policies in place.

The problem of providing flexible access control solutions that would overcome many known RBAC limitations is not a simple replacement of Roles-Based Access Control with Rules-Based Access Controls (using the RBAC analogy, we will abbreviate Rules-Based Access Control as RuBAC). Indeed, RuBAC can implement and enforce arbitrary complex access rules and thus offers a viable approach to providing fine-grained access control to data. However, RuBAC does not scale well with the growth of the rule set. Managing large rule sets is at least as complex a problem as the one we showed during the RBAC discussion.

Therefore, a hybrid roles-and-rules-based access control (RRBAC) may be a better approach to solving access control problems. This hybrid approach to defining access controls uses more complex and flexible *policies* and processes that are based on *user identities, roles, resource entitlements,* and *business rules.* The semantics and grammar of these policies can be quite complex, and are the subject of a number of emerging standards. Examples of these standards are the OASIS WS-Security[2] standard and W3C WS-Policy.[3] The latter is a Web Services standard allowing users to create an XML document that unambiguously expresses the authorization rules.

Entitlements Taxonomy

As we just stated, the key concepts of the hybrid approach are policies, identity-based entitlements, roles, and rules. We already discussed roles in the preceding sections of this chapter. However, the discussion on the hybrid approach to access controls would not be complete if we don't take a closer look at policies and entitlements.

Policies

In the context of authorization and access control, we will define a *policy* as the encoding of rules particular to a business domain and its data content, and the application systems designed to operate in this domain on this set of data.

Whenever a user requests an access to a resource, an appropriate policy acts as a "rule book" to map a given request to the entitlements of that user.

Entitlements

An *entitlement* is an expression stating that a *party* has *permission* to do something with respect to some *entity* or an *object when certain conditions are met.*

For example, you may create an entitlement for your college-age daughter stating that she has permission to withdraw money from your checking account as long as the withdrawal amount does not exceed $500. In this example, we established the party (daughter), object (checking account), nature of the permission or the action (withdrawal), and the condition of the permission ($500 limit).

It is easy to see that entitlements contain both static and dynamic components, where static components tend to stay unchanged for prolonged periods of time. The value of the dynamic component (for example, a $500 limit), on the other hand, may change relatively frequently and will most likely be enforced by applying business rules at run time.

Another interesting observation about entitlements is the fact that, on one hand, they can be categorized as functional and data entitlements, and on the other hand as coarse- and fine-grained entitlements (see Figure 11-1).

This entitlements taxonomy has interesting implications for the complexity of the business rules and the applicability of the already-discussed ACL and RBAC approaches.

Indeed, at a coarse level of granularity, there are many situations where ACL or RBAC solutions would provide an adequate level of access controls. But given their shortcomings in terms of scalability and manageability, a different approach had to be found for fine-grain entitlements. This different approach is based on a relatively recent set of technologies known as policy authorization servers, or policy servers for short. As the name implies, policy servers evaluate all access control requests against the appropriate set of polices and business rules in the context of identities, roles, and entitlements of the authenticated users. To state it differently, policy servers help ensure proper alignment of access control enforcement with the security policies of the enterprise. Policy servers avoid the scalability and manageability issues of ACL and RBAC by combining the roles-based and rules-based approaches to authorization. As important, policy servers abstract the authorization decisions away from the application. Specifically, the network administrators or security managers define users, authentication methods (such as passwords, token-based authentication, or X.509 certificates), and access controls. The applications no longer handle access control directly. Instead, they interact with the policy server whenever a user issues a request to use a resource.

Typically, a policy server answers the question "Can user U perform action A on object O?" A number of commercial products offer robust policy server functionality. Some products use a group-based policy, where a user's group might be determined by user role (for example, cashiers), or the group's placement in an enterprise authentication directory (for example, LDAP tree). Other products support policies of higher complexity, where user privilege may

Figure 11-1
Entitlements taxonomy

	Coarse Grain	Fine Grain
Functional Entitlements	Service or Application Entitlements	Transaction, Method Level, Interface Level
Data Entitlements	URL/URI, File, Database, Table	Record, Attribute, Field

be based on certain attributes (for example, a policy defines the authorization level of 1 to 5, where 1 is the highest level of access or similar privilege). Role- or attribute-based policies place users into groups based on user attributes. For example, greater access may be granted to the holder of an American Express Platinum card, or an airline upgrade entitlement is determined by the status and level of the frequent flyer.

Yet, more advanced approaches use complex policies where the policy paradigm is extended to drive access control decisions based on events. For example, if a user is not registered for a particular service, the policy can redirect the user to the enrollment/registration page. Conversely, trying to enter an invalid password more than a predetermined number of times can redirect the user to a customer service page. All of these decisions can be further enhanced by using user attributes as factors in the policy evaluation.

Transactional Entitlements

Event-based access controls can be used to support coarse-grained and fine-grained entitlements as well as *transactional* entitlements—an interesting approach to policy-based authorization designed to solve complex access control problems in real time.

Transactional entitlements allow authenticated users to check their permissions against specific parameters by evaluating business policy rules in real time on an individual basis. For example, a transactional entitlement can control a user's ability to execute a requested transaction such as perform a funds transfer, update a log, or search a particular database. Transactional entitlements can control various business-defined actions, including updates to a personnel file, execution of a particular transaction only on a certain day and/or at a certain time, in a given currency, and within a specified spending/trading limit. In our college student example earlier, checking for a $500 withdrawal limit is a transactional component of the entitlement structure.

In transactional entitlements, logical expressions can be arbitrarily complex to address real-world requirements. And ideally, the expressions are strongly typed and reusable, written once to support similar transactions, not just one transaction at a time.

The key differences between transactional and non-transactional entitlements are twofold:

- Transactional entitlements are evaluated (and can be updated) in real time.
- Transactional entitlements can support the transactional semantics of atomicity, consistency, isolation, and durability (ACID properties) by performing their actions within transactional brackets.

Transactional entitlements are vital to providing just-in-time authorization decisions for real-time applications such as online banking, trading, purchasing, and similar activities. Transactional entitlements are especially useful when business applications rely on dynamic policy-driven access controls to a Master Data Management environment and its information, which represents the authoritative system of records.

Entitlements and Visibility

The definition of entitlements makes it clear that the entitlements, being a resource-dependent expression, have to be *enforced locally*, close to the target resources. This enforcement should be done in the context of the access request, user credentials, and resource attributes. Moreover, the resource access request *should not* be decided and enforced by a central, resource-agnostic authority because of performance, scalability, and security concerns. As mentioned in previous sections, technology solutions that provide entitlement enforcement are known as policy servers. These servers are designed to be resource-aware and thus can enforce entitlement rules in the context of the specific access requests.

Policy servers can support fine-grained access controls, but are especially well-suited to support functional-level authorization at the method and interface level, since the policy semantics are easily adaptable to include the access rules.

However, fine-grained access control for data access and fine-grained data entitlements represent an interesting challenge. The area of fine-grained data access, shown in the lower-right corner of Figure 11-1, is known as *data visibility challenge*. It is the primary data access control concern for Master Data Management platforms such as Data Hub systems. This challenge is a direct result of the complexity of the business rules defining who can access what portion of the data, what kind of access (for example, Create, Read, Update, or Delete) can be granted, and under what conditions. Solving this data visibility challenge requires a new policy evaluation and policy enforcement approach that should complement the functional entitlement enforcement provided by the current generation of policy servers. The following sections look more closely at this data visibility challenge and a potential architecture of the visibility solution in more detail. This chapter also discusses approaches that allow for effective integration of functional and data entitlements in the context of the overarching enterprise security architecture framework.

Customer Data Integration Visibility Scenario

Let us illustrate the data visibility challenges with an example of a Data Hub solution for a hypothetical retail brokerage. As we stated previously, one of the key goals of an MDM solution is to enable transformation of the enterprise from an account-centric to an entity-centric (in our example, customer-centric) business model.

To that end, a retail brokerage company has embarked on the initiative to build an MDM platform for Customer Domain (the Customer Data Hub) that eventually would become a new system of record for all customer information. The data model designed for the new Data Hub will have to satisfy the specific business need to support two types of entities—customers with their information profiles, and the brokers who provide advisory and trading services to the customers. In order for this scheme to work, the project architects decided to build a reference facility that would associate a broker with his or her customers.

To improve customer experience and to enforce broker-customer relationships, the company has defined a set of business policies that state the following access restrictions:

- A customer may have several accounts with the company, and have relationships with several brokers to handle the accounts separately.
- A broker can see and change information about his or her customer but only for the accounts that the broker manages. The broker cannot see any customer account data owned by another broker.
- A broker's assistant can see and change most but not all customer information for the customers that have relationships with this broker.
- A broker's assistant can support more than one broker and can see the customer data of all of the brokers' customers but cannot share this information across brokers, nor can this information be accessed at the same time.

- A customer service center representative can see some information about all customers but explicitly is not allowed to see the customers' social security numbers (SSN) or federal tax identification numbers (TIN).

- A specially appointed manager in the company's headquarters can see and change all data for all customers.

It is easy to see that this list of restrictions can be quite extensive. It is also easy to see that implementing these restrictions in the Data Hub environment where all information about the customers is aggregated into customer-level data objects is not a trivial task. Specifically, the main requirements of data visibility in Data Hub environments are twofold:

- Create customer and employee/broker entitlements that would be closely aligned with the authorization policies and clearly express the access restrictions defined by the business (for example, the restrictions described in the preceding list).

- Implement a high-performing, scalable, and manageable enforcement mechanism that would operate transparently to the users, be auditable to trace back all actions taken on customer data, and ensure minimal performance and process impact on the applications and the process workflow used by the business.

The first requirement calls for the creation of the entitlement's grammar and syntax, which would allow the security and system administrators to express business rules of visibility in a terse, unambiguous, and complete manner. This new grammar has to contain the set of primitives that can clearly describe data attributes, conditions of use, access permissions, and user credentials. The totality of these descriptions creates a *visibility context* that changes as the rules, variables, and conditions change. This context allows the designers to avoid an inflexible approach of using hard-coded expressions, maintenance of which will be time-consuming, error-prone, and hard to administer. The same considerations apply to the functional permissions for the data services (for example, a permission to invoke a "Find Customer by name" service), as well as usage permissions for certain attributes based on the user role (for example, SSN and TIN restrictions for customer service representative). Another consideration to take into account is that the role alone is not sufficient—for example, a broker's assistant has different permissions on data depending on which broker that assistant supports in the context of a given transaction.

The second requirement is particularly important in any online business, especially in financial services: Performance of a system can be a critical factor in a company's ability to conduct trading and other business activities in volatile financial markets. Thus, the enforcement of the visibility rules has to be provided in the most effective and efficient manner that ensures data integrity but introduces as little latency as technically feasible.

Policies, Entitlements, and Standards

One way to define the policy and entitlement language and grammar is to leverage the work of standards bodies such as the Organization for the Advancement of Structured Information Standards (OASIS) and the World Wide Web Consortium (W3C). Among some of the most relevant standards to implement policy-enforced visibility are eXtensible Access Control Markup Language (XACML),[4] eXtensible Resource Identifier (XRI),[5] and WS-Policy,[6] a component of the broader WS-Security framework of standards for Web Services security.

XACML

XACML is designed to work in a federated environment consisting of disparate security systems and security policies. In that respect, XACML can be very effective in combination with the Security Assertion Markup Language (SAML)[7] standard in implementing federated Roles-Based Access Control. We briefly discussed SAML standard in Chapter 9.

> ### XACML and XRI
> The XACML standard provides a clear and unambiguous syntax and grammar to express permissions for the user to perform certain actions on a specific resource (defined in XRI), and *obligations* of how to enforce a given permission.

These standards can be used to encode the policies and entitlements and therefore design policy evaluation systems that can provide clear and unambiguous access control decisions. For example, XACML policy can define a condition that allows users to log in to a system only after 8 A.M. A fragment of this policy in XACML that uses standard references to XML schema for the "time" data type may look like this:

```
<Condition FunctionId="urn:oasis:names:tc:xacml:1.0:function:and">
      <Apply FunctionId="urn:oasis:names:tc:xacml:1.0:function:time-
greater-than-or-equal"
…..
AttributeId="urn:oasis:names:tc:xacml:1.0:environment:current-time"/>
      </Apply>
      <AttributeValue
DataType="http://www.w3.org/2001/XMLSchema#time">08:00:00</AttributeValue>
      </Apply>
</Condition>
```

While XACML offers a vehicle to clearly express access policies and permissions, XRI, on the other hand, allows users to create structured, self-describing resource identifiers. For example, XRI can describe the specific content of the library of research documents where the documents and books are organized by author, title, ISBN number, and even the location of the library, all in one comprehensive expression. To illustrate this power of XRI, consider a book search application that would allow users to find a book on a given subject that is available from one or more bookstores and library branches. Using XRI we can define the following resources:

```
xri://barnesandnoble.store.com/(urn:isbn:0-123-4567-8)/(+new)
xri://borders.store.com/(urn:isbn:0-123-4567-8)/(+used)
xri://NY.Public.Library.org/(urn:isbn:0-123-4567-8)/(+used)
```

In this example, XRI is used to identify the same book title (identified by its ISBN number), which is available from three different sources, two of which are bookstores—Barnes and Noble, and Borders—and the third one is the New York Public Library. Furthermore, XRI allows fine-grained resource definition attributes such as new or used book types.

Additional Considerations for XACML and Policies

The OASIS XACML technical committee (TC) has defined a number of details about XACML language, policies, rules, the way the policies are to be evaluated, and the decisions to be enforced. While these details are beyond the scope of this book, we will briefly look at some key XACML constructs, components, and features that can help MDM architects, designers, and implementers to protect access to the information stored in the MDM Data Hub systems.

Using the definition of the Policy as the encoding of Rules particular to a business domain, its data content, and the application systems designed to operate in this domain on this set of data, we can review several basic XACML components:

- XACML specifies that each Policy contains one or more Rules, where each Policy and Rule has a *Target*.

- XACML Target is a simple predicate that specifies which *Subjects, Resources, Actions,* and *Environments* the Policy or Rule has to apply to.

- XACML is designed to support policy expressions across a broad range of subject and functional domains known as *Profiles*.

Profiles and Privacy Protection   The notion of XACML profiles is very useful and provides for a high degree of reuse and manageability. For example, among several XACML-defined profiles there is a Profile for Access Control and a Profile for Privacy Protection. The latter should be particularly interesting to MDM designers since it shows the power and extensibility of XACML as a policy language even for privacy policies that, unlike most traditional access control policies, often require a verification that the purpose for which information is accessed should match the purpose for which the information was gathered.

> **XACML Privacy Profile**
>
> The *XACML Privacy Profile* defines standard attributes for describing the purpose for which information was gathered and the purpose for which information is being accessed. A Privacy policy may require that in order to gain access to data, these two values must match.

In addition to defining the privacy attributes, the XACML Privacy Profile describes how to use them to enforce privacy protection. This is a very important argument in favor of using XACML in defining and enforcing policies in the MDM environments for Customer Domain, where customer privacy preferences have to be captured, maintained, and enforced according to the explicit and implicit requests of the customers.

The XACML standard offers a flexible, useful, and powerful language that allows organizations to implement systematic creation, management, and enforcement of security and privacy policies. What follows is a brief discussion on how to use XACML to help MDM architects, designers, and implementers to address complex issues related to information security and data visibility in MDM environments.

Integrating MDM Solutions with Enterprise Information Security

The challenge of implementing data visibility and security in Master Data Management environments is twofold:

- First, it is a challenge of enforcing the access restriction rules in a new system of record.
- Second, it is a challenge of integrating new visibility controls with the existing enterprise security infrastructure using a comprehensive and overarching security architecture.

Many commercially available MDM solutions on the market today support these requirements to a varying degree by adding the data visibility functionality to their core products. Leveraging Policy servers could be problematic because not all Policy server products used in the enterprise can enforce the visibility rules of required complexity and granularity in high-performance, low-latency environments.

However, experience shows that the visibility problem can be solved when you architect the solution (for example, a Data Hub) using a component-based, services-oriented architecture approach and extending the key principle of the "separation of concerns" to include a key concept relevant to information security—*separation of duties,* or *SoD.*

We discussed some basics of the "separation of concerns" principle in Part II of this book. Let's define the companion principle, the separation of duties, since it has direct applicability to information security by stating that no single actor should be able to perform a set of actions that would result in a breach of security.

> **Separation of Duties and Data Visibility**
> In the context of security and visibility, separation of duties principle means that making policy-based access control decisions is a general function that is different and should be separated from the actions related to the enforcement of these access decisions.

Looking at the conceptual data visibility architecture that is based on XACML and the separation of duties principle, we can identify three major components (we omitted a detailed discussion of all components, such as Policy Information Point, or PIP, for the sake of simplicity). The decision maker in this context is called a *Policy Decision Point* (*PDP*), and the decision enforcement is performed by one or more *Policy Enforcement Points* (*PEPs*). The third component is a policy administration facility known as a *Policy Administration Point* (*PAP*), sometimes referred to as a Policy Management Authority (PMA). As the name implies, the role of a PAP is primarily to perform out-of-band policy creation, administration, editing, and reporting—functionality that is clearly separate and distinct from run-time decision making and enforcement.

The benefits of separating the actions and responsibilities (duties) of policy administration, decision making, and access decision enforcement into separate components and services include better security posture against a threat of a compromise by a single user, the ability to better manage the complexity of fine-grained access control enforcement, and the ability to change policy or add additional resources or new entitlements without requiring any changes to the consuming applications that issue data access requests.

The conceptual distributed security architecture that shows the roles of the PDP, PEP, and PAP components is shown in Figure 11-2.

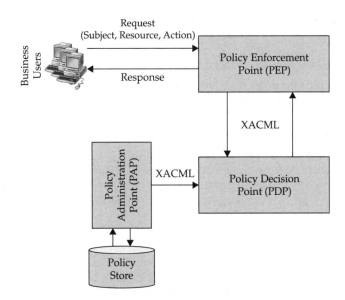

Figure 11-2
Conceptual OASIS distributed security architecture

The details of the PDP, PEP, and PAP roles and responsibilities are defined by the OASIS distributed security standard described in detail in the OASIS document library available on www.oasis.org.

Overview of Key Architecture Components for Policy Decision and Enforcement

The OASIS standard defines a Policy Enforcement Point (PEP) that is responsible for intercepting all attempts to access a resource (see Figure 11-2). It is envisioned to be a component of the request-processing server such as a Web server that can act as an interceptor for all requests coming into the enterprise through a network gateway.

Since resource access is application-specific, the PEP is also application- or resource-specific. The PEP takes its orders from the Policy Decision Point (PDP), a component that processes resource access requests and makes authorization decisions.

The PDP is divided into two logical components. The *Context Handler* is implementation-specific. It knows how to retrieve the policy attributes used in a particular enterprise systems environment. The PDP *Core* is implementation independent and represents a common, shared facility. It evaluates policies against the information in the access request, using the Context Handler to obtain additional attributes if needed, and returns a decision of *Permit, Deny, Not Applicable,* or *Indeterminate*. The last two values are defined as follows:

- *Not Applicable* means that there is no policy used by this PDP that can be applicable to the access request.

- *Indeterminate* means that some error occurred that prevents the PDP from knowing what the correct response should be.

Policies can contain *Obligations* that represent actions that must be performed as part of handling an access request, such as "Permit access to this resource but only when an audit record is created and successfully written to the audit log."

The PDP exchanges information with PEP via XACML-formatted messages. The PDP starts evaluating a decision request in the following sequence:

- Evaluate the Policy's Target first.
- If the Target is *FALSE,* the Policy evaluation result is *Not Applicable,* and no further evaluation is done of either that Policy or of its descendants.
- If the Target is *TRUE,* then the PDP continues to evaluate Policies and Rules that are applicable to the request.
- Once all levels of Policies are evaluated to *TRUE,* the PDP applies the Rule's *Condition* (a Boolean combination of predicates and XACML-supplied functions).
- Each Rule has an *Effect,* which is either *Permit* or *Deny.* If the Condition is *TRUE,* then the Rule returns a valid *Effect* value. If the Condition is *FALSE,* then *Not Applicable* is returned.

Each Policy specifies a *combining algorithm* that says what to do with the results of evaluating multiple *Conditions* from the Policies and Rules. An OASIS-defined example of such an algorithm is *Deny Override.* Here, if any detail-level Policy or Rule evaluates to *Deny,* then the entire high-level Policy *set* that contains these detail policies and rules evaluates to *Deny.* Of course, other combining algorithms are also possible, and should be defined based on the business requirements and business-level security policies.

NOTE *Several implementations of this XACML-based data visibility architecture are available today. These include vendor products such as Oracle Entitlement Server (OES) and custom implementations using various Java or Microsoft .NET frameworks, such as the Spring Framework.*

The Spring Framework

The *Spring Framework*[8] is an open-source application framework for the Java platform and .NET Framework (Spring.NET). Spring Security supports Interceptors that can be inserted into application code using Spring's "dependency injection" mechanism. Spring Security Interceptors can be used to intercept and evaluate access requests in a manner similar to XACML-defined PDP-PEP interaction flows.

Integrated Conceptual Security and Visibility Architecture

The foregoing brief discussion offers an insight into how PDP and PEP components operate and communicate with each other. We also discussed how policies, rules, and obligations have to be expressed in order to provide a clear set of directives for access control decisions. Together, these components represent building blocks of the Data Hub *Visibility and Security Services.* Let's apply the principles of separation of duties, separation of concerns, and service-oriented architecture framework to these Data Hub visibility and security services in order to define a comprehensive end-to-end security and visibility architecture that would enable policy-based, fine-grained access control to the information stored in a Data Hub system.

First, let's adjust the architecture shown in Figure 11-2 to accommodate the following enterprise requirements:

- To ensure appropriate performance and transaction latency requirements, the policy enforcement has to be performed as "close" to the resource being protected as possible. For example, when a Data Hub is built on a relational database platform, a Policy Enforcement Point may be implemented as a stored procedure or other appropriate SQL-based technique.

- Most enterprise environments contain a large number of heterogeneous resources, each of which may implement a different, resource-specific PEP. We'll reflect this concern by introducing additional resources and PEP components as shown in Figure 11-3.

- Given a potentially large number of heterogeneous resources that require PEP-based protection, we can optimize the information and control flows in such a way that a resource-independent PDP will receive a data request, make a *Permit* or *Deny* decision based on the user entitlements and the security policy, and send the result to the appropriate PEP component as part of the XACML obligations.

- Finally, since a global enterprise data environment typically contains a large variety of data stores, it is reasonable to assume that a business application may request data not just from the Data Hub but from multiple, often heterogeneous data stores and applications. Such complex requests have to be managed and *orchestrated* to support distributed transactions including compensating transactions in case of a partial or complete failure. Therefore, let's introduce a conceptual Request Management Service Component that would receive data requests from consuming applications, communicate with the Policy Decision Point, and in general, manage and orchestrate request execution in an appropriate, policy-defined order. Note that we're defining

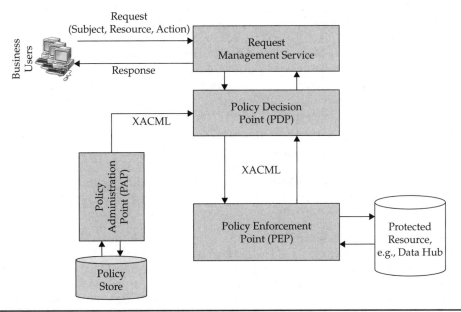

FIGURE 11-3   Policy enforcement architecture adjusted to enterprise requirements

the Request Management function as a service in accordance with the principles of the service-oriented architecture. Thus, as the enterprise adds additional resources and develops new workflows to handle data requests, the business applications will continue to be isolated from these changes since all authorization decisions are performed by the PDP.

The resulting architecture view is shown in Figure 11-3.

Let's define specific steps aimed at implementing this architecture of a distributed, enterprise-scale data visibility solution:

- Define business visibility requirements and rules.

- Design a Data Hub data model that can enable effective visibility-compliant navigation (for example, by introducing data tags that can be used for highly selective data retrieval).

- Decompose data visibility rules into decision logic and decision enforcement components.

- Develop an entitlements grammar (or extend the existing policy grammar) to express visibility rules.

- Map visibility rules to user credentials and roles.

- Design and/or install and configure a Policy Decision Point (PDP) engine—a component of the architecture that would analyze every data request to the Data Hub and evaluate it against the policies and entitlements of the requester (user). The PDP can be an implementation of a specialized proprietary or a commercial rules engine.

- Design and develop a Policy Enforcement Point (PEP) as a data-structure and data-content-aware component that performs requested data access operations in the most technically efficient manner. For example, in the case of a Data Hub implementation that is using a Relational Database Management System (RDBMS), the PEP can be a library of stored procedures, a set of database triggers, built-in functions, or an extension to the Data Hub data model that would include a "security table." A security table approach includes a purpose-built data object that is populated (provisioned) using the content of the policies and entitlements; this security table will be joined with Data Hub tables by the PEP to produce the required result set or an empty set, depending on the values of security attributes in the security table.

- Ensure that all policies are created, stored, and managed by a Policy Administration Point (PAP). This component stores the policies and policy sets in a searchable policy store. PAP is an administration facility that allows an authorized administrator to create or change user entitlements and business rules. Ideally, if the enterprise has already implemented a policy database that is used by a Policy server, a visibility policy store should be an extension of this existing policy store.

However, data visibility is only a part of the overall data security and access control puzzle. Therefore, while these steps can help develop a policy-based Visibility Architecture, we need to extend this process and the architecture itself to integrate its features and functions with the overall enterprise security architecture. It is reasonable to assume that the majority of functional enterprises have no choice but to implement multilayered "defense-in-depth" security architecture that includes perimeter defense, network security, enterprise-class authentication, roles-based or policy-based authorization, a version of a single-sign-on (SSO) facility, and an automated provisioning, deprovisioning, and certification of user entitlements (see Chapter 9 for additional discussion on these topics).

Let's add the following steps to the architecture definition and design process outlined in the preceding list. These steps are designed to ensure that the resulting architecture can interoperate and be integrated with the existing enterprise security architecture:

- Develop or select a solution that can delegate authentication and coarse-grained authorization decisions to the existing security infrastructure including Policy Servers.

- Similarly, ensure that user credentials are captured at the point of user entry into the system and carried over through the PDP and PEP components to the Data Hub, thus supporting the creation and management of the auditable log of individual user actions.

- Make sure that the PDP, PEP, and the Enterprise Audit and Compliance system can interface with each other and interoperate in supporting business transactions so that all data access actions can be captured, recorded, and reported for follow-on audit analysis.

Applying these additional steps to the architecture shown in Figure 11-3 may result in the high-level conceptual integrated enterprise security and visibility architecture shown in Figure 11-4.

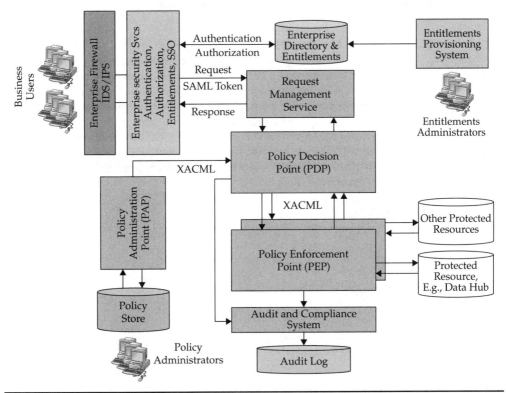

Figure 11-4   Integrated enterprise visibility and security conceptual architecture

This architecture shows how major components of the visibility and security services can be integrated and configured to provide seamless and transparent access control to the data stored in the MDM platform (that is, a Data Hub). As we stated earlier, the core components in this architecture include:

- Policy Administration Point (PAP)
- Policy Store that contains visibility and entitlements policies and rules
- Policy Decision Point (PDP)
- Policy Enforcement Point (PEP)

These components are integrated with the enterprise security architecture that includes but is not limited to

- Perimeter defense and firewalls
- Enterprise directory
- Entitlements and access control policy store that supports policy authorization server
- Enterprise authentication and authorization service (possibly including enterprise-class single-sign-on solution)
- Enterprise provisioning and certification system
- Regulatory and compliance auditing and reporting system

Visibility and Security Architecture Requirements Summary

The foregoing discussion of the visibility and security components and services helps illustrate the complexity of the integrated visibility design. This complexity is one of the drivers for making the "buy vs. build" decision for PDP, PEP, PAP, and other components and services. This decision must be made very carefully in order to protect the entire MDM initiative from the risk of embarking on a complex, unproven, error-prone, and extensive implementation. To help make this decision, we would like to offer the following list of functional requirements that MDM and security architects should consider during the evaluation of the available products and solutions. At a high level, the PDP and PEP components of the architecture should support

- XACML properties
- Domain independence
- Protection of XML documents
- Distributed policies
- Optimized indexing of policies
- Rich set of standard functions and data types
- Profiles
- Policy administration and delegation

These functional requirements are listed here as a template and a reference. Specific implementation requirements may differ and should be evaluated in a formal, objective, and verifiable fashion like any other enterprise software purchase decision.

Visibility and Security Information Flows

The integrated security and visibility architecture shown in Figure 11-4 is designed to support user requests to access data stored in the MDM platform by implementing a number of run-time interaction flows. These flows have been adapted from the OASIS-defined PDP and PEP interaction patterns briefly mentioned in the previous section. We discuss these flows in this section to illustrate the key processing points:

- The user gains access to the MDM environment by supplying his or her credentials to the network security layer.

- After passing through the firewall the user interacts with the enterprise authentication and authorization service, where the user credentials are checked and the user is authenticated and authorized to use the MDM platform (this is a functional authorization to use MDM services that is enforced by a Policy Server).

- The authenticated user issues the request for data access, probably invoking a high-level business service (*Find Party, Edit Product Reference*, and so on).

- The authorization system reviews the request and makes an authorization decision for the user to *permit* or *deny* invocation of a requested service and/or method (in this case, a service method that implements *Find Party* or *Edit Product Reference* functionality).

- Once the affirmative decision is made, the user credentials and the request are passed to the Policy Decision Point, where the request is evaluated against user entitlements in the context of the data being requested. If the PDP decides that the user is allowed to access or change the requested set of data attributes, it will assemble an XACML-formatted payload using one of the standard message formats (possibly an SAML message). This message would include user credentials, authorization decision, and obligations containing enforcement parameters and the name of the enforcement service or interface (for example, the name of the stored procedure and the value for the predicate in the SQL WHERE clause). The authorization decision and corresponding parameters comprise policy obligations that can be expressed in XACML and XRI.

- If the decision evaluates to *Permit*, the PDP sends the message with the XACML payload to the appropriate Policy Enforcement Point (PEP).

- The PEP parses the payload, retrieves the value of the obligation constraints that should form data access predicates (for example, a list of values in the SQL WHERE clause), and invokes the appropriate PEP service or function.

- Once the PEP-enforced data access operation completes successfully, the query result set is returned to the requesting application or a user.

- The PEP retrieves the user credentials and uses them to create a time-stamped entry in the audit log for future analysis and recordkeeping.

- If necessary, the PEP will encrypt and digitally sign the audit log record to provide nonrepudiation of the actions taken by the user on the data stored in the MDM/ Data Hub.

For these steps to execute effectively at run time, several configuration activities need to take place. These configuration flows may include the following:

- Use the Enterprise Provisioning System to create and deliver user credentials and entitlements from the authoritative systems of user records (for example, an HR database for employees) to all consuming target applications including the Enterprise Directory.

- If necessary, extend, modify, or create new entries in the Visibility and Rules Repository.

- Use an Enterprise Access Certification system to configure and execute audit reports and to obtain regular snapshots of the list of active users, their entitlements, and a summary of their actions, so that system administrators can detect and correct conflicting or improper entitlements and tune the overall system to avoid performance bottlenecks. At the same time, the security administrators can use the activity logs to integrate them with the enterprise intrusion detection and protection systems.

While these steps may appear simple, the task of architecting and integrating data visibility and user entitlements into the overall enterprise security framework is very complex, error-prone, and time-consuming, and will require a disciplined, phased-in approach that should be managed like any other major enterprise integration initiative.

We conclude this part of the book with the following observation: Master Data Management environments are designed to provide their consumers with an accurate, integrated, authoritative source of information. Often, Master Data Management environments deliver radically new ways to look at the information. For example, in the case of a Data Hub for Customer domain, the MDM platform can deliver an authoritative and accurate customer-centric operational data view. However, an MDM Data Hub can deliver much more. Indeed, it may also make integrated data available to users and applications in ways that extend and sometimes "break" traditional processes and rules of the business that define who can see which part of what data. Therefore, the majority of MDM implementations need to extend the existing policy grammar and policy servers or develop and deliver new capabilities that support fine-grained functional and data access entitlements while at the same time maintaining data availability, presentation flexibility, and alignment with the legacy and new improved business processes. To sum up, the entitlements and data visibility concerns of Master Data Management represent an important challenge. To solve this challenge, the demands of data security and visibility have to be addressed in an integrated fashion as a key part of the MDM architecture and in conjunction with the enterprise security architecture.

References

1. Coyne, Edward J. and Davis, John M. *Role Engineering for Enterprise Security Management (Information Security and Privacy).* Artech House (2008).

2. http://www.oasis-open.org/committees/download.php/16790/wss-v1.1-spec-os-SOAPMessageSecurity.pdf.

3. http://www.w3.org/TR/2006/WD-ws-policy-primer-20061018/.

4. http://www.oasis-open.org/committees/tc_home.php?wg_abbrev=xacml.

5. http://www.oasis-open.org/committees/tc_home.php?wg_abbrev=xri.

6. http://www.w3.org/TR/2006/WD-ws-policy-primer-20061018/.

7. http://www.oasis-open.org/committees/tc_home.php?wg_abbrev=security.

8. Johnson, Rod, Jürgen Höller, Arendsen, Alef, Risberg, Thomas, and Sampaleanu, Colin. *Professional Java Development with the Spring Framework (First Edition).* Wrox Press (2005).

Implementing and Governing Master Data Management

U p to this point, our discussion was focused on issues and concerns surrounding the architecture and design of Master Data Management systems. We took a close look at the business and technology drivers for MDM, discussed architecture considerations and design concerns, and offered an architected approach to addressing some of the key challenges presented by the MDM goal of integrating data across the enterprise, and especially the challenges related to data security and visibility.

This part of the book deals with the practical aspects of implementing MDM solutions as complex, multidisciplined, enterprise-wide projects or programs. The complexity and multidisciplined nature of MDM systems are such that implementing these solutions requires an approach that may be broader than a single project, and should be managed as an initiative-level, enterprise-wide program that consists of multiple projects, phases, steps, tasks, and activities that are organized into a cohesive set of concurrent but interdependent work streams. The terms "project," "program," and "initiative" are often defined according to the rules, structures, processes, and standards of an individual organization, and are frequently treated as synonyms. Therefore, to avoid confusion related to the appropriate use of these terms, we will use the familiar term "project" when discussing the implementation concerns of MDM systems.

We begin this discussion with a focus on creating and justifying a compelling business case and defining the roadmap for Master Data Management implementation.

Building a Business Case and Roadmap for MDM

W hen an enterprise entertains the idea of a Master Data Management (MDM) program, it has to create a justifiable business case and successfully complete an MDM investment funding request phase in order to initiate the program. The successful business case is critically dependent on securing executive management commitment and organizational stakeholder buy-in. This is the reason why so many publications have been devoted to the business case, value proposition, and justification of MDM and other information- and data-centric initiatives.

Importance of the MDM Business Case and the Current State of the Problem

A business case for MDM remains a significant challenge for many organizations. Many MDM initiatives are entertained and discussed for years and fail to get started because key stakeholders are not able to develop a common vision and reach consensus on the business case for MDM and justify the investment. This lack of clarity and consensus costs a lot to the organizations in terms of the time spent on the discussions and in terms of a lost opportunity due to the failure to execute a program that could provide a competitive advantage. The cost of such a failure can have reputational implications for the individuals who championed the initiative and were on point to develop the business case.

Many publications and presentations are available in the public domain that discuss and teach how to justify MDM and calculate the return on investment (ROI). Oftentimes these publications and presentations are not actionable and present an overly simplistic picture of the business case justification and MDM funding phase without taking into account the variety and complexity of scenarios and factors that impact the business case justification process. Many publications are written with the thought in mind that an MDM initiative is always a good idea. A reality is that for some organizations an enterprise MDM may not be the right priority at a given point in time or, even more, the costs of the program may exceed the benefits that can be realized as a result of the program. The devil is in the details, and the quality of the business case analysis or lack thereof can result in a highly profitable MDM initiative or make it a total waste.

Hypothetical MDM business case estimations representing an "average" company may not apply to your organization. A real cost-benefit analysis in your enterprise may show significant deviations (up or down) from the average estimated for a hypothetical company. It is highly probable that the deviation will exceed the average, which tells us that it is critically important to understand the challenges of business case justification of MDM and the techniques that can help your organization to build a compelling business case.

This chapter intends to help program managers, planners, solution architects, and other MDM stakeholders tasked by executive management or compelled on their own to develop a business case for MDM. It is important to understand that there are no shortcuts in approaching business case development for MDM. Hence, we will not even try to provide a "silver bullet" recipe for the MDM business case conundrum. Instead, this chapter aims at to provide the reader with an analysis of a variety of scenarios, considerations, and factors that should be understood and taken into account in order to build the business case for MDM properly.

Once these factors, scenarios, and their impacts are understood, MDM stakeholders are in a much better position to determine the risks of the funding phase and mitigation strategies. We will discuss what works and what does not work to help the reader avoid some common mistakes made by some practitioners during MDM business case justification efforts. This discussion is critical to the success of a strong business case that will move an MDM program into execution mode.

MDM Sponsorship Scenarios and Their Challenges

The idea that an organization needs an MDM environment comes and is incubated within organizations as a combination of two primary sponsorship scenarios:

- Business strategy–driven MDM
- IT strategy–driven MDM

Both scenarios are quite common and can result in successful business case justification and the overall success of the MDM initiative. Having said that, it is much easier to justify MDM when there is a solid business strategy behind it, and oftentimes what drives the business case is a combination of business and IT factors.

Business Strategy–Driven MDM

When MDM is driven by a business strategy, the imperative for a change comes from executive management (CEO, CFO, or divisional leadership). In this scenario, executive management is sick and tired of operational inefficiencies as well as the lack of the enterprise's ability to interact with the customer holistically and report on master entity–centric metrics, where master entity is customer, product, location, supplier, service, and so on. Executive management has a strategic business vision of a change and demands it.

The initiative is typically executed under mottos and mantras such as "Customer Experience," "One Organization, One Customer," "Customer 360 Strategy," "Global Account Opening and Management," "Global Policy Issuance and Management," "One View of a Guest," "Health Electronic Record," and other names that vary by industry.

It is quite common that IT is not able to recommend a quick fix to support the new business strategy. Legacy processes and platforms may create formidable obstacles and preclude any attempts to quickly fix the problem without significant investments and structural changes that require a new IT vision and strategy to support the change.

The new IT strategy and its elaboration may include a number of priority projects:

- A new core operational system to replace the existing legacy platform that has been in production for 20–30 years

- Development of service-oriented architecture (SOA) that includes an Enterprise Service Bus (ESB) for messaging, interoperability, and increased agility of business processes

- Selection of a Business Rules Engine software

- Development of a new conceptual master data model

- Other foundational changes related to MDM and data quality.

Considering these projects could become a pivotal point in the program life-cycle when business executives may learn about the existence of the term "MDM" for the first time, even though it turns out to be one of the core foundational components required to execute the business strategy. This is not always a bad thing; the goal here is not to complicate the business strategy with detailed IT aspects too early.

To sum up, in the business strategy–driven scenario, business executives have a vision that implicitly points to the need for MDM. In this scenario, MDM is a critical part of a larger initiative that supports or implements the business strategy. Clearly, this scenario makes the development of the business case for MDM and the overall MDM justification much easier because it is subsumed in the larger vision for change in the business.

IT Strategy–Driven MDM

About 50 percent of MDM programs are driven by IT organizations as an IT strategy initiative. This scenario makes the MDM business case more challenging because typically IT management cannot approach the business case problem with the same degree of power and authority as business executive management in the business strategy–driven MDM scenario.

IT strategy–driven MDM efforts sometimes focus mostly on implementations of MDM software and the creation of a "golden" record in the MDM Data Hub, while leaving the analysis of consuming applications and processes that will be enabled by MDM for the consequent phases. This approach may cause problems in relationships with the business, negatively impact end user adoption, and can even cause the initiative to fail.

If this view prevails in the enterprise, an MDM initiative can be perceived by many as a massive infrastructure improvement project that requires significant efforts and investments while lacking tangible business and operational benefits. This is a common challenge for many MDM initiatives driven by IT organizations, and this perception of MDM as an infrastructure-driven investment should be addressed as a part of business case development.

Some MDM experts have even expressed an opinion that MDM initiatives driven by IT are doomed. In reality, many IT strategy–driven initiatives succeed if they engage the business properly and in a timely manner. Some IT leaders, especially those who have spent over 15–20 years with the company, have acquired a broad understanding of business and operational issues and are well positioned to champion the initiative.

What MDM Stakeholders Want to Know

The challenges of the MDM business case grow with the number of stakeholders. Different groups of stakeholders see MDM from different perspectives and approach the funding/ no-funding decision with different criteria and agendas. Thus, individuals responsible for a justification of MDM also have to approach the business case from multiple perspectives and explore a variety of methods to tackle the business case justification problem properly.

Managers responsible for MDM business case justification should have a mindset of a salesperson engaged in complex technical sales. The book *Hope Is Not a Strategy*, by Rick Page, introduces the concept of a "Shark Chart" that describes a variety of stakeholder levels and roles.[1] The overall approach and methodology in this book is a good example of what the individuals responsible for MDM business case justification should adopt.

At the very strategic level, the board of directors and CEO want to know how the equity value, market capitalization, and competitive posture of the company would change as a result of the initiative that includes MDM. Executive management wishes to know which divisions/ lines of business (LOBs) will benefit from the MDM initiative and how. They want to hear that divisional leadership supports the initiative and understands its benefits, risks, and costs.

A CFO may require ROI and NPV (Net Present Value) calculations. Oftentimes, for a CFO the cost of the initiative is more important than the benefits, even though the CFO may rely on the business leadership opinion that the change promised by the initiative is indeed required. The CFO wants to have a solid understanding of the initiative's costs to prevent a potential long-term cash flow problem. To make the CFO a supporter of the initiative, the business case justification team needs a solid understanding of what type of MDM solution will be implemented, what components will be used, what processes will change, and what resources will be required. Then the team can develop an implementation roadmap that is detailed enough to substantiate cost estimates with a reasonable certainty.

For large (Fortune 1000) firms, a division can be considered an enterprise in its own right. Then an enterprise MDM may be limited to the division or even a line of business. In this scenario, the head of the LOB is considered to be in the role of the CEO from the MDM sponsorship perspective.

Even if the LOB management does not sponsor the initiative championed by their superior executive management, the LOB support is absolutely critical. LOB leaders are looking to understand tactical changes in the LOB processes and user interfaces that the initiative will bring in. They want to understand what resources from their organization will be engaged in the initiative and thus distracted from their current functions and responsibilities.

Information strategists and enterprise architects are looking to see how well the new MDM architecture will comply with applicable architecture standards and fit their enterprise architecture vision. Operations management, database administrators, and individuals who will be responsible for the maintenance of MDM components have significant stakes in the MDM solution, too. In Chapter 13 we will discuss in more detail the key questions a typical organization has to understand for MDM program initiation.

Business Processes and MDM Drivers

Business processes that will be improved as a result of MDM vary by industry, company, program, and even by the phase of the MDM initiative. Still, there are common areas and processes that are typically improved by MDM.

We discussed the predominant MDM drivers and the areas that benefit from MDM in Figure 2-2 of Chapter 2. The most common beneficiaries of MDM are listed there. This list can help an MDM team charged with the responsibility to define the business case and justify the investment. Leveraging the table in Figure 2-2 as a starting point, the business case definition team can prioritize the drivers as needed and adjust the list of drivers to better reflect the business context of the MDM program in their organization.

One of the considerations for prioritization is based on economic conditions: In the time of economic downturns, we see an increased focus on operational efficiency. Conversely, when the economy grows fast, MDM initiatives tend to focus more on the enablement of new business opportunities and processes.

Benefits and Their Estimation

Benefits are often divided into two categories: quantitative and qualitative. *Quantitative benefits* (that is, "hard" benefits) are those that can be estimated from cost savings, the enablement of new revenue opportunities, or the avoidance of scenarios in which a revenue opportunity will be lost (for example, due to customer attrition). *Qualitative benefits* deal with "softer" aspects such as reputation risks, company competitiveness, potential compliance issues that may be very significant for business but not easily quantifiable, and so on.

In reality, there is no wall between qualitative and quantitative benefits. Some benefits that are considered quantitative may be difficult to evaluate for a given company in the context of its current business processes. On the other hand, benefits traditionally placed in the qualitative category can sometimes be evaluated and measured. For instance, benefits of improved compliance[2] are sometimes estimated in terms of avoided penalties that an enterprise can be subjected to without the improvements promised by MDM. It is difficult, however, to quantify the cost of corporate scandals and ruined reputation of a company and its top executives, along with the potential legal consequences these executives might be subjected to.

From the business case methodology perspective, two high-level approaches can be used to estimate an MDM impact:

- **A traditional bottom-up approach**   This approach quantifies MDM benefits by performing an in-depth analysis of the current-state processes, identifying their inefficiencies, and developing an ROI model by showing how MDM can reduce costs and increase the revenue.

- **A less traditional Economic Value (EV) approach**   This approach provides a high-level estimate for the business impact of MDM and other information-centric initiatives (this is different from a more traditional Economic Value Added or EVA metric, which is a measure of the financial performance of the company that represents an estimate of economic profit).

Traditional Methods for Estimation of Business Benefits

As well explained by David Linthicum in his online article "Defining the ROI for Data Integration,"[3] the business case begins with the definition of the problem domain. The drivers outlined in the previous section define the most common high-level problem domains for MDM.

If your organization's ROI and NPV estimations require a more detailed list of problem domains and processes, you can benefit from a number of articles where a variety of benefits achieved through improved data quality and improved management of master data are discussed in detail.[4,5,6,7,8]

Let's consider a simple business case scenario where an enterprise seeks to implement MDM because its current process heavily relies on a third-party supplier of customer data. The enterprise pays $4 million to the supplier annually. In addition to being on a continuous cash outflow, the enterprise suffers from a lack of agility to support changing business requirements. The enterprise makes a decision to implement an MDM solution and discontinue the subscription to the third-party data.

The initial implementation costs, including the MDM software license cost, integration services, acquisition of new hardware, training, and other initial expenses are estimated at $3 million. On completion of the MDM implementation, the total of on going annual expenses is estimated at $400,000, which may include the annual software license fee, cost of data stewardship resources, maintenance, and other on going costs.

In this example, in the first year after implementation the enterprise will spend $3.4 million on MDM. Because the third-party data subscription is canceled, the $4 million cost was avoided, which results in a total cost savings of $0.6 million in the first year. Every consequent year will provide an additional $3.6 million in savings. In five years after implementation, the $5 million total investment will result in $20 million of cost avoidance, which translates into the following:

(20 – 5) / 5 * 100% = 300% ROI over five years and $15M Net Present Value (NPV)

Even though we didn't put a dollar tag on the increased agility to support changing business needs, we identified inefficiency ($4 million annually) and found a way to eliminate it by making a profitable investment in MDM products and services. In this example, the problem domain was very well defined and the ROI model was simple. Unfortunately, these simple ROI scenarios for MDM are rather limited.

Let's discuss another example of the MDM business case typical for marketing applications that are often addressed by analytical MDM. A company runs several mail marketing campaigns annually with a total of 10,000,000 mailings. The company has estimated that 10 percent of the mailings are sent with at least one of the following errors:

- The mailing address is incorrect and as a result the mailing does not reach the recipient.
- More than one letter is sent to the same person.
- More than one letter is sent to the same household because the enterprise lacks the capabilities to identify households, even though the business would like to be able to market to households rather than to individuals.

The company decides that if it implements MDM for its Customer domain, the 10-percent error rate will be practically eliminated. This yields estimated savings of $500,000 annually, assuming each mailing costs 50 cents. In this scenario, assuming the cost of the MDM implementation is the same as described in the previous example, the company will save only $100,000 annually: $500,000 savings less $400,000 spent on the on going expenditures. In order to offset the initial MDM investment ($3 million) and to break even, the company will need 30 years! This is too long for any reasonable investment return, especially if you consider an impact of inflation that would drive the real value of the currency (for example, U.S. dollar) to drop significantly over this period of time.

In this case, the estimate cannot justify the MDM investment. It does not mean, however, that the enterprise has considered all of the benefits that can be realized from the MDM implementation. For instance, the marketing department considering an MDM investment may want to develop an advanced market segmentation model, which requires MDM as a component of the solution. Indeed, by definition, the MDM system will integrate customer information from multiple systems and possibly third-party sources and will create and maintain one holistic view of the customer and household. This holistic view is the basis that would enable marketing segmentation software to deliver accurate segmentation models, thus justifying the need for MDM as the enabler and the catalyst of improved marketing efficiency.

The preceding scenario highlights some of the challenges typical for business case estimations:

- The company estimated a 10-percent error rate in mail delivery. In reality, it is often a challenge to determine the actual error rate. Ten percent is most likely a guess. The real rate can be significantly higher or lower.

- If market segmentation is one of the applications planned for the implementation, the invested amount should be calculated for the whole market segmentation project, with MDM being only one of its components. Hence, the baseline project cost will be higher than $3 million and the annual cost will be higher than $400,000.

- The total value of the benefits should be calculated as a sum of the mailing savings and the savings and/or revenue opportunities associated with the new market segmentation capabilities and processes.

- A number of books and numerous articles discuss the metrics estimating efficiency of marketing campaigns. These metrics require accurate measurements of the outcomes of marketing campaigns, which is not a simple task.[9] Many companies do not measure the efficiency of marketing campaigns, which complicates the quantification of the MDM business case because the impact of MDM cannot be measured in business terms. If the business itself does not measure its efficiency, it is difficult to estimate the incremental business impact of MDM on the business.

In the marketing segmentation scenario, we noted that cost savings from improved mailings did not provide enough savings to make an MDM project profitable. It is not unusual that in addition to cost savings, the business case has to take into account the new revenue opportunities to justify the investment.

Cost savings can be achieved through the reduction of resources involved in the process. The top resources that can provide savings include:

- **Employees (measured as full-time equivalents, or FTEs)**   This includes not just headcount reduction but also reduced administrative overhead, better process automation, organization, and improved productivity.

- **IT infrastructure (hardware) cost through better architected data management with improved data redundancy**   This will increase the efficiencies and reduce the costs of systems where master data may reside.

The team responsible for the MDM business case should be prepared to answer the CFO's questions, such as the following: "OK, you say that we will be able to reduce the number of people engaged in the current process. Can you be more specific on how many employees, fixed price and time and material consultants, and other temporary workers the company will be able to free or reassign to fill other openings? What infrastructure components can we save on if we purchase a vendor MDM Data Hub product?" These questions can put the MDM business case team in a politically difficult situation, especially as it relates to the opportunity of FTE reduction. Indeed, let's estimate how many FTEs should be released from the process to make an MDM investment profitable. Assuming the annual FTE cost of $50,000 per employee, in order to break even with the MDM investment defined earlier, we will need to reduce the workforce by 23 employees immediately in order to break even in four years! Indeed, the savings from reducing the number of employees by 23 yield 23 * 50,000 = $1,150,000 annually or $4,600,000 for 4 years. The same amount will be spent by the enterprise on MDM: $3 million for the initial investment and $1.6 million on the maintenance ($400,000 annually for 4 years). This perspective may put you at odds with many people in your organization and defeat the idea of MDM.

This emphasizes an important point: In many scenarios cost savings may not be able to justify the investment. You should be prepared to inspire the organization with new revenue opportunities enabled by MDM to develop a sound business case. The business should be willing to champion the ideas of new revenue opportunities enabled by MDM. This may bring a new business strategy that will help MDM business case justification.

It should be pointed out that in a number of projects similar to our marketing mailing scenario, a business case was originally defined in terms of savings achieved through a reduction of mailings. Later, when the project went into production, the enterprise chose to keep the number of mailings the same while benefiting from significantly improved quality of marketing campaigns (lift) that brought in significant incremental revenue.

Some companies, after an in-depth analysis of their processes, came up with the cost of a duplicate master record between $20 and $60 per record, which is two orders of magnitude higher than the cost estimated from the model based on the duplicate mailing scenario. This is another indication that those easily quantifiable benefits provide only a small fraction of the real value that MDM can provide. The cost of $40 per duplicate can be used as a rule of thumb for high-level estimates if a detailed business process analysis has not been performed by the enterprise. In the authors' experience, this estimate works well for enterprises where the number of customers is high (for instance, greater than 15 to 20 million records).

As we can see from this discussion, the complexity of a bottom-up business case can range from a relatively simple scenario when one or a few specific and easily quantifiable problem domains justify an investment, to a variety of complex scenarios where only a long list of cost avoidance areas in combination with multiple revenue opportunities can justify the business case for MDM.

Economic Value of Information as MDM Business Case Estimation Technique

Robert Hillard and Sean McClowry[10] formulated an alternate approach to business case justification for information-centric initiatives such as MDM. Instead of tackling the business case challenges bottom-up through an in-depth analysis of business process inefficiencies that can be cured by MDM, the top-down approach introduces the notion of an EV of information and applies a Capability Maturity Model (CMM) approach.

It is always a challenge to put a dollar value on information without knowing its content and the context in which it can be used. The EV model approaches this challenge by establishing a relationship between the market value of the enterprise and the value of the enterprise information. The EV of information is defined as

$$EV \text{ of Information} = P(\text{Information}) * \text{Market Capitalization}$$

where P(Information) is a parameter of the model that indicates what fraction of the corporate market capitalization falls under informational assets. Hillard and McClowry recommend P = 0.2, even though they report that this estimate is fairly conservative. This value was obtained as a result of a number of workshops and interviews with corporate executives.

We have adapted this method to MDM. The preceding EV can be rewritten for MDM as

$$\text{EV of Master Data} = \text{P(MDM)} * \text{Market Capitalization}$$

where P(MDM) indicates what fraction of the corporate market capitalization falls under MDM assets.

This formula has been used on a number of practical MDM implementations. The results show that the value of parameter P(MDM) is typically in the range of 0.03–0.06. For example, let's apply this approach to an enterprise with a market capitalization of $3 billion. Assuming P(MDM) = 0.04, then the dollar equivalent of the enterprise master data will be equal to $120 million. This is what the enterprise master data would be worth if the Master Data Management initiative was executed perfectly.

MDM Capability Maturity Model

To use the EV approach effectively, the enterprise should define 15–30 capabilities, processes that are to be enabled, and problem domains that are to be fixed by the enterprise via MDM. For each capability, the current state, the expected target state, and the relative importance of the capability are identified as depicted in Figure 12-1.

- Market Cap = (Shares)x(Share Price).
- Economic Value of Information Overall (between 20% and 50%).
- Economic Value is Estimated 3%-6% for MDM

CMM \ Capability	Level 0 New	Level 1 Chaotic	Level 2 Repeatable	Level 3 Defined	Level 4 Managed	Level 5 Optimized	Weight (1-10)
Capability 1	0%	20%	40%	60%	80%	100%	8
Capability 2	0%	20%	40%	60%	80%	100%	5
Capability 3	0%	20%	40%	60%	80%	100%	3

- *Level 0:* New – Capability does not Currently Exist
- *Level 1:* Chaotic – Undocumented, Manual, does not Meet Business Requirements
- *Level 2:* Repeatable – Mostly Repeatable but Reactive, does not Meet Business Requirements
- *Level 3:* Defined – Meets Minimum Current Business Requirements, Partly Automated
- *Level 4:* Information Managed Enterprise-Wide as well-Engineered Effort with Established Metrics and Controls
- *Level 5:* Optimized, Managed as Strategic Asset, Best in Class, Data Issues Prevented at the Source
- Can be 100+ Capabilities for Information Management, 15-30 for MDM

FIGURE 12-1 Economic Value approach to information and MDM

PART IV

Generic guidance on the definitions of maturity levels (1–5) can be found in numerous books and articles on CMM and IMM. Rob Karel[2] recommends definitions of five maturity levels of MDM, along with typical enabling technologies and usage scenarios for each MDM maturity level. Karel's definitions can be leveraged as a guide to define maturity levels for each of the capabilities. David Loshin[11] has defined MDM maturity levels by grouping MDM capabilities into the following categories:

- Architecture
- Governance
- Management
- Identification
- Integration
- Business Process Management

The MDM management team should understand the overall approach to CMM and the definition of capabilities, evaluation categories, and tactical views for MDM benefits. You can read more on these in the references given at the end of the chapter.[2,4,8,10]

Using this information as a guide, MDM stakeholders can make informed decisions on which capabilities best fit their MDM objectives and organizational culture. The process of evaluating the current state for each of the categories identified for a given MDM initiative and understanding the expected target state and the incremental releases in terms of CMM for MDM is a great exercise that helps key MDM stakeholders to get on the same page and agree on their views on what drives their MDM initiative (readers who would like to find additional information on this topic can review the series of blogs titled "Estimating the Benefits for MDM").[12]

In discussing CMM for MDM, we extend the traditional CMM model by adding maturity level 0 to denote the capability that currently does not exist but is on the enterprise wish list, which means that the enterprise is planning to develop this new capability that can be a new business process or even a line of business.

The arrows in Figure 12-1 indicate that a given capability would be created and/or enhanced across several maturity levels. For example, Capability 1 will be enhanced from Maturity Level 1 to Maturity Level 4, while Capability 2 will be increased from Level 0 to Level 3.

The following formula defines an incremental increase in the market cap of the enterprise when the target capabilities enabled by MDM are achieved:

$$\Delta EV = \frac{\text{Market Cap} * \sum W_i * \Delta L_i}{5 * \sum W_i}$$

In this formula, $\sum$ stands for the summation over all capabilities that will change, and W_i and ΔL_i are the relative importance and expected maturity level change as a result of the MDM implementation.

One of the benefits of the EV approach is that a quantitative model can be built relatively quickly. The capabilities, their current and target states, as well as their relative values are defined in a few workshops with MDM stakeholders. The workshops are followed by an analysis of the obtained results. The EV approach can estimate the values that are practically impossible to obtain by the traditional bottom-up evaluation method. Even soft MDM benefits such as corporate reputation can be accounted for within the EV method. Indeed, the market capitalization depends on the company's reputation, and therefore the incremental economic value obtained through MDM will take this factor into account.

MDM Economic Value workshops with broad representations of key stakeholders bring a great value as a technique that helps the enterprise to develop a common view on why they are pursuing MDM, to socialize the value of MDM, and to build organizational consensus.

A weakness of the EV method is that it provides only high-level estimates. Some companies and their CFOs get used to and require more traditional ROI and NPV estimates. They may be skeptical about the accuracy of the EV method.

For some capabilities, both approaches may be applicable. The quantitative values obtained from the two approaches can be compared to ensure reasonable consistency. The incremental increase in EV due to MDM is expected to be three to ten times greater than the total estimated value of the annual benefits calculated by the traditional bottom-up method. This rule of thumb can be used to validate the model and refine its parameters.

The best results are obtained when both approaches (EV and the traditional bottom-up approach) are used in concert. We believe that a combination of these methods will become the mainstream technique for MDM business case evaluations in the future.

Key Takeaways About MDM Business Case

- Business case justification should be approached with a solid understanding of MDM drivers, challenges, scenarios, and techniques. This understanding should be applied in the context of the enterprise problem domains.

- MDM is usually driven by some combination of business and IT strategies. Both scenarios can produce successful business case justification. It is easier, however, when the need for MDM is mostly driven by a business strategy. The best way to sell MDM to the business is not to mention MDM at all but rather focus on the business strategy or processes that MDM enables.

- A number of techniques exist that help justify MDM initiatives even when a well-defined business strategy is not available at the beginning of the MDM program.

- A combination of traditional ROI and NPV estimates with the Economic Value approach produces the best results and helps justify MDM business cases based on a variety of benefits that an enterprise can obtain through MDM.

- An MDM business case is not only about the "hard" benefits. MDM justification requires organizational and executive buy-ins based on the consensus of the multiple stakeholder groups. Each of these groups should be able to understand how it will benefit and be impacted by the planned MDM implementation.

- Data governance policies that clearly identify information as a key enterprise asset and require accountabilities and metrics are important in building an organizational consensus on business case justification. We started the discussion on data governance in Part I of the book and offer a more detailed discussion on this topic in Chapter 17.

The content presented thus far focuses mostly on the business benefits of MDM and the methods of their estimation. The benefits define the numerator in the ROI equation. For the ROI and NPV calculations, the cost structure is equally important. Thus, to complete the business case, a detailed analysis of the key early decision points that significantly impact the MDM roadmap, costs, risks, and mitigation strategies is also critical. These decision points and a high-level MDM roadmap must be developed as part of the business case to position the enterprise for a balanced and comprehensive cost-benefit analysis. The MDM roadmap should include a number of views critical for scope and costs estimations.

The importance of a balanced and properly defined MDM roadmap, along with the MDM development techniques, will be discussed in the remainder of this chapter.

Importance of the MDM Roadmap

In the previous sections of this chapter, we discussed MDM business benefits, methods of their estimation, and factors important to understand in order to successfully initiate an MDM program. Even if business benefits are estimated and understood by the enterprise, the business case for MDM is incomplete and cannot be quantified if the costs and risks are not estimated.

When an enterprise embarks on an MDM program, it is critical for the stakeholders to understand the key decision points that determine the initiative's costs, risks, and risk mitigation strategies. An enterprise that begins an MDM program without a properly defined implementation roadmap will not be able to proactively understand the target state of MDM and its evolution from release to release. This will adversely impact planning and the ability to execute the program. Without proper understanding of the "what," "when," and, at a high level, "how," it is impossible to articulate what benefits will be realized and when, what areas of the enterprise will be impacted when and how, and what resources (people, hardware, software, and so on) will be required.

Consequently, in the absence of a comprehensive MDM roadmap, it is not feasible to intelligently estimate the program costs and when they will be incurred. Without cost estimates, even if the benefits of MDM are clear, the enterprise cannot complete a cost-benefit analysis and estimate ROI and NPV. Ultimately the MDM stakeholders cannot make a substantive go/no-go decision about the MDM initiative. In the absence of a properly developed MDM roadmap, understanding and estimating the dependencies and risks is not feasible either.

A properly developed MDM roadmap, at a high level, defines program releases for the MDM evolution over one to five years. For a multiphase MDM program, the immediate phase is planned in more detail. The phases that follow are planned with decreasing levels of detail, while including enough information to drive the most important decisions.

For a multiphase MDM implementation, the MDM roadmap document is a "living summary" that evolves as the initiative progresses rather than a document created once at the beginning of the program and is never touched later.

Experience shows that on a number of MDM projects, the teams responsible for the program claimed to have an MDM roadmap. The analyses that followed showed that in many cases the roadmaps had been defined in a very superficial way and lacked critical details. The MDM roadmap definition was often limited by a single dimension: the data domains that will be addressed by MDM (for example, Phase 1: Customer, Phase 2: Location,

Phase 3: Product, Phase 4: Other). Such a superficial roadmap does not provide enough information to estimate costs and resources, evaluate risk, and establish confidence among the stakeholders that they as a team have developed as a common MDM vision.

Some enterprises initiating MDM programs tend to fall to the other extreme. They try to envision many lower-level details that may not be predictable because the answers depend on factors that can be refined only in the future. The desire to understand and include too many details may result in an "analysis paralysis" scenario, where discussions that are supposed to refine questions generate many other unanswered questions and uncertainties. As a result, the initiative fails to start for months or even years.

The challenge of the MDM roadmap resides in prioritizing the most critical questions that greatly impact costs and risks while postponing other questions that are less important. Some questions are critical enough to be impactful, but they cannot be answered at the time of program commencement. In this case, it may be a good idea to identify potential solution options and the associated uncertainties and risks.

This section discusses the areas of the roadmap and decision points that are crucial for a typical MDM roadmap. The section provides recommendations on how to define a comprehensive MDM roadmap in terms of 20 MDM roadmap views that are discussed in the following subsections. Note that in our online blog series[13] we introduced the term "MDM roadmap domains." In this book we will consistently use the term "MDM roadmap views" instead to avoid the usage of the term "domain" in different contexts throughout the book, which may cause some confusion.

Basic MDM Costs

An MDM program's cost can vary drastically. Some low-end home-grown solutions are built and maintained by one or two people. These types of solutions, although rudimentary in terms of their capabilities and industrial strength, can be well tailored to the business needs and valuable for the business, and thus are easy to understand and manage. Let's consider an enterprise-scope MDM program and review the cost components of such a program.

We will assume that the reader is a stakeholder in an enterprise program that includes MDM Data Hub software purchased from one of the established MDM vendors.

Then the primary cost components include:

- Software
- Professional services for software installation, analysis, configuration, training, and on going support
- Hardware
- Initial integration
- On going maintenance and integration
- Data stewardship (optional)
- Subscription for third-party data providers (optional)

Some basic costs for a hypothetical company with 5 million customers were estimated[14] by Rob Karel of Forrester Research, Inc. The total estimated cost of $3 million was incurred by the hypothetical company over the initial implementation and three years of production.

This included roughly 20 percent spent on the MDM Data Hub software license, 40 percent on the professional services work (installation, configuration, analysis, and integration), and 12 percent on the hardware. The remaining 28 percent was spent on the full-time resources—annual cost of IT maintenance ($270,000) and the annual cost of data steward resources ($81,000). These annual on going costs become predominant over the years in the described scenario. The estimate was performed for a single domain (Customer). No third-party data costs were included in the estimates.

Many MDM initiatives incur costs an order of magnitude higher than $3 million, whereas some other MDM initiatives are implemented with a fraction of the $3 million budget. Historically, some companies invested more in the initial product but ended up with significantly lower ongoing IT maintenance costs that determine the annual cash flow and the MDM cost of ownership from the longer-term perspective. Thus, the stakeholders of any MDM initiative should understand the factors responsible for cost variations of MDM initiatives through the analysis of the target state and the roadmap.

MDM Roadmap Views

In order to make the target state of MDM and the MDM roadmap reasonably comprehensive, the following roadmap views should be included in the roadmap development plan:

1. Business Benefits
2. Systems and Applications in Scope of MDM
3. Data Domains, Entities, and High-Level Data Model
4. Relationships, Hierarchies, and Metadata
5. Third-Party Data Sources
6. Systems Decommissioning Strategy
7. Data Hub Usage Style
8. Data Hub Architecture and Data Ownership Style
9. Data Volume, Performance, and Scalability Considerations
10. Reference Data Management
11. Deployment Strategies and User Groups
12. Related Initiatives
13. Master Data Governance Maturity
14. Master Data Quality Processes, Metrics, and Technology Support
15. Integration with Unstructured Data
16. Multilingual Requirements
17. Complexity of Cross-Domain Information Sharing
18. Complexity of Data Security and Visibility Requirements
19. People Resources and Skills
20. Enabling Technologies: ETL, SOA, and ESB

As you can see from this list, these roadmap views address MDM project concerns holistically and touch upon business drivers, data architecture, systems architecture, organization and governance, security and compliance, development life cycle, and system and master data maintenance. One of the key values of the roadmap view approach is its ability to make the roadmap agile and active, so it can be easily adjusted as business requirements change.

Some views may be more important than others for a specific enterprise. Still, it is a good idea to look at all of them first, prioritize some of them, and possibly de-prioritize some others based on your enterprise's needs.

Business Benefits

The Business Benefits view tops the list of roadmap views. As we stated earlier in this chapter, the business case cannot be considered complete without a sound roadmap that determines the primary cost parameters. The reverse statement is also valid. An MDM roadmap should consider business benefits by release or implementation phase. MDM stakeholders want to know what groups will benefit from the program, how, and when. Some groups may be enthusiastic about the coming change promised by MDM. Some others can be cautious and even reluctant to accept the coming changes and the new business processes enabled by MDM. The reluctance to adopt MDM represents a risk for the initiative, and the motivations of this reluctance need to be understood. Business benefits, their priorities, and timing can indirectly impact the costs. For instance, if the initial phase of the initiative is focused on marketing, this focus is an indication that an analytical MDM solution will be implemented. The cost and implementation risks of an analytical MDM are typically lower than those for an operational MDM. We will focus on this aspect over the discussion of the Data Hub Usage Style roadmap view.

Systems and Applications in Scope of MDM

It is not unusual to have 20–40 systems and even more in the scope of a long-term MDM data and systems integration. Significant cost savings can be achieved by standardizing systems' on-boarding procedures. Even though different systems may have different integration modes that depend on the latency requirements, data exchange attributes, merge and split requirements, and other solution characteristics, it is important to define a finite number of standard systems' on-boarding procedures that the enterprise will leverage for MDM integration. Once these standard procedures are established during the first MDM implementation phase, they can be reused to effectively contain the cost of the subsequent phases. The enterprise cannot afford a scenario where every additional system is integrated with the Data Hub as an independent project that does not leverage the previously developed systems' on-boarding procedures, standards, and data and systems integration techniques.

Data Domains, Entities, and High-Level Data Model

Although early MDM implementations were primarily focused on a single MDM domain (for example, Customer or Product), the current trend is shifting to multidomain MDM solutions. Thus, the majority of recent and current MDM implementations have a multidomain perspective, even though the initial phase oftentimes concentrates on a single domain. An MDM team that approaches MDM with a multidomain perspective must make sure that the MDM product they select can handle multiple domains. The recommended way of doing this is to select an MDM product with a data domain–agnostic data model and services.

Standardization of systems' on-boarding procedures will help here, too. This standardization approach will help constrain future per-phase costs in which new data domains are added to the MDM scope. This can make investments in the integration of new data domains an order of magnitude lower than the costs of the first MDM data domain.

When evaluating the complexity and potential cost of the implementation, it is important to understand the complexity of the key data domains. A master data model can greatly help in the understanding of the level of MDM complexity. Even when a single-domain MDM is being implemented (for example, Customer), the overall party model can be fairly complex and consist of 20–30 entities in the 3NF representation. The complexity of the model grows with the introduction of multiple entity definitions (customer, client, and so on) that can coexist within each of the domains. More specifically, it is not unusual for an enterprise to have 10–15 definitions of a customer that depend on the context, department, or function. For instance, the term "customer" can apply to an individual, a household (which can be defined in multiple ways), a trust fund, or a commercial institution. For shipping and logistics applications, the intersection of a customer and location attributes can represent a new definition of a customer. Marketing, billing, and compliance departments can have very different definitions of a customer. A combination of this variety of customer views can result in a complex party model. Availability and reasonable completeness of the master model helps reduce uncertainties in planning and cost estimations. It is not expected from the model to be complete for early estimates. Still, the change in scope between a single entity with 20 attributes that later unexpectedly evolves into a relatively complex data model with 20–30 entities and many hundreds of attributes can impact the accuracy of planning, resources, and the cost estimates. As we showed in Chapter 7, the size and maturity of the MDM data model are important parameters for the planning of an MDM solution.

Relationships, Hierarchies, and Metadata

The value of MDM greatly depends on what the program does to manage relationships between master entities. See the discussions on the importance of relationships on the online resources given at the end of the chapter.[13,14,15]

Any mature MDM solution includes strong support for relationship management. A holistic and panoramic view of a customer includes a comprehensive view of relationships. As we discussed in the previous section, various enterprise functions require different views and definitions of entities. The same applies to relationships. Understanding relationships between parties and products as well as customer and product hierarchies is critical for enterprises. It is quite common for an MDM program to begin with one or a few master entities and then evolve into a multidomain MDM with a strong focus on relationships. At a high level, three techniques are used to build entity relationships and hierarchies:

- Use an external trusted source of relationships (or multiple trusted sources) and build relationships and hierarchies by comparing in-house master data with external trusted sources.

- Define the rules that will be used to algorithmically infer relationships. These rules can be based on common attribute values (for example, people sharing the same home address are defined as a household). The attributes can be matched exactly or probabilistically by applying the same probabilistic and fuzzy methods that are used for entity resolution (we discussed this process in Part II of the book).

- Link relationships manually by using graphical interfaces. This method requires additional data stewardship resources and therefore additional costs associated with data stewardship.

Each method has its inherent benefits, areas of applicability, and limitations. In full-scale MDM implementations, enterprises can benefit from using all three methods to create and maintain a comprehensive view of relationships.

The use of each of these methods can, on the one hand, increase the value of the MDM solution while increasing the MDM implementation cost.

Organizing data domains into hierarchies and providing capabilities to create, change, manage, and link hierarchies is a critical and complex area of an MDM solution that needs to be well understood and carefully estimated depending on the number and complexity of business requirements for hierarchy management and its proposed applicability to downstream systems. In addition, both the relationship and hierarchy management require the support of a metadata repository and a metadata management facility, a complex area of technology that should be considered as a key part of the MDM roadmap. (See the discussion on hierarchy management in Chapter 4 and the discussion on metadata in Chapter 5.)

Third-Party Data Sources

An MDM solution can greatly benefit from the use of third-party data. A Data Hub matches enterprise master data with the third-party data, which helps to improve the quality of the matching process and enhances entity and relationship resolution. Third-party data also helps in the development of customer and product hierarchies. External trusted sources can improve data quality and enrich enterprise master data.

There are costs associated with third-party data. These include the costs of data subscriptions and the costs of integration with trusted sources. Specifics of the third-party source or sources, their usage, and integration modes will impact the total cost.

Decommissioning of Systems and Applications

Significant long-term cost savings can be achieved if some systems or applications are decommissioned as a result of an MDM program. Systems decommissioning can free people and system resources. It can also result in cost avoidance if there exists a license maintenance cost associated with the decommissioned systems. For the most part, companies tend to add MDM Data Hub systems to their existing environments. An addition of any system, no matter how well it is architected, causes some incremental complexity in the overall system and data management. It is important to look at what workflows can be improved or eliminated and what systems can be decommissioned as a result of the MDM implementation.

Therefore, if systems decommissioning is a part of the program, the decommissioning and related activities should be looked upon as a roadmap dimension. The decommissioning effort can be responsible for some additional costs in the short term but can provide significant long-term operational and cost-reduction benefits.

If systems decommissioning is planned only in the future phases, a decommissioning strategy is still an important consideration that may impact MDM solution design decisions. If the strategy is to phase out a legacy system, the enterprise may not be willing to invest in new integration interfaces for the legacy system that is planned to be decommissioned.

PART IV

Data Hub Usage Style

As we discussed in Part II of this book, three primary MDM usage styles determine the usage focus of MDM:

- Analytical
- Operational
- Collaborative

Analytical MDM concentrates on data warehousing, business intelligence, reporting, and analytical applications. Within an analytical MDM implementation, the Data Hub obtains data from operational systems, processes the data to resolve entities and relationships, and sends high-quality data to the consuming analytical systems. An integration style where the data flows in one direction and bidirectional synchronization is not required results in lower risks and costs. Analytical MDM has the lowest costs and implementation risks.

Operational MDM typically requires bidirectional synchronization between the Data Hub and operational systems, which increases the cost and risk. And Collaborative MDM supports complex workflows and can include the needs to support a supply chain application with multiple branching points that depend on the actions and choices of the workflow stakeholders. This process is quite typical for Product Information Management (PIM) and can be fairly complex.

When the benefits of MDM are estimated, all of the usage styles should be considered. They can collectively contribute to the total value of the benefits of an MDM program. Similarly, the total cost depends on the usage styles and when/where in the MDM roadmap these styles are deployed. The MDM usage style can evolve over phases of the MDM program. From the cost and risk perspectives, a practical approach is to consider beginning the initiative with Analytical MDM. Of course, this is just an option; business requirements can change the focus and usage style implementation sequence (for example, the business prefers an operational MDM focus from the very beginning). This is likely to cause an increase of the implementation cost.

Data Hub Architecture and Data Ownership Style

We have discussed Data Hub architecture and data ownership styles in Part II of this book. The three primary Data Hub styles are

- Registry
- Coexistence
- Hybrid Transaction

Typically, the Registry style, with possibly some hybrid features, is the least risky and the most efficient way to implement the Data Hub while maximizing business benefits and minimizing risks and costs. The Registry style arbitrates the data across multiple operational systems that retain the ownership of the master data.

Contrast this with two scenarios that work in favor of the Transaction style:

- The master entity that is to be managed by the Data Hub has not been supported by the present operations. For instance, an organization wants to build an entity called "Provider" that has not been managed before.

- The other scenario that favors the Transaction Hub choice for implementation applies to projects where the existing processes are already entity-centric (for example, customer centric). The MDM project objective is to replace the existing customer-centric database with a new industrial-strength MDM Data Hub while preserving the entity-centric flows.

For either style, the complexities of the match, merge (attribute survivorship), and split rules should be taken into account; solution options should be analyzed, and associated costs should be estimated.

Data Volumes and Performance Considerations

A Master Data Hub can manage millions and even billions of records. The cost of the hardware depends on these volumes and a variety of performance requirements, such as average transaction rates for reads, writes, and peak transaction rates. The number of physical servers, disc space, and other hardware components needed to support all of the required architectural tiers and components of the solution depends on the data volumes, transactional rates, and availability requirements. This can drastically impact the hardware cost.

Even more importantly, the MDM Data Hub license costs typically depend on the number of records that will be stored in or processed by the Data Hub. The number of records in the Data Hub grows over time. This roadmap view should reflect this consideration to determine how the hardware configuration and price will change over time, and to develop a recommendation and a cost mitigation strategy to establish a vendor agreement that supports an enterprise-acceptable pricing structure.

Reference Data

A typical list of master data domains includes Party, Product, Location, Supplier, Account, Organization, and other entities that may contain many thousands of records.

Each of these domains may include informational attributes (account value, customer credit score, and so on) and reference attributes. For the most part, reference data is represented by relatively static codes created and managed by the enterprise. These codes are important characteristics of master entities. From the application perspective, these codes are found in the lookup tables or displayed in drop-down menus for users to select, or are referenced in some other ways. For instance, accounts managed by the enterprise are characterized by account type. Products are tagged by class, category, type, and brand. Customers can be categorized by marketing segment, category, classification, gender, country of citizenship, and so on. Reference lists are defined and managed, and their codes reconciled for consistent use by the data governance team and the business owners of the data. Reference data reconciliation is an important problem that must be addressed as part of an MDM initiative. Reference code reconciliation can be approached as a work stream of an MDM program or managed as a separate project. Reference data may or may not be managed by the same software as master data. To sum up, if reference data is a part of the MDM program, it is an important view of the MDM roadmap that impacts the MDM initiative's cost.

Deployment Strategy

This roadmap view defines what users will be impacted by the new processes and applications enabled by MDM, as well as when and how.

Significant user acceptance risks are associated with MDM deployment. For instance, bank tellers or customer support representatives may not be involved early enough in the

MDM process. When the business process changes, the end users may be taken by surprise and learn that every time they intend to create a new customer they have to search the Data Hub first. They may also be instructed that every time they speak with a customer they have to verify certain pieces of information and that their performance will be measured by how well they perform these data quality functions.

This type of change, its timing, and user training should be well thought out and properly orchestrated. When end users are impacted, it may be a good idea to deploy the MDM solution for a small but representative group of users first. This partial deployment can represent a challenge, though. It may not be easy to deploy the new solution to some end users while still keeping the other users on the old system and business processes. Thus, deployment is an important view of an MDM roadmap.

Related Initiatives

Some enterprise-wide and even business-specific initiatives can be dependent on MDM. Conversely, the MDM program can be dependent on some other initiatives. These dependencies can represent significant risks and must be addressed by the MDM roadmap.

Some of the related efforts may include:

- A data warehouse project
- Client and Product Hierarchy Management
- CRM initiative
- SOA infrastructure
- Reference Data Management
- Core Banking System
- Trust Accounting System
- Patient Registration System
- Claim Processing System

Each enterprise has its own portfolio of projects that may or may not include some of the projects from this list. This portfolio should be reviewed from the MDM roadmap perspective. A project dependency review can drive changes in MDM planning and impact the vision of MDM priorities. The MDM roadmap document must include a discussion of the key related initiatives, the nature of the dependencies, and how they will be addressed.

Master Data Governance Maturity

Enterprise MDM is built for the benefit of multiple lines of business and therefore has a cross-functional context. An enterprise data governance organization typically represents cross-functional business requirements and brings them to a common set of standards and controls. The maturity of the data governance organization is critical for a successful MDM implementation; in fact, some practitioners call MDM and data governance "siblings."

If the data governance organization is not mature, the absence of data governance policies and a lack of data governance support can increase risks and cause additional costs of the MDM implementation. If the individuals responsible for the MDM program implementation identify weaknesses in data governance, they should ensure that the MDM roadmap includes proper support and evolution of the data governance capabilities required to enable MDM, develop and socialize master data policies, establish a properly functioning data governance council, and define master data quality processes and controls (a detail discussion on data governance is offered in Chapter 17).

Master Data Quality Processes, Metrics, and Technology Support

Whether an MDM initiative has an operational or an analytical focus, master data quality processes are to be established and data quality metrics are to be introduced and continuously measured. These processes must be established by the business and the data governance group.

Master data quality processes, metrics, and technologies supporting these processes and metrics (for example, via a data governance dashboard) should be included in the MDM roadmap as one of its views (see Chapter 17 for a further discussion of MDM and data quality).

Integration with Unstructured Data

A vast majority of MDM initiatives do not include integration with the systems managing unstructured data. The unstructured data includes images, contracts, memos, documents, Microsoft Excel spreadsheets, and similar data. Some industry-specific MDM variants are integrated with unstructured data. For example, EMPI (Enterprise Master Patient Index) implementations, which represent a hospital or medical center variant of MDM, normally include integration of the MDM Data Hub with patients' test results, images produced by X-rays, CT scans, MRI data, and other imaging technologies. This integration is accomplished by a cross-reference between EMPI and the indexes referencing documents, tests, and images. Similarly, pharmaceutical companies are interested in cross-references between the products the company is developing or has developed and the tremendous amount of unstructured data accumulated over the years of laboratory experiments.

Other industries can also benefit from integration between MDM and document management systems. For instance, a mortgage company can benefit from MDM integration with loan contracts and other documents associated with the loan. An enterprise embarking on an MDM initiative should consider the benefits and costs associated with the inclusion of unstructured data in the scope of MDM integration.

If, after careful consideration, an enterprise makes a decision to include integration between MDM and document management systems in the scope of MDM, this integration becomes an important MDM roadmap view.

Multilingual Requirements

So far, the majority of Master Data Management products have been developed in North America, and English is the predominant language these MDM products use. When MDM is implemented in an environment where another language is important, this roadmap view helps understand and estimate the impact of this challenge. The multiple-language–support requirement may result in additional costs and risks of the MDM implementation.

On global MDM projects, multiple languages are used within a single program. This may also apply to bilingual countries such as Canada. A number of areas of complexity are caused by multilingual requirements in MDM. Some of them include the following:

- Matching of records in different languages.
  - By default, the majority of MDM products' phonetic functions work only for English and possibly a few other languages.

- The same applies to the list of equivalencies. For instance, Rob is a likely nickname for Robert, and Bill for William. The Data Hub libraries contain the lists of equivalencies in English. The most established libraries may not include similar equivalency libraries in Russian, Chinese, or Korean.

- Address information is commonly used for matching. The accuracy of matching algorithms and address standardization algorithms can significantly depend on the language and local country standards and customs.

- The use of multiple character sets can create additional complications.

- Oftentimes reference data is altered from one language to another.

Complexity of Cross-Domain Information Sharing

Most MDM implementations are built using a single Data Hub that cross-references the records loaded from multiple source systems. In a number of scenarios, all records cannot be placed in a single database, and even the creation and maintenance of a single index that cross-references all records may not be an option. For instance, when MDM is implemented for multiple countries, country-specific regulations may prevent the storage and processing of their country data in databases maintained in other countries. Similarly, different branches of government are not allowed to store their data in systems managed by other organizations or agencies. Healthcare (patient) information cannot be placed in the same database as social security information.

Even when formally defined regulations do not exist, operational realities and risks associated with the placement of data managed by multiple agencies in a single database (MDM Data Hub) can be significant. This drives nontraditional MDM designs with multiple Data Hubs. These designs may rely on dynamic cross–Data Hub processes and information exchanges. These types of nontraditional implementations represent additional challenges that may result in extra costs. The MDM management team should be able to recognize and articulate requirements for multiple regulatory rules and regulations that restrict data sharing and the storage of data from multiple domains in a single Data Hub.

Complexity of Data Security, Visibility, and Access Control Requirements

Most MDM Data Hubs contain sensitive, private, or confidential information about enterprise business, customers, and products. Therefore, an extensive set of data security, visibility, and access control requirements is applicable to the majority of MDM Data Hub implementations. It is a common practice that an MDM Data Hub must support role-based, policy-driven secured access to data and independent audit capabilities.

For some MDM implementations, data security, visibility, and access control requirements are more stringent than for others. For instance, for wealth management organizations, multiple teams of financial advisors operate under the umbrella of a single financial services company. The majority of corporate and independent financial advisors serve their clients with only limited data sharing, as required by the nature of this business. Advanced needs for data security and visibility in these organizations create significant complexities that become a factor driving the complexity of the MDM program overall and the initiative's cost. We offered an extensive discussion on data security and visibility in MDM environments in Part III of this book.

Resources and Skills

We will list typical work streams of an MDM initiative in Chapter 13. Each MDM program should define these work streams early in the life cycle of the initiative. It is important to follow the principle that one and only one individual should be responsible for a work stream to ensure accountability for planning and execution purposes. The role of program management is to follow and resolve inter–work stream dependencies and conflicting priorities.

Each of the work streams should be staffed with the right resource levels and skills. It may make a significant cost difference whether these skills are available in-house or should be filled with temporary employees or consultants.

Data governance is one of the often underestimated work streams. The data governance organization leads the work stream that includes data stewardship resources. The data governance work stream is responsible for the definition of data stewardship needs, data stewardship responsibilities, and other requirements that drive the number of data stewards, their activities, their functions, and the incremental costs.

Testing is another work stream that has been often underestimated on large MDM initiatives. Testing for an MDM Data Hub project requires skills that go beyond the traditional testing of application logic. MDM Data Hub testing may require comprehensive data testing and Web Services testing skills.

Enabling Technologies: ETL, SOA, and ESB

If MDM requires real-time or near-real-time integration with operational systems, the attention to and reliance on service-oriented architecture and technologies such as SOA infrastructure and Enterprise Service Bus (ESB) is very important. These technologies can significantly facilitate an MDM implementation from the integration perspective. On the other hand, the absence of a real-time integration infrastructure can become a considerable impediment for an MDM program.

Similar considerations apply to data quality technologies and ETL. Most companies embarking on MDM had previously acquired ETL and some data quality software. If this assumption does not hold, it is important to consider these technologies and their integration in the scope of MDM.

Conclusion

To sum up, in this chapter we discussed two related topics:

- MDM business case and justification of MDM
- Development of an MDM roadmap

We started with a discussion of the importance of the business case for MDM, as well as its challenges, methods, and techniques that can be used for MDM justification. Then we focused on the importance of the MDM roadmap. We explained why the MDM business case and roadmap should be considered together. The MDM roadmap defines the evolution of MDM and critical architectural and organizational decisions that impact the MDM initiative's cost, risk, risk mitigation strategies, and ultimately the ROI and NPV.

We have identified and described 20 critical MDM roadmap views. Each of these views should be considered at the inception, when an MDM initiative is planned, and then reviewed periodically as the program evolves. The 20 MDM roadmap views provide a fairly comprehensive framework of the most critical MDM areas. A periodic review of the critical MDM roadmap views and their refinement can help significantly to properly initiate and execute MDM programs. Clearly, the relative importance of the roadmap views varies from one MDM initiative to another. Even within a single MDM program, the relative importance of the roadmap views can change as the program evolves.

We will continue our discussion of key MDM implementation aspects in the subsequent chapters.

References

1. Page, Rick. *Hope is Not a Strategy: The 6 Keys to Winning the Complex Sale.* (March 2003).

2. Karel, Rob. "The ROI for Master Data Management." Forrester Research, Inc., October 29, 2008. (Available online from Forrester Research, Inc.)

3. Linthicum, David. "Defining the ROI for Data Integration." http://blogs.informatica .com/perspectives/index.php/2009/09/23/defining-the-roi-for-data-integration/.

4. Jones, Nathan. "20 Reasons for Data Quality in Charts of Accounts and Internal Organisation." Information and Decisions, December 16, 2009. http://nathanjones .wordpress.com/2009/12/16/20-reasons-for-data-quality-in-charts-of-accounts-and-internal-organisation/.

5. Liliendahl Sorensen, Henrik. "55 Reasons to Improve Data Quality." Liliendahl on Data Quality, http://liliendahl.wordpress.com/2009/11/22/55-reasons-to-improve-data-quality/.

6. Africa, Andrew. "Rely on Data Quality to Survive." InfoManagement Direct, August 20, 2009. http://www.information-management.com/infodirect/2009_135/ data_quality_economy_it_business_intelligence_bi-10015920-1.html?ET=informatio nmgmt:e1080:2188289a:&st=email.

7. Joshi, Nitin. "Quantifying Business Value in Master Data Management." InfoManagement Direct, September 3, 2009. http://www.information-management .com/infodirect/2009_137/master_data_management-10016016-1.html.

8. Jones, Dylan. "Using Metrics to Assert a Business Case for Data Quality." Data Quality Pro, November 2009. http://www.dataqualitypro.com/data-quality-home/ using-metrics-to-assert-a-business-case-for-data-quality.html.

9. Berson, Alex, Smith, Stephen, and Thearling, Kurt. *Building Data Mining Applications for CRM.* McGraw-Hill (December 1999).

10. Hillard, Robert and Sean McClowry. "Economic Value of Information." Mike 2.0. http://mike2.openmethodology.org/wiki/Economic_Value_of_Information.

11. Loshin, David. *Master Data Management.* The MK/OMG Press (September 2008).

12. Dubov, Lawrence. "Estimating the Benefits for MDM." Mastering Data Management, February 23, 2010. http://blog.initiate.com/index.php/2010/02/23/ estimating-the-benefits-of-mdm/.

13. Dubov, Lawrence. "Master Data Management: Importance of Relationship Management." Information Management, March 19, 2009. http://www.information-management.com/specialreports/2009_132/10015070-1.html. TMCNet.com, April 8, 2009. http://callcenterinfo.tmcnet.com/Analysis/articles/53858-master-data-management-importance-relationship-management.htm.

14. Linthicum, David. "The Importance of Relationship Management with MDM." Ebiz, April 16, 2009. http://www.ebizq.net/blogs/linthicum/2009/04/the_importance_of_relationship.php.

15. Isler, Adam. "MDM and Relationship Linking." Intelligent Database Marketing, March 25, 2009. http://pntblog.com/2009/03/25/mdm-and-relationship-linking/.

16. Dubov, Lawrence. Series: Building and MDM Roadmap. April 13, 2010. http://blog.initiate.com/index.php/2010/04/13/series-building-an-mdm-roadmap/.

PART IV

13

Project Initiation

I n the previous chapter we showed the approaches to building a robust and compelling business case for the MDM initiative, and also demonstrated the value and the scope of the MDM roadmap. At this point, let's assume that the business case, the initial definition of the MDM roadmap, and the business drivers, objectives, and value propositions for the overall MDM program or specific MDM projects have been established and agreed upon within the organization. This agreement should result in senior management's issuing marching orders to the Information Technology organization to proceed with the project.

Senior management will want to know how the project is to be organized and planned and the major project or program milestones. Senior management will also want to know how much this project would cost to develop and deploy. What should the IT organization do to translate business objectives and the roadmap into IT vision, strategy, and resource-loaded project plans, in order to successfully implement the project? Senior management will want to see the end-state vision across all business and technology domains, and will ask a number of key questions, such as how the currently ongoing projects should be modified, aligned, and prioritized in the context of the MDM project. Many of the questions have been answered to some extent by the business case and MDM roadmap definitional activities. In this chapter we concentrate on the further details and specifics of starting and running an already approved MDM project.

Implementation Begins

As we stated in Chapter 12, one of the key management challenges of MDM projects is the need to define the project's success criteria. When asked informally, IT executives may provide very different answers to the question of how to decide if the project is successful, including answers such as "Have better quality data," "Improve application functionality," "Achieve regulatory compliance faster," and "Keep the end users happy." In practice, MDM projects should be based on a compelling, business strategy–driven and/or IT strategy–driven, agreed-upon and approved business case, and follow an MDM capabilities roadmap with a sound release strategy that defines what will be implemented and deployed, and when. Key components of this roadmap are clearly defined short-term and long-term success criteria that need to be understood and agreed upon by all stakeholders.

Of course, the tasks of defining the road map and success criteria would be so much easier to accomplish if there were a single strategy and solution architecture that works for all MDM implementations. Unfortunately, that is not the case. As we mentioned earlier, MDM projects address multiple, often diverse business requirements, involve a broad spectrum of technical disciplines, and can be extremely complex.

Addressing the Complexity of MDM Projects

At a high level all MDM projects are quite similar. For example, all MDM projects that focus on Customer domain have common goals of delivering an authoritative system of record for customer data that represents a complete, 360-degree view of customer including the totality of the relationships the customer has with the organization. At this high level, project management and all key stakeholders are enthusiastic and are in "violent" agreement about the capabilities and opportunities offered by the MDM Customer system.

The devil is in the details. And there are *many* details to consider. At the beginning and in the course of an MDM project, the wide variety of questions, issues, and dependencies may appear so overwhelming that the initiative's stakeholders feel like the fishermen in the movie *The Perfect Storm*. The characters of the film were practically helpless before the fury of the ocean. The situation may seem similarly unmanageable for the participants of some MDM projects. Many large MDM projects failed with dire consequences for the company and people who worked on the project. We will discuss risks and reasons for project failure in Chapter 19.

To illustrate the diversity and criticality of the expectations of the MDM project stakeholders, let's briefly recap key questions and concerns of senior management relevant to the MDM:

- How will the equity value and market capitalization of the company change as a result of the MDM project?
- What is the first set of applications and business functions that would become the early adopters and beneficiaries of the MDM project?
- What are the phase-by-phase and total project costs, ROI, and/or NPV?
- How will the new business processes be different?
- What will it take to accomplish the transition to the new business processes?
- What additional skills, both business and technology, will the organization's staff members have to acquire and how?
- Will the organizational structure be affected, and to what extent?
- What legacy systems and functions will be affected and how?
- How will the project be organized and planned?
- What are the major milestones and releases?
- Does the technology organization have adequate knowledge, resources, and understanding of industry best practices in order to translate business objectives into IT vision, strategy, actionable road map and project plans, and successfully implement the project?
- What are the investment and delivery risks and mitigation strategies?
- What is the end-state vision that would impact business and technology domains?

- How should the current in-flight initiatives be modified, aligned, and prioritized in light of starting an MDM project?
- What are the success criteria for each phase and for the project overall?

MDM Ecosystem

From the overall program/project management perspective, it becomes increasingly clear that due to the variety of conditions and the complexity of MDM projects, it is difficult to define a single one-size-fits-all set of recommendations. Moreover, we showed in the previous chapter that a comprehensive MDM project roadmap includes at least 20 roadmap domains:

1. Business Benefits
2. Systems and Applications in Scope of MDM
3. Data Domains, Entities, and High-Level Data Model
4. Relationships, Hierarchies, and Metadata
5. Third-Party Data Sources
6. Systems Decommissioning Strategy
7. Data Hub Usage Style
8. Data Hub Architecture and Ownership Style
9. Data Volume, Performance, and Scalability Considerations
10. Reference Data Management
11. Deployment Strategies and User Groups
12. Related Initiatives
13. Master Data Governance Maturity
14. Master Data Quality Processes, Metrics, and Technology Support
15. Integration with Unstructured Data
16. Multilingual Requirements
17. Complexity of Cross-Domain Information Sharing
18. Complexity of Data Security and Visibility Requirements
19. People Resources and Skills
20. Data Quality Technologies: ETL, SOA, and ESB

All these factors and considerations contribute to the overall complexity of any MDM project. Experience shows that an effective working approach to manage this complexity and address broadly diverse problems such as the ones presented by MDM is to define a comprehensive solution framework that is designed around sound problem-solving design patterns and architecture principles, including separation of concerns, layered architecture, federation, and service orientation (please see Part II for more details on the architecture framework and design principles). Such a framework allows us to use industry best practices for particular areas of concern, and to break down the problem domain into smaller and more manageable pieces. At a more granular level the tasks and decision-making points are much more common and manageable across MDM projects. We will follow this approach and break down the MDM problem domain into work streams and components that support and are supported by what we define as the MDM "ecosystem." The areas of concerns and key components that constitute a general MDM "ecosystem" are shown in Figure 13-1. We discuss most of them throughout this book in more detail.

The MDM "ecosystem" is a layered construct that includes business processes and technical domains of change. In the case of MDM for Customer domain, the core MDM functional area includes:

- Customer identification, matching, correlation, hierarchies, relationships, and grouping
- Information quality
- External data providers

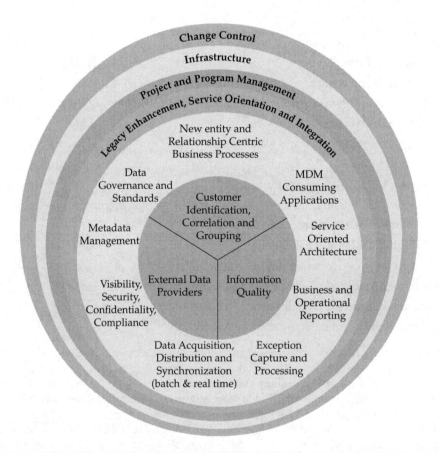

Figure 13-1   MDM "ecosystem": high-level areas of the solution

---

NOTE *The first area in this list is specific to the MDM for Customer domain. It is easy to see that this focus on the customer can be substituted or complemented by other domains such as Products, Organizations, Locations, and so on.*

The layer immediately surrounding the MDM core is a key part of the MDM "ecosystem" even though it includes some components that support both MDM and non-MDM environments. We discuss various aspects of these components throughout the book.

As we continue to "peel" the layers of the MDM "ecosystem," we can see the components and services that do not necessarily represent "pure" MDM functionality, but are affected and/or required by the MDM system to function. For example, the legacy layer demonstrates these dual properties—it is usually the source of MDM data and is a key consumer of new functionality enabled by the MDM platform.

Similarly, the outer layers of the MDM "ecosystem" cover Infrastructure, Project/Program Management, and Change Control. These areas of concern are vital for any successful project, including MDM implementations. Indeed, it is hard to imagine a project of MDM magnitude that can be successful without considering infrastructure issues or providing adequate program management and change control.

MDM-related areas of the "ecosystem" contain components that have to be acquired or built. Thus, the MDM "ecosystem" also provides a framework for "buy vs. build" decisions. These decisions are not easy to make, especially considering that many vendor products in the MDM space provide similar, often overlapping capabilities, and the resulting market focus and positioning of many MDM vendors continues to change. For example, ETL and data synchronization vendors are moving into the Information Quality space, and Information Quality vendors are extending their capabilities toward MDM Data Hubs. A discussion of the vendor landscape and their product features can be found in Chapter 18.

Socializing the MDM Project with the Stakeholders

The complexity of the MDM problem space requires the participation of multiple stakeholders. This, in turn, creates a formidable socialization problem. The idea of bringing all people onto the same page on all issues can easily paralyze any initiative. While consensus building is a good strategy, we need to remember that both unlimited democracy and military-style Command and Control decision making can cause large initiatives to fail. Best practices suggest to set up a small leadership group that can successfully combine principles of strong management control and decision making with principles of sharing information and keeping all participants on common ground in key areas.

Sample Workshop Agenda

- State project goals and senior management concerns.
- Define and agree on the end-state of the solution and what it means from both business and technology points of view.
- Discuss the types of partners and vendors that will be required to achieve the objectives.
- Define and socialize the project's organizational structure and project governance.

(continued)

PART IV

- Discuss a high-level roadmap.
- Determine project success criteria.
- Analyze cost and business benefits of the project.
- Discuss the timeline, content, and the deliverables of the project on a phase-by-phase basis.
- Build consensus between the business and technology teams as the decision on "What should the first release look like?" is made.

Of course, every time you want diverse groups such as business and technology teams to agree, you have to overcome the challenge of each group looking at the problem from its own perspective. Using the comprehensive solution framework described throughout this book should help the reader to manage the discussions about the project and to make decisions that each project team can be comfortable with.

It is a good idea to start an MDM project with a well-structured workshop where the business vision and technology approach will be discussed. Two or three days spent as a team can be very beneficial to jump-starting the project by getting high-level agreement on a number of key issues.

Using a multi-phased approach to an MDM project is clearly a good strategy. The outcome of the first phase (first release of the MDM solution) should be thought of as a trade-off between what the business and executive management ultimately need and what is achievable in a single release. A practical rule of thumb is that each phase should not exceed six to eight months and should deliver tangible, business-recognizable benefits. Credibility of the project will be at stake if a year has gone by and no changes have been implemented. Enterprise-level planning should be in place to ensure successful cross-departmental delivery.

When an MDM project is initiated, the IT group should have access to business-sponsored documents that define the business case by business function and line of business. This set of business requirements documents should include the following:

- Formulation of business problems as they relate to MDM
- Definition of the business scope, including articulations of the new business processes
- Strategic business vision and objectives
- Business drivers and priorities
- ROI or Economic Value estimation for MDM implementation

Considering the complexity and potential breadth of the impact an MDM solution may have on the organization, defining the scope is one of the key factors that determines the actual or perceived success or failure of the MDM project.

Scope Definition

When we discuss MDM projects, we should realize that the scope of these projects is a multidimensional matter. The most important dimensions are shown in Figure 13-2 and discussed in this section.

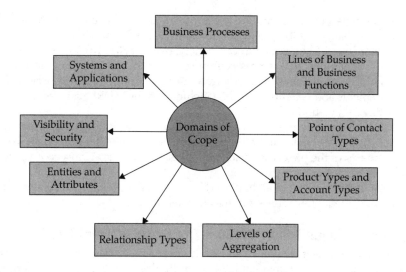

FIGURE 13-2
Domains of scope

Figure 13-2 contents: Business Processes; Lines of Business and Business Functions; Point of Contact Types; Product Yypes and Account Types; Levels of Aggregation; Relationship Types; Entities and Attributes; Visibility and Security; Systems and Applications; Domains of Ccope

Business Processes

It is critically important to understand what business processes need to be improved. Without a clear understanding of what business processes will be improved and how, the entire effort may turn into a costly and most likely useless endeavor. Starting from the business objectives, drivers, and value propositions, the technology group should work with the business team to document the current state of the business processes that need to be improved. There are many methodologies on how to define and document business processes. The Rational Unified Process (RUP) is one of the better-known methodologies used for this purpose. RUP uses a concept of use cases as the core of business process analysis and definition. There are a number of excellent tutorials and references describing RUP, such as Philippe Kruchten's book.[1]

Once the current state of the business processes and their weaknesses are defined and documented, the target-state business processes need to be determined. There are many techniques and methodologies on business process improvement and reengineering.[2]

What level of granularity in the business process definition is sufficient? If you need to describe the process of lawn mowing, you can do it at a high level, for example, get the lawn mower, turn it on, mow the lawn, clean the lawn mower, and put it back. Alternatively, you can describe this process with more granularity and show decision points, for example, what happens if you do not have enough gas, or what you do if the tool breaks, or how do you trim corners that cannot be reached by the lawnmower. The required granularity of the business process should be at the level of detail that is sufficient to define the logical data model of the MDM solution. This brings us to an important point. The data modelers should work closely with the business process development team to provide input and pose questions driving the depth of the business process coverage. Refer to the discussion on data modeling aspects of the MDM solution in Chapter 7 of this book.

Lines of Business and Functions

One of the outcomes of the creation and analysis of the business requirements for the project is the determination of new and impacted legacy business processes. At the same time, the requirements should specify the needs of key lines of business and business functions that drive the change. At that point, the requirements analysis should determine whether there are other lines of business that can benefit from the MDM-driven change. The perspective of these other lines of business is important for the enterprise in order to understand that additional benefits can be realized from implementing the MDM project. These additional requirements and benefits should be included in the MDM business case and may strengthen its value proposition.

In addition, a comprehensive view presented by all lines of business and functions early in the project life cycle can help understand constraints that otherwise would be revealed at later phases of the project with additional risks and costs always accompanying late changes in project planning and execution.

An understanding of all impacted lines of business should also help in building a project team that adequately represents all interested parties.

Customer Touch Points, Product Types, and Account Types

Modern enterprises frequently use multiple channels that support various customer touch points, where the customer could be an individual, an institutional customer, a partner, a supplier, and so on. For instance, individual customers can interact with a hotel chain by phone, personally in the hotel lobby, online over e-mail and the Internet, by mail, and so on. The same channels may provide additional touch points for customers who participate in hotel membership clubs or are hotel credit card holders; alternatively, the same channels can be used by travel agencies or the company's travel department. Similar variety in the touch points exists in the financial services and other industries.

Analyzing the channel and touch point requirements helps bring into focus additional perspectives and questions that can impact the scope of the MDM project. Specifically, the customer data presented at different touch points may vary significantly, and as a result may impact the identification and matching process, data visibility, and security approaches. More generally, the channel and touch point properties have an impact on any master data entities that are available and accessible via these channels. We will discuss entity identification and matching in more detail in Chapter 14. Visibility and security are discussed in depth in Part III of the book.

A typical enterprise normally offers and serves many product types to its customers. In the financial services industry, for example, products are often linked to or represented by account types such as Wealth Management Account, Cash Management Account, 401K Retirement Account, and so on. Other industries also have a strong emphasis on products. For example, a telecommunications company can offer and provide local, long distance, and international phone service; Internet connectivity; wireless connectivity services; satellite or cable TV services; and so on. They may also offer their private label credit card and other financial instruments.

As industries define their specific portfolios of products and services, this view is very important to adequately define the scope and priorities of the planned MDM effort. This understanding can help bring a valuable perspective from the groups of existing or new stakeholders of the MDM project.

Levels of Aggregation and Relationship Types

This dimension of scope defines how the data should be aggregated. Typically data aggregation is an area discussed within data warehousing projects. If a data warehouse has already been built, the MDM project scope should answer the question of whether the MDM Data Hub will feed the data warehouse in the future and how the existing processes will be impacted. If the data warehouse is not yet available, we do not recommend mixing the MDM Data Hub project and a data warehousing effort, even though interdependencies between the two efforts should be well understood.

Although the creation of multiple data aggregation layers is not the primary focus of the MDM Data Hub, we should consider a data aggregation view that is directly associated with MDM Data Hubs. This particular data aggregation view is also known as a "single version of truth" for master data. We defined this new, MDM-inspired and -managed data aggregation view in Parts I and II of the book.

Indeed, a typical enterprise does not want to get rid of all of its customer records, even though some of them may exist in multiple versions. Thus, customer data aggregation enabled by an MDM Data Hub may reveal an enterprise's intent to preserve and maintain the existing redundant customer records along with the new single version of truth for customer data. This is true for other data domains as well, so we'll try to generalize these discussions by referring to master data entities throughout this chapter, and will revert to specific data domains such as Customer or Product only when the differences between the domain-related concerns warrant such specificity. Because by definition an MDM platform integrates all available data about the master entities into the authoritative system of record, this single version of truth represents an aggregated data view. We discuss MDM data aggregation in more detail in Chapter 14.

A discussion of relationship types that have to be supported and managed by the MDM platform is another important dimension of scope. MDM and entity relationships are discussed in Chapter 15.

Entities and Attributes

As the MDM project is initiated, an initial logical/canonical data model of the integrated solution should include all entities, key attributes, and other attributes (to the extent possible at this early project stage) required by the integrated solution regardless of which systems these data elements reside in at present. The canonical data model, described in Chapter 7, defines the entities in scope, and the relationships between the entities and data attributes in scope no matter where they physically reside.

Clearly, to enable proper MDM functionality, the data attributes used for entity resolution should be included in the model. However, some of the data attributes and entity types may not be available in any of the existing systems at all. Such a logical data model provides the organization with a technique to abstract their analysis from the complexities of the existing data structures and develop a desired consolidated data model that represents the business vision correctly.

It is not always easy to conceptualize the enterprise vision and abstract it from the organizational realities. Therefore, we highly recommend finding the right external partners specializing in logical data modeling, preferably with deep expertise in an appropriate subject area domain (that is, customer, product, subscriber, and so on.). Some domain-specific data models are published by their owners or vendors. As an example, see *The Data Model Resource Book* by Len Silverston.[3,4,5] If you feel that the data models recommended by your partners do not entirely fit your organizational needs, which is not uncommon, your organization would still benefit from the experience of data modelers who have built proven industry-specific models. It is also very useful for project direction to get a clear understanding of why the industry model does not fit your organization's business model. Whether you buy a data model from an external source or decide to develop it internally, discussions about the choices you need to consider in developing and deploying the data model for the MDM platform will enable the organization to establish a logical data model that defines the scope of the solution from the data attributes' perspective.

There are other considerations that drive the scope of the canonical model. In addition to the initial scope, the team should determine the scope of the incremental data model changes as the MDM platform evolves from one release to the next.

Systems and Applications in Scope

Systems and applications are another important dimension of scope. Specifically, in a typical MDM Data Hub the data is sourced from multiple systems. A key question to answer is, when the MDM Data Hub is in production, how will the current systems be affected? Some applications and systems may have to be phased out, which is a significant scope issue that also determines the end-state of the solution and the work in the legacy system areas that must be planned.

Alternatively, existing legacy systems may have to coexist with the Data Hub. The discussion of what such a coexistence means will lead us to the topic of the next section about the MDM Data Hub solution architecture.

MDM Data Hub Solution Architecture

As the process of the project scope definition reaches a point where the team gains a consensus about entities, data attributes, products/account types, and other business requirements, the MDM project can move into the next phase to decide upon architectural choices for the MDM Data Hub. MDM products and solutions known as MDM Data Hubs are designed to support data structures, functions, and services that enable rationalization, integration, and delivery of master data across multiple data domains. A conceptual MDM Data Hub architecture, described in detail in Part II of the book, recognizes a number of options that can be used to solve master data creation and continuous integration problems in the context of the business requirements of a given enterprise. Let's review these architecture options as they have been defined by several industry analysts, most notably by the industry research firm The Gartner Group. Although the extensive discussion on the MDM architecture viewpoints, and specifically on the Design and Deployment architecture dimension (sometimes referred to as MDM data ownership and architecture styles) has been provided in Part II of this book, the follow-on section in this chapter provides an implementation analysis of the MDM architecture styles and offers some insights into and variations of the architecture options for these styles, which are based on the authors' practical experience implementing MDM solutions.

Data Hub Architecture Styles

Using the architecture framework approach introduced in Part II of the book, we can recognize some generally accepted architecture "styles" as the architecture viewpoints that determine the way the MDM system is intended to be used and kept reliably in sync with its data providers (data sources) and data consumers. These viewpoints represent an intersection of the functional and data dimensions of the enterprise architecture framework at the logical, conceptual, and contextual levels. Specifically, let's review the three most popular MDM architecture styles.

Registry Hub

The Registry-style Data Hub uses a metadata repository, or a stand-alone Data Attribute directory that points to the locations of the data attributes using specialized Data Hub services called the Attribute Locator service and the Metadata service (see Chapters 4–6 for more details on the Data Hub services). Figure 13-3 illustrates the way the Registry-style Hub operates. For instance, the metadata repository should store the rules about the retrieval of the "best" entity attributes (for example, a customer name), the "best" (that is, authoritative) source for entity type (for example, account type), and so on. The rules can be complex enough to take into account multiple conditions and scenarios. The Data Hub of this style stores only key identifiers and links them to the fragments of master data in source systems. In addition, the Registry-style Data Hub supports data transformations necessary to achieve semantic consistency and reconciliation. The Registry-style Data Hub provides a real-time reference by dynamically assembling an integrated but read-only master data view from the source systems.

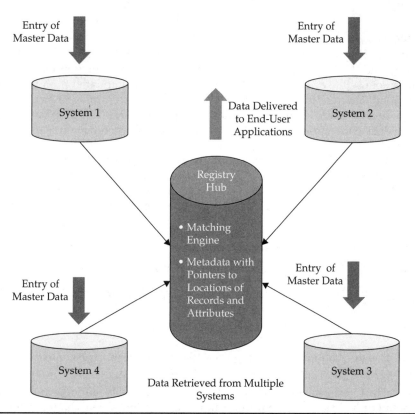

FIGURE 13-3   Registry Hub

The Registry Hub is the right choice if the company's strategy is to preserve the existing systems and invest their development funds to fix and enhance legacy systems over time. Considerations for and against a Registry-style Data Hub are shown in the following list.

Pros:

- The lowest-cost master data integration solution.
- The data flow changes are limited and implementation risks are minimized.
- Only limited data reconciliation between the legacy and the new Data Hub systems is required.

Cons:

- If the Data Hub has to support complex business rules including data survivorship, the data access (query) performance of the Hub can be an issue. The term "data survivorship" refers to the rules defining how to assemble a single record from two or more records with overlapping attributes that may contain conflicting values. In this case the attributes "compete" for survivorship to resolve the conflicts.
- Query performance represents an even bigger concern when multiple systems must be accessed to retrieve the data.

Coexistence Hub

The Coexistence Hub architecture style of the Data Hub (see Figure 13-4) physically stores some master data along with referencing some other data in the source systems. This Data Hub style is not used to directly originate transactions, but is updated from the source systems that initiate transactions. The Data Hub is used as a central reference point for master data. In addition to the master entities, this style of MDM Data Hub can also store relationship data, entity grouping, and so on, with specifics dependent on the industry and organizational needs.

The Coexistence Hub bridges some gaps in the existing systems. It is the right choice if the company's strategy is to partially preserve the existing systems and decommission at least some of the legacy systems. The Coexistence Hub style is sometimes used as a step toward a Transaction Hub. Its advantages and disadvantages are summarized in the following list.

Pros:

- The Coexistence Data Hub solution cost is relatively low.
- Data flow is limited to unidirectional synchronization.
- Data retrieval performance issues are resolved by storing certain data attributes in the Data Hub. The complexity of data transformation is moved to ETL.

Cons:

- ETL transformations that are required to maintain Data Hub content can be fairly complex.
- Since the Coexistence-style Data Hub assumes some data redundancy, its design should provide for synchronization and reconciliation of data changes between the source systems and the Data Hub.

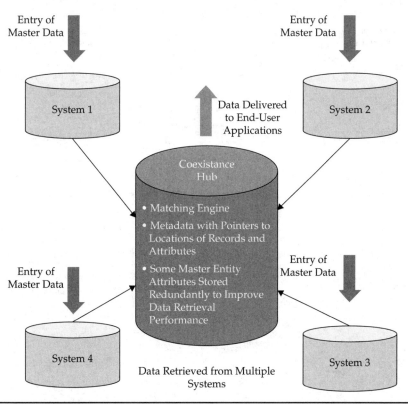

Entry of
Master Data

Entry of
Master Data

System 1

Data Delivered
to End-User
Applications

System 2

Coexistance
Hub

- Matching Engine
- Metadata with Pointers to Locations of Records and Attributes
- Some Master Entity Attributes Stored Redundantly to Improve Data Retrieval Performance

Entry of
Master Data

Entry of
Master Data

System 4

System 3

Data Retrieved from Multiple
Systems

FIGURE 13-4   Coexistence Hub

Transaction Hub

This Data Hub style physically stores the master entities and is used as the authoritative system of record for master data, as shown in Figure 13-5. This style of Data Hub supports services that apply data access transactions directly to the Data Hub and generate messages or batch files that publish the results of the transactions to the systems external to the Data Hub. The Transaction Hub is the right choice when the organization does not intend to invest additional money and resources in the source systems for the data domains where the Data Hub must become the master. In this case, a prudent approach is to prepare to support significant data flow changes in the existing system structure, including the decommissioning of some of the legacy systems. Transaction Hub advantages and disadvantages are shown in the following list.

Pros:

- This is a comprehensive solution that can be used to phase out obsolete legacy systems.

- This architecture style of the Data Hub allows organizations to achieve at least one of the major MDM goals—the creation of an accurate, timely, and complete system of record that maintains just-in-time data accuracy and integrity.

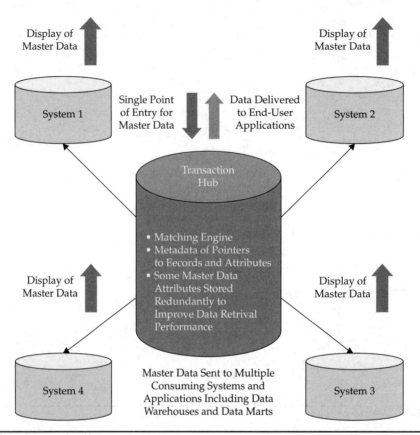

Cons:

- This architecture style of the Data Hub results in the highest complexity of ETL implementation.

- This style requires complex real-time synchronization and reconciliation. Therefore, it usually demands the highest cost and implementation risk. The complexity of data synchronization is discussed in Chapter 16.

- This style requires that careful attention is paid to the extensibility and scalability aspects of the Data Hub design by including MDM services and components such as a robust metadata repository and Record and Attributor Location services so that on-boarding new systems and data sources does not require a significant or complete overhaul of the MDM system.

The taxonomy of the three architecture styles illustrates an interesting pattern: The richness of the Data Hub functionality and the complexity and the associated risks of MDM implementations increase as the Hub stores and manages more and more entities and attributes of master data. Therefore, MDM projects need to carefully evaluate the benefits and risks associated with each approach and decide on the appropriate balance of these factors for implementing an MDM solution in a phased, risk-managed fashion.

Phased Implementation of Customer Data Hub

Even if an ultimate goal of the MDM project is to develop a Transaction Hub solution, in order to achieve this goal and to manage the risks and impact of implementing a Transaction Hub, an MDM project typically begins with a "slim" Data Hub implementation. The plan should be to evolve the Data Hub by increasing the number of data attributes for which it acts as a master. As the Data Hub data scope grows, so does the value that the Data Hub provides to the organization. From the project management point of view, this evolutionary change should be organized into well-defined project phases, starting with the Project Initiation phase, which is the subject of this chapter.

Using this approach as a guide, we recommend a somewhat different categorization of the MDM Data Hub styles that are more aligned with phased implementation as shown in Figure 13-6.

Phase 1: Hub "Slave"	Phase 2: Hub "Slave" Enhanced	Phase 3: Hub "Master"
Data Governance • Reference Data • Data Cleansing in Source • Data Cleansing during Transformations Buy vs Build and Client Hub Vendor Selection • Data-Model Specific • Data-Model-Agnostic Entity Identification (matching) and Data Quality Vendor Selection • Deterministic Match • Probabilistic Match Key Generation Cross-Reference Loading and Synchronizing the Hub Visibility and Security at the Record Level Limited to View Only	Additional Attributes, LOBs, and Systems Attribute Level Visibility and Security Solution All Entity Types (Account, Party, Product, Organization, etc.) Globalization Enhanced Entity Identification Capabilities Based on Improved Data Quality and Stewardship Comprehensive Reference Data Translations Visibility and Security at the Attribute Level Legacy System/Functionality Phase-Out Road map	Direct Updates against the Hub Inverse Data Flows to Support Hub Master Scenario for Selected Fields Entity Identification Enhanced by End-User Input • Merge • Split • Data Enrichment Comprehensive Visibility and Security Implementation Legacy Dystem/Functionality Phase-Out Comprehensive Transactional Semantics Comprehensive Visibility and Security Solution Including Support for Direct Data Changes in the Hub

FIGURE 13-6 Data Hub phased implementation

Artifacts That Should Be Produced in the Project Initiation Phase

Typical artifacts that are to be produced at the end of the Project Initiation phase are shown in the following list:

- Business process analysis (current state)
- Requirements for business process improvement and re-engineering (desired target state of the business processes)
  - Incremental business process changes by release
  - Incremental benefits by business function and line of business
- State of the solution architecture by release
- Conceptual and logical data model of the integrated solution and how it ties back to the business processes
- Scope and priority definitions in terms of data attributes, entity/products/account types, and lines of business
- Solution architecture and the architecture roadmap indicating how the architecture evolves with the implementation releases
- Vendor product evaluation criteria, buy vs. build decision, and tool recommendation/ selection for the key areas of MDM Data Hub functionality

Project Work Streams

In the beginning of this chapter we mentioned that an effective methodology to managing complex projects such as a MDM Data Hub is to use a phased approach and organize the work and resources into a number of interconnected and interdependent work streams. The following work streams typically represent the body of work that needs to be planned and executed:

- Entity resolution—Entity (for example, customer/account, legal entities) groups and relationships
- Data governance, standards, quality, and compliance
- Data architecture
- Metadata and related services, including Record Locator service, Attribute Locator service, and Metadata Repository service
- Initial data load
- Inbound data processing (batch and real-time)
- Outbound data processing (batch and real-time)
- Changes to legacy systems and applications
- Visibility and security
- Exception processing
- Infrastructure

- Data Hub applications
- Reporting requirements of a stratified user community
- Testing
- Release management
- Deployment
- Training
- Project management

To sum up, if you are planning to embark on an MDM effort, this list can be used as a guide to build a detailed project plan including appropriate resources and the project team composition. Each of these work streams should have clearly defined deliverables that have to be aligned at the entire project level in order to produce a cohesive and comprehensive solution. Although these work streams define different interdependent efforts that prevent the work streams from being executed in a totally parallel fashion, many of these work streams can be structured so that their dependency on each other is minimized and the overall project timeline is optimized to parallelize as much work as possible. We will cover the areas addressed by these work streams in the chapters that follow.

References

1. Kruchten, Philippe. *The Rational Unified Process: An Introduction, Third Edition.* Addison-Wesley (2003).

2. Jeston, John and Johan Nelis. *Business Process Management: Practical Guidelines to Successful Implementations.* Butterworth-Heinemann (2006).

3. Silverston, Len. *The Data Model Resource Book, Vol. 1: A Library of Universal Data Models for All Enterprises.* Wiley Computer Publishing (March 2001).

4. Silverston, Len. *The Data Model Resource Book, Revised Edition, Vol. 2: A Library of Universal Data Models For Specific Industries.* Wiley Computer Publishing (March 2001).

5. Silverston, Len and Angew, Paul. *The Data Model Resource Book, Vol. 3: Universal Patterns for Data Modeling.* Wiley Computer Publishing (January 2009).

PART IV

14 CHAPTER

Entity Resolution: Identification, Matching, Aggregation, and Holistic View of the Master Objects

As we already mentioned in Part I and discussed in more detail in Part II of this book, entity resolution—and in particular the ability to recognize, uniquely identify, match, and link entities—is at the heart of MDM. Specifically, we showed that a conceptual MDM data model that can support a customer-centric business such as retail banking, institutional banking, personal insurance, or commercial insurance is known as a *party-centric* model, and it may consist of a number of entities and attributes, including party/customer, party profile, account, party group, location, demographics, relationships, channels, products, events, and privacy preferences. Some of the key attributes of this model include identity attributes used to uniquely identify the party entities as a collection or cluster of individual detail-level records.

We also showed that when we deal with the Product domain, the challenge of identifying, matching, and linking entities is much harder, and not just for managing hierarchies of product entities, but for the fundamental activities of matching product entities that appear to be at the same levels in a given hierarchy. Moreover, we showed that the techniques and approaches to entity resolution in the Product domain are often based on semantics-driven rather than syntax-driven analysis. The semantics analysis is much more complex, and would make our discussion of entity identification harder to present within a single chapter. Therefore, in this chapter we focus our attention on discussing approaches, techniques, and concerns of the key aspect of entity resolution—entity identification—where the entity is the customer or a party.

The goal of entity identification is to enable and support accurate and timely information about each master entity. In the case of MDM for the Customer domain, entity identification enables the MDM system to create and maintain accurate and timely information about the customer (an individual or an organization) that has past, current, or potential future relationships with the enterprise regardless of what business unit actually owns those relationships. Clearly, the sales and marketing department will want to know the nature of interested parties that have or had some relationships or points of contact with the company but may never have been the company's customer. Furthermore, a party may have multiple relationships with the enterprise. These relationships should be tracked across channels, lines of business, and contact types. In a variety of businesses, for legal and compliance reasons the company may need to know about the employees who are also the company's customers.

A more complex question the company may want to answer is whether its employee or an existing customer has a professional relationship with other existing customers, for example, their attorney, accountant, or any other interested party.

Generally speaking, the first step in entity identification is the ability to identify an entity in the most granular way that makes sense for the enterprise. The granularity level also depends on the way the source data is stored in legacy systems. Reconciling various degrees of granularity represents one of the challenges that needs to be addressed for efficient entity identification. Although this general approach can be applied to all types of entities, we want to turn our attention to the specifics of the MDM for the Customer domain because most of the challenges, approaches, and concerns of entity identifications can be effectively illustrated in the context of customer identification. More often than not, customer data resides in multiple systems that represent different business area silos. Figure 14-1 illustrates the integration of multiple disparate systems around the concept of a party. In the enterprise environment, it is quite common that the number of systems that need to be integrated ranges from 10 to 30 and sometimes even higher. Customer data in these systems is formatted, stored, and managed differently since these application systems tend to be highly heterogeneous because they are created and maintained by different departments and used for different purposes. Often various application systems maintain overlapping attributes and may support different levels of granularity and different data structures—for example, account-centric data vs. customer-centric data, household-level data, different touch points, channels, and so on.

FIGURE 14-1
System integration and a 360-degree view of customer/party

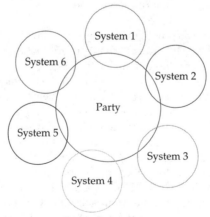

Matching attributes link customer records across disparate
systems to create an enterprise-wide notion of a party

Holistic Entity View and a 360-Degree View of a Customer: Frequently Used Terms and Definitions

In order to recognize entities representing those individuals or parties that have one or more relationships with the firm, the granular-level information about the individuals or corporate customers must be assembled from all relevant records across the enterprise. This comprehensive view of the party entity is frequently referred to by business as a "360-degree view of a customer." What are some key challenges in creating this view?

It is not always clear if the records that read Mike Johnson and M. Johnson represent the same individual entity even if the records show the same address, home phone number, and credit card number, as in Figure 14-2. Two records with the name M. Johnson at the same address may still belong to different people (for example, father and son). Indeed, if we consider Mike's son Mack Johnson, then M. Johnson may represent Mike Johnson or Mack Johnson. Other scenarios are also possible.

On the other hand, two records for Mike Johnson at two different addresses may still represent the same individual who moved from one address to another. In this scenario one of the addresses was occupied by this individual in the past; see Figure 14-3.

In the case of customers residing in the United States, a service that can access National Change of Address (NCOA) information, which is maintained by the U.S. Postal Service, may be required to link the records in Figure 14-3 and associate them with the same individual. Similar address maintenance service exists in many other countries. Another variation on the theme could be a situation where Mike Johnson may have two or more addresses at a time (for example, the primary residence and a vacation home). In addition, both names and addresses can have different spellings, aliases, and so on.

An important concern to consider when creating a comprehensive 360-degree view of an entity such as a customer is the concern of *overmatching*. This scenario occurs when the records belonging to two or more customers are mistakenly assigned to a single individual. If the matching data is used for a marketing campaign, such an error may result in the marketing department not sending a marketing letter to a customer. However, when data is used for legal, medical, or financial purposes, a customer can be incorrectly linked to legal documents, financial statements, or medical records, which can have serious consequences for both the customer and the firm. For example, the firm may send a dividend check to a wrong individual or disclose sensitive information to a stranger.

Naturally, the reverse outcome of treating two or more records about the same entity as different entities is also possible, thus failing to deliver a comprehensive 360-degree entity

Full Name	Address	Phone Number	Credit Card Number	
Mike Johnson	123 Main St. Bordentown, NJ 08513	(609) 987-6543	4213 0001 1234 6789	Do these two records represent the same individual?
M. Johnson	123 Main St. Bordentown, NJ 08513	(609) 987-6543	4213 0001 1234 6789	

FIGURE 14-2 Two records for Mike Johnson and M. Johnson with the same phone number and credit card number

Full Name	Address	Phone Number	Credit Card Number	
Mike Johnson	123 Main St. Bordentown, NJ 08513	(609) 987-6543	4213 0001 1234 6789	Do these two records represent the same individual?
M. Johnson	767 Central Ave. Bordentown, NJ 08513	(609) 987-6543	4213 0001 1234 6789	

FIGURE 14-3   Two records for Mike Johnson at different addresses

view, and the matching process should have appropriate safeguards built into it to handle both scenarios.

> **Errors in Matching**
> Two or more records erroneously matched to the same master entity record are frequently referred to as *false positives*. Conversely, two or more records that are not matched even though they do belong to the same master entity record are referred to as *false negatives*.

The business must identify the required match accuracy in terms of the level of confidence for both false negatives and false positives. Legal, financial, medical, and certain other applications of customer data integration typically require high-confidence data with the primary focus of avoiding false positives at any cost. Some compliance applications are relatively tolerant of false positives but need to avoid false negatives, for example, identifying suspects potentially involved in money laundering, drug trafficking, terrorism, and other criminal activities. In the latter case, the law enforcement officer wants to see all suspects who meet given suspect criteria, while realizing that some records may be false matches. False negatives in this scenario would mean an exclusion of potential criminals from the list of suspects. Once the initial "wide-net" list of records is produced systemically, a manual effort and analysis will be required to exclude false positives and finalize the list.

The sections that follow summarize some common reasons responsible for producing false positives and false negative matches.

Reasons for False Positives in Party Matching

With a typical match for individuals based on the name, address, phone number, and some other attributes, the primary reasons for false positives are as follows:

- Family members living at the same address with the same or similar first names or initials and possibly having joint accounts or trusts on which they have different roles (for example, Mike Johnson Sr. vs. Mike Johnson Jr.).

- Lack of differentiation between party types. For instance, if a customer Tom Kent opened a checking account with a firm, created a trust where he is a trustee, and has an account for his small business called "Tom Kent Associates," the system may not be able to recognize the three parties as distinct entities (individual, trust, and small company).

- The use of invalid or incorrect data for multiple records—for example, records with an anonymous social security number (SSN) of 999-99-9999, which is often used when some entry is required but the right value is unknown.

- The use of a phone number as a personal number when it is shared by many people because it is a general number for a large organization.

Reasons for False Negatives in Party Matching

There are many reasons for false negative matches, most of them being related to data quality:

- The use of multiple versions of the same name
  - Nicknames and aliases (Bill vs. William, Larry vs. Lawrence are the most common)
  - Misspelled names
  - Use of acronyms in organization names
  - Names for international entities, such as individuals that may not fit the English-standard First Name–Middle Initial–Last Name structure
- Entity name changes
  - As a result of marriage
  - As a result of the naturalization process
  - Organizational name changes as a result of rebranding, mergers, acquisitions, and company spin-offs
- Addresses
  - Incorrect spelling
  - Different abbreviations and spellings, including full spellings (Street vs. St., Avenue vs. Ave, Ave vs. Rd, St vs. Ct., and so on)
  - Inability to parse certain formats
  - Vanity addresses (multiple towns associated with a single ZIP code; the towns are used interchangeably in the mailing address)
  - Address changes
- Phone numbers
  - Inability to systemically parse some of the phone number formats

Attributes and Attribute Categories Commonly Used for Matching and Identification

The attributes used for matching and entity identification can be divided into the following three major categories:

- **Identity attributes** Used for direct matching
- **Discriminating attributes** Used to disqualify similar records
- **Record type or record qualification attributes** Used to determine which identification rules to apply

Identity Attributes

Identity attributes are the primary attributes used by the matching algorithm to directly identify an entity—for example, a name or SSN can be used to directly identify a customer. If identity attributes match two or more records, there is a good chance that the party/customer records are matched correctly. If a high-confidence match is required, a match on a single identity attribute may not be sufficient and multiple attributes should be taken into account. Good candidates for identity attributes include:

- **Name**   Individual names (first, last, and middle initial) for persons and full business names for organizations are the most well-known identity attributes. Indeed, names were invented for identification purposes. From this perspective, the identification problem for individuals is as old as humankind.

- **Key identifiers**   Since the vast majority of individuals' names are not universally unique, people invented key identifiers such as social security numbers, tax identification numbers, driver's license numbers, passport identifiers, patient numbers, student IDs, employee IDs, and so on, to identify individuals and organizations.

- **Address**   The customer's address is frequently used for identification purposes. It is not uncommon for a marketing campaign to target households (typically a family living in the same physical location) rather than individual customers or prospects.

- **Phone**   Home phone numbers and cell phone numbers are frequently used for identification. Automated interactive customer service systems shortcut security questions when they recognize the customer phone number.

- **Online identity attributes**
  - IP address
  - Internet provider
  - E-mail address
  - Other online identifiers

- **Product type, account number, and role**   In account-centric enterprises (the majority of businesses across all industry segments today belong to this category), the most credible customer information is stored and maintained at the account level. The firm recognizes a customer by examining the product type (for example, mortgage), account number, and the customer's role (for example, co-borrower) on the account. Typically, account information is maintained by multiple systems across the enterprise, which makes these attributes good candidates for matching.

- **Customer affiliations**   Customer affiliation information is frequently used as additional identity information. A typical example of an affiliation is customer's employment information.

- **Customer relationships and hierarchies**   This information is particularly critical and frequently used by organizations servicing high-net-worth customers. Every customer in these organizations is defined through a relationship with the firm or with other customers (individuals or groups) and then by name, address, and so on. Customer relationships can also be used as additional identification information. Hierarchies of institutional customers may also be important as identification attributes. We will discuss this in more detail in Chapter 15.

Note that most of the identity attributes can change over time, due to life events and normal business activities. Support for changes in identity attributes represents one of the key MDM requirements. Indeed, people and businesses move and change addresses, phones, and professional affiliations. For institutional customers, mergers and acquisitions cause additional complexities. Name changes are not unusual either. And they not limited to the name change as a result of marriage. The immigration and naturalization process in many countries includes a name change as part of the naturalization process.

Discriminating Attributes

Discriminating attributes are the attributes that are not typically used to match two entities. Instead, they are used to disqualify two or more similar records. For example, in the Customer domain, a father and son with the same name and address can be differentiated by the discriminating attribute "Date of Birth." Typically, a strong discriminating attribute candidate should be static and have a well-defined set of distinct values (for example, Date of Birth or Gender).

Even if some identity attributes match across two or more records, there is a chance that the records still belong to different customers. Discriminating attributes help to distinguish between similar records that may or may not belong to the same customer. Typical discriminating attributes are:

- Individuals
  - Date of birth (DOB)
  - Date of death
  - Gender
- Organizations
  - Date of incorporation/establishment
  - Date of closure

Discriminating attributes are often utilized in combination with identity attributes to reduce the probability of false positive matches. Typical situations in which discriminating attributes help include the following scenarios:

- Husband and wife or a parent and a child with the same first initial and last name— for example, J. Smith can be John Smith or Jane Smith, or, using our Johnson family example, M. Johnson can be Mike or Mack Johnson.
- Similarly, J. Smith can represent two brothers partnering in business. Assuming they were not born on the same date, the Date of Birth (DOB) attributes will help.

Unlike identity attributes, discriminating attributes typically have lower cardinality. From this perspective, Gender is a common discriminating attribute with a customary cardinality of 2. However, note that the cardinality of Gender is sometimes defined by a number greater than 2. There are local variations where, for example, a common discriminating attribute such as Gender can assume up to six distinct values. The cardinality of the DOB attribute is much higher in a typical customer data store that covers 50 years of customer life span for active customers, and using 365 days in a year, the cardinality of the DOB attribute is 18,250. While this number may appear large, for a multimillion-customer file this translates into hundreds or even thousands of individuals with the same date of birth.

Additional characteristics of discriminating attributes that are also important in terms of entity identification include:

- Stability
  - Unlike identification attributes, which are made up by people and can change over time, in real time, or in one mass change operation (for example, a group of customers from the same retirement plan was reassigned to a new plan with different account numbers), the discriminating attributes for individuals are much less volatile. Indeed, your first name and middle initial are normally given by your parents, and the last name can change as a result of marriage or some other events. The DOB attribute should never change. Even though gender can be changed by modern medical science, it is still a relatively rare event.
  - Similarly, when we deal with organizations, the Incorporation Date and Business Closure date do not change. This applies at least to formal organizations that are registered with the appropriate government agencies and assigned tax identifiers.
- Universality
  - By their nature, every individual, regardless of the country of residence, citizenship, occupation, and other characteristics, has such attributes as Date of Birth and Gender, and they can be used for global identification. On the other hand, identification attributes such as social security numbers that are used as unique identifiers for individuals in the U.S. most likely cannot be used to identify individuals outside the U.S. To make it even more interesting, there are some exceptions when U.S. residents do not have an SSN either.
- Availability
  - Gender is one of the most easily available attributes. Most customers do not keep their gender secret.
  - Date of Birth is more difficult to obtain than Gender, but it is still easier to obtain than the social security number. Certain data privacy regulations discussed in Part III prohibit the disclosure and use of social security numbers for identification purposes.
- Ease of validation
  - For Gender, the process is straightforward; for example, a typical rule allows for only "F" (Female), "M" (Male), and "U" (Unknown) values.
  - Date validation routines are well known and are widely available in multiple products, including commonly used relational databases. It is important to note that common calendar and date formats are accepted and used globally. However, it is not easy to establish global validation rules for names and addresses. Indeed, multiple attempts to apply rules such as "Last Name must have more than one character" have been defeated. Even though such last names are infrequent, they do exist.

It is our recommendation to maintain the discriminating attributes in the best possible conditions in terms of data quality. Best of all, discriminating attributes should be defined as mandatory fields that have assigned values. In other words, in terms of database technology, the discriminating attributes should be defined as NOT NULL if possible. If this is not possible, data profiling and data quality maintenance on these attributes should be a priority task for data stewards.

The attributes of "Date of Birth" and "Business Incorporation/Establishment Date" are particularly important and attractive from the identification perspective. Even though these attributes are considered to be discriminating attributes (this is how they are commonly perceived), they can be successfully used for identification purposes as well.

Record Qualification Attributes

The *record qualification or type attributes* are used to provide additional metadata about the entity records. This information helps the matching algorithm to determine which identification rules should be applied to the record. The following attributes are typically used as record type identifiers:

- Party Type
- Country Attribute and Domestic vs. International Identifiers
- Leading Relationship (if a customer has multiple relationships with the enterprise, the most important relationship from the enterprise perspective is referred to as a Leading Relationship)

The need for record qualification attributes reinforces the assertion that the quality of an MDM solution depends not only on the narrow set of identification and discriminating attributes but also on a wider set of attributes that are typically included in the data scope of MDM projects. Consequently, for many organizations, MDM projects become drivers for enterprise-wide data quality improvement initiatives.

Party Type

Data about master entities such as customer often exists in different data stores within a firm and tends to be very heterogeneous, both from the format and the system representation perspectives. Consequently, from the matching perspective, it is important for the matching algorithm to qualify the record type to determine appropriate matching rules for that record type. The Party Type attribute characterizes the type of party/customer this record belongs to. The most common Party Types are Individual (retail customers, citizen, patient) and Organization (wholesale, commercial, business, government agency). Typical attributes for individuals are quite different from those for organizations. The most obvious example illustrating this distinction is the set of the name attributes. For an individual, first name, last name, and middle initial are typical while businesses are characterized by full business names that usually include the type of the business entity (for example, "Inc." for Incorporated entity, "LLC" for Limited Liability Corporation, "Ltd." for Limited, and so on)

Some attributes, such as Gender, provide information about a person but do not apply to businesses. Social Security numbers for living individuals are unique within the U.S. Unfortunately, this uniqueness does not hold true if the matching record set includes both individuals and businesses. Even the Business Tax Identification Number can be the same as an individual SSN. The list of examples illustrating the differences between individual and organizational records can be significantly extended. The bottom line here is that the matching algorithm needs the Party Type as an important record-qualifying attribute since different matching rules apply to different Party Type entities.

We have to point out that individual customers are somewhat easier to identify since, in general, individuals can be better "defined." For example, each individual is identified by his or her unique DNA. Even though the DNA data is not typically available for most MDM systems, this does not change the fact that, conceptually, individuals are better defined for recognition than organizations are. The latter can frequently be viewed as subjects of fuzzy matching and identification. Indeed, the Party Type of "Organization" is often subcategorized, where the subcategories depend on the industry segment in which the "Organization" operates. In financial services organizations, the subcategory list may include such party types as trust, fund, estate, annuity, association, and so on. A party subcategory might be important in refining the rules on how the customer record should be processed by the matching algorithm.

As we stated before, product matching is even more complex than organization matching, and it involves a variety of sophisticated approaches and algorithms that are often based on semantics processing.

Country Attribute and Domestic vs. International Identifiers

The country attribute is important for correct name and address recognition. As we discussed in Part I of the book, different rules apply to names with different ethnic backgrounds. Accordingly, advanced customer matching and recognition algorithms that use probabilistic models can take advantage of the country and geography information (for example, state or province data) to improve the accuracy of matching.

In the case of an address, the address structure and ultimately the party recognition and identification depend on the way addresses are defined in a given country. Therefore, it is important to determine the country type for each record that has to be matched. In many cases, when the country data is not reliable, it is important to differentiate between U.S. domestic addresses and international addresses. This distinction is important for U.S.-centric MDM solutions because U.S. domestic addresses are normally better defined and therefore can be processed in a more automated fashion, while international addresses require more manual intervention. Even if the MDM system is designed to access an external knowledge base from a "trusted" data provider such as Acxiom or Dun & Bradstreet, it is important to know that the commercially available U.S. domestic name and address information are more accurate and complete than international name and address data for most foreign countries.

Leading Relationship and Relationship Level

Another important piece of the entity identification metadata is the information about the details of a customer's relationships with the firm. This information can be used by the MDM system to identify the most profitable low-/high-risk customers (individuals and institutional customers) and the relationship managers who are responsible for maintaining the corresponding customers' accounts. The Leading Relationship information is particularly important since it can help prioritize the way customer records have to be cleansed up and processed for identification.

When we consider an individual Customer domain (as opposed to institutional customers), we see that the personal information about the individual customers is typically more complete and accurate than data about the prospects. It is a good practice to maintain a special attribute that indicates whether the party is a customer or a prospect. A person is considered to be a customer if he or she has at least one relationship (for example, account) with the firm. In the case of a customer, some minimum information is not just required but is in fact mandatory in order to open an account. For prospects that are only potential customers, minimum data requirements can be much less restrictive. Consequently, the expected accuracy of matching for prospects is lower than that for customers. Similarly, the expected accuracy for primary customers is higher than that for secondary customers (for example, a spouse listed on the account as a beneficiary), third-party vendors, and so on.

The identification accuracy of the most profitable customers is a business imperative that is aimed at increasing the customer's level of satisfaction, so it is not unusual to invoke a manual identification process to reduce the number of identification errors. In order to support a manual customer identification effort, it is critical to know who in the firm is primarily responsible for the relationship. Thus, an MDM system must maintain the attributes that link customer information with the relationship owners. For example, a financial services firm would have to know and maintain information about customer relationship managers, financial advisors, agents, and account managers who manage the relationship with the customer.

Customer Identification, Matching Process, and Models

Let's continue our discussion on customer identification by taking a closer look at the identification processes and concerns as they apply to individual customers and prospects.

Minimum Data Requirements

A prerequisite to effective customer identification and matching is the consideration of minimum data requirements for any record to be included as a matching candidate. This notion is reflected in Figure 14-4.

If the minimum data requirements are not met, the record may require additional manual processing (for example, additional data must be collected, entered, or changed). Data change is required if an attribute value is determined to be invalid. Figure 14-4 shows six combinations of attributes. If a record does not meet any of the requirements specified here, the matching algorithm will exclude the record from the matching process and report it as a data quality exception.

An alternative approach to the minimum data requirements is based on the probabilistic self-scoring of an entity record. A matching score that is typically used to quantify a similarity or dissimilarity of two records can be used in self-scoring when a record is scored to itself. Higher self-scores indicate that the record contains a higher amount of identifying information. An advantage of this method is in that it doesn't require any deterministic business rules.[1] The method takes into account not only what attributes are populated but

FIGURE 14-4
An example of a minimum requirements definition

No	Full Name	Address	Home Phone	Date of Birth	SSN
1	+				+
2		+			+
3			+		+
4				+	+
5	+	+		+	
6	+		+	+	

also recognizes the frequency of the values (or the uncertainty of randomly matching the values). For instance, in the U.S., "John Smith" as a name will self-score lower than any other less frequent name. Consequently, a record with a rare name will score higher than a record with more commonly used names.

Matching Modes

From a systemic perspective, the identification process consists of two high-level steps: *record match* and *record merge*.

Merge and split processing is discussed in some detail in Chapter 15. This chapter is focused on the implementation issues of record matching. The goal of the record match process is to create Match Groups. Each group contains one or more records that represent the same party. Typically, once the Match Groups are identified, the goal is to eliminate duplicate records and create a unique "Golden copy" of each entity (in this case, customer) record. Depending on the business requirements, the creation of a Golden copy may not be mandatory. Moreover, some MDM implementations require keeping multiple linked records without removing duplicates.

The Match Group is used to systemically identify parties. This may or may not be identical to Party ID, which is the ultimate "Golden copy" identifier for a Party. If an end-user input is required to assert the Match Group value, then the terms Party and Match Group may have different meanings. In this context, the Party identifier represents a true single holistic customer view created by an matching process, possibly with the assistance of a subject matter human expert while the Match Group identifier is the best the system could do to automatically identify the customer in order to assist the expert.

Operationally, we can distinguish between batch and online matching modes. *Batch matching* applies to a process in which a large number of records must be processed to cluster individual records and assign a unique Party ID to each Match Group. Note that the Party ID is a unique identifier for each cluster representing a single customer. During the initial "unseeded" match, all records are assigned to Match Groups (see Figure 14-5). It is not unusual for the batch-matching process to process a complete multimillion-record customer database and to run for extended period of time.

Online matching is part of daily ongoing activities when new party records are created, deleted, deactivated, or updated (see Figure 14-6). Online matching is a "seeded" process,

Figure 14-5
Initial match process

Record	Match Group
Customer Record 1	
Customer Record 2	
Customer Record 3	
Customer Record 4	
Customer Record 5	
Customer Record 6	
Customer Record 7	

During the initial "unseeded" match process all match groups are assigned

Record	Match Group
Customer Record 1	1
Customer Record 2	2
Customer Record 3	1
Customer Record 4	2
Customer Record 5	3
Customer Record 6	3
Customer Record 7	2

Record	Match Group
Customer Record 1	1
Customer Record 2	2
Customer Record 3	1
Customer Record 4	2
Customer Record 5	3
Customer Record 6	3
Customer Record 7	2

Customer Record 8

A new record is matched against the existing customer base and assigned to match group 2

Record	Match Group
Customer Record 1	1
Customer Record 2	2
Customer Record 3	1
Customer Record 4	2
Customer Record 5	3
Customer Record 6	3
Customer Record 7	2
Customer Record 8	2

FIGURE 14-6   An Online, real-time, or near-real-time match

where each new record is matched against the existing records with assigned Match Groups identifiers and/or Party IDs.

In this example, the addition of a record does not cause any Match Group changes. However, this is not always true. As we will discuss later in this chapter, a new record can "chain" two or more other records, which results in changes of the Match Group assignment for the existing records.

Defining Matching Rules for Customer Records

This section lists the typical steps used to define matching rules for customer records. Note that at a high level, these rules apply to the matching of any entities that carry identifying attributes and support syntax-based or pattern-based matching (for example, contacts or institutional customers).

First, we need to identify the matching attributes. All attributes that should be used for matching need to be identified. This includes all types of the attributes previously discussed:

- Identity attributes
- Discrimination attributes
- Record qualification attributes

Defining Matching Rules at the Attribute or Attribute Group Level

This section discusses factors that need to be considered when two attributes are compared for matching, and how to quantify them. The types of match operations that we need to consider in order to understand the factors affecting the match outcome include the following:

- **Exact match**   Within this comparison model, two attributes are considered to be matched if they are represented by two equal attribute values, for example, character strings after the removal of padding spaces, carriage returns, and other characters that are not meaningful for string comparisons in the context of customer matching.

- **Match with the use of "common sense" standardization rules**   These standardization rules cover a number of "common sense" rules about individual names and addresses—for example, match Steve to Steven, Ave. to Avenue, St. to Street, and names that sound similar (for instance, Stacy matches with Stacey).

- **Match with the use of knowledge-based intelligence**   This category of matching involves rules that can be implemented based only on the facts available in the knowledge databases and data libraries. For instance, a knowledge base can hold data about the streets available in each town, valid ranges for street addresses, vanity addresses, and the National Change of Address (NCOA) data.

- **Probabilistic attribute match**   A Probabilistic Attribute Match algorithm utilizes frequency-based data analysis for attribute value distribution on the attributes in the customer database. For instance, a probabilistic approach will take into account that the first name "John" is much more frequent in the database than the first name "Dushan." From the probabilistic approach perspective, a match on a less frequent attribute value is statistically more significant than a match on an attribute value that is very frequent in the database. It should be pointed out that customer locality or geography can affect and even reverse the attribute frequency ratio. Indeed, the first name "Dushan" will be more frequent in the Balkans than the first name "John." Frequency-based matching typically improves the accuracy of matching by 4–10 percent. An advantage of a probabilistic approach is the transparency of explicitly defined deterministic rules. In a probabilistic approach, matching results are more difficult to interpret because the matching engine does its "magic" under the covers.

Matching Quantification   Once all factors driving a match decision are established, the model should also define how the attribute match will be quantified. The simplest case is a binary decision. The result of an attribute-to-attribute comparison can be presented as

$$Match = True$$

or

$$Match = False$$

More complex algorithms take into account various degrees of the confidence level of an attribute match. The confidence is at the maximum level for exact matches and decreases as the match becomes "fuzzier." The confidence parameters need to be set and tuned in terms of the rules that define match outcome values. In clustering or K-nearest neighbor[2] algorithms, the attribute match confidence is expressed through the "distance" between the two attribute values. The exact match would be characterized by the distance value of zero (distance = 0). As the match becomes less certain, the distance between the two values grows. There are several variations of these algorithms where, for example, different match weights are used to reflect different confidence levels.

Record-Level Match
Once the attribute-level match has been performed, it is time to expand the matching process to include the record-level match. There are a few ways to combine attribute-level matches and convert them into a record-level match.

Binary Rules for the Attribute and Record Match   In this scenario, based on the attribute match defined as binary, the record match is defined by a number of explicitly specified matching rules. These rules can be simply codified in the "*M*" of "*N*" model (*M* of the total attributes *N* match). Figure 14-7 illustrates this approach.

The match criteria shown in Figure 14-7 require a match of any three attributes or attribute groups (*M* = 3) out of the five available (*N* = 5). The "*M*" of "*N*" model requires that in order for two records to be considered a match, *M* out of *N* attributes or groups of attributes should match. In the following example, there are five attribute groups or individual attributes:

- Full Name
- Address
- Phone
- Date of Birth
- SSN

Since three of them match within this rule, the two records match.

Typically, a simple rule such as "*M*" of "*N*" will not hold true from a match accuracy perspective when the record structures are complex and include many descriptive attributes that don't have strict domain constraints. Moreover, given the complexity of enterprise data, the number of explicitly defined match rules can easily reach several hundreds, which further complicates the matching process. Lastly, in order to achieve the desired accuracy, the rules can become fairly complex and include conditional logic with dependencies on multiple attributes. Overall, the result of the computation is expressed in terms of a binary match/no match decision for the records. For instance, a rule may read: *If the social security numbers match and the last names match, then the records are determined to be a match unless two valid and different dates of birth are found in the records.*

Binary Rule for the Attribute Match and Score for Record Match   In this scenario, assuming that the Binary Attribute match is true, the Record Match is defined through a score. First, we define attribute match weights for each attribute. Then the overall record-to-record matching score is computed as a total over the field of matching scores. Then, the calculated record score is compared with the matching threshold. If the computed value exceeds the threshold, the two records are considered to be a match.

Full Name			Address				Phone			Date of Birth	SSN
First	M.	Last	Street	City	State	ZIP Code	Area Code	Phone #	Date of Birth	SSN
Tom	J	Jones	231 Main St	Blue Sky	XY	12345	512	123-1010	03/12/1961	111-22-3333
Tom	J	Jones	12 Mercer St	Blue Sky	XY	12345	512	123-1010	03/12/1961	
Match							Match		Match	

FIGURE 14-7   A simple "M" of "N" attributes match scenario

Scoring for Both the Attribute Match and the Record Match   In this scenario, the scores obtained from the attribute-level calculations and optionally weighted by the relative attribute weights are used to compute the record-level score. If the computed value exceeds the threshold, then the two records are considered to be a match.

It should be pointed out that one of the advantages of scoring methodologies is based on the fact that the matching requirements can be defined in a more compact form than the requirements defined explicitly in term of a great number of complex business rules. The scoring models allow for ease in defining matching iterations and testing procedures. This is particularly important since any matching process requires multiple iterations to reach the required level of accuracy.

Defining the Thresholds

As we discussed in the preceding section, the scoring models require a definition of match accuracy threshold. A higher threshold will make the matching more conservative, which means that the procedure will minimize false positive matches. A higher threshold will also result in a higher tolerance to false negatives. This is a disadvantage of any single-threshold model. A more flexible model should include two thresholds, as shown in Figure 14-8. In the figure, the scoring values are segmented into three areas: confident match, confident mismatch, and the "gray" area where additional information or human input is required to determine the match.

Effect of Chaining

Another important consideration in the matching process is the effect of chaining. *Chaining* is a situation where two or more records are assigned to the same Match Groups even though they should not be matched by using the rules defined by a direct record-to-record match. Instead, the records are "chained" by a third record that is directly matched to the first two records.

The accuracy of matching and performance may be impacted by how the matching algorithm handles chaining. A chaining scenario is illustrated in Figure 14-9.

In this example, we assume that the matching rule requires three attribute group matches for the records to be linked to the same party. The second record is linked to the first one on the Full Name, Phone, and Date of Birth. The third record is linked to the second one on the Full Name, Address, and Phone. Since three matching attributes are required to directly link records, the third record is not directly linked to the first one because only two attribute groups, Full Name and Phone, are matched for these records. Nevertheless, the first record and the third record are linked to each other indirectly through the second record.

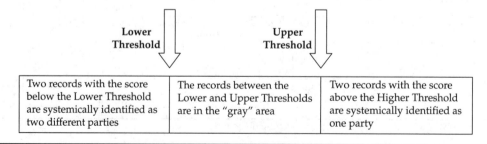

Lower Threshold	Upper Threshold	
Two records with the score below the Lower Threshold are systemically identified as two different parties	The records between the Lower and Upper Thresholds are in the "gray" area	Two records with the score above the Higher Threshold are systemically identified as one party

FIGURE 14-8   Two thresholds segment the scoring values into three areas

Full Name			Address				Phone		Date of Birth	SSN
First	M.	Last	Street	City	State	ZIP Code	Area Code	Phone #	Date of Birth	SSN
Tom	J	Jones	231 Main St	Blue Sky	XY	12345	512	123-1010	03/12/1961	111-22-3333
Tom	J	Jones	12 Mercer St	Blue Sky	XY	12345	512	123-1010	03/12/1961	
Tom	J	Jones	12 Mercer St	Blue Sky	XY	12345	512	123-1010		

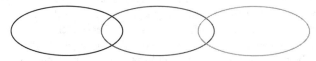

Figure 14-9   Effect of chaining for customer records

In order to understand the potential difficulties with chaining, we should note that the result of chaining depends on the order in which the records were processed. If Record 3 is processed after Record 1 but before Record 2, then Record 3 will not be linked to Record 1 and therefore will be assigned a different Party ID. When Record 2 is processed, it will be assigned its own Party ID. Consequently, three records will not be linked in the first pass. This may create matching accuracy and/or performance and scalability issues. Today, advances in developing matching algorithms allow MDM systems to achieve reliable scalability characteristics by aligning the processing time with the number of matching records.

As we pointed out earlier, there are situations where a new record can cause a Match Group recalculation in other records. Figure 14-10 illustrates this point.

In this figure, Customer Record 8 is found to match a record from Match Group 2 and a record from Match Group 3. This results in the merge of Match Groups 2 and 3. From a

Customer Record 8

Record	Match Group
Customer Record 1	1
Customer Record 2	2
Customer Record 3	1
Customer Record 4	2
Customer Record 5	3
Customer Record 6	3
Customer Record 7	2

A new record is matched against the existing customer base and assigned to match group 2. customer record 8 is also matched to customer record 3 to result in merge of match groups 1 and 2

Record	Match Group
Customer Record 1	2
Customer Record 2	2
Customer Record 3	2
Customer Record 4	2
Customer Record 5	3
Customer Record 6	3
Customer Record 7	2
Customer Record 8	2

Figure 14-10   An example where a new record cause Match Group changes in existing records

business perspective, this means that an addition of a new record led the matching algorithm to a conclusion that Match Groups 2 and 3 represent the same entity record.

Similarly, an update or a deletion of a customer record can cause changes in Match Group assignments of other records. For instance, if Customer Record 8 is deleted, the process in Figure 14-10 may be reversed and the three Match Groups may be created.

Break Groups and Performance Considerations

In practice, performance concerns about matching records in a very large data set can be addressed effectively if we apply a matching algorithm on smaller sets of records called *break groups*. There are other optimization techniques that allow MDM systems to achieve acceptable levels of performance and scalability. Many of these techniques are the subject of published and ongoing research, and are well beyond the scope of this book. Nevertheless, the performance of the matching process, in combination with its accuracy, is one of the topics presented by practically all MDM vendors as their competitive "differentiator." Many claims have been made that a particular proprietary technique can match hundreds of millions or even billions of records in practically near-real time. While we're not going to dispute these claims, we want to turn the reader's attention to a set of considerations designed to separate the reality of match scalability from the marketing hype. The discussion that follows describes an analytical approach to matching performance that is based on the concept of break groups.

When a matching algorithm runs against a data set, in general, it has to evaluate match/ no match conditions for all records in the data set in a pair-wise fashion. The total time spent on matching depends to a large degree on the time spent on the match/no match evaluation for the record pairs.

Using this as a base, let's consider a simple model where the data set contains N records. Assume that M attributes are used for the match. Let t be the time required to evaluate the matching conditions for a given attribute for a given pair of records. The number of pairs of records can be evaluated through the number of combinations of N divided by 2, which yields $N \times (N-1)/2$. The time required to perform the match/no match decisions for all record pairs is

$$T = t \times M \times N \times (N-1)/2$$

Given that $N \gg 1$, we arrive at

$$T \approx t \times M \times N^2/2$$

The value of t depends on a number of factors such as hardware, complexity of comparison, and so on. For this evaluation we will use $t = 10^{-8}$ s. For typical values of $M = 20$ and $N = 30,000,000$, the factor $M \times N^2/2$ evaluates to 10^{16}. Assuming a single process, with this number of comparison operations, the time required to complete matching is $T = 10^8$ s, which is over three years. This indicates that it is practically impossible to get a reasonable matching performance on a very large data set using the current state of the art in conventional computing platforms. Of course, this process can be parallelized into multiple parallel streams using grid/cloud computing platforms, the MapReduce[3] computing paradigm, and other approaches. In general, the optimization goal is to decrease the number of comparisons in each comparison job stream by orders of magnitude to get meaningful performance results. This can be achieved by using break groups that segment the data set into smaller sets of records so that record matches are possible only within the break groups and never across them.

Let's evaluate the change in the number of comparisons as a result of creating B break groups. For simplicity, let's assume that all break groups are equal and hence each of the groups contains N/B records. Then the time required to perform the match/no match decisions for all record pairs within each group is

$$T_B \approx t \times M \times N^2/(2 \times B^2)$$

If matching is performed in break groups sequentially, the total computation time is

$$T \approx t \times M \times N^2/(2 \times B)$$

We can conclude that the number of comparisons is inversely proportional to the number of break groups. Using parallel processing platforms, parallel database systems, and/or approaches such as MapReduce in conjunctions with the break groups approach can drastically improve the total match time for large data sets. The break group algorithm supports software- and hardware-based parallelism since matching within each of the break groups does not depend upon matching in all other break groups.

Regardless of the particular choice of parallel processing system option, we can define the optimum configuration for the break groups. Let's assume that out of M critical attributes used for matching, some attributes are more important than others. From the matching-engine configuration perspective, this means that higher weights were assigned to these attributes than to other attributes. In this case, we can select a small subset of the most important attributes $K \ll M$ so that any two records cannot possibly match if none of the K attributes match. We will also assume that since the selected K attributes are so important, at least one of the K attributes must contain a value; otherwise, the record does not meet the minimum data requirements and will be excluded from the matching process. We can define a break group on the K attributes as follows: Any two records belong to the same break group if and only if they have a match on at least one attribute of the K selected attributes. From the performance perspective, it is important to realize that the number of break groups defined this way is high, which is caused by the high cardinality of the values in the selected K fields.

To illustrate these points, assume that $K = 3$ and the three selected attributes are the credit card number, full name, and the phone number. The data is loaded from multiple systems and not all of the three attribute values are available for each record. However, at least one of the three attributes must have a value to meet the minimum data requirements. The number of break groups B defined this way is very high, and the match engine should be able to perform the first pass of the match process to assign break group keys based on simplified matching conditions that include only the selected K fields. The second pass will be performed within a large number B of break groups.

We can now summarize the findings of this section as follows:

- For a multimillion-record data set, a matching process can achieve a reasonably good performance if it can identify break groups with high cardinality—that is, the number of break groups is high and the average number of records in each group is low.

- The matching engine should be selected with the break-group matching capability in mind.

- The matching engine should be able to support hardware- and software-based parallel processing to perform matching within break groups in parallel.

Similarity Libraries and Fuzzy Logic for Attribute Comparisons

Individuals use different names such as legal names, aliases, nicknames, and so on. The matching algorithm should take into account the connections between names like "Bill" and "William" or "Larry" and "Lawrence." Name alias libraries (these aliases are also known as "equivalencies") that are based on human knowledge must be built and made available to the matching engine to link this type of string values. Such a library should maintain only commonly used names. Otherwise, if unusual aliases are in the library, the probability of overmatching increases. For instance, if John Michael Smith wants to use an alias JM, such an alias should not be placed in the library.

A similar problem exists for addresses. It is not unusual for multiple small towns to be served by one postal office. In this case the town names can be used interchangeably. The mail will be delivered anyway. From the MDM perspective this means that two town aliases can be used for a given address. A similar condition exists for street names. This situation is known as vanity addresses. For example, a 5th Avenue address in Manhattan, New York, USA, sounds better than 86th Street, Lincoln Center sounds more prestigious than West 66th Street, and so on. Such vanity addresses are used as aliases for locations that are close to the "real" address but are used because they sound prestigious and expensive. As in the name libraries, address-alias libraries based on human knowledge must be built to link this type of string values. The National Change of Address (NCOA) database is a good example of where additional libraries should be used to achieve good matching results.

Similarity libraries cannot resolve the matching problems when the names or addresses are misspelled. Phonetic conversion algorithms (many of them based on fuzzy logic) are used in this case. Typically, fuzzy logic is required when comparing names, addresses, and other textual attributes. This type of comparison is one of the greatest MDM challenges. The fuzzy logic algorithms provide inexact match comparisons. SOUNDEX[4] is the most widely known phonetic algorithm, developed in the beginning of the twentieth century. There are many modifications of this algorithm. They convert character strings into digital codes in such a way that phonetically similar strings acquire the same code values. These routines are included in many libraries of standard string-comparison functions.

NYSIIS is another phonetic algorithm, which was developed in 1970. The acronym NYSIIS stands for "New York State Identification and Intelligence System." This algorithm is said to improve SOUNDEX matching capabilities by 2.7 percent. For details please refer to the website of the National Institute of Standards and Technology.[5]

A more recent sophisticated inexact string comparison algorithm known as Bipartite Graph Matching (BGM)[6] is based on mathematical modeling that simulates the human notion of similarity. We will touch on BGM in vendor products again in Chapter 18 of this book.

Summary of Data-Matching Requirements and Solutions

Let us summarize the key considerations that should be used to evaluate data-matching solutions and engines. This summary can be also used as a decision-making checklist for MDM designers and product evaluators. As a base we will use the list originally published by Initiate Systems (2004) in the white paper, "Initiate Customer Data Integration and Customer Data Matching: Achieving a 360-Degree Customer View," and make some changes and additions that come from our implementation experience.

- Accuracy and key characteristics of matching algorithm:
  - Support probabilistic and/or deterministic matching algorithms.
  - Support for history of attribute changes as they relate to matching.
  - Support for single- and/or dual-threshold capabilities.
  - Support for a "human similarity" match that utilizes learning algorithms. Instead of defining matching rules explicitly, which sometimes is not easy, the end users do manual matching on a "training" set. The matching engine infers the rules from the training set and provides a "human similarity" match.
  - Ability to use National Change of Address and other reference data services for matching accuracy.
- Batch load
  - Support for initial load with required performance
  - Implementation of chaining scenarios and how the scenarios affect performance
  - Scalability: time of processing as a function of the number of records
- Real time
  - Real-time processing for new customer records and record updates, merges, splits, and so on.
  - Implementation of chaining scenarios in real time
- Architecture
  - SOA compliance and support for Web services
  - Data exchange solution architecture between the matching engine and the primary database
  - Platforms supported: operating systems and databases
  - Support for parallel processing
  - Openness of the solution and support for integration and iterative improvements
- Flexibility of configuration and customization
  - Matching parameters supported
  - Solution customization; languages supported, if any
- Merge and split (these points are discussed in more detail in Chapter 15)
  - Support for data merge and data survivorship rules
  - Support for symmetric split
  - Support for asymmetric spit
- Solution change control
  - Solution change-control capabilities are important to support the history of configuration changes. It is important in some cases to review what configuration was used at some point in the past.
- Operational complexity
  - Matching file preparation

- Match/merge configuration setup
- Creation of the matching data set
- Reporting
  - Change configuration reporting
  - Reporting in support of operational processing
- Error processing
  - Automatic error processing
  - Support for manual entry to resolve errors and conditions when the algorithm cannot resolve matching
- Ability to work with country-specific plug-ins for data matching, including name and address aliases, phonetic and string similarity algorithms, transliteration problems, and differences in the character set codes
  - Two different competing approaches can be used here. The first approach assumes that name and address standardization is performed first. Then a match is executed against persistently stored standardized names and addresses and other attributes participating in the match process. This approach is most common. It generates standardized names and addresses that are beneficial for other purposes beyond matching.
  - There is an alternative approach. It suggests that higher match accuracy can be achieved if the record is matched as is with all fuzziness and the library issues resolved dynamically in a holistic manner for all attributes participating in the matching process.

To sum up, this chapter discusses key issues and approaches associated with entity identification and matching, with the specific focus on the Customer domain. This topic is one of the core requirements and benefits of any MDM project and has profound implications for the way business processes and applications are affected by a new authoritative system of record created and managed by an MDM Data Hub.

References

1. Dubov, Lawrence. "Quantifying Data Quality with Information Theory: Information Theory Approach to Data Quality for MDM." http://mike2.openmethodology.org/blogs/information-development/2009/08/14/quantifying-data-quality-with-information-theory/.

2. Berson, Alex, Smith, Stephen, and Thearling, Kurt. *Building Data Mining Applications for CRM*. McGraw-Hill (December 1999).

3. Dean, Jeffrey and Ghemawat, Sanjay. "MapReduce: Simplified Data Processing on Large Clusters." Google, Inc., 2004.

4. http://www.archives.gov/publications/general-info-leaflets/55.html.

5. http://www.itl.nist.gov/div897/sqg/dads/HTML/nysiis.html.

6. http://www.mcs.csueastbay.edu/~simon/handouts/4245/hall.html.

Beyond Party Match: Merge, Split, Party Groups, and Relationships

T he previous chapter provided an in-depth discussion of how an MDM solution enables entity identification using various attribute- and record-level matching techniques. Although we discussed entity identification in general terms, we concentrated on the easier-to-explain Customer domain to describe the process of identification in a sufficient level of detail.

Merge and Split

We use the same approach and continue this discussion by taking a closer look at the complementary operations of entity merge and split, and will try to explain these operations both in general terms as well as using the specifics of merging and splitting entities in the Customer domain.

Merge

Chapter 14 showed how to match records and link them into match groups or clusters of affinity. Figure 15-1 illustrates how a match and link process can uniquely identify a Match Group 100.

Matching and linking operations represent a critical step in entity identification, but as the example in Figure 15-1 illustrates, in the case of customer identification, the records describing the individual contain some contradictions. For example, it is unclear what name, residential address, SSN, and so on, represent the "right" data about the individual. The MDM Data Hub has to solve this problem and decide what attributes should "survive" when the Hub *merges* records in the match group in order to create a single integrated customer record that represents a 360-degree view of the individual, including an integrated view of key customer metrics such as a complete and accurate net-worth or risk exposure of the customer.

Full Name	Address	SSN	Match Group	The Records are Assigned to the Same Match Group "100". How to Merge these Records? Which Name and Address is Right?
Thomas Wilson	67 Main Street. Ocean View, CA 91765	123-456-7890	100	
Tom Wilson	61 Main St. Ocean View, CA 91765	123-456-7890	100	

FIGURE 15-1   Linked records—candidates for merge

In general terms, a successful and flexible approach to merging match group records calls for the development and implementation of a hybrid automatic and manual user-guided process. This process should allow the user to select the correct attribute values for the entity in question. For example, when you look at the information about an individual, the "correctness" is typically determined by a human operator familiar with the individual, a data steward applying data governance guidance to attribute survivorship, or a systemic, automated process that can make this determination based on some predefined rules and certain additional information. Such information may include individual preferences captured via a service channel or reference information acquired from a trusted external data provider (for example, National Change of Address [NCOA]). In the latter case, an MDM system can assist the user in making the right decision by providing some default merge recommendations that can then be validated or overridden by the end user. The attribute survivorship decisions can be driven by simple rules or arbitrary complex business logic. For example, the survivorship of a particular attribute can be based on the source systems that hold the record, the value the record displays, the end user who entered the attribute value, and other factors. This indicates that the MDM Data Hub solution must maintain attribute-level data about the record's source, time stamp of creation and modification, and certain user information, including user role and other identity attributes (often referred to as user credentials). Figure 15-2 shows a sample spreadsheet that can be used as a template for specifying default survivorship rules.

A pragmatic approach to developing merge capabilities for MDM Data Hub solutions states that each survivorship candidate attribute should be defined and uniquely identified

Entity Name	Field Name	Survivorship Rule
Individual	Individual Name	• Is to be sourced from system A provided that the value in system A is not blank. • Otherwise use the value from system B
Individual	Individual Date of Birth	• Is to be sourced from system A if the individual is an active or former client. • For prospective clients the attribute value should be sourced from system C. • If systems A and C do not provide valid attribute values or the values are blank, the attribute value should be sourced from system B or system D. • If both systems contain valid data, the latest assigned value should prevail.

FIGURE 15-2   A template defining attribute survivorship rules

in the Data Hub's logical data model. If the project requirements call for the creation of a persistent merge history, we can extend the Data Hub data model by creating a history entity as shown in Figure 15-3.

This model supports the notion of inheritance of records merged from the same system or multiple legacy sources.

If two records are merged, the new "golden" record is created. The "golden" record may or may not inherit CUSTOMER_ID from one of the existing records. The attribute MERGED_TO_CUSTOMER_ID in the Customer History table points to the record created as a result of the merge in the table Customer (where the MERGED_TO value is equal to 1000).

As we have noted before, the creation and maintenance of a high-confidence "golden" record requires user input for practically any data domain that is managed in the MDM system. The technology organization supporting the MDM project should develop a user-friendly interface that allows end users to create entity groupings, display the duplicates, and choose the attribute values for the "golden" record.

Merge operations can be rather complex and impact other systems that are using or are used by the Data Hub. The changes in the data content that result from performing a merge operation should be propagated to other systems in order to synchronize their data content with the Data Hub as the master of the content. Additional complexity of the merge operation for the Party domain may be caused by the need to merge relationships, agreements, and other documents that have been tied to two or more separate party records before the merge. When two or more records are merged in the Data Hub, a merge transaction is sent to the consuming data warehouses and data marts. Often, merge processing can be automated and additive facts processed automatically; for instance, the total value of sales or total of all outstanding credit balances will be summarized over all merged customer records.

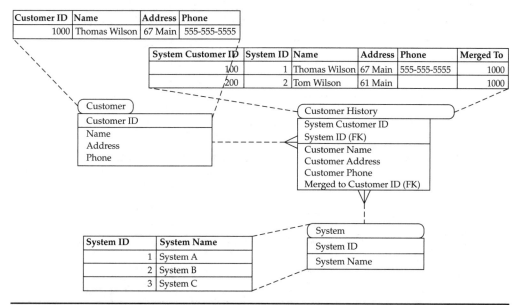

FIGURE 15-3   A model supporting merge history

The complexity of the merge processing is not the only challenge for entity management in an MDM Data Hub. The process of entity split can be even more complex.

Split

A *split* is an MDM process that is functionally opposite to a merge. Using the party model as the context, we can say that a split is required if information gathered from two or more parties has been mistakenly stored in a single party record. Figure 15-4 displays an example in which a record that was thought to represent one individual, Bill Johns, in reality represents two individuals, Bill Johns, Sr., and his son Bill Johns, Jr., with different dates of birth. Procedurally, the split would "undo" a merge operation provided that the appropriate information to perform the split is available even after the merge is done.

In this example, as soon as the mistake of the merge decision has been discovered, a corrective action is taken. Typically, this is a manual action that requires inputting additional information. In the example shown in Figure 15-4, Bill Johns, Sr., retains the Party ID (100) while a new Party ID (110) is created for Bill Johns, Jr. The MDM project's technology team should plan on providing a user-friendly interface that allows the business user to perform the split process. Similarly, in order to merge, if the project requirements include split history support, we can further extend our MDM logical data model as shown in Figure 15-5. If documents, relationships, and other information had been tied to a party record before the split, all pieces of this information must be distributed between the records formed as a result of the split. This adds to the complexity of splits.

Unlike a merge, where additive information can be summarized automatically, automation may not be feasible for a split. Indeed, a split transaction requires a clear definition of the post-split state that may not be available in the system before the split.

Party ID	Name	Address	Phone Number	Gender	Date of Birth
100	Bill Johns	467 Mercer Street. Ocean View, CA 19765	(818) 456-7890	M	Unknown

Split

Party ID	Name	Address	Phone Number	Gender	Date of Birth
100	Bill Johns, Sr	467 Mercer Street. Ocean View, CA 91765	(818) 456-7890	M	04/25/1954
110	Bill Johns, Jr	467 Mercer Street. Ocean View, CA 91765	(818) 456-7890	M	09/25/1992

FIGURE 15-4   An example of a split

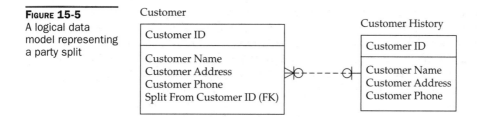

FIGURE 15-5
A logical data
model representing
a party split

Customer

Customer ID
Customer Name Customer Address Customer Phone Split From Customer ID (FK)

Customer History

Customer ID
Customer Name Customer Address Customer Phone

NOTE *As described in the Merge and Split sections above, the project team should plan for an additional modeling effort if the business functional requirements include support for merge and split within a single model. For the implementation to be successful, it is important to develop guidance principles about how to store and maintain enterprise entity identifiers generated by the Data Hub. In order to facilitate message exchanges between enterprise systems, it may be beneficial to develop a Key Lookup service that is capable of returning a system-specific identifier or translate master data identifiers across systems.*

Relationships and Groups

Although solving entity identification problems is key to creating any MDM solution, it is not the end of the road for an MDM project. Indeed, the newly created MDM Data Hub contains the superset of entities from multiple source systems. Again, let's use Customer and Party as entity types in order to illustrate a number of key concerns related to identification, merge, split, and other entity resolution operations.

Some of the party entities in the MDM Data Hub are current customers while others are still prospects or past customers who terminated their relationships with the firm for any number of reasons. Moreover, some of the parties may not be customers but are important to the organization since they are related to the current customers or provide some service to them. For example, an MDM Data Hub may contain information about spouses and children named as beneficiaries on customer accounts, trustees of the customer, or powerful and influential individuals who are designated as having power of attorney for some customers.

These relationships may represent a very attractive opportunity for the enterprise that is looking to increase its customer base and grow the share of its customers' wallets. In order to take advantage of this opportunity, an MDM Data Hub has to support the notion of explicit and implicit party relationships and party groups. Specific requirements to support these features as well as their implementation priorities depend on the industry, line of business, and particular needs of the organization as defined in the business scope documentation for the project. Thus, we limit the discussion on these topics to a generic overview of the issues, concerns, and approaches to solving the party relationships and grouping challenge.

Direct Business Relationships with an Individual

We will use an example of retail financial services industry that includes brokerage, banking, and insurance to explain the notion of direct relationships. In this case, a relationship with an individual begins when the individual becomes a prospect (potential customer). Depending on the channel used, a financial services enterprise would create a party record for this individual that points to a new relationship between the enterprise and the individual. Depending on the architecture style of the MDM Data Hub, this party record for the individual is created either in the Hub or in one of the source systems. If the sales process was successful (for example, the individual decides to establish one or more relationships [for example, open an account] with the firm), the prospect becomes a customer. Depending on the individual situation and set of preferences, this newly created customer may have different roles on his or her accounts. In the example shown in Figure 15-6, John S. Smith is in the role of "Primary" on account 4736922239.

The attribute "Date Closed" in the Account table is blank, which identifies John Smith as an active customer. When the account is closed, this attribute is updated with the actual or effective event date. If this happens with all of John's accounts, he assumes the role of a "Former Customer."

Another type of direct relationship between an individual and an organization is an agreement according to which the individual provides services to some of the customers or works with prospects. The individuals can be employees of the firm or work on a contractual basis (for example, consider external consultants that provide some very specialized services, such as jumbo insurance policies, to a small group of enterprise customers). The individuals

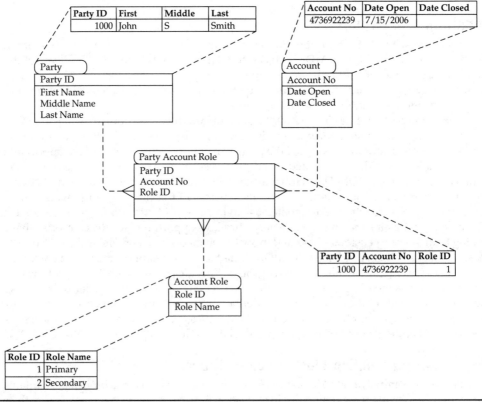

Figure 15-6 Data model and example illustrating a direct relationship between the enterprise and an individual

responsible for servicing accounts or interacting directly with customers or prospects can also be customers or prospects of the same enterprise, which means that, depending on the functions/services they perform, the individuals can have multiple roles and relationships with the enterprise.

The importance of the relationships is not limited to financial services. Companies that provide products and services to customers either directly or through an intermediary want to get a greater share of each customer's wallet, enable more compelling and higher value cross-sell and up-sell opportunities, and increase customer retention rates. However, they want to do so while gaining better control, and limiting, or even eliminating, relationships that are risky or not cost effective. Service and product provider companies may use multiple names to do business with your organization. Understanding relationships would help the organization to identify all the names a single company is using, which would reduce their risk exposure by better controlling how much credit is being extended to a single entity or closely related individuals, or individuals and organizations. For example, a small business owner could lease or purchase a computer under his own name and then lease or purchase another one under the company's name. It may be important for the computer company to understand that this is the same person, especially if that same person were to apply for credit multiple times using different identity profiles, and the company were to issue credit multiple times to that same individual, which would create a high level of risk exposure.

Energy companies and other utilities that provide services to consumers and organizations face similar risks from customers they call "spinners." Spinners are people who are notoriously bad customers, ordering service under different names and never paying for it. For example, an electric company might first put service in the husband's name, then the wife's, and then another household member's name—and they don't pay again and again. The same situation could occur with a company that uses different names. With spinners, it is extremely important to know how customers are related to each other, and how/if people and organizations are related.

For hospitality business and travel companies that operate loyalty programs, it is important that they develop a good understanding of the behavior of individual customers and also their spouses, partners, and other family members. This knowledge will help companies to develop better and more attractive offers to loyalty club members. It is not uncommon for people to buy hospitality and travel services based on family preferences rather than their individual preferences, so the companies having more information about how people are related will ultimately improve the bottom line.

In healthcare, it is obvious that understanding how patients are related would be helpful for better understanding genetic diseases. Understanding relationships between patients and providers is also critical to support online portals and self-service applications. These solutions require data visibility, security, and eligibility, which can be effective only if the system "understands" what individual or organization is authorized to have access to a patient's health record, the type of access, and so on. By providing physicians with an information portal that has complete patient detail—including how physicians are related to patients, how physicians are related to hospitals, how physicians are related to their offices, and what kind of plans they offer in each office—hospitals make it more convenient for physicians to interact with them, which ultimately results in more physician referrals and more revenue for the hospitals.

Relationship data is also critical for government agencies looking for criminals. For example, when the Homeland Security Agency is tracking terrorists or the police are looking for organized crime suspects, they need to see how people are related and who is connected to whom. Often, members of organized crime rings and terrorist groups operate behind some kind of a legitimate-appearing legal entity (façade), so understanding relationships, not only between people, but also between people and different kinds of associations, funds, and organizations, can be critically important.

Symmetric and Asymmetric Relationships

When dealing with individual customers and prospects, the enterprise needs to know the potential and actual "value" of the individual and his or her specific assets along with the roles the individual plays relative to the assets. To provide an effective personalized customer service, the enterprise needs to be able to recognize all of the individual's assets managed by the firm across all lines of business. This goal can be achieved when the MDM Data Hub solves the party identification problem. As a result, the enterprise gains a clear view of its direct customers. The missing component of the equation is the assessment of the relationships between customers, particularly high-value customers. The fragment of a data model shown in Figure 15-7 represents a structure that can be used to support *symmetric* relationships between individuals—siblings, spouses, partners in business, and so on.

Figure 15-7 illustrates the relationship between John Smith and Mary Smith. Relationship ID = 1 points to "Spouse" for the relationship between John and Mary with Party IDs equal to 1000 and 1100 respectively.

We can also use the example of John and Mary to illustrate *asymmetric* relationships. If, for example, Mary is a high-value customer and John has no accounts with the firm, the enterprise will be able to recognize John only as an "indirect" customer through his relationship with Mary. The relationships that can be supported by the data structure shown in Figure 15-7 are limited to symmetric relationships where the result will not change if the columns in the table "Individual to Individual Relationship" are swapped. Indeed, if "John is Mary's spouse" is a valid statement, the reverse statement is valid too: "Mary is John's spouse."

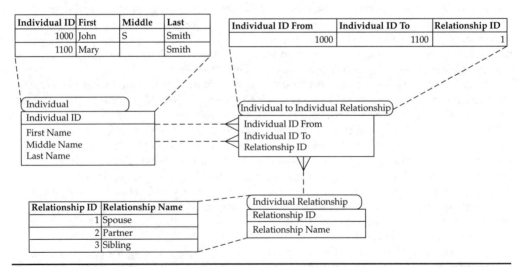

Figure 15-7   Data model and example illustrating a symmetric relationship between two individuals

Such symmetry does not hold for other types of relationships (for example, parent/child relationships or service provider/customer relationships). To support these relationship types, the two columns "Individual ID" in the table "Individual to Individual Relationship" should be changed to "Individual ID From" and "Individual ID To" to create an asymmetric relationship. This transformation is shown in Figure 15-8, where Larry Smith is John Smith's father and Tom Logan is John's accountant.

As per Lawrence Dubov's article,[1] there exist three MDM techniques to build entity relationships and hierarchies:

- Use an external trusted source of relationships or multiple trusted sources ("tree of truth") and build your internal relationships and hierarchies comparing in-house data with the trusted sources.

- Define rules that will be used by the systems automatically to infer entity relationships. These rules can be based on common attribute values—for example, people sharing the same location are defined as a household. The locations can be matched exactly or probabilistically.

- Develop relationship matches and links manually using graphical interfaces enabling the user to perform the relationship building work with ease and efficiency.

These methods can be used individually or in combination to achieve varying levels of success in terms of identifying and understanding symmetric and asymmetric, one-to-many and many-to-many relationships. Each of these three methods has its benefits, areas of applicability, and limitations. In full-scale enterprise MDM implementations, all three methods can be beneficially used to create a comprehensive view of relationships.

When an organization is using an external trusted source, it relies on that source's data and matches its internal records against the external data to help establish which of its records are related. This approach is frequently used to establish and maintain the hierarchies of customer

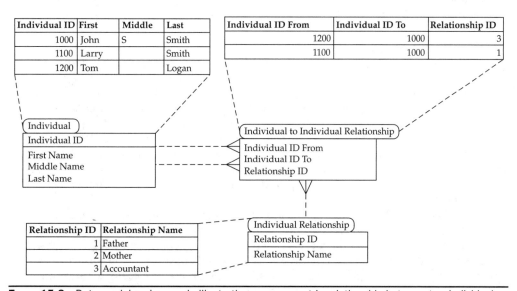

FIGURE 15-8   Data model and example illustrating an asymmetric relationship between two individuals

or product data. Maintenance of corporate hierarchies is a critical task from the credit risk perspective, marketing, territory alignment, and so on. Structurally, each of the hierarchies is represented by a single root with an unlimited number of layers below. Applications typically display and manage these hierarchies in a tree view.

For global MDM implementations, it is often important to build a solution capable of using multiple country-specific data providers and decision tree logic. This logic can "decide" which of the trusted external sources is the best to use for a given internal record.

The second approach to establishing relationships includes creating rules for matching algorithms to determine which records are related and how. Rules can be used to algorithmically infer relationships and to validate relationship rules. For example, a Data Hub should be able to define the rules for the identification of people who work for the same employer, belong to the same professional group, or are part of the same household. These rules can be simple or quite complex to include fuzzy and probabilistic matching. Relationship validation rules can be used to specify that a company is allowed to have only one parent or a patient must be associated with at least one provider. When a validation rule is violated, an alert is generated and human review of the data exception is required. If, for example, a company is found to have two parent companies, a validation rule is violated, which causes the rules engine to generate a data exception that will be sent in a data stewardship queue for review and processing.

Human intervention is often necessary to resolve rule violations and other data anomalies. However, there are also instances where organizations want to determine how data is related but cannot use an external source or create a specific rule to establish a relationship. In those situations organizations must rely on manual methods to establish relationships and links between data. For this reason, data stewardship processes and technologies should be seamlessly integrated with MDM technologies in organizations that want to establish a relationship-centric view of the enterprise.

A sound relationship management strategy that combines all three approaches enables enterprises to build comprehensive MDM solutions with a balanced use of advanced algorithms and business user input.

Households and Groups

MDM capabilities that support the discovery of relationships between parties should include the ability to recognize customers' Households or Party Groups. Indeed, the members of these entities are related or connected in some way, and although they may or may not be direct customers at present, they certainly represent an opportunity for the enterprise to convert them into direct customers. The term *Party Group* is used to denote a group of individuals or business partners that are connected in some implicit or explicit way and should be considered as a customer from the firm's relationship perspective (when the relationships are based on the family structures, these Party Groups are sometimes referred to as "Family Groups"). The term "Household" is typically limited to the family members residing at the same address.

If the MDM Data Hub can recognize Households and Party Groups, the enterprise can offer customized products and services to the group's members proactively even before they are recognized as high-value individual customers. Understanding these relationships provides the enterprise with a competitive advantage and opportunity to improve overall customer experience, strengthen customer relationships, and reduce customer attrition.

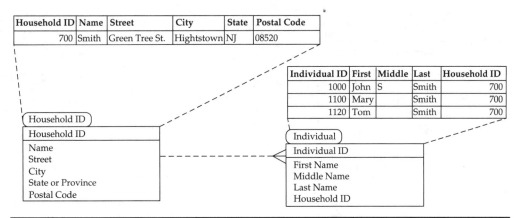

FIGURE 15-9 Data model and example illustrating the concept of Household or Party Group

Recognizing the totality of customer relationships allows organizations to create cross-sell and up-sell opportunities and increase the share of wallet within each Household and a Party Group. The association between individuals and households is depicted in Figure 15-9. The Household/Party Group structure shown in Figure 15-9 is limited in that one individual cannot cross Household/Party Groups.

Customer Groups

The notion of a *Customer Group* avoids the single-group limitation by defining a structure in which an individual can belong to multiple groups. For example, a group of individuals having a common interest can open an account and by doing so establishes a direct relationship with the enterprise, where the newly created Customer Group is playing the role of a customer. Members of a Customer Group don't have to be related to each other in the same way the members of the Family Group are. In fact, Customer Groups could be considered as artificial constructs created for a particular, often transient business purpose. A Customer Group can be formal (that is, includes businesses, organizations, legal entities, and associations that have a legal status and are recognized as legal entities) or informal. Figure 15-10 illustrates the notion of a Customer Group.

It follows from the example that Mary Turner and Larry Goldberg serve on the "ABC Board of Directors," Larry as the "Chair" and Mary as a "Member."

NOTE *The notion of a Customer Group represents a special case of the entity-grouping capability of an MDM solution. It is easy to imagine that many entity classes can be grouped together in order to enable certain business-driven features—for example, a group of accounts can allow a special tax treatment; a group of products can be created to provide specialized, dedicated support and preferential pricing; and so on.*

Relationship Challenges of Institutional Customers and Contacts

The Basel Committee[2] and other regulatory bodies require that corporations, shareholders, signatories, and other decision-making individuals and groups in positions of power and

Record	Match Group
Customer Record 1	1
Customer Record 2	2
Customer Record 3	1
Customer Record 4	2
Customer Record 5	3
Customer Record 6	3
Customer Record 7	2

Customer Record 8

A New Record Is Matched against the Existing Customer Base and Assigned to Match Group 2. Customer Record 8 Is Also Matched to Customer Record 3 to Result in Merge of Match Groups 1 and 2

Record	Match Group
Customer Record 1	2
Customer Record 2	2
Customer Record 3	2
Customer Record 4	2
Customer Record 5	3
Customer Record 6	3
Customer Record 7	2
Customer Record 8	2

FIGURE 15-10   Data model and example illustrating the concept of a Customer Group

control be identifiable with the required degree of reliability. These requirements have direct implications on how an MDM Data Hub should recognize individuals who represent institutions and act on their behalf. In this discussion, we are using the term "institutional contact" to define individuals who represent institutions and act on their behalf. This is different from a situation where the customer is an institution and the MDM Data Hub manages legal entities, their relationships, groupings, and hierarchies as customers in their own right. We call these customers "institutional customers."

The recognition challenge in the case of institutional contacts is complicated by the fact that these individuals may use the identification attributes provided to them by their institution. For example, a trader working for a major brokerage house may be identified by his or her exchange registration number rather than by name and social security number. When such an institutional contact interacts with the enterprise on his or her firm's behalf, the enterprise must recognize these types of relationships and the role the individual and the firm can assume in the relationships. This is a difficult problem that can be addressed differently depending on the set of business rules and allowed roles that vary from industry to industry and from one institution type to another. For example, the roles and rules may depend on whether the corporation represented by an individual is listed on a recognized stock exchange. In general, these complex relationships can be maintained by the structure shown in Figure 15-11.

In the preceding example, Mary Turner and Larry Goldberg work for ABC Corporation. Mary's role is "Decision Maker" (could be CEO, CFO, and so on). while Larry is an employee.

Relationship Challenges of Institutional Customers

Dealing with institutional customers (institutions), their contacts, and their inter-relationships is extremely challenging. In addition to the data quality and clerical issues common to both individual and institutional customers, there is frequently a lack of a solid definition of what constitutes an institutional customer. This is particularly true in cases where a firm has

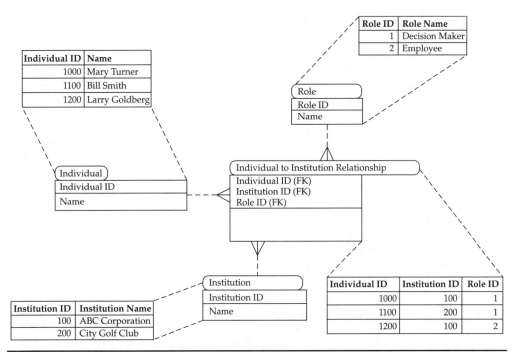

Figure 15-11   Data model and example illustrating relationships between institutional contacts and individuals

multiple relationships with the institutions represented by various individuals. In this case, the firm may have multiple customers with the same customer tax identifier. This indicates that the tax identification number may not be granular enough to uniquely identify the customers representing institutions. As we stated in the previous section, separate relationships can exist between individuals acting on behalf of different corporations, lines of business, geographic locations, divisions, and departments. Likewise, separate relationships can exist between the enterprise and the institution at the parent company level, the subsidiary level, line of business, division, and so on. In general, the notion of customer relationship can become very uncertain and would depend on how the customer relationship managers wish to define the customer. Different units within the organization may have different granularity needs for customer relationship definition. Moreover, when dealing with large institutional customers, MDM solutions face additional challenges that result from merger and acquisition activities. For example, corporations, their business units, and their lines of business may change names as a result of mergers and acquisitions, rebranding, internal reorganizations, and so on. The relationships between parent companies and their subsidiaries are also unstable. The same applies to the organizational hierarchies of institutional customers and, consequently, to their relationships with the enterprise. Institutional customers may require different customer definitions for the same customer depending on the line of business, a channel, or other conditions. For example, a business unit responsible for shipping is likely to identify customers by a mailing label that includes the name of the organization and its address.

From the sales organization's perspective, each customer relationship is identified through the relationship's contacts. As a result, institutional relationships require more complex and, at the same time, more flexible data models than those built for individual customers. Of course, we recognize that in general the number of institutional customers is much smaller than the number of individual customers, and that fact helps MDM Data Hub systems to effectively manage institutional relationships.

Another challenge presented by institutional customers is the need to correlate customer records in order to remediate customer hierarchy changes. Left unmanaged, hierarchy changes can create a perception that the hierarchy of institutional customers is incorrect, incomplete, and unreliable. Incorrect institutional customer hierarchy data can negatively affect the enterprise in multiple ways. For financial services companies that deal with the institutional customer (for example, investment banks), incorrect customer hierarchy data may cause failures in trading, erroneous financial reporting, lost marketing opportunities, failure in Anti-Money Laundering (AML) and Know Your Customer (KYC) processing, and other business and regulatory issues. This challenge is rapidly coming to the forefront of business concerns for any enterprise that supports institutional customers, and many MDM solutions are being developed or modified today to address this concern.

To illustrate the problem in its simplest form, consider an institutional hierarchy where each node is either the root with no parents or a leaf that can have only one parent. Figure 15-12 illustrates this situation by showing two institutions, ABC and ABD, that are in fact the subsidiaries of one parent company.

However, if we apply a customer-level matching process, it may identify ABC and ABD as likely to be the same institutional customer whose name was changed or misspelled. This happens because the institutional customer hierarchy and the associated relationship data represent a new piece of information never used by the matching process designed to handle individuals. In principle, this problem can be addressed in one of two ways: modifying the matching process to include hierarchy-based relationship data, or changing the relationship hierarchy traversal to leverage the results of the matching process.

In either situation, an MDM system should be extended to accommodate additional business rules and workflows that can handle institutional customer hierarchies. Then the modified MDM-system will be able to identify, profile, quantify, and remediate errors in matching the institutional hierarchy data by mapping hierarchy nodes to integrated customer entities.

Figure 15-12
A simple institutional hierarchy that conflicts with institutional customer identification

Institution Name	Match Group
ABC Inc.	200
ABD Inc.	200

According to the Institutional Hierarchy "Parent Corp" Has Two Subsidiaries While, According to the Match Process, Both Company Records Belong to the Same Match Group

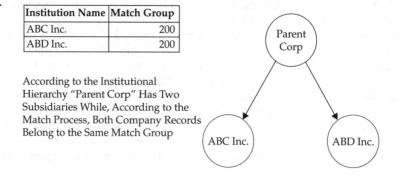

Need for Persistent Match Group Identifiers

Match Groups may or may not have to be persisted. If a match engine is used to find potential matches in a few party records, it is not necessary to persist a match group even though such persistence may be beneficial from the search performance perspective. There are maintenance cost trade-offs in implementing this. As soon as we persist something that can change, we have to capture and manage the change, which is a complex task. Indeed, match groups can change if critical match attributes change. This can trigger a chain of events within and outside the matching process. What if legal documents have already been tagged by the Match Group Identifiers? Can we allow a systemic change of the identifier? The answer is most likely negative.

Generally speaking, Match Group Identifiers should be persisted but carefully managed when the records representing individuals and/or organizations are linked to other entities. The creation and maintenance of relationships and hierarchies are typical situations that require the Match Group Identifier to be persisted.

There are scenarios where the Match Group Identifiers do not need to be persisted. For instance, if a match process is used only to eliminate duplicates and create merged records that will be used for a stand-alone marketing campaign, the goal can be achieved without storing and therefore managing the Match Group Identifiers. Another typical scenario occurs when the matching process is only used for computer-assisted manual data de-duping. In some situations with very conservative requirements for match and merge, only the end users can provide the ultimate match, link, and merge decisions. In these situations the Match Group Identifier is not equal to the "golden copy" Party ID, but is treated as an intermediate attribute assisting the end user with customer identification key assignment.

Even though some specific needs may not require the generation and storage of the Match Group Identifiers, the general intent to create and maintain a single unique "golden copy" of the Party ID across the enterprise is a good idea that aligns the MDM Data Hub design with the strategic intent of the Master Data Management initiative.

Additional Considerations for Customer Identifiers

Whether you operate in an account-centric enterprise and are planning for a transition to a customer-centric enterprise, or a transition to a customer-centric business is already under way, the majority of data access requests still rely on the account numbers for inquiries, updates, deletes, and other operations. It probably makes no sense to try to get rid of account numbers as entity identifiers and a communication exchange vehicle that all participants are familiar with and clearly understand.

So what will happen when the migration to the customer-centric view is complete? Would it be a good idea to maintain account numbers and associated entities in the customer-centric world? So far, we presented the customer identifier solely as a technical artifact, a key that is generated, maintained, and used by the system with no exposure to the end user. Depending on a given project's requirements, this may continue to be the case. Alternatively, the customer identifier may be exposed to end-user applications and users may be trained to use the customer identifier in conjunction with or even instead of the traditional account number in order to search for customer groups, family groups, relationships, customer agreements, and other related entities. If the business requirements specifically ask for customer identifiers to be exposed to end-user applications, then the project team needs to carefully plan and design the rules for generating and using customer identifiers prior to the first MDM Data Hub deployment.

Here are some considerations related to the generation of customer identifiers:

- The key must be unique. This sounds obvious, but we do not want to miss this critical requirement here.

- The key should have a check digit or other data integrity check rule so that the integrity of the key can be confirmed.

- We do not recommend defining key ranges unless there are very compelling reasons, such as established business processes and an inflexible technology infrastructure.

- Generally speaking, the use of intelligent (meaningful) keys is not a good practice because it limits the solution's flexibility and adaptability to changing business conditions.

- The key length should be sufficient to provide unique identification for all entities in the MDM Data Hub.

An identifier that conforms to the technical requirements in this list is referred to as a "well-formed identifier" and is a primary vehicle that enables entity identification.

To reiterate, entity identification is a key component of entity resolution and represents one of the primary functional requirements for any MDM Data Hub solution. As the scope and size of master data managed by the MDM Data Hub increases over time, the requirement to create and maintain well-formed identifiers may be extended to include relationships, entity groups, and other attributes and constructs that are selected to act as enablers of the enterprise-wide deployment of a Master Data Management environment that provides meaningful business benefits, including the ability to transform the enterprise into an entity relationship–centric model.

References

1. Dubov, Lawrence. "Master Data Management: The Importance of Relationships Management," Information Management, March 19, 2009. http://www.information-management.com/specialreports/2009_132/10015070-1.html.

2. http://www.bis.org/list/bcbs/index.htm.

Data Synchronization, MDM System Testing, and Other Implementation Concerns

This chapter deals with several complex implementation concerns facing MDM designers. We will discuss batch and real-time synchronization issues, MDM system testing concerns, options to consider when designing MDM application and presentation layers components, as well as concerns related to the MDM deployment infrastructure. Combined with the previous discussions on MDM architecture, design, key functional requirements, and specific features, as well as the in-depth review of how to build the MDM business case and define the MDM roadmap, this chapter should prepare readers to fully appreciate not just the complexity and magnitude of MDM, but also the need, the value, and the critical nature of data governance as a key enabler and a necessary component of any successful MDM initiative. We discuss key aspects of data governance in Chapter 17.

Goals of Data Synchronization

Data synchronization is one of the most difficult and frequently underestimated areas of Master Data Management. The purpose of this section is to describe a typical implementation of an MDM synchronization solution in the context of the following use case.

NOTE *The discussion that follows offers a hypothetical implementation approach where many technical details/components represent a conceptual or logical view of the implementation solution rather than a specific vendor product or custom-built code. For consistency and continuity, wherever possible we tried to map these logical components to the various MDM Data Hub architecture components and services that we described in Parts II and IV of the book.*

> **Use Case: Delivering Customer Information to the Touch Point in Real Time**
>
> The ABC Company has multiple applications and systems used across multiple lines of business to provide services to customers. The company faces a significant business challenge—its inability to integrate information about customers and their relationships across different lines of business in a timely manner. Due to the heterogeneous and disconnected nature of these legacy systems, an integrated customer view can only be delivered using the existing customer data warehouse. Unfortunately, the data warehouse is updated only once a day using overnight batch processing. Given the real-time nature of the company's sales and servicing channels (that is, customers have the ability to buy products and services on the company Web Portal as well as invoke many self-service actions and requests), the resulting latency of customer information seriously impacts the company's ability to gain better insight into customer behavior, including the propensity to buy products and services, the probability of default (for example, on a loan), and other traits available through the use of customer analytics. At the same time, senior management wants to preserve the existing applications while making customer information available in real time to all applications and all customer touch points.

Technology Approach to Use Case Realization

When a customer initiates contact with the ABC Company, the customer has to provide some pieces of identification information. Depending on the customer service channels supported by the ABC Company, the identification information may vary from officially issued credentials such as SSN, driver license, or passport, to authentication credentials the user has to possess in order to access the website or a customer service call center. Regardless of the authentication method, the MDM Data Hub would have to map user credentials to the identification attributes that are required to perform user identification and matching (see Chapter 14 for details). The MDM Data Hub services are capable of recognizing the user as an existing or a new customer. The ABC Company business requirements specify that for existing customers, all relevant customer information and recent contact history are available for viewing and editing to the appropriate company personnel subject to the constraints imposed by the data visibility and security policy. Transactional information at each point of contact is captured in the legacy systems, while all updates and new pieces of identity information for the existing customers are captured and stored in the MDM Data Hub. At the same time, new customers will be recognized by the appropriate Data Hub service, and all relevant information will also be captured and stored in the MDM Data Hub using the transformation rules defined in the MDM Metadata Repository (see Chapter 5 for a discussion on the role of a metadata repository in MDM systems).

Given this overall process view, we will discuss the technology approach to developing an MDM solution in the context of the MDM design classification dimension, and specifically will focus on the MDM Data Hub architecture styles discussed in Chapter 4. Let's start with the reconciliation engine style Hub, and then look at the additional considerations relevant to an MDM Data Hub style known as the Transaction Hub. Just to recap, in discussing MDM design classification dimensions and the corresponding architecture styles, we have shown that an MDM Data Hub system can act as a registry of key master attributes (Registry-style Hub), a pass-through "slave" (reconciliation engine) of the legacy systems, or it can be a master of some or all entity attributes (in our use case scenario, this entity represents customer profile data).

MDM Data Hub with Multiple Points of Entry for Entity Information

As stated in our use case scenario, a customer can interact with the ABC Company across a variety of different channels, including Web self-service, Interactive Voice Response (IVR) telephone system, customer service representative access via telephone or in person, in-branch interactions, and so on.

The ABC Company's stated goal of the MDM project is to enable and ensure a consistent customer experience regardless of the channel or the interaction mode, and this experience should be achieved by creating a unified, holistic view of the customer and all of his or her relationships. Further, this holistic view has to be available on demand, in real time, to all channels supported by the ABC Company.

Let's start with the reconciliation engine style design approach. This architecture style positions the MDM Data Hub as a "slave" (reconciliation engine) for the existing data sources and applications. With this background, let's consider the specific process steps and Data Hub components involved when a customer interacts with one of the ABC Company's customer touch points. Figure 16-1 illustrates the key logical steps of the integrated solution.

NOTE *We focus on the process steps that involve or require Data Hub services directly. External systems interactions such as authentication and authorization actions to gain access to the channel via integration with or delegation to the enterprise security system are implied but not elaborated on for the sake of simplicity.*

1. At the point of contact, the customer provides his or her identification information (for example, name and address or the user ID established at the time of enrollment in the service). The information is scanned or entered using a customer identification application (login) interface that should be designed to enforce data entry formats and attribute values whenever possible. In the case of a self-service channel, the information is entered by the customer; otherwise, it is done by an authorized employee of the ABC Company. The identification application uses one of the published Data Hub services to initiate a check to verify whether the customer record exists in the Data Hub. The service forms a message with the received identification information using a standard matching message format. The message is published to the Enterprise Message Bus (EMB)—a middleware technology that is often present as a component of the service-oriented architecture and frequently referred to as the *Enterprise Service Bus (ESB)*. The first functional component to receive the message is the EMB Message Validator, which analyzes the message and confirms the correctness of the format. It also validates that the message context meets minimum data requirements. For flexibility and manageability, the MDM Data Hub system provides a management facility that allows users to configure minimum data requirements based on the appropriate metadata definitions.

2. The message is forwarded to the EMB Transaction Manager. The message gets assigned a unique transaction ID by the EMB Transaction Manager's Key Generator.

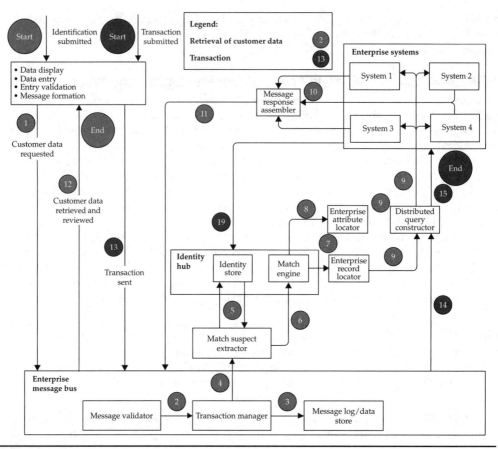

FIGURE 16-1   Data synchronization and key synchronization components

3. The Transaction Manager can optionally log transaction information, including the transaction type, transaction originator, time of origination, and possibly some other information about the transaction.

4. The Transaction Manager forwards the message to the Match Suspect Extractor.

5. The Match Suspect Extractor reads the identification parameters in the message and creates an MDM Data Hub extract with suspect matches. It can also contain records that were selected using various fuzzy matching algorithms.

6. The Match Suspect Extractor sends the extract message to the Match Engine. The Match Engine is an MDM Data Hub component that performs the match. It can return zero, one, or multiple matches. The engine computes the confidence level for the matched records. We assume that the matching engine is configured for two thresholds: T1 < T2 (the two-threshold model is discussed in Chapter 14).

a. If the confidence level is above T2 and only one match is found, then the Match Engine returns a unique customer ID along with additional data obtained from the Data Hub and/or external vendor knowledge bases. To improve the confidence of the match process, our ABC Company can choose to purchase and integrate an external information file (a knowledge base) that contains "trusted" information about the customer.

b. If the match confidence level is between T1 and T2 and multiple suspect matches are found, the identification application may initiate a workflow that prompts the user for additional identification information, or alternatively can ask the user to select the right customer record from the returned suspect match list. The latter can trigger another iteration of matching, usually described as a part of the information quality loop.

c. If the match confidence is below T1, the match service returns a notification that the customer record is not found. The user may choose to modify the identification information and resubmit the modified record for identification.

7. The Transaction Manager orchestrates other MDM Data Hub services to gather additional information about the identified customer. The customer identifier is sent to the Enterprise Record Locator, which contains a cross-reference facility with linkage information between the Data Hub keys and the source system keys. The source system keys are returned to the Transaction Manager (see Chapter 6 for a discussion on MDM Data Hub keys and services).

8. The Transaction Manager invokes the Enterprise Attribute Locator service to identify the best sources of data for each attribute in the enterprise data model.

9. The Transaction Manager sends inquiry messages to the source systems through the EMB, where it invokes the Distributed Query Constructor service, which generates a distributed query against multiple systems.

10. The source systems process the query request messages and send the messages to the Response Assembler. The Response Assembler assembles the messages received from the Data Hub and source systems into the Response Message.

11. The assembled message is published to the EMB. The Transaction Manager recognizes the message as part of the transaction that was initiated by the request in step 2. The Transaction Manager returns the message to the requestor and marks the transaction complete.

12. The ABC Company customer service employee who initiated this transaction in the first place can review the returned message and take advantage of the accurate and complete information about the customer and his or her transactions, which gives the customer service employee the required intelligence. Because the customer is identified with the appropriate degree of confidence, the customer service employee can initiate a business transaction to serve a customer request. For example, this could be a transaction that involves data changes to the customer information. Changes generated by the transaction are sent to the corresponding legacy system, whereas the customer identification information message is sent to the MDM Data Hub via the EMB.

13. The Data Hub initiates a *change transaction* by sending a transaction message to the EMB. The transaction may result in changes to the critical attributes used for matches. As we discussed in previous chapters, this in turn can trigger merges and splits in the MDM Data Hub. Splits can cause the creation of new customer IDs, whereas merges result in the deletion of some customer records.

    a. Every time the customer keys stored in the MDM Data Hub change, the corresponding changes in the Enterprise Record Locator (also referred to as the Cross-Reference Record Locator) must be applied as a single transaction.

    b. When the Data Hub and the Cross-Reference Record Locator are updated, the ABC Company's auditors may request a detailed record of these changes. A sound practice is to design the MDM Data Hub to preserve the history and change activity of all updates to the Data Hub, including archiving business events that triggered the change in the first place. Thus, a good MDM Data Hub design should provide for configurable archival and purge components and services. Typically, operational needs for archival and logging are relatively short term and limited to a few days or a few weeks maximum. Audit requirements are driven by regulatory compliance and legal requirements and typically specify relatively long data retention terms that can cover a span of several years. Active access, retention, archival, and purge requirements could be quite significant and thus must be defined based on the needs of all stakeholder groups and accounted for in the MDM business case and the roadmap.

14. The EMB makes messages available to the source systems in either a push or pull mode. In either case, operational source systems can accept or reject a change. The data governance group, working with the business systems owners, should establish rules around the level of control each system will have in terms of the ability to reject the changes coming from the Data Hub. Because customer identity updates can come from multiple systems, the project design team must establish a set of rules that can resolve data synchronization conflicts for each attribute. Typically, the source and the date/time of the change at the attribute level are the most important factors that must be taken into account.

Considerations for the Transaction Hub Master Model

If our ABC Company plans to transition the MDM solution from the Hub Slave model to the Hub Master model, the resulting impact on the information flows and processes can be quite profound. In the Hub Master scenario, in order to support our use case, all customer profile data (whatever attributes are determined to constitute the customer profile) is entered through a new Customer Profile Management application pointed directly to the MDM Data Hub. Customer profile attributes that were previously editable through multiple legacy applications should now be protected from changes through these applications and should become read-only attributes. A typical scenario implementing this approach may be as follows:

- The end users can search for a customer using identity attributes.
- As soon as a customer is found and selected by the end user, all customer profile information may be retrieved from the Data Hub and displayed in the legacy application screen.

- With a single point of entry into the MDM Data Hub, data synchronization in the Hub Master scenario is easier, but in order to achieve this state, some significant work in legacy applications must be performed to ensure that they do not enter or change customer information. This may not be what the enterprise is willing to do.

Therefore, overall Hub Master implementations are quite difficult, particularly in organizations with large and heterogeneous legacy environments, multiple generations of legacy systems, and complex delta processing and synchronization that involves many legacy systems. In practice, legacy-rich organizations should start implementing MDM solutions in a Hub Slave (reconciliation engine) style, with the Data Hub providing identification services as discussed in the previous section. Conversely, for new organizations or brand-new business units, the legacy is not as big an issue, and a Transaction Hub (Hub Master) might be a viable option. Serious analysis is required to determine the right end-state of the MDM solution and the actionable implementation roadmap.

Real-Time/Near-Real-Time Synchronization Components

The ABC Company use case we described in the previous sections is useful to show not only the synchronization data flows but also MDM Data Hub components and services that should be in place to implement an enterprise-scale data synchronization solution. Let's take a closer look at these components and services.

Legacy System Data Entry Validation Component   This component serves as the first barrier preventing erroneous data entry into the system. Good information management practice shows that it is important to bring data validation upstream as close to the point of data entry or creation as possible. Data validation components restrict the formats and range of values entered on the user interface screen for a data entry application (for example, an account opening or user registration applications). Ideally, the MDM designers should strive to make data entry validation in the legacy systems consistent with the Data Hub validation requirements.

Legacy System Message Creation and Canonical Message Format Component   Each legacy system that needs to be integrated into the real-time synchronization framework must have components responsible for creating and publishing the message to the Enterprise Message Bus. The message must conform to the canonical message format—that is, an enterprise standard message used for application-independent data exchange (the canonical data model and formats are discussed in Part II of the book). The canonical message format and the canonical data model are the enablers of effective data synchronization.

Legacy System Message-Processing Components   Each legacy system should be able to receive and process messages in a canonical format. The processing includes message interpretation and orchestration in terms of native legacy system functions and procedures.

Message Validation and Translations   Message validation components must be able to validate the message structure and message content (payload). These components should also be "code translation aware" in order to translate system-specific reference code semantics into enterprise values, and vice versa.

Transaction Manager and Transaction Logging Service   As the name implies, the Transaction Manager is responsible for the execution and control of each transaction. The Transaction Manager registers each transaction by assigning a transaction identifier (transaction ID).

All transactions in the transaction life cycle are recorded in the Transaction Log using Transaction Logging Service, regardless of whether they are successful or not. Transaction Log structures, attributes, and service semantics are defined in the MDM Metadata Repository. The Transaction Manager orchestrates and coordinates the transaction processing of composite, complex transactions, and interfaces with the exception-processing and compensating transaction management components and services if a transaction fails for any reason.

Match Suspect Extractor   When a new piece of customer information arrives (new customer record, change in the existing customer record, or deletion of an existing record), the matching engine needs to receive an extract with suspected records for which the match groups must be recalculated. It is a challenge to construct this extract to be small enough to support real-time or near-real-time match calculations and at the same time to capture all impacted records. Because the match rules and the attributes used for matching have a tendency to evolve over time, it is a good practice to make the Match Suspect Extractor a configurable component that uses metadata definitions provided and maintained in the MDM Metadata Repository through an administrative application interface.

Identity Store   The Identity Store maintains the customer data with the superset of records that includes records from all participating systems in scope. The attributes are limited to the critical attributes needed for matching (see Chapter 14 for a detailed discussion on critical data attributes). Also, the Identity Store includes the Match Group keys. In a typical MDM system for a large enterprise, the Identity Store may have hundreds of millions of records. A lot of computer power and advanced performance optimization techniques are required to enable high throughput for both reads and updates. In addition, the Identity Store holds some amount of historical information. Typically, it is limited to recent history that enables error recovery and the resolution of operational issues.

Change Capture   This component is responsible for capturing the record or records that have been changed, added, or deleted. Pointers to these records are the entry information required by the Match Suspect Extractor to begin match processing.

Purge, Archival, and Audit Support   Purge and archival components are responsible for purging records to get rid of history records that exceeded the predefined retention threshold. The audit features allow MDM Data Hub solutions to archive purged records for potential audit or investigation purposes. More importantly, though, audit features are a required functionality to comply with regulatory requirements such as those of GLBA, the Sarbanes-Oxley Act, and many others. Similar to the Transaction Log Store described earlier, we recommend using a separate Data Store to maintain audit records and to support audit reporting. It should be noted that regulatory requirements for purging may apply to former customers whose records reside in multiple systems. In order to correctly tell present customers from former customers, a holistic cross-system view of a customer must be maintained to meet the purge requirements, which is the core MDM objective.

Enterprise Record Locator   The Enterprise Record Locator contains information about all system source keys and the Identity Store keys. The Enterprise Record Locator is the key component that stores cross-system reference information to maintain the integrity of the customer records. The Enterprise Record Locator can be implemented as a dedicated subject area of the Metadata Repository, and should support many-to-many relationships between source system keys. Services built around this component should cross-reference keys from all involved systems, including the Data Hub, and deliver this service with high throughput, low latency, and high concurrency.

Enterprise Attribute Locator   This component enables the data governance group to specify the best trusted source of data for each attribute in the canonical data model. The Enterprise Attribute Locator stores pointers to the best source of data, and can be implemented as a subject area within the Metadata Repository. An administrative interface is required to maintain these pointers. The Enterprise Attribute Locator information can be defined at different levels of trust:

- System-level trust, when a certain system is selected as the trusted source for all profile data.
- Attribute-level trust, when a single trusted source is defined for each attribute in the canonical data model.
- Trust at the level of attributes and record types, when a single trusted source is defined for each attribute in the canonical data model with additional dependencies on the record type, account type, and so on.
- Trust at the level of attributes, record types, and timestamps is similar to the trust level defined in the previous bullet, except that it includes the timestamp of when the attribute was changed. This timestamp attribute is an additional factor that can impact the best source rules.

Race Condition Controller   The Race Condition Controller is responsible for defining what change must prevail and survive when two or more changes conflict with each other. This component should resolve the conflicts based on the evaluation of business rules that consider, among other factors, the source of change by attribute and the timestamp at the attribute level. This component should be configurable, metadata driven, and have an administrative application interface for ease of administration.

Distributed or Federated Query Constructor   When the customer data is distributed or federated across multiple data stores, this component should be able to parse a message and transform it into a number of queries or messages against legacy systems.

Message Response Assembler   Once each of the source systems participating in creating a response successfully generates its portion of the response message, the complete response message must be assembled for return. This is the job that the Message Response Assembler is responsible for.

Error Processing, Transactional Integrity, and Compensating Transactions   At a high level, there are two ways to handle transactional errors. The conservative approach enforces all-or-nothing transactional semantics of atomicity, consistency, isolation, and durability (ACID properties) and requires the entire distributed transaction to complete without any errors in order to succeed. If any step in this transaction fails, the entire transaction fails and all its uncommitted changes are rolled back to the pre-transaction state. The other transaction model is to support a complex multistep transaction in such a way that even though some steps may fail, the entire transaction may continue depending on the transactional context and the applicable business rules. Typically, these are long-running complex and composite business transactions that are more difficult to design and manage. The integrity of these transactions is not ensured via an automatic rollback and usually requires a design of what is known as "compensating transactions."

Hub Master Components   In the case of the Hub Master, such as the Transaction Hub, all attributes that are maintained in the Hub Master must be protected from the changes in the source systems. In this scenario, the Data Hub becomes the authoritative source, the point of entry, and the system of record for the data it manages. The MDM Master Data Hub should include a set of services, components, and interfaces designed to maintain the Master Hub attributes centrally. In other words, all other applications and systems in the scope of the MDM Customer Master (for example, supporting our use case scenario) should access customer data from the Data Hub. The Hub Master will typically require the maintenance of relationships, groups of customers, and other associations and aggregations (these topics are discussed in Chapter 15).

Batch Processing

In the previous section, we concentrated on a real-time data synchronization solution that works for both the slave and the master models of the MDM Data Hub. Let's consider the question of whether the MDM system still needs a batch data synchronization facility that may use Extract, Transformation, and Load (ETL) processes and components. One way to think about this question is to decide whether the real-time messaging infrastructure and the appropriate MDM Data Hub services can be used to process large sets of data synchronization messages as a single large batch. The answer to this question consists of at least two parts.

The first part of the answer is based on the fact that almost any established enterprise must maintain reliable, mission-critical batch processes that are aligned with the business models of the industry the enterprise operates in (for example, nightly updates of inventory levels, trade settlements, insurance claim processing, and so on). This means that there will continue to be the need to process some aspects of Master Data Management in batch mode.

The second part of the answer is that in cases where the MDM Data Hub has to process millions of data changes at a time, batch processing is the right operational and technical approach, although the process itself has to be carefully designed and optimized to fit the available batch window. The latter point can be addressed effectively and efficiently by using mature technology such as ETL.

Indeed, the primary goal of ETL is to support large-scale batch transformations from one form of input data (for example, account-centric structure) to another, potentially higher level of the output or target data (for example, a customer-centric structure). Contemporary ETL technologies can parallelize the majority of transform and load operations and thus can achieve very high throughput and performance. This is particularly important for initial data load processing and for rapidly bringing additional data sources into the Data Hub. Very large batches are required not only to seed the Data Hub initially; mergers and acquisitions, changes in branch office hierarchies, new lines of business that have to be included in the scope of the MDM Data Hub, and other business events may result in creating very large data files that have to be cleansed, transformed, and loaded into the Data Hub. In other

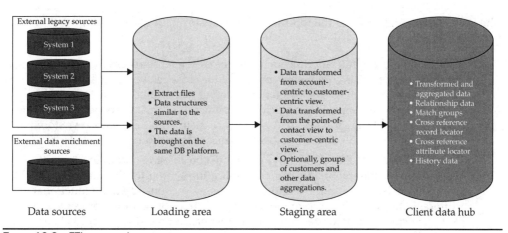

FIGURE 16-2   ETL processing

words, ETL-style batch data processing—including data load and, by extension, data synchronization—are required for any enterprise-scale MDM implementation. We discussed the architectural approach to data loading in Chapter 5, where we introduced the Data Zone architecture approach to data management (refer to Figure 5-2). A simplified high-level view of ETL processing from the data sources through the loading and staging areas to the Data Hub is shown in Figure 16-2.

The process begins with file extraction from legacy systems. The file extracts are placed in the Loading Area and loaded into tables. The purpose of this area is to bring all the data onto a common platform. The Loading Area preserves the data in its original structure (in our example, account centric) and makes the data available for loading into the staging ares.

The following types of transformations occur when the data is loaded into the staging area:

- Core transformations to the customer-centric view. In addition, the staging area must preserve legacy system keys. They will be used to build the cross-reference Record Locator Service.

- Reference code translations are used to bring the codes into the Data Hub–specific format.

- Data validation occurs and the beginning of exception processing for records that do not comply with established standards. The records enter the exception processing framework from the staging area.

- The data defaults are checked against declared definitions.

- If data enrichment processing from an external vendor or vendors is in scope, it can optionally be done in the staging area. Otherwise, data enrichment occurs in the Data Hub.

From the staging area, the data is loaded into the MDM Data Hub. The Data Hub data load performance has to be compatible with the processing throughput maintained by ETL.

PART IV

The Data Hub should support the following data transformations and manipulation functions:

- One of the most significant functions is the cross-reference record locator (Enterprise Record Locator). This component consists of the cross-reference registry and services that manage the linkages between the customer keys stored in the Data Hub and legacy systems in scope. In the batch-processing mode, this component must be able to generate the Data Hub keys, cross-reference them with the legacy keys stored in the staging area, and persist the cross-reference information in the Data Hub.

- The Match Suspect Extractor component must be able to work in batch mode. Besides this requirement, this component is quite similar to the match extract component described in the real-time processing section. The main functional difference between the two component types is that for real-time processing, the Match Suspect Extractor generates an extract based on a single record change, while the batch version of the Match Extractor operates on multiple records caused by processing changes in the batch.

- Matching is one of the core functions of the MDM Data Hub. This function should be available in real-time and batch modes, and it should support batch mode for the initial data load and delta processing.

- As mentioned earlier, if data enrichment processing from an external vendor or multiple vendors is in scope, data enrichment is typically performed in the MDM Data Hub. Initial data load and batch delta processing have to support processing of the enriched customer records.

- Batch processing has to be able to resolve the race conditions mentioned earlier in this chapter. The Data Hub also provides support for data aggregation, merging of matching records, and other data consolidation activities, including processing of entity groups and relationships.

The distribution of MDM data manipulation functions and components between the staging area and the Data Hub often depends on the business requirements, legacy data landscape, and infrastructure requirements. The demarcation line is therefore flexible, and it can be moved.

A significant practical consideration for designing and deploying these components is the type of vendor solutions that the project team selected. The choice is usually between an ETL and an MDM vendor's products. Some MDM vendors offer functionality that traditionally belongs to the ETL and/or messaging vendor space. For instance, some MDM vendors offer their own staging area implementation and the corresponding procedures. A question that has to be answered is whether it is a good idea to bundle ETL transformation inside the MDM vendor solution. What follows is a list of considerations that have to be taken into account when answering this question.

Pros:

- Some MDM vendors provide a common framework, metadata, and component reuse capabilities for both batch ETL and real-time processing. In general, however, ETL vendor products can complement but do not replace real-time data transformation vendor products. Therefore, we can recommend that data validation components, match extractors, race condition components, and others must be evaluated, designed, and developed for both real-time and batch modes.

- This common synchronization framework offers a shared standard exception-processing facility.

Cons:

- Most of the MDM vendor products are relatively young and the Data Hub solution space has lots of room to mature. It is not unreasonable to assume that even if the organization is building an MDM solution today using a particular technology choice, it may decide to replace it tomorrow. Given this level of uncertainty, we believe it'll be preferable to use an industry-proven ETL vendor solution to handle the functions that are native to ETL.

- It is reasonable to assume that the performance of ETL tools and real-time components will not be equal, leading to a decision to use these tools and techniques separately to satisfy specific business and operational requirements.

Synchronization and Considerations for Exceptions Processing

Real-life operational data processing often encounters conditions different from the expected outcome of "normal" processing. These conditions can be caused by unexpected data values, violations of referential integrity, violations of sequence of record processing, access problems, system or object availability problems, and so on. These conditions are known as *exceptions*. Exceptions can impact and even disrupt operations. Thus, the MDM Data Hub architecture should include exception capture, management, and root-cause impact analysis and reporting.

Having a common standard framework for exception processing is a great idea. In its absence, different development groups may create their own disparate exception-processing solutions. A systematic approach to exception processing that will include batch and real-time operations will pay off multiple times. This framework should be able to create and maintain an exception-processing flow by orchestrating exception-processing scenarios. Like many other Data Hub services and processes, the exception-processing framework has to be metadata driven, and, at a minimum, the framework should define a number of steps that have to be performed for each exception or error capture. In addition, such a framework should define a common format for the exception messages that contains:

- The process type and identifier (real time or ETL)
- The transaction identifier
- The module where the error occurred (for example, staging area, matching engine, Data Validator)
- The error message

Once the exceptions are captured, they have to be presented to the appropriate users and applications designed for exception handling and resolution. Exception handling and resolution may require separate administrative applications and exception-processing workflows.

An interesting concern about the exception-processing framework and its boundaries has to do with the scope of the exceptions—for example, should the exception framework go beyond the synchronization components? We believe that it should. For example, consider exceptions caused by unauthorized users or invalid requests.

It is true that data visibility and security (discussed in detail in Part III of the book) can significantly impact the processes surrounding an MDM Data Hub by applying additional constraints to the already complicated Data Hub services, ad-hoc queries, and predefined access routines. To state it differently, many data exceptions are caused by data security controls. In this case, exception processing needs to capture all relevant information about the user identity, the content of the request, and a statement of the security policies and rules that the system has to follow to process the request. The result of this analysis could indicate not a technology failure but rather an attempt at the unauthorized request or an incorrect, incomplete, or contradictory set of policies and rules.

The variety of exception types leads to the creation of numerous exception-processing workflows and organizational roles that are to be involved in exception handling. Therefore, exception processing requires robust and configurable mechanism distributing and routing the exceptions to the right organizational roles. Data exceptions may also contain sensitive information requiring visibility and security constraints to be imposed on the access to exception processing data.

As we discussed in Chapter 14, the MDM Data Hub supports many attributes that can be used to identify an individual and/or organization. From the synchronization perspective, a decision must be made as to when an identity of the party must be reevaluated. For example, if a name, phone number, address, and credit card number are used for identification, should we recompute the Match Group identifiers every time one of these attributes changes? If a phone number change occurs because the phone number was initially incorrect, then this may be a reason for the match group recomputation. On the other hand, if a correction has been made because a well-known customer changes his or her phone number, there is no need to trigger the match group identifier recomputation. A good practice in this case is to make sure that attribute changes are tagged with the reason for the change, a timestamp of the change, and other decision-driving attributes. These attributes should be used by the MDM Data Hub to help make a decision about whether the change should trigger the match process. Typically, as soon as a customer record is identified with a sufficient level of confidence, it should not change the associated identity. This simplifies data synchronization considerably.

Given that large companies have many systems that are to be integrated within the MDM framework, a significant milestone from the data synchronization perspective would be a detailed definition of *system on-boarding.* This term refers to a set of standards and processes that determine what applications and attributes each system should adjust, modify, or extend as a prerequisite to being integrated into the enterprise MDM solution. These standards and processes should typically cover multiple scenarios—for example, real-time vs. batch integration, service integration using SOA principles vs. native APIs, integration in a pure "slave" scenario or as a master for certain attributes, and so on.

The granularity of the standard messages for inter-application exchange of master data must also be considered. In general, a standard message is typically defined at the entity (for example, customer) level. This message is represented by multiple data model entities that, in the case of a Customer or Party Domain, may include customer name, address, and many other entities and attributes comprising the customer profile. Similar considerations apply to other domains (for example, Products). If some entity or entities are updated much more often than others, it may be a good idea to consider a separate message that handles only the frequently changing entities. It is always a trade-off between the simplicity of having a single standard message and enterprise MDM system performance considerations, and the decision has to be made only after a careful analysis of the nature of the attribute change, attribute change frequency, number of applications/components/services that consume these attributes, the throughput of the messaging infrastructure, and so on. In some cases, the analysis may indicate that more complex hierarchies of standard synchronization messages may be required.

Testing Considerations

Testing is a critical work stream that is often underestimated, especially in the context of an MDM Data Hub. When we discuss the topic of testing, we include several testing categories and dimensions. On the one hand, testing should include functional testing, data testing, and nonfunctional testing (the latter includes performance, scalability, throughput, manageability, resilience to failure, interface compliance, and so on). On the other hand, testing is an iterative process that should be defined and implemented as a sequence of iterative steps that may include a unit test, a system test, an integration test, a QA test, and a user acceptance test (UAT). When embarking on an MDM project, the project team has to make sure that the scope of testing is clearly defined and mapped to the business requirements for traceability, and to the project acceptance criteria for project management and stakeholder buy-in.

We further suggest that regression testing be performed for each testing type (there are numerous definitions and published works related to regression testing[1]). Testing activities should begin very early in the project's life cycle. The testing team should develop a comprehensive test strategy as soon as the business requirements are defined and some initial technical elaboration is complete. Best practices suggest that the test cases should be developed in parallel with the software requirement and design specifications. For example, when the team uses a Rational Unified Process[2] and defines use cases to articulate software requirements, the test cases can be (and should be) developed at the same time as the use cases.

MDM technologies and MDM use cases introduce additional complexities to the test strategy. In order to illustrate this complexity, let's consider the following categories of test-related issues:

- MDM testing of data and services
- Match group testing
- Creation and protection of test data

Testing of MDM Data and Services

The high-level approach to testing MDM data and services has to follow a standard testing methodology that at a minimum defines the following test levels:

- **Unit testing**   This testing is performed by developers, who verify and certify their own work. They have to come up with their own test cases. Typically, these test cases are executed automatically. Some manual testing may also be involved. Unit testing is limited in scope and often tests only individual components rather than the end-to-end solution. Unit testing also addresses the validity of internal components that may not be included in other test groups (for example, internally called functions, procedures, and services).

- **System testing, also known as integration testing or system integration testing (SIT)**   This process tests multiple components of a system in an integrated fashion, with the test cases defining initial conditions, test sequences, and expected outcome from executing all of the components required to implement a complete business function or a service. Integration testing provides an insight into the overall system behavior as well as performance and throughput characteristics.

- **Quality assurance (QA) testing**   This level of testing provides the technology organization and the business community with an assessment and measurement of the quality of the developed system. QA testing can be further broken down into Technical QA and Business QA. These tests are executed independently from each other, and by different groups:

  - Technical QA is performed by a Technology QA group that uses independently developed test cases. The goal of the Technical QA is to certify that the solution is developed in compliance with approved technical requirements. Technical QA testing is focused primarily on the technical behavior of the system under test, and does not test technical features and functions at the same level as unit testing. The intent of Technical QA is to test end-to-end applications and systems in accordance with the technical software requirements documentation and based on the testers' interpretation of the requirements. The Technology QA group interacts closely with the development organization in order to resolve issues discovered during testing. From the process point of view, defects identified by the Technology QA group should be formally logged into the dedicated system used for defect resolution. If defects are found and fixed by the development group, regression testing may be required to validate the corrected code. On completion of regression testing, the results are documented and certified by Technology QA.

  - Business QA tests are performed by a dedicated Business QA team. The Business QA team executes end-to-end test cases and compares the results with the business requirements as well as with specific examples derived from running real-life production applications. In addition to validating test results against business requirements, the Business QA team works closely with the Technology QA team and business stakeholders to refine both the business requirements and their technical interpretations. The resulting changes have to be retested, which, in turn, may require a cycle of regression testing at the Unit, System, and QA levels.

  - Joint Technical QA/Business QA testing is especially important when the MDM Data Hub data security and visibility implementation are being tested (see the detailed discussion on data security and visibility in Chapter 11). The project team has to work closely with the enterprise security organization and the policy administration team to make sure that access controls are implemented and enforced according to the policy statements and users' roles and entitlements, and that every authorization decision can be traced back to the appropriate policy. In addition, when developing testing scenarios for data visibility, the team has to make sure that these scenarios include both necessary and sufficient conditions. To state it differently, when a visibility engine allows access to a particular set of Data Hub data, the QA teams have to make sure that all data that was supposed to be accessed based on the policy is granted such an access, and that there are no additional records or attributes that can be accessed by mistake.

MDM solutions put additional emphasis on testing not only services and components, but often the data itself. Not surprisingly, one of the key testing targets of an MDM system is data quality. If the data quality of the source system is a part of the testing process, it should include definition, measurement, and defect-resolution steps. The entire test suite should include clearly defined assumptions, pre- and post-conditions, defect-tracking tools and procedures, and acceptance criteria. At a minimum, testing deliverables should include test cases, reports used for testing, test scripts, test execution results, traceability matrices, and defect-management logs.

Typically, data testing is performed using either or both of the following approaches:

- **Bulk statistical analysis executed against all data**   The fact that all data is covered by the analysis contributes to its strength. A common weakness is that it is not easy to resolve abnormalities if and when they are found.

- **Scenario-based testing performed on a small subset of records**   It is always a question of how many records need to be tested and how to select the subset optimally to cover a representative set of scenarios. Because we are dealing with projects where the number of records is typically in excess of seven digits, manual processing is not an option and automation is not always feasible either.

When we perform data testing in the MDM environment, we have to select the source and the target data files for testing. Let's use a typical data transformation sequence that the data undergoes during the initial load process into the Data Hub. We discussed this topic in the beginning of this chapter, and Figure 16-2 illustrates the process. An important choice facing the MDM designers is whether the testing routines should be performed at each data migration step (the loading area, staging area, record locator metadata store, and so on). If the decision is negative, then all test cases should compare the initial source (the legacy source systems) with the content of the ultimate, post-transformation target (the MDM Data Hub). This amounts to the end-to-end testing that is typically a province of Technical and/ or Business QA.

However, end-to-end data testing is somewhat different from functional testing in that it requires a low level of detail in order to discover data defects and trace their origins. This can be a very complex task given the variety and scope of various data transformation steps. Therefore, an effective approach to Technical QA and Business QA testing is to implement it as a step-wise process, where testing of some steps could be quite complex.

Bulk Statistical Testing Challenges

Let's consider a "simple" example of testing one-step data transformations between the loading and staging areas of the Data Hub, using bulk statistical testing to confirm the number of records where a certain attribute is blank (see Figures 16-3 and 16-4). As before, we'll use the example of testing data from a Customer domain to illustrate the details of the problem.

The goal is to reconcile the number of records where the ZIP Code is blank (NULL). The account-centric structure shown in Figure 16-3 (the source) contains three customer records and two different account numbers.

The customer-reporting application would show three customer records: Mary Turner, Mary L. Turner, and Paul Turner, with three addresses, two of them having ZIP Code NULL (we assume that two records for Mary Turner belong to the same individual).

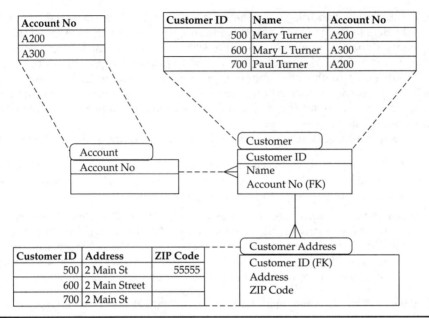

FIGURE 16-3   An account-centric data model

In contrast, the customer/account data in the customer-centric structure, shown in Figure 16-4, has a single address that belongs to the aggregated customer.

As a result of the transformation to a customer-centric model and customer and address de-duping, the two records indicate that one person (Mary Turner) and the three addresses are recognized as one. In the customer-centric structure there are no records with ZIP Code equal to NULL. Therefore, a direct comparison of NULL counts in the two data structures would not provide meaningful testing results.

Even this simple example taken in the context of the Customer domain shows that records that are rejected during the transformation operation drive additional complexity into the process of bulk statistical testing. This complexity may be even higher for other master data domains.

In order to reconcile record counts where a certain attribute is blank (NULL), the source should be compared with the target corrected by the rejected records. A combination of data transformation, data cleansing, de-duping, and record rejection makes bulk comparison difficult. We are not trying to discourage the reader from using this approach, but rather want to make sure that the difficulties of bulk testing are correctly understood.

Looking at the problem of attribute testing in more general terms, we suggest the following attribute transformation categories that have to be tested:

- Attributes that are expected to be unchanged after the transformation
- Attributes that changed only due to the code translation
- Attributes created in new entities due to new levels of aggregation

Testing should cover both real-time/near-real-time processing and batch processing.

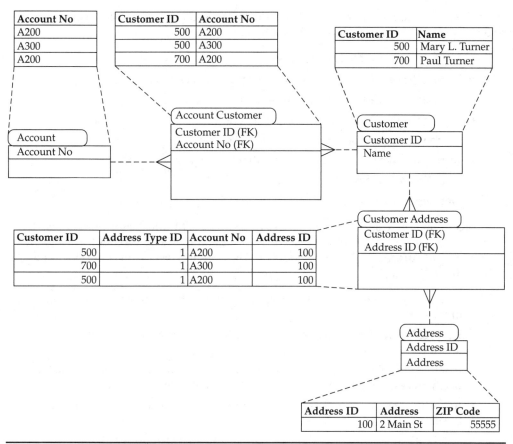

FIGURE 16-4   A customer-centric data model

Scenario-Based Testing

This approach requires very tedious analysis and specifications for all transformation scenarios. In a typical MDM environment, hundreds or even thousands of scenarios have to be tested. In some cases, if there is no data in the test data set to support certain test conditions, these conditions and the corresponding test data have to be created.

Testing MDM Services

MDM testing is not limited to data testing. Because an MDM Data Hub is built on the foundation of a service-oriented architecture (SOA), testers must be able to test Data Hub services, especially Web Services (see Chapter 4 on the SOA approach to MDM architecture). Testing Web Services is a challenge because the testing processes, procedures, and test cases should take into account the different styles of Web Services (SOAP based or REST based), the disconnected nature of the services, the protocols used to publish and consume services, and many other concerns, including the following:

- Testing SOAP[3] and REST[4] messages
- Testing WSDL[5] files and using them for test plan generation
- Web Service consumer and producer emulation
- Testing the Publish, Find, and Bind capabilities of an SOA-based solution
- Testing the asynchronous capabilities of Web Services
- Testing the dynamic run-time capabilities of Web Services
- Web Services orchestration testing
- Web Services versioning testing

Considering these and other challenges of testing MDM solutions, components, data, and services, we have to conclude that the skill set that the Technical QA team should possess is quite diverse and hard to come by. The Technical QA team skill set should include the following:

- Test-strategy development skills that cover both data-testing capabilities and testing of services.
- Knowledge and hands-on experience with best-in-class testing methodologies and tools.
- Ability to develop test cases that require strong data analysis skills. This includes batch processing and real-time/near-real-time data flows.
- Reporting and query-building skills that require experience with reporting and business intelligence tools.
- Application and process testing for new customer-centric applications.

These testing qualifications can be difficult to find. Usually, the variety of skills required for testing leads to very little overlap in experience among the Technical QA team members, which in turn leads to a necessarily large Technical QA team. The rule of thumb for MDM projects is that the number of testing resources should be about 75 percent of the number of developers.

Match Group Testing
Another MDM-specific functional area of testing is the verification of Match Group assignments. As we discussed in previous chapters, the Match Groups are created to identify and link the records that belong to one Party (that is, an individual or an organization). The process of creating and testing Match Groups is critical for any MDM project. Because typical matching algorithms are iteratively tuned throughout the testing cycles in order to optimize matching accuracy and performance, it is very important to have a process that verifies the results of matching and discovers errors and issues.

We suggest a simple process successfully used by the authors on multiple projects. Assume that the Match Groups have been computed as a result of the matching process and the Match Group identifier has been assigned to each record in the Data Hub.

- The process begins with a search for false positives. In order to do that, the match results are sorted by the Match Group. If the match is based on scoring, the match score should be displayed next to the Match Group ID. In this case, the correctness of the score could be verified for each combination of attributes that should be treated as a test case. Alternatively, if the match is based on business rules defined as conditional statements, the match results should also be tested for each scenario. From the testing perspective, the use of scoring systems for matching is more convenient and enables faster test processing.

- False negatives are tested as soon as the analysis of false positives is complete. Assume that there are a few attributes such that at least one of them must match in order for two records to acquire the same match identifier. If fuzzy logic is used for attribute comparison, the index generated by fuzzy logic should be used instead of the attribute value. Let's assume that three attributes are most critical: credit card number, phone number, and address. Thus:
  - Only records for which the credit card number is the same but the Match Group identifiers are different are included. The results are sorted by credit card number and analyzed.
  - Only records for which the phone number is the same but the Match Group identifiers are different are included. The results are sorted by phone number and analyzed.
  - Only records for which the address is the same but the Match Group identifiers are different are included. The results are sorted by address and analyzed.

In order to come up with conclusive results on match testing, the test must cover a representative set of scenarios. Scenarios should be defined on a case-by-case basis. Unlike transformation test processing, where most scenarios are at the record level, match-testing scenarios, by their nature, include multiple records, which may result in an unmanageably high number of scenarios. If matching requirements are clearly defined, they can be used to construct appropriate test scenarios. A report representing the results of match testing should include an analysis of what attributes and matching conditions have been covered within the test data set.

Some vendors and MDM practitioners question the value of the detailed scenario-level or attribute-level requirements. We recommend that business users identify matching requirements and guidelines at a high level, and leave the matching details to the implementation team. Once the matching design is completed and the tool is selected and/or configured, a match audit process should be invoked to assess the accuracy of the match. This match audit process usually involves an independent, often external, match audit provider. Responsibilities of a match audit provider include the following:

- Perform an independent match and identify the Match Groups.
- Compare the results with the results obtained by the match process under audit.
- Recommend improvements in business rules, data quality, profiling by attributes, and so on.

Creation and Protection of Test Data

Today, companies have to comply with numerous global and local data privacy and confidentiality rules and regulations. Many organizations treat the need to protect sensitive data such as material nonpublic financial information and personally identifiable customer information very seriously. These organizations develop information security strategies and implement the appropriate auditable security controls as required by regulations such as the Sarbanes-Oxley Act and the Gramm-Leach-Bliley Act. These steps are designed to protect sensitive data from external attacks. However, a slew of recent security breaches shows that the threat to data privacy and confidentiality comes from outside the corporation as well as from internal users (disgruntled employees, lack of security awareness, improper sharing of access privileges, and so on). What makes this data security problem even more alarming is the large number of incidents where a security-aware organization focused on protecting sensitive production data may allow copies of that data to be used for testing of new systems and applications, even though it is a known fact that test environments are rarely protected as strongly as the ones used for production. OCC Regulation 2001-47 and other regulations have been developed specifically to address the issue of third-party data sharing, because many companies are outsourcing large-data-volume system testing to third-party service or solution providers.

All these concerns lead many organizations to adopt processes that protect test data from potential compromise. And these concerns and processes apply directly to MDM solutions: MDM test data tends to "look" almost like production data in its content and volumes. To avoid the security exposure discussed earlier, an MDM project team has to recognize test data security issues at the beginning of the project, and develop approaches to protect not just production data but also test data. These approaches usually fall into two major categories: protecting or hardening the test environment, and protecting or sufficiently modifying the test data content to avoid security compromise.

Let's look at the latter because it deals with the data content and thus may affect the way the MDM testing is performed. Test data protection can be achieved by anonymizing (obfuscating or cloaking) data at the file, record, or attribute level. The level of obfuscating is determined by the company's security and privacy policy and the nature of the data. In the case of customer data protection, the goal is to protect those PII attributes that can directly or indirectly identify individuals (that is, names, social security numbers, credit card numbers, bank account numbers, medical information, and other personal information). From the regulatory compliance point of view, companies should be aware that if material nonpublic information (MNPI) and personally identifiable information (PII) is compromised even outside the company walls (for example, the data security is breached at the outsourced third-party vendor site), the company is still responsible for data confidentiality protection. But because the security violation happened outside the company walls, the risk to the company's reputation is even greater.

The key challenges in using data anonymization techniques include:

- The ability to preserve logic potentially embedded in data structures and attributes to ensure that application logic continues to function.

- The ability to provide a consistent transformation outcome for the same data. In other words, many obfuscation techniques transform a particular attribute value into a different but predictable value consistently (for example, "Alex" always gets converted into "Larry").

In some situations, however, the data sensitivity is so high that the transformations are designed to provide random, nonrepeatable values.

- Support for enterprise-scale data sets at the required levels of performance, scalability, and throughput.

The most popular anonymization techniques include the following:

- **Nullification**   All attribute values are replaced with NULL. The solution is simple and easily implementable. The primary disadvantage is that the data is lost and cannot be tested.

- **Masking data**   All attribute values are replaced with masking characters. The solution is also simple and easily implementable. Only limited testing is possible (for instance, on the number of characters). The primary disadvantage is that the logic embedded in the data or driven by the data is lost, and thus application or functional testing may be infeasible.

- **Substitution**   Replace the data values with similar-looking data created in separate stand-alone tables. For instance, if last names must be anonymized, all last names will be replaced with different last names in a cross-reference table. The algorithm is reasonably fast and preserves consistency across records; for example, if the last name Smith is replaced with the last name Johns, this replacement will occur consistently for all records with the last name Smith. The last name lookup table serves as the key and must be protected. This approach allows for testing of entity matching, although fuzzy matching may require additional in-depth analysis of the testing outcome.

- **Shuffling records**   This method is similar to substitution, but, unlike the substitution method where the lookup table stores the cross-reference values, the record-shuffling method stores cross-reference pointers that randomly point to the records in the table that contains the anonymized data.

- **Number variance**   The algorithm multiplies each value by a random number.

- **Gibberish generation**   This is often accomplished by the random substitution of characters. The length of the data will be preserved. One-to-one relationships between the original code values and the anonymized code values can be preserved.

- **Encryption/decryption**   This is a classical approach, and many vendor solutions that perform encryption/decryption of data are available. The biggest challenge of this approach is related to the performance and key management of the crypto algorithm. Indeed, if the encryption/decryption keys are lost or destroyed, the data may not be useable at all.

Many organizations decide to implement a combination of various techniques in order to meet all anonymization requirements.

Considerations for the MDM Application and Presentation Layers

Once the MDM system is ready to be deployed, we have to consider MDM implications on the design of Data Hub Management, Configuration, and Administration applications as well data-consuming applications and reporting solutions.

The data-consuming applications include those applications that can be designed to take advantage of the data and services provided by the MDM Data Hub, including applications that can leverage new entity-centric (for example, customer-centric) views of the master and reference data both for traditional entity management functionality (such as customer on-boarding and reporting applications) as well as new applications that are designed specifically to use and support entity centricity. The availability of aggregated, cleansed master data may not only have some impact on the existing applications but can also drive the development of new, purpose-built business applications that can impact and/or take advantage of new workflows and business processes. In general, an MDM Data Hub enables new entity-centric (for example, customer-centric) applications to search, access, and manage entity information not just via an account number, invoice number, confirmation number, and so on, but via relevant entity identifiers. The choice of identifiers and the overall design impact on these existing and new applications are highly dependent on the business purpose of a given application, the enterprise system architecture, and a number of other factors, and are usually assessed and considered in the context of business requirements by the application development teams that work together with the MDM development team. In all cases, though, these applications leverage published Data Hub services such as Entity Resolution, Search services, Authoring services, Interfaces services, and others. In general, business applications using an MDM Data Hub have to be designed as instances of a service-oriented architecture that interact with the MDM Data Hub via a well-known set of coarse-grained and fine-grained Data Hub services (see Chapters 4–6 for more details on these services).

The Data Hub Management, Configuration, and Administration applications, on the other hand, are directly influenced by the MDM system capabilities, work with and manage MDM Data Hub services, and therefore have to be designed to make the MDM Data Hub system manageable, configurable, and an operation-ready platform.

Let's briefly look at the types and requirements of the Data Hub Management, Configuration, and Administration applications. We'll conclude this section with a short discussion on the approach to designing and deploying business intelligence and reporting applications.

Data Hub Management, Configuration, and Administration Applications

In order to understand the requirements for the MDM Management, Configuration, and Administration applications, let's review once again the conceptual MDM architecture framework discussed in Chapter 4 and illustrated in Figure 4-6 and, for ease of reference, repeated again as in Figure 16-5.

The Data Management layer of the framework contains components that are typically managed by a suite of administrative applications and user interfaces regardless of whether we consider an MDM vendor product or internally developed MDM Data Hub. Key components in this layer that are managed by the administrative application suite include Identification Configuration services (part of the Entity Resolution and Lifecycle Management Service), Search services, Master Entity Authoring services, Metadata Management services, and Hierarchy Management services. The suite of administration and configuration applications that manages these components is designed to manage the configuration complexity of the Data Hub environment by making Data Hub operational parameters "data driven." Some of the applications in this suite are briefly discussed next:

- **Master Data Authoring** This is a specialized application that manages MDM Authoring services and provides MDM administrators and data stewards with the

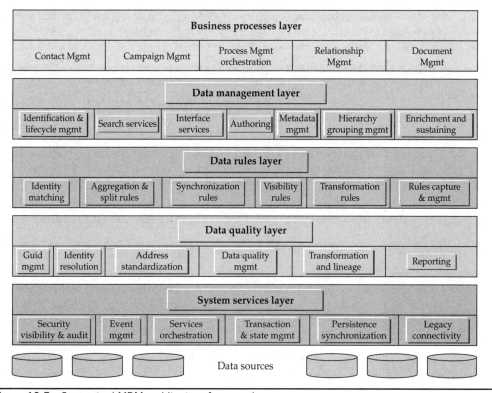

Business processes layer				
Contact Mgmt	Campaign Mgmt	Process Mgmt orchestration	Relationship Mgmt	Document Mgmt

Data management layer							
Identification & lifecycle mgmt	Search services	Interface services	Authoring	Metadata mgmt	Hierarchy grouping mgmt	Enrichment and sustaining

Data rules layer					
Identity matching	Aggregation & split rules	Synchronization rules	Visibility rules	Transformation rules	Rules capture & mgmt

Data quality layer					
Guid mgmt	Identity resolution	Address standardization	Data quality mgmt	Transformation and lineage	Reporting

System services layer					
Security visibility & audit	Event mgmt	Services orchestration	Transaction & state mgmt	Persistence synchronization	Legacy connectivity

Data sources

FIGURE 16-5   Conceptual MDM architecture framework

capabilities to create (author), manage, customize/change, and approve definitions of master data (metadata) as well as to create, read, update, and delete (for example, support CRUD services) specific instances of master data.

- **Adjustment application**   This is a user-friendly component of the Authoring application designed specifically to enter and apply adjustments to either specific instances of master entities or to some attributes of reference data. Usually, an adjustment application supports a purpose-build user interface that allows for effective navigation of adjustment activities and seamless integration with appropriate workflow to receive adjustment approval (if appropriate), apply the adjustment, and create a record of the adjustment action for audit and traceability purposes.

- **Reference code maintenance application**   This application is a subset of the more general-purpose Adjustment application and is designed specifically to maintain allowed code values in the MDM Data Hub.

- **Hierarchy management application**   This is a very important component of the MDM Management, Configuration, and Administration suite. The design and implementation approaches for hierarchy management vary widely, based on the ability to support single vs. multiple data domains as well as support for alternate hierarchies, custom aggregation, groupings, and other factors (an additional discussion on hierarchy management is offered in Part II of the book). In principle, though, we can describe a conceptual hierarchy management application in terms of commonly recognized functional and user interface (UI) requirements as follows:

- The hierarchy management UI should present a reference data hierarchy using a tree metaphor (perhaps similar to the popular Windows Explorer).

- The UI should allow users to copy, cut, paste, move, drag, and drop nodes of a given hierarchy in order to change an existing hierarchy or create an alternative hierarchy.

- The UI should allow users to perform a "one-click" action to see or change properties and definitions of the nodes in the hierarchy, including editing of the metadata rules describing the content of each node (for example, the value of a given node can be defined via a simple or complex formula).

- The application should allow for the creation of a view of the hierarchy that includes data lineage that can be traced back to the source of the reference data.

- The tool should support the creation of a data change capture record that could be used to deliver hierarchy changes as instructions or data manipulation statements to the downstream systems.

- The application should support and make available the change log and audit trail for all actions performed on a given hierarchy, including the identity of the user who performed these actions.

- **Operations/scheduling controller**   This application allows the MDM Data Hub system administrator to request, initiate, or control certain operational activities such as running on-demand reports, creating file extracts that are used as input into downstream systems, loading or reloading the Data Hub, and changing the location of a particular data source.

- **Metadata Management application**   This is a user-facing composite application that is focused on managing various aspects of the Data Hub metadata facility.

  - **Matching Attributes Maintenance application**   This application defines what attributes are used as critical data attributes. The extract for the matching engine is generated based on the entries from this application.

  - **Rules Configurator**   This is an application that allows an authorized administrative user or an MDM steward to author, change, or delete data management rules that govern certain Data Hub services, such as the establishment of the match threshold or the rules of attribute survivorship.

  - **Data Locator and Attribute Locator Registry Editor**   As the name implies, this application provides a rich user interface to define, create, or change the content of the data and attribute locator registries that are implemented as dedicated areas of the MDM Data Hub metadata store.

  - **Exception-Processing support**   This application allows an MDM system administrator to define new error types and exception-processing flows and create appropriate metadata records.

  - **Default Value Management application**   This application allows MDM administrators and data stewards to define and maintain default values.

- **Master Search application**   This is an administrative application that allows data stewards and other authorized users to effectively search for master data entities or reference data records based on fully qualified search criteria or by using a fuzzy, generic, or proximity search. If desired, this application or its variant can be made available to all authorized MDM Data Hub users as a business application focused on searching entities (for example, customers, parties, products) that are maintained in the Data Hub.

Reporting

MDM solutions tend to be optimized for real-time/near-real-time operations but not necessarily for batch reporting. Experience in implementing large data warehouses and business intelligence applications proves that running complex queries against very large databases (and, of course, an MDM solution usually ends up having to support a very large data store known as a Data Hub) may have serious performance and throughput implications on the technical infrastructure and end-user application response times.

If the MDM project specifies the need for extensive entity-centric reporting, the project architects may consider implementing a separate reporting environment that loads a performance-optimized reporting data mart from the Data Hub and makes its data available to the end-user BI and reporting application suite. This approach is valid for any MDM Data Hub architecture style because Data Hub design is rarely optimized for data warehousing–type queries.

These considerations apply to end-user BI-style reporting. Of course, there are other types of reports that need to be developed to support Data Hub and application testing and operations. In fact, testing relies heavily on reporting. The good news is that the majority of the reports developed for testing can be leveraged and sometimes reused for operational controls when the MDM system is deployed in production.

Additional Technical and Operational Concerns

In addition to the issues discussed in the previous sections, we have to mention a few technical considerations that MDM projects need to take into account when building Data Hub systems.

Environment and Infrastructure Considerations

In general, building and deploying an MDM Data Hub platform should be done using the same approaches, processes, and procedures that are common in any large enterprise initiative. Here are some examples:

- The Enterprise Database Administrator (DBA) and the infrastructure team should be adequately staffed. DBAs and infrastructure architects should work proactively to gather, understand, document, and integrate requirements from all work streams participating in the MDM project (the list of typical work streams is discussed in Chapter 13).

- Given the number of work streams, the diversity of software, the requirements for parallel processing, and the need to support multiple system environments (for example, test, QA, production), each of which should be able to store very large amounts of data, the success of the MDM project would depend on the availability of a dedicated and appropriately resourced infrastructure and architecture work stream.

- Some or all of the following infrastructure environments have to be set up:
  - Development
  - Unit testing
  - Integration testing
  - Technology QA
  - Business QA
  - Performance testing
  - UAT environment
  - Production
  - Disaster recovery (DR)

Typically, one or two additional environments are required specifically for data testing. These environments support snapshots of data and provide basic data management capabilities but may not include all MDM services and application components.

The following logical components must be acquired, installed, and configured as part of the MDM technical architecture definition step (these logical components may be represented by a different number of physical infrastructure components):

- **Database servers**   These servers support the relational database management systems used by the MDM project (for example, an enterprise may decide to use Oracle DBMS for the Data Hub, and SQL Server for the loading and staging areas of the data architecture). Regardless of the DBMS technology, these servers should be able to support the operations and recovery of very large volumes of data, possibly on the terabyte or even petabyte scale.

- **Message server (Enterprise Message Bus)**   This server supports real-time or near-real-time messaging and data synchronization requirements.

- **ETL servers**   These servers are focused on supporting Extract, Transform, and Load data flows and corresponding processes.

- **Core MDM Data Hub and Entity-Matching server**   This is a type of an application server that supports core MDM services, including record matching.

- **Web and Application servers**   These servers provide traditional functionality required to process web interactions and application services.

- **Test Management server**   This server is used for test planning, execution, and defect management.

- **Reporting server**

- **Change Management server**

- **Knowledge Management server**   This server would support project documentation and a searchable shared knowledge library for the project (for example, an internal Wiki server).

Deployment

As we have stated repeatedly throughout the book, Master Data Management is an enterprise-wide initiative that may have a profound impact on how an enterprise manages its core data. The deployment of any enterprise-wide structural change that impacts established business processes is a significant technical, organizational, and political challenge. The deployment complexity grows as the MDM solution evolves from the Registry Hub to the Transaction Hub, and begins to support more than one master data domain. Indeed, we have shown in the previous chapters that the Transaction Hub requires more invasive modifications of the data structures and radical changes to established business processes. Managing change and managing expectations of an MDM project should go hand in hand. Thus, the MDM project team should consider these typical deployment options:

- The "Big Bang" scenario includes MDM and new applications deployment across the entire enterprise in a single system release.
  - **Pros:** The enterprise-wide change avoids potential inconsistencies that are inevitable if only some of the processes and systems are migrated to the new customer-centric world.
  - **Cons:** High implementation risk of changing the entire organization at once. If the transition to entity centricity runs into any kind of problem (organizational, technical, budgetary, and so on), the resulting risk of project failure will be high.
- Deployment by line of business or geography.
  - **Pros:** This deployment strategy makes sense if the entire MDM master file (for example, a customer base) can be partitioned, and if the new applications can process smaller segments of data independently from each other. Partitioning the data files allows for more manageable chunks of data to be handled by new applications. Moreover, smaller data partitions allow for smaller groups of users to be trained on their familiar data segments in parallel.
  - **Cons:** During the deployment rollout, some parts of the enterprise will be transitioned onto a new MDM platform while others may still be using legacy systems. If not planned and carefully coordinated, this coexistence of the two modes of operations can cause significant problems. Multiple releases may be required to complete the enterprise-wide transition.
- Deployment for new transactions only.
  - **Pros:** This deployment strategy involves the entire enterprise and completes the transition in a single release.
  - **Cons:** This deployment strategy has similar implementation and management issues as the LOB and geography deployment options discussed earlier. The main concern is the necessity to manage both new and old environments and transactions concurrently until the migration to the new systems is completed.

Considerations for the MDM Data Hub Data Model and Services

This section offers a brief discussion on what to look for if the organization decides to acquire an MDM product instead of building one in-house.

An important consideration in evaluating MDM Data Hub products deals with the Data Hub data model. We discussed MDM data model concerns and approaches extensively in Chapter 7 of this book. One school of thought on this topic states that a business-domain–specific, proven data model should be at the top of the MDM Data Hub selection criteria list. Is that always the right approach?

There are two competing MDM Data Hub product approaches as they relate to the Data Hub data model:

- The first one is based on a vendor-developed, out-of-the-box data model. It is very attractive for most firms to have the "right" data model. The "correctness" of the data model is a point-in-time decision because data models tend to evolve over time. The majority of MDM solutions available in the marketplace today provide a mechanism by which the model can be customized, but these customizations may be quite complex, and the resulting data model may have to be tuned and customized again and again until all business and technical requirements are met. This is particularly true if the core MDM data model includes hundreds or even thousands of entities, whereas only 10 to 30 entities (that is, tables) are required to support an MDM implementation that is based on the enterprise canonical data model.

- The second approach is "data-model agnostic." A chosen MDM product can instantiate any data model that better fits the organization. When the data model is instantiated, the MDM Data Hub automatically generates prerequisite core Hub services. Such products provide a higher level of flexibility, but the data model needs to be defined separately. Also, the set of services generated automatically is often limited to low-level services. More complex composite services have to be developed by the project team and the enterprise application developers where appropriate. These data-model-agnostic products are in fact tools designed for accelerated MDM development. Figure 16-6 illustrates the idea of the data model for the Data Hub data-model-agnostic solution architecture.

In reality, some vendors of MDM solutions offer a hybrid approach where a product is data-model-agnostic but also offers several "out-of-the-box" data models that can be used with some customizations. We offer additional discussion on various categories and types of the MDM Data Hub products in Part V of the book.

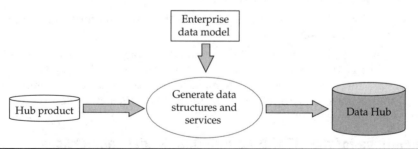

FIGURE 16-6 Data-model-agnostic solution architecture

To sum up, this chapter offered a brief discussion of several implementation considerations for MDM solutions. We started this discussion with the example of a use case that defined the need for real-time and batch data synchronization across various customer touch points. The use case helped us to illustrate typical components that system designers should be considering when developing an MDM data synchronization solution. We showed that the synchronization, although vitally important to the success of the MDM project, is not the only concern of the MDM implementers. We showed that other, equally important considerations include issues related to building Data Hub Management applications, reporting, testing, and other operational and deployment concerns. The major takeaway from these discussions is that these concerns are some of the keys to a successful MDM implementation, and, if underestimated, these areas of concerns can represent significant project risks and can ultimately cause a project to fail. We discuss some of the key reasons for MDM project failures in Chapter 19.

References

1. http://en.wikipedia.org/wiki/Regression_testing.

2. Kruchten, Philippe. *The Rational Unified Process: An Introduction, Second Edition.* Addison-Wesley Longman Publishing Co., Inc. (2000).

3. http://www.w3schools.com/SOAP/soap_syntax.asp.

4. http://java.sun.com/developer/technicalArticles/WebServices/restful/.

5. http://www.w3schools.com/wsdl/wsdl_intro.asp.

Master Data Governance

I n the previous chapters of Part IV, we concentrated on various implementation aspects of MDM. We have noted a few times throughout the book that Data Governance is a critical area that must be addressed to ensure a successful MDM implementation. Practically every description, reference, and discussion document published about MDM emphasizes the criticality of Data Governance for MDM. Without Data Governance it is impossible to successfully implement and operate an MDM program or solution.

In this chapter we will do a "deep dive" into Data Governance. We will seek to understand Data Governance challenges in more detail, especially as they relate to an implementation of complex MDM programs, and will recommend some solutions to the key Master Data Governance problems.

This chapter is organized into two major sections. The first section concentrates on the basics of MDM Data Governance definitions and frameworks. The second section concentrates on Data Governance as it relates to MDM and proposes some new advanced approaches to the Master Data Governance focus area. We conclude the chapter with a summary of recommendations on how to organize an MDM Data Governance program for effective adoption in a way that helps avoid common mistakes that may adversely impact a Data Governance program. Because of the importance and criticality of Data Governance we capitalize the spelling of this term throughout the book.

Basics of Data Governance

Let's start this discussion with an overview of the history behind Data Governance.

Introduction to and History of Data Governance

Industry experts, practitioners, and analysts are all in agreement on the importance of Data Governance. Unfortunately, despite such a universal support for Data Governance, not many organizations have reached a Data Governance maturity or are on a fast track to it. At the same time, we often see that information governance is discussed ever more frequently by enterprise executive committees and boards of directors.

Data Governance initiatives cross functional, organizational, and system boundaries and are enormously challenging in creating and aligning an effective and efficient program within the current organizational culture, programs, and maturity level. Despite its challenges,

Data Governance is increasingly viewed as an authoritative strategic initiative, mobilizing organizational resources to leverage data as an enterprise asset.

In contrast to this growing interest in Data Governance at the leadership level, many field data professionals, operations managers, and business managers often express some level of frustration in private discussions that the term "Data Governance" and the appreciation of the Data Governance as a discipline remain elusive. There are a number of reasons for this attitude toward Data Governance. To start with, Data Governance is perceived by many as a new umbrella buzzword for well-known terms from the past, such as business analysis, business process improvement, data quality improvement, program management, and so on. Moreover, many Data Governance programs are often too large, inefficient, and bureaucratic, even though they started as focused activities that were organized according to the recommendations of Data Governance thought leaders. But this perception of Data Governance as too abstract and bureaucratic can and does get addressed by following proven best practices and approaches to Data Governance. Examples of effective approaches to Data Governance programs include establishment of Data Governance boards or councils that have been holding regular (typically monthly) Data Governance meetings. Another effective approach is based on establishing communities of practices in data quality, data protection, data modeling, metadata, and other areas under the umbrella of Data Governance. For example, developing risk-based milestones for any Data Governance initiative will foster the early detection and mitigation of issues that would be costly in terms of opportunities and threats had they materialized later. These approaches often result in some degree of success in setting up Data Governance programs; however, most stakeholders are not satisfied with where they presently are in the area of Data Governance.

As per research work by David Waddington,[1] only 8 percent of enterprises estimate their Data Governance as comprehensive. For the most part, companies report that their Data Governance exists in some specific areas—for example, data security, data protection, support for Basel II, and so on. Most enterprises do not see a way or don't feel they have a need to reach higher levels of Data Governance maturity. These research results are consistent with what we see in the field.

It is difficult to pin down a specific point in time when the terms "Data Governance" and "Information Governance" were first introduced. As per Gwen Thomas, the founder of the Data Governance Institute (DGI),[2] in 2003 an Internet search on "Data Governance" returned only 67 references. Since 2003, Data Governance is on an increasingly fast track to be adopted as a discipline. According to the InformationWeek, IBM will offer Data Governance consulting.[3] IBM Corporation formed the IBM Data Governance Council[4] in 2004. Interestingly enough, the MDM-CDI Institute was founded by Aaron Zornes, also in 2004. Whether it was a coincidence or not, some analysts call Data Governance and MDM "siblings" not just because of the timing but mostly due to considerable synergies between MDM and Data Governance. We believe that these synergies are not accidental. Both disciplines seek to bring better control over data management through an establishment of enterprise-wide authoritative sources, controls, good policies, sound practices, and ultimately establish methods of transition to information development–enabled enterprise.

Definitions of Data Governance

There exist numerous definitions of Data Governance. These definitions represent various views and program focus areas, which in turn yield multiple perspectives of what Data Governance is. Here are a few examples:

- In the first edition of our book,[5] Data Governance is defined as "a process focused on managing data quality, consistency, usability, security, and availability of information."

- The MDM Institute[6] defines Data Governance as "the formal orchestration of people, processes, and technology to enable an organization to leverage data as an enterprise asset."

- Jill Dyche and Evan Levy[7] define Data Governance through the goal "to establish and maintain a corporate-wide agenda for data, one of joint decision-making and collaboration for the good of the corporation rather than individuals or departments, and one of balancing business innovation and flexibility with IT standards and efficiencies."

- As per the IBM Data Governance Council,[8] "Data Governance is a quality control discipline for accessing, managing, monitoring, maintaining, and protecting organizational information."

- As per the Data Governance Institute,[9] "Data Governance is the exercise of decision-making and authority for data-related matters." A slightly longer definition from the same source reads as follows: "Data Governance is a system of decision rights and accountabilities for information-related processes, executed according to agreed-upon models which describe who can take what actions with what information, and when, under what circumstances, using what methods."

The list of definitions for Data Governance can be easily expanded. There exist a number of great books on Data Governance and/or MDM[10,11] and each of these books provides a somewhat different definition of Data Governance, which indicates that each of the definitions focuses on a different aspect of Data Governance. Most definitions concentrate on the cross-functional role of Data Governance. This is important because the cross-functional aspects of Data Governance are the primary differentiators between Data Governance and departmental business-driven data analysis and rules.

Data Governance Frameworks, Focus Areas, and Capability Maturity Model

The primary challenge of Data Governance is in that often it is too big to be approached holistically without a focus on a specific program, area, or need. Indeed, Data Governance overlaps with so many functions, processes, and technologies that it makes it practically impossible to embrace its scope holistically. Therefore, there is a pressing demand to break down the Data Governance discipline and program and to present them as a set of more manageable pieces that can be prioritized, aligned with organizational goals and economic impacts, and executed upon and scaled up over time with successful incremental adoption and growing organizational maturity. The key point here is that Data Governance is not optional and must be organized in a measurable, timely, compliant, and repeatable manner to realize true material value of enterprise data assets.

Data Governance frameworks serve this need. They break down Data Governance into more manageable pieces, which allow us to approach Data Governance in a structured, methodological way and improve communication and compliance around complex subjects.

Mike2.0 Framework

The open-source Mike2.0 methodology concentrates on Information Development.[12] The methodology breaks down a Data Governance program into the following segments:

- **Data Governance Strategy**   This area concentrates on the mission, charter, and strategic goals of the Data Governance program and aligns the Data Governance program with business and operational imperatives, focus areas, and priorities. These imperatives, focus areas, and priorities can change over time. The Data Governance strategy will evolve with the changes.

- **Data Governance Organization**   The key part of the Data Governance organization is the Data Governance Board. Some organizations use the term "Data Governance Council" or "Data Governance Committee." This body is responsible for the direction of the Data Governance program and its alignment with business imperatives. The participants of the Data Governance Board can change as Data Governance focus areas and priorities are changing. Some roles and stakeholders should be considered as permanent members of the Data Governance Board—for example, the Chief Data Officer, Data Stewardship Managers, and the Chief Data Architect. Some other roles can vary based on the current focus area of the program; for example, different business stakeholders can be involved in different aspects of Data Governance and be area-specific representatives on the Data Governance Board. As the Data Governance journey evolves, the permanent members of the Board secure the continuity of the Data Governance development while area-specific Board members participate as needed based on the topics on the agenda of a specific Data Governance Board discussion. There are a number of good resources describing the challenges and methodology of building a Data Governance Board; see, for instance, publications by Gwen Thomas[13] and Marty Moseley.[14]

- **Data Governance Policies**   The need for Data Governance policies exists at two levels. At the executive level, Data Governance strategic corporate policies are articulated as principles and high-level imperatives. Some typical examples of principle-level policies are discussed by Malcolm Chisholm.[15] A policy that declares that information is a key corporate asset and possibly defines roles accountable for this asset is a good example of a principle-based policy. More specific tactical policies are defined in the form of rules, standards, and high-level metrics. These policies represent "how-to" realizations of the strategic policies. This is more consistent with our tactical use of the term "policy" in Part III, when we discussed data security, visibility, and the privacy aspects of MDM.

- **Data Governance Processes**   This segment of Data Governance defines the processes and procedures established by Data Governance in order to direct and control the proliferation of Data Governance strategies, policies, and directions across the enterprise. The processes can focus on specifics associated with critical entities and data elements. This area establishes accountabilities for Data Governance metrics and data stewardship functions in the context of specific Data Governance processes.

- **Data Investigation and Monitoring**   This area concentrates on specific data issues that cause failure to comply with Data Governance policies and metrics. This area may need to establish more detailed processes and a data stewardship level to monitor, track, and resolve data issues.

- **Technology and Architecture**   In this area, Data Governance stakeholders work closely with IT management and enterprise architects. The Data Governance role is to ensure open and common standards in data management. This is the area where Data Governance functions may overlap with corporate IT. As we will see later, Data Governance as an enterprise function can have its own specific tools and architectural components that enable Data Governance operations.

The Data Governance Institute Framework

The Data Governance Institute's framework[16] recognizes a number of Data Governance focus areas that a typical Data Governance program can align with. The list of typical focus areas includes:

- Policy, Standards, and Strategy with the primary concentration on Enterprise Data Management (EDM) and Business Process Reengineering (BPR)
- Data Quality
- Privacy/Compliance/Security
- Architecture/Integration
- Data Warehousing and Business Intelligence

The Data Governance Institute's methodology is very thorough and easy to follow. It decomposes the framework into components and provides detailed descriptions to key Data Governance components.

That said, it should be noted that the Data Governance Institute's framework places MDM under the umbrella of "Architecture/Integration." As we will see later, MDM offers its own unique Data Governance aspects and characteristics that take Data Governance for MDM far beyond the "Architecture/Integration" focus area.

The IBM Data Governance Council Framework and Maturity Model

The IBM Data Governance Council has developed many sound and very detailed materials on how to componentize Data Governance. The methodology's framework contains 11 categories that are somewhat similar (no surprise here) to what we have seen previously in the Mike2.0 and the Data Governance Institute frameworks. The categories defined by the IBM Data Governance Council are as follows:

- Organizational Structure and Awareness
- Stewardship
- Policy
- Value Generation
- Data Risk Management and Compliance
- Information Security and Privacy
- Data Architecture
- Data Quality Management
- Classifications and Metadata

- Information Lifecycle Management
- Audit Information, Logging, and Reporting

The IBM Data Governance Council has also developed and introduced a Data Governance maturity model in 2007.[17] The model helps organizations understand where they stand in their Data Governance journey and provides a common measure that enables organizations to compare their Data Governance readiness with the readiness in other organizations.

The Data Governance maturity model follows the Capability Maturity Model developed by the Software Engineering Institute (SEI) in 1984. The IBM Data Governance Council's model measures Data Governance maturity by placing the state of Data Governance of the evaluated organization on one of the following levels:

- **Level 1: Initial**   Ad hoc operations that rely on individuals' knowledge and decision making.

- **Level 2: Managed**   Projects are managed but lack cross-project and cross-organizational consistency and repeatability.

- **Level 3: Defined**   Consistency in standards across projects and organizational units is achieved.

- **Level 4: Quantitatively Managed**   The organization sets quantitative quality goals leveraging statistical/quantitative techniques.

- **Level 5: Optimizing**   Quantitative process improvement objectives are firmly established and continuously revised to manage process improvement.

As we can see from the definitions of Data Governance maturity for levels 4 and 5, properly defined metrics are absolutely critical if an organization seeks to reach high levels of Data Governance maturity. We will refer to this important point in the next section, when we discuss the need for MDM metrics and how these metrics should be defined from the Information Theory perspective.

Data Governance for Master Data Management

In the previous section of this chapter we discussed some basic, foundational topics of Data Governance. These included definitions of Data Governance, Data Governance frameworks, Data Governance focus areas, and the Capability Maturity Model for Data Governance.

In this section we will concentrate on Data Governance in the context of Master Data Management, which is the primary focus of this book, and will introduce the term "Master Data Governance" (MDG).

Master Data Governance Definition

Master Data Governance (MDG) is the governance discipline and the framework that are the result of the intersection and unification of MDM and Data Governance. Master Data Governance can be described as a Data Governance version that applies to MDM implementations, especially enterprise implementations with complex cross-functional, cross-departmental, and cross-divisional solution needs. Master Data Governance includes some unique characteristics and challenges.

We will leverage the basics we discussed in the first section of this chapter and use them as a guide to get deeper into some new advanced areas of MDG.

> **Master Data Governance Mission**
> The mission of the Master Data Governance program is to define processes, controls, organizational structures, metrics, and tools enabling continuous data quality improvement, security, privacy, timeliness, compliance, and adaptability of master data across the enterprise.

As we mentioned in the previous sections, Master Data Management and Data Governance as disciplines formed almost at the same time (2003–2004), but in addition to this common timing, both disciplines make the definition of the authoritative sources of data one of the top priorities. This commonality reveals profound synergy between Data Governance and MDM.

Data Governance came into existence in order to address the complexity of enterprise data management. The need for cross-functional, cross-LOB, and cross-divisional standards and consistency in data management resulted in growing demand for Data Governance. Similarly, MDM reconciles data inconsistencies accumulated over the years in application silos by focusing on master data such as customer, product, location, and so on. As we learned from Part I of this book, master data is highly distributed across the enterprise, which is one of the key challenges that MDM resolves.

The synergies and similarities between strategic Data Governance goals and MDM objectives make MDG a great point of entry to start a comprehensive Data Governance program. Once MDG problems are addressed, it is much easier to resolve Data Governance problems in other focus areas.

In this section we will leverage our understanding of the Data Governance frameworks presented in the previous section and the Capability Maturity Model developed by the IBM Data Governance Council. For some of the categories we will limit our discussion to a brief summary and references, whereas other Data Governance categories, such as the data quality for master data (that is, master data quality, or MDQ) and MDQ metrics and processes, will be discussed in more detail. The focus and structure of this chapter is driven by the need to present some new areas and characteristics of MDG that have not been extensively discussed in other publications.

Data Quality Management

Let's look at the area that is often at the very top of Data Governance priorities—Data Quality Management—and discuss it in the context of MDM (see also Lawrence Dubov's series of blogs[18] on this topic).

We have stated throughout the book that MDM Data Hub is an architectural concept and technology that is at the very core of most MDM implementations. At a high level, the MDM Data Hub's function is to resolve the most important master entities that are distributed across the enterprise, and to understand their intra- and inter-relationships.

Modern MDM Data Hubs have grown into powerful, multifaceted service-oriented toolkits that match, link, merge, cleanse, validate, standardize, steward, and transform data. Modern MDM systems accomplish this by leveraging advanced algorithms and master data modeling patterns, and a variety of services, techniques, and user-friendly interfaces.

In order to unleash the power of the MDM Data Hub systems, MDG programs need to be implemented at the enterprise level. The MDG's goal is to refine a variety of cross-functional business requirements that cannot be originated from individually focused business groups. Often, MDG should be able to understand and summarize cross-LOB business requirements and articulate them in the form of a sound enterprise-wide Data Governance strategy for master data. This strategy should be able to reconcile cross-departmental inconsistencies in rules, requirements, and standards in a timely, effective, and measurable manner.

One of the key questions MDG should address is how the MDM Data Hub will be leveraged to ensure the creation, maintenance, and proliferation of high-quality master data across the enterprise. In the absence of strong MDG thought leadership, MDM Data Hub technologies may be underused, never be able to achieve the expected ROI, and ultimately be perceived as a failed effort.

With the advances of MDM, we observe a growing confusion around the commonalities and differences between MDM and data quality programs. This confusion manifests itself in questions such as the following:

- Will an MDM initiative resolve our data quality issues? Is this the right approach to data quality?

- We are not sure where the boundaries are between MDM and data quality. How are these two related?

- We are confused and don't know which of these two projects—MDM and MDG— we need. If we need both, then what are the dependencies and the recommended implementation sequence?

- We already have data quality tools. Do we still need MDM?

- Is data quality part of MDM, or is MDM part of data quality?

A list of these type of questions can be easily expanded, and no simple answer can resolve the confusion expressed by these questions. What is required is a comprehensive discussion and a blueprint on how MDM and MDG can help develop an effective data quality program along with the appropriate methods, techniques, metrics, and other considerations. Let's discuss how MDG can effectively define the role of the MDM Data Hub as a tool and technique to prioritize data quality problems.

Data quality is an age-old problem for almost every enterprise. The sheer number and variety of data quality issues makes it difficult even to list and prioritize them. This may result in analysis-paralysis scenarios, where the needs and requirements for a data quality program are discussed for years and the program fails at inception.

MDG can help solve the question about data quality vs. data management by clearly stating its Master Data Management focus. MDM concentrates on master entities that are, as defined by the MDG and business, more important than others because they are widely distributed across the enterprise, they reside and are maintained in multiple systems and application silos, and they are used by many application systems and users. In other words, although master data entities may comprise only 3%–7% of an enterprise data model, their significance from the information value and data quality perspectives is disproportionally high. Bringing master data into order often solves 60%–80% of the most critical and difficult-to-fix data quality problems. These considerations define the MDG position that MDM is a great way to prioritize data quality problems and focus resources properly to maximize the return on a data quality effort. Although data quality priorities vary from system to system, MDG takes a lead in aligning data quality efforts and priorities across the enterprise.

Expressed differently, MDM is an efficient approach to addressing enterprise data quality problems, enabling organizations to cherry pick their biggest data quality and data management battles that will ensure the highest ROI.

Data Quality Processes

At a high level, MDM approaches data quality by defining two key continuous processes:

- **MDM benchmark development**   The creation and maintenance of the data quality Benchmark Master—for example, a benchmark or high-quality authoritative source for customer, product, and location data. The MDM benchmark also includes the relationships between master entities.

- **MDM benchmark proliferation**   Proliferation of the benchmark data to other systems, which can occur through the interaction of the enterprise systems with the MDM Data Hub via messages, Web Service calls, API calls, or batch processing.

In most modern MDM solutions, Data Hub technologies focus on the MDM benchmark development process and its challenges. This process creates and maintains the MDM benchmark record in a Data Hub. The process focuses not only on data integrity, completeness, standardization, validation, and stewardship but also on the record timeliness and accuracy. Data accuracy often requires verification of the content with the individuals who know what the accurate values for certain attributes are.

Data timeliness is treated slightly differently. When a new record is created or an existing record is changed in one of the operational systems, the Data Hub receives an update message with the shortest possible delay. The Data Hub processes the change by applying an update to the benchmark record based on the attribute survivorship rules defined by the business as part of its Data Governance. This process is designed to ensure that data timeliness meets the criteria specified by Data Governance, and thus at any point in time the Data Hub maintains the most current benchmark record for the master entity. This makes the Data Hub the benchmark or authoritative source for all practical purposes.

The benchmark proliferation process is equally important for data quality. It is no doubt a great accomplishment for an enterprise to define, create, and maintain the golden (benchmark) record in the Data Hub. That said, from the enterprise data quality perspective, a critical challenge remains. Enterprise stakeholders are looking to establish and maintain data quality in numerous systems across the enterprise. They care about the quality of data in the Data Hub mostly because it helps them solve their data quality problems in other data sources, applications, and systems. In this case, the Data Hub is viewed as just a technique helping to establish and maintain master data quality across the enterprise rather than the key component and ultimate goal of an MDM initiative.

MDG for Operational and Analytical MDMs

It is important for the MDG team to understand that analytical systems and operational systems interact with the MDM Data Hub differently. In analytical MDM, the data warehouse "passively" takes the content created and maintained by the MDM system to load and manage complex data warehousing dimensions. From this perspective, the quality of the data warehousing dimensions built from an MDM Data Hub inherits the quality of the master data, and is mostly a data-integration problem that requires relatively limited Data Governance involvement.

The operational MDM requires an integration of an MDM Data Hub with operational systems. The operational systems' owners wish to retain control over each record in their application areas. Consequently, these systems cannot accept data feeds from the Data Hub in bulk, which would override the existing data. These systems can still benefit from the MDM Data Hub by leveraging the ability to search the Data Hub before a new record is created or edited in the source system (this is often referred to as a "lookup before create" capability) or by listening to the Data Hub messages and selectively accepting or rejecting the changes sent by the MDM Data Hub.

The operational MDM implementations are much more efficient than their analytical counterparts from the data quality perspective and require a much higher level of Data Governance involvement. Indeed, an operational MDM solution effectively addresses data quality issues at the point of entry, whereas the analytical MDM tackles data quality downstream from the MDM Data Hub. The "dirty" data created at the point of entry, once spread to multiple enterprise applications and systems, is next to impossible to cleanse. Hence, operational MDM is a real remedy for enterprise data quality problems.

Operational MDM reduces administrative overhead of redundant data entries, eliminates duplicates and inconsistencies, facilitates information sharing across enterprise applications and systems, and ultimately improves data quality by addressing the root cause of bad data.

From the MDG perspective, the operational MDM is a powerful technique that enables the enterprise to bring its master data to an acceptable high-quality state without necessarily storing all master entities in a single data repository, keep the data in a high-quality state continuously, and avoid periodic cleansing projects that consume significant resources and have been often proven ineffective. To paraphrase the previous point, an operational MDM helps solve the Data Governance problem of ensuring a continuous data quality improvement in the operational systems while the operational systems' users retain control over each record.

Data Governance also helps answer another hard question of maintaining data quality—how do we synchronize the source systems with the Data Hub without explicitly synchronizing them through data integration? These are some of the most foundational questions Data Governance and its MDM-focused variant—MDG—must address to achieve advanced Data Governance maturity levels.

In order to maintain a continuous synchronization with the Data Hub, a data quality improvement processes must be defined and built, progress measured, and accountabilities for the progress established. This consideration is very important but certainly not new. Any data framework and methodology, including those we discussed in the beginning of this chapter, require this process to be in place.

Let's concentrate on two critical components of the quality improvement process that represent significant challenges but, once defined, enable continuous data quality processes for master data across the enterprise and ultimately lift the overall data quality. These components are

- Master Data Governance Policies for Data Quality
- Master Data Governance Metrics for Data Quality

Master Data Governance Policies for Data Quality

As we discussed in the first section, the Data Governance organization can have a variety of Data Governance focus areas and categories under the Data Governance umbrella. Often, for a given enterprise, some areas of Data Governance are more developed than others. For instance, to comply with increasingly stringent regulatory requirements, corporate executives of established firms have addressed certain key aspects of Data Governance as it relates to data security and privacy.

This is not necessarily true with respect to the quality of the master data. Although Data Governance organizations of large companies typically have a number of data-related policies, it is essential to develop a new policy or augment the existing policies to focus on data quality for key master data domains, such as Customer or Party data. Such a policy or policy augmentation should be brief and specifically define, at the executive level, the enterprise position on Customer/Party or Product data in the context of data quality. It is important to make sure that the policy states clearly whether the data will be viewed and managed as a local resource for some systems and applications or as an enterprise asset.

If the enterprise's data and information philosophy states that enterprise data is just a resource for some applications, your organization is doomed to be reactive and address data issues after they had been discovered. If the corporate policy sees data only as an application resource, this policy does not position the organization to initiate and successfully execute a Master Data Governance (MDG) program and/or MDM. In terms of the Capability Maturity Model levels developed by the IBM Data Governance Council, it is impossible to reach advanced Data Governance levels if the organization looks at data (especially Party, Account, and Product data) as just a resource for departmental systems and applications.

It is much better for the firm if its master data policy defines data as a strategic enterprise asset that can be measured and have economic value. Indeed, if data is an enterprise asset, the asset's metrics and accountabilities for these metrics must be established. This is similar to any other enterprise function, department, or LOB, such as sales, call center, marketing, risk management, and so on. For instance, for a sales organization, the revenue is typically the primary metric used to measure the success. For a call center, one of the primary metrics is the number of calls the organization processed monthly, quarterly, or annually. Marketing targets may include the number of campaigns, the number of marketing letters sent, and the quantitative outcomes of the campaigns.

When an enterprise forms a Data Governance organization responsible for master data, what is an equivalent of the metrics used by sales organizations, call centers, or any other enterprise functions? How will the success of the MDG be measured? This is the most fundamental question that represents a significant challenge for many Master Data Governance organization. Indeed, no organization can be given an executive power if there are no metrics quantifying the organizational success. Therefore, the master data–centric policy must mandate relevant, quantifiable metrics that are sponsored at the executive level of the enterprise.

It is important to note that no one department or function can articulate a comprehensive set of requirements for an enterprise MDM, and some departmental requirements may be in conflict with each other. An MDG organization needs an executive power to execute MDG and contribute to a successful implementation of MDM. To a certain degree, it is MDG's requirements that play the role of business requirements for an enterprise MDM. MDG reconciles a variety of often contradictory and incomplete departmental requirements for MDM and brings these requirements to a common denominator across the enterprise.

Once the policy is defined at the executive level, the MDG organization receives a mandate to define the Data Governance metrics for master data quality.

Master Data Governance Metrics for Information Quality

Over the past decade, data quality has been a major focus for data management professionals, data governance organizations, and other data quality stakeholders across the enterprise. If we look back at the advanced levels of the IBM Data Governance Council's CMM, its Level 4 (Quantitatively Managed) explicitly calls for "quantitative quality goals leveraging statistical / quantitative techniques." Level 5 emphasizes the need for "...quantitative process improvement objectives firmly established and continuously revised to manage process improvement." One more data point—on December 2, 2009, Gartner Research published an article titled "Predicts 2010: Enterprise Information Management Requires Staffing and Metrics Focus." Gartner Research provides this article on request.

Demands for Master Data Governance metrics are growing not only in the minds of industry analysts. This need is recognized by the majority of data professionals implementing MDM solutions. Still, the quality of data remains low for many organizations. To a considerable extent this is caused by a lack of scientifically or at least consistently defined data quality metrics. Data professionals are still lacking a common methodology that would enable them to measure data quality objectively in terms of scientifically defined metrics and compare large data sets in terms of their quality across systems, departments, and corporations to create industry-wide standards. MDG should be able to report the results of data quality measurements to executive committees and even at the Board of Directors level in a way that is clearly understood and can be trusted.

In order to define the right executive level metrics we will start with a brief discussion of the existing data quality and data profiling metrics to understand why these metrics are not optimal for executive Data Governance reporting. Then we will discuss the characteristics of the metrics we are looking for to support executive Data Governance. Finally, we will define the model and the metrics that meet the requirements.

Even though many data profiling metrics exist, their usage is not scientifically justified. This elusiveness of data quality metrics creates a situation where the job performance of enterprise roles responsible for data quality lacks consistently defined criteria, which ultimately limits the progress in data quality improvements.

Clearly, we need a quantitative approach to data quality that, if developed and adopted by the data management and Data Governance communities, will enable data professionals to better prioritize data quality issues and take corrective actions proactively and efficiently.

The Existing Approaches to Quantifying Data Quality

At a high level there are two well-known and broadly used approaches to quantifying data quality. Typically both of them are used to a certain a degree by every enterprise.

The first approach is mostly application driven and often referred to as a "fit-for-purpose" approach. Oftentimes business users determine that certain application queries or reports do not return the right data. For instance, if a query that is supposed to fetch the top ten Q2 customers does not return some of the customer records the business expects to see, an in-depth data analysis follows. The data analysis may determine that some customer records are duplicated and some transaction records have incorrect or missing transaction dates.

This type of finding can trigger additional activities aimed at understanding the data issues and defining corrective actions. Measured improvement in outcomes of marketing campaigns is another example of a "fit-for-purpose" metric.

An advantage of the fit-for-purpose approach to data quality is that it is aligned with specific needs of business functional groups and departments. A disadvantage of this approach is that it addresses data quality issues reactively based on a business request, observation, or even a complaint. Some data quality issues may not be easy to discover, and business users cannot decide which report is right and which one is wrong. The organization may eventually draw a conclusion that their data is bad but would not be able to indicate what exactly needs to be fixed in the data, which limits IT's abilities to fix the issues. When multiple LOBs and business groups across the enterprise struggle with their specific data quality issues separately, it is difficult to quantify the overall state of data quality and define priorities of which data quality problems are to be addressed enterprise-wide and in what order.

The second approach is based on data profiling. Data-profiling tools intend to make a data quality improvement process more proactive and measurable. A number of data-profiling metrics are typically introduced to find and measure missing and invalid attributes, duplicate records, duplicate attribute values that are supposed to be unique, the frequency of attributes, the cardinality of attributes and their allowed values, standardization and validation of certain data formats for simple and complex attribute types, violations of referential integrity, and so on. A limitation of data-profiling techniques is in that an additional analysis is required to understand which of the metrics are most important for the business and why. It may not be easy to come up with a definitive answer and translate it into a data quality improvement action plan. A variety of data-profiling metrics are not based on science or a sound principle but rather driven by the ways relational database technologies can report on data quality issues.

Even though each of these two approaches has its advantages and value, a more strategic approach should be considered by Data Governance organizations. This approach should be able to provide a solid scientific foundation, principles, and models for data quality metrics inline with the requirements for levels 4 and 5 of the CMM developed by the IBM Data Governance Council. Later in this chapter we define such an approach that quantifies the value of master data quality for data sources as percentage points relative to the data quality in the MDM Data Hub.

Enterprise data analysts who know their data well often recognize that the data quality is low, but can't identify ten top data quality issues. A data analyst may indicate that some customer records are lacking names, that the date of birth is often unavailable, or filler values are broadly used for the phone numbers and date of birth attributes and nonpublic information is inadequately protected from unauthorized users. The analysts may be able to name a few issues like that, which would point to the candidates to address within the fit-for-purpose approach. However, if data analysts are required to define a comprehensive set of data quality issues, the sheer number of known issues and the effort to discover them overall quickly becomes overwhelming. Indeed, even to define record-matching attributes for a deterministic MDM matching algorithm may typically require an evaluation of many hundreds of rules. The number of rules that would need to be defined and implemented to measure and improve the enterprise data quality overall is absolutely overwhelming, and approaches limited *only* to deterministic techniques to data quality are not viable. Therefore, there is a pressing demand for generic, sound scientific principle- and model-driven approaches to data quality that must coexist with deterministic rule-driven fit-for-purpose approaches. Jim Harris discussed somewhat similar needs and trends using the terms "The Special Theory of Data Quality" and "The General Theory of Data Quality."[19]

Information Theory Approach to Data Quality for MDM

Previously, we identified the two primary data quality improvement processes:

- MDM Benchmark Development
- MDM Benchmark Proliferation

Let's first assume that the MDM Benchmark Development process has succeeded and the "golden" record set G for master data (for example, Customer) is established and continuously maintained in the Data Hub. This "golden" record can be created dynamically or be persistent. There exist a number of data sources across the enterprise, each containing some Customer data attributes. This includes the source systems that feed the Data Hub and other data sources that may note be integrated with the Data Hub. We will define an external dataset g, such that its data quality is to be quantified with respect to G. For the purpose of this discussion, g can represent any data set, such as a single data source or a collection of sources. For more discussions on the applications of Information Theory to data quality for MDM, you can refer to the references at the end of this chapter.[20,21]

Our goal is to define metrics that compare the source data set g with the benchmark data set G. The data quality of the data set g will be characterized by how well it represents the benchmark entity G defined as the "golden view" for the Customer data.

At the end of the 1940s, Claude Shannon, known as the "Father of Information Theory," published a few foundational articles on Information Theory.[22] We will leverage the model that Shannon developed and applied to the transmission of a telegraph code. Figure 17-1 illustrates the idea and shows the similarity between the telegraph transmission problem and the benchmark proliferation model.

Shannon analyzed a scenario in which a telegraph code generated by a transmitter is sent through a channel that generates some noise as any real-life channel. Due to the noise in the transmission channel, the telegraph code received by the receiver can be distorted and therefore different from the signal originally sent by the transmitter. The theory

FIGURE 17-1
Transmission of telegraph code— the classic problem of Information Theory

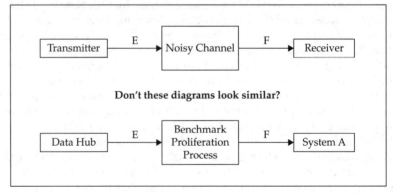

- Information Theory helps to measure transmission quality.

Don't these diagrams look similar?

developed by Shannon provides a solution that quantifies the similarity of the signal on the receiver end with the signal sent by the transmitter. The quality of the transmission channel is high if the received signal represents the original signal sent by the transmitter well. Conversely, if the quality of the transmission channel is low, the channel is considered noisy and its quality is low.

The two telegraph code transmission scenarios in Figure 17-2 illustrate two transmission channels: high quality (good) and noisy (bad).

The first example, in the top part of the figure, illustrates a high-quality channel. The receiver generates signals E1, E2, and E3 with probabilities 0.5, 0.3, and 0.2, respectively. The diagonal matrix in the top part of the figure represents a perfect quality transmission channel. The transmitter signals E1, E2, and E3 are translated into F1, F2, and F3, respectively. A good transmission channel requires consistency between the signals generated by the transmitter and the signals on the receiver end. The signals E and F do not have to be equal, but rather the transmission outcomes (F) must be consistent and predictable based on the original signals (E). But that's exactly what we want for enterprise data quality: consistency and predictability!

We will apply the same transmitter/receiver model to the quality of the MDM Benchmark Proliferation process.

Information Theory is heavily based on probability theory and other concepts, with the notion of *information entropy* being the most important.

NOTE *The term* entropy *is not unique to the Information Theory; it plays a key role in physics and other branches of science. Because this discussion is about information, we'll use the term* entropy *to refer to Information Entropy. Shannon's definition of entropy in Information Theory is a measure of the uncertainty over the true content of a message and is measured by a specific equation he stipulates.*

Readers familiar with probability theory concepts and the meaning of the term *entropy* can skip the next few paragraphs and explanations pertaining to Figures 17-3 though 17-6. For those who are interested in an introduction to the notion of entropy, we provide a brief illustrative explanation of the term. This explanation will be helpful in better understanding the material in the remainder of this chapter.

Figure 17-3 introduces the term *entropy* for a simple example of a symmetrical coin.

FIGURE 17-2
An illustration of a good vs. bad transmission channel

- Three signals E1, E2, and E3 result in F1, F2, and F3, respectively.
- The transition matrix is diagonal: E1 → F1, E2 → F2, and E3 → F3.

	F1	F2	F3	Total
E1	0.5	0	0	0.5
E2	0	0.3	0	0.3
E3	0	0	0.2	0.2
Total	0.5	0.3	0.2	

- In this scenario the entry signal E1 can result in F1 and F3, etc.
- Information Theory helps to tell good transmission quality from bad transmission quality.

	F1	F2	F3	Total
E1	0.4	0.0	0.1	0.5
E2	0.1	0.1	0.1	0.3
E3	0.0	0.2	0.0	0.2
Total	0.5	0.3	0.2	

PART IV

FIGURE 17-3
The entropy of a
symmetrical coin

- $H = -\Sigma\,(P_k * Log_2 P_k),$
  - where H is the entropy and P_k is probability
- Two Outcomes:
  - $E_1 = 0$ and $E_2 = 1$
  - $H = -[\frac{1}{2} * (-1) + \frac{1}{2} * (-1)] = 1$

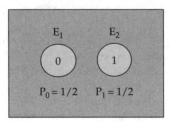

Once the coin is tossed and flipped, it can display two possible outcomes: 0 or 1, with equal probabilities of 0.5.

The entropy **H** is defined as $-\Sigma\,P_k\,log\,P_k$, where the logarithm's base is 2 and the symbol Σ signifies a summation over all possible outcomes. The entropy calculation yields **H = 1** for a symmetrical coin, which is the maximum entropy for one coin.

In Figure 17-4 a similar scenario applies to an asymmetrical coin.

For the asymmetrical coin, the probability of displaying "1" (0.7) is higher than the probability to display "0" (0.3). As we can see in Figure 17-4, the entropy **H = 0.881**, which means that a more predictable result corresponds to a lower value of entropy.

If we make the result of our experiment even more predictable, as in Figure 17-5, where the coin always displays "1," the entropy **H = 0**. This scenario represents minimum entropy and therefore minimum uncertainty.

Conversely, when we make our experiment less predictable by introducing two symmetrical coins, as in Figure 17-6, the entropy increases.

In this scenario, the increase of the entropy reflects the independence of the two coins and four possible outcomes of the experiment: (0,0), (0,1), (1,0), and (1,1), with a probability of 0.25 each, which shows that the result of tossing two coins is more difficult to predict. The joint entropy in this scenario **H = 2**, which is the theoretical maximum entropy for two coins.

FIGURE 17-4
The entropy of an
asymmetrical coin

- $H = -\Sigma\,(P_k * Log_2 P_k),$
  - where H is the entropy and P_k is the probability
- Two Outcomes:
  - $E_1 = 0$ and $E_2 = 1$
  - $H = -[0.3 * (Log_2\,0.3) + 0.7 * (Log_2\,0.7)] = 0.881$

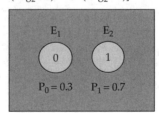

FIGURE 17-5
An extreme case:
the entropy of a
single outcome
coin

- $H = -\sum (P_k * \text{Log}_2 P_k)$,
  - where H is the entropy and P_k is the probability
- an outcome with probability 1 corresponds to
  a fully predictable scenario:
  - $E_0 = 1$ (on both sides of the coin)
  - $H = -[1.0*(\text{Log}_2 1.0)] = 0.0$

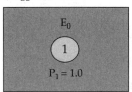

FIGURE 17-5
An extreme case:
the entropy of a
single outcome
coin

We can generalize this discussion and arrive at the conclusion that the entropy is a measure of the predictability and uncertainty of the system's behavior. Low entropy indicates that the system is easily predictable and orderly, while high entropy indicates that it is difficult to predict the system's behavior because it is more chaotic.

Information Entropy
Information entropy is a measure of uncertainty associated with the predictable value of information content. The highest information entropy is when the ambiguity or uncertainty of the outcome is the greatest.

The preceding paragraphs offered a brief explanation of how Information Theory measures the value of the information content by using the concept of entropy. Now we are in a position to review how this theory can be applied to quantify the information quality as a measure of uncertainty.

FIGURE 17-6
The joint entropy of
two symmetrical
coins

- Four outcomes with probability 0.25 each:
  - (0,0)
  - (0,1)
  - (1,1)
  - (1,0)

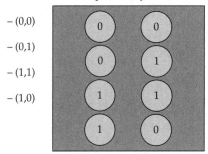

$$H = -\sum (P_k * \text{Log}_2 P_k),$$

- $H = -4 * \frac{1}{4} * \text{Log}_2 (1/4) = 2$
- For independent events, the joint entropy is equal to the sum of individual entropies
- $H(x,y) \leq H(x) + H(y)$ (equality when independent)

As mentioned, Information Theory says that the information quantity associated with the entity *G* is expressed in terms of the information entropy as follows:

$$H(G) = - \sum P_k \log P_k, \tag{1}$$

where P_k are the probabilities of the attribute (token) values in the "golden" data set *G*. The index *k* runs over all records in *G* and all attributes. *H(G)* can also be considered the quantity of information in the "golden" representation of entity *G*.

Similarly, for the source data set *g*, the quality of which is in question, we can write the following:

$$H(g) = - \sum p_i \log p_i, \tag{2}$$

We will use lowercase *p* for the probabilities associated with *g* whereas the capital letter *P* is used for the probabilities characterizing the "golden" data set *G* in the MDM Data Hub. The mutual entropy, which is also called mutual information, *J(g,G)*, is defined as follows:

$$J(g,G) = H(g) + H(G) - H(g,G) \tag{3}$$

In equation (3), *H(g,G)* is the joint entropy of *g* and *G*. It is expressed in terms of probabilities of combined events; for example, the probability that the last name equals "Smith" in the golden record *G* and the last name equals "Schmidt" in the source record *g* both represent the same customer, and in IT terms are linked by a single customer identifier. The behavior of the mutual entropy *J* qualifies this function as a good candidate for (?) quantifying the data quality of *g* with respect to *G*. When the data quality is low, the correlation between *g* and *G* is expected to be low. In an extreme case of a very low data quality, *g* doesn't correlate with *G* and these data sets are independent. Then

$$H(g,G) = H(g) + H(G) \tag{4}$$

and

$$J(g,G) = 0 \tag{5}$$

If *g* represents *G* extremely well (for example, *g* = *G*), then *H(g)* = *H(G)* = *H(g,G)* and

$$J(g,G) = H(G) \tag{6}$$

To make equations more intuitive, let's apply them to the scenarios in Figure 17-2. We will obtain the following outcomes:

- **Scenario 1**   High-quality transmission with no noise in Figure 17-2:

    H(E) = 1.485
    H(F) = 1.485
    H(E,F) = 1.485
    J(E,F) = 1.485

- **Scenario 2**   Transmission with noise in Figure 17-2:

    H(E) = 1.485
    H(F) = 1.485
    H(E,F) = 2.322
    J(E,F) = 1.485 + 1.485 − 2.322 = 0.648

As we can see, the mutual entropy demonstrates a very interesting and useful property. The mutual entropy is equal to the entropy of the individual golden data set G when the data source g is entirely consistent with G. Conversely, for the noisy channel in the second scenario in Figure 17-2, the mutual entropy $J(g,G) = 0.648$, which is significantly lower than the entropy of the golden source $H(G)$ in the MDM Data Hub.

Let's leverage this property and define transmission quality DQ as $J(E,F)/H(F)*100\%$. An application of this formula to the noisy channel scenario yields the following:

$$DQ(E,F) = 0.648/1.485 *100\% = 27.9\%$$

Because we seek to apply the same model to data quality, we can now define the data quality of g with respect to G by the following equation:

$$DQ(g,G) = J(g,G)/H(G)*100\% \tag{7}$$

Using this definition of data quality, we observe that DQ can change from 0 to 100%, where 0 indicates the data quality of g is minimal with respect to G (g does not represent G at all). When $DQ = 100\%$, the data source g perfectly represents G and the data quality of g with respect to G is 100%.

The beauty of this approach is not only in its quantifiable nature, but also in the fact that it can be used to determine partial attribute/token-level data quality, a feature that can provide additional insights into what causes most significant data quality issues.

From the data quality process perspective, the data quality improvement should be performed iteratively. Changes in the source data may impact the golden record. Then equations (1) and (7) are applied again to recalculate the quantity of information and data quality characteristics.

To sum up, this section offers an Information Theory–based method for quantifying information assets and the data quality of the assets through equations (1) and (7). The proposed method leverages the notion of a "golden record" created and maintained in the MDM Data Hub, with the "golden record" used as the benchmark against which the data quality of other sources is measured.

Simple Illustrative Examples of Data Quality Calculations

Let's apply our definition of data quality to a few simple examples to see how equation (7) works and what results it produces. In Figure 17-7, the records in the data source F differ from the benchmark records in the MDM Data Hub by only one attribute value, the state code where Larry resides.

The application of equation (7) yields $DQ = 85.7\%$.

In Figure 17-8, a duplicate record with an incorrect value of the state in source system F causes a data quality issue, which yields $DQ = 84.3\%$.

As Figure 17-9 shows, equivalencies applied consistently do not cause any data quality penalties within the proposed model. Even though all state codes are substituted with fully spelled state names, $DQ = 100\%$ if it is done consistently.

The Use of Matching Algorithm Metrics

If an organization has already acquired or developed software that can score two individual records for the purpose of probabilistic matching, the same software can be used for a comparison of the data sets g and G in the spirit of our Information Quality discussion.

Benchmark Records E   Records in System F   The Difference in State
Causes DQ Problems

EID	Name	State
1	Larry	NJ
2	Jim	GA
3	Scott	CA
4	Marty	CA

EID	Name	State
1	Larry	GA
2	Jim	GA
3	Scott	CA
4	Marty	CA

E

Value	Probability	Sk
Larry	0.25	0.5
Jim	0.25	0.5
Scott	0.25	0.5
Marty	0.25	0.5
NJ	0.25	0.5
GA	0.25	0.5
CA	0.5	0.5
H(E)		3.5

F

Value	Probability	Sk
Larry	0.25	0.5
Jim	0.25	0.5
Scott	0.25	0.5
Marty	0.25	0.5
GA	0.5	0.5
CA	0.5	0.5
H(F)		3

E,F

Value	Probability	Sk
Larry, Larry	0.25	0.5
Jim, Jim	0.25	0.5
Scott, Scott	0.25	0.5
Marty, Mary	0.25	0.5
NJ, GA	0.25	0.5
GA, GA	0.25	0.5
CA, CA	0.5	0.5
H(E,F)		3.5

DQ(E,F) = (3.5 + 3–3.5)/3.5*100% = 85.7%

Figure 17-7   Data quality for discrepancy in the state value

The following equation yields results similar to equation (7):

$$DQ(g,G) = 1/N_G \sum_{j=1}^{N_G} \sum_{i=1}^{n_s} 1/n_{i,j} Score(g_{i,j},G_j)/Score(G_j,G_j),$$ (8)

where the index j runs over all golden records in the Data Hub; index i runs over all source system records that are linked to the benchmark record and reside in the system, the quality of which is measured; N_G is the number of benchmark golden records in the MDM Data Hub; $n_{i,j}$ is the number of source records linked to the benchmark record j; and $Score(a,b)$ stands for the matching score function that matches record a to record b. Similarly to

Benchmark Records E   Records in System F   The Duplicate Record with
Incorrect State Causes DQ Problems

EID	Name	State
1	Larry	NJ
2	Jim	GA
3	Scott	CA
4	Marty	CA

EID	Name	State
1	Larry	NJ
2	Jim	GA
3	Scott	CA
4	Marty	CA
1	Larry	CA

E

Value	Probability	Sk
Larry	0.25	0.5
Jim	0.25	0.5
Scott	0.25	0.5
Marty	0.25	0.5
NJ	0.25	0.5
GA	0.25	0.5
CA	0.5	0.5
H(E)		3.5

F

Value	Probability	Sk
Larry	0.4	0.528771238
Jim	0.2	0.464385619
Scott	0.2	0.464385619
Marty	0.2	0.464385619
GA	0.2	0.464385619
CA	0.6	0.442179356
NJ	0.2	0.464385619
H(F)		3.292878689

E,F

Value	Probability	Sk
Larry, Larry	0.4	0.5288
Jim, Jim	0.2	0.4644
Scott, Scott	0.2	0.4644
Marty, Mary	0.2	0.4644
NJ, CA	0.2	0.4644
GA, GA	0.2	0.4644
CA, CA	0.4	0.5288
NJ, NJ	0.2	0.4644
H(E,F)		3.8439

DQ(E,F) = (3.5 + 3.293 – 3.844)/3.5*100% = 84.3%

Figure 17-8   Effect of a duplicate value with an incorrect state value

Scenario 4: Effect of Equivalencies

Benchmark Records E   Records in System F   Consistent Use of Equivalencies
do Not Cause DQ Problems

EID	Name	State
1	Larry	NJ
2	Jim	GA
3	Scott	CA
4	Marty	CA

EID	Name	State
1	Larry	New Jersey
2	Jim	Georgia
3	Scott	California
4	Marty	California

E Value	Probability	Sk
Larry	0.25	0.5
Jim	0.25	0.5
Scott	0.25	0.5
Marty	0.25	0.5
NJ	0.25	0.5
GA	0.25	0.5
CA	0.5	0.5
H(E)		3.5

F Value	Probability	Sk
Larry	0.25	0.5
Jim	0.25	0.5
Scott	0.25	0.5
Marty	0.25	0.5
New Jersey	0.25	0.5
Georgia	0.25	0.5
California	0.5	0.5
H(F)		3.5

E,F Value	Probability	Sk
Larry, Larry	0.25	0.5
Jim, Jim	0.25	0.5
Scott, Scott	0.25	0.5
Marty, Mary	0.25	0.5
NJ, New Jersey	0.25	0.5
GA, Georgia	0.25	0.5
CA, California	0.5	0.5
H(E,F)		3.5

$DQ(E,F) = (3.5 + 3.5 - 3.5)/3.5*100\% = 100\%$

FIGURE 17-9   Effect of equivalencies

equation (7), equation (8) yields 1 when the data quality is very high and scores lower than 1 when the data quality is less than perfect.

Note that the self-score $Score(G_i,G_i)$ is a great metric for record completeness and can be used in multiple practical scenarios, including the evaluation of the completeness of the golden record in the MDM Data Hub. Figure 17-10 shows an illustrative distribution.[23]

The illustrative self-score distribution shows that a significant percentage of the records reside in the right part of the graph, which indicates that there are many records with a high level of completeness, corresponding to the self-scores between 16.5 and 19.5. In the left part of the graph there are some records on the tail of the distribution that show relatively low self-scores between 11.0 and 12.0. The average self-score of the distribution is around 17.5, while the 10 percent quintile is close to 13.0. The Data Governance Board can establish the target thresholds for the average self-score (for example, at 18.0, and 15.0 for the 10 percent quintile). This should initiate data stewardship activities. Most likely the low-scoring records on the left side of the distribution will be the data stewardship targets. Once additional data is provided, the completeness metrics will meet the Data Governance requirements. This example illustrates how the Data Governance organization can enable continuous master data quality improvement processes through a few aggregated Data Governance metrics for data quality.

Organizations can leverage equations (1), (7), and (8), as well as the self-score metrics in Figure 17-10, to augment the Data Governance policies for MDM and enable processes that will lead to advanced maturity levels of the CMM for Data Governance.

By using this quantitative approach consistently across organizations and industries, over time Data Governance organizations will accumulate valuable insights into how the metrics apply to real-world data characteristics and scenarios. Good Data Governance

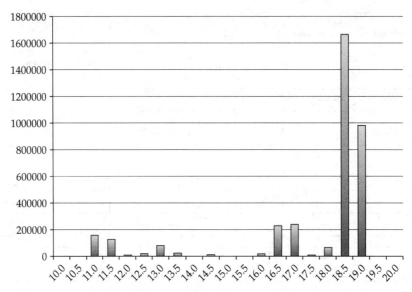

• Metric 1: Average self-score (17.5 in this example)
• Metric 2: 10% quintile (13 in this example)

Figure 17-10 An illustrative self-score distribution

practices defining generally acceptable data quality thresholds will be developed. For instance, Data Governance may define an industry-specific target policy for, let's say, P&C insurance business, to keep the quality of customer data above the 92 percent mark, which would result in the creation of additional, clearly articulated Data Governance policies based on statistically defined metrics. This methodology seems promising if the idea of the inclusion of the data quality in corporate books of records will ever come true. As per the IBM Data Governance Website, "IBM Council predicts data will become an asset on the balance sheet."[24] This scenario is likely to require the metrics discussed in this chapter.

The described approach can be incorporated into future products such as executive-level Data Governance dashboards and data quality analysis tools. MDG will be able to select information sources and assets that are to be measured, quantify them through the proposed metrics, measure the progress over time, and report the findings and recommended actions to executive management.

Even though we are mainly focusing on data quality in this chapter, there are other applications of data quality metrics. The quantity of information in equation (1) represents the overall significance of a corporate data set from the Information Theory perspective. From the M&A perspective, this method can be used to measure an additional amount of information that the joint enterprise will have compared to the information owned by the companies separately. The approach just described will measure both the information acquired due to the difference in the customer bases and the information quantity increment due to better and more precise and useful information about the existing customers. It may also determine the data migration and integration level of effort that will be required as part of M&A, as well as the integration of any authoritative external data.

How to Make Data Governance More Focused and Efficient

As we noted in the introductory part of this chapter, the primary challenge of Data Governance is in its elusiveness, ambiguity, and lack of clearly defined boundaries. This creates a market perception that "Data Governance" is an umbrella term for a new enterprise bureaucracy. Let's summarize some good Data Governance practices that tackle this challenge and make Data Governance better defined, more manageable, and valuable.

Agile Data Governance

Marty Moseley has introduced agile Data Governance in a number of blogs and publications.[25, 26] These publications recognize the challenge of an all-encompassing "top-down" approach to Data Governance and propose an alternative "bottom-up" approach that focuses on a single Data Governance area first and approaches Data Governance in more manageable chunks. Here are the seven agile Data Governance steps proposed and described by Moseley:

1. Selecting the project implementation team
2. Defining the size and scope of the data problem
3. Drafting the data steward team
4. Validating or disproving project assumptions
5. Establishing new policies for handling data
6. Enlisting internal IT groups and kicking off implementation
7. Comparing results, evaluating processes, and determining next steps

Similar considerations are brought by Rob Karel et al.[27] of Forrester Research and expressed slightly differently by Mark Goloboy.[28]

Any team engaging in Data Governance should think about applying an agile, bottom-up, lightweight approach to Data Governance while preserving the longer term vision and objectives of strategic Data Governance.

Overlaps with Business Requirements Generated by Departments and Business Functions

Any team engaging in Data Governance should understand that their role is in finding a common denominator of cross-functional business requirements and standards as opposed to stepping on the toes of departmental business analysts. It is certainly a challenge to find the right balance between enterprise policies and standards on the one hand and giving enough flexibility to the departmental requirements with their business rules on the other.

The Data Governance initiative must add true measurable and accepted value. It must not be perceived as an impediment for changes needed at the accelerating speed of business to respond to market threats, market opportunities, and regulatory mandates.

Overlaps with the Enterprise IT

A Data Governance team should work closely with enterprise data, systems, and application architects to ensure that they are on the same page and, at the same time, see the boundaries separating Data Governance functions from those of the enterprise architects. Both groups are responsible for establishing and enforcing enterprise standards and consistent good practices. The best remedy to make it right is to develop a solid communications plan that includes all stakeholders and maintains continuous interactions between the groups. Communications and socialization of the MDG vision and strategy are key remedies for making Data Governance successful.

Data Governance and Data Governance Frameworks

A Data Governance team should choose one of the Data Governance frameworks and follow it as closely as feasible. We briefly described three Data Governance frameworks; many more frameworks are available. We are not recommending any particular framework over the others, just strongly suggesting that the Data Governance team selects a framework and uses it in practice. This will make their objectives and activities better defined and streamlined.

Processes and Metrics

We put a lot of focus in this chapter on Data Governance processes for master data quality and the corresponding metrics. The metrics we discussed are certainly a subset of metrics a Data Governance organization can use and should rely on. Both aggregate metrics and lower level detail metrics are important. The aggregate metrics provide visibility at the executive level, whereas more granular metrics are used on a daily basis to investigate the issues.

Data Governance Software

There is a significant difference in how the two "siblings" (MDM and Data Governance) have formed and evolved over the last seven years. MDM has shaped a software market with the MDM Data Hubs as the core new technologies. Master Data Management software products are continually evaluated by industry analysts such as the Gartner Group and Forrester Research. Unlike MDM, Data Governance has not evolved as a software market. Data Governance is not associated with any specifically defined type of software products, although, as per Gwen Thomas,[29] a variety of software products such as ETL tools, metadata tools, information quality tools, and so on, can be considered under the umbrella of Data Governance software.

With this extremely broad field of Data Governance–related software solutions, it is fairly clear why many IT managers and practitioners call the term "Data Governance" elusive and ambiguous. Indeed, when an area is defined too broadly, it doesn't seem actionable.

A number of software companies have approached Data Governance within the roadmaps of their product strategy perspectives rather than by developing new tools from scratch.[30–32] This is an interesting trend that recently formed in Data Governance, and it appears that this trend may eventually start changing the face of Data Governance by making the area better defined through association with certain core software capabilities.

Data Governance and Edward Deming Principles

W. Edwards Deming,[33] one of the founders of the quality control discipline, developed 14 principles that have been considered by many a basis for the transformation of American industry and the economic miracle with the Japanese economy after WWII. Some of the principles are highly applicable to information quality and Data Governance. This is especially true for the following principle (principle #3):

> "Cease dependence on inspection to achieve quality. Eliminate the need for inspection on a mass basis by building quality into the product in the first place."

In the context of MDG, this principle mandates continuous data quality improvement processes embedded in everyday operations as opposed to massive data-cleansing exercises that are proven ineffective.

Conclusion

We started this chapter with a description of Data Governance basics, including definitions, frameworks, and the Capability Maturity Model. We tried to avoid broad general discussions on the topic, as these are readily available in numerous publications and through a variety of online sources.

Instead, we focused on the areas that, we believe, are critical for the success of Data Governance and, at the same time, are insufficiently developed and/or covered in the industry. Given the focus of this book on MDM, we concentrated our discussions on Master Data Governance. We strongly believe that this is the area of Data Governance that will become the next breakthrough in helping organizations achieve advanced levels of Data Governance maturity.

The next Data Governance challenge is in the translation of Data Governance metrics into direct and indirect financial impact on the organization. This is a very challenging and critically important area that is currently still in the embryonic stage, even though some research work has been done in this direction.[34]

References

1. Waddington, David. "Adoption of Data Governance by Business." Information Management Magazine, December 1, 2008. http://www.information-management .com/issues/2007_54/10002198-1.html.

2. http://www.datagovernance.com/.

3. http://www.informationweek.com/news/global-cio/showArticle .jhtml?articleID=196603592.

4. http://www.ibm.com/ibm/servicemanagement/data-governance.html.

5. Berson, Alex and Dubov, Lawrence. *Master Data Management and Customer Data Integration for a Global Enterprise.* McGraw-Hill (July 2007), p. 382.

6. http://www.tcdii.com/whatIsDataGovernance.html.

7. Dyche, Jill, Levy, Jill, and Levy, Evan. *Customer Data Integration: Reaching a Single Version of the Truth.* John Wiley (2006).

8. http://www.ibm.com/ibm/servicemanagement/data-governance.html.

9. http://www.datagovernance.com/glossary-governance.html.

10. Sarsfield, Steve. *The Data Governance Imperative.* IT Governance, Ltd. (April 23, 2009).

11. Loshin, David. *Master Data Management.* The MK/OMG Press (September 28, 2008).

12. http://mike2.openmethodology.org/wiki/Information_Governance_Solution_ Offering.

13. The Data Governance Institute. "Governance Roles and Responsibilities." http:// www.datagovernance.com/adg_data_governance_roles_and_responsibilities.html.

14. Moseley, Marty. "Building Your Data Governance Board." March 18, 2010. http:// www.datagovernance.com/adg_data_governance_roles_and_responsibilities.html.

15. Chisholm, Malcolm. "Principle Based Approach to Data Governance." http:// www.b-eye-network.com/channels/1395/view/10746/.

16. http://www.datagovernance.com/dgi_framework.pdf.

17. ftp://ftp.software.ibm.com/software/tivoli/whitepapers/LO11960-USEN-00_10.12.pdf.

18. Dubov, Lawrence. "Confusion: MDM vs. Data Quality." http://blog.initiate.com/ index.php/2009/12/01/confusion-mdm-vs-data-quality/.

19. Harris, Jim. "The General Theory of Data Quality." August 12, 2009. http://www .linkedin.com/news?viewArticle=&articleID=73683436&gid=45506&articleURL= http%3A%2F%2Fwww%2Eocdqblog%2Ecom%2Fhome%2Fpoor-data-quality-is-a-virus%2Ehtml&urlhash=-0w3&trk=news_discuss.

20. Dubov, Lawrence and Jim Cushman. "Data Quality Reporting for Senior Management, Board of Directors, and Regulatory Agencies," October 20, 2009. http://blog.initiate .com/index.php/2009/10/20/data-quality-reporting-for-senior-management-board-of-directors-and-regulatory-agencies/.

21. Dubov, Lawrence. "Quantifying Data Quality with Information Theory: Information Theory Approach to Data Quality for MDM," August 14, 2009. http://mike2 .openmethodology.org/blogs/information-development/2009/08/14/quantifying-data-quality-with-information-theory/.

22. Shannon, C.E. "A Mathematical Theory of Communication," *Bell System Technical Journal*, 27, July and October, 1948. pp. 379–423, 623–656.

23. The authors are grateful to Dr. Scott Schumacher for the illustrative self-score distribution materials.

24. http://www.ibm.com/ibm/servicemanagement/us/en/data-governance.html

25. Moseley, Marty. "Agile Data Governance: The Key to Solving Enterprise Data Problem." Information Management, September 18, 2008. http://www.information-management.com/specialreports/2008_105/10001919-1.html.

26. Moseley, Marty. "Seven Steps to Agile Data Governance." Information Management, November 20, 2008. http://www.information-management.com/spec ialreports/2008_105/10001919-1.html.

27. Karel, Rob, et al. "A Truism For Trusted Data: Think Big, Start Small. A Bottom-Up Valuation Approach For Your Data Quality Initiative." Forrester, July 28, 2008. http://www.forrester.com/rb/Research/truism_for_trusted_data_think_big%2C_ start/q/id/46308/t/2.

28. Goloboy, Mark. "Lightweight Data Governance: The Starting Point." Boston Data, Technology and Analytics. June 22, 2009. http://www.markgoloboy. com/2009/06/22/lightweight-data-governance-a-starting-point/.

29. http://www.datagovernance.com/software.html.

30. http://www.informatica.com/solutions/data_governance/Pages/index.aspx.

31. http://www.initiate.com/services/Pages/BusinessManagementConsulting.aspx.

32. http://www.dataflux.com/Solutions/Business-Solutions/Data-Governance .aspx?gclid=COe8g_elvqECFRUhDQod0x6UhQ.

33. http://en.wikipedia.org/wiki/W._Edwards_Deming.

34. Wende, Kristin and Otto, Boris. "A Contingency Approach to Data Governance." In Proceedings of the Twelfth International Conference on Information Quality (ICIQ-07).

Master Data Management: Markets, Trends, and Directions

I n the previous parts of the book, we described the goals, principles, benefits, architecture, design, data governance, data quality, and implementation concerns of MDM solutions in a way that was independent of specific vendors and their products. This independence from vendors and products allowed us to concentrate on defining Master Data Management and Master Data Governance and how they should be designed, enabled, and implemented.

This part of the book addresses two additional topics and is organized into two chapters. Chapter 18 offers an overview of the key MDM vendors and their products, whereas Chapter 19 provides a brief summary of all the topics discussed in the book from a more prescriptive point of view by focusing on the major reasons why MDM projects fail. Chapter 19 concludes with a discussion on the MDM industry, market, and technical trends and directions of Master Data Management. This discussion is aimed at providing readers with the authors' insight into what may lie ahead for us on this long and winding road to creating, managing, and effectively using information assets in a global enterprise.

CHAPTER

MDM Vendors and Products Landscape

U p until this point in the book, we have discussed the architecture, design, and implementation approaches of MDM solutions in a vendor- and product-agnostic way. This was done in order to have a better focus on the essence of MDM from inception and justification, to design, implementation, and deployment, covering major domain areas, concerns, issues, and risks. This vendor-agnostic approach is effective in helping MDM practitioners with common tasks and activities (such as building the business case and the roadmap), the architecture and design for an MDM solution, decisions related to buy vs. build, what vendor to partner with, in which area, and how. In other words, we need to know what features and functions are available today from what vendor, what is the vendor product roadmap, what pitfalls to look for when planning to establish a partnership with a particular vendor, and a host of other very relevant questions. Therefore, this book would be incomplete without an overview of the primary MDM vendors and their products.

NOTE We recognize that the information about specific vendors and their products is extremely volatile, and most of it may become quickly outdated. We also recognize that the list of vendors discussed in this chapter is far from complete. We focused on several key players that were either leading or gaining market share at the time of this writing. Nevertheless, we believe that the choice of vendors discussed here provides a good snapshot of the current MDM market landscape for a reader who wants to get to the key pieces of information quickly, which may lead to more detailed research in some specific area of MDM interest.

NOTE This overview is presented in the context of major MDM product/vendor categories, including MDM Data Hub products for the Customer domain, MDM Data Hub products for the Product domain, information quality vendors, data providers, and delivery accelerators. However, even this high-level categorization of vendors and their solutions may be somewhat misleading.

Indeed, as we show in Chapter 19, several key market trends in the MDM space, including market consolidation and multidomain MDM engines, result in a situation where a given vendor may provide solutions in several of the listed categories, depending on the point in time when a particular vendor is reviewed. Examples of these multifaceted evolving vendors include IBM, Oracle, SAP, Informatica, SAS, Tibco, and D&B Purisma. Of course, the MDM market is large and new entrants arrive on a reasonably regular basis, thus increasing market diversity and growing the number of specialist vendors that focus on a particular aspect of MDM. Most of these new entrants are not discussed here to maintain our focus on the major direction-setting MDM players.

MDM Market Consolidation

Over the three years that passed since the first edition of this book, the MDM product market has matured significantly. A wave of acquisitions that peaked in the first half of 2010 brought a significant consolidation of the market around a few key players in the MDM space. For example, let's look at what happened with major vendors that were considered in the leadership position at the time when the first edition of this book was published in 2007. Key acquisitions in the MDM space include a new home for Initiate and Exeros, which have become IBM companies, and Siperian, which is now part of Informatica. Also, Business Objects (First Logic) was acquired by SAP, Purisma was acquired by D&B, and Sun's SeeBeyond is now a part of Oracle. Finally, Netrics was acquired by Tibco Software.

This consolidation, however, does not change the fact that Master Data Management is a complex, multicomponent integrated platform that involves numerous technical, organizational, and business process areas of concerns (refer to Figure 13-1, which shows the MDM "ecosystem"). Like any large and complex computer system, MDM solutions represent an attractive and lucrative target to large and small vendors, some of whom attempt to develop integrated product suites that are designed to provide an "MDM in the box," whereas others concentrate on particular aspects of the MDM challenge or focus on providing supporting or enabling functionality. The MDM market opportunity continues to be strong, and drives the technology innovators and established vendors to actively participate in this market. Thus, we fully expect more players and more consolidation activities driven by MDM. But, to understand the long-term view of the MDM vendor landscape, we need to establish a baseline of where various types of MDM vendors and their products are today. Clearly, discussing all vendors that offer MDM-related products is well beyond the scope of this book. Therefore, the sections that follow discuss only a few leading MDM Data Hub vendors and their products. In doing so, and where appropriate, we'll indicate whether a given product addresses a single MDM data domain or an MDM-specific feature, or has a broader, multidomain and multifunctional coverage.

Lastly, the information presented in this chapter has been synthesized from various sources, including vendor briefings, analysis of publicly available research reports, and the authors' practical experience implementing MDM solutions using a number of mature and new vendor products. However, this chapter is not intended to be a substitute for comprehensive, in-depth analysis of the MDM vendor market and the products available from these sources.

The Gartner Group and Forrester Research provide excellent industry market overviews of the vendors and products in these areas.[1-5]

Major MDM Vendors

As stated earlier, recent market consolidation has caused a significant landscape shift, and as a result relatively few established companies dominate the MDM market. The list of these companies includes IBM, Oracle, Informatica, SAP, SAS, Tibco, and D&B Purisma. We added to this list Acxiom as a leading provider of reference data for MDM solutions primarily in Customer domain. These companies and their products are discussed in the sections that follow.

IBM

After the acquisition of Initiate Systems in 2010, IBM ended up with three key MDM products: InfoSphere Master Data Management Server (MDM Server), InfoSphere MDM Server for PIM (Product Information Master), and Initiate Master Data Service (MDS).

MDM Server evolved from Web Sphere Customer Center (WCC), which in turn was developed based on a CDI product from DWL, which IBM acquired in 2005. WCC and the MDM Server inherited their party domain focus with out-of-the-box data structures for customer, account, and product domains.

MDM Server for PIM evolved from the MDM product built by Trigo, a company that IBM acquired in 2004. MDM Server for PIM concentrates on the product data domain and focuses on support for workflows critical for PIM. Hence, even though both MDM Server products can deal with product data, they focus on different aspects of MDM. Rob Karel of Forrester Research compared PIM with an "Enterprise Application,"[5] and MDM Server for PIM's capabilities can serve as an illustration of Karel's point.

Both MDM Servers are considered leaders in Gartner's Magic Quadrants for Customer and Product Data Hubs, respectively, which points to the niches each of the MDM Servers occupies. Although highly desirable, it is less obvious to many experts how the MDM Server and Initiate MDS will coexist if left unchanged. Despite the fact that the MDM Server and Initiate MDS had been fighting in the same MDM space prior to Initiate's acquisition by IBM, the products pursue very different MDM philosophies. It is appropriate at this point to refer the reader to Chapter 7, where we described different data-modeling styles that dominate the MDM market. The Initiate MDS does not have any business data model out of the box. A business data model is built by the meta-model configuration. This yields the Initiate solution optimized for entity resolution and relationship management. In Initiate architecture, business data services and other types of services have to be developed by MDM implementers or vendor-supplied expert consultants.

In contrast, the MDM Server comes with a pre-built data model and a few layers of packaged services on top of the data model out of the box. It is logical to assume that rather than aim for coexistence, an approach that merges the capabilities from both products will create a combined product with strong probabilistic matching and data services capabilities. For complex MDM projects, both products can work jointly within a single MDM solution that requires strong probabilistic matching, entity resolution, relationship resolution, flexibility of the data model, and business services for customer, account, and product domains. These services support real-time transactions such as managing core customer data, address and contact information, customer grouping and aggregation, financial information, customer roles and relationships, alerts, matching, and duplicate suspect processing. More complex services known as "composite transactions" can be built using the basic MDM Web Services.

Key points regarding the three IBM MDM products follow.

The InfoSphere MDM Server

This solution suite includes several levels of services and components to support the flexibility of the business service model:

- Coarse-grained business services
- Fine-grained business services
- Business object model
- Database

The InfoSphere MDM Server offers multiple access methods, such as Web Services, EAI publish-subscribe interfaces, and object-level interfaces. The ability to build composite transactions by calling coarse-grained, fine-grained, and business object components at run time makes this product even more flexible.

The InfoSphere MDM Server provides data visibility functionality using its Rules of Visibility (RoV) engine. This includes a menu-driven interface for managing Rules of Visibility that determine what data end users can see and what they can do with that data in the system. Batch Framework is available to support batch processing when real-time synchronization is not required or not feasible.

Initiate's MDS

This product was rated as a "leader" by the Gartner Group's "Magic Quadrant for Customer Data Integration Hubs," in the second quarter of 2009. Initiate provides strong matching capabilities that enable its clients to create a single trusted view of the customer profile data. Initiate supports management of organizational hierarchies for institutional customers, and provides a set of APIs and Web Services that can effectively support application integration. The main components of the Initiate solution include:

- **Initiate Master Data Service**   The core MDM engine designed to deliver a single master data view
- **The Workbench (Eclipse based)**   Used as a Data Hub management and administration tool
- **Initiate Inspector**   Used as a data stewardship web-client interface
- **Initiate Enterprise Viewer**   Enables users to view linked records across lines of business and systems

InfoSphere MDM Server for PIM

This product's key components and capabilities include the following:

- Data model flexibility to support product categories and hierarchies/taxonomies
- Data aggregation, syndication, and standard protocols for the import and export of product data
- Collaborative MDM functionality and workflows for PIM
- Granular access to product data

In addition to core MDM products, IBM offers a comprehensive suite of data quality and ETL tools, including WebSphere ProfileStage and WebSphere QualityStage, which provide data profiling and data quality capabilities, and the WebSphere DataStage ETL suite. These tools are often used in conjunction with the MDM Data Hub products for MDM implementations.

Oracle

Oracle approaches the market with Oracle Master Data Management Suite. The suite includes a number of data-domain-specific MDM Data Hub products:

- Oracle Customer Hub
- Oracle Site/Location Hub
- Oracle Supplier Hub
- Oracle Product Hub
- Oracle Higher Education Constituent Hub

In addition to the pure MDM Data Hub products, Oracle's MDM suite addresses master data quality with domain-specific cleansing and standardization tools. On specific project implementations, one or more Oracle MDM Data Hub products can be used. Oracle Corporation positions its Data Hub products as part of its open architecture middleware family of products. Each of the Oracle Data Hub products operates as a Transaction Hub with appropriate data structures and services customized and configured to support particular data domains. Oracle MDM Data Hubs are integrated through services to ensure the integrity of the MDM solution across data domains.

Oracle's MDM Products for Customer Domain

Let's start with an Oracle product that is based on Siebel UCM, which was often rated by analysts as the leader in the CRM space. After Oracle's acquisition of Siebel, the company was identified as a leader in the MDM for Customer domain by the Gartner Group's "Magic Quadrant for Customer Data Integration Hubs" in the second quarter of 2009. Oracle/Siebel Universal Customer Master (UCM) has well-developed customer-centric data structures and modules for a number of industries. Oracle/Siebel's MDM solution consists of three modules:

- **Universal Application Network (UAN)**   Enables organizations to deploy business processes. UAN includes UAN Integration Processes, UAN Common Objects, and UAN Transformations.
- **The Data Quality module**   Provides matching capabilities in real-time and batch modes. It supports integration with other data-cleansing tools. These capabilities are available for multiple countries, languages, and character sets.
- **Universal Customer Master (UCM)**   A Customer Data Hub that provides prebuilt components that integrate customer data from multiple systems.

Oracle Customer Data Hub (CDH) is another MDM product for the Customer domain. It assembles a broad set of components, including data quality, matching, customer key management, data enrichment, data synchronization, and analytics. The product was ranked as a niche player by the Gartner Magic Quadrant for the second quarter of 2009. CDH is primarily positioned for and used by E-Business Suite customers that focus on manufacturing products, often in combination with Oracle Product Data Hub and Oracle Site Hub.

Other MDM Products in Oracle Portfolio

Oracle offers and supports several additional products in its MDM portfolio:

- Oracle Financial Consolidation Hub integrates financial data from multiple sources.

- Oracle Product Information Management Data Hub integrates product data by creating a centralized product database. This product is known as Oracle Product Hub (Oracle PH).

   It was ranked a "leader" by the Gartner Magic Quadrant published in the third quarter of 2009. Oracle PH enables its customers, especially those leveraging Oracle E-Business Suite, to achieve a single view of product data across the enterprise.

- Oracle data quality solution for the product domain includes sophisticated semantic-based technology required to properly parse poorly structured product data.

Data Relationship Manager

Oracle's acquisition of Hyperion enhanced its MDM portfolio by adding the Data Relationship Management (DRM) tool, which is a full-function, comprehensive hierarchy management tool that supports a wide variety of hierarchy management operations, including support for alternative hierarchies, custom aggregations, data lineage, and many other features required for complex hierarchy manipulations typical for global, multinational, geographically distributed, and diverse organizations.

Informatica

Informatica, a leader in the data integration space, has been moving to the MDM market gradually. With the acquisition of Similarity Systems in January of 2006, Informatica took a significant step toward getting a leadership position in data quality as it relates to the MDM, especially the Customer domain. Similarity Systems expanded the traditional Informatica offering in the ETL and data integration areas by bringing strong data profiling, data standardization, and matching capabilities. The Informatica Data Quality Suite is built on Similarity Systems' ATHANOR product, and it delivers data standardization, data matching, and data quality monitoring capabilities to its users.

The acquisition of Identity Systems in 2008 continued Informatica's expansion into the MDM market.

Siperian

With the recent acquisition of Siperian in 2010, Informatica has become one of the leading players in the MDM space. The Siperian solution was considered "visionary" by Gartner Group's "Magic Quadrant for Customer Data Integration Hubs" for the second quarter of 2009. The Siperian Hub is designed as a metadata-driven J2EE application that can work with any data model. This flexibility positions Siperian not only as a customer-centric solution but also as a platform applicable to wider MDM data domain coverage. The Siperian Hub includes the following primary high-level components:

- **Master Reference Manager (MRM)**   Creates and manages record location metadata to support data synchronization in batch and real-time modes.
- **Hierarchy Manager (HM)**   Manages relationships and hierarchies.
- **Activity Manager (AM)**   Manages a unified view of transaction and reference data across systems. It is used to continually monitor and evaluate data and act on data events.

The Siperian Hub has its own cleanse and match capabilities. Alternatively, external engines can be used to cleanse and standardize the data (for example, Business Objects/ First Logic or Trillium). Typically, a data-cleansing engine, whether internal or external, cleanses and standardizes the data whereas Siperian Hub performs matching and linking. Siperian licenses MetaMatrix Data Services Solution (acquired by Red Hat in 2007), which supports on-demand federated access to associated customer activity data not stored in the customer master. MetaMatrix provides Siperian with additional capabilities to implement the Registry-style solution even though initially the Siperian Hub was developed with the Transaction-style Hub in mind.

Informatica Data Quality Suite

This set of products enables enterprise data stewards and data governance officers to establish and maintain data quality rules. These rules and associated capabilities cover name and address parsing and validation for all countries, and data validation and corrections for various business domains such as Product, Inventory, Assets, and so on. The product provides robust matching and householding capabilities. In addition, the Informatica Data Quality Suite offers industry-specific libraries of data quality content for financial services and consumer packaged goods (CPG) companies. The suite provides Unicode-compliant technologies important for global projects because Unicode allows all writing systems and languages of the world to be represented and handled consistently.

Informatica Data Quality Suite uses an integrated data repository shared by the following components:

- **Informatica Data Quality Designer**   Provides an interface used to build information quality rules and plans.
- **Informatica Data Quality Server**   Provides the platform for the development, testing, and execution of the information quality rules and plans.
- **Informatica Data Quality Runtime**   Enables the enterprise to schedule and run data analysis, profiling, and other information quality processes.
- **Informatica Data Quality Realtime SDK**   Provides real-time capabilities for information quality processes such as data validation, corrections, standardization, and enrichment.
- **A library of reference data**   This is a section of the repository that maintains synonyms, aliases, and other data required to support the tool's navigational capabilities.

SAP

SAP started out as a premier vendor in the Enterprise Resource Planning (ERP) market. It has rapidly evolved into a major player in Master Data Management. SAP offers a well-known and widely deployed suite of business applications. One of them, MySAP Customer Relationship Management, is designed for customer-centric solutions, including MDM capabilities that are optimized for Transaction-style implementations. SAP solutions provide an integrated set of information management capabilities, including catalog and content management as well as product life-cycle management (PLM), with a particular focus on marketing, merchandising, and promotions (these features came from the acquisition of A2i in 2004).

The Gartner Magic Quadrants for Product and Customer data published in 2009 ranked SAP MDM as a "challenger" in the product domain and a "niche player" in the customer domain. SAP MDM solutions are based on NetWeaver technology, which provides a service-oriented architecture approach to integrating business processes, software components, information, and organizational entities. NetWeaver is designed to be "platform agnostic" and thus can interoperate with Microsoft .NET and a J2EE platforms such as IBM WebSphere. In recent years, SAP has made significant improvements in its NetWeaver MDM technologies by integrating data-domain-specific repositories and enhancing data model management flexibility. The power and flexibility of the NetWeaver platform and the size and influence of SAP as a leader in ERP solutions help position SAP to become one of the leaders in the MDM space. In the product domain, SAP leverages its ERP installed base. In the customer domain, the primary SAP focus is B2B MDM solutions.

With the acquisition of Business Objects and First Logic, SAP strengthened its positions in MDM data quality, matching, and BI capabilities. Acquired by Business Objects in April 2006, First Logic is a specialist data quality product vendor. Its solution is designed to integrate with most leading Data Hub vendors. The capabilities commonly used for customer-centric MDM implementations include data cleansing and standardization for names and addresses, and entity match and merge (consolidate).

With the acquisition of Sybase in 2010, SAP has further improved its position in data management space, and we may see a Sybase-based MDM engine from SAP that can fully leverage Sybase and Sybase IQ capabilities.

SAS DataFlux

DataFlux is a division of SAS. DataFlux complements SAS core competencies in business intelligence software and services by providing solutions aimed at information quality and data profiling.

As per the 2009 Gartner Magic Quadrant for Data Quality tools, DataFlux was a recognized leader in the data quality space. DataFlux "officially" entered the MDM space in 2008 with the introduction of the qMDM product. The product has a primary focus on the MDM for Customer domain. Its data modeling flexibility has the potential to expand in the Product domain and other MDM areas.

DataFlux focuses on some foundational MDM capabilities such as reference data, code semantics reconciliation, pattern recognition and standardization, and data standardization. Key DataFlux components used in its MDM suite include:

- **Master Customer Reference Database**   Stores customer information.

- **dfPowerStudio**   Enables data stewards and Data Governance professionals to monitor and profile data across the enterprise, analyze the data quality, and take corrective actions using a single interface. Data quality features are based on libraries that enable address standardization and enrichment in line with U.S. Postal Service standards, party-type recognition (individual vs. organization), gender recognition, and other critical MDM data quality functions. Data integration features allow users to match, link, and merge records across systems.

- **DataFlux Integration Server**   Provides a single mechanism for batch and real-time data synchronization. It reads the business rules from the metadata created by dfPowerStudio and enforces the rules for data synchronization, taking advantage of parallel processing to support higher throughput. The product is capable of running batch jobs and exposes interfaces to its data quality functions and algorithms, which can be called from many languages. Otherwise, the functions and algorithms can be invoked as Web Services.

Being a part of SAS, the DataFlux products are well positioned to leverage their data quality and MDM strengths with SAS's capabilities in the business intelligence and marketing analytics areas.

Tibco

Tibco has entered the MDM market with a position of strength in Enterprise Information Integration based on its recognized name in SOA and ESB technologies. These areas of strength determined Tibco's focus on collaborative MDM and PIM. In the 2009 Gartner's Magic Quadrant for Product data, Tibco was placed high in the "visionary" quadrant, almost on the border with the "leader" quadrant occupied by IBM and Oracle.

Tibco Collaborative Information Manager (CIM) serves mostly the Product data domain. Its flexible data model positions CIM for penetration into other domains, especially when collaborative MDM capabilities are stated as business and technical goals. CIM was originally based on a PIM product developed by Velocel, acquired by Tibco in 2005.

Tibco demonstrates a high focus on MDM in conjunction with SOA, which, as we discussed throughout the book, benefits both MDM and SOA. SOA-enabled MDM solutions are agile and can accommodate real-time data management requirements and a hub-and-spoke solution architecture, whereas SOA benefits from MDM implementations due to an alignment with core data strategies—an alignment that is key to ensuring a meaningful business impact and positive ROI of SOA.

Tibco augments the collaborative MDM capabilities of CIM with a B2B gateway functionality. Tibco has been continuously growing its Customer domain MDM and data quality capabilities by integration with leading data quality technologies such as Trillium. Tibco's investments in the Customer domain include the open-source Lucene fuzzy matching technology.

In 2010, Tibco reemphasized its focus on MDM by acquiring Netrics. Netrics provides unique matching capabilities based on graph theory, specifically on the Bipartite Graph Matching (BGM) algorithm. This algorithm makes it possible to incorporate a human-like intelligence into the matching process.

These matching capabilities significantly exceed the capabilities provided by more traditional fuzzy algorithms such as SOUNDEX and NYSIIS. The algorithm scales as $N*logN$, where N is the number of records in the matching record set. Also, the algorithm works well with sparse data. Sparse data is a common problem when matching heterogeneous records sourced from multiple systems and lines of business. Most traditional algorithms are not optimized to handle this problem.

With the Netrics acquisition, Tibco can utilize a learning algorithm that can accept manual user input to refine the matching rules. This empowers the user to manually change match groups for a small sample data set and use the learning algorithm that will automatically interpret the manual input and define it internally as a generic rule that it will apply on the next matching iteration.

Dun & Bradstreet Purisma

Dun and Bradstreet (D&B) maintains a global commercial database that contains over 100 million business entity records. Therefore, a partnership with D&B can make a difference for MDM projects focusing on commercial customers. Such a partnership can be particularly helpful for sales and marketing, credit management, and managing the company's suppliers.

Technically speaking, D&B entered the MDM software market in 2007 with its acquisition of Purisma. Purisma Customer Registry is a "thin" Registry-style Customer Data Hub solution that enables the company to align multiple applications from the perspectives of customer data accuracy and data quality. The product offers strong matching capabilities and supports complex hierarchical relationships between customers with a focus on institutional entities. The support for hierarchical relationships includes systemic relationship correlation capabilities. Purisma stores relevant data in a module known as the Master Customer Identity Index. The product consists of the following three tightly integrated components:

- **Purisma Correlation Engine**   This component is at the core of the solution. It manages matching and association metadata, and ultimately maintains customer identity.

- **Purisma Data Stewardship Engine**   This component provides views and user interfaces that allow the user to analyze the data, manage exceptions, and perform audit, hierarchy management, and other manual control functions.

- **Purisma Integration Services**   This component provides Web Services–based utilities for third-party integration.

Purisma supports Transaction Hub capabilities that enable enterprises to use the Purisma Hub as the Master Data Hub that provides bidirectional synchronization with multiple systems.

Purisma technology is combined with the D&B database that contains global business profile information. This creates a powerful combination of D&B database and Purisma software in the B2B market. The information includes company name, headquarters address, phone and fax, primary office or site locations, corporate executives, stock index, parent company information, year of establishment, approximate or reported net worth, current financial information, credit risk information, lawsuits against the company, history of slow payments, and many other data attributes. D&B creates and maintains a unique global identifier (DUNS number) for each entity (company) that it recognizes and maintains information on. D&B also maintains the company's credit ratings and D&B PAYDEX scores.

In addition to its MDM-related offerings, D&B offers a number of packaged solutions, including Risk Management Solutions (which assists in mitigating project risks), Sales and

Marketing Solutions, E-Business Solutions (which help in market research), and Supply Chain Management Solutions.

D&B continues to improve its market position in the MDM space, especially in MDM for Customer domain. The company established a Product and Technology Outsourcing Agreement with Acxiom on August 2, 2006. This agreement is aimed at improving matching rates by using Acxiom technology.

Acxiom

Acxiom is the leading MDM data provider with a unique customer knowledge base for individual customer data. This is a significant solution player in the MDM space for the Customer domain, and although it is more a data than a software provider, our discussion of the MDM vendor market would not be complete without at least a brief look at Acxiom.

Acxiom's primary focus is customer information management and customer data integration. Acxiom's Knowledge Base contains records of customer information collected from and verified by multiple sources. Acxiom's Command Center supports over 850 terabytes of customer information. Acxiom provides a very broad coverage of individuals residing in the United States, the United Kingdom, and Australia. It licenses U.S. Postal Service information, and in particular its National Change of Address (NCOA) file. This enables the company to store and maintain up-to-date name and address information. Therefore, if a company is going to implement an MDM solution that needs to use name and address to match its corporate or individual customer data, a partnership with Acxiom can provide significant benefits to data quality and confidence of the match process. Some of the Acxiom products frequently used on MDM projects are as follows:

- **AbiliTec**   This product provides batch and near-real-time matching and data enrichment information. AbiliTec receives an information request for customer name and address and returns the AbiliTec links that represent the event of matching this name and address data against Acxiom's Knowledge Base. Specifically, if the match has been found, the link type is referred to as "maintained." Otherwise, a "derived" AbiliTec link is returned.

- **AddressAbility**   This product verifies, corrects, and standardizes addresses to USPS specifications, which includes ZIP codes, city names, state abbreviations, resolution of vanity addresses, and so on.

- **DSF[2]**   This product stores all valid addresses recognized by the USPS. The product can also differentiate between residential and business addresses. This product can assist in party type identification. We discussed the importance of party identification in Chapter 14.

- **NCOA (National Change of Address)[6]**   Provides change of address information. From the MDM perspective, this information can be used to bring together two individual records at different addresses, recognizing them as one individual record.

- **LACS (Locatable Address Conversion System)[7]**   Provides information about permanent address conversions resulting from renumbering, street or city name changes, and so on. This is a critical piece of information that helps in matching customer records.

References

1. Radcliffe, John. "Magic Quadrant for Master Data Management of Customer Data." Gartner Research, June 16, 2009.

2. Friedman, Ted and Bitterer, Andreas. "Magic Quadrant for Data Quality Tools." Gartner Research, June 9, 2009.

3. White, Andrew. "Magic Quadrant for Master Data Management of Product Data." Gartner Research, July 9, 2009.

4. Wang, Ray. "The Forrester Wave: Customer Hubs." Forrester Research, August 4, 2008.

5. Karel, Rob, et al. "Product Information Management (PIM)." Forrester Research, July 21, 2009.

6. http://www.usps.com/ncsc/addressservices/moveupdate/changeaddress.htm.

7. http://www.usps.com/ncsc/addressservices/addressqualityservices/lacsystem.htm.

CHAPTER 19

Where Do We Go from Here?

W e have finally arrived at the point in the book that allows us to talk about the future of Master Data Management. Throughout the book, we have used various ways to describe MDM and to articulate the business drivers and technical challenges of implementing MDM initiatives. We showed the complexities surrounding MDM architecture, paid close attention to often-overlooked issues of data security and visibility, and shared the authors' personal experiences in addressing implementation concerns on a number of MDM projects across several industries.

Review of the Key Points Covered in the Preceding Chapters

We have stated in the beginning of the book that MDM is a broad, complex, and multidiscipline set of technologies organized into a policy-driven comprehensive framework that can be viewed from several business and technical perspectives. We introduced the notion of MDM classification dimensions that allows us to better understand how to consider, design, deploy and obtain benefits from an MDM system. As MDM continues to mature and attract attention of enterprise decision makers across a wide spectrum of industries, the amount of available information about MDM continues to grow as well, and in order to make sense of various, sometimes contradictory assertions about MDM, we need to apply a proven approach to the reduction of complexity—an approach of decomposition and classification or categorization. This approach allows us to organize available information and discuss various aspects of MDM according to a well-defined structure. The MDM classification dimensions that we introduced in Chapter 1 enable us to better understand the relevance and importance of various factors affecting the product selection; architecture, design, and deployment choices; impact on the existing and new business processes; and overall MDM strategy and readiness for the enterprise. The latter is based on a number of variations of the capability maturity model including the Capability Maturity Models for MDM introduced in Chapter 12 and the Capability Maturity Model for data governance that we discussed in detail in Chapter 17. The sections that follow provide a brief summary of lessons that we learned up to this point.

A Brief Summary of Lessons Learned

Let's quickly review all major points that are relevant to any MDM initiative regardless of the data domain, industry, geography, and other deployment requirements.

Lesson Learned: MDM Classification Dimensions

Several commonly accepted MDM classification schemes or dimensions that we introduced in Chapter 1 include the Design and Deployment dimension, the Use Pattern dimension, and the Information Scope or Data Domain dimension. We showed these dimensions as persistent characteristics of any MDM solution regardless of the industry or master data domain. Let's recap the key classification dimensions here:

- **Design and Deployment**   This classification describes MDM architecture styles that support a full spectrum of MDM implementations—from a thin MDM reference-only layer to a full Master Data platform (or MDM Data Hubs). The entire range of the MDM Data Hub variations (from thin to thick) can support all business processes including transaction processing. These styles—Registry, Coexistence, and Transaction Hub—were discussed in greater detail in Part II of the book.

- **Use Pattern**   This classification differentiates MDM solutions based on how the master data is used. We see three primary use patterns for MDM data usage—Analytical MDM, Operational MDM, and Collaborative MDM.

  - *Analytical MDM* supports business processes and applications that use master data primarily to analyze business performance and provide appropriate reporting and insight into the data itself, perhaps directly interfacing with Business Intelligence suites; Analytical MDM tends to be read-mostly, in that it does not change/correct source data in the operational systems, but does cleanse and enrich data in the MDM Data Hub; from the data warehousing perspective, Analytical MDM builds complex data warehousing dimensions.

  - *Operational MDM* allows master data to be collected, changed, and used to process business transactions; Operational MDM is designed to maintain semantic consistency of master data affected by the transactional activity. Operational MDM provides a mechanism to improve the quality of data in the operational systems, where the data is usually created.

  - *Collaborative MDM* allows its users to author master data objects and collaborate in the process of creation and maintenance of master data and associated metadata.

- **Information Scope or Data Domain**   This dimension describes the primary data domain managed by the MDM solution; in the case of Customer MDM, the resulting solution is often called Customer Data Integration or CDI; in the case of product MDM, the solution is known as Product Information Management or PIM; other data domains may not have formal definitions yet, but could have an impact on how the MDM solution is designed and deployed.

Lesson Learned: Key Requirements of a Successful MDM Initiative

In addition to the introduction of the MDM classification dimensions, we extensively discussed two major requirements of any MDM initiative, and showed that in many cases failing to address either of these requirements would most likely result in a failure of the MDM project. These two major requirements of a successful MDM project are

- The creation and acceptance of a compelling, justifiable, and comprehensive business case

- The establishment and continuous involvement of an enterprise-wide Data Governance framework and a dedicated Data Governance team that is empowered and accountable for the implementation and enforcement of data governance policies and procedures

These two major MDM requirements are continuously confirmed not just by the authors' extensive experience in developing MDM solutions, but also by a number of industry analysts that conduct large-scale surveys and publish interesting and compelling statistics. For example, according to Forrester's August 2009 Global Master Data Management/Data Quality Online Survey,[1] 68 percent of surveyed organizations that embarked on the MDM journey require either a formal, detailed business case with a clearly articulated ROI, or a more high-level business case that defines the MDM blueprint in the context of the overall enterprise business and technical architecture but does not have to include a detailed analysis. And likewise, according to the same Forrester Research report, 95 percent of organizations rate data governance as important, very important, or critical to the successful implementation and rollout of MDM solutions.

Lesson Learned: MDM Is a Global, Industry-Agnostic Enabler of Enterprise Transformation

There are many MDM implementation challenges, and they span organizational, business, and technical aspects of the MDM. Let's briefly summarize some of these key points of MDM that often drive the implementation challenges. We discussed these points in detail throughout the book.

- The ability to recognize individual entities as members of arbitrary complex groups (for example, households and extended families for individuals, holding companies and other organizational hierarchies for business entities such as corporations, product bundles for product components, and so on) is one of the key properties of Master Data Management, and it applies equally well to MDM for Customer Data domain, Reference Data Management, Product Master Hubs, and so on, with the complexity of the associations and grouping depending in large part on the completeness and accuracy of the data and the business rules driving the resolution of conflicting or undetermined links.

- Master Data Management is a horizontal technology that applies equally well to all industries and markets and is global in nature. This point has two equally important aspects:

  - MDM in general, with its variants such as the customer-centric version known as Customer Data Integration or CDI and the product master version sometimes called Product Information Master or PIM, is especially effective in modernizing a global enterprise.

  - The need for an authoritative, accurate, timely, and secure "single version of the truth" is pervasive and is not particular to a specific industry, data domain, country, or geography.

- At the time of this writing, Master Data Management for Customer domain continues to be the predominant MDM variant. While evolutionary from the pure technological point of view, it is revolutionary in its potential business impact of transforming the enterprise into a customer-centric model. In that, MDM Customer (CDI) represents a particularly interesting opportunity to any customer- or citizen-facing organizations including commercial businesses and government agencies alike.

- Master Data Management can enable an enterprise to achieve a sustainable competitive advantage by improving the levels of customer service and overall customer experience, reducing the attrition rates, growing customer-based revenue as a share of their wallet by understanding and leveraging the totality of customer relationships with the enterprise, and helping the enterprise to be in a better position to achieve regulatory compliance, to name just a few.

- MDM benefits extend well beyond the Customer domain. For example, MDM can significantly improve enterprise efficiencies where a holistic view of the products can help streamline various business processes, enable effective innovation, and improve new products, competitiveness and time-to-market metrics.

- MDM can be extremely beneficial to various government agencies and businesses not only from a customer service point of view but also in helping law enforcement agencies in threat detection and prevention.

Key Lessons Learned about MDM Technical Approaches

In addition to the organizational, process-related, and business challenges, MDM presents a number of challenges that are driven by the complexity of its technology framework and the variety of approaches designed to address them. Throughout the book, we discussed key MDM technical approaches and challenges. Among them are the following:

- Building an MDM solution as an instance of a service-oriented architecture (SOA)

- Building MDM solutions to utilize Web Services as the insulation vehicle between new master data, legacy data stores, business processes, and applications

- Addressing data governance and data quality issues with a high focus on data quality metrics to achieve advanced levels of data governance

- Defining and applying accurate matching algorithms for batch and real-time processing

- Building an MDM solution as a policy-driven framework, with the policies providing context and directions for defining and applying survivorship rules for the "single version of the truth" records, solving complex data synchronization and reconciliation issues, and in general governing MDM system behavior

- Considering the complexity of new, MDM-enabled business transactions that span systems and applications not only within the enterprise but also across system domains of its business partners

- Addressing the scalability challenges of data volumes, transactional throughput, and structured and unstructured data types

- Enabling robust process controls to support audit and compliance reporting

- Designing effective approaches to protecting access to the integrated data as well as to the services and applications that can access that data—fine-grained access controls and policy—and entitlements-driven data visibility and security

Key MDM Technical Capabilities

The following MDM technical capabilities should be considered for any MDM solution that creates and maintains a reliable trusted single version of the truth.

- Entity resolution (Client/Prospect/Product)—recognition, identification, matching, and linking
- GUID (globally persistent unique identifiers) generation and management, where the scope of uniqueness can be limited to a particular data domain
- Identification of associations, roles, and relationships
- Data lineage
- Hierarchy management
- Entity (for example, Account, Legal Entity, Customer) grouping
- Probabilistic and rules-driven arbitration among data sources
- Direct, proximity, and association-based search of master entities
- Metadata-driven X-Ref Data Locator registry
- Alias management
- Entity change capture, maintenance, notification, distribution, and reconciliation
- Data validation, de-duping, hygiene, standardization, and enrichment
- Entity assembly, aggregations, splits
- Data security and visibility

Most of these capabilities are governed by a rich set of technology-agnostic policies.

Main Reasons MDM Projects Fail

It should come as no surprise that addressing the points in the preceding sections does not guarantee that an MDM project will be a success.

Master Data Management projects represent significant enterprise-wide undertakings that rely on and impact four pillars of successful MDM initiatives: business processes, people, organizational structure, and technology. These four pillars of MDM are needed to maintain the balance—break one pillar, and the entire MDM "house" may fall! In almost all cases, these four pillars depend heavily on the MDM maturity level of the organization. We discussed a few flavors of the MDM maturity model throughout the book and in Chapter 12, while Chapter 17 discusses CMM for Data Governance. These CMM models are very useful and in combination can profile the current state of MDM and Data Governance maturity and define the target state.

However, even higher levels of maturity may not prevent an MDM initiative from failure. We can see several predominant reasons why MDM initiatives fail, and many of these reasons apply to any MDM or Data Governance CMM level organization. We discuss these reasons in the following sections.

Review of the Key Reasons for MDM Project Failure

The following represents just some of the key reasons why MDM projects may fail

Lack of Justifiable, Business-Driven Business Case,
Lack of Executive Support and Budgetary Commitment

As we mentioned several times, MDM initiatives can succeed only if there is executive-level support. This is the key since many MDM projects tend to become very large very quickly and last longer than a few months. Even though signing checks is critical, senior management commitment must go beyond that. Senior management must understand the key benefits, dependencies, release scope and timing, high-level risks, and trade-offs the project is facing. A formal business case is the primary vehicle to ensure this understanding and enterprise buy-in.

Lack of Coordination and Cooperation
Between Business and Technology Organizations

The complexity, size, and the implementation risk of MDM initiatives require close coordination and cooperation between business and technology organizations involved in the MDM initiative not only in order to achieve the goals of the project but also to reach an agreement that these goals have been met. All too often a business unit defines high-level business requirements for an MDM solution and passes them on to the technology team to implement. The technology team analyzes the requirements and their technical feasibility, and defines the plan, the approach, the architecture, the infrastructure, and the tools required to deliver what has been requested by the business. However, sometimes the requirements are expressed in such high-level terms that their technical implications are not apparent to the business and technology organizations. Without a continuous joint effort to address the potential ambiguity of the requirements, the technology team may create a project plan that, from the business-unit point of view, is too long, too expensive, and does not deliver what the business sees as a timely value proposition. Without proper cooperation and coordination, this disconnect may be "discovered" several months into the project with the money already spent and no recognizable return on investment. A potential outcome might be the withdrawal of business support and funding that would lead to the cancellation of the project for failure to deliver. The business case must include a comprehensive MDM roadmap that is bound to define the target state vision as well as intermediate releases of MDM.

Lack of Consuming Applications

The old adage "if we build it they will come" does not always work in the case of Master Data Management. MDM projects are often positioned as infrastructure projects, and here lies the danger. Typically, an infrastructure initiative becomes "visible" only when the organization experiences an infrastructure-related problem, for example, the enterprise network is not available and a major application or customer channel is down, and so on. Successful infrastructure projects keep enterprises "alive" but are rarely appreciated unless a problem occurs. MDM projects hold a promise of significant business benefits and thus should not be invisible. To put it another way, it is very difficult to demonstrate the value and the benefits of an MDM solution if there are no applications and no end users that can take advantage of these new capabilities. Inability to demonstrate value may result in a negative perception of a project as a failure, with the project stakeholders withdrawing their support and looking for alternative solutions. For example, bundling MDM with customer on-boarding and account opening process can clearly demonstrate significant value and at the same time improve the quality of MDM-enabled applications and processes. In this case, the added value becomes clear since the business community obtains a new, more efficient and highly-visible account opening application that leverages higher quality customer data, reduced data entry errors, and streamlined processes.

Lack of User Adoption

This reason is closely related to the preceding one. One of the impacts of an MDM project is the ability to view, use, and manage critical enterprise data differently, possibly using different applications and business processes. That requires not only the availability of new consuming applications that can take advantage of the MDM solution, but also an educated and trained end-user community. End-user education should start as soon as the project is approved. Training is another critical area of user adoption. Training performed too early is not effective since the end users may forget what they learned by the time the system is in production. In addition, training should be flexible enough to accommodate users with different levels of computer literacy, from novices to "power" users.

Underestimating or Not Considering Impact of Legacy

Many MDM implementations have to be developed and deployed into already-established enterprise system environments, and therefore have to deal with existing data sources and applications. While the need for an accurate, timely, and authoritative system of record is understood and shared by both the business and technical teams, it is often the case that an application area in charge of an existing data store such as a data warehouse, CRM system, or a reference database would consider extending existing data stores and consuming applications as well as attempting to improve data quality in a tactical fashion by focusing on the local data stores. In addition, the legacy system owners may put forward an argument that since their legacy solution is already in place, there is no need for additional system integration work. In short, a legacy extension and modernization approach may present a tactical alternative to an MDM solution that can be perceived by the management as a lower risk approach. The MDM project team needs to assess the impact of the incremental system integration effort required to deploy a new MDM platform into the existing system environment, understand the potential shortcomings of legacy-based tactical solutions, and develop an MDM business case that would create compelling strategic arguments for a MDM solution.

Failing to Socialize MDM Throughout the Enterprise

MDM projects can affect practically every department in an enterprise. Therefore, MDM project owners must be also MDM evangelists and social champions who continuously work toward obtaining and maintaining enterprise-wide support, making sure that the project plan is built using realistic timelines and appropriate resources and budget. Effectively socializing the project's goals and benefits would ensure the proper level of stakeholder involvement, from awareness to understanding and ownership.

Lack of the Data Governance Strategy That Includes Well-Defined Data Stewardship and Formally Managed Metrics-Driven Data Quality Program

This reason is practically self-explanatory; without proper measurable data quality metrics the MDM solution would be an integration point of inaccurate or incomplete data, which makes its usefulness questionable. We put a lot of focus on this aspect of Data Governance in Chapter 17.

PART V

Lack of a Comprehensive, Service-Oriented MDM Architecture

As MDM projects grow up from their initial pilot implementations, they need to be architected to be easily integrated with the enterprise architecture. This requirement is easy to understand if you consider that the goal of any MDM project is to create an authoritative, accurate, and, most importantly, enterprise-wide system of record. So, leveraging enterprise legacy infrastructure and applications and designing for interoperability, performance, scalability, and security are only a few aspects that have to be addressed. Using a comprehensive architecture framework to build service-oriented MDM solution helps decouple end-user business applications from the structure and the physical location of the existing and new data stores and thus helps reduce data and functional redundancy, and provides the flexibility, scalability, and adaptability of the MDM solution.

Choosing the MDM Data Model Poorly

A choice between a vendor-provided data model and a custom data model developed in-house could spell the difference between success and failure of the project. This choice has to be made carefully and in the context of the enterprise business strategy and capability requirements.

Project Staffing

The complexity and multidisciplinary nature of Master Data Management initiatives requires the availability of a properly trained, knowledgeable cross-functional project team that has the appropriate number and the correct mix of subject matter experts, managers, planners, system architects, application developers, data analysts, database administrators, infrastructure designers, security experts, testers, and representatives of the business teams. Such a complex undertaking can be successful only if the project team has a respected, strong project leader who can also act as a visionary and evangelist who continues to reinforce the business value messages and to maintain effective collaboration and socialization among the team members.

MDM Guiding Principles

The reasons for MDM project failure that we discussed above should help MDM practitioners to avoid some obvious pitfalls on the road to MDM implementation. To further help readers to navigate turbulent MDM project waters successfully, we put together a concise set of MDM guiding principles that apply to practically any MDM initiative across any industry segment regardless of the specific MDM data domain or the architecture style. Some of these principles are conceptual while others are more focused on the specific technical issues and directions that help make an MDM initiative both useful and successful. These guiding principles are listed below:

- The MDM initiative has to start with well-defined, business-driven, and clearly justifiable business case.
- The MDM scope, design, architecture style, degree of federation and/or centralization, and the deployment roadmap shall be driven by sufficiently articulated business requirements and properly documented business processes.
- The MDM project approach, structure, and implementation roadmap shall include and be based on well-defined Data Governance rules and policies administered and enforced by an Enterprise Data Governance group.

- MDM and business processes are intrinsically linked: The MDM project team should design and deploy an MDM system in a way that can benefit, improve or optimize business processes.

- Whenever possible, make sure that the MDM system can support multiple data domains.

- Data that is mastered by an MDM system shall be captured once and validated at the source to the extent possible within the context.

- Any data modifications/corrections to the master data can be made only by the Master Data System according to the rules and policies established by the business, including the rules of resolving data change conflicts.

- Changes to the master data have to become available to all downstream systems at the time and in the form defined by the enterprise policies and business-specific SLAs.

- Every data item shall have an identified business owner and a steward (custodian).

- The quality of the master data shall be measured in accordance with information quality standards established by the organization. Whenever possible, the Data Governance/Data Quality Management team should apply Data Science and Information Theory principles to define measurable information quality standards.

- The MDM system architecture shall be designed from the ground up to ensure data security, integrity, visibility, and appropriate enterprise access controls.

- MDM shall be designed to support the appropriate versioning and retention of data at the appropriate level of granularity.

- The MDM system shall provide for and leverage standardization of sources, definitions, structures, and usage of shared and common information.

- MDM shall leverage consistent and validated metadata definitions for all data under management.

- At a minimum, the MDM architecture shall support key foundational MDM capabilities including but not limited to entity resolution; management of entity identifiers for all master entities; management of entity taxonomies, hierarchies, groups, and relationship; and entity data change capture, maintenance, notification, distribution, and reconciliation.

Master Data Management: Trends and Directions

Master Data Management solutions are still relatively new, and the road ahead has unexpected turns, peaks, and valleys. At the time of this writing, the market for MDM solutions continues to grow fast, and there are numerous research reports and surveys indicating current and future market sizes in terms of total expenditure and vendor revenue. According to the report published by Forrester Research, interest in MDM and a number of MDM initiatives continues to grow, and MDM is growing rapidly and becoming a clear priority for many organizations.[2] For example, "2008 Forrester's Enterprise and SMB Software Survey for North America and Europe"[3] found that 49 percent of organizations were planning to implement or expand their use of MDM software in 2009, a 9 percent increase from the previous year. We believe that the 2009–2010 economic recovery will help drive this trend to even higher numbers across industries and geographic locations.

However, the financial side does not necessarily indicate the direction that MDM would take going into the future.

It is hard to predict the future, and this is certainly true in the case of Master Data Management. Nevertheless, there are a number of research reports from various industry analysts that attempt to define market trends with various degrees of accuracy. In order to present a cohesive picture of MDM trends, we synthesized many of these predictions and analyses; supplemented them with our personal insights and observations based on practical, hands-on involvement in the MDM projects across different industry segments; and put together a compact and hopefully provocative list that takes into account not just MDM-specific trends but also major disruptive technology trends we are observing and experiencing in the second decade of the twenty-first century. We separate the discussion about the MDM trends into two categories: MDM market trends and MDM technical capabilities trends.

MDM Market Trends

These are the trends that we see developing in the MDM marketplace:

- Even though MDM is a multidomain discipline, two major domains—Party/Customer and Product—will continue to dominate enterprises' MDM agendas. Specifically, in the case of Party/Customer domain (this domain includes customer, prospect, patient, citizen, supplier, and employee data), many MDM initiatives will be positioned to lead enterprises toward customer-centric transformations. In that, MDM project scopes will become more broadly defined and include not just the implementation of an MDM Data Hub but also activities focused on business process management and applications reengineering with the end goal of developing new, more agile, comprehensive, customer-centric, and user-friendly processes and applications.

- Many MDM initiatives will be defined and implemented specifically to address the growing issue of managing a diverse set of externally sourced and internally maintained reference data, with a particular focus on managing reference data hierarchies and building enterprise-wide reference data distribution service solutions that operate according to the terms of generally accepted data governance policies, rules, and service contracts.

- External reference data providers and their "trusted" data sources and services will play a more prominent role in MDM implementations. Companies such as Dun & Bradstreet, Acxiom, Lexus-Nexus, Transunion, and Experian are a few examples of these data providers. Although these companies may not offer complete MDM solutions, they will certainly be positioned to become key players in the data cleansing, rationalization, enrichment, and linking and matching space.

- Master Data Management solutions will proliferate throughout various industry segments but will be subjected to two opposing forces: one is to develop industry-specific or business-specific implementations that emphasize each enterprise's strongest and differentiating competencies, while the other is the desire to implement MDM using newer, more flexible, multidomain-capable technology solutions to avoid creating numerous, possibly incompatible MDM platforms that would be difficult to integrate and may eventually result in higher development, maintenance, and, where appropriate, license costs.

- While the majority of MDM implementations will follow a service-oriented model, we see that both near-real-time (for example, near-real-time complete customer view) and batch designs (for example, a master file of pharmaceutical company customers—physicians and other healthcare providers) are going to co-exist in an enterprise, mostly dependent on the particular use case, data and application domain, and MDM architecture choices.

- Vendor solutions will evolve to concurrently support multiple domains, for example, delivering solutions such as Product Data Hub, Reference Data Hub, Location Data Hub, Account Data Hub, Privacy Data Hub, and others, using the same MDM engine. This is going to be especially true for the MDM solutions that focus on managing multidomain hierarchies and entity groups.

- The MDM vendor marketplace will continue to consolidate aggressively, with large system vendors acquiring smaller MDM specialty vendors. Given the typical size and complexity of MDM initiatives, the willingness of companies to partner with a larger vendor is part and parcel of the implementation risk mitigation strategy. The latest examples of such consolidation are the acquisition of Siperian by Informatica and the acquisition of Initiate Systems by IBM.

- Master Data Governance capabilities will grow and partly become embedded in the MDM Data Hub systems, including support for Data Governance metrics at different levels; organizations using these metrics will be able to establish a Master Data Governance group as an organizational unit with defined performance targets.

MDM Technical Capabilities Trends

We have seen the following technical capabilities in MDM emerging in the recent years:

- MDM solutions and vendor products will continue to extend master data capabilities along several dimensions:
  - "Organically," by evolving core functionality within the MDM engine
  - Through integration with new complementary technologies such as advanced data quality and matching solutions
  - Leveraging new computing paradigms such as virtualization, cloud computing (cloud computing is Internet-based computing model where shared computing resources such as CPU cycles, memory, software, and information are available to consumers such as application systems, devices and appliances on-demand, transparently and securely, based on the previously established service contracts), and cloud-related technologies such as Software-as-a-Service (SaaS), Platform-as-a-Service (PaaS), Data-as-a-Service (DaaS) and so on. These computing paradigms dramatically and often positively change the cost, scalability, manageability, and deployment factors of the MDM project equation.

- MDM becomes available as an Open Source solution. Open Source MDM is a new direction, and while the viability of this approach in the MDM space needs to be evaluated on the case-by-case basis, the promise of Open Source includes such benefits as improved development cycle, shorter time to market, and reduced cost.

Moreover, Open Source MDM, by definition, can leverage the open source community as a collective requirements generator, idea generator, and diversified tester. The resulting Open Source MDM solutions may deliver robust, collaboratively developed data models and effective, shared, and broadly tested technology components and algorithms such as sophisticated entity resolution algorithms that are often proprietary and are controlled by a single vendor owner.

- The majority of today's MDM solutions deal with structured data that can be represented in fixed tabular formats supported by relational database technology. An emerging trend in MDM technology is the support for unstructured and semi-structured data. This category of data represents at least 80 percent of all data under management, and having a single version of the truth of a large collection of semi-structured objects, images, XML documents, and other data types represents an interesting and exciting opportunity for MDM, for example, to enable rich content analysis; robust semantics processing; proximity and semantic searching; and management of such master objects as business, compliance, and security policies.

- A direct consequence of MDM support for the unstructured and semi-structured data is positioning MDM as a potential platform to centrally manage privacy policies and thus to help enforce trusted relationships between the enterprise and its customers.

- We stated repeatedly that master data managed by an MDM system must be protected not only from unauthorized, fraudulent use, but also from any attempt to access it that is against corporate business and security policy. These concerns are the subject of data security and visibility components of the MDM architecture. As the MDM market continues to mature, enterprises and vendors alike are developing standards-based policy enforcement mechanisms that can protect data and preserve existing business processes, while at the same time positioning the enterprise to be ready for verifiable, auditable compliance with government and industry regulations and laws concerning data security, visibility, confidentiality, and privacy protection.

- An obvious and easy prediction: MDM matching and linking technology will continue to evolve, will become much more sophisticated and powerful, and will support data matching for both structured and unstructured content, as well as support deep ontology-based semantic matching for complex objects in product domain.

- Business demands and vendor consolidation are already resulting in the availability of integrated MDM solutions that include sophisticated data quality components, flexible rules engines, metadata repositories, reporting and business intelligence tools, and even audit and compliance-monitoring capabilities in componentized service-based product suites. We believe that this trend will continue at least for the next several years.

Of course, this is far from a complete list of MDM trends. There are others, some more tactical and others that may be viewed as too radical or strange. Let's consider the following examples:

- Current thinking in the MDM world is to build MDM systems as Data Hubs. But we know from networking technologies that there are better, more efficient topologies than hubs and spokes. Would it be possible to build the next generation of MDM solution as a secure "switch" or "data grid" fabric that scales effectively and intelligently as an infinitely flexible cloud?

- Current Analytical MDM solutions are designed to support downstream data warehouses and BI systems that become primary consumers of master data. However, if an MDM system can effectively manage the structures and contents of dimensional hierarchies, this can allow future data warehousing environments to contain only facts or measures, and manage the dimensions directly in the MDM Data Hub. This architecture appears to be more flexible, more federation-friendly, and thus offers higher affinity to various cloud computing and virtualization models.

- Because MDM relies on the availability and effective execution of various rules and policies, it may be possible to extend the current view of MDM to support the new MDM information domain type—the domain of policies and rules—thus creating MDM Policy Hub systems that can "govern" other MDM Data Hubs.

We may not be able to answer questions like this today, but we're confident that collectively we will be able to see the answers emerging from the mist of the not-so-distant future. And then we can even find an answer to the *big* question: What is the next "disruptive" thing after MDM?

References

1. "Global Master Data Management/Data Quality Online Survey." Forrester Research, August 2009.

2. Karel, Rob. "Trends 2009: Master Data Management." Forrester Research (2009).

3. "Enterprise and SMB Software Survey, North America and Europe," Q4 2008.

PART V

VI PART

Appendixes

APPENDIX

List of Acronyms

3NF, 4NF, 5NF   The Third, Fourth, and Fifth Normal Forms, respectively

ACL   Access Control List

AJAX   Asynchronous JavaScript and XML

AML   Anti-Money Laundering

B2B   Business-to-Business

B2C   Business-to-Consumer

BGM   Bipartite Graph Matching algorithm

BI   Business Intelligence

CDI   Customer Data Integration

CFR   Code of Federal Regulation

CIF   Customer Information File

CMM   Capabilities Maturity Model

CPNI   Consumer Proprietary Network Information

CRM   Customer Relationship Management

CRUD   Create, Read, Update, Delete operations

CSIO XML   The Centre for Study of Insurance Operations standard XML

DNC   Do Not Call

DQ   Data Quality

ebXML   Electronic Business using eXtensible Markup Language

EDI   Electronic Data Interchange

EDM   Enterprise Data Management

EDW   Enterprise Data Warehouse

EIGG   Enterprise Information Governance Group

EII   Enterprise Information Integration

EIM   Enterprise Information Management

EMB   Enterprise Message Bus

EMF   Extensible Message Format

ETL   Extract, Transform, and Load

EV   Economic Value

EVA   Economic Value Added

FDA   U.S. Food and Drug Administration

FDIC   Federal Deposit Insurance Corporation

FFIEC   Federal Financial Institutions Examination Council

FixML   Financial Information Exchange Markup Language

FpML   Financial Product Markup Language

FSI   Financial Services Institution

G2B   Government-to-Business

G2C   Government-to-Customer

GLBA   Gramm-Leach-Bliley Act

HHS   Health and Human Services

HIPAA   Health Insurance Profitability and Accountability Act

HL7   Health Level Seven

HTNG   Hotel Technology Next Generation standard

IAA XML   Insurance Application Architecture XML

IAM   Identity and Access Management

ISO   International Standards Organization

IT   Information Technology

JAAS   Java Authentication and Authorization Service

JCA   J2EE Connector Architecture

JDBC   Java Database Connectivity

JMS   Java Message Service

KYC   Know Your Customer

LOB   Line of Business

MDDL   Market Data Definition Language

MDG   Master Data Governance

MDM   Master Data Management

MDQ   Master Data Quality

MNPI   Material Non-Public Information

NASD   National Association of Securities Dealers

NHI   National Health Index (New Zealand)

NPV   Net Present Value

NYSIIS   New York Sate Identification and Intelligence algorithm

OASIS   Organization for the Advancement of Structured Information Standards

OCC   Office of the Comptroller of the Currency

ODBC   Open Database Connectivity

ODS   Operational Data Store

OFAC   Office of Foreign Asset Control

OIG   Office of Inspector General

OLTP   On-Line Transaction Processing

OTA   OpenTravel Alliance standard

PAP   Policy Administration Point

PDP   Policy Decision Point

PEP   Policy Enforcement Point

PII   Personally Identifiable Information

QA   Quality Assurance

RBAC   Roles-Based Access Control

REST   Representational State Transfer

RFID   Radio Frequency Identification

RIXML   Research Information Markup Language

ROI   Return On Investment

RUP   Rational Unified Process

SAML   Security Assertion Markup Language

SB 1386   California Database Security Breach Notification Act

SDN   Specially Designated Nationals

SEC   Security and Exchange Commission

SCD   Slowly Changing Dimension

SOA   Service-Oriented Architecture

SOAP   Simple Object Access protocol

SOX   Sarbanes-Oxley Act

SQL   Structured Query Language

SPML   Service Provisioning Markup Language

SSN   Social Security Number

STP   Straight Through Processing

TIN   Tax Identification Number

UML   Unified Modeling Language

W3C   World Wide Web Consortium

WCC   WebSphere Customer Center

XACML   eXtensible Access Control Markup Language

XBRL   eXtensible Business Reporting Language

XCRL   eXtensible Customer Relationships Language

XRI   eXtensible Resource Identifier

Glossary

Account-centric view A physical or virtual representation of customer information that is limited only to the data affiliated with a particular customer account.

AJAX (Asynchronous JavaScript and XML) A web development technique for creating interactive web applications.

Authentication A process designed to verify that an individual or a party are who they claim they are.

Authorization A process of determining what information and computing resources the authenticated party is allowed to access.

Business rule A statement that defines or constrains some aspect of the business. It is intended to assert business structure or to control or influence the behavior of the business.

Business Rules Engine (BRE) A software application or a system that is designed to manage and enforce business rules based on a specified stimulus, for example, an event such as a change of an attribute value. Business Rules Engines are usually architected as pluggable software components that separate the business rules from the application code.

Coexistence-style Hub The hub style that combines features of the Registry Hub and the Transaction Hub. For some data attributes the Coexistence Hub maintains the system of record data; some other data attributes are managed by the metadata that points to data attributes in external systems.

Compliance risk Risk resulting from having inaccurate or untimely data related to consumer compliance disclosures, or an unauthorized disclosure of confidential customer information.

Confidentiality In information security, a business requirement that defines the rules and processes that can protect certain information from unauthorized use.

Counterparty Each party to a (financial) transaction.

Cryptography The process of converting data into an unreadable form via an encryption algorithm. Cryptography enables information to be sent across communication networks that are assumed to be insecure, without losing confidentiality or the integrity of the information being sent.

Cryptanalysis The study of mathematical techniques designed to defeat cryptographic techniques. Collectively, a branch of science that deals with cryptography and cryptanalysis is called cryptology.

Customer In the context of this book, "Customer" is used as a generic term that indicates an entity that requires and consumes an organization's products and services. The term "customer" can be replaced by industry- or line of business–specific terms such as Client, Contact, Party, Counterparty, Patient, Subscriber, Supplier, Prospect, Service Provider, Citizen, Guest, Legal Entity, Trust, Business Entity, and other terms.

Customer-centric view An aggregated physical or virtual record of customer information spanning all customer accounts and anchored around customer identity.

Customer Data Integration (CDI) A Master Data Management framework focused on the Customer Data domain; it is a comprehensive set of technology components, services, and business processes that create, maintain, and make available an accurate, timely, integrated, and complete view of a customer across lines of business, channels, and business partners.

Customer Relationship Management (CRM) A set of technologies and business processes designed to understand a customer, improve customer experience, and optimize customer-facing business processes across marketing, sales, and servicing channels.

Data Hub A common approach for a technical implementation of a service-oriented MDM solution. Data Hubs store and manage some data attributes and the metadata containing the location of data attributes in external systems in order to create a single physical or federated trusted source of information about customers, products, and so on.

Data governance A framework of processes aimed at defining and managing the quality, consistency, usability, security, and availability of information with the primary focus on cross-functional, cross-departmental, and/or cross-divisional concerns of information management.

Data profiling A process focused on generating data metrics and measuring data quality. The data metrics can be collected at the column level (for example, value frequency, nullity measurements, and uniqueness/match quality measurements), at the table level (for example, primary key violations), or in cross-table relationships (for example, foreign key violations).

Data Quality (DQ) A set of measurable characteristics of data that define how well the data represents the real-world construct to which it refers.

Data security An area of information security focused on the protection of data from either accidental or unauthorized intentional viewing, modification, destruction, duplication, or disclosure during input, processing, storage, transmission, or output operations. Data security deals with data that exists in two modes: data-in-transit and data-at-rest.

Data-at-rest   Data residing in memory caches, locally attached or networked data stores, as well as data in archives (for example, tape backup).

Data-in-transit   Any data moving between systems over network connections as well as data transferred between applications using file transfer mechanisms, messaging and queuing mechanisms, and/or ETL tools.

Data warehouse   "A data warehouse is a subject-oriented, integrated, time-variant, nonvolatile collection of data in support of management decisions." —W. H. Inmon

Economic Value of Information   The economic value of information, in the context of this book, expressed in terms of a fraction of the market capitalization of the company.

Encryption algorithm   A process that transforms plain text into a coded equivalent, known as the cipher text, for transmission or storage.

Enterprise Architecture Framework   Pioneered by John Zachman, an Enterprise Architecture Framework is an abstraction that helps to solve the complexity of the enterprise architecture by decomposing the problem into two main dimensions, each of which consists of multiple subcategories. The first dimension defines the various levels of abstraction that represent the business scope, business, systems, and technology models. The second dimension consists of key decision-driving questions: *what, how, where, who, when,* and *why?*

Enterprise Rights Management (ERM)   A set of technologies designed to manage and enforce information access policies and use rights of electronic documents within an enterprise. ERM enables the protection of intellectual property embedded in electronic documents, and provides protection persistence that enforces information access policies to allow an organization to control access to information that needs to be secured for privacy, competitive, or compliance reasons, and prevents users and even administrators from disabling the protection mechanisms.

Enterprise Service Bus (ESB)   A middleware software architecture construct that provides foundational services for more complex architectures via an event-driven and standards-based messaging engine (the bus). An ESB generally provides an abstraction layer on top of an implementation of an enterprise messaging system.

Entitlement   An expression meaning that a party has permission to do something with respect to some entity or an object.

Hierarchy   In the context of MDM, we can define a *hierarchy* as an arrangement of entities (parties, accounts, products, cost centers, and so on) where entities are viewed in relationship to each other as "parents," "children," or "siblings/peers" of other entities, thus forming a conceptual tree structure where all leaf nodes in the hierarchy tree can be rolled into a single "root."

Identity and Access Management   An organizing principle, a framework, and a set of technologies designed to manage the flow, consumption, security, integrity, and privacy of identity and business data across the enterprise in line with its business demands.

Information entropy A measure of uncertainty associated with the predictable value of information content. The highest information entropy is when the ambiguity or uncertainty of the outcome is the greatest.

Information Theory The area of applied mathematics founded by Claude Shannon that is focused on the quantification of information. Data quality for master data in this book is quantified by applying key principles of Information Theory.

Integrity In information security, integrity is a business requirement that data in a file or a message traversing the network remains unchanged or that any data received matches exactly what was sent; data integrity deals with the prevention of accidental or malicious changes to data or message content.

Intrusion detection The process of monitoring the events occurring in a computer system or network and analyzing them for signs of intrusion.

Java Authentication and Authorization Service (JAAS) A Java security facility that defines a pluggable, stacked authentication scheme. Different authentication schemes can be plugged in without having to modify or recompile existing applications.

Loss Data Warehouse (LDW) In the context of the Basel II Capital Accord, LDW is a primary vehicle to provide accurate, up-to-date analysis of capital adequacy requirements, and is also a source of disclosure reporting.

Loose coupling An architecture and design principle that avoids rigid, tightly coupled structures in which changes to one component force that change to be propagated throughout the system, and where the failure or poor performance of one component may bring the entire system down. Service-oriented architectures and Web Services support and promote loose coupling.

Master Data Governance (MDG) The area of Data Governance focusing on master data processes, metrics, controls, and accountabilities.

Master Data Management (MDM) A discipline that resolves master data to maintain the golden record, the holistic and panoramic view of master entities and relationships, and the benchmark for master data that can be used across the enterprise, and sometimes between enterprises to facilitate data exchanges.

Matching A highly specialized set of technologies that allows users to derive a high-confidence value of the party identification that can be used to construct a total view of a party from multiple party records.

Matching algorithm An algorithm that scores cross-record similarities and relates records by linking them with a common enterprise identifier.

Match Group In MDM, this is a group of master-type entity records determined to belong to a single master entity. The determination can be done systemically through the use of a matching algorithm or manually by end-user input.

Material Non-Public Information (MNPI) Information about a company or a market condition or an event that will have a material effect on the stock price(s) if it becomes known to the public.

Merge   An operation of creation of a single master entity record from two or more source systems' records.

Network Security   A security discipline that deals with authenticating network users, authorizing access to the network resources, and protecting the information that flows over the network.

Non-Public Personal Information (NPI)   Personally identifiable legal and financial information that is provided by a customer to the enterprise; derived from any transaction with the customer, or any service performed for the customer; or obtained by the enterprise via other means.

Nonrepudiation   In information security, the ability to confirm the fact that an action in question was undertaken by a party in question, and that the party in question cannot legally dispute or deny the fact of the action.

Obligations   In defining and evaluating XACML policies, obligations refer to actions that must be performed as part of handling an access request.

Opt-in   A privacy option that prohibits the sharing or sale of customer data *unless* the customer explicitly agreed to allow such actions.

Opt-out   This privacy option means that *unless and until* the customers inform their financial institution that they do not want them to share or sell customer data to other companies, the company is free to do so. The implication of this law is that the initial burden of privacy protection is on the customer, not on the company.

Party   A uniquely identified collection or cluster of individual detail-level records; the notion of the party supports multiple types, including organizations, customers, prospects, and so on.

Perimeter Security   This security discipline deals with security threats that arrive at the enterprise boundary via a network.

Personally Identifiable Information (PII)   Information that can be used to uniquely identify, contact, or locate an individual.

Policy   The encoding of rules particular to a business domain, its data content, and the application systems designed to operate in this domain on this set of data.

Provisioning   A set of management activities, business processes, and technologies governing the creation, modification, and deletion of user credentials and entitlements. It provides assured delivery and removal (deprovisioning) of the identity and entitlement data from all affected applications and systems.

Privacy   Proper handling and use of personal information (PI) throughout its life cycle, consistent with data-protection principles and the preferences of the subject.

Registry-style Hub   An MDM Data Hub architecture style that stores metadata with pointers to data elements in external systems.

Reputational Risk   Risk to the reputation of the business that arises from errors, delays, omissions, and information security breaches that become public knowledge or directly affect customers.

Risk   In general, *risk* is the probability that a threat agent will be able to exploit a defined vulnerability that would adversely impact the business.

Roles-Based Access Control (RBAC)   The processes and technologies of providing access control based on user credentials and roles.

Security   In the context of information security, a set of standards, processes, and technologies that include authentication, authorization, access control, and auditability of user actions in order to protect access to and use of the information resources only by authorized users. Information security goals are to ensure the integrity, confidentiality, and availability of the information.

Separation of Concerns   A process of breaking a program or a system into distinct features that overlap in functionality as little as possible.

Separation of Duties (SoD)   In the context of security and visibility, the separation of duties principle means that making policy-based access control decisions is a general function that is different and should be separated from the actions related to the enforcement of these access decisions.

Service-Oriented Architecture (SOA)   The software design and implementation architecture of loosely coupled, coarse-grained, reusable services that can be integrated with each other through a wide variety of platform-independent service interfaces.

Single Sign-On (SSO)   The technology that enables users to access multiple computer systems or networks after logging in once with a single set of authentication credentials.

Split   An operation of creating two records from a single record when new information becomes available and reveals the existence of two customers mistakenly represented by a single record. Typically this event occurs when two customers have many similar data element values—for example, a father and son living at the same address and having the same name.

Spyware   A type of malicious software that installs itself onto a user's computer and sends information from that computer to a third party without the user's permission or knowledge.

Transaction Risk   Risk that may arise from fraud, error, or the inability to deliver products or services, maintain a competitive position, or manage information.

Transaction-style Hub   A Data Hub solution that treats the Data Hub as a master system of record for master data. Other systems receive updates from the Transaction Hub.

Visibility   Ability to enforce fine-grained access to and operations on data at the record, attribute, and attribute-value levels based on user entitlements and data usage and access policies.

Web Services   Encapsulated, loosely coupled, coarse-grained, and contracted software objects offered via standard protocols.

Index